Advances in Generative Lexicon Theory

TEXT, SPEECH AND LANGUAGE TECHNOLOGY

VOLUME 46

Series Editor

Nancy Ide, *Vassar College, New York*

Editorial Board

Emily M. Bender, *University of Washington, USA*
Mona Diab, *Columbia University, USA*
Pascale Fung, *The Hong Kong University of Science and Technology,*
    Hong Kong SAR
Roberto Navigli, *Sapienza University of Rome, Italy*
Virach Sornlertlamvanich, *NECTEC, Thailand*
Fei Xia, *University of Washington, USA*

For further volumes:
http://www.springer.com/series/6636

James Pustejovsky • Pierrette Bouillon
Hitoshi Isahara • Kyoko Kanzaki • Chungmin Lee
Editors

Advances in Generative Lexicon Theory

Springer

Editors

James Pustejovsky
Computer Science Department
Brandeis University
Waltham Massachusetts
USA

Pierrette Bouillon
Faculté de Traduction
Université de Genève
Geneva
Switzerland

Hitoshi Isahara
Information and Media Center
Toyohashi University of Technology
Toyohashi
Japan

Kyoko Kanzaki
Dept. of Ling Theory & Structure
Nat. Inst. f. Japanese Lang. and Ling.
Tachikawa
Japan

Chungmin Lee
Dept. Linguistics
Seoul National University
Seoul
Korea, Republic of (South Korea)

ISSN 1386-291X
ISBN 978-94-007-9586-0   ISBN 978-94-007-5189-7 (eBook)
DOI 10.1007/978-94-007-5189-7
Springer Dordrecht Heidelberg New York London

Printed on acid-free paper

Springer is part of Springer Science+Business Media (www.springer.com)

Contents

Contributors

Nicholas Asher IRIT, Université Paul Sabatier Toulouse, Toulouse, France

CNRS, Toulouse, France

Department of Philosophy, University of Texas, Austin, TX, USA

Toni Badia Translation and Language Sciences Department, Pompeu Fabra University, Barcelona, Spain

Christian Bassac CRTT & INRIA, Université de Lyon2, Lyon, France

Université Michel de Montaigne Bordeaux 3, Pessac, France

Sabine Bergler Computer Science and Software Engineering Department, Concordia University, Montreal, QC, Canada

Francesca Bertagna Università di Pisa, Pisa, Italy

Pierrette Bouillon FTI/TIM/ISSCO, University of Geneva, Geneva, Switzerland

Nicoletta Calzolari Istituto di Linguistica Computazionale – CNR, Pisa, Italy

José M. Castaño Departamento de Computación, Facultad de Ciencias Exactas y Naturales, Universidad de Buenos Aires, Buenos Aires, Argentina

Brandeis University, Waltham, MA, USA

Vincent Claveau IRISA, Rennes, France

University of Montréal, Montreal, QC, Canada

Ann Copestake University of Cambridge Computer Laboratory, University of Cambridge, Cambridge, UK

Irena Drašković Department of Primary Care Medicine, Radboud University, Nijmegen, The Netherlands

Nijmegen Medical Centre, Nijmegen, The Netherlands

UMC, Nijmegen, The Netherlands

Christiane Fellbaum Department of Computer Science, Princeton University, Princeton, NJ, USA

Berlin-Brandenburgische Akademie der Wissenschaften, Berlin, Germany

Seohyun Im Department of Computer Science, Brandeis University, Waltham, MA, USA

Hitoshi Isahara Information and Media Center, Toyohashi University of Technology, Toyohashi, Japan

Evelyne Jacquey UMR 7118 ATILF CNRS & Université de Lorraine, Nancy, France

Kyoko Kanzaki Department of Linguistic Theory and Structure, National Institutes for Japanese language and Linguistics, Tokyo, Japan

Christopher Kennedy Department of Linguistics, University of Chicago, Chicago, IL, USA

Yoon-shin Kim Silla University, Busan, South Korea

Chungmin Lee Seoul National University, Seoul, South Korea

Alessandro Lenci Università di Pisa, Pisa, Italy

Louise McNally Department of Translation and Language Sciences, Universitat Pompeu Fabra, Barcelona, Spain

Monica Monachini Istituto di Linguistica Computazionale, Pisa, Italy

Kentaro Nakatani Department of English and American Literature and Language, Konan University, Kobe, Japan

Fiammetta Namer UMR 7118 ATILF CNRS & Université de Lorraine, Nancy, France

Naoyuki Ono Graduate School of International Cultural Studies, Tohoku University, Sendai, Japan

James Pustejovsky Department of Computer Science, Brandeis University, Waltham, MA, USA

Roser Saurí Voice and Language Group, Barcelona Media, Barcelona, Spain

Rob Schreuder Radboud University, Nijmegen-Midden, The Netherlands

Pascale Sébillot IRISA, Rennes, France

Robert D. Van Valin Jr. Department of Linguistics and Information Science, Heinrich Heine University, Düsseldorf, Germany

Department of Linguistics, University at Buffalo, Buffalo, NY, USA

The State University at New York, Albany, NY, USA

Chapter 1
Introduction

James Pustejovsky, Pierrette Bouillon, Hitoshi Isahara, Kyoko Kanzaki,
and Chungmin Lee

This volume collects some of the most recent papers addressing models of linguistic
composition from the perspective of Generative Lexicon Theory. Generative Lexicon (henceforth GL) developed out of a goal to provide a compositional semantics
for the contextual modulations in meaning that emerge in real linguistic usage.
Since it was first proposed, GL has developed to account for a broad range of
phenomena involving argument alternation, polysemy, type coercion, as well as
discourse phenomena and metaphor. Many of the observations from GL regarding
the importance of non-verbal meaning towards determining the semantic shifts
and alternations in sentence composition have been adopted by other grammatical
frameworks and researchers.

The works collected here address the relationship between compositionality
in language and the mechanisms of selection in grammar that are necessary to
maintain this property. There are two great challenges to the traditional view on
compositionality in language:

- The Interpretation of Context: this includes quantifier interpretation, definiteness,
  modal scope, and adverbial modification;

J. Pustejovsky (✉)
Department of Computer Science, Brandeis University, Waltham, MA, USA
e-mail: jamesp@cs.brandeis.edu

P. Bouillon
FTI/TIM/ISSCO, University of Geneva, Geneva, Switzerland

H. Isahara
Information and Media Center, Toyohashi University of Technology, Toyohashi, Japan

K. Kanzaki
Department of Linguistic Theory and Structure, National Institutes for Japanese language
and Linguistics, Tokyo, Japan

C. Lee
Seoul National University, Seoul, South Korea

J. Pustejovsky et al. (eds.), *Advances in Generative Lexicon Theory*, Text,
Speech and Language Technology 46, DOI 10.1007/978-94-007-5189-7_1,
© Springer Science+Business Media Dordrecht 2013

- The Mechanisms of Selection: this involves the phenomenon of polymorphism at all levels, including type shifting and polysemy more broadly.

The first challenge above has been addressed by linguists for decades, and is now the focus of two debates, "direct compositionality" (cf. Barker and Jacobson, 2007) and dynamics in semantics (Heim, 1982, Kamp and Reyle, 1993, Chierchia, 1995). The former issue relates to whether syntax reflects any artifice of the semantics in a transparent manner, giving rise to predictable, if not deterministic interpretations. From the perspective of direct compositionality researchers, surface syntax is a fair reflection of the semantic complexity and richness in the language. As a result, syntactic categories and their combinations in syntax are subject to a variety of type shifting and category changing mechanisms. The latter issue relates to how context is modeled in the logical form for an utterance in a discourse.

The second challenge also concerns direct compositionality in the syntax as well as the interpretation of context. Characterizing the nature of argument and type selection is at the core of semantic theory, since it determines the projection of lexical semantic information to compositional interpretations in the sentence, as well as the mutability of meaning through contextual modulations. Much of the work in the GL tradition over the past 10 years has focused on this problem: namely, what information structures and associated mechanisms are necessary in the grammar to allow for creative and novel meanings to emerge in context. This challenge will be the main focus of the present volume.

Generative Lexicon attempts to provide a compositional semantics for the contextual modulations that occur in language in two respects: first, it enriches the data structures associated with the lexical encoding of semantic information; secondly, it enhances the means by which this information is exploited in composition. These two changes result in a semantic theory with a distributed view on what linguistic units are responsible for determining meaning and selection. In recent work, this distinction has been identified as *inherent* versus *selectional* polysemy (Pustejovsky 2011, this volume). In fact, polysemy cannot truly be modeled without enriching the various compositional mechanisms available to the language. In particular, lexically driven operations of coercion and type selection provide for contextualized interpretations of expressions, which would otherwise not exhibit polysemy. This is in contrast with Cruse's (2000) view that it is not possible to maintain a distinction between semantic and pragmatic ambiguity. Cruse suggests that polysemy is best viewed as a continuous scale of sense modulation. The view within GL is generally that a strong distinction between pragmatic and semantic modes of interpretation should be maintained if we wish to model the complexity and provenance of the contributing factors in compositionality.

The notion of context enforcing a certain reading of a word, traditionally viewed as selecting for a particular word sense, is central both to lexicon design (the issue of breaking a word into word senses) and local composition of individual sense definitions. However, most lexical theories continue to reflect a static approach to dealing with this problem: the numbers of and distinctions between senses within an entry are typically frozen into a grammar's lexicon. This sense enumerative approach has inherent problems, and fails on several accounts, both in terms of what information is made available in a lexicon for driving the disambiguation process, and how a sense selection procedure makes use of this information.

The issues mentioned above are addressed from four distinct perspectives in the present volume:

1. Basic Theoretical Mechanisms of GL
2. Analysis of Linguistic Phenomena within GL
3. Interfacing with a GL Lexicon
4. Building GL-related Resources

Part I of the volume presents some of the recent theoretical developments in Generative Lexicon Theory. Pustejovsky's chapter, "Type Theory and Lexical Decomposition" (Chap. 2), explores the relation between methods of lexical decomposition and the theory of types. He identifies two approaches to lexical decomposition in grammar: parametric and predicative strategies. He then outlines how the predicative approach to decomposition can be realized within a type theory using richer selectional mechanisms such as those in GL. These mechanisms include two methods of type coercion (introduction and exploitation), operating over a basic three-way type distinction over the domain of interpretation.

In their contribution, "A Type Composition Logic for Generative Lexicon" (Chap. 3), Asher and Pustejovsky discuss the integration of discourse-sensitive logics with the compositional mechanisms available from lexically-driven semantic interpretation, such as that provided in GL. They outline a composition logic required to model complex types within GL, for which they employ SDRT principles. This logic provides a set of techniques governing the type shifting possibilities for various lexical items so as to allow for the combination of lexical items in cases where there is an apparent type mismatch. These techniques themselves follow from the structure of the lexicon and its underlying logic.

Finally, Van Valin's chapter, "Lexical Representation, Co-composition, and Linking Syntax and Semantics" (Chap. 4), addresses the question of whether semantic representation of a sentence is projected from the lexical properties of the verb or is constructed based on the structure of the sentence. This is an ongoing area of research, and both projectionist and constructionist approaches have been proposed. His chapter examines the alleged opposition between these approaches and argues that they are in fact complementary rather than contrasting explanations for semantic interpretation.

Part II of this volume turns to the analysis of specific linguistic phenomena. In "The Telic Relationship in Compounds" (Chap. 5), Bassac and Bouillon study a construction known as Purposive or Telic Compounds in French and Turkish. They propose some interesting generalizations regarding the formation of such compounds, accounted for here by the exploitation of the qualia structure of the compound elements, specifically the telic role. Their analysis also explains various syntactic properties associated with these compounds, such as those involving anaphoric reference and coercion.

Bergler's contribution, "Metonymy and Metaphor: Boundary Cases and the Role of a Generative Lexicon", addresses the question whether structure-based approaches to metonymy resolution can be combined with wider treatments of non-literal language comprehension, with particular emphasis on the co-occurrence and interaction between metonymy and metaphor. She examines data from the Wall Street Journal for this phenomenon and discusses different approaches to illustrate the tradeoffs and shortcomings of models that are built on the notion of either metaphor or metonymy in isolation.

In his chapter "Spanish Clitics, Events, and Opposition Structure" (Chap. 7), Castaño presents a unified account of the Spanish clitic *se*, specifically addressing the issue of the so called non-argument clitics, and the multiplicity of thematic roles these clitics are able to participate in. Castaño develops an interesting application and extension to the notion of Opposition Structure and the Qualia role values carried by the predicates in opposition.

Drašković, Pustejovsky and Schreuder, in their chapter "Adjective-Noun Combinations and the Generative Lexicon" (Chap. 8), report on two experimental studies on cognitive processing of adjective-noun combinations in which lexical semantic representations and processes are modeled within GL. They investigate the effects of adjectival qualia structure and the compatibility of semantic interpretation with the head in the adjective-noun combination. Three types of adjective-noun combinations were distinguished namely, intersective (e.g., yellow car), subsective compatible (e.g., interesting car), and subsective incompatible (e.g., fast car). Generally, the findings support a model of semantic interpretation of adjective-noun combinations where generative, type-driven computational processes are emphasized.

The next chapter discusses how compositional processes from GL can help model a kind of light verb construction in Korean. In "Combination of the Verb HA-'Do' and Entity Type Nouns in Korean: A Generative Lexicon Approach" (Chap. 9), Im and Lee aims to account for direct combination of an entity type noun with the verb HA- 'do' (e.g. piano-rul ha- 'piano-ACC do') in Korean. The verb HA- 'do' coerces some entity type nouns (e.g. pap 'boiled rice') into an event by virtue of the noun's qualia. This chapter extends the qualia of GL by adding an *engagement telic* role. Qualia are, nevertheless, not pragmatic but composed of information necessary to explain lexical meaning and co-occurrence constraints. Type coercion of the verb HA- 'do' has certain constraints related with the qualia of coerced nouns. Finally, they consider co-composition as an alternative to simple type coercion for the crucial operation of type shifting.

In their chapter, "Generative Lexicon Approach to Derived Inchoative Verbs in Korean" (Chap. 10), Kim and Lee present the lexico-semantic structure of the Korean inchoative verbs and their generative mechanism by means of a GL approach. The Korean inchoatives can be classified into three groups, the gradable, the semi-gradable and the ungradable one, considering their aspectul interpretation, semantic properties of their arguments and their opposition structures reflected in their event structures. Also, gradable and semi-gradable inchoatives show the generativity of the lexicon by the type coercion. Their typology and the associated lexico-semantic structures of Korean inchoatives is just a starting point in a larger study of a comprehensive classification of change-of-state verbs.

On a related topic, McNally and Kennedy also address the phenomenon of scale modification in their chapter "Degree vs. Manner *Well*: A Case Study in Selective Binding" (Chap. 11). They present a semantic analysis of the adverb well which captures its degree and manner readings in a principled fashion via the Generative Lexicon Selective Binding composition rule. Their analysis integrates Kennedy and McNally's (2005) treatment of scale structure with GL, and embeds the resulting semantics in HPSG.

Nakatani's chapter, "V-Concatenation in Japanese" (Chap. 12), examines the semantic properties of a type of Japanese verbal complex, the *V-te V* predicate, and argues that a non-derivational approach to the semantics of the *V-te V* predicate is inadequate both descriptively and explanatorily. A generative theory that derives the semantics of this predicate from its parts is explored within GL. The complex predicate formation is characterized as a process of collapsing two or more qualia structures into a single one, a process in which at least three operations and one well-formedness condition on semantic representations are involved.

In the next contribution, "Change of Location and Change of State" (Chap. 13), Lee provides parallels between change of location and certain change of state verbs. Argument reduction is proposed for the link. The GL event structure and headedness are employed to explain the polysemy of *spray*-verbs in Korean and Japanese. Headedness, along with extensions to the classic GL theory of event structure, allows for a novel and expressive solution to a distinction between certain motion verbs in Korean and Japanese. Lee's analysis advances the expressiveness of GL by incorporating the phenomenon of quantization in variable degree accomplishments (which has been absent from GL) with GL's subeventual structure. It elaborates the mechanisms at work in co-composition to derive multiple interpretations of change of state and creation predicates in Korean, thereby providing an expressive analysis of these data.

The Theory of Event Structure is also discussed and developed in Ono's chapter, "Event Structure and the Japanese Indirect Passive" (Chap. 14). This chapter presents a description and analysis of indirect passives in Japanese in terms of event structure and qualia structure proposed in the framework of the generative lexicon. On the assumption that the event structure of the indirect passive construction is based on the default causative paradigm, the present analysis accounts for the adversative interpretation of indirect passive sentences, the selection restriction on verbs, and the obligatory presence of the adjunct phrase.

In Part III of this volume, "Interfacing the Lexicon", the theme shifts to how lexical information represented with GL data structures, and compositional operations enriched with GL-like type-shifting mechanisms, can be integrated and interfaced to other linguistic theories. The first chapter to address this theme is Badia and Saurí's "Developing a Generative Lexicon within HPSG" (Chap. 15). This contribution discusses how to enrich the semantic treatment normally assumed in HPSG in order to deal with several issues not adequately solved, concerning the representation of: verbal and nominal complement optionality, non-intersective uses of adjectives, selection restrictions imposed by predicates to their arguments, and the implication of syntactically non-expressible participants and events as part of the denotation of lexical items. They enrich the content description level of HPSG as well as its governing principle. The resulting framework, they demonstrate, is implementable in LKB.

Fellbaum's chapter, "Purpose Verbs" (Chap. 16), illustrates how theoretical mechanisms from GL can be integrated with some conventional WordNet classification distinctions. Analogous to the distinction between TYPE and ROLE nouns, she differentiates between MANNER and PURPOSE verbs. Purpose verbs like *exercise*, *treat*, and *cheat* can conflate with manner verbs and contribute an additional, telic meaning component to these verbs. Conflation is triggered by contextual factors that create an "expectation" favoring a purpose interpretation over a pure manner reading. She compares and contrasts purpose verbs with Functional Events in GL. Some Functional Events are also purpose verbs, but Functional Events comprise a much larger and more loosely defined class, so the mapping is not exact.

In their chapter, "Word Formation Rules and the Generative Lexicon: Representing Noun-to-Verb Versus Verb-to-Noun Conversion in French" (Chap. 17), Namer and Jacquey focus on the interface between lexical semantics and word formation, working within the formalism called Morphological Structure Composition Schema (MS-CS), designed within GL. This interface is illustrated in French by the representation of the word formation processes of Noun-to-Verb (NtoV) versus Verb-to-Noun (VtoN) conversion. The relevance of this for lexical semantics is twofold: it's a non-conventional, affix-free, and semantics-driven mechanism; and it is both a productive and frequent phenomenon, observed in several languages. On the basis of a frequency-ranked, semantics-based classification over a large corpus, a unified GL-inspired model is proposed and illustrated through several examples.

The final section of this volume, Part IV, deals with building resources using GL data structures and principles. The first contribution is "Boosting Lexical Resources for the Semantic Web: Generative Lexicon and Lexicon Interoperability" (Chap. 18) by Calzolari, Francesca, Bertagna, Lenci, and Monachini. This chapter confronts two issues involved in making linguistic interoperability and the semantic web a reality: which involves two issues: (i) linguistic content must be dealt with in a multilingual environment; (ii) linguistic standards are needed to achieve interoperability and integration. Within the Semantic Web, ontologies are the key components for managing knowledge, while in Human Language Technology, semantic descriptions are captured within computational lexicons, such as GL-inspired lexicons. They describe how such resources can account for the complex, multidimensional and multifaceted nature of meaning in lexicon and ontology design, while also representing an essential interface between advanced research in the field of multilingual lexical semantics and the practical task of developing resources for HLT.

The chapter by Claveau and Sébillot, "Automatic Acquisition of GL Resources, using an Explanatory, Symbolic Technique" (Chap. 19), presents a symbolic machine learning method that automatically infers, from descriptions of noun-verb pairs found in a corpus in which the verb plays (or not) one of the qualia roles of the noun, where corpus-specific morpho-syntactic and semantic patterns that convey qualia relations. They demonstrate that these patterns are explanatory and linguistically motivated, and can be applied to a corpus to efficiently extract GL resources and populate Generative Lexicons. The linguistic relevance of these patterns is examined, and the N-V qualia pairs that they can detect is discussed. Comparisons to other methods for corpus-based qualia extraction are also presented.

In the final contribution to the volume, Copestake addresses the limits to productivity in her chapter "The Semi-Generative Lexicon: Limits on Productivity" (Chap. 20). She argues that, although there are clear motivations for generative devices in the lexicon, there are limits to productivity that must be accounted for. Her article provides an overview of several different classes of semi-productivity, including both lexical and phrasal examples. She then outlines a probabilistic approach to account for these phenomena, which relies on GL devices, but only in part.

References

Barker, C., & Jacobson, P. (2007). *Direct compositionality*. Oxford: Oxford University Press.

Chierchia, G. (1995). *Dynamics of meaning*. Chicago: University of Chicago Press.

Cruse, A. (2000). *Meaning in language*. Oxford: Oxford University Press.

Groenendijk, J., & Stokhof, M. (1991). Dynamic predicate logic. *Linguistics and Philosophy, 14*(1), 39–100.

Heim, I. (1982/1988). *The semantics of definite and indefinite noun phrases*. New York: Garland Publications.

Kamp, H., & Reyle, U. (1993). *From discourse to logic*. Dordrecht: Kluwer Academic.

Kennedy, C., & McNally, L. (2005). Scale structure and the semantic typology of gradable predicates. *Language, 81*, 2.

Pustejovsky, J. (2011). Coercion in a general theory of argument selection. *Journal of Linguistics, 49*(6).

Chapter 2
Type Theory and Lexical Decomposition

James Pustejovsky

2.1 Introduction

In this paper, I examine the relation between the type of an argument as selected by
a predicate, and the role this argument subsequently plays in the computation of the
sentence meaning. The thesis that I will put forth is that there is an important
connection between the nature of the type that a predicate selects for as its
argument, and the subsequent interpretation of the predicate in the model. In
order to understand this connection, I explore the logical structure of decomposition
as used in linguistic theory. Two basic models of word meaning are discussed,
parametric and *predicative* decomposition. These are then compared to selection
within a rich type theory.

Type theoretic selection can be viewed as *partial decomposition*. The advantage
over a full decomposition model such as predicative is that, in defining a predicate,
one is not forced to identify the distinguishing features (as in Katz and Fodor) in the
model. However, the types used as assignments to the arguments of the predicate are
a recognizable and distinguished subset of possible predications over individuals.

In the first two sections, I explore the relation between methods of lexical
representation involving decomposition and the theory of types as used in linguistic semantics and programming semantics. I first distinguish two approaches
to lexical decomposition in language, *parametric* and *predicative* decomposition.
I demonstrate how expressions formed with one technique can be translated into
expressions of the other. I then discuss argument selection within a type theoretic

---

The framework developed here is extended to a broader classes of coercion types in the context of
argument selection in Pustejovsky (2011).

J. Pustejovsky (✉)
Department of Computer Science, Brandeis University, Waltham, MA, USA
e-mail: jamesp@cs.brandeis.edu

J. Pustejovsky et al. (eds.), *Advances in Generative Lexicon Theory*, Text,
Speech and Language Technology 46, DOI 10.1007/978-94-007-5189-7_2,
© Springer Science+Business Media Dordrecht 2013

approach to semantics, and show how type theory can be mapped to the predicative approach of lexical decomposition. I argue that a type theoretic framework results in an interpretative mechanism that is computationally more tractable than with either atomic expressions or simple parametric decomposition. In the final three sections, Generative Lexicon (GL) is illustrated as a constrained model of type selection and predicative decomposition. I outline three basic mechanisms of argument selection for semantic composition, and demonstrate how these mechanisms interact with the type system in GL.

2.2 Methods of Lexical Decomposition

Typically, linguistically sensitive theories of lexical structure tend to focus on how verb meanings relate to syntactic forms within a sentence; that is, linking lexical-semantic form to syntax (van Valin 2005; Levin and Rappaport Hovav 2005; Jackendoff 2002; Davis and Koenig 2000). To accomplish this, much of the work on the structure of lexical items in language over the past 10 years has focused on the development of type structures and typed feature structures. The selectional behavior of verbal predicates, on this view, follows from the type associated with the verb's arguments. There is, however, a distinction in the way that verbs select their arguments that has not been noticed, or if it has, has not been exploited formally within linguistic theories; namely, argument structure and decomposition are intimately connected and typically inversely related to one another.

Before we examine the various models of lexical decomposition, we need to address the more general question of what selection in the grammar is, and what exactly the formal nature of an argument is. We begin by reviewing informally what characteristics may comprise the predicative complex that makes up a verb's meaning. These include, but are not limited to:

(1)   a. Specific properties of the participants of the event;
       b. Change of being, state, location, relation;
       c. Causation and agency;
       d. Manner and means of an activity;
       e. Temporal and spatial constraints;
       f. Intentionality of the actor;
       g. Instrumental information;
       h. Psychological state of the participants;

The question that I wish to address in this paper is the following: which of these aspects can be abstracted as selectional restrictions to arguments, and which of these can be abstracted as arguments in their own right? To answer this question, I will first examine the role that lexical decomposition plays in the theory of grammar. I will characterize four approaches to decomposition that have been adopted in the field, and illustrate what assumptions each approach makes regarding selectional restrictions on the arguments to a verb.

Linguists who do adopt some form of lexical decomposition do not typically concern themselves with the philosophical consequences of their enterprise. Still, it is hard to ignore the criticism leveled against the field by Fodor (1998), who claim that any model of semantics involving decomposition is without support and leads to the anarchy of conceptual holism. In fact, however, most linguists assume some kind of decompositional structure for the semantic representations associated with lexical items, including, as it happens, Fodor and LePore themselves.[1]

How do we decompose the meaning of a verb? In order to categorize the various techniques of decomposition, I will assume that a predicative expression such as a verb has both an *argument list* and a *body*. This is schematically illustrated in (2) below.

(2) $\overbrace{\lambda x_i}^{Args}\ \overbrace{[\Phi]}^{Body}$

Intuitively, the question is the following: if the semantics of a predicate can convey any or all of the components of meaning mentioned above in (1), then how are they represented, if at all, in the semantic form adopted for the lexical representation of this predicate? How explicit is the predicative decomposition over Φ, and how many arguments does the predicate carry underlyingly? What I hope to demonstrate here is the way in which the *args-body* structure is modified by different approaches to lexical decomposition in order to account for these separate components of a predicate's meaning.

We will consider four possible strategies for reconfiguring the *args-body* structure of a predicate.[2] We begin first with the null hypothesis, what I refer to as *atomic predication*. In this approach, the parameter structure of the underlying semantic representation of an expression α is mirrored directly by the realization of the verb's arguments in the surface syntax.

(3)   ATOMIC DECOMPOSITION: The expression α has a simple atomic body, Φ, and a parameter list matching the arguments in syntax.

       $\lambda x_n \ldots \lambda x_1 [\Phi] \Rightarrow \text{Verb}(\text{Arg}_1, \ldots, \text{Arg}_n)$

This is illustrated in the sentences in (4)–(5), where each argument in the semantic form is expressed syntactically.

---

[1] The admission that mentalese appears to be a first order language is already an acceptance that some sort of decomposition is desirable or necessary for describing language. But beyond this, we will see that the vocabulary accepted as standard to discuss verb behavior is a further commitment to types or categories as part of lexical descriptions.

[2] Each of these strategies has been thoroughly explored in the literature. What I hope to illustrate here is the organization of these approaches according to the above classification. The focus in the discussion below will be on verbs and their projection to syntactic form.

(4)   a. $\lambda x[\text{die}(x)]$
      b. The flower died.

(5)   a. $\lambda y \lambda x[\text{hit}(x, y)]$
      b. The car hit the wall.

   To ensure the correct mapping to syntax from the lexical representation of the predicate, a mechanism of *argument identification* must be assumed.[3]
   From the basic representation in (3), four distinct strategies for the decomposition of lexical information have been proposed in the literature.[4]

(6)   a. PARAMETRIC DECOMPOSITION: The expression α
         has a simple atomic body, Φ, but the parameter list
         adds additional arguments for interpretation in the
         model:

         $$\lambda x_m \ldots \lambda x_{n+1} \lambda x_n \ldots \lambda x_1[\Phi]$$

      b. SIMPLE PREDICATIVE DECOMPOSITION: The
         expression α has a complex expression of
         subpredicates, $\Phi_1, \ldots \Phi_k$, over the parameter list:

         $$\lambda x[\Phi_1, \ldots \Phi_k]$$

      c. FULL PREDICATIVE DECOMPOSITION: The
         expression α has a complex expression of
         subpredicates, $\Phi_1, \ldots \Phi_k$, while also adding
         additional arguments to the parameter list, binding
         into the subpredicates:

         $$\lambda x_m \ldots \lambda x_{n+1} \lambda x_n \ldots \lambda x_1[\Phi_1, \ldots \Phi_k]$$

      d. SUPRALEXICAL DECOMPOSITION: The expression
         α does not change, but the parameter structure is
         enriched through mechanisms of additional
         operators such as R (associated with functional
         categories); the interpretation of α is enriched by an
         extra compositional operation:

         $$\lambda f_\sigma \lambda x_1[R(f)(x_1)](\lambda x[\Phi_1, \ldots \Phi_k])_\sigma$$

---

[3]This is the θ-theory in varieties of Chomsky's framework from the 1980s, and the Functional Uniqueness Principle from LFG.

[4]For the present discussion, I assume that the subpredicates in the expressions below are related by means of standard first order logical connectives.

For each of these approaches, the representation adopted for the predicate meaning will have consequences for the subsequent mapping of its parameters to syntax, namely, the problem of argument realization. To better illustrate the nature of these strategies, let us consider some examples of each approach, beginning with parametric decomposition. Within this approach, the intuitive idea is to motivate additional parameters over which a relation is evaluated in the model. These can be contextual variables, parameters identifying properties of the speaker, hearer, presuppositional information, and other pragmatic or domain specific variables. Perhaps the most widely adopted case of parametric decomposition is Davidson's proposed addition of the event variable to action predicates in language (Davidson 1967). Under this proposal, two-place predicates such as *eat* and three-place predicates such as *give* contain an additional argument, the event variable, e, as depicted below.

(7) a. $\lambda y \lambda x \lambda e[\text{eat}(e)(y)(x)]$
     b. $\lambda z \lambda y \lambda x \lambda e[\text{give}(e)(z)(y)(x)]$

In this manner, Davidson is able to capture the appropriate entailments between propositions involving action and event expressions through the conventional mechanisms of logical entailment. For example, to capture the entailments between (8b–d) and (8a) below,

(8) a. Mary ate the soup.
     b. Mary ate the soup with a spoon.
     c. Mary ate the soup with a spoon in the kitchen.
     d. Mary ate the soup with a spoon in the kitchen at 3:00 pm.

In this example, each more specifically described event entails the one above it by virtue of and-elimination (conjunctive generalization) on the expression.

(9) a. $\exists e[\text{eat}(e, m, \text{the} - \text{soup})]$
     b. $\exists e[\text{eat}(e, m, \text{the} - \text{soup}) \wedge with(e, a\_\text{spoon})]$
     c. $\exists e[\text{eat}(e, m, \text{the} - \text{soup}) \wedge with(e, a\_\text{spoon}) \wedge in(e, \text{the\_kitchen})]$
     d. $\exists e[\text{eat}(e, m, \text{the} - \text{soup}) \wedge with(e, a\_\text{spoon}) \wedge in(e, \text{the\_kitchen}) \wedge$
        $at(e, 3:00\text{pm})]$

There are of course many variants of the introduction of events into predicative forms, including the identification of arguments with specific named roles (or partial functions, cf. Dowty 1989; Chierchia 1989) such as thematic relations over the event. Such a move is made in Parsons (1990).[5]

---

[5]The neo-Davidsonian position adopted by Kratzer (1994) does not fall into this category, but rather in the supralexical decomposition category below. Reasons for this will become clear in the discussion that follows.

Within AI and computational linguistics, parameter decomposition has involved not only the addition of event variables, but of conventional adjunct arguments as well. Hobbs et al. (1993), for example, working within a framework of first-order abductive inference, models verbs of change-of-location such as *come* and *go* as directly selecting for the "source" and "goal" location arguments. As a result, directional movement verbs such as *follow* will also incorporate the locations as direct arguments.

(10)   a. $\lambda z \lambda y \lambda x \lambda e[go(e, x, y, z)]$
         b. $\lambda z \lambda y \lambda x \lambda e[follow(e, x, y, z)]$

Generalizing this approach, we see that parametric decomposition involves the addition of logical parameters to the body of the expression without enriching the "descriptive content" of the predicate itself. Furthermore, on this strategy, the one-to-one correspondence from the semantic representation to syntactic expression of an argument is not explicitly maintained.

(11)   parametric decomposition:
         $\lambda x_m \ldots \lambda x_{n+1} \lambda x_n \ldots \lambda x_1[\Phi] \Rightarrow \text{Verb}(\text{Arg}_1, \ldots, \text{Arg}_n)$

Because some parameters are not always expressed, such a theory must take into consideration the conditions under which the additional parameters are expressed. For this reason, we can think of parametric decomposition as requiring both argument identification and *argument reduction* (or Skolemization) in the mapping to syntax. That is, something has to ensure that an argument may be elided or must be expressed.

We turn next to *simple predicative decomposition*. Perhaps the best known examples of lexical decomposition in the linguistics literature are the componential analysis expressions proposed in Katz and Fodor (1963), as well as in Lakoff (1965), McCawley (1968), Lyons (1968), and others. Under this strategy, concepts such as *bachelor* are seen as conjunctions of more "primitive" features[6]:

(12) $\forall x[bachelor(x) \Rightarrow [male(x) \wedge adult(x) \wedge \neg married(x)]]$

Independent of the syntactic or semantic motivations for such a definition, it is clear that (12) is an instance of the simple predicative decomposition. For the present discussion, notice that neither the argument structure nor the type of the variable has changed in the expression in (12) for *bachelor*; only the body of the expression has been effected.

Verbs have also been expressed as simple predicative decompositions in the literature; for example, the representation for the verb *die*, as (13) illustrates (cf. Lakoff 1965; Dowty 1979).

---

[6]Whether the concept of *married* is any less complex than that of the definiendum *bachelor* has, of course, been a matter of some dispute. Cf. Weinreich (1972).

(13) $\forall x[\text{die}(x) \Rightarrow [\text{Become}(\neg\text{alive}(x))]$

Again, using our simple *args-body* description of the expression, the predicative content in the *body* of (13) has become more complex, while leaving the arguments unaffected, both in number and type. The mapping to syntax from a simple predicative decomposition structure can be summarized as the following relation:

(14) simple predicative decomposition:

$\lambda x_n \ldots \lambda x_1[\Phi_1, \ldots \Phi_k] \Rightarrow \text{Verb}(\text{Arg}_1, \ldots, \text{Arg}_n)$

In addition to argument identification, this strategy requires that the subpredicates, $\Phi_1, \ldots \Phi_k$, get collapsed into one syntactically realized verbal element.[7]

When the predicative and parametric approaches to decomposition are combined we arrive at what I will refer to as *full predicative decomposition*. This is generally the approach taken in Generative Lexicon Theory (Pustejovsky and Boguraev 1993; Pustejovsky 1995), Jackendoff's Conceptual Structure (Jackendoff 2002), Pinker (1989), and Levin and Rappaport's work on predicate decomposition (Levin and Rappaport Hovav 1995, 2005).

For example, ignoring aspects of named functional roles (e.g., qualia structure or thematic relations), the decomposition for a causal predicate such as *kill* includes reference to the subevent involving the activity proper (Moens and Steedman's (1988) preparatory phase) and the culminating state. This is represented in (15).

(15) a. **kill**:

$\lambda y\lambda x\lambda e_1\lambda e_2[\text{act}(e_1, x, y) \land \neg\text{dead}(e_1, y) \land \text{dead}(e_2, x) \land e_1 < e_2]:$

b. The gardener killed the flower.

The correspondence between lexical structure and syntactic realization for this strategy can be schematically represented as follows:

(16) full predicative decomposition:

$\lambda x_m \ldots \lambda x_{n+1}\lambda x_n \ldots \lambda x_1[\Phi_1, \ldots \Phi_k] \Rightarrow \text{Verb}(\text{Arg}_1, \ldots, \text{Arg}_n)$

Note that, as with parametric decomposition, both argument identification and argument reduction are required for the mapping to syntax. As with the simple predicative strategy, a condition is required to ensure that the subpredicative structure is adequately expressed in the syntax.

Finally, it should be noted that the effects of decomposition can be reconstructed through composition in a more abstract syntax, as proposed, for example, by Kratzer (1996). Following Marantz's (1984) analysis of verbs as lacking external arguments in their lexical encoding of argument structure, Kratzer proposes that the external

---

[7]Recall that such collapsing operations were an important process prior to lexical insertion in Generative Semantics, cf. McCawley 1972; Dowty 1979.

argument is introduced through a functional category of *voice*, which adds the argument that was otherwise missing from the verbal structure. The event associated with the agent and that of the main predicate are composed through an operation she terms *Event Identification* (Kratzer 1996).

(17)   supralexical decomposition:
        a. $\lambda x_n \ldots \lambda x_1[\Phi] \Rightarrow \text{Verb}(\text{Arg}_1, \ldots, \text{Arg}_n)$
        b. $v \Rightarrow \lambda f_\sigma \lambda x_1[R(f)(x_1)]$
        c. $\lambda f_\sigma \lambda x_1[R(f)(x_1)](\lambda x[\Phi])_\sigma$

Thus, in the sentence in (18), the external argument along with the semantics of agency and causation are external to the meaning of the verb *build*.

(18)   John built a house.

This view has broad consequences for the theory of selection, but I will not discuss these issues here, as they are peripheral to the current discussion.

2.3   Types and the Selection of Arguments

Having introduced the basic strategies for semantic decomposition in predicates, we now examine the problem of argument selection. We will discuss the relation between selection and the elements that are assumed as part of the type inventory of the compositional semantic system.

In the untyped entity domain of classical type theory as conventionally adopted in linguistics (e.g., Montague Grammar), determining the conditions under which arguments to a relation or function can "be satisfied" is part of the interpretation function over the entire expression being evaluated. The only constraint or test performed prior to interpretation in the model is the *basic typing* carried by a function. For example, to determine the interpretations of both sentence (19a) and (19b), the interpretation function, $[[.]]^{M,g}$ tests all assignments according to g within the model M.

(19)   a. A rock fell.
           $\exists x \exists e[\text{fall}(e, x) \wedge \text{rock}(x)]$
        b. A rock died.
           $\exists x \exists e[\text{die}(e, x) \wedge \text{rock}(x)]$

Hence, our assignment and model will determine the correct valuation for the proposition in (19a). As it happens, however, there will be no assignment that satisfies (19b) in the model. We, of course, as speakers of language, intuit this result. The model does not express this intuition, but does evaluate to the same answer. The valuation may always be correct (the correct truth-value universally assigned), but the computation required to arrive at this result might be costly and unnecessary: costly because we must evaluate every world within the model with the appropriate assignment function; and unnecessary because the computation could effectively be avoided if our system were designed differently.

This can be accomplished by introducing a larger inventory of types and imposing strict conditions under which these types are accepted in a computation. A richer system of types works to effectively introduce the test of "possible satisfaction" of an argument to a predicate. The types in the entity domain encode the possible satisfaction of the argument. We can think of argument typing as a *pre-test*. If an expression fails to past the pretest imposed by the type, it will not even get interpreted by the interpretation function.[8] This is what we will call a "fail early" selection strategy. Hence, the domain of interpretation for the expression is reduced by the type restriction.

In the discussion above, we distinguished the argument list from the body of the predicate. To better understand what I mean by a "fail early" strategy of selection, let us examine the computation involved in the interpretation of a set of related propositions. Consider the following sentences.

(20)   a. The woman slept soundly.
        b. The soldier died in the street.
        c. The child dreamt of Christmas.

Imagine *tracing* the interpretation of each sentence above into our model. Given a domain, for each sentence, the assignment function, g, and interpretation function, I results in a valuation of each sentence. What is notable about the sentences in (20), is that the trace for each sentence will share certain computations towards their respective interpretations. Namely, the argument bound to the subject position in each sentence is *animate*. How is this common trace in the interpretation of these predicates represented, if at all, in the grammar?[9]

Consider the λ-expression for a two-place predicate, Φ, which consists of the subpredicates $\Phi_1, \ldots, \Phi_k$. The variables are typed as individuals, i.e., e, and the entire expression is therefore a typical first-order relation, typed as $e \rightarrow (e \rightarrow t)$.

$$
\overset{\textit{Args}}{\overbrace{\lambda x_2 \lambda x_1}} \ \overset{\textit{Body}}{\overbrace{[\Phi_1, \ldots \Phi_k]}}
$$

(21)

---

[8] In programming languages, the operation of semantic analysis verifies that the typing assignments associated with expressions are valid. This is essentially done in compilation time, as a pre-test, filtering out arguments that would otherwise have the wrong type. In a model that does not perform predicate decomposition to incorporate typing constraints, sentences like (19b) are just false.

[9] Regarding argument selection, there are two possible strategies for how the argument accommodates to the typing requirement. Given that the type requirement is a pretest, the argument expression can fail (strict monomorphic typing), or coerce to the appropriate type (polymorphic typing). We will not discuss coercion in the context of the fail early strategy in this paper.

A richer typing structure for the arguments would accomplish three things: first, it acts to identify specific predicates in the body of the expression that are characteristic functions of a given argument;

(22) $\lambda x_2 \lambda x_1 [\Phi_1, \ldots \overbrace{\Phi_{x_1}}^{\tau}, \ldots \overbrace{\Phi_{x_2}}^{\sigma}, \ldots, \Phi_k]$

Secondly, it pulls this subset of predicates out of the body;

(23) $\lambda x_2 \, \lambda x_1 [\Phi_1, \ldots, \Phi_k - \{\Phi_{x_1}, \Phi_{x_2}\}]$

Finally, it takes the set of predicates associated with each argument and *reifies* them as type restrictions on the λ-expression, i.e., as the types τ and σ.

(24) $\lambda x_2 : \sigma \, \lambda x_1 : \tau [\Phi_1, \ldots, \Phi_k - \{\Phi_{x_1}, \Phi_{x_2}\}]$

The typing restriction on the arguments can be seen as a *pretest* on the λ-expression, where they act as restricted quantification over a domain of sorts, denoted by that set of predicates. So, in terms of the computation, we see that the test for each argument is performed before the predicate is considered for evaluation.

Returning to the examples in (20), we can identify one distinguishing predicate over each subject argument as *animate*. This suggests that the verbs *sleep*, *die*, and *dream* are members of the natural class of predicates taking an animate argument as logical subject. This aspect of the computation that the sentences share can be captured within the model by means of a structure such as a semi-lattice. Hence, if $anim \sqsubseteq e$, then, *sleep* and the related predicates from (20) are typed as in (25a):

(25)   a. *sleep*: $anim \rightarrow t$
       b. $\lambda x : anim[sleep(x)]$

Under such an interpretation, the expression makes reference to a type lattice of expanded types, such as that shown in (26) below (cf. Copestake and Briscoe 1992; Pustejovsky and Boguraev 1993).

(26)

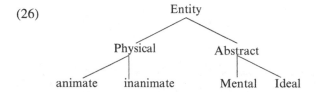

Thus, instead of representing the verb *sleep* as the λ-expression

(27) $\lambda x[animate(x) \wedge sleep(x)]$

we can interpret predication of animacy over the subject directly as a *pre-test condition* on the typing of that argument, $\vdash xanim$. This will be denotationally equivalent to the previous expression in (27), but would be operationally distinct. Namely, the computation performed to determine whether the subject satisfies the condition on animacy is done before the λ-reduction is even computed.[10]

What this correspondence suggests more generally is that a semantic expression in one decomposition strategy may be translated (and perhaps equivalent) to an expression in another strategy. Of particular interest is the relation between predicate decomposition and strategies involving richer inventories of types. There is an obvious trade-off in expressiveness between these two strategies. Where decomposition posits specific predications over its argument, an enriched typing strategy will make many of those predications part of the typing assignment to the argument itself, cf. below.

(28)   Types for the verb *sleep*:

APPROACH	Type	Expression
atomic	$e \to t$	$\lambda x[sleep(x)]$
predicative	$e \to t$	$\lambda x[animate(x) \wedge sleep(x)]$
enriched typing	$anim \to t$	$\lambda x : anim[sleep(x)]$

Similar remarks hold for the semantics of nouns, and in particular, the predicative decomposition of relational nouns (cf. Borschev and Partee 2001) and agentive nouns (Busa 1996).

In the remainder of this paper, I will examine in more detail the consequences of enriching the inventory of types. First, however, we examine what linguistic motivations exist for such a move.

2.4   Enriching the Type System

2.4.1   Semantic Transparency

Researchers in linguistics typically assume that language meaning is compositional, and that a theory of semantics for language should model this property. There appear to be, however, many phenomena in language that are non-compositional and which are not directly accounted for by conventional models of compositionality (Partee 1992; Kamp and Partee 1995). This gap in descriptive power has motivated several views of richer representation and semantic operations, one of which is Generative Lexicon Theory (Pustejovsky 1995). Generative Lexicon (GL) is concerned in part with explaining the creative use of language. On this view, our ability to categorize and structure the world is an operation of generative categorization and

---

[10]This brings up the issue of how a pre-test is related to the presuppositional interpretation of argument selection. Although an important question, I will defer discussion to a forthcoming treatment of selection mechanisms, Pustejovsky (forthcoming).

compositional thought, and the lexicon is seen as a dynamic component, responsible for much of the information underlying this phenomenon. Language, therefore, is the natural manifestation of our generative construction of the world through the categories it employs. This has been an implicit guiding principle within much of linguistic semantic research, from Chomsky (1986) to Ginzburg and Sag (2000) and Jackendoff (2002).

In Pustejovsky (2005) I refer to this informally as the *Principle of Semantic Transparency*. From a GL perspective, this states that the syntactic realization of an argument is directly dependent on: (a) the semantic type imposed by the selecting predicate; and (b) the coercion transformations available to that type in the grammar. What this says is that there is a direct mapping from semantic representations and their types to specific syntactic effects. Specifically, it states that such a mapping must be a property of semantic categories generally, and not merely selectively. The thesis as stated may in fact be too strong, and indeed there appear to be areas of grammar where direct semantic transparency seems to fail (such as the syntactic realization of mass and count terms cross-linguistically). Nevertheless, I will adopt semantic transparency to help structure our intuitions regarding the linguistic modeling of types for selection in grammar.

The standard theory of selection in grammar can be viewed as follows. There is some inventory of types, T, associated with the entities in the domain, along with t, a Boolean type. Verbs are analyzed as functional types, meaning that they are functions from this set of types to t (i.e., employing a functional type constructor such as $\rightarrow$). The selectional constraints imposed on the arguments to a verb are inherited from the type associated with that argument in the functional type that the verb carries. This is generally quite weak and if any further constraints are seen as being imposed on the semantics of an argument, then they would be through some notion of selectional constraints construed as a presupposition during interpretation.

The approach taken here differs from the standard theory in two respects. First, we will aim to make the selectional constraints imposed on a verb's arguments transparently part of the typing of the verb itself. This entails enriching the system of types manipulated by the compositional rules of the grammar. Following Pustejovsky (2001) and Busa et al. (1999), I will assume the theory of type levels, where a distinction is maintained between *natural*, *artifactual*, and *complex* types for all major categories in the language. Secondly, the mechanisms of selection available to the grammar are not simply the application of a function to its argument (function application, argument identification, θ-discharge), but involve three type-sensitive operations: type *matching*, *coercion*, and *accommodation*. These will be introduced in subsequent sections.

2.4.2   The Notion of Natural Type

There has been a great deal of research that depends on the concept of *natural kind*, much of it in developmental psychology (Rosch 1975; Keil 1989), presupposing the discussion of the problem as presented in Putnam (1975) and Kripke (1980). Although the problem emerges in a superficial manner in the semantics and knowledge representation literature (Fellbaum 1998), there is surprisingly little discussion of the conceptual underpinnings of natural kinds and how this impacts the linguistic expression of our concepts. This section addresses the linguistic and conceptual consequences of the notion of natural kind. Particularly, I will examine what it means, from the perspective of linguistic modeling, for the grammar to make reference to a natural or unnatural kind in the conceptual system.

The world of entities inherited from Montague's theory of semantics is, in many respects, a very restricted one. In that model, there is no principled type-theoretic distinction made between the kinds of things that exist within the domain of entities. Similarly, the only distinctions made in the domain of relations pertains mostly to the number of arguments a relation takes, or the intensional force introduced over an argument (cf. Dowty et al. 1980; Heim and Kratzer 1998). Many enrichments and modifications have been made to this model over the past 30 years, including the addition of stages and kinds (cf. Carlson 1977), but interestingly enough, no extensions have ever been made for modeling natural kinds.

From a linguistic point of view, this might not seem surprising, since the grammatical behavior of natural kind terms doesn't noticeably distinguish itself from that of other nominal classes. In fact, there has never been sufficient evidence presented for making such a grammatical distinction. Consider, for example, the sentences in (29) below. The natural kind terms *dog*, *man*, and *bird* behave no differently as nominal heads than the artifactual nouns *pet*, *doctor*, and *plane*.

(29)   a. Mary saw every *dog/pet*.
       b. John visited a *man/doctor*.
       c. *Birds/planes* can fly.

Similarly, no discernible difference between nominal classes is present with the adjectival constructions below.

(30)   a. a sick *dog/pet*
       b. an American *man/doctor*
       c. white *birds/planes*

In this section, however, I discuss three linguistic diagnostics which appear to motivate a fundamental distinction between natural and unnatural kinds. These diagnostics are:

(31)   a. *Nominal Predication*: How the common noun behaves predicatively;
       b. *Adjectival Predication*: How adjectives modifying the common noun can be interpreted;
       c. *Interpretation in Coercive Contexts*: How NPs with the common noun are interpreted in coercive environments.

Let us first consider the nominal predicative construction, illustrated in (32) with natural kind terms.

(32)   a. Otis is a dog.
        b. Otis is a poodle.
        c. Eno is a cat.

As is apparent, natural kind terms permit singular predication: what is interesting, however, is that they appear to require predicative uniqueness. Note that the nominal co-predication in (33a) is odd, while that in (33b) is ill-formed ('!' here indicates semantic anomaly).

(33)   a. ?Otis is a dog and an animal.
        b. !That is a dog and a cat.
        c. Otis is a dog and therefore an animal.

While (32a) identifies the individual, Otis, as belonging to a particular natural kind, *dog*, the predication in (33a) would apparently violate a pragmatic principle on redundant typing (Gricean informativeness). The predication in (33b), on the other hand, is contradictory.

Observe that the *and-therefore*-construction in (33c) is acceptable with the nominal sortal terms *dog* and *animal*. This construction is valid when the first nominal term is a subtype of the second nominal term; hence, since dogs are a subtype of animals, the construction is valid.

The property of predicative uniqueness does not hold for adjectives, however. Something can obviously be both "big and red", "long and thin", or "flat and smooth". Note, however, that co-predications from the same domain are ill-formed, as shown in (34).

(34)   a. !This box is large and small.
        b. !Your gift is round and square.

Such examples illustrate the inherent complementarity of the predicative space being alluded to in each example; *size* in (34a) and *shape* in (34b). The restriction on co-predication suggests that natural kind terms are structured in a taxonomy, somehow obeying a complementary partitioning of the conceptual space, in a similar manner to the adjectival cases in (34).

The question that immediately arises is how prevalent the restriction on nominal predication is. The fact is that most co-predication with nominals is acceptable, and natural kind terms are the exception. Observe the sentences in (35), with nominals from the class of artifacts.

(35)   a. This is both a pen and a knife.
        b. The substance is a stimulant and an anti-inflammatory.

Occupational terms and agentive nominals also easily co-predicate, as seen in (36).

(36)　a. Mary is a housewife and a doctor.

　　　 b. Bernstein was a composer and a conductor.

Not surprisingly, the *and-therefore*-construction is acceptable with both artifacts and human agentive nominals.

(37)　a. This object is a knife and therefore a weapon.

　　　 b. Emanuel Ax is a pianist and therefore a musician.

Knives are a subtype of weapon, and pianists are a subtype of musician. Notice, however, that the *and-therefore*-construction in (38) is also acceptable.

(38)　Emanuel Ax is a pianist and therefore a human.

While it is true that pianists are humans, this subtyping relation is different from that with musicians in (37b). We return to this distinction below in the next section.

While natural kinds terms seem to distinguish themselves from other sortal terms with nominal predicative constructions, the same holds for certain adjectival predications as well. Consider the adjectival modifications in (39), with natural kind terms as head.

(39)　a. very old gold

　　　 b. a new tree

　　　 c. a young tiger

　　　 d. such a beautiful flower

The adjectives in (39) behave in a conventional subsective manner and are unambiguous in their modification of the nominal head. That is, there is one distinct semantic aspect of the head that they modify. Compare these examples to those in (40) and (41), with artifacts and agentive nominals as head, respectively.[11]

(40)　a. a blue/Swiss pen

　　　 b. a bright/expensive bulb

　　　 c. a long/shiny CD

---

[11]This class of adjectives has been studied extensively. Bouillon (1997) analyzes such constructions as subselective predication of a qualia role in the head. Larson and Cho (2003) provide a more conventional interpretation without the need for decompositional representations.

(41)   a. a very old friend
        b. a good professor
        c. such a beautiful dancer

   With the NPs in (40), observe that the adjectives can modify aspects of the
nominal head other than the physical object: *blue* in (40a) can refer to the color
of the object or the color of the ink; *bright* in (40b) most likely refers to the bulb
when illuminated; and *long* in (40c) can refer only to the length of time a CD will
play.[12]
   Turning to the agentive nominal heads in (41), a similar possibility of dual
adjectival modification exists. The adjective *old* in (41a) can refer to the individual
as a human or the friendship; *good* in (41b) can refer to teaching skills or humanity;
and *beautiful* in (41c) can refer to dance technique or physical attributes.
   From this brief examination of the data, it is clear that not all kind terms
are treated equally in nominal predication and adjectival modification. As a final
diagnostic illustrating grammatical distinctions between natural and unnatural kind
terms, let us consider the selection of NPs in type coercive contexts. Verbs that select
for multiple syntactic frames for the same argument can be viewed as polymorphic
predicates. In Pustejovsky (1993, 1995), it is argued that predicates such as *believe*
and *enjoy*, as well as aspectual verbs such as *begin* and *finish* can *coerce* their
arguments to the type they require. For example, consider the verb-object pairs in
(42)–(43):

(42)   a. Mary enjoyed drinking her beer.
        b. Mary enjoyed her beer.

(43)   a. John began to write his thesis.
        b. John began writing his thesis.
        c. John began his thesis.

   Although the syntactic form for each sentence is distinct, the semantic type
selected for by *enjoy* and *begin*, respectively, remains the same. For the readings
in (42b) and (43c), following Pustejovsky (1995), we assume that the NP has
undergone a type coercion operation to the type selected by the verb. For example,
in (43c), the coercion "wraps" the meaning of the NP "his thesis" with a controlled
event predicate, in this case defaulting to "writing".
   What is interesting to note is that artifactual nouns seem to carry their own default
interpretation in coercive contexts. This property is completely absent with natural
kind terms, however, as shown below.

---

[12]In both (40b) and (40c), interpretations are possible with modification over the object, but they
are semantically marked with *bright* and contradictory with *long*.

(44)   a. !John finished the tree.
       b. !Mary began a tiger.

There are, of course, legitimate readings for each of these sentences, but the interpretations are completely dependent on a specific context. Unlike in the coercions above, natural kinds such as *tree* and *tiger* carry no prior information to suggest how they would be "wrapped" in such a context.

In sum, we have discovered three grammatical diagnostics distinguishing natural kind terms from non-natural kind terms. They are:

(45)   a. *Nominal Predication*: How the common noun behaves predicatively;
       b. *Adjectival Predication*: How adjectives modifying the the common noun can be interpreted;
       c. *Interpretation in Coercive Contexts*: How NPs with the common noun are interpreted in coercive environments.

Given this evidence, it would appear that natural kinds should be typed distinctly from the class of non-naturals in language. The latter, however, is itself heterogeneous, and deserves further examination. As explored in Pustejovsky (2001), there are specific and identifiable diagnostics indicating that the class of non-natural entities divides broadly into two classes, what I call *artifactual types* and *complex types*. Because this distinction largely mirrors that made in Pustejovsky (1995) between unified and complex types, I will not review the linguistic motivations in this chapter.

In the next section, I show how the representations and mechanisms of Generative Lexicon (GL) theory can account for these distinctions. These facts can be accounted for by establishing a fundamental distinction between natural types and non-natural types within our model. We first review the basics of GL and then present our analysis.

2.5   Types in Generative Lexicon

Generative Lexicon introduces a knowledge representation framework which offers a rich and expressive vocabulary for lexical information. The motivations for this are twofold. Overall, GL is concerned with explaining the creative use of language; we consider the lexicon to be the key repository holding much of the information underlying this phenomenon. More specifically, however, it is the notion of a constantly evolving lexicon that GL attempts to emulate; this is in contrast to currently prevalent views of static lexicon design, where the set of contexts licensing the use of words is determined in advance, and there are no formal mechanisms offered for expanding this set.

One of the most difficult problems facing theoretical and computational semantics is defining the representational interface between linguistic and non-linguistic
knowledge. GL was initially developed as a theoretical framework for encoding
selectional knowledge in natural language. This in turn required making some
changes in the formal rules of representation and composition. Perhaps the most
controversial aspect of GL has been the manner in which lexically encoded knowledge is exploited in the construction of interpretations for linguistic utterances.
Following standard assumptions in GL, the computational resources available to
a lexical item consist of the following four levels:

(46) a. **Lexical Typing Structure**: giving an explicit type for a word
         positioned within a type system for the language;
      b. **Argument Structure**: specifying the number and nature of the
         arguments to a predicate;
      c. **Event Structure**: defining the event type of the expression and any
         subeventual structure it may have; with subevents;
      d. **Qualia Structure**: a structural differentiation of the predicative force
         for a lexical item.

The qualia structure, inspired by Moravcsik's (1975) interpretation of the *aitia* of
Aristotle, are defined as the modes of explanation associated with a word or phrase
in the language, and are defined as follows (Pustejovsky 1991):

(47) a. **formal**: the basic category of which distinguishes the meaning of a
      b. word within a larger domain;
      c. **constitutive**: the relation between an object and its constituent parts;
         telic: the purpose or function of the object, if there is one;
      d. **agentive**: the factors involved in the object's origins or "coming into
         being".

Conventional interpretations of the GL semantic representation have been as
feature structures (cf. Bouillon 1997; Pustejovsky 1995). The feature representation
shown below gives the basic template of argument and event variables, and the
specification of the qualia structure.

$$
\begin{bmatrix}
\alpha \\
\text{ARGSTR} = \begin{bmatrix} \text{ARG1} = x \\ \dots \end{bmatrix} \\
\text{EVENTSTR} = \begin{bmatrix} \text{E1} = e_1 \\ \dots \end{bmatrix} \\
\text{QUALIA} = \begin{bmatrix} \text{CONST} = what\ x\ \textbf{is made of} \\ \text{FORMAL} = \textbf{what } x \textbf{ is} \\ \text{TELIC} = \textbf{function of } x \\ \text{AGENTIVE} = \textbf{how } x \textbf{ came into being} \end{bmatrix}
\end{bmatrix}
$$

It is perhaps useful to analyze the above data structure in terms of the *args-body* schema discussed in previous sections. The *argument structure (AS)* captures the participants in the predicate, while the *event structure (ES)* captures the predicate as an event or event complex of a particular sort (Pustejovsky 2001). The body is composed primarily of the *qualia structure* together with temporal constraints on the interpretation of the qualia values, imposed by event structure. This is illustrated schematically below, where QS denotes the qualia structure, and C denotes the constraints imposed from event structure.

$$
(48) \quad \overbrace{\underbrace{\lambda x_n \ldots \lambda x_1}_{AS} \underbrace{\lambda e_m \ldots \lambda e_1}_{ES}}^{Args} \quad \overbrace{[Q_1 \wedge Q_2 \wedge Q_3 \wedge Q_4; C]}^{Body:\ QSUC}
$$

Given this brief introduction to GL, let us return to the problem of argument selection. I propose that the selection phenomena can be accounted for by both enriching the system of types and the mechanisms of composition. I will propose three mechanisms at work in the selection of an argument by a predicative expression. These are:

(49) a. *Pure Selection* (Type Matching): the type a function requires is directly satisfied by the argument;
b. *Accommodation*: the type a function requires is inherited by the argument;
c. *Type Coercion*: the type a function requires is imposed on the argument type. This is accomplished by either:
    i. *Exploitation*: taking a part of the argument's type to satisfy the function;
    ii. *Introduction*: wrapping the argument with the type required by the function.

Following Pustejovsky (2001), we will separate the domain of individuals into three distinct type levels:

(50) a. *natural types*: Natural kind concepts consisting of reference only to
b. Formal and Const qualia roles;
    artifactual types: Concepts making reference to purpose or function.
c. *complex types*: Concepts making reference to an inherent relation between types.

The level of a type will be modeled by its structure, following Asher and Pustejovsky (2006) *Type Composition Logic*. The set of types is defined in (51) below.

(51) a. e the general type of entities; t the type of truth values.
           (σ, τ range over all simple types, and subtypes of e; cf. the semilattice
           in (26) above).
       b. If σ and τ are types, then so is $\sigma \rightarrow \tau$.
       c. If σ and τ are types, then so is $\sigma \otimes_R \tau$, where R can range over
           Agentive or *Telic*.
       d. If σ and τ are types, then so is $\sigma \bullet \tau$.

In addition to the conventional operator creating functional types ($\rightarrow$), we introduce a type constructor $\bullet$ ("dot"), which creates dot objects from any types σ and τ, deriving $\sigma \bullet \tau$. This is essentially identical with the construction of complex types in Pustejovsky (1995). We also introduce a type constructor $\otimes$ ("tensor") which can be seen as introducing qualia relations to a base type.

To illustrate how the type system here is a natural extension of that in Pustejovsky (1995), consider a classic GL type feature structure for a term α, ignoring const for now:

$$
(52) \quad
\begin{bmatrix}
\alpha \\
\text{QUALIA} =
\begin{bmatrix}
\text{FORMAL} : \beta \\
\text{TELIC} : \tau \\
\text{AGENTIVE} : \sigma
\end{bmatrix}
\end{bmatrix}
$$

In Pustejovsky (1995), the type specification for an expression α, (i.e., the formal qualia value β) is distinct from the other qualia values in the semantic representation for α. The qualia structure, on this view, is the entire feature structure associated with the expression.

What we will do here is conceptually not that different but has some interesting consequences for how compositionality is modeled. We will identify the entire qualia structure as the typing assignment for the expression itself. That is, we integrate the formal type specification with the qualia values to create a richer typing structure. Assume that the formal role is always present in the qualia, and hence will be considered the *head* type of the assignment; that is, [formal $= \beta$] is simply written β.

The additional qualia values can be seen as structural complementation to the head type. Each quale value will be introduced by a tensor operator, $\otimes$. To differentiate the qualia roles, we will subscript the operator accordingly; e.g., [telic $= \tau$] can be expressed as $\otimes_T \tau$, [agentive $= \sigma$] can be expressed as $\otimes_A \sigma$.

Now the feature structure for the expression α from (52) can be represented as a single composite type, as in (53), or written linearly, as $\beta \otimes_T \tau \otimes_A \sigma$.

$$
(53) \quad
\begin{bmatrix}
\alpha \ \beta \\
\otimes_T \tau \\
\otimes_A \sigma
\end{bmatrix}
$$

Given these assumptions for how qualia structures can be interpreted as types, let us return to our previous discussion of natural versus non-natural types. We can see the expression of natural typing throughout the major linguistic categories in the language:

(54) a. **Nouns**: rock, water, woman, tiger, tree
      b. **Verbs**: fall, walk, rain, put, have
      c. **Adjectives**: red, large, flat, big

These will be our atomic types, from which we will construct our $\otimes$-types and •-types (artifactual and complex types, respectively).

We will assume that the natural entity types, N, are just those entities formed from the Formal qualia value i.e., atomic types. The natural types are formally structured as a join semi-lattice (Pustejovsky 2001), $\langle N, \sqsubseteq \rangle$ (cf. the structure in (26)).

Now consider the predicates that select for just these natural types. Once natural type entities have been defined, we are in a position to define the natural predicates and relations that correspond to these types. The creation of functions over the sub-domain of natural types follows conventional functional typing assumptions: for any type τ in the sub-domain of natural types, $\tau \in N$, $\tau \rightarrow t$ is a *natural functional type*.

First, let us review some notation. I assume a *typing judgment*, $g \vdash \alpha : \tau$, with respect to a grammar to be an assignment, g, an expression, α, and a type, τ, such that under assignment g, the expression α has type τ. In the case of the natural types, I will also assume the following equivalence:

(55) $g \vdash x : \tau \in \mathcal{N} =_{df} g \vdash x : e_n$

Hence, all of the predicates below are considered *natural predicates*, since each is a functional type created over the sub-domain of natural entities.[13]

---

[13]It is worth noting that the propositions formed by the composition of a natural predicate with natural type entities have a special status, since they form the basis of what we will call natural propositions. Examples of such propositions are given below:

The rabbit died.
The rock touches the water.
The ants are under the tree.

It is interesting to compare this to Anscombe's (1958) discussion and Searle's (1995) extension regarding "brute facts" as opposed to "institutional facts.". The natural predication of a property over a natural entity is a judgment requiring no institutional context or background. Facts (or at least judgments) can be classified according to the kinds of participant they contain; in fact, as we shall see, the qualia and the principle of type ordering will allow us to enrich this "fact classification" even further.

(56)   a. *die*: $e_N \rightarrow t$
       b. *touch*: $e_N \rightarrow (e_N \rightarrow t)$
       c. *be under*: $e_N \rightarrow (e_N \rightarrow t)$

These predicates can be expressed as λ-expressions with typed arguments as in (57):

(57)   a. $\lambda x{:}e_N[die(\mathrm{x})]$
       b. $\lambda y{:}e_N \lambda x{:}e_N[touch(\mathrm{x,y})]$
       c. $\lambda y{:}e_N \lambda x{:}e_N[be\text{-}under(\mathrm{x,y})]$

Before we look at how natural types are exploited in composition in the language, we will illustrate how non-natural types are constructed in GL's Type Composition Logic.

2.5.1   Artifacts and Artifactual Types

One of the innovations introduced by GL is the idea that conceptual differences in the mental lexicon are reflected in the qualia structures for the lexical items associated with those concepts. Hence, the nouns *person, typist, water*, and *wine*, all have distinct qualia structures reflecting their conceptual distinctions. This has always been at the core of GL's view of lexical organization. What I wish to do here is demonstrate how these differences are accounted for directly in terms of the structural typing introduced above.

In the previous section, natural entities and natural functions were defined as the atomic types, involving no $\otimes$- or $\bullet$-constructor syntax. Artifactual objects, that is, entities with some function, purpose, or identified origin, can now be constructed from the tensor constructor and a specific value for the telic or agentive role. I will adopt the term *artifact*, in a broad sense, to refer to artifactually constructed objects, or natural objects that have been assigned or assume some function or use.[14] Following the discussion above, then, composing a natural entity type, e_N, with a Telic value by use of the $\otimes$-constructor results in what we will call an *artifactual type*.[15]

(58)   ARTIFACTUAL TYPE (Version I): For an expression α, whose head type, $\beta \in \mathcal{N}$, then for any functional type γ, the $\otimes_R$-construction type, $\beta \otimes_R \gamma$, is in the sub-domain of *artifactual types*, $\mathcal{A}$.

---

[14]Dipert makes a similar move in his 1993 book *Artifacts, Art Works, and Agency*.

[15]The judgments expressed by the predication of an artifactual predicate of an artifactual subject results in an artifactual proposition. This is formally similar to Searle's notion of institutional fact.

To illustrate how the qualia structure of artifacts can be modeled in this fashion, observe the type structures for a selection of artifactual entity types:

(59)   a. *beer*: $liquid \otimes_T drink$
       b. *knife*: $phys \otimes_T cut$
       c. *house*: $phys \otimes_T live\_in$

As it stands, the definition in (58) is not general enough to model the set of all artifacts and concepts with function or purpose. As argued in Pustejovsky (1995), the head type (the formal quale role) need not be an atomic type (natural), but can be arbitrarily complex itself. As a result, we will broaden the type for the head to include artifactual types as well:

(60)   ARTIFACTUAL TYPE (Final Version): For an expression α, whose head type, $\beta \in \mathcal{N} \cup \mathcal{A}$, and any functional type γ, the $\otimes_R$-construction type, $\beta \otimes_R \gamma$, is in the sub-domain of *artifactual types*, $\mathcal{A}$.

As with the naturals, the creation of functions over the sub-domain of artifactual types is straightforward: for any type τ in the sub-domain of artifactual entity types, $\tau \in A$, $\tau \rightarrow t$ is a *artifactual functional type*. Below are some examples of such functional types, expressed as λ-expressions with typed arguments:

(61)   a. $\lambda x{:}e_A[spoil(x)]$
       b. $\lambda y{:}e_A \lambda x{:}e_N[fix(x,y)]$

Before we examine the specific mechanisms of selection accounting for strong (enriched) compositionality in the grammar, we review the final level of types generated by the Type Construction Logic, that of the Complex Types (Dot objects).

2.5.2 Dots and Complex Types

Because the behavior of complex types has been studied in a number of works (Pustejovsky 1995, 1998), I will concentrate on how they are constructed in GL's Type Construction Logic. To account for the inherent polysemy in nouns such as *book*, where distinct ((62a) and (62b)) and contradictory (62c) selectional environments are possible, GL introduces a type constructor, •, which reifies the two elements into a new type.

(62)   a. Mary doesn't believe the book.
       b. John bought his book from Mary.
       c. The police burnt a controversial book.

(63)   COMPLEX TYPE: For any entity types α, $\beta \in \mathcal{N} \cup \mathcal{A}$, the $\bullet$-construction
       type, $\alpha \bullet \beta$, is in the sub-domain of *complex types*, $\mathcal{C}$.

Creating functions over the sub-domain of complex types is similarly straightforward: for any type τ in the sub-domain of complex entity types, $\tau \in C$, $\tau \to t$ is a
complex functional type. Below is an example of the verb *read*, a complex functional
type, since it selects a complex type as its direct object.

(64)   a. *read*: $phys \bullet info \to (e_N \to t)$
       b. $\lambda y{:}phys \bullet info\ \lambda x{:}e_N[read(x,y)]$

The concept of *reading* is sui generis to an entity that is defined as "informational
print matter", that is, a complex type such as $phys \bullet info$. In a selective context
such as (65), the predicate directly selects for a complex type, *a magazine*.

(65)   Mary read *a magazine* on the plane.

How exactly this is accomplished we will explain below. In the next section, we
turn finally to the mechanisms of selection at work in ensuring that predicates and
their arguments are compatible in semantic composition.

2.6   Mechanisms of Selection

In this section, we examine the compositional processes at work in communicating
the selectional specification of a predicate to its arguments. In particular, we analyze
domain-preserving selection between a predicate and its arguments. As a result, we
will not discuss type-shifting rules across domains, such as the classic type coercion
rules invoked in aspectual and experiencer verb complementation contexts (e.g.,
enjoy the beer, finish the coffee). How these operations are analyzed in terms of the
compositional mechanisms presented here is described elsewhere (cf. Pustejovsky
2006).
   There are three basic mechanisms available in the grammar for mediating the
information required by a predicate, F, and that presented by the predicate's
argument. For a predicate selecting an argument of type σ, $[\_\_\_\_]_\sigma F$, the following
operations are possible:

(66)   a. PURE SELECTION: The type a function requires of its argument, A, is directly satisfied by that argument's typing:

$[A_\alpha]_\alpha\ F$

b. ACCOMMODATION: The type a function requires is inherited through the type of the argument:

$[A_\beta]_\alpha\ F,\ \alpha \sqcap \beta \neq \bot$

c. COERCION: The type a function requires is imposed on the argument type. This is accomplished by either (where $\odot$ represents the disjunction of the two constructors, $\otimes$ and $\bullet$):

i. *Exploitation*: selecting part of the argument's type structure to satisfy the function's typing:

$[A_{\alpha\odot\tau}]_\beta\ F,\ \alpha \sqsubseteq \beta$

ii. *Introduction*: wrapping the argument with the type the function requires:

$[A_\alpha]_{\beta\odot\sigma}\ F,\ \alpha \sqsubseteq \beta$

The table below illustrates what operations are available in which selectional contexts. Obviously, *pure selection* is only possible when both the type selected and the argument type match exactly. Also, *accommodation* is operative only within the same type domain.

The remaining cases are varieties of coercion: *exploitation* is present when a subcomponent of the argument's type is accessed; and *introduction* is operative when the selecting type is richer than the type of its argument.[16]

(67)

	Type Selected		
Argument Type	Natural	artifactual	Complex
Natural	Sel/Acc	Intro	Intro
artifactual	Exploit	Sel/Acc	Intro
Complex	Exploit	Exploit	Sel/Acc

To better understand the interactions between these operations, let us walk through some examples illustrating each of these selectional operations. We start with the set of predicates selecting for a natural type argument. Consider the intransitive verb *fall*, as it appears with natural, artifactual, and complex arguments, respectively. The typing on the head noun for each example is given in parentheses.

---

[16]It might be possible to view pure selection as incorporating the accommodation rule as well, which would result in a more symmetric distribution of behavior in the table. Whether this is computationally desirable, however, is still unclear.

(68)   a. *N*: The rock fell to the floor. (*phys*)
      b. *A*: The knife fell to the floor. ($phys \otimes_T cut$)
      c. *C*: The book fell to the floor. ($phys \bullet info \otimes_T read \otimes_A write$)

The mechanism at work in (68a) is pure selection, as illustrated below in (69).

(69)

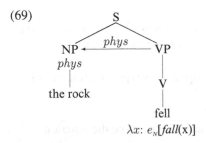

For the second and third examples, exploitation applies to provide access to the physical manifestation of the type appearing in the argument position. Below is the derivation for (68c); the exploitation in (68b) is similarly derived.[17]

(70)

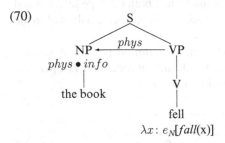

Now let us consider artifactual type selecting predicates. We take the verb *spoil* as an example. Again, we look at each type possibility in argument position. The selected type of the complement is in parentheses.[18]

---

[17]Exploitation on the info element of the dot object for book occurs in examples such as

(i)   below:

(i)   I don't believe this book at all.

Here the verb is selecting for propositional content, which is present by exploitation in the dot object of the direct object.

[18]For the present discussion, we ignore selection of a dot object in an artifactual type context. In general, the analysis will follow the introduction rule seen in (71a) below, but there are complications in some cases. These are discussed in Pustejovsky (2011).

(71)   a. *N*: The water spoiled. (*phys*)

　　　 b. *A*: The food spoiled. (*phys⊗$_T$eat*)

Consider first the case of pure selection in (71b). Here the predicate is selecting for an artifactual entity as subject, and the NP present is typed as one. Hence, the typing requirement is satisfied.

(72)

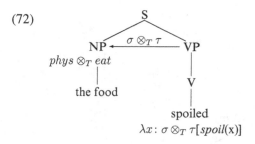

$$\lambda x : \sigma \otimes_T \tau[spoil(\text{x})]$$

Now consider the presence of a natural entity in a subject position selecting for an artifactual type. This is the case in (71a); to satisfy the typing requirements on the predicate, the coercion rule of *Introduction* is required to wrap the natural type with a functional interpretation; that is, this water was going to be used for something, it had some function intended for it. The derivation is shown below.

(73)

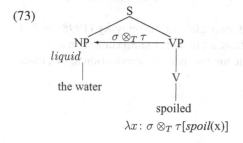

$$\lambda x : \sigma \otimes_T \tau[spoil(\text{x})]$$

Finally, let us examine the selectional mechanisms at work when the predicate selects for a complex type. As discussed in Pustejovsky (1998, 2001), these include verbs such as *read*.

(74)   a. *N*: Mary read a rumor about John. (*info*)

　　　 a′. *N*: The bathers read the sand on the beach. (*phys*)

　　　 b. *A*: The passengers read the walls of the subway. (*phys⊗$_T$τ*)

　　　 c. *C*: Mary read the book. (*phys • info⊗$_T$read⊗$_A$write*)

In this case, sentence (74c) is the example of pure selection. The predicate *read* requires a dot object of type *phys • info* as its direct object, and the NP present, *the book*, satisfies this typing directly. This is shown in (75) below, where $p \bullet i$ abbreviates the type $phys \bullet info$.

(75)

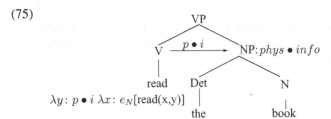

(76)

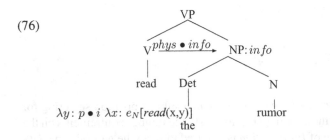

For all of the other cases, (74a), (74a′), and (74b), the NP in direct object position is wrapped with the intended type by the rule of Introduction, as shown below for sentence (74a).

The consequences of this type shifting, as argued in Pustejovsky (1998), is that this information object (*the rumor*) must have a physical manifestation, in order for it to be read. This follows directly from the mechanism of Introduction in this case.

2.7 Conclusion

In this paper, I have examined the relationship between decomposition and argument typing in semantics. What emerges from the interplay of these two formal strategies is a clearer understanding of some of the mechanisms of compositionality in language. I outlined a model of argument selection for natural language involving two major components: a three-level type system consisting of natural, artifactual, and complex types; and three compositional mechanisms for mediating the type required by a predicate and the type present in the argument. These are: pure selection (matching), accommodation, and coercion. There are two kinds of coercion, exploitation and introduction, and we illustrated each of these operations at work in the syntax.

References

Anscombe, G. E. M. (1958). On Brute facts. *Analysis, 18*, 69–72.

Asher, N., & Pustejovsky, J. (2005). *Word meaning and commonsense metaphysics*. ms. Brandeis University and University of Texas.

Asher, N., & Pustejovsky, J. (2006). A type composition logic for generative lexicon. Journal of Cognitive Science.

Borschev, V., & Partee, B. (2001). Genitive modifiers, sorts, and metonymy. *Nordic Journal of Linguistics, 24*(2), 140–160.

Bouillon, P. (1997). *Polymorphie et sémantique lexicale: le cas des adjectifs*. Lille: Presses Universitaires du Spetentrion.

Busa, F. (1996). *Compositionality and the semantics of nominals*. Ph.D. dissertation, Brandeis University.

Busa, F., Calzolari, N., Lenci, A., & Pustejovsky, J. (1999). Building a semantic lexicon: Structuring and generating concepts. In *Proceedings of IWCS-III*, Tilberg, The Netherlands.

Carlson, G. (1977). *Reference to Kinds in English*, Ph.D. dissertation. Amherst: University of Massachusetts.

Chierchia, G. (1989). Structured meanings, thematic roles, and control. In G. Chierchia, B. Partee, & R. Turner (Eds.), *Properties, types, and meaning* (Vol. 2, pp. 131–166). Dordrecht: Kluwer Academic.

Copestake, A., & Briscoe, T. (1992). Lexical operations. In a unification-based framework. In J. Pustejovsky & S. Bergler (Eds.), *Lexical semantics and knowledge representation*. Berlin: Springer.

Chomsky, N. (1986). *Knowledge of language, its nature, origin, and use*. New York: Praeger.

Corblin, F. (2003). Presuppositions and commitment stores in Diabruck. *7th Workshop on the semantics and the pragmatics of dialogue, 2003*. Saarbruecken, Germany.

Cruse, D. A. (1986). *Lexical semantics*. Cambridge: Cambridge University Press.

Davis, A., & Koenig, J.-P. (2000). Linking as constraints on word classes in a hierarchical lexicon. *Language, 76*, 56–91.

Davidson, D. (1967). The logical form of action sentences. In N. Rescher (Ed.), *The logic of decision and action*. Pittsburgh: Pittsburgh University Press.

Dipert, R. R. (1993). *Artifacts, art works, and agency*. Philadelphia: Temple University Press.

Dowty, D. R. (1979). *Word meaning and Montague grammar*. Dordrecht: Kluwer Academic.

Dowty, D., Wall, R., & Peters, S. (1980). *Introduction to montague semantics, Synthese Language Library*. Dordrecht: Kluwer.

Dowty, D. R. (1989). On the semantic content of the notion 'thematic role'. In G. Chierchia, B. Partee, & R. Turner (Eds.), *Properties, types, and meaning* (Semantic issues, Vol. 2). Dordrecht: Kluwer.

Fodor, J. (1998). *Concepts*. New York: Oxford University Press.

Fodor, J., & Lepore, E. (1998). The emptiness of the lexicon. Critical reflections on J. Pustejovsky's 'The generative lexicon'. *Linguistic Inquiry, 29*, 269–288.

Fellbaum, C. (Ed.). (1998). *WordNet: An electronic lexical database*. Cambridge, MA: MIT Press.

Ginzburg, J., & Sag, I. (2000). *Interrogative investigations: the form, meaning, and use of English interrogatives*. Stanford: CSLI Publication.

Heim, I., & Kratzer, A. (1998). *Semantics in generative grammar*. Oxford: Blackwell.

Hobbs, J., Stickel, M., Martin, P., & Edwards, D. (1993). Interpretation as abduction. *Artificial Intelligence, 63*, 69–142.

Jackendoff, R. (2002). *Foundations of language*. Oxford: Oxford University Press.

Kamp, H., & Partee, B. (1995). Prototype theory and compositionality. *Cognition, 57*(2), 129–191.

Katz, J., & Fodor, J. (1963). The structure of a semantic theory. *Language, 39*, 170–210.

Keil, F. (1989). *Concepts, kinds, and cognitive development*. Cambridge, MA: MIT Press.

Kratzer, A. (1994). On external arguments. In J. Runner & E. Benedicto (Eds.), *Functional projections* (pp. 103–129). Amherst: GLSA.

Kratzer, A. (1996). In J. Rooryck & L. Zaring (Eds.), *Severing the external argument from its verb. Phrase structure and the lexicon* (pp. 109–137). Dordrecht: Kluwer.

Lakoff, G. (1965/1970). *Irregularity in syntax*. New York: Holt, Rinehart, and Winston.

Larson, R., & Cho, S. (2003). Temporal adjectives and the structure of possessive DPs. *Natural Language Semantics, 11*, 3.

Levin, B., & Rappaport Hovav, M. (2005). *Argument realization*. Cambridge: Cambridge University Press.

Levin, B., & Rappaport Hovav, M. (1995). *Unaccusatives: At the syntax-lexical semantics interface*. Cambridge: MIT Press.

Lyons, J. (1968). *Introduction to theoretical linguistics*. Cambridge: Cambridge University Press.

Marantz, A. P. (1984). *On the nature of grammatical relations*. Cambridge: MIT Press.

McCawley, J. D. (1968). The role of semantics in a grammar. In E. Bach & R. T. Harms (Eds.), *Universals in linguistic theory*. New York: Holt, Rinehart, and Winston.

Moens, M., & Steedman, M. (1988). Temporal Ontology and Temporal Reference. *Computational Linguistics, 14*, 15–28.

Moravcsik, J. M. (1975). Aitia as generative factor in Aristotle's philosophy. *Dialogue, 14*, 622–36.

Parsons, T. (1990). *Events in the semantics of English*. Cambridge, MA: MIT Press.

Partee, B. (1992). Syntactic categories and semantic type. In M. Rosner & R. Johnson (Eds.), *Computational linguistics and formal semantics*. Cambridge: Cambridge University Press.

Partee, B., & Borshev, V. (2001). Genitives, relational nouns, and argument-modifier ambiguity. In C. Fabricius-Hansen, E. Lang, & C. Maienborn (Eds.), *Modifying adjuncts* (Interface explorations). Berlin: Mouton de Gruyter.

Pinker, S. (1989). *Learnability and cognition: The acquisition of argument structure*. Cambridge: MIT Press.

Pustejovsky, J. (1991). The generative lexicon. *Computational Linguistics, 17*, 409–441.

Pustejovsky, J. (1993). Type coercion and lexical selection. In J. Pustejovsky (Ed.), *Semantics and the lexicon*. Dordrecht: Kluwer Academic.

Pustejovsky, J. (1995). *The generative lexicon*. Cambridge: MIT Press.

Pustejovsky, J. (1998). The semantics of lexical underspecification. *Folia Linguistica, 32*, 323–348.

Pustejovsky, J. (2001). Type construction and the logic of concepts. In P. Bouillon & F. Busa (Eds.), *The syntax of word meaning*. Cambridge: Cambridge University Press.

Pustejovsky, J. (2005). Natural kinds in linguistics. In *Festschrift for Chungmin Lee*. Hankook Munhwasa Publishers.

Pustejovsky, J. (forthcoming). *Language meaning and the logic of concepts*. Cambridge: MIT Press.

Pustejovsky, J. (2011). Coercion in a general theory of argument selection. *Journal of Linguistics, 49*(6).

Pustejovsky, J., & Boguraev, B. (1993). Lexical knowledge representation and natural language processing. *Artificial Intelligence, 63*, 193–223.

Putnam, H. (1975). *Mind, language and reality* (Philosophical papers, Vol. 2). Cambridge: Cambridge University Press.

Rosch, E. (1975). Cognitive representations of semantic categories. *Journal of Experimental Psychology: General, 104*(3), 192–233.

Searle, J. (1995). *The construction of social reality*. New York: Free Press.

Van Valin, R. (2005). *Exploring the syntax-semantics interface*. Cambridge: Cambridge University Press.

Weinreich, U. (1972). *Explorations in semantic theory*. The Hague: Mouton.

Chapter 3
A Type Composition Logic for Generative Lexicon

Nicholas Asher and James Pustejovsky

3.1 Introduction[1]

Recent work in discourse semantics has focused on modeling the determinants of meaning for linguistic utterances beyond the level of a single clause. As more parameters of interpretation have been incorporated into our model of meaning, the assumption sregarding compositionality have become much more complex (cf. Groenendijk and Stokhof 1990; Kamp and Reyle 1993; Asher 1993; Asher and Lascarides 2003). Similarly, at the level of the clause, richer notions of composition and lexical structure have surfaced to explain the systematic variation in meaning involved in polysemies and polymorphisms (cf. Nunberg 1995; Moravcsik 1975; Pustejovsky 1995; Copestake and Briscoe 1995; Jackendoff 1997). This tradition in lexical semantics argues that we need a notion of composition for which, combining the meanings of two words may result in a change to those meanings themselves. We concentrate here on one problem in particular, that of *copredication*, where apparently incompatible types of predicates are applied to a single type of object. As argued in Nunberg (1995), Pustejovsky and Boguraev (1993), and Copestake and Briscoe (1995), to handle such cases some context-sensitive notion of composition is needed, which is not what one finds in the standard theory of

---

[1]This work forms the basis for more extensive discussion of the Type Composition Logic, presented in Asher (2011), and its application in Pustejovsky (2006, 2011).

N. Asher (✉)
CNRS, Toulouse, France

Department of Philosophy, University of Texas, Austin, TX, USA
e-mail: nasher@bertie.la.utexas.edu

J. Pustejovsky
Department of Computer Science, Brandeis University, Waltham, MA, USA
e-mail: jamesp@cs.brandeis.edu

J. Pustejovsky et al. (eds.), *Advances in Generative Lexicon Theory*, Text, Speech and Language Technology 46, DOI 10.1007/978-94-007-5189-7_3,
© Springer Science+Business Media Dordrecht 2013

compositionality exemplified in classical Montague Grammar (Montague 1973). We believe these shifts in meaning during composition to be a matter of lexically-governed shifts in *semantic type*—in a manner similar to earlier work on "type shifting" (Partee and Rooth 1983; Klein and Sag 1985; Hendriks 1993). In this paper, we develop a method of composition that adds to the contents contributed by lexical elements when certain word meanings combine. At the end of this paper, we extend our method to treat other phenomena like the *qualia* that Moravcsik (1975) and Pustejovsky (1991, 1995) introduced to explain phenomena that are difficult to account for on a simple context-insensitive method of building sentence meanings.

In a similar vein, recent advances in discourse interpretation have furnished a way of integrating pragmatics and semantics together into a context sensitive theory of discourse interpretation. SDRT is one such approach (Asher 1993; Lascarides and Asher 1993; Asher and Lascarides 2003); exploiting the rhetorical function of information, it introduces a context-sensitive method of calculating the *discourse update* of a discourse with new information—viz., new information may be added to the context in a number of different ways reflecting distinct rhetorical functions. In the pair of examples in (1), for example, two very different rhetorical functions create coherent interpretations, but with different temporal and causal structures:

(1)   a. John entered. Max greeted him.
      b. John fell. Max pushed him.

The interpretation of *Narration* in (1a) is consistent with the updates and lexical information associated with *enter* and *greet*. This relation is not consistent with (1b), however, while the relation *Elaboration* is.

Both GL and SDRT are reactions to theories of the lexicon and discourse update (i.e., an atomistic Fodorian lexicon (Fodor and Lepore 1998), and standard dynamic semantics, respectively), that fail to account adequately for a wide variety of phenomena having to do with the pragmatics/semantics interface. What earlier theories lack is an account of how the "composition" of new information in context could in fact alter the information as well as the elements in the context, in ways not predictable within a framework countenancing only operations like *lambda conversion* or *merge*. GL and SDRT make this the core of their approach to meaning.

Broadly speaking, context-sensitive approaches to both lexical composition and discourse interpretation have a common view about meaning, some of the same formal tools, and some of the same problems. GL and SDRT both use nonstandard formalisms to compute logical forms, for which model theoretic interpretations can be supplied. SDRT makes use of a special purpose "glue" logic with limited access to various information sources for building up logical forms of discourses from underspecified logical forms for clauses. This glue logic has a limited and partial access to the information content of discourse constituents, Asher and Fernando (1997) and Asher and Lascarides (2003) argue, because full access to information content would render the task of computing logical forms hopelessly complex. Though we do not believe all of linguistic understanding should necessarily be computationally simple, computing logical forms, which is the prerequisite to any deeper understanding, should be a simple matter. This in turn leads to a strong distinction in SDRT between information available to the linguistic system, of which the glue logic is part, and nonlinguistic information or world knowledge. This separates SDRT and us from competing approaches (e.g., Hobbs et al. 1993), which assume that a general purpose reasoning system makes no distinctions between linguistic and nonlinguistic knowledge.

The distinction between lexical and world knowledge as made in GL has strong linguistic motivation, as argued in Pustejovsky and Boguraev (1993), Jackendoff (2002), and Moravcsik (1998). The task of a lexicon is, at the very least, to supply the semantic material introduced by each word into the logical form of a clause. We suppose further that this information must be capable of model theoretic interpretation though we will not examine any of those details here. Secondly, this information must be able to combine compositionally, insofar as this is possible, to yield the logical form for a clause. There are constraints, or selectional restrictions, involved in this information that the lexical entry for each word must carry. For instance, the verb *weigh* takes a degree phrase or something denoting a quantity of weight as its second argument while its first argument must be a physical object of some sort. The verbs *recount* or *describe*, on the other hand, cannot take *merely* physical objects as first arguments. The fact that these verbs cannot take arguments of a certain kind leads to semantic anomaly when we attempt to violate these constraints, as can be seen from the examples below '!' indicates for us semantic anomaly.

(2)   !Bob's idea weighs five pounds.

(3)   !Bob's sack of fertilizer recounts the events leading up to the Civil War.

Hence, one can view the semantic component of a lexical entry as consisting of one part determining the model-theoretic content and another part carrying information that enables it to combine with other bits of lexical information to give a meaning for a whole clause. This latter sort of information should state constraints about the types of arguments the lexical entry either requires or introduces in the logical form.

Typed unification grammars and type calculi are the two main frameworks in which to carry out such a project in a way consonant with current approaches to syntax. GL's rich approach to lexical meaning was originally couched within a unification like framework (Pustejovsky 1995), but many of the formal mechanisms were not spelled out in complete detail. One of our tasks here is to provide some of those details. We believe that a natural deduction style type calculus with complex types of the sort we present here is quite suitable to this task. This approach is inspired by Howard's (1980) seminal paper and the topic of current work in polymorphic typed calculi (Amadio and Curien 1998; Crole 1993) (see also Crouch and van Genabith 2000). Thus, as in Montague Grammar and other standard frameworks, we will take a lexical entry to consist in a lambda term and a type assignment to the variables in the term. This will then determine via the standard interpretation for the lambda term a functional type for the whole expression. Unlike Montague Grammar, however, our *type composition logic* (TCL) will have a much richer system of types reflecting the information conventionally associated with a word in the GL approach, and correspondingly more complex rules for manipulating these types. Like SDRT's glue logic, the type composition logic builds up logical forms; but the composition logic builds up clausal logical forms (CLFs), whereas SDRT's glue logic builds discourse logical forms (DLFs) from CLFs. Like the construction of DLFs, the process for constructing CLFs is also quite simple. But again like SDRT's glue logic, the type composition logic has partial access to common sense information or world knowledge, which ultimately determines the compatibilities and incompatibilities between semantic types. With partial access to common sense knowledge, the type composition logic can exploit this information in guiding shifts in type during semantic composition more efficiently. Nevertheless, word meaning is distinct from non-linguistic or world knowledge at least in form and scope. Metaphysical information is drastically simplified into conventionalized type information; as a result, the type composition logic will be a drastically simplified reflection of certain ontological principles that underlie general reasoning. Hence, SDRT's approach to computing logical form will thus be reflected in the type composition logic for GL developed in this paper.

While SDRT's approach to discourse meaning and GL's approach to lexical meaning share many features, we believe it is important, to keep discourse interpretation and lexical semantic modules distinct. Many people have advocated dispensing with this distinction, where one general purpose pragmatic engine handles all reasoning operations homogeneously (e.g., Hobbs et al. 1993). We believe this approach is misguided for two reasons. First, the glue logic and the type composition logic have very different tasks. The type composition logic primarily checks the lexical type assignments in applying one lambda term to another and resolves type conflicts when they arise, as in cases of type coercion and co-composition. SDRT's glue logic, on the other hand, resolves elements left underspecified by lexical elements in the compositional process; it computes the optimal attachment points for new information in a discourse structure as well as the rhetorical roles for this information. The second reason for keeping lexical and discourse processes distinct is that the two systems interact in subtle and interesting ways, and merging these two modules would make it more difficult to formulate these distinctions systematically. Discourse structure and context, for example, can obviously affect lexical interpretation in context. Here we see an example of how it affects "logical metonymy".

(4)   The goat hated the film but enjoyed the book.

Depending on whether the context is a fairy tale or not, (4) will convey the same or different sense of *enjoy* as that assumed in (5).

(5)   The boy hated the film but enjoyed the book.

That is, discourse context can alter types: in a fictional interpretation, goats can become talking, thinking and reading agents, thereby assuming characteristics that they would not normally have, due to their sortal typing. Thus, conventional and lexical associations such as those encoded in the interpretation for (5) can be overturned by new or more specific information in a particular discourse context.[2] Furthermore, lexical ambiguities can be resolved by discourse in ways that override lexical preferences (Asher and Lascarides 1995).

In this paper, we begin to explore generally the integration of GL and SDRT processes, the problems that such an integration faces, and what advantages it might offer. Specifically, we concentrate on developing the type composition logic required to model one of the complex types of GL, for which we employ the various SDRT principles and strategies we've already outlined. As we are interested in the composition of information to construct logical forms, we will build on the standard way of getting logical forms, namely, the lambda calculus in which functional types are exploited. By relating types in the lexicon we can give partial, implicit definitions, which will help together with how the items compose, to determine inferences based on truth conditional contents. Secondly, by developing a strongly typed theory of lexical items and a theory of how such lexical items combine and interact in the process of semantic composition and of discourse interpretation, we can constrain the lexical semantics with predictions of semantically well-formed or ill-formed predications and word combinations. We outline a new type calculus that captures and extends one of the fundamental ideas of GL: providing a set of techniques governing type shifting possibilities for various lexical items so as to allow for the combination of lexical items in cases where there is an apparent type mismatch. These techniques themselves should follow from the way the lexicon is organized and its underlying logic.

3.2 Polysemy and Sense Extension

While the Generative Lexicon is perhaps best known for its development of the notion of *qualia* (based on Moravcsik's 1975 interpretation of *aitia*) another enrichment to the type system proposed in the Generative Lexicon is a complex type introduced to explain *copredications* in the context of polysemy. Copredications involve two or more predications on the same object. Many syntactic constructions give rise to copredications—relative clauses, and small clauses, for instance—but the classic cases of copredication are those that involve coordinated verbs or verb phrases as shown below.

---

[2]For a fuller discussion and a theory of this interaction using default unification and the glue logic DICE of SDRT see Asher and Lascarides (1995) or Lascarides and Copestake (1995).

(6)   a. <u>The book</u> was a huge pain to lug home and turned out to be very
          uninteresting.
      b. Mary picked up and mastered <u>three books on mathematics</u>.
      c. <u>The bottle</u> has a nice label and is a merlot.
      d. <u>The temperature</u> is ninety and rising.
      e. <u>Lunch</u> was delicious but took forever.
      f. <u>The bay</u> curves from the lighthouse to a sandy spit and is lovely to
          swim in.

The copredications that interest us involve predicates that select for two different, even incompatible types. In GL the underlined nouns receive a complex type; the so-called *dot objects* of GL first introduced by Pustejovsky (1994) are, in effect, best understood as objects of a particular complex type with two constituent types. The constituent types pick out aspects of the object, and the object's complex type reflects the fact that it may have several, distinct, even incompatible aspects. The term *dot object* thus refers to objects with a complex type (*not* to complex objects— whatever those might be—or to pairs of objects),[3] with several aspects, which have become part of the meanings of the words that denote such objects. Such dot objects allow for predications that are licensed over either of the two dot element types (see Pustejovsky 1995, 1998 for details).

Another mark of dot objects and the copredications that interest us is that neither typing required by each of the coordinated verbs or verb phrases of (6) fits fully comfortably as a dependent type of the other. For example, the verb *pick up* types its object as physical, whereas the verb *master* types its object as informational. Similarly, the figure and ground aspects inherent in the meaning of *bay*, like the physical aspect and informational aspect of a book are mutually interdependent; you cannot have one without the other. The intuition is that copredication requires these two types to be accessible *simultaneously* during composition; the function of dot objects is to make this possible.[4]

---

[3] Here the notation of earlier work on dot objects suggested these interpretations; but our approach here is resolutely different from those older attempts at description. We are very explicit that • is a type constructor and has nothing to do with the construction of a complex object.

[4] Not all copredications need involve dot objects. Some may exploit events that are conventionally associated with the types of the subjects, like those described in qualia structure. In (7), for example, it appears as though some predicates make reference to aspects having to do with the so called telic qualia role of the subject NP they are predicating i.e., the smoking and drinking events, respectively.

(7)   a. <u>Arnold's cigar</u> is Cuban and lasted the whole afternoon.
      b. <u>Your last glass of wine</u> was a Merlot and lasted half an hour.

Hence, copredication does not uniquely identify NPs typed as dot objects. Similarly, it is unclear whether *grinding* operations, which also license copredications, should be analyzed as

There are of course constraints on what dot objects can be formed. We see this when copredications become odd, zeugmatic or just unacceptable. Thus, as in (8) below, we see that contrastively ambiguous words (Pustejovsky 1995) do not introduce a dot object, where two distinct senses are simultaneously accessed. Hence, such words cannot support copredications.

(8)   !The bank specializes in IPO's and is being quickly eroded by the river.

On the other hand, we see that many words appear to give rise to complex types, though not all copredications are equal (cf. (9b)). We believe that this has to do with the fact that a dot object's existence may depend not only on commonsense metaphysical intuitions, that are conventionalized as typing information in the lexicon, but also on discourse context and the rhetorical connections between the two predications.[5] For example, a noun such as *newspaper* denotes an object that has both physical and informational characteristics and so would have a complex type consisting of the type of physical objects and the type of informational objects. *newspaper* actually can denote a related entity, the organization that produces the objects of physical • informational type, but this type doesn't combine very well with the physical type, as copredications like (9b) are semantically anomalous, even though copredications involving the organization *as an agent* and the information in the newspaper are acceptable (9c).[6]

(9)   a. The Sunday newspaper weighs 5 lbs and documents in depth the economic news of the week.
       b. !The newspaper was founded in 1878 and weighs 5 lbs.
       c. The newspaper contains some really useful information about restaurants and concerts but publishes a lot of useless junk as well.

What these examples demonstrate is the polysemous (and apparently polymorphic) nature of nouns such as *newspaper*. A dot object is a packaging of both types, reified through a coherence relation as one complex type, with the ability to exploit aspects of its type structure in diverse predicative contexts.[7]

---

involving dot objects, type-changing operations, or involve the exploitation of lexical information from the qualia structure. See Pustejovsky (1995) for discussion.

[5]The felicity of copredications often depends on the order of the predications as well. This again we feel is due to discourse factors. We don't go into this here, as it would involve bringing in too much of the SDRT framework, obscuring our restricted aim here to provide a type composition logic. In any case, we will keep such rhetorical constraints on felicitous copredications with dot objects separate from the composition logic.

[6]As a result, such concepts are actually double dot objects, but we ignore this point for now, cf. Pustejovsky 1995.

[7]We note as well that such types may be subject to discourse effects like parallelism; for instance, (9b) improves if we shift the second event to the past:

(9b')   The newspaper was founded in 1878 and weighed 5 lbs in its first edition.

An alternative approach to these cases of copredication is not to postulate complex types for the argument of the predicates, but rather to change the types involved in the individual predications. Thus, we might try changing the type of the verb *document* so that it takes a physical object as a subject, but the verb phrase means roughly "instantiates an informational object that documents in depth the economic news of the week."[8] This approach, however, runs into immediate trouble, because we can't explain then why such a type shift works only with certain arguments, which on this view are all of some simple type. While newspapers, books, and theories can document something in the relevant sense, walls, windows, flowers, rocks and trees cannot. This selectivity is immediately explained, however, if we require all arguments of *document* to be of, or to have as a constituent type, the informational type. Under this analysis the verbs do not shift; and since *document* requires an informational object as its subject, sentences like *The wall documented the news of the week* will not yield a felicitous logical form because of the typing mismatch. On the other hand, certain nouns like *newspaper* introduce lambda terms whose main variable has a complex type containing both informational and physical types as constituents. In predication, *newspaper*'s type can be adjusted to one of its simpler constituent types so that the types match and predication succeeds. This is not to say of course that verbs *cannot* undergo type shifting; verbs of creation such as *bake* do appear to have distinct but related meanings, depending on the exact nature of their arguments. However, the copredications that we are interested in cannot be treated adequately by shifting the types of the predicates.

Copredications involving relative clauses and adjectival modification also sometimes require their arguments to be of complex type. For example, as pointed out in Pustejovsky (1998), some lexical items denote both an event and a participant in this event, as with the noun *dinner*. Both aspects of this complex type may be predicated, as witnessed in the sentence below.

(10)   John stopped by during our delicious dinner.

The preposition *during* selects for a temporal object of type event or interval, while *delicious* selects a comestible substance. The noun *dinner* satisfies both these typing restrictions by virtue of its type, namely, its status as a dot object denoting both event and substance.

Further, we have evidence that this information is so far conventionalized that it even affects the case system in some languages. There is considerable consensus

---

But we will not attempt to integrate such discourse effects with our story about complex types here.

[8] Klein and Sag (1985) take this approach to multiple subcategorization phenomena. However, as discussed in Pustejovsky (1995), type-shifting the predicate in such cases does not change the basic meaning of the predicate, but only the surface typing. Both Klein and Sag's analysis of *believe* and Godard and Jayez's (1993) treatment of coercion predicates involve meaning postulates to relate verb senses. The alternative analysis here is similar to the sense transfer operation proposed in Nunberg (1995). As we see, however, this is an inappropriate use of transfer.

that languages distinguish types for places (fixed elements in the terrestrial reference frame) and types for objects (elements that have a complex internal structure and can move with respect to the terrestrial reference frame). Evidence for these distinct types comes from Dutch, for example, where there are special pronouns for referring to locations.[9]

(11)   a. Dat is een mooi weiland.
            Daarin houd ik mijn koeien.
            *In het houd ik mijn koeien.
        b. That's a nice field.
            Therein I keep my cows.
            *In it I keep my cows.

Further evidence for this distinction comes from Basque, where the grammar encodes differences between location and objects via two genitive cases -*ko* and -*ren*; locations in general easily take the genitive -*ko* but not -*ren*, while objects in general do the reverse (Aurnague 2001). Aurnague (2001) distinguishes the following sortals: *places* (e.g., valley, field, river, mountain, hill), *objects* (e.g., apple, glass, chair, car), and *mixed objects* (e.g., house, church, town hall). Of particular interest are the "mixed objects" and the behavior of their expressions in Basque: they readily accept both forms of the Basque genitive. So if we accept the encoding hypothesis for Basque, mixed objects would appear to belong to two types, or two ontological categories, at the same time, PLACE and PHYSICAL-OBJ, neither of which is a subtype of the other (it is neither the case that the properties associated with physical objects are inherited as properties of places nor that the properties associated with places are inherited as properties of physical objects).

(12)   Maite dut etxe<u>ko</u> atea ha<u>ren</u> paretak harriz eginak direlariak.
        (Michel Aurnague p.c.)
        I like the door of the house the walls of which are made of stone.

More motivating data for the existence of dot objects comes from the following minimal pairs, involving quantification over different aspects of the meaning of the nouns *book* and *question*. Consider the sentences below.

(13)   a. The student *read* every book in the library.
        b. The student *carried* off every book in the library.

(14)   a. The teacher *answered* every student's question.
        b. The teacher *repeated* every student's question.

---

[9]This point is due to Melissa Bowerman, pc.

The quantification over books in (13) is sensitive in one case to its informational aspect, and in the other to its physical aspect. In (13a), we simply quantify over all informationally distinct individuals without reference to the instantiations of these informational units; it is not necessary, for example, for the student to have read every distinct copy of every book in the library. In (13b), however, every physical individual must have been taken in order to be true. Similar remarks hold for the distinction in (14b): an answer to the same question posed on multiple occasions will count as an answer to each question; this is not the case with the act of repeating the question, however, since this refers to copying the speech act rather than providing the informational content of the answer.

One might think that a simple account of these examples would just involve coercing *book* to be, in some cases, a physical object, and in other cases, an informational one. Such an analysis, however, makes it difficult to explain the copredication data. Furthermore, as with the construction in (10) above, we need access to both types simultaneously, in order to explain the predications for cases such as (15) and (16) below.

(15)   John's mother burned the book on magic before he mastered it.

(16)   Mary bought a book that contradicts everything Gödel ever said.

Since the verb *master* in (15) involves selecting for the informational sense of book, we cannot "use up" the dot object *book* when predicating burning of it in the first sentence. Otherwise we will be unable to bind the anaphor in the second clause; alternatively, if we try to coerce the object of *master* back to an informational object, we get a typing conflict with the typing requirements of *burn*).

In addition to copredication constructions, there are other grammatical and lexical devices that introduce or select dot objects. Pustejovsky (1998) argues that the verb *read* is a predicate that requires a dot object as its complement; it can even coerce its direct object into something of just this complex type, namely, an informational entity with physical manifestation.

(17)   a. Mary read the book.
         b. John read the rumor about his ex-wife.
         c. Mary read the subway wall.

The coercion phenomenon in (17) involves a subtle shift in meaning. One can hear rumors and spread rumors, which one cannot do with books (even if you're listening to a book on tape); on the other hand, one can't see or look at rumors whereas one can see or look at a book. On the other hand, one can see a subway wall or look at it, without getting any informational content. However, in (17b, c) the arguments of *read* change their meaning. For instance, (17c) implies that the subway wall is a conveyor of information, and the only way to understand (17b) is to assume that the rumor has been printed or exists in some physical medium. One explanation of this phenomenon is that *read* coerces its arguments into objects of the same type as *book*. For both (17b) and (17c) the predicate coerces its complement to the appropriate type, that of an informational object with physical manifestation. In each of these cases, there is a "missing element" to the complex type: for (17b) the coercion effects the introduction of the physical manifestation to the otherwise informational type; for (17c) the coercion results in the introduction of an informational component to an otherwise merely physical type.

Barbara Partee has suggested (p.c.) that one might handle the quantificational ambiguity seen above with *read* and *carry off* by treating the entire phenomenon as an instance of the type/token distinction. According to this suggestion, (13a) makes reference to the type while (13b) refers to the token. While not discounting this approach completely, there appear to be two problems with this solution. First, simply reducing the above phenomenon to a type/token distinction does not solve the problem of how the copredication works; if the type/token suggestion were right, we could envision using that distinction along with our dot object apparatus in the analysis, but without the latter, it is not clear what the analysis would be. Furthermore, there are cases where reference seems to be made to more objects than are available under a simple type/token analysis. For example, in (18b), quantification is over informational tokens that are distinct from the actual physical object tokens that would be available.

(18)   a. John hid every Beethoven 5th Concerto score in the library.

         b. John mastered every Beethoven 5th Concerto score in the library.

Hence, for a dot object, if there are type and token interpretations available for each component type of the dot, then the underlying typing is more complex than originally countenanced.

One final argument against a type/token distinction for cases of dot object subselection can be seen in examples such as (19) below.

(19)   a. John has stolen every book there is.

         b. Frances has grown every wildflower in Texas.

While there are (improbable) interpretations exploiting the token reading of the quantified expression in each example above, the type interpretation is more felicitous. However, the interpretation of the generalized quantifier in (19a) makes clear that the type reading of *every book* is distinct from the informational content interpretation of the dot object in sentence (13). That is, the verb *steal* selects for physical instantiations of kinds of books. This is the true "kind interpretation", but it is distinct from that seen with the exploitation of part of a dot object from the verb *read* in (13).

We will re-examine much of these data from the perspective of the type composition logic we develop, later in the paper. First, however, we wish to turn to the metaphysical picture suggested by complex types and what in general should be the relation between commonsense metaphysics and the lexicon.

3.3   Constraints on the Mapping to Semantics

Thus far, we have seen evidence that common sense metaphysics and contextual factors constrain the construction of complex types—that is, which arguments we consider as having a complex •-type or, equivalently, of being dot objects. Common sense metaphysics informs lexical semantics by providing the basic types and basic relations between types. It also acts as one constraint on whether certain complex types are admissible (discourse context is another). The general metaphysical picture is that objects of complex type have non-necessarily spatio-temporal parts or aspects to them that fall under the simple types that are constitutive of the complex type. The information encoded in metaphysical categories is "lifted" conventionally into the type structure and then exploited in semantic composition. Predication, the application of a property to an object, may sometimes be restricted to a particular aspect of an object, something known in scholastic philosophy as *qua predication*, where philosophers speak of an X qua Y as having the property *P*. We think that such restricted predication need not be overtly marked in ordinary language, though it can be (see Asher 2004). When we need to look only at one aspect of a (dot) object of complex type, we assume that the predication involving the simple aspect is an "object-elaboration" of the dot object—it's elaborating on one aspect of the object.[10] For short, we will call this link *O-Elab*. O-Elab is a not necessarily physical, antisymmetric and transitive proper-part-of relation.[11]

The way predications behave actually tells us something about the metaphysical relation between aspects and things that have them. Aspects are mysterious, metaphysical beasts—they are some sort of individual trope perhaps. From the perspective of lexical semantics, however, aspects are atoms, and objects of •-type are just mereological sums of their aspects; •-types are hence idempotent, associative and commutative. We'll assume in addition that x is of type σ and y is of type τ and we have $O\text{-}elab(z,x)$ and $O\text{-}elab(z,y)$, then $x = y$; i.e. parts of an object singled out for predication that are of the same aspect are identical.

There is a further connection between commonsense metaphysics and the lexicon, but it is not a direct one. Metaphysics permits the construction of some complex types but not others. We represent this simply as a condition in the composition logic as, $\diamond x\colon \sigma \bullet \tau$, which states that it is consistent with information sources that are relevant to the lexicon, for the variable x to have the complex type $\sigma \bullet \tau$. This imposes, in effect, a *fence* or filter from commonsense metaphysics to lexical information.[12] One reason to distinguish commonsense metaphysics from the lexicon is that metaphysics is only one contributory factor to the logic of

---

[10]The name is intended to evoke an analogy to a similar relation in discourse. But the development of that analogy is for another time.

[11]In Asher (2004), the O-Elab relation is assumed to be asymmetric, but the work that is supposed to do there is perhaps better explained on pragmatic grounds than by stipulating a strange part of relation.

[12]For more on fences and their usefulness in discourse semantics, see Asher and Fernando (1997).

composition. Clearly both syntax and morphology contribute to the construction of semantic argument structures, while discourse context can also affect the semantic types in the lexicon. Hence, the fence $\diamond x: \sigma \bullet \tau$ may also function as a purveyor of information from context.

Our main reason for distinguishing between the lexicon and metaphysics is to distinguish the conventional aspects of word meaning from general world knowledge. If the lexicon is distinct from metaphysics, we open up the possibility that complex types only attach to some words and not others. Conventions will decide what words introduce complex types and what those complex types are. We will show how to account for such cases below in detail, but our point here is that by distinguishing metaphysics from the lexicon, we can both maintain that something like a person may have many aspects that are not part of the lexical entry. For instance, Nicholas Asher may have an aspect of which he is a philosopher, to which we can refer in language by means of the *qua* construction: *Nicholas as a philosopher* (Asher 2004). Nevertheless, there is no evidence that such aspects enter into the dot types for lexical entries.

But of course word meaning, at least the typing information that we are interested in, also in some sense reflects the way the world is and our commonsense metaphysics. The way we distinguish between lexical meaning and world knowledge is primarily a difference in the way this knowledge is presented. The type language of the lexicon is less expressive than that of commonsense metaphysics. The lexicon simplifies information that percolates up to it from commonsense metaphysics in many ways. First, type information is quantifier free, whereas it is hard to imagine any formalization of commonsense metaphysics doing without quantification—typically such formalizations exploit higher-order quantification. A second way our type logic will be simpler is that it will exploit type hierarchies, in which for instance incompatibilities are already precomputed (given by metaphysics). This makes the knowledge of the meaning of words much simpler and computationally much easier; and further, as our composition logic will use some default rules, the simplicity of the basic language is technically needed to make our logic tractable at all. Building logical forms, which is what we are trying to account for, should be relatively easy; it is, after all, a minimum standard of semantic competence for speakers of a language. Building logical forms is different and easier than grasping their full content.

3.4 A Type Composition Logic for GL

3.4.1 The Type Language

In the discussion above, we presented the notion of the complex •-type and related notions. We now need a logic for manipulating these types that will allow us to construct logical forms for interpretation that capture the motivating data from the first section. The data our logic addresses are those that arise from the process of combining meanings. In general this means building a logical form for an entire discourse, thus combining both the type composition logic and the glue logic; we will concentrate on the composition logic here, leaving the interactions with discourse contexts for another venue (see, however, Lascarides and Copestake 1995).

Our logic extends the lambda calculus for functional types with rules for manipulating •-types. These types resemble conjunctive types, and our natural deduction rules for exploiting and introducing them will resemble something like conjunction elimination and introduction. We need sometimes to exploit these complex types when a predicate applies to only one aspect of an object of complex type. But our rules are quite a bit more complicated than the introduction and elimination rules for simple conjunctive types, as they add material to logical form, as well as revise the types of variables. The reason for this is that when we predicate something of an aspect of a thing, we need to encode the information in logical form that the aspect is an aspect of some particular object—we don't want to lose that information since we may refer back to the object or the aspect of it in future discourse.

Besides these rules, we will assume the presence of a type hierarchy with a subtyping relation $\sqsubseteq$ that defines a partial order on the set of types and a greatest lower bound operation $\sqcap$ on the set of types. $\sqcap$ has the usual properties—e.g., idempotence, associativity, commutativity, and $\alpha \sqsubseteq \beta$ iff $\alpha \sqcap \beta = \alpha$. We will capture incompatibility between types in terms of their common meet, $\perp$.

Our type language takes as fundamental the notion of a term together with a typing context or type assignment that our rules can revise or extend. A typing context for a term t determines an assignment of types to all subterms of t. A term together with a typing context represents all the information contained in a typed feature structure. Our rules manipulate these type assignments. Our logic of the lexicon and of logical form construction at the clause level is like that of unification (Carpenter 1992) and other forms of logic manipulating types (Morrill 1992; Hendriks 1993); its complexity is no worse than simple unification, given that its operations are all driven by type adjustments and information about types in the lexicon.

This is not the only way one could go about implementing a composition logic to account for GL representations. Since most of the work on coercion and other generative operations has used the framework of typed feature structures together with the operation of unification (Pustejovsky 1995; Pustejovsky and Boguraev 1993; Copestake and Briscoe 1992; 1995), one might ask why we are proposing a new formalism. But as we have already argued, there are conceptual and computational advantages for our decision. As regards unification, the operation of unification is an efficient way of representing the replacement of one element with another that is determined to be more specific via some partial ordering. But with coercion, subselection, and co-composition, we must *transform* types during semantic composition.

Coercions and co-compositions can be captured via lexical rules (Godard and Jayez 1993; Copestake and Briscoe 1995). Such rules allow us to rewrite given feature structures as new ones. But this approach has several drawbacks. First, these rules allow us to change feature structures in an arbitrary way, whereas for us coercion is precisely the exploitation of something already in the given type structure. Such lexical rules don't discriminate between destructive type shifts like grinding (as in *Rabbit is good to eat and is all over my windshield right now*) and the ampliative inferences that are part of logical metonymy and copredication. In the latter, we *add* information about objects that are the typical denotata of the expressions involved. In the system of type rules to be introduced below, these two types of rules will be distinguished. Logical metonymy and copredication involve ampliative rules like dot and qualia exploitation. Type structures with these rules are not transformed; they are preserved but trigger the addition of new information to logical form. Finally, our framework allows a more flexible relation between world knowledge and the lexicon than that for unification. While head types are typically stable, we imagine that values for qualia structures may be highly contextually dependent, and as such we may be able to form such types dynamically in discourse. Given the standard treatment of qualia structure, these are taken to be universal features in typed feature structures and so are much more rigidly construed.

3.4.2   The Set of Types

We will first define the set of types for the logical system in general terms. We will assume there are *simple* types and complex types, *dot types*, for which we'll use the type forming operator • and functional types for which we'll use the type forming operator $\multimap$ to distinguish this from the material implication $\rightarrow$.

(20)   a.   PRIMITIVE TYPES: e the general type of entities and $\underline{t}$ the type of
              truth values. Below σ, τ range over all simple types, the subtypes of e
              as well as $\underline{t}$.[13]
       b.   FUNCTIONAL TYPES: If σ and τ are types, then so is $(\sigma \multimap \tau)$.
       c.   DOT TYPES: If σ and τ are types, then so is $(\sigma \bullet \tau)$.

We assume that the lexicon contains a library of types that determines the type for each lexical item. This library may also evolve as the discourse proceeds, in ways that we will not explore in detail for the present discussion.

The subtyping relation $\sqsubseteq$ affects functional types in the following way. The functional type from a more specific type of object α into β is itself a subtype of the functional type from α' into β' if α is a subtype of α'. Formally this means that: if $\alpha \sqsubseteq \alpha'$, then $(\alpha \multimap \beta) \sqsubseteq (\alpha' \multimap \beta)$. We also will assume that if $\beta \sqsubseteq \beta'$, then $(\alpha \multimap \beta) \sqsubseteq (\alpha \multimap \beta')$. Similar subsumption relations hold for the complex •-types.

Our Type Composition Logic (TCL) has the usual lambda terms familiar from compositional semantics, together with a set of type assignments, of the form $t\!: \sigma$

---

[13]The details of the relationship between e and its subtypes, as a join semi-lattice, in the simple type domain are spelled out in Pustejovsky (2001,2011).

where σ is some type and t is some term. Constraints on types will also be available; for instance, we may need to know that σ is a subtype of τ, something we express as $\sigma \sqsubseteq \tau$ or that two types are compatible, which we write as $\sigma \sqcap \tau \neq \bot$. We also have (minimal) information about syntactic structure that we will exploit in our rules; for instance, we will have a formula *head* ψ, where ψ is a term telling us that ψ is derived from some projection of the head or the head itself of the syntactic structure whose meaning we are currently trying to build up. We'll discuss this in more detail below. We also need our "fence" formula from discourse context and metaphysics $\Box x\colon \sigma \bullet \tau$. Most likely we will need formulas that allow us to put constraints on what types variables may be, like the reentrancy equations of unification, but we will not use such rules in the present paper.

In order to introduce the specific characteristics of the composition logic, let us examine what is involved in type coercion and subselection phenomena involving a dot object, i.e., a $\bullet$-type. Consider, for example, the compositional interpretation of the noun phrase in (21).

(21)   a heavy book

The interpretation of interest is predication of the book *qua* physical object as being heavy. Let us suppose that the adjective *heavy* is understood as an intersective adjective and so yields the lambda term in (22).

(22) $\lambda P \lambda x[\text{heavy}(x) \wedge P(x)]$

where x:PHYSICAL-OBJECT, or $x : p$ for short, is the type assignment to x. This of course implies that P is assigned type $p \multimap t$. The adjective phrase itself has type $(p \multimap t) \multimap (e \multimap t)$. This must combine with the semantic expression for *book* to create a full noun phrase in the DP analysis of syntax that will then combine with the determiner. Let us suppose that *book* introduces a predicate whose argument is conventionally determined to be an object with both a physical and an informational aspect. Thus, it yields the term $\lambda v \text{book}(v)$ together with the typing context $x :$ physical $-$ object $\bullet$ information, or $x : p \bullet i$ for short. This implies that $\lambda v \text{book}(v)$ has type $(p \bullet i) p \multimap t$. This, however, presents us with a type clash between the adjective's type and the noun's type; that is, we cannot combine these two lambda terms via lambda conversion because the type of the lambda abstracted variable P and the term that is to replace P don't match. Three questions arise in the context of this mismatch. First, should we make a type adjustment? If so, where should the type adjustment in this construction take place, on the type of the adjective itself, on the noun, or on some lower variable?[14] Finally, what sort of type adjustment should be made?

The first question has an obvious answer: since a phrase like *heavy book* is clearly felicitous, some sort of type adjustment should be made to allow lambda conversion

---

[14]Classic GL analyses (Bouillon 1997; Pustejovsky and Boguraev 1993; Pustejovsky 1995) have argued that adjectival subselection selects for a particular qualia role or the corresponding type for a quale within the feature structure of the nominal semantics. That is, they are typed to modify the particular qualia role of the noun in a specific construction. We compare this analysis to the present one below.

to take place so as to construct a logical form for the NP. For the second question there also seems to be a principled answer, which we state below as (23). The idea of (23) is that the syntactic head of any environment X should determine the typing of X. To be more precise, let's first define a *type clash* between two constituents A and B to occur whenever: if A is function that is supposed to apply to B, then the greatest lower found of the type τ of lambda abstracted variable in A and the type of B is $\perp$ or if B is function that is supposed to apply to A, then the greatest lower found of the type τ of lambda abstracted variable in B and the type of A is $\perp$. For example, A and B will have a type clash, when A is $\lambda x F x$ where $x : p$ and B is y where $y : i$ and $p \sqcap I = \perp$. Next, let's define the *tail* of any functional type $\alpha \multimap \beta$ to be β.

(23) **Head Typing Principle:** Given a compositional environment X with constituents A and B, and type assignments A: α and B: β in the type contexts for A and B respectively that clash, if A is the syntactic head in the environment, then the typing of A must be preserved in any composition rule for A and B to produce a type for X.

This means that in the case of (21), we should adjust the adjective's type, given that the noun is the relative head in the construction. Similarly, when we combine a DP in object position with a governing verb to form a VP or a VP or NP with an adjoined modifying phrase, we want the verb's categorization to affect the way the NP is interpreted, given our principle that the head of the category should win out. For subjects of a sentence, given the Head Typing Principle, we need to establish what the head of the IP is. If we take standard $\bar{X}$-syntax as our guide, it is the inflection node which introduces an event to saturate the VP, which is its complement. By Type Accommodation, the result will then have the type phys $\multimap t$. So the Head Typing Principle tells us that we must change the type of the subject DP in order for it to conform to the typing of the I'.[15] It appears as though the VP's type will win out, forcing us to change the type of the subject if there is a type clash. Finally, for coordinate constructions, the Head Typing Principle doesn't determine how types should adjust, but a slight extension of it would dictate that in coordinate constructions *both* coordinated constituents will undergo a typing change. Thus, coordinate constructions may give rise to the introduction of complex •-types, each coordinated constituent supplying one of the constituent types to the complex type.

The Head Typing Principle dictates where we should make typing adjustments, should there be conflicts involving the type of a complement and the selectional context within which it appears. But what should those adjustments be? If we go back to our metaphysical underpinnings, then what complex types allow us to do is to predicate properties of aspects of individuals. But if an aspect of a thing exists, then the thing itself must exist as well; in this respect, aspects differ from parts.

---

[15]Results are largely equivalent if we choose HPSG as our syntactic guide; there the verb will be the lexical head and will once again force us to change the NP's type.

So in retyping a variable to represent an aspect of a thing, we should also have a variable representing the thing itself, and we need to make sure that we link the variable representing the aspect to the variable representing the thing via our parthood relation, O-Elab. Thus, type adjustments with complex •-types typically add more information into the logical form; that is, our type inferences actually change the formula.

The last issue concerns which of the two variables we need to be the argument to the predicate. For instance, for (21), we want to say that it is the physical aspect of the book that is heavy, but we don't want this type to percolate up into the main predication. So we introduce a new variable of complex type that is the argument of the property variable and that will end up being the argument to *book*, and we close the variable typed PHYS off existentially in the lambda term for *heavy* before the adjective and the noun combine. Formally for (21), this amounts to rewriting the lambda term for the adjective as:

(24) $\lambda P \lambda y \exists z[\text{heavy}(z) \wedge O - \text{elab}(z, y) \wedge P(y)]$

where the typing context for the formula is, $z : \text{phys}$, $y : p \bullet i$. By adjusting the type of the argument of P, the adjectival phrase can now combine with the translation of the noun phrase, carrying the appropriate typing on the head variable. It turns out that conjoining this information with the predicate variable P in either the DP or adjectival phrase gives the quantificational closure just the right scope. If we follow our principle that the head type should be preserved on the main argument, then the proper treatment for (21) must introduce a dot typed variable within the adjectival phrase. This leads us then to posit two sorts of rules, a rule of •-Exploitation, and a rule of •-Introduction. In each case we will want to rewrite the term whose type needs to be changed in the way we've just discussed.

Type conflicts involving a complex dot type and a constituent type may occur not only when we attempt to apply a quantifier or property of properties to a property as in (21), but also when we apply a higher order property to a quantifier. We will state the rules for each of these cases in the discussion that follows.

3.4.3   The Basic Rules for Type Composition Logic

In our discussion above, we've seen how the type composition logic may change the types of terms during the construction of a logical form. Thus, our rules may call for the revision of a type context; when a type context is revised with the assignment $t : \alpha$, which we write as $c * (t : \alpha)$, then the revised context contains $t : \alpha$ and all the types of terms that involve t have their functional types changed accordingly. If t does not occur in c then $c * (t : a)$ just extends c with the assignment of a to t; i.e., $c * (t : a) = c + (t : a)$. $c(t : a)$ simply means that the type assignment c includes the assignment of a to t. We'll write $c + c'$ to denote the merging of two typing contexts or the extension of c by c'.

With this notation out of the way, we now introduce the rules for our Type Composition Logic (TCL). As usual a lambda expression denotes a functional type, i.e., a $\alpha \multimap \beta$ type. Such rules should be understood as reduction rules, thereby giving rise to equivalent term expressions. Application is defined in terms of a context, c, which provides typing assignments to both the variable in the applicand and the argument.

(25) **Application:**
$$\frac{\lambda x \phi[t], \quad c(x : \alpha, t : \alpha)}{\phi[t/x], c}$$

In terms of the type calculus itself, application corresponds to a rule of modus ponens for $\multimap$. The type calculus of course also has lambda abstraction which corresponds to a rule of conditional proof for $\multimap$.

The contexts that accompany the rule of Application and other operations may be updated or combined, as the result of a rule being applied. We will refer to this rule as *Merging Contexts*. We will write {.} braces around the function and [.] brackets around the argument for readability.

(26) **Merging Contexts:**
$$\frac{\{\lambda x \phi, c\}[t, c']}{\lambda x \phi[t], (c + c')}$$

This is a bookkeeping rule and does not really correspond to any properties of any of the type constructors.

As with the types available in the type semi-lattice from the lexicon (cf. Pustejovsky 1995; Copestake and Briscoe 1992), we have the rule of *Type Accommodation*. Type accommodation covers what results in type unification, in which a supertype can unify with a subtype yielding the subtype as the result. This rule allows us to shift the types in the case of compatible types, which we write as $\alpha \sqcap \beta \neq \perp$, to the meet of the two.

(27) **Type Accommodation:**
$$\frac{\lambda x \phi[t], c(x : \alpha, t : \beta), \quad \alpha \sqcap \beta \neq \perp}{\lambda x \phi[t], c * (x, t : \alpha \sqcap \beta)}$$

Type Accommodation corresponds to a limited strengthening of the antecedent for $\multimap$ (limited, because Type Accommodation works only when we are to trying to apply one term to another). By the axiom on the subsumption relation, Type Accommodation applies to higher functional types defined from simple types that stand in the proper subtyping relations. For instance, if a determiner of type $(e \multimap t) \multimap ((e \multimap t) \multimap t)$ takes a physical property as an argument—i.e. something of type $(plimpt)$, then the axiom on subtypes will tell us that being a physical property is a subtype of being a property, and Type Accommodation will adjust the type of the determiner to $(p \multimap t) \multimap ((e \multimap t) \multimap t)$. This will allow us then to use Application to combine the meaning of the determiner and the physical property.

3.4.4 ● Types and Dot Objects

As discussed above, there are strong motivations for enriching the domain of entity types. In addition to simple types of e and its associated semi-lattice of subtypes, we introduced the domain of dot objects (●-types). In this section we develop the rules allowing us to exploit a ●-type during composition.

Let us look again at a representative example of a type mismatch involving a dot object, where the subject is a complex type and the predicate selects for one of the constituent types. Consider the predication in (28) below.

(28)   The book is heavy.

The Head Typing Principle tells us that we have to change the type of the subject DP, while the type of the VP remains unchanged. Confirmation of the Head Typing Principle comes from this implication about changing the type of the DP. To see why, suppose that the quantification in the DP in (28), and more importantly in (29) is over dot objects. Suppose that we assert (29) in a context in which some books from the library have been stolen and others borrowed.

(29)   Every book is now back in the library.

Suppose in addition that there are five copies of *Anna Karenina*, six copies of *The Possessed* and four copies of *Madame Bovary* but only one copy of each has been returned. Assuming that the head of the construction is the subject DP and universally quantifying over dot objects implies that (29) is true in that case. Indeed dot objects are difficult to "count", but it seems that we can individuate at least some of them, viz. books, in terms of the individuation conditions of either constituent type. Our intuitions, however, dictate that (29) is neither ambiguous nor indeterminate but false in this context. To avoid such "sloppy" individuation conditions, we need to resort to simple types. The Head Principle dictates that we need to type the DP in (29) so that it quantifies over physical objects. If we quantify over every physical book in the library, then this will make (29) false in the context we have specified. This means that we need to shift the type of the DP so that it has a simple type by shifting the type of the head variable in the DP; i.e., if our DP looks like

(30) $\lambda P \forall x (\psi \rightarrow P(x))$

where x has a complex type, then we need to shift the type of x, and that will in turn shift the type of P to the appropriate type.

In fact if we attend to the Head Typing Principle and to the lexical categories elements of which may type their arguments as having a complex or simple subtype of e (the type of all entities), then we can get an idea of exactly what sort of exploitation rules we need for complex types. Lexical elements that fall under the determiner (D), inflection (I) or Adverb (Adv) categories may impose type requirements on their arguments but they do not involve complex types, as far as we have been able to determine. Hence, our rules will not apply to type conflicts between a determiner and its complement NP, or between an Inflection morpheme and its complement VP, for example. The categories whose elements do have selectional restrictions involving complex types are verbs, nouns, adjectives and prepositions. The Head Typing Principle dictates that our rules must change the types in the cases of type clash that interest us of: DPs when combining with a verb or VP, DPs when combining with a preposition, and adjectives when combining with an NP. It turns out that for all of these cases, we need only two sorts of rules: one where an argument to a DP meaning forces a shift in the DP's meaning, and one where a functor taking a DP meaning as an argument forces a shift in the meaning of the DP. The case we just considered is one where a DP argument forces a shift in the DP meaning. Below we consider cases of the second type.

Let us now formalize these observations. For an expression, ϕ, in which there is a λ-bound property variable whose type is a function from objects of a complex type to objects of some other type, we will suppose that the property variable in ϕ takes an argument x that is of complex type, something we will write as $\lambda P \phi(P(x))$. We introduce a new existentially bound variable v with type $\alpha \bullet \beta$ and replace x with v within the part of the predication, call it Δ, in ϕ that is responsible for the original typing of x. Intuitively, Δ is the main predication in ϕ. We also shift the type of x to a constituent type of the $\bullet$-type, thus changing the property variable's type to be a function of type α or β. Finally, we add the relevant parthood connection between x and v to Δ by conjoining to Δ, $O\text{-}elab(x, v)$. To this end, we designate $\Delta(\phi, x)$ to be the smallest subformula of the term ϕ containing predications responsible for assigning x the type it has in ϕ and such that no predications in ϕ outside of $\Delta(\phi, x)$ impose that complex typing on x. Given this definition $\Delta(\phi, x)$ must be a formula with x free, since neither quantification nor lambda abstraction imposes any typing requirements on the variables they bind. Furthermore, $\Delta(\phi, x)$ will not include the property variable itself, since it inherits its type from its argument x, not the other way around. This allows us to make our variable substitution, to retype x, and to add the $O\text{-}elab$ condition without any problem. To illustrate Δ, we look to some particular constructions. For instance, in the case of the logical form for a simple, adjectival phrase, Δ would constitute the material contributed to the lambda term from the adjective, as we saw in the previous section. In the case of a DP, Δ would be the formula in the restrictor of the generalized quantifier logical form.

We can now state this version of $\bullet$-Exploitation with a pair of substitutions, which look like the expression, $\chi\{\frac{\phi}{\psi}\}$. One other bit of notation has to do with the square brackets; they represent an application that hasn't yet taken place. That is with $P[x]$ we haven't yet applied the property that P stands for to x; similarly the lambda expression with its typing context, $[\psi, c']$ hasn't yet been integrated with the lambda expression with its context on its left. We enclose the complex expression that is to apply to $[\psi, c']$ in curly brackets to help for readability. Below $\phi(P[x])$ represents the fact that the property variable P is to apply to x in the expression ϕ, and ψ : $\begin{bmatrix} \alpha' \\ \beta' \end{bmatrix} \multimap \gamma$ represents the fact that ψ is typed either as $\alpha \multimap \gamma$ or as $\beta \multimap \gamma$. In this rule and the following rules concerning $\bullet$-types, we will assume that $\alpha \sqcap \alpha' \neq \bot, \beta \sqcap \beta' \neq \bot$.

(31)   •-**Exploitation (•E):**

$$\{\lambda P\phi(P(x)),\ c(P:(\alpha\bullet\beta)\multimap\gamma)\}\left[\psi,\ c'(\psi:\begin{bmatrix}\alpha'\\\beta'\end{bmatrix}\multimap\gamma)\right],\text{head}(\psi)$$

$$\overline{\left\{\lambda P\phi\left[\frac{\exists v(\Delta(\phi,x)[\frac{v}{x}]\wedge O-\mathrm{Elab}(x,v))}{\Delta(\phi,x)}\right],\ c*\left(x:\begin{bmatrix}\alpha\sqcap\alpha'\\\beta\sqcap\beta'\end{bmatrix},v:\alpha\bullet\beta\right)\right\}[\psi,c']}$$

•-Exploitation does two things; it adds material to the logical form of the lambda term to which it applies and it also revises the type contexts to reflect a shift in the typing of some of the variables in the altered lambda term. If we look just at what happens to the type for x, •-Exploitation corresponds to something like a conjunction elimination rule for •-types, but it is more complicated than that since it forces us in reintroduce a variable of •-type. It is in fact an *ampliative* rule.[16]

Let us look at an example of •E at work. Consider the sentence in (28), where the VP in effect predicates only of the physical aspect of a $p\bullet i$.[17]

1. $[[\text{the}]]=\lambda Q\lambda P\exists x(Q[x]\wedge P[x]),\langle P,Q:e\multimap\underline{t},x:e\rangle$[18]
2. $[[\text{book}]]=\lambda v\text{book}(v),\langle v:p\bullet i\rangle$
3. $[[\text{the book}]]=\lambda Q\lambda P\exists x(Q[x]\wedge P[x]),\langle P,Q:e\multimap\underline{t},x:e\rangle\,[\lambda v\text{book}(v),\langle v:p\bullet i\rangle]$
4. As $e\sqcap(p\bullet i)=p\bullet i$, by Accommodation, which revises the typing context, we get:

   $\lambda Q\lambda P\exists x(Q[x]\wedge P[x]),\langle P,Q:(p\bullet i)\multimap\underline{t},x:p\bullet i\rangle\,[\lambda v\text{book}(v),\langle v:p\bullet i\rangle]$
5. Now we use Application and Merging Contexts to get a term for *the book*:

   $\lambda P\exists x(\text{book}(x)\wedge P[x]),\langle x:p\bullet i,\ P:(p\bullet i)\multimap\underline{t}\rangle$
6. The logical form for *is heavy*, and the interpretation in this sentence is the following: $\lambda u\text{heavy}(u),\ \langle u:p\rangle$
7. The syntax dictates:

   $\lambda P\exists x(\text{book}(x)\wedge P[x]),\langle P:e\multimap\underline{t},x:p\bullet i\rangle\,[\lambda u\text{heavy}(u),\ \langle u:p\rangle]$
8. By•-Exploitation:

   $\{\lambda P\exists x(\exists v(\text{book}(v)\wedge O-\mathrm{Elab}(x,v))\wedge P[x])\,\langle v:p\bullet i,x:p\rangle\}[\lambda u\text{heavy}(u),\langle u:p\rangle]$

---

[16]For some cases we may have to treat the existential quantifier on v as having its force determined by the original over x. As in DRT, we would have to treat such quantifiers over x as unselective. The cases we have in mind would be those where ϕ is of the form $Qx(\psi(x),\chi(x))$, and both restrictor and nuclear scope have material that is responsible for typing x originally as being of complex type. We will not deal with this complexity here.

[17]This effectively replaces the *Dot Object Subtyping* rule, $\dot{\Theta}^{llet}$, as developed in Pustejovsky (1995) pp. 150–151.

[18]We assume for illustration purposes that the computation will accommodate the presuppositions of definiteness locally in the composition.

9. By Merging Contexts and Application,

$$\exists x\,(\exists v(\text{book}(v)\land O-\text{Elab}(x,v))\land\lambda u\text{heavy}(u)[x]),\,\langle x:p,\,u:p,\,v:p\bullet i\rangle$$

10. By Application:

$$\exists x\,(\exists v(\text{book}(v)\land O-\text{Elab}(x,v))\land\text{heavy}(x)),\quad\langle v:p\bullet i,x:p\rangle$$

The rule of •-Exploitation lets us take any modifier of a noun that would force a dot type (the adjective *readable* would be one such example) and apply it to a noun with a simple type that is the constituent of the modifier's type. We could then combine the two together to get a noun phrase of the simple type as required. Thus if we have a sentence such as (32) below:

(32) John turned off every readable screen.

our rule will produce a noun phrase that looks like the following, before the determiner meaning is applied:

(33) $\lambda x(\exists v(\text{readable}(v)\land O-\text{Elab}(x,v)\land\text{screen}(x)),\langle x:p,v:p\bullet i\rangle$

When the determiner meaning is applied, we will get a quantification over all physical screens, which is what is intuitively required.

Our rule of •-Exploitation makes the quantification over objects of the constituent types always have scope over the quantification over objects of • type. But is this right? Consider for instance, the following.

(34) Three books by Tolstoy are heavy.

Following the derivation above, we would get a logical form for this sentence according to which on a distributive reading there are three physical aspects p_1,p_2,p_3 each of which have to satisfy the formula $\exists v(\text{book by Tolstoy}(v)\land O-\text{Elab}(x,v))$, where $x:p$ and $v:p\bullet i$, and each of which are heavy. Nothing in our semantics forces the three aspects to be part of the *same* book. In fact, quite the opposite. Our semantics for O-elab makes such an interpretation incoherent, for if we have O-elab(p_1,b) and O-elab(p_2,b), $p_1=p_2$, which contradicts the meaning of the quantifier. In our semantics of O-elab, this subformula of the logical form of (34) can only be satisfied if there is a distinct book for each distinct physical aspect. Though there is a collective reading of the DP(the three books together are heavy), our semantics precludes having a collective reading of the formula in the restrictor of the quantifier.[19] Thus, we end up predicting that (34) is true only if there are three distinct books each with its own physical aspect that is heavy. Because of the particular dependency of aspects on the substances to which they belong, there is a quantificational dependency between variables for aspects and variables ranging over the substances of which they are parts.

---

[19]For details on how such distributive and cumulative readings together are possible, see Asher and Wang 2003.

There is one other case of •-exploitation to consider, namely, the one where the complex type/simple type conflict occurs between an expression that has a generalized quantifier as an argument and a generalized quantifier. This is the second type of rule we alluded to above. This could occur for instance when a verb types its argument as a physical object but the noun in the complement types its argument as a complex type, say $p \bullet i$. This situation can be illustrated by the following example.

(35)   John's mother <u>burned</u> the book on magic before he <u>mastered</u> it.

The verb *burn*'s object argument must be a physical object, and as the Head Typing Principle dictates, although the object DP enters the composition with type $p \bullet i$, there must be some way to coerce it into having the right type, to satisfy the typing context and thereby allow the λ-conversion from the verb to go through. The way we do this is to apply a kind of •-Exploitation on the generalized quantifier to coerce it into the right type.

Let us look at the details. In (35), we see a problem with the typing of the expressions we are trying to compose (recall that p (physical-object) in this context is a subtype of e in the semi-lattice structured domain of entities, i.e., $p \sqsubseteq e$):

(36) $\lambda \mathcal{P} \lambda w \mathcal{P}[\lambda u(\mathrm{burn}(w, u))], \langle \mathcal{P} : (p \multimap \underline{t}) \multimap \underline{t}, u : p, w : p \rangle$

$[\lambda P \exists x (\mathrm{book}(x) \wedge P(x)), \langle P : (p \bullet i) \multimap \underline{t}, x : p \bullet i \rangle]$

Because we are not changing the sense of the predicate in any way (that is, *burn* should still mean *burn*) it is undesirable to change the type of the variable $\mathcal{P}$ over DP denotations; rather, we want to change the type of the object itself. In that case, •E won't apply directly, but we can invoke a type shifted version of it, which we call •-Exploitation^{TS} (•E^{ts}). As before, we assume $\alpha \sqcap \alpha' \neq \bot, \beta \sqcap \beta' \neq \bot$.

(37)   **•-Exploitation:**^{TS}

$$\frac{\left\{ \lambda \mathcal{P} \phi, c(\mathcal{P} : \left(\left[{\alpha' \atop \beta'} \right] \multimap \gamma \right) \multimap \delta) \right\} [\lambda P \psi(P[x]), c'(P : (\alpha \bullet \beta) \multimap \gamma)], \mathrm{head}(\phi)}{\left\{ \lambda \mathcal{P} \phi, c \right\} \left[\lambda P \psi \left\{ \frac{\exists v(\Delta(\psi, x)\{\frac{v}{x}\} \wedge O - \mathrm{Elab}(x, v))}{\Delta(\psi, x)} \right\}, c' * \left(v : \alpha \bullet \beta, x \left[{\alpha \sqcap \alpha' \atop \beta \sqcap \beta'} \right] \right) \right]}$$

The type shifted version of •-Exploitation applies to (35'), and we can now rewrite the object DP so that λ-reduction can take place, as illustrated below.

(38) $\lambda \mathcal{P} \lambda w \mathcal{P}[\lambda u(\mathrm{burn}(w, u))], \langle \mathcal{P} : (p \multimap \underline{t}) \multimap \underline{t}, u : p, w : p \rangle [\lambda P \exists x$

$(\exists v(\mathrm{book}(v) \wedge O - \mathrm{Elab}(x, v)) \wedge P[x]), \langle P : p \multimap \underline{t}, x : p, v : p \bullet i \rangle]$

Applying *Merging* and *Application*, we get the following expression:

(39) $\lambda w \, \lambda P \, \exists x (\exists v(\mathrm{book}(v) \wedge O - \mathrm{Elab}(x, v) \wedge P[v]))[\lambda u(\mathrm{burn}(w, u))],$

$\langle P : p \multimap \underline{t}, x : p, v : p \bullet i, u : p, w : p \rangle$

We can now continue the λ-reductions with Application to get:

(40) $\lambda w \exists x \exists v (\text{book}(v) \wedge O - \text{Elab}(x, v)) \wedge \text{burn}(w, v), \langle w : p, x : p, v : p \bullet i \rangle]$

When we apply this to the subject DP, we get the desired reading: namely, that the physical manifestation of the book has been burned, though the dot object book remains for discourse binding. Given the Head Typing Principle, we do not need any other •-Exploitation rules.

3.4.4.1   •-Introduction

Whereas •-Exploitation merely selects as an argument a constituent type of a •-type to facilitate application, sometimes predicates will force the introduction of a variable of • type. This happened in our discussion of the phrase *a heavy book*. As illustrated earlier, a verb such as *read* can also select a dot object (17a) or coerce a lower type to dot object status (17b–c).

(17)   a. Mary <u>read</u> the book.
        b. John <u>read</u> the rumor about his ex-wife.
        c. Mary <u>read</u> the subway wall.

The mechanism for performing this shift is already implicit in our •E rule. To turn that rule into a • introduction rule, we need merely to readjust which variable is introduced and ends up being lambda bound, and which variable is existentially quantified over. Instead of existentially binding the dot-typed variable as in •E, we will existentially quantify over the constituent-typed variable, allowing the dot-typed variable to combine with its dot-typed property. This rule, •-introduction or •I, applies when the head of the construction is the argument (in the rule below the argument is ψ). Once again, we assume $\alpha \sqcap \alpha' \neq \bot, \beta \sqcap \beta' \neq \bot$.

(41)   •-**Introduction** (•**I**):

$$\frac{\left\{\lambda P\phi(P[x]), c\left(P: \begin{bmatrix} \alpha' \\ \beta' \end{bmatrix} \multimap \circ \gamma\right)\right\} [\psi, c'(\psi:(\alpha\bullet\beta)\multimap\circ\gamma)], \text{head}(\psi)}{\left\{\lambda P\phi\left[\frac{\exists v(\Delta(\phi,x)[\frac{v}{x}]\wedge O-\text{Elab}(v,x))}{\Delta(\phi,x)}\right], c*(v: \begin{bmatrix} \alpha \sqcap \alpha' \\ \beta \sqcap \beta' \end{bmatrix}, x:\alpha\bullet\beta)\right\} [\psi, c']}$$

•-Introduction is needed to construct the properly typed lambda term for (2), *a heavy book*. Recall that *heavy* has a logical form $\lambda P \lambda x (\text{Heavy}(x) \wedge P(x))$ where

$x : p$ and $P : p \multimap \underline{t}.book$ yields the term $\lambda v book(v)$ together with the typing context $v : p \bullet i$. Using $\bullet$-Introduction on the lambda term for *heavy* we get

(42) $\lambda P \lambda x \exists z((Heavy(z) \wedge O - elab(z, x) \wedge P[x]),$

where $x : p \bullet i\ z : p$ and $P : p \bullet i \multimap \underline{t}$.
This can now combine with the head noun *book* to give us:

(43) $\lambda x \exists z((Heavy(z) \wedge O - elab(z, x) \wedge Book(x))$

and this will combine with the determiner to give the right meaning for the whole DP.

The only other case we need to consider is where a higher order λ-abstracted variable carries the complex type and it is a head with respect to its argument. Such is the case in a sentence such as (44).

(44)   John read every wall.

In this example, the verb *read* takes a DP as its object that it must coerce into a dot type. This is done through a variant of the type shifted version of $\bullet$-Introduction. It looks very similar to $\bullet$-Exploitation^{TS}, and we'll assume once again that $\alpha \sqcap \alpha' \neq \bot$, $\beta \sqcap \beta' \neq \bot$.

(45)   **$\bullet$-Introduction with Type Shifting ($\bullet\mathbf{I}^{TS}$):**

$$\frac{\{\lambda \mathcal{P}\phi,\, c(\mathcal{P}:((\alpha\bullet\beta)-\diamond\gamma)-\diamond\delta) \left[\lambda P\psi(P[x]),\, c'\left(P:\begin{bmatrix} \alpha \\ \beta \end{bmatrix}-\diamond\gamma \right) \right],\, head(\phi)}{\{\lambda \mathcal{P}\phi,\, c\} \left[\lambda P\psi \left\{ \frac{\exists v(\Delta(\psi,x)\{\frac{v}{x}\}\wedge O - Elab(v,x))}{\Delta(\psi,x)} \right\},\, c' * \left(x:\alpha\bullet\beta,v:\begin{bmatrix} \alpha \sqcap \alpha' \\ \beta \sqcap \beta' \end{bmatrix} \right) \right]}$$

The rule of $\bullet$-I^{TS} transforms the logical form for the DP *every wall* into:

(44') $\lambda P\ \forall x[\exists v[wall(v) \wedge O - elab(v, x)] \rightarrow P(x)],\quad \langle x : p \bullet i,\ \ v : p \rangle$

The DP in (1) may now combine with the verb, while allowing the verb's argument type to win out and get the appropriate quantificational force from the DP, which is what is desired.

3.5   Conclusion

In this paper, we have outlined a type theoretic interpretation of Generative Lexicon Theory. This involved developing an extension to the lambda calculus, Type Composition Logic, with rules for exploiting and introducing complex types.

These rules suffice to handle much of the data about these types that has come to light in work on the Generative Lexicon. But we think there are many extensions to this work. Rules for complex types have already been shown to be useful in the analysis of indirect speech acts (Asher and Lascarides 2001). On the other hand, complex types and their exploitation have proved useful in reasoning about discourse structure (Asher and Lascarides 2003); verbs with a causative structure often yield complex types that support certain discourse connections. We think this work can also further be extended by extending the notion of complex types, beyond those we have considered here. For instance, a verb like *buy* may introduce in fact a complex type, in which one type of eventuality serves as a Background to the other. And the same anaphoric mechanisms for further specifying these types that we referred to earlier and discussed by Danlos (1999) might apply here:

(46)   Kim sold her truck. Sandy bought it.

By merging concerns of the lexicon with those of discourse interpretation together, we can explore these hypotheses further.

Acknowledgment We would like to thank Sheila Asher, Pascal Denis, Tim Fernando, Ivan Sag, Stan Peters, David Israel, Alex Lascarides, Ann Copestake, José Castaño, Roser, Saurí, and Johanna Seibt for helpful comments on earlier drafts. This work was partially supported by NIH Grant DC03660, to James Pustejovsky.

References

Amadio, R., & Curien, P. L. (1998). *Domains and lambda calculi*. Cambridge: Cambridge University Press.
Asher, N. (1993). *Reference to abstract objects in discourse*. Dordrecht: Kluwer.
Asher N. (2004). Things and their aspects, manuscript.
Asher, N. (2011). *The web of words*. Cambridge: Cambridge University Press.
Asher, N., & Fernando, T. (1997). Effective labeling for disambiguation. In *Proceedings of the second international workshop in computational linguistics*, Tilburg, The Netherlands.
Asher, N., & Lascarides, A. (1995). Lexical disambiguation in a discourse context. *Journal of Semantics, 1*, 69–108, Oxford University Press.
Asher, N., & Lascarides, A. (2001). Indirect speech acts. *Synthese, 128*, 183–228.
Asher, N., & Lascarides, A. (2003). *Logics of conversation*. Cambridge: Cambridge University Press.
Bouillon, P. (1997). *Polymorphie et sémantique lexicale: le cas des adjectifs*. Lille: Presses Universitaires du Spetentrion.
Carpenter, B. (1992). Typed feature structures. *Computational Linguistics, 18*, 2.
Copestake, A., & Briscoe, T. (1992). Lexical operations in a unification-based framework. In J. Pustejovsky & S. Bergler (Eds.), *Lexical semantics and knowledge reperesentation*. Berlin: Springer.
Copestake, A., & Briscoe, T. (1995). Semi-productive polysemy and sense extension. *Journal of Semantics, 15*.
Crole, R. (1993). *Categories for types*. Cambridge: Cambridge University Press.

Crouch, D., & van Genabith, J. (2000). *Linear logic for linguists*, ESSLLI-00 Course material manuscript.

Danlos, L. (1999). Event coherence in causal discourses. In P. Bouillon & F. Busa (Eds.), *The syntax of word meaning*. Cambridge: Cambridge University Press.

Fodor, J., & Lepore, E. (1998). The emptiness of the lexicon: Critical reflections on J. Pustejovsky's "The Generative Lexicon". *Linguistic Inquiry, 29*, 269–288.

Godard, D., & Jayez, J. (1993). Towards a proper treatment of Coercion Phenomena. In *Proceeding of the 1993 European ACL*.

Groenendijk, J., & Stokhof, M. (1990). Dynamic predicate logic. *Linguistics and Philosophy, 14*.

Hendriks, H. (1993). *Flexible Montague Grammar, LP-1990-09*. Logic, Philosophy and Linguistics (LP) Series: ILLC Publications.

Hobbs, J., Stickel, M. E., Appelt, D. E., & Martin, P. (1993). Interpretation as abduction. *Artificial Intelligence, 63*, 69–142.

Howard, W. A. (1980). The formulas-as-types notion of construction. In J. P. Seldin & J. R. Hindley (Eds.), *To H. B. Curry: Essays on combinatory logic, lambda calculus and formalism*. New York: Academic.

Jackendoff, R. (1997). *The architecture of the language faculty*. Cambridge: MIT Press.

Jackendoff, R. (2002). *Foundations of language*. Oxford: Oxford University Press.

Kamp, H., & Reyle, U. (1993). *From discourse to logic*. Dordrecht: Kluwer Academic.

Klein, E., & Sag, I. (1985). Type-driven translation. *Linguistics and Philosophy, 8*, 163–202.

Lascarides, A., & Asher, N. (1993). Temporal interpretation, discourse relations and commonsense entailment. *Linguistics and Philosophy, 16*, 437–493.

Lascarides, A., & Copestake, A. (1995). The pragmatics of word meaning. In *Proceedings SALT V*.

Levin, B., & Hovav, M. R. (1995). *Unaccusatives: At the syntax-lexical semantics interface*. Cambridge, MA: MIT Press.

Montague, R. (1973). The proper treatment of quantification in ordinary English. In K. Hintikka, J. Moravcsik, & P. Suppes (Eds.), *Approaches to natural language* (pp. 221–242). Dordrecht: Kluwer. (Reprinted in Thomason 1974, pp. 247–270).

Moravcsik, J. (1975). Aitia as generative factor in Aristotle's philosophy. *Dialogue, 14*, 622–36.

Moravcsik, J. (1998). *Meaning, creativity, and the partial inscrutability of the human mind*. Stanford: CSLI Publications.

Morrill, G. (1992). *Type-logical grammar*. Utrecht: Onderzoeksinstituut voor Taal en Spraak.

Nunberg, G. (1995). Transfers of meaning. *Journal of Semantics, 12*.

Partee, B., & Rooth, M. (1983). Generalized conjunction and type ambiguity. In S. Bäuerle & A. von Stechow (Eds.), *Meaning, use, and interpretation of language*. Berlin: Walter de Gruyter.

Pustejovsky, J. (1991). The generative lexicon. *Computational Linguistics, 17*, 409–441.

Pustejovsky, J. (1994). Semantic typing and degrees of polymorphism. In C. Martin-Vide (Ed.), *Current issues in mathematical linguistics*. Holland: Elsevier.

Pustejovsky, J. (1995). *The generative lexicon*. Cambridge, MA: MIT Press.

Pustejovsky, J. (1998). The semantics of lexical underspecification. *Folia Linguistica, XXXII*.

Pustejovsky, J. (2001). Type construction and the logic of concepts. In P. Bouillon & F. Busa (Eds.), *The Syntax of Word Meaning*.: Cambridge University Press.

Pustejovsky, J. (forthcoming). *Meaning in context: Mechanisms of selection in language*. Cambridge: MIT Press.

Pustejovsky, J. (2011). Coercion in a general theory of argument selection. *Journal of Linguistics, 49*(6).

Pustejovsky, J., & Boguraev, B. (1993). Lexical knowledge representation and natural language processing. *Artificial Intelligence, 63*, 193–223.

Chapter 4
Lexical Representation, Co-composition, and Linking Syntax and Semantics

Robert D. Van Valin, Jr.

4.1 Introduction

A fundamental issue dividing theories of the syntax-semantics interface is whether the semantic representation of clauses is projected from the lexical representation of the verb which determines to a large extent the syntactic structure of the clause or whether it is constructed or composed based on the NPs and PPs co-occurring with the verb in a clause; in the latter view, the verb has a very general or underspecified meaning. The empirical problem underlying this dispute concerns the ability of a single verb to occur in a variety of morphosyntactic contexts, as illustrated with the English verb *shatter* in (1).

(1) a. The window shattered.
     b. The burglar shattered the window.
     c. The burglar shattered the window with a crowbar.
     d. The crowbar shattered the window.
     e. *The window shattered with a crowbar.

This verb occurs as an intransitive verb in (1a), as a transitive verb in (1b–d), with an optional instrumental PP in (1c), and with an instrumental subject in (1d); the optional instrumental PP is only possible with the transitive version, as (1e) shows. Are the verbs in (1a–d) represented in distinct lexical entries in the lexicon, or is there a single lexical entry underlying all four uses? If there is only one lexical entry, then how are the various patterns to be accounted for? Are the four patterns

R.D. Van Valin, Jr. (✉)
Department of Linguistics and Information Science, Heinrich Heine University, Düsseldorf, Germany

Department of Linguistics, University at Buffalo, Buffalo, NY, USA
e-mail: vanvalin@ling.uni-duesseldorf.de

J. Pustejovsky et al. (eds.), *Advances in Generative Lexicon Theory*, Text, Speech and Language Technology 46, DOI 10.1007/978-94-007-5189-7_4,
© Springer Science+Business Media Dordrecht 2013

related by means of lexical rules? Or are they a function of an underspecified lexical representation plus the information supplied by the NPs and PPs in the clause?

The first approach mentioned above, which has been dubbed the 'projectionist approach,' has been advanced by Foley and Van Valin (1984), Pinker (1989), Levin and Rappaport Hovav (1994), Rappaport Hovav and Levin (1998), Van Valin (1993, 2005), and Van Valin and LaPolla (1997), among others, while the second, which has been termed the 'constructionist approach,' has been championed by Goldberg (1995), Pustejovsky (1995) and Michaelis and Ruppenhofer (2001), among others.[1] The two approaches have often been viewed as conflicting and incompatible with each other, but in this paper it will be argued that they are in fact complementary and therefore not necessarily in conflict with each other. In the discussion, the projectionist view will be represented by Role and Reference Grammar [RRG] (Van Valin 1993, 2005; Van Valin and LaPolla 1997) and its theory of semantic representation and theory of linking between syntax and semantics, and the constructionist perspective will be represented by the Generative Lexicon [GL] theory and in particular its notion of co-composition (Pustejovsky 1995, 1998).

The discussion will proceed as follows. In Sect. 4.2, two different verbal alternations will be presented, the activity-active accomplishment alternation and the causative alternation; in addition, the ability of the same forms to license optional PPs such as instruments and comitatives will be taken as a further issue for the two approaches. In Sect. 4.3, the RRG projectionist analysis of these alternations will be explicated, and then in Sect. 4.4 the GL analysis of them will be laid out. In Sect. 4.5 the two approaches will be reconciled with each other, and in Sect. 4.6 an RRG account of co-composition will be developed. Conclusions will be presented in Sect. 4.7.

4.2 The Verbal Alternations

4.2.1 The Activity-Active Accomplishment Alternation

The first alternation to be discussed concerns the atelic and telic use of activity verbs such as *run, walk, eat, drink,* and *write.* These two uses can be distinguished by their co-occurrence with the temporal adverbial PPs *for an hour* (atelic) and *in an hour* (telic). This is exemplified in (2)–(4).

---

[1]Rappaport Hovav and Levin (1998) contrast projectionist accounts with what they call 'constructional' approaches, which derive sentence meaning from a general verb meaning plus the meaning of the syntactic construction in which the verb occurs. The term 'constructionist' as used here is meant to cover both constructional approaches as well as other approaches which attempt to derive the meaning of sentences from the verb plus co-occurring elements, regardless of whether they posit constructional meanings or not. Goldberg (1995) and Michaelis and Ruppenhofer (2001) would be an example of the first approach, which may also be termed 'enriched compositionalist' (Jackendoff 1997), and Pustejovsky (1995) of the second.

(2) a. The soldiers marched (in the park) for an hour/*in an hour.   Atelic
     b. The soldiers marched to the park in an hour.[2]   Telic

(3) a. Sandy wrote (poetry) for an hour/*in an hour.   Atelic
     b. Sandy wrote the poem in an hour.   Telic

(4) a. Chris drank (beer) for an hour/*in an hour.   Atelic
     b. Chris drank the beer in an hour.   Telic

With atelic motion activity verbs, as in (2a), the locative PP is optional, and only *for an hour* is possible. When there is a goal PP, as in (2b), the verb behaves like a telic verb; the PP cannot be omitted, if the telic reading is to be maintained, and an *in* temporal PP is possible. With atelic creation activity verbs, as in (3a), the object is non-referential and omissible, and only a *for*-temporal PP is possible. When the object is specific or quantified, as in (3b), the verb behaves like a telic verb, and *in an hour* is possible. Finally, with a consumption activity verb, as in (4a), the object is likewise non-referential, just as in (3a), and only a *for* temporal PP is permitted. Again, as in (3b), when the object is specific or quantified, as in (4b), the verb behaves like a telic verb, and an *in* temporal PP may appear with it. In RRG, the telic uses of activity verbs are termed 'active accomplishments', and this term will be used hereafter to refer to the *Aktionsart* of the verbs in sentences like (2b)–(4b).

Early discussions of the alternations in (3) and (4) attributed the crucial difference to the referential status of the object NP, e.g. Verkuyl (1972), but if this were the case, then such an analysis would predict that the contrast observed in (3) and (4) would not be found in languages without articles indicating the referentiality of NPs. But this is not the case. In Russian and Georgian, for example, this contrast is signalled by changes in the verb, not by changes in the object NP. This is exemplified in (5) for Russian[3] and (6) for Georgian (Holisky 1981).

---

[2]With some of these verbs a *for* PP is possible, e.g. *The soldiers marched to the park for an hour*. However, the meaning here is either that the soldiers marched back and forth from somewhere to the park for an hour, which is an iterative, atelic reading, or it means that they marched to the park and stayed there for an hour, in which case the for PP modifies the result of the action and not the action itself. The crucial distinction is that the atelic uses of these verbs can only take *for* and not *in*, while the telic uses take *in*.

[3]Russian data are from Viktoriya Lyakh (personal communication).

(5) a. Ja   jë-l   (kaš-u)   decjat' minut.   Atelic
        1sgNOM eat.IMPF-PAST kasha-ACC ten   minutes
        'I ate (kasha) for ten minutes.'[4]

     b. Ja   s"-jë-l   kaš-u   za decjat' minut.   Telic
        1sgNOM PRFV-eat-PAST kasha-ACC in ten   minutes
        'I ate the kasha in ten minutes.'

(6) a. K'ac-i   (c'eril-s)   c'er-s   xuti saati.   Atelic
        man-NOM (letter-DAT) write.PRES-3sg five hours
        'The man is writing (letters) for five hours.'

     b. K'ac-i   c'eril-s   da-c'er-s   at c'ut-ši.   Telic
        man-NOM letter-DAT PRV-write.PRES-3sg ten minutes-in
        'The man will write the letter in ten minutes.'[5]

In both pairs of sentences, there is no difference in the coding of the direct object, despite the differences in interpretation. There is, however, a difference in the verb in both languages: the telic form of the Russian verb for 'eat', *jest'*, takes the prefix *s-*, and the telic form of the Georgian verb for 'write', *c'er-*, takes the preverb *da-*. In both languages, as in English, the object NP is optional with the atelic verbs but obligatory with the telic verbs.

Further examples can be found in languages from other parts of the world. The Amazonian language Pirahã (Everett 1986) has distinct telic and atelic suffixes for verbs, as illustrated in (7).

(7) (*xápiso*) *xaho-aí-*   'eat (bark)'   *xápiso xaho-áo-*   'eat the bark'
        (bark)   eat-ATELIC   bark   eat-TELIC

In some syntactically ergative languages, the base form of verbs like 'eat' and 'drink' appears to be telic, and in order to get the atelic reading, the verbs must be antipassivized. The examples in (8) are from Dyirbal (Dixon 1972), an Australian Aboriginal language, and the ones in (9) are from Sama (Walton 1986), a Philippine language.

---

[4]Abbreviations: ABS 'absolutive', ACC 'accusative', ANTI 'antipassive', COM 'comitative', DAT 'dative', ERG 'ergative', IMPF 'imperfective', IND 'indicative', INST 'instrumental', LOC 'locative case', MR 'macrorole', NFUT 'non-future tense', NM 'noun marker', NMR 'non-macrorole', NOM 'nominative', PAST 'past tense', PRES 'present tense', PRFV 'perfective', PRT 'particle', PRV 'preverb'.

[5]The reason this sentence has a future interpretation is that despite being present tense, it is also telic, which entails completion of the action. Since the action cannot be both in progress and completed at the moment of speaking, it is given a future interpretation. Also, in this sentence 'in ten minutes' refers to the length of time it will take to write the letter, not the length of the interval until the writing begins.

(8) a. Balam   wudyu-Ø baŋgul   yaṛa-ŋu   dyaŋga-ɲu.   Telic
         NM.ABS fruit-ABS NM.ERG man-ERG eat-NFUT
         'The man is eating the fruit.'

     b. Bayi   yaṛa-Ø   dyaŋgay-mari-ɲu   (bagum wudyu-gu).   Atelic
         NM.ABS man-ABS eat-ANTI-NFUT   NM.DAT fruit-DAT
         'The man is eating (fruit).'

(9) a. Inum na d'nda   kahawa.   Telic
         drink PRT woman coffee
         'The woman already drank the coffee.'

     b. N-inum   na d'nda   (kahawa)   Atelic
         ANTI-drink PRT woman   coffee
         'The woman is now drinking (coffee).'

In (8a) and (9a), the verb has a telic interpretation, the patient NPs are interpreted
as referentially specific, and they are obligatory. In the antipassive forms in (8b) and
(9b), the verb has an atelic interpretation, the patient NPs are interpreted as non-
referential, and they are omissible.

Thus, in all five of these languages the locus of the coding of the activity-active
accomplishment alternation is on the verb, not on the patient NP. Only in Dyirbal,
in which the patient shifts from absolute to dative case, is there any change in
the morphosyntactic coding of the patient, and it is not related to the referential or
quantification status of the NP. Hence the claim that this alternation is primarily
related to and signaled by the referential or quantification status of the object NP
is incorrect. In these five languages, changes in the marking of the verb results in
changes in the interpretation of the object NP.

4.2.2 The Causative Alternation

The basic causative alternation in English was illustrated in (1a, b), repeated in (10)
below.

(10)   a. The window shattered.
        b. The burglar shattered the window.

There are at least five ways the verbs in these two sentences could be related
to each other. First, one could claim that they are listed separately in the lexicon,
on the analogy of semantically similar pairs like *die* and *kill* which bear no
formal resemblance to each other. Second, one could claim that there is a single
representation in the lexicon which is underspecified for transitivity underlying both
forms (Pustejovsky 1995). Third, one could claim that there is an alternating stem
form from which the two are derived; in such an analysis, neither form is considered
to be basic (Piñón 2001). Fourth, one could claim that the transitive form in (1b) is

derived from the intransitive form in (1a) by a causativization rule, on the analogy of languages like Huallaga Quechua (Weber 1989); the operation of this rule is exemplified in (11).

(11)   a. *hatunya:-*   *hatunya:-chi-*
            become.big   become.big-cause
            'become bigger'   'make something bigger'
       b. *wañu-*   *wañu-chi-*
            die   die-cause
            'die'   'kill'
       c. *yacha-*   *yacha-chi-*
            learn   learn-cause
            'learn'   'teach'

Fifth, one could claim that the intransitive form is derived from the transitive form, on the analogy to languages like Russian, French and Yagua (Payne and Payne 1989), in which such a derivational relationship is explicit in the morphology of the two forms. This is sometimes referred to as the 'anticausative alternation'.

(12)   a. Russian   *razbit'* 'break [TR]'   *razbit'sja* 'break [INTR]'
       b. French   *briser* 'break [TR]'   *se briser* 'break [INTR]'
       c. Yagua   *-muta-* 'open [TR]' -   *muta-y-* 'open [INTR]'

In Russian and French the addition of reflexive morphology yields the intransitive equivalent of the transitive, causative verb, and in the Peruvian language Yagua the suffix *-y-* serves the same function. See Haspelmath (1993) for a cross-linguistic survey of the morphological patterns that verbs in this alternation exhibit. The English verbs that enter into this alternation do not show any morphological differences; they are often referred to as 'labile' verbs. Given this lack of any overt morphological derivation, it is not obvious which, if any, of these derivational analyses applies appropriately to the English situation.

It should be noted that these first two alternations can combine to generate up to four possible interpretations for a single English verb. Consider *march* in (13).

(13)   a. The soldiers marched in the field.   Activity
       b. The sergeant marched the soldiers in the field.   Causative activity
       c. The soldiers marched to the field.   Active accomplishment
       d. The sergeant marched the soldiers to the field.   Causative active
                                                             accomplishment

Since English marks neither alternation overtly, the questions raised in this section and the last apply jointly to the verb *march* and others like it.

4.2.3 Optional Instruments and Comitatives

The last issue to be discussed is the occurrence of optional instrumental and comitative PPs with certain verbs. The interaction of instrumental PPs with the causative alternation was shown in (1c–e), repeated in (14).

(14)   a. The burglar shattered the window with a crowbar.
       b. The crowbar shattered the window.
       c. *The window shattered with a crowbar.

The instrumental NP *crowbar* can appear with the transitive form of *shatter*, either as a part of an optional PP or as subject. It cannot, however, occur with the intransitive form of the verb. This raises the issue of what licenses the occurrence of an instrumental NP, especially as an optional PP. Similar issues arise with respect to comitative NPs, as shown in (15).

(15)   a. Chris and Pat went to the movies.
       b. Chris went to the movies with Pat.
       c. Pat went to the movies with Chris.

(16)   a. The gangster robbed the bank (together) with the corrupt policeman.
       b. The bank was robbed by the gangster (together) with the corrupt policeman.
       c. *The bank was robbed (together) with the corrupt policeman.

The NP in a comitative PP can also appear as part of a conjoined subject in sentences like (15). Here again there is an NP that can occur either in an optional PP or as subject.

The question that is relevant for this discussion is, how are these optional instruments and comitatives licensed? Are they adjuncts, in which case they are not directly tied to the verb's argument structure, or are they a kind of optional argument? If they are adjuncts, then how are (14c) and (16c) to be explained?

4.2.4 Summary

None of the alternations discussed in this section are normally coded on the verb in languages like English, but there are languages in which there are overt morphological indicators of the alternation. In the next section the relevant aspects of Role and Reference Grammar will be introduced along with an analysis of these phenomena. Then the Generative Lexicon co-composition analysis will be presented.

4.3   The Role and Reference Grammar Theory of Lexical Representation and Linking

Role and Reference Grammar is a monostratal theory of syntax which posits a single syntactic representation for each sentence, which is linked to a semantic representation by means of a set of linking rules called the linking algorithm. Discourse-pragmatics may play a role in the linking, but it will not be discussed in this paper. The organization of the theory is given in Fig. 4.1.

   The arrow on the linking algorithm is double-headed, because the linking system maps a semantic representation into the appropriate syntactic representation, and also maps a syntactic representation into the appropriate semantic representation.

4.3.1   Basic Principles of Role and Reference Grammar[6]

Little will be said about the nature of the syntactic representation in RRG, since the focus in this paper is on semantic representation and linking. Termed 'the layered structure of the clause', the syntactic representation of clauses is based on the set of semantic contrasts summarized in Table 4.1.

   An example of the layered structure of a simple English sentence is given in Fig. 4.2.

   The verb *show* is the predicate in the nucleus of the clause, and its three arguments, *Scully*, *the photo* and *Mulder*, are all arguments in the core of the clause. The two adjuncts, *at the office* and *yesterday*, occur in the periphery of the clause. Syntactic structures are stored as 'syntactic templates' in the syntactic inventory, and these templates are combined to create the structure of a sentence.

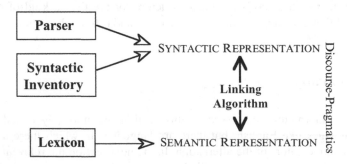

Fig. 4.1 The organization of Role and Reference Grammar

---

[6]Detailed presentations of RRG can be found in Van Valin (2005) and Van Valin and LaPolla (1997). A bibliography of work in the theory, along with copies of recent papers, dissertations and theses can be found on the RRG web site: http://linguistics.buffalo.edu/research/rrg.html.

Table 4.1 Semantic units underlying the syntactic units of the layered structure of the clause

Semantic element(s)	Syntactic unit
Predicate	Nucleus
Argument in semantic representation of predicate	Core argument
Non-arguments	Periphery
Predicate + arguments	Core
Predicate + arguments + non-arguments	Clause (=core + periphery)

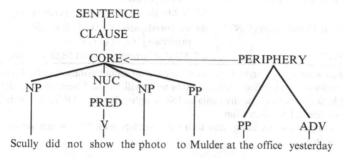

Fig. 4.2 The layered structure of the clause in English (Grammatical categories such as tense and negation, called 'operators' in RRG, are represented in a separate projection of the clause. It is not included, since it is not directly relevant to the topic of this paper. Also, the internal structure of PPs and NPs will not be represented unless relevant to the point at hand)

The semantic representation in RRG is built around the lexical representation of the predicate in the nucleus, which is an *Aktionsart*-based decompositional representation. The *Aktionsart* classes together with examples from English are given in (17).

(17) a   State: The boy is scared.
      a′ Causative state: The dog scares the boy.
      b. Achievement: The balloon popped.
      b′ Causative achievement: The cat popped the balloon.
      c. Semelfactive   The cane tapped on the tabletop.
      c′. Causative semelfactive   The man tapped the cane on
                                        the tabletop.
      d. Accomplishment: The ice melted.
      d′. Causative accomplishment: The hot water melted the ice.
      e. Activity: The soldiers marched in the field.
      e′. Causative activity: The sergeant marched the
                                          soldiers in the field.
      f. Active accomplishment: The soldiers marched to the field.
      f′. Causative active accomplishment: The sergeant marched the
                                          soldiers to the field.

Table 4.2 Lexical representations for *Aktionsart* categories

Logical structure	Verb class
STATE	**predicate´** (x) or (x, y)
ACTIVITY	**do´** (x, [**predicate´** (x) or (x, y)])
ACHIEVEMENT	INGR **predicate´** (x) or (x, y), or
	INGR **do´** (x, [**predicate´** (x) or (x, y)])
SEMELFACTIVE	SEML **predicate´** (x) or (x, y)
	SEML **do´** (x, [**predicate´** (x) or (x, y)])
ACCOMPLISHMENT	BECOME **predicate´** (x) or (x, y), or
	BECOME **do´** (x, [**predicate´** (x) or (x, y)])
ACTIVE ACCOMPLISHMENT[a]	**do´** (x, [**predicate₁´** (x, (y))]) & INGR
	predicate₂´ (z, x) or (y)[b]
CAUSATIVE	α CAUSE β, where α, β are LSs of any type

[a]The telic use of activity verbs is often classified as an accomplishment in the literature, and accordingly, a modified version of this term will be used here, despite the fact that the logical structure actually contains INGR rather than BECOME. See Van Valin (2005), section 2.1 for discussion

[b]'&' is a connective meaning 'and then'; it contrasts with '∧', which means 'and simultaneously'

The decompositions for the different *Aktionsart* categories are given in Table 4.2. These representations are called 'logical structures' [LSs].

Examples of verbs and their LSs from English are given in (18).

(18)   a. STATES

Pat is a fool.	**be´** (Pat, [**fool´**])
The window is shattered.	**shattered´** (window)
Kim is in the library.	**be-in´** (library, Kim)
Dana saw the picture.	**see´** (Dana, picture)

      b. ACTIVITIES

The children cried.	**do´** (children, [**cry´** (children)])
Carl ate pizza.	**do´** (Carl, [**eat´** (Carl, pizza)])

      c. ACHIEVEMENTS

The window shattered.	INGR **shattered´** (window)
The balloon popped.	INGR **popped´** (balloon)

      d. SEMELFACTIVES

Dana glimpsed the picture.	SEML **see´** (Dana, picture)
The light flashed.	SEML **do´** (light, [**flash´** (light)])

      e. ACCOMPLISHMENTS

The snow melted.	BECOME **melted´** (snow)
Mary learned French.	BECOME **know´** (Mary, French)

f. ACTIVE ACCOMPLISHMENTS
    Chris ran to the park.
> do´ (Chris, [run´ (Chris)]) & INGR be-at´ (park, Chris)

    Carl ate the pizza.
> do´ (Carl, [eat´ (Carl, pizza)]) & INGR consumed´ (pizza)

g. CAUSATIVES
    The dog scared the boy.
> [do´ (dog, Ø)] CAUSE [feel´ (boy, [afraid´])]

    The burglar shattered the window.
> [do´ (burglar, Ø)] CAUSE [INGR shattered´ (window)]

    Sam flashed the light.
> [do´ (Sam, Ø)] CAUSE [SEML do´ (light, [flash´ (light)])]

    Max melted the ice.
> [do´ (Max, Ø)] CAUSE [BECOME melted´ (ice)]

    Felix bounced the ball.
> [do´ (Felix, Ø)] CAUSE [do´ (ball, [bounce´ (ball)])]

    Mary fed the pizza to the child.
> [do´ (Mary, Ø)] CAUSE [do´ (child, [eat´ (child, pizza)]) &
> INGR consumed´ (pizza)]

The semantic representation of a clause is based on these LSs; a full representation contains information about operators like illocutionary force, tense, negative and aspect (see Van Valin and LaPolla 1997:171–2). The selection of the syntactic template for the core is determined by the following general principle (Van Valin and LaPolla 1997:173).

(19)   Syntactic template selection principle:
       The number of syntactic slots for arguments within the core is equal
       to the number of distinct specified argument positions in the semantic
       representation of the core.

There are a number of language-specific and construction-specific qualifications for this principle, but it underlies the projection of the syntactic structure of the clause from its semantic representation, as it determines which syntactic template is appropriate.

The semantic representation of nominals is based on the theory of nominal qualia proposed in GL in Pustejovsky (1991, 1995). Four qualia are posited: constitutive, which is the relation between an object and its constituents, or proper parts; formal, which distinguishes the object within a larger domain; telic, which is the purpose and function of the object; and agentive, which includes factors involved in the origin or creation of an object. Pustejovsky gives the following representation for the noun *novel*; the values of the qualia are given using the RRG representational system.

(20)   **novel** (x)
    a.   Const: **narrative´** (x)
    b.   Form: **book´** (x), **disk´** (x)
    c.   Telic: **do´** (y, [**read´** (y, x)])
    d.   Agentive: **artifact´** (x), **do´** (y, [**write´** (y, x)]) & INGR **exist´** (x)

Qualia may also be linked to argument positions in LSs, in order to express the selectional restrictions of the predicate.

The most important component of the RRG theory of semantic roles is the two semantic macroroles, actor and undergoer.[7] They are the two primary arguments of a transitive predication, and an intransitive verb may take an actor or an undergoer as its single argument, depending on its semantics. This is illustrated in (21).

(21)   a.   Maria [Actor] closed the door [Undergoer].
        b.   The door [Undergoer] was closed by Maria [Actor].
        c.   Maria [Actor] sang.
        d.   Maria [Undergoer] died.

Transitivity in RRG is defined in terms of the number of macroroles that a verb takes: a transitive verb takes two, an intransitive verb takes one, and an atransitive verb has no macrorole arguments. The transitivity of verbs and other predicates is determined by the following macrorole assignment principles.

(22)   Default Macrorole Assignment Principles
    a. Number: the number of macroroles a verb takes is less than or equal to the number of arguments in its logical structure

      1. If a verb has two or more arguments in its LS, it will take two macroroles.
      2. If a verb has one argument in its LS, it will take one macrorole.
    b. Nature: for verbs which take one macrorole,
      1. If the verb has an activity predicate in its LS, the macrorole is actor.
      2. If the verb has no activity predicate in its LS, the macrorole is undergoer.

These are default assignment principles, because there are many exceptions to (22a); transitivity is, as has long been recognized, a very idiosyncratic lexical property of verbs.

The selection of actor and undergoer in a LS is governed by the Actor-Undergoer Hierarchy given in Fig. 4.3.

This hierarchy says that given the LS for a transitive verb, the leftmost argument in it will be the actor and the rightmost will be the undergoer. Hence in the LSs in (18g), *the dog* is the actor of *scare* and *the boy* the undergoer, *the cat* the actor of *pop*

---

[7]See Van Valin (1999, 2004) for more detailed discussion of semantic macroroles, including a comparison of them with analogous notions in other theories.

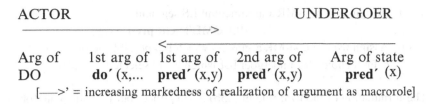

ACTOR   UNDERGOER

————————————————————————>

<———————————————————————

Arg of	1st arg of	1st arg of	2nd arg of	Arg of state
DO	**do**′ (x,...	**pred**′ (x,y)	**pred**′ (x,y)	**pred**′ (x)

[———>' = increasing markedness of realization of argument as macrorole]

Fig. 4.3 The Actor-Undergoer Hierarchy

and *the balloon* the undergoer, *Sam* the actor of *flash* and *the light* the undergoer, *Max* is the actor of *melt* and *the ice* the undergoer, *Felix* is the actor of *bounce* and *the ball* is the undergoer, and *Mary* is the actor of *feed* and *the pizza* is the undergoer.

With three-place LSs, such as those with verbs like *give*, *show*, and *present*, the lowest ranking argument in the LS is only the default choice for undergoer with many verbs in English. It is possible to select the second-lowest ranking argument to function as undergoer, which is a marked selection.[8] This is illustrated in (23) and (24) with the verbs *give* and *present*.

(23) a [**do**′ (Pat, Ø)] CAUSE [BECOME **have**′ (Kim, book)]
      b. Pat [Actor] gave the book [Undergoer] to Kim.   Default choice
      c. Pat [Actor] gave Kim [Undergoer] the book.   Marked choice

(24) a [**do**′ (Pat, Ø)] CAUSE [BECOME **have**′ (Kim, book)]
      b. Pat [Actor] presented the book [Undergoer] to Kim.   Default choice
      c. Pat [Actor] presented Kim [Undergoer] with the book.   Marked choice

Thus, the highest ranking argument in the LS in terms of the Actor-Undergoer Hierarchy is always the actor, whereas the lowest ranking argument is the undergoer with two-place predicates but the default or unmarked choice with three-place predicates.

Actor and undergoer are always direct arguments, when they occur in the core. In languages like English, non-macrorole core arguments are typically marked by prepositions; they are termed oblique core arguments. The primary exception is the non-macrorole direct core argument *the book* in (23c). There are preposition assignment rules in RRG (Jolly 1991, 1993, Van Valin and LaPolla 1997), and the ones for *to* and *with* are given in (25).

---

[8]Primary object languages (Dryer 1986) work somewhat differently; see Guerrero and Van Valin (2004) for an analysis of primary-object languages in RRG terms.

(25)   a. Assign *to* to non-MR *x* argument in LS segment:
       ... BECOME/INGR **pred´** (x, y)
       b. Assign *with* to non-MR argument which is a possible actor or the
           default choice for undergoer but which is not selected as a MR.

The formulation of the *with* rule in (25b) is simplified, but it is adequate for the purposes of this discussion; see Van Valin and LaPolla (1997:381). In (23b) and (24b) the second argument of BECOME **have´** is selected as undergoer, and this leaves the first argument (*Kim*) as a non-macrorole core argument. The conditions for the rule in (25a) are met, and accordingly *Kim* is assigned the preposition *to*. In (23c) and (24c), on the other hand, the first argument of BECOME **have´** is selected as undergoer. The default choice for undergoer, the second argument of BECOME **have´** is a non-macrorole core argument, and the conditions for the application of the *with* rule in (25b) are met. It applies with most verbs in English but not with the group of dative shift verbs like *give* and *show*. Hence the non-macrorole core argument is marked by *with* in (24c) but not in (23c). The rule in (25b) also applies to verbs taking instrumental arguments. Consider the sentence in (1c), repeated in (26a), and its LS in (26b).

(26)   a. The burglar shattered the window with the crowbar.
       b. [**do´** (burglar, Ø)] CAUSE [**do´** (crowbar, Ø)] CAUSE
           [INGR **shattered´** (window)]

Both *the burglar* and *the crowbar* are potential actors, as (1c) and (1d) show, but only *the burglar* can be selected as actor, as it is the highest ranking argument in the LS. *The crowbar* has been outranked for actor, and the rule in (25b) applies, assigning *with*.

It is important to distinguish instrument-like NPs which can serve as actor and those that cannot. Contrast (1d) with (27b).

(27)   a. Chris ate the soup with the spoon.
       b. *The spoon ate the soup.

The crucial difference between the *with* PP in (26a) and the one in (27a) is that there is no causal chain in the event in (27), whereas there is one in (26). That is, in (26), the burglar acts on the crowbar, and the crowbar does something to the window which causes the window to shatter. It is the crowbar that actually does the shattering action. This is not the case in (27): it is not the case that Chris acts on the spoon, the spoon acts on the soup, which causes the soup to be eaten. The soup does not do the eating action; Chris does. Because there is no causal chain, the spoon is not an argument of **do´** and therefore cannot be an actor. The LS for (27) is given in (28).

(28)   **do´** (Chris, [**eat´** (Chris, soup) ∧ **use´** (Chris, spoon)]) &
       INGR **consumed´** (soup)

In (27a), *Chris* would be the actor and *soup* the undergoer, and because *spoon* has been outranked for both macroroles and the conditions for the *to* rule are not met, the *with* rule applies, yielding *with the spoon*. In Van Valin and LaPolla (1997) the two types of *with* PPs are distinguished as 'instrument' PPs (e.g. *with the crowbar* in (26a), which is part of a causal chain) versus 'implement' PPs (e.g. *with the spoon* in (27a), which is not part of a causal chain).

It is important to note the fundamental difference between the two prepositions in these examples: *to* has a LS associated with it, while *with* does not. All locative prepositions have a LS, but *with* is associated with the outcome of certain linking options, rather than a specific LS. Hence it can occur more than once in a single core, as in (29).

(29)   The man loaded the truck *with* hay *with* a pitchfork *with* Bill.

This sentence contains optional implement and comitative PPs, both headed by *with*.

In syntactically accusative languages like English, the default choice for subject (the privileged syntactic argument [PSA], in RRG terms) with a transitive verb is the actor, and the undergoer may function as subject in a passive construction, as (21a, b) illustrate.[9] In syntactically ergative languages like Dyirbal, on the other hand, the undergoer is the default choice for subject.

The linking between syntax and semantics is governed by the Completeness Constraint, which is stated in (30).

(30)   Completeness Constraint:
        All of the arguments explicitly specified in the semantic representation of a sentence must be realized syntactically in the sentence, and all of the referring expressions in the syntactic representation of a sentence must be linked to an argument position in a logical structure in the semantic representation of the sentence.

The main components of the RRG linking system are summarized in Fig. 4.4. The actual steps in the linking algorithm for simple sentences, both for linking from semantics to syntax and from syntax to semantics, are given in Van Valin (2005), sections 5.1.2 and 5.1.3.

4.3.2   The Role and Reference Grammar Account of Verb Alternations and Optional PPs

In Sect. 4.1, RRG was described as a 'projectionist' theory in which the semantic representation of the clause is projected from the lexical representation of the

---

[9]RRG does not posit the traditional grammatical relations of subject and direct object as theoretical constructs, but because this paper is not concerned with grammatical relations, the traditional terms will be used for ease of presentation.

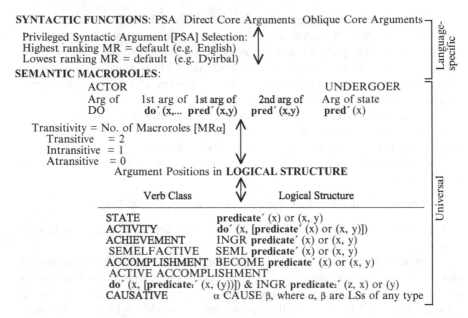

SYNTACTIC FUNCTIONS: PSA Direct Core Arguments Oblique Core Arguments

Privileged Syntactic Argument [PSA] Selection:
Highest ranking MR = default (e.g. English)
Lowest ranking MR = default (e.g. Dyirbal)

SEMANTIC MACROROLES:

	ACTOR				UNDERGOER
	Arg of	1st arg of	1st arg of	2nd arg of	Arg of state
	DO	do´ (x,...	pred´ (x,y)	pred´ (x,y)	pred´ (x)

Transitivity = No. of Macroroles [MRα]
  Transitive   = 2
  Intransitive = 1
  Atransitive = 0

Argument Positions in **LOGICAL STRUCTURE**

Verb Class	Logical Structure
STATE	**predicate´** (x) or (x, y)
ACTIVITY	**do´** (x, [**predicate´** (x) or (x, y)])
ACHIEVEMENT	INGR **predicate´** (x) or (x, y)
SEMELFACTIVE	SEML **predicate´** (x) or (x, y)
ACCOMPLISHMENT	BECOME **predicate´** (x) or (x, y)
ACTIVE ACCOMPLISHMENT	
do´ (x, [**predicate₁´** (x, (y))]) & INGR **predicate₂´** (z, x) or (y)	
CAUSATIVE	α CAUSE β, where α, β are LSs of any type

Language-specific

Universal

Fig. 4.4 Summary of components of RRG linking system

verb, and this semantic representation determines to a large extent the syntactic representation of the clause. The lexical representations for the verbs in the activity-active accomplishment and the causative alternations are those given in Table 4.2 and (18). Simplified semantic representations for the pairs of sentences in (2), (4) and (10) are given in (31)–(33).

(31) a. The soldiers marched in the park.   Activity
      a´. **be-in´** (park, [**do´** (soldiers, [**march´** (soldiers)])])
      b. The soldiers marched to the park.   Active accomplishment
      b´. **do´** (soldiers, [**march´** (soldiers)]) & INGR **be-at´** (park, soldiers)

(32) a. Chris drank (beer).   Activity
      a´. **do´** (Chris, [**drink´** (Chris, (beer))])[10]
      b. Chris drank the beer.   Active accomplishment
      b´. **do´** (Chris, [**drink´** (Chris, beer)]) & INGR **consumed´** (beer)

---

[10]A complete semantic representation of the NPs filling the argument positions would include their definiteness, quantification, and other values. See Van Valin and LaPolla (1997:194-5).

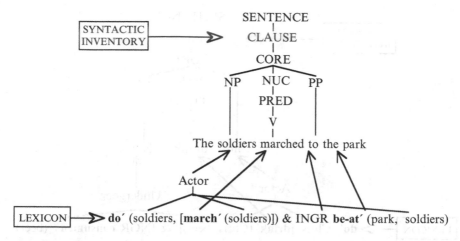

Fig. 4.5 Linking from semantics to syntax in (31b)

(33) a. The window shattered.   Non-causative
     a´ INGR **shattered´** (window)
     b. The burglar shattered the window.   Causative
     b´. [**do´** (burglar, Ø)] CAUSE [INGR **shattered´** (window)]

Together with the syntactic template selection principle in (19) and the RRG linking algorithm, these representations determine the syntactic form of a sentence. The linking to the syntax for (31b) is given in Fig. 4.5.[11]

Because the LS has two arguments in it, namely *the soldiers* and *the park*, a core template with two argument slots is selected from the syntactic inventory. *March* is an intransitive verb, and therefore it has only one macrorole, an actor, following (22b).[12] The actor NP, *the soldiers*, will be the subject and linked to the initial argument position in the core. The NP *the park* is a non-macrorole argument, and the conditions for the *to* rule in (25a) are met; consequently it is assigned *to*, yielding the PP *to the park*. This PP is a kind of argument, not an adjunct, because its LS shares the argument *the soldiers* with the LS for *march*; contrast this LS with the one for the adjunct PP *in the park* in (31a´), in which the entire LS for *march* is an argument of the prepositional LS.

The linking from semantics to syntax for (32b) is given in Fig. 4.6.

This LS has two arguments in it, namely *Chris* and *the beer*, and consequently a core template with two argument positions is selected from the syntactic inventory.

---

[11]Certain aspects of the syntactic representation have been simplified; and these simplifications are irrelevant to the points under discussion.

[12]Note that if the verb has been *reach*, as in *The soldiers reached the park*, then two macroroles would have been assigned, because *reach* is transitive. The LS is basically the same for both verbs, however, with *reach* having an unspecified verb of motion in the activity part of the LS.

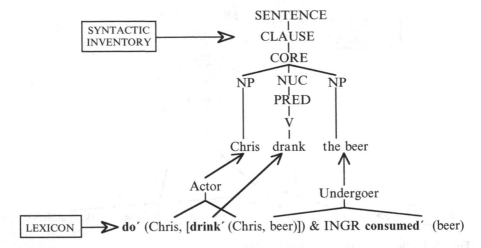

Fig. 4.6 Linking from semantics to syntax in (32b)

Fig. 4.7 Linking from semantics to syntax in (33a)

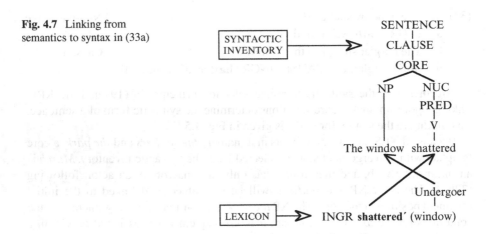

The active accomplishment form of *drink* is transitive, and accordingly it takes two macroroles. In terms of the Actor-undergoer Hierarchy in Fig. 4.3, *Chris* as the highest ranking argument will be the actor, and *the beer*, as the lowest ranking argument, will be the undergoer. These macroroles are then linked to the subject and direct object positions in the core.

The linking in (33a) is given in Fig. 4.7.

This LS has only one argument in it, and therefore a core template with only one argument position is selected from the syntactic inventory. *Shatter* is here an intransitive verb, which means that it has only one macrorole, and following the principles in (22b), it must be undergoer. It is the only macrorole argument, and consequently it appears as subject, as in Fig. 4.7.

These three examples have illustrated the projectionist nature of RRG: starting from the semantic representation of a clause, based on the lexical representation of the verb or other predicating element, a syntactic template is selected, macroroles are assigned, and the core arguments are linked into the syntactic representation. The next question to be asked is, how are the variant forms of *march, drink* and *shatter* in (31)–(33) related to each other? RRG expresses the relationship between these forms by means of lexical rules (see Van Valin and LaPolla 1997, section 4.6). The lexical rule which relates the two uses of *march* in (31) is given in (34a), while the one which relates the two uses of *drink* in (32) is given in (34b); along with the rule in (34c) for the two uses of *write* in (3), these rules capture the three alternations between activity and active accomplishment verbs presented in (2)–(4).

(34) a. Activity [motion] ⇒ Active Accomplishment:
          do´ (x, [**pred´** (x)]) ⇒ **do´** (x, [**pred´** (x)]) & INGR **be-LOC´** (y, x)
      b. Activity [consumption] ⇒ Active Accomplishment:
          do´ (x, [**pred´** (x, y)]) ⇒ **do´** (x, [**pred´** (x, y)]) & INGR **consumed´** (y)
      c. Activity [creation] ⇒ Active Accomplishment:
          do´ (x, [**pred´** (x, y)]) ⇒ **do´** (x, [**pred´** (x, y)]) & INGR **exist´** (y)

These rules embody the claim that verbs like *march, drink* and *write* are basically activity verbs and that their active accomplishment uses are derivative. In this, these two verbs contrast with *reach* (cf. fn. 12) and *devour*, which are non-derived active accomplishment verbs.

What kind of evidence is there that a verb is basically one type or the other? One fact that helps to distinguish lexically telic verbs from lexically atelic verbs concerns the behavior of such verbs with mass noun or bare plural objects. It has long been known that telic verbs behave like atelic verbs when they have a mass noun or bare plural object, but unlike inherently atelic verbs, telic verbs necessarily have a iterative interpretation in this case. This contrast is exemplified in (35).

(35) a.   Pat crushed the can in ten seconds.   Telic
      a´. Pat crushed cans (over and over again) for/*in ten minutes.   Atelic
      b.   Chris ate the spaghetti in five minutes.   Telic
      b´. Chris ate spaghetti ((*)over and over again) for an hour.   Atelic
      c.   Sandy devoured the spaghetti in five minutes.   Telic
      c´. Sandy devoured spaghetti (over and over again) for an hour.   Atelic

The verb *crush* is a causative accomplishment verb, and its telic nature is shown in (35a). When it occurs with a bare plural object, as in (a´), it takes a *for* rather than an *in* time adverbial, which is indicative of an atelic use. However, this sentence has a necessarily iterative reading, i.e. there must be serial events of can crushing, not a single, temporally unbounded event of can crushing. The crucial contrast for this discussion is between (35b´) and (c´), in which the objects are mass nouns. The sentence with *eat* is compatible with two readings, an iterative one, in which Chris eats plate after plate of spaghetti, and a non-iterative one, in which there is a single large plate of spaghetti from which she eats for an hour with no implication that she finished it. The iterative adverb *over and over again* is compatible only with the iterative interpretation. With *devour* in (c´), on the other hand, only the iterative reading is possible: Sandy eats plate after plate of spaghetti, and the eating of each plateful constitutes a distinct event in the sequence. Hence *devour* is inherently telic, while *eat* is not.[13]

Thus, RRG would posit one entry for *march* and one entry for *drink* in the lexicon, with the active accomplishment uses derived by the lexical rules in (34). If one assumes that overt derivational morphology signals the operation of a lexical process, then the postulation of such rules is supported by languages like Georgian and Russian, as exemplified in (5) and (6), in which the base form of verbs like *eat* and *write* are activities and the derivation of their active accomplishment uses is indicated overtly morphologically. In languages like Dyirbal and Sama, as illustrated in (8) and (9), on the other hand, it appears that the base form of verbs like *eat* and *drink* are telic, hence active accomplishments, and therefore their atelic (activity) uses would be derived; in these languages, the direction of the arrow in the rules in (34) would be reversed. In these languages too, special morphology marks the derived forms.

The contrast in interpretation with mass noun or bare plural objects obviously does not apply to motion verbs, which are intransitive for the most part in English. However, the behavior of these verbs when they occur without any kind of accompanying PP suggests that they are basically activity verbs. This is shown in (36).

(36)   a.   Pat walked for/*in an hour.
        b.   The soldiers marched for/*in an hour.
        c.   Kim ran for/*in an hour.

All three verbs are perfectly fine when cooccurring with a *for* time adverbial but not with an *in* PP. This follows, if they are activity verbs. Thus, the lexical rules in (34) serve to derive the active accomplishment uses of activity verbs.

The other alternation discussed in Sect. 4.2 is the causative alternation, as in (33). Because the verbs undergoing this alternation in English show no morphological marking, unlike Huallaga Quechua in (11) and French, Russian and Yagua in (12), there is no obvious evidence as to which of the two forms is basic. Positing one form as basic raises a couple of problems, as Piñón (2001) points out. First, there is the fundamental issue of justifying the selection of the basic alternant, and different analyses have proposed different choices. For example, Levin and Rappaport Hovav (1994) and Rappaport Hovav and Levin (1998) propose an analysis in which the

---

[13] A consequence of the fact that these atelic uses of telic verbs are necessarily iterative, as in (35a´, c´), is that there is no change in their LS in the two uses. Hence there is no need to posit a lexical rule to relate these pairs of sentences.

causative version is basic, while Van Valin and LaPolla (1997) argue that the non-causative form is basic. Second, whichever form is taken as basic, it is necessary to account for the verbs which fall into one class or the other but do not alternate, e.g. *dirty* has only a causative form, while *disappear* has only a non-causative form.

The approach that will be taken here follows a suggestion of Piñón (2001), although it is implemented rather differently. The idea is that there is no basic form; rather, there is a general rule expressing the alternation, which is given in (37).

(37)   General lexical rule for causative alternations

   $[$**do**$'$ $(x, \emptyset)]$ CAUSE $[$BECOME/INGR **pred**$'$ $(y \, (,z))]$

   $\Longleftrightarrow$ BECOME/INGR **pred**$'$ $(y \, (,z))$

The lexical entry for a verb like *shatter* in (33) would not contain a LS; rather, it would contain a pointer to the rule in (37) along with the specifications 'INGR', '**pred**$'$ $(y \, (,z))$' = '**shattered**$'$ (y)'. In the linking for (33a) the right-hand element of the rule would be selected, while in the linking for (33b) the left-hand element would be selected. Neither is considered to be basic or derived. For non-alternating verbs, their lexical entry would simply have the appropriate LS, causative or non-causative, and because there was no reference to (37), the verbs would not alternate.[14]

In languages like Huallaga Quechua and Yagua in which there is clear evidence of derivation from the morphology, the rule in (37) can be interpreted directionally. In Huallaga Quechua the causative morpheme $-chi-$ signals the operation of the rule, deriving the left-hand LS from the right-hand one, while in Yagua the anti-causative morpheme $-y-$ indicates the operation of the rule in the reverse direction, deriving the right-hand LS from the left-hand one.

There is an interesting and striking asymmetry between the two verb classes listed above and activity and active accomplishment verbs with respect to the causative alternation: there seems to be a clear basic form, namely, the activity form, because the majority of activity verbs do not alternate with a causative counterpart. Furthermore, there appear to be far more active accomplishments than causative active accomplishments. The simplest solution is to analyze causative activity and active accomplishment verbs as being derived from their non-causative counterparts by means of the rule in (38); in this rule '...' refers to the '& INGR **be-at**$'$ (z, y)' component of active accomplishments.

(38)   Lexical rule for causative alternations involving activity verbs

   do$'$ $(y, [$**pred**$'$ $(y)])$ ... $\Rightarrow$ $[$**do**$'$ $(x, \emptyset)]$ CAUSE $[$**do**$'$ $(y, [$**pred**$'$ $(y)])$ ...$]$

Since only a minority of activity verbs undergo this alternation, the simplest way to account for those verbs which alternate and those which do not is to adopt the

---

[14]The question of why verbs fail to alternate is an important and much discussed issue; see e.g. Levin and Rappaport Hovav (1994), Piñón (2001). It is beyond the scope of this discussion and will not be addressed here.

approach proposed above for the causative alternation: non-alternating verbs would have the appropriate LS in their lexical entry, and alternating verbs would not have a LS in their lexical entry, only a pointer to the rule in (38), along with a specification of the value of '**pred´**'.

It might seem odd to posit no basic form for the causative alternation involving achievement and accomplishments verbs and a causativization rule for activity verbs, but in fact when one looks at languages in which there is overt morphology expressing this relationship, causativization is far more common than decausativization with activity verbs. In Russian and French, the reflexivization pattern illustrated in (12a, b) is not generally found with activity verbs. In French, for example, the causative equivalents of *bondir* 'bounce', *marcher* 'walk' and *courir* 'run' are created by combining *faire* 'make, cause' with these verbs, which are intransitive, in a complex construction; these verbs do not have transitive causative versions. Analogous morphological derivations are illustrated in (39).

(39)   a. Mparntwe Arrernte (Australia; Wilkins 1989)
            unthe- 'go walkabout'   *unthe-lhile* 'make someone go walkabout'
       b. Tepehua (Totonacan, Mexico; Watters 1988)
            pu:pu- 'boil [intransitive]   *ma-pu:pu-* 'make something boil'

Thus, it seems reasonable to postulate that activity verbs undergo the causativization rule in (38), rather than a decausativization rule.

There are two lexical rules involving activity verbs, and their interaction yields the four possible interpretations of verbs like *march*, as shown in (40).

(40) a. *march* activity, as in (13a)   Basic, underived LS
      b. *march* causative activity, as in (13b)   (38)
      c. *march* active accomplishment, as in (13c)   (34a)
      d. *march* causative active accomplishment, as in (13d)   (34a) + (38)

The final issue raised in Sect. 4.2 is optional instrument, implement and comitative PPs, as in (14a), (27a) and (15b, c). Each of these is handled differently in RRG. As discussed in Sect. 4.3.1, instrument arguments are part of a causal chain, and therefore the full LS for the causative version of a verb like *shatter* would be as in (26a), repeated in (41).

(41)   [**do´** (x, Ø)] CAUSE [**do´** (y, Ø)] CAUSE [INGR **shattered´** (z)]

In this LS, the x and y variables have important selectional restrictions: the x variable must be filled by animate, normally human argument, while the y variable must be filled by an inanimate argument. If the y variable is lexically filled, the result is a sentence with an instrument PP like (26a), *The burglar shattered the window with a crowbar*. As discussed in Sect. 4.3.1, the NP *a crowbar* is a non-macrorole core argument which has been outranked by *the burglar* for actor selection, and therefore the *with* rule in (25b) applies. If it is not lexically filled, then the result is a sentence like (1b), *The burglar shattered the window.* Finally, if the *x* argument is not lexically filled but the *y* argument is, then the result is a sentence like (1d), *The crowbar shattered the window.* These LSs are given in (42).

(42)   a. [**do´** (burglar,Ø)] CAUSE [**do´** (crowbar, Ø)] CAUSE
           [INGR **shattered´** (window)] = (26a)
       b. [**do´** (burglar, Ø)] CAUSE [**do´** (Ø, Ø)] CAUSE
           [INGR **shattered´** (window)] = (1b)
       c. [**do´** (Ø,(Ø)] CAUSE [**do´** (crowbar, Ø)] CAUSE
           [INGR **shattered´** (window)] = (1d)

In addition to instruments, at least one other kind of intermediate LS is possible, as illustrated in (43).

(43)   a.   Max shattered the teacup against the wall.
       a´. [**do´** (Max, Ø)] CAUSE [INGR **be-against´** (wall, teacup)]
            & [INGR **shattered´** (teacup)]
       b.   The teacup shattered against the wall.
       b´. [INGR **be-against´** (wall, teacup)] & [INGR **shattered´** (teacup)]

In both (43a, b) the undergoer comes into contact with something and undergoes a change of state. The sentence in (43a) treats this contact as induced by the actor *Max*, while (b) makes no reference to the cause of the teacup coming into contact with the wall.

This analysis of the LS of *shatter* as containing a causal chain with an instrument or location argument requires a modification of the lexical rule in (37); it is given in (44).

(44)   Lexical rule for causative alternations (revised)
       [**do´** (x, Ø)] CAUSE {[...]} [BECOME/INGR **pred´** (y (,z))]
       $\Longleftrightarrow$ BECOME/INGR **pred´** (y (,z))

The '{[...]}' represents the optional intermediate cause and the instrument or location argument, which some verbs of the kind may have.[15] These optional arguments may be represented by the following lexical templates. In (45a), the *w* argument must be inanimate, as noted with respect to (41).

(45)   a. Lexical template for optional instrument: ... [**do´** (w, Ø)] CAUSE ...
       b. Lexical template for optional location: ...
                                  [INGR **be-LOC´** (v, w)] & ... w = y

---

[15]The notation is taken from Wunderlich (1997).

The primary part of the rule is unaffected, and this rule provides an explanation for the ungrammaticality of (1e), *The window shattered with a crowbar. The *with a crowbar* PP requires the full LS; the BECOME/INGR **pred´** (y (, z)) output LS has no place for an instrument argument. It should be noted, however, that a middle construction like *The window shatters easily with a crowbar* has a different LS; it is given in (46).[16]

(46)   **be´** ([[**do´** (Ø, Ø)] CAUSE [**do´** (crowbar, Ø)] CAUSE
                    [INGR **shattered´** (window)]],[**easy´**])

This LS contains the full causative achievement LS for *shatter*, which is why the instrument PP is possible.

Implement PPs, as argued in Sect. 4.3.1, have a different semantic representation. The earlier example in (27a) is repeated in (47a) together with its LS from (28).

(47)   a. Chris ate the soup with the spoon.
        b. **do´** (Chris, [**eat´** (Chris, soup) ∧ **use´** (Chris, spoon)])
                                                    & INGR **consumed´** (soup)

The occurrence of implement PPs is restricted to activity verbs (and their active accomplishment counterparts), and it may be accounted for by the following lexical rule.

(48)   Lexical rule for implement PPs
        do´ (x, [**pred´** (x, (y)) . . . ⇒ **do´** (x, [**pred´** (x, (y)) ∧ **use´** (x, z)]) . . .

This rule adds **use´** (x, z) to the LS of an activity predicate, z being the implement argument. Because it is not selected as actor or undergoer, the *with* rule in (25b) applies. Two things follow from this rule: first, implement PPs can only occur with activity or active accomplishment verbs, and second, because the implement is not part of a causal chain, it cannot function as actor; as the second argument of a two-place predicate, it is not a candidate for actor selection in terms of the Actor-Undergoer Hierarchy.

Comitative PPs do not require any kind of special rule; they follow from linking possibilities already available in the theory. The relevant examples from (15) and (16) are repeated below.

(49)   a. Chris and Pat went to the movies.
        b. Chris went to the movies with Pat.
        c. Pat went to the movies with Chris.

---

[16]See Van Valin and LaPolla (1997: 416-7) for justification of this LS for middle constructions.

(50) a. The gangster robbed the bank (together) with the corrupt policeman.
　　　 b. The bank was robbed by the gangster (together) with the corrupt
　　　　　 policeman.
　　　 c. *The bank was robbed (together) with the corrupt policeman.

The LS for all of the sentences in (49) is given in (51).

(51) **do´** (Chris $\wedge$ Pat, [**go´** (Chris $\wedge$ Pat)]) & INGR **be-at´**

(movies, Chris $\wedge$ Pat)

There are three linking possibilities: if both *Chris* and *Pat* are selected as actor, i.e. as a conjoined NP, then the result is (49a); if only one of them is selected as the actor, then the other is left as a non-macrorole core argument, and the *with* rule in (25b) applies, yielding (49b) or (c). The LSs for the examples in (50) are given in (52).

(52) a. [**do´** (gangster $\wedge$ corrupt policeman, $\emptyset$)] CAUSE
　　　　　 [BECOME NOT **have´** (bank, $\emptyset$)]
　　　 b. [**do´** ($\emptyset$ $\wedge$ corrupt policeman, $\emptyset$)] CAUSE
　　　　　 [BECOME NOT **have´** (bank, $\emptyset$)]

In (50a, b), which have (52a) as their LS, *the gangster* is selected as actor, leaving *the corrupt policeman* as a non-macrorole core argument to be marked by with, following (25b). It does not matter whether the linking is active voice, as in (50a), or passive voice, as in (50b). If both arguments had been selected as actor, the result would have been *The gangster and the corrupt policeman robbed the bank*. However, in an agentless passive like (50c), the actor argument is unspecified in the LS, and this yields the impossible LS in (52b) for the ungrammatical (50c). That this is impossible can be seen straightforwardly in the ungrammaticality of *$\emptyset$ and the corrupt policeman robbed the bank*. Hence the fact that a comitative PP is only possible with a specified actor follows naturally from this account.

In this section the RRG projectionist account of these verb alternations and three types of optional PPs has been given. Lexical rules relating one LS to another are an essential part of the analysis. In the account of the causative alternation and of optional instrument PPs, the different possibilities, as in (1) are analyzed as the result of a selecting one of the alternants, based on (44), of instantiating certain optional argument variables in the LS, or of leaving certain variable lexically unspecified, as in (42). Mairal and Faber (2002) show how this approach can successfully account for the different morphosyntactic patterns associated with English verbs of cutting, which exhibit a much more complex set of forms than what has been considered here. In the next section, a constructionist account of the same phenomena will be given, based on Pustejovsky's Generative Lexicon theory.

4.4 The Generative Lexicon and Co-composition

The GL approach to these phenomena exemplifies the constructionist perspective on verbal alternations, and the crucial theoretical tool is the notion of co-composition. It is well illustrated by the GL analysis of the activity-active accomplishment alternation with motion verbs. Pustejovsky (1995) analyzes the active accomplishment clause *The bottle floated into the cave* as the result of co-composing the directional PP *into the cave* with the verb *float*, and he states explicitly that "the conflated sense for the verb float exists only phrasally and not lexically"(1995:126). The semantic representations for *float* and *into the cave* are given in Fig. 4.8.

When the verb and PP cooccur in the syntax, an interpretive process, co-composition, combines their representations to yield the active accomplishment interpretation of *float into the cave*. The resulting representation is in Fig. 4.9.

Thus, an active accomplishment predication like *float into the cave* is not derived from an activity predication in the lexicon, as in the projectionist RRG account, but rather it is the result of semantic interpretive processes applying to a combination of verb plus PP in the syntax.

The activity-active accomplishment involving consumption and creation verbs like *drink* and *write* would also be handled via co-composition. The lexical representations for the verb *drink* and the noun *beer* are given in Fig. 4.10.

For a language like English, a constructionist approach like GL would have to take the quantificational properties of the object NP as the decisive factor in

$$
\begin{bmatrix}
\textbf{float} \\
\text{ARGSTR} = \begin{bmatrix} \text{ARG1} & = \boxed{1} & [\text{ physobj }] \end{bmatrix} \\
\text{EVENTSTR} = \begin{bmatrix} E_1 & = e_1\text{:state} \end{bmatrix} \\
\text{QUALIA} = [\text{AGENTIVE} = \textbf{float}(e_1, \boxed{1})]
\end{bmatrix}
$$

$$
\begin{bmatrix}
\textbf{into the cave} \\
\text{ARGSTR} = \begin{bmatrix} \text{ARG 1} & = \boxed{1} & [\textbf{physobj }] \\ \text{ARG 2} & = \boxed{2} & [\textbf{the\_cave }] \end{bmatrix} \\
\text{EVENTSTR} = \begin{bmatrix} E_1 & = & e_1 : \textbf{state} \\ E_2 & = & e_2 : \textbf{process} \\ \text{RESTR} & = & <_\infty \\ \text{HEAD} & = & e_2 \end{bmatrix} \\
\text{QUALIA} = \begin{bmatrix} \text{FORMAL} & = \textbf{at}(e_2, \boxed{1}, \boxed{2}) \\ \text{AGENTIVE} & = \textbf{move}(e_1, \boxed{1}) \end{bmatrix}
\end{bmatrix}
$$

Fig. 4.8 Semantic representations for *float* and *into the cave* in GL (Pustejovsky 1995)

$$
\begin{bmatrix}
\text{float into the cave} \\[4pt]
\text{ARGSTR} = \begin{bmatrix} \text{ARG1} & = & \boxed{1}\ [\ \text{physobj}\ ] \\ \text{ARG2} & = & \boxed{2}\ [\ \text{the\_cave}\ ] \end{bmatrix} \\[20pt]
\text{EVENTSTR} = \begin{bmatrix} \text{E}_1 & = & e_1 : \textbf{state} \\ \text{E}_2 & = & e_2 : \textbf{process} \\ \text{E}_3 & = & e_3 : \textbf{state} \\ \text{RESTR} & = & <_{\propto} (e_2, e_3),\ o_{\propto} (e_1, e_2) \\ \text{HEAD} & = & e_3 \end{bmatrix} \\[28pt]
\text{QUALIA} = \begin{bmatrix} \text{FORMAL} & = & \textbf{at}(e_3, \boxed{1}, \boxed{2}\ ) \\ \text{AGENTIVE} & = & \textbf{move}(e_2, \boxed{1}\ ),\ \textbf{float}(e_1, \boxed{1}\ ) \end{bmatrix}
\end{bmatrix}
$$

Fig. 4.9 Semantic representation of *float into the cave* in GL

$$
\begin{bmatrix}
\textbf{beer} \\
\text{ARGSTR} = \begin{bmatrix} \text{ARG1} = \textbf{x:liquid} \end{bmatrix} \\[8pt]
\text{QUALIA} = \begin{bmatrix} \text{FORMAL} = \textbf{x} \\ \text{TELIC} = \textbf{drink(e,y,x)} \end{bmatrix}
\end{bmatrix}
$$

$$
\begin{bmatrix}
\textbf{drink} \\[4pt]
\text{ARGSTR} = \begin{bmatrix} \text{ARG1} & = & \boxed{1}\ [\ \text{anim\_ind}\ ] \\ \text{ARG2} & = & \boxed{2}\ [\ \text{mass}\ ] \end{bmatrix} \\[18pt]
\text{EVENTSTR} = \begin{bmatrix} \text{E}_1 & = & e_1 : \textbf{process} \\ \text{E}_2 & = & e_2 : \textbf{state} \\ \text{HEAD} & = & e_1 \end{bmatrix} \\[22pt]
\text{QUALIA} = \begin{bmatrix} \textbf{consume lexical conceptual paradigm} \\ \text{FORMAL} = \textbf{consumed}\ (e_2, \boxed{2}\ ) \\ \text{AGENTIVE} = \textbf{drink\_act}\ (e_1, \boxed{1}, \boxed{2}\ ) \end{bmatrix}
\end{bmatrix}
$$

Fig. 4.10 Lexical representations for *drink* and *beer*

determining whether the verb is to be interpreted as telic or atelic. When the verb takes a mass noun object, it receives an activity, i.e. process without a result state, interpretation. That is, only E_1 in the event structure and the agentive quale are realized. The telic use of *drink* would be represented basically the same way, except on the telic interpretation E_2 and the formal quale are also realized. Exactly how this follows from the quantification properties of ARG 2 is not clear (Fig. 4.11).

Co-composition does not figure into the GL analysis of the causative alternation; it takes a projectionist approach and assumes that alternating verbs like *shatter* have a single, underspecified lexical representation. The event structure of such a verb can be represented as in Fig. 4.12.

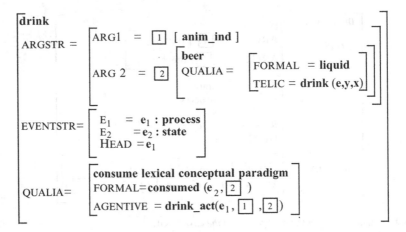

Fig. 4.11 Semantic representation for *drink (a) beer*

Fig. 4.12 Event structure of
English verb *shatter*

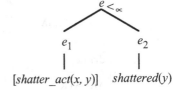

$[shatter\_act(x, y)]$ $shattered(y)$

The event structure of shatter has two subevents, a shattering action and a result state, and either may be selected as the 'head' of the structure. If e_2, the result state, is taken as the head, then the result is a sentence like (1a), *The window shattered*. If e_1, the shattering action is taken as the head, then the full causative structure is involved, and the result is a sentence like (1b), *The burglar shattered the window*. Hence the verb *shatter*, and other verbs like it, has a single lexical representation underlying both its causative and non-causative uses; it is given in Fig. 4.13.

The first argument of *shatter* is an event (J. Pustejovsky, p.c.), which may be expressed directly as in *John's throwing a rock shattered the window* or metonymically as in *John shattered the window*. Since this representation does not specify a head in the event structure (compare it with the one for *drink* in Fig. 4.11), either e_2 with just the formal quale or both e_1 and e_2 with both formal and agentive qualia may be expressed, yielding the two possibilities in (1a) and (1b). This contrasts with the RRG approach, in which the verb *shatter* has distinct lexical representations in these two sentences, which are related by the lexical rule in (37).

The three types of arguments discussed in previous sections are handled in different ways. Instruments are not distinguished from implements, and they would be the optional argument 4 in semantic representations like those in Fig. 4.13. Comitatives, on the other hand, would be derived via co-composition, analogous

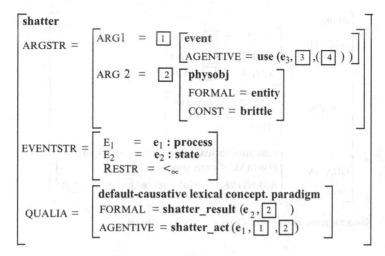

Fig. 4.13 Semantic representation for causative/non-causative verb *shatter*

$$
\begin{bmatrix}
\textbf{with Pat} \\
\text{ARGSTR} = \quad \text{ARG1} = \boxed{1}
\begin{bmatrix}
\textbf{Pat} \\
\text{ARGSTR} = [\ \text{ARG1} = [\textbf{x: human}\ ] \\
\text{QUALIA} = \begin{bmatrix} \text{CONST} = \textbf{male(x)} \\ \text{TELIC} = \textbf{act}(\text{e}_1, \boxed{1}\ ) \end{bmatrix}
\end{bmatrix} \\
\text{EVENTSTR} = [\ \text{E}_1 = \textbf{e}_1 \textbf{:process}\ ]
\end{bmatrix}
$$

Fig. 4.14 Semantic representation of comitative PP *with Pat*

to the treatment of *float into the cave* in Fig. 4.9. Crucial to the interpretation of a comitative PP like *with Pat* in a sentence like *Chris drank beer with Pat* are the qualia properties of the NP; the relevant ones for a human referent are given in (53).

(53) **Pat (x)**
   a. Const: **male (x)**
   b. Telic: **act (e_1, x**

With presents an interesting problem for lexical semantics because of all of its uses, e.g. comitative, instrument, implement, manner adverb (e.g. *with enthusiasm*), and oblique object (e.g. *presented Mary with flowers*). GL is opposed to simply listing an item multiple times in the lexicon, each with a different sense (Pustejovsky 1995), and so it may be assumed that some kind of underspecified entry for this preposition would be required, and the particular interpretation would be derived from the qualia properties of its object along with the verb with which it cooccurs. It would occur with a human referent normally only in a comitative sense. A partial semantic representation for *with Pat* is given in Fig. 4.14.

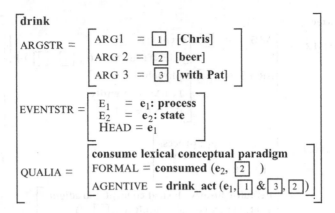

Fig. 4.15 Semantic representation for *Chris drank beer with Pat*

This PP co-composes with the semantic representation for *drink beer* from Fig. 4.11, yielding the representation in Fig. 4.15 (aspects of the argument structures have been simplified).

Pat is added as a third argument, and thanks to its telic quale it is interpreted as a co-agent with *Chris*. As with *float into the cave*, this representation exists only phrasally, not lexically.

The GL approach to the phenomena under consideration has employed co-composition, a quintessentially constructionist mechanism, as well as underspecified lexical entries for both verbs and prepositions. This contrasts with the RRG approach presented in the previous section, which is consistently projectionist. The two approaches appear to make quite contradictory claims with respect to some of these phenomena: GL claims that active accomplishment predications and comitative expressions do not exist in the lexicon and are created from the syntactic structure via co-composition, whereas RRG maintains that both are projected from the lexicon, and that the alternations involve the application of lexical rules to derive the lexical forms from which they are projected. But are these two approaches as different and incompatible as they appear?

4.5   The Place of Lexical Rules and Co-composition in the Grammar

Lexical rules and co-composition are different ways at arriving at semantic representations; they relate to different parts of the grammar. Lexical rules, by definition, operate in the lexicon, while co-composition operates on syntactic phrases. One way of conceptualizing the distinction runs as follows. A speaker has a message that she or he wants to communicate, and the first step in the construction of an appropriate expression for it is the constitution of a semantic representation, made

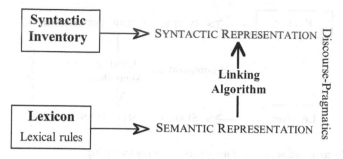

Fig. 4.16 Lexical rules as part of the semantics-to-syntax linking

up of the lexical representations of the predicate, the arguments and modifiers to be used. This means that if a speaker wants to say *Chris ran to the park*, he or she puts together a semantic representation for that sentence, which means, in RRG terms, constituting a logical structure like the one in (18f). This semantic representation is then mapped into the appropriate syntactic representation, as in Fig. 4.5. The projectionist perspective thus represents what the speaker does in putting a sentence together.

The hearer, on the other hand, does not know what the speaker is going to say, and in particular does not know, having heard *Chris ran*, whether it will be followed by *in the park* or *to the park*. That is, the hearer does not know whether *ran* is an activity or active accomplishment until he or she has heard the PP which follows it. Consequently, the hearer must arrive at the meaning via co-composition. Thus, the constructionist perspective represents what the hearer does in determining the meaning of a sentence.

Because the linking algorithm in RRG goes both from the semantic representation to the syntactic representation and from the syntactic representation to the semantic representation (see Fig. 4.1), it provides a natural way to capture this contrast. Lexical rules are part of the semantics-to-syntax linking, as in Fig. 4.16.

The role of lexical rules in the linking from semantics to syntax is illustrated in the analysis of the sentences in (31)–(33), as presented in Figs. 4.5, 4.6, and 4.7. They are crucial to the formation of the lexical representation of the verb. There is also a lexical rule for adding an implement argument to activity verb LSs.[17]

Co-composition, on the other hand, is part of the syntax-to-semantics linking. Here the hearer has to rely on overt morphosyntactic cues in the sentence in order to determine its meaning. Whether a verb is being used as causative or non-causative is directly a function of whether it has two arguments or one in a language like English

---

[17]This raises an interesting issue about the structure of the lexicon. The LSs created by the lexical rules are not stored in the lexicon, unlike the input LSs, and therefore it appears that the lexicon must be divided into at least two parts, one in which lexical items and morphemes are stored, and another in which lexical rules operate and create items which are not stored permanently in the lexicon.

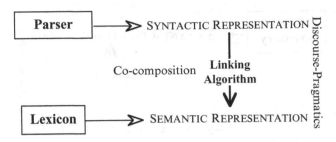

Fig. 4.17 Co-composition as part of the syntax-to-semantics linking

with no overt (anti-)causative morphology on alternating verbs. Whether a verb is being used as an activity or active accomplishment is directly a function either of the quantification of the object NP (consumption and creation verbs) or of the PP that accompanies it (motion verbs). This is represented as in Fig. 4.17.

Thus from this perspective, lexical rules and co-composition are not incompatible concepts at all; rather, they complement each other, in that they play roles in different aspects of the linking.

GL employs co-composition but not lexical rules; where lexical rules are used in RRG to capture the contrast between causative and non-causative verbs, GL uses underspecified lexical entries, as in Fig. 4.13. Pustejovsky (1995) leaves open the possibility that lexical rules could be used in GL in certain cases.

All of the RRG machinery introduced in Sect. 4.3.1 is described in terms of its role in the linking from semantics to syntax; it is purely projectionist. The interpretation issue addressed by co-composition is crucial for syntax-to-semantics linking in RRG, and therefore an RRG approach to co-composition is needed. It will be developed in the next section.

4.6 Co-composition in Role and Reference Grammar

Before a notion of co-composition can be implemented in RRG, it is first necessary to present the syntax-to-semantics linking algorithm as developed in Van Valin and LaPolla (1997) and Van Valin (2005).

4.6.1 Linking from Syntax to Semantics in Role and Reference Grammar

For a language like English, the syntax-to-semantics linking algorithm works basically as follows. The first step is that the parser outputs a labeled tree structure of

Fig. 4.18 Syntax to
semantics linking in simple
English sentence

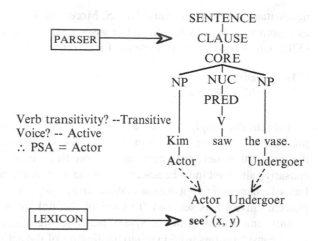

the type in Fig. 4.2.[18] The next step is to identify the predicate, usually a verb, in the
nucleus and determine its transitivity. If the predicate is intransitive, then the subject
is a macrorole argument. If the predicate is a transitive verb, then it is necessary
to determine its voice: if it is active voice, then the subject is an actor, and if it is
passive voice, the subject is an undergoer. If it is active voice, then the other direct
core argument is an undergoer. At this point it is necessary to go to the lexicon and
access the LS of the predicate; the number and nature of the macroroles associated
with the LS is determined by the principles in (22), and macroroles are assigned
following the Actor-Undergoer Hierarchy in Fig. 4.3. At this point, the actor in the
sentence is linked to the actor in the LS, and the undergoer in the sentence is linked
to the undergoer in the LS, completing the linking and satisfying the Completeness
Constraint in (30). This is illustrated in Fig. 4.18 for the English sentence *Kim saw
the vase*.

4.6.2 Co-composition

Suppose the sentence were *Kim shattered the vase* instead of the one in Fig. 4.18.
One of the major issues of concern in this paper arises in this example at the point
at which the LS of the verb is accessed in the lexicon. *Shatter* can be transitive
(causative) or intransitive (non-causative), and the analysis of the alternation
presented in Sect. 4.3.2 has no full LS in the lexical entry for *shatter*, only a pointer
to the rule in (44) and the specifications 'INGR' and **'pred´** (y (,z))' = **'shattered´**
(y)'. Which of the alternants should be selected? Here is where co-composition
comes into play. First, the fact that there are two direct core arguments in the clause

---

[18]See Van Valin (2006) for discussion of how a parser based on RRG could be constructed.

necessitates selecting the causative LS. Moreover, Kim has already been identified as a human noun, and the telic quale associated with a human being was given in (53b), which would be formulated in RRG terms as in (54).

(54)   a. **Kim** (a)
        b. Telic: **do´** (a, [...])

This means simply that humans act, do things, are potential actors. Given the presence of a human referent in the sentence in the position where actors occur, this means that there must be an activity predicate in the LS, and consequently the causative alternant must be selected.[19] If the sentence were *The vase shattered*, the lack of a human referent does not invoke an activity predicate, and consequently the non-causative LS is selected. The rest of the linking is straightforward, as there is only one argument in the syntax and one argument position in the LS. The same considerations would go into the linking of the activity and causative activity versions of verbs like *march* in (13a,b).

If the sentence being linked were *The rock shattered the window*, the causative LS would have to be selected, because there are two arguments in the sentence. However, the inanimate NP *the rock* could not be linked to the x argument, because it is incompatible with the selectional restrictions of the first **do´** in the LS, which requires an animate, sentient x argument. Moreover, it could not be linked to the y argument, because the undergoer *the window* would have priority for that linking. The only way to satisfy the Completeness Constraint is to invoke one of the optional lexical templates in (45); because the preposition in the sentence is *with*, which is not a locative preposition, the template in (45b) is ruled out. In addition, it is reasonable to assume that part of the telic quale for *rock* would be the idea that one can use them in some way to do something, and this could be represented as in (55).

(55)   Telic quale for **rock** (a): ..., **do´** (x, [**use´** (x, a)]) $\wedge$ **do´** (a, [...]), ...

If the telic quale for *rock* contained information like this, then it would invoke the lexical template for an optional instrument in (45a). This would create an argument position for the rock to be linked to, thereby satisfying the Completeness Constraint. The x argument in (44) would be marked as unspecified, yielding the LS in (42c). If the sentence to be linked were *The teacup shattered against the wall*, the intransitive LS in (44) would be selected, and the locative preposition in the sentence would invoke the lexical template in (45b).

The case used to present co-composition in Pustejovsky (1995) is the active accomplishment use of activity verbs, and this is a good candidate for a co-composition analysis in RRG. In RRG terms, the LS of the verb in the nucleus

---

[19]The crucial role of the telic quale of the subject NP in the interpretation of this example was pointed out by James Pustejovsky (personal communication).

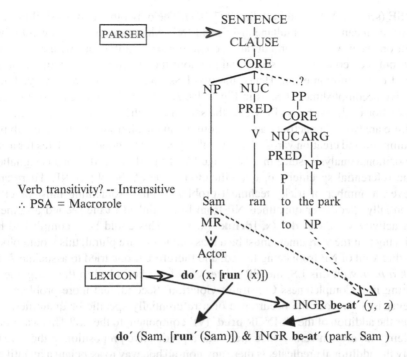

Fig. 4.19 Co-composition in the syntax-to-semantics linking of an active accomplishment

would combine with the LS of the preposition marking the goal PP to yield the appropriate active accomplishment LS. The linking in Sam ran to the park is given in Fig. 4.19.

The linking of *Sam ran* is straightforward. The complications involve the linking of the PP. Since the LS of *run* is fully linked, the preposition must be predicative, and therefore it is necessary to go to the lexicon and access the LS of the preposition, in this case, *to*. The LS for *to* is INGR **be-at´** (y, z); the y argument must be a location, and, crucially, the z argument must be an individual. This contrasts with the LS for prepositions like *in* and *on*, e.g. **be-in´** (y, z), in which the second argument may be either an individual or an event.[20] In the linking in Fig. 4.19, the object of *to* links to the first argument position in its LS, but what links to the second argument position? There are only two candidates: the NP *Sam* or the LS for *run*. Since *to* takes only an individual and not an event for its second argument, the only possibility is *Sam*. The final question concerns how the two LSs combine. Since the verb is intransitive, this cannot be a causative construction, and accordingly they cannot be linked by

---

[20]The reason for the '?' in the syntactic representation is that the PP cannot be correctly attached to the core until its meaning is determined. That is, if the PP is headed by *to*, then it would be an argument in the core, whereas if it were headed by *in*, as in *Sam ran in the park*, then it would be an adjunct in the periphery.

CAUSE (see Van Valin and LaPolla 1997:101). The only other two possibilities are '∧', which means 'and simultaneously', and '&', which means 'and sequentially'. A motion event with temporal duration could not be simultaneous with a punctual event, but they could be in a sequential relation: the punctual event could indicate the end of the motion event. Hence the two LSs must be joined by '&', yielding an active accomplishment LS, as in Fig. 4.19. Appropriately, the result of this co-composition of the verb plus PP yields the same LS as the lexical rule in (34a).

There are two other activity-active accomplishment alternations, those involving consumption and creation verbs. These would appear to be good candidates for a co-compositional analysis, since in a language like English the difference is signalled by the referential specificity or quantification value of the object NP. There are, however, a number of tricky technical problems. First, something must block a referentially specific or quantified NP from being linked to the second argument of an activity verb, e.g. **do**´ (x, [**drink**´ (x, y)]). This could be accomplished by specifying that the y argument must be a mass noun or bare plural; this would block any other kind of NP from being linked, and therefore if one tried to associate *John drank a beer* with this LS, the NP *a beer* could not be linked to the y argument, resulting in a Completeness Constraint violation. Second, and more problematic, however is: how does the occurrence of a referentially specific or quantified NP trigger the addition of the '& INGR **pred**´ (y)' component to the LS? This was not a problem with motion verbs, since there was a predicative preposition in the core to supply the additional predicate. Is there any non-ad hoc way to associate a quantified NP object with an additional predicate? How is the nature of the additional predicate specified? The answer seems to be 'no' to the first question, at least in terms of the system of semantic representation as it currently stands. The solution proposed for the causative alternation is a possible answer to these questions: there would be a pointer in the lexical entry for consumption and creation verbs pointing to the lexical rules in (38b, c), with specifications that the activity form is used with a mass noun or bare plural y argument and the active accomplishment form with a quantified or specified y argument. In languages like Georgian, Russian, Pirahã, Dyirbal and Sama, on the other hand, the fact that the telic and atelic forms of these verbs are distinct means that each alternant would be correlated with a different form of the verb.

The other potential cases of co-composition involve optional arguments: implements and comitatives. Implement arguments are associated with activity verbs, and activity verbs do not have the complex causal structure of verbs like *shatter*. Consequently, there is no ready-made slot available for them in the LS of the verb, and co-composition must come into play. For a sentence like *Chris wrote the letter with a pen*, the problem is immediate: the LS for *write* has only two arguments, but this sentence has three. The source of the third argument position cannot be *with*, because it is never predicative in the RRG analysis (see (25b)). Rather, the source is the telic quale of the third NP, *a pen*: it specifies that the function of a pen is that one uses it for writing. The LS in the telic quale of *pen* merges with the LS of the verb *write*, yielding a LS which can accommodate the additional argument; it matches the output of the lexical rule in (48). This is represented in Fig. 4.20.

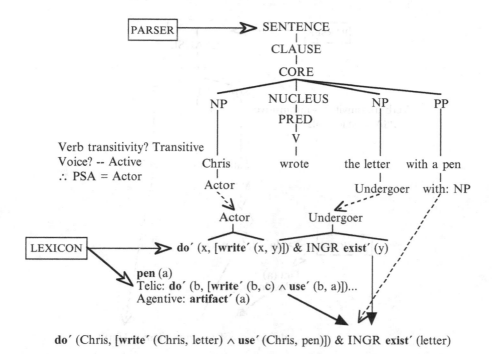

do′ (Chris, [write′ (Chris, letter) ∧ use′ (Chris, pen)]) & INGR exist′ (letter)

Fig. 4.20 Co-composition in sentence with an implement PP

Comitative PPs are handled in a similar fashion: the telic quale of the NP object of *with* supplies the crucial information for the interpretation. In this case, the object of with is a human, e.g. *Sam ran with Tim*, and as indicated earlier in (53b), the telic quale for a human individual is that they act, they do things; in other words, they are potential actors. This means that the interpretation of the NP *Tim* in this sentence is that it is a doer, a potential actor, and this generates a comitative interpretation. The linking from syntax to semantics for *Sam ran with Tim* is given in Fig. 4.21 above. Thus for both implement and comitative PPs, their interpretation depends upon the telic quale of the *with* NP. Again, in languages like Dyirbal and Swahili, in which the presence of instrument, implement and comitative arguments are coded on the verb, there would be little need for co-composition in the syntax-to-semantics linking.

It was mentioned in Sect. 4.3.1 that because *with* is never predicative it can occur multiple times in a single clause. The example of a clause with three *with* PPs is repeated from (29).

(56)   The man loaded the truck with hay with a pitchfork with Bill.

The object of the first *with*, *hay*, is an argument of *load* and links to an argument position in the basic LS of the verb; the other two PPs are implement and comitative PPs, and their interpretations are derived via co-composition. As in the previous two examples, it is the telic quale of the NP object of *with* that underlies the NP's

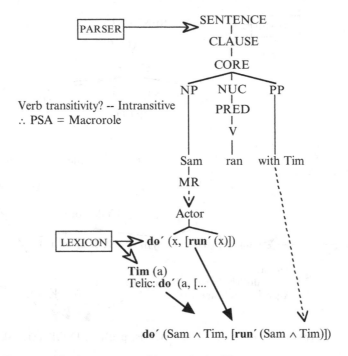

Fig. 4.21 Co-composition in a sentence with a comitative PP

interpretation. The linking from syntax to semantics of (56) is given in Fig. 4.22 below. The basic syntax-to-semantics linking algorithm can account for only the first three arguments; the other two are left unlinked, leading to a potential Completeness Constraint violation. However, by using co-composition and taking information from the telic qualia of the NPs, the additional LS components can be derived which allow the NPs to be linked, thereby avoiding a Completeness Constraint violation.

4.7 Conclusion

This paper has contrasted projectionist and constructionist views of the syntax-semantics interface, and it has been argued that, far from being incompatible and contradictory, the two approaches represent different perspectives on the construction of sentence meaning: the projectionist approach represents the speaker's perspective, while the constructionist approach represents the hearer's perspective. In RRG terms, the former fits naturally with the linking from semantics to syntax (Fig. 4.16), whereas the latter fits naturally with the linking from syntax to semantics (Fig. 4.17). The recognition of the constructionist notion of co-composition as part of the linking from syntax to semantics led to an attempt to incorporate it into

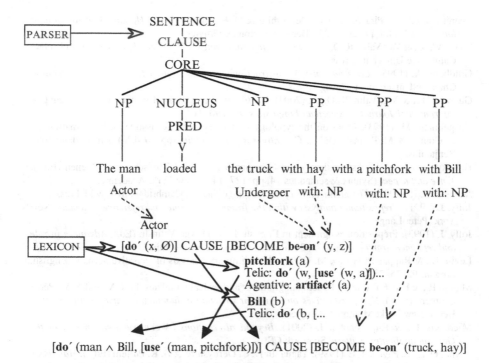

Fig. 4.22 Syntax-to-semantics linking with multiple *with* PPs

the RRG linking system. Co-compositional analyses of the causative alternation and optional instrument, implement and comitative arguments were developed for languages like English in terms of the RRG syntax-to-semantics linking system. In languages in which these alternations are coded overtly on the verb, the need for co-composition in the syntax-to-semantics linking is less obvious.

Acknowledgements Versions of this paper have been presented at the First International Work-shop on Generative Approaches to the Lexicon, Université de Genève (April, 2001), at the 2002 International Conference on Role and Reference Grammar, Universidad de La Rioja, Spain (July, 2002), at the Heinrich-Heine Universität, Düsseldorf (December, 2002), and the University of Colorado (February, 2003). I would like to thank Elizabeth Guest, Jean-Pierre Koenig, Anja Latrouite, Laura Michaelis, Christopher Piñón, and James Pustejovsky for comments on earlier drafts.

References

Dixon, R. M. W. (1972). *The Dyirbal language of North Queensland*. Cambridge: Cambridge University Press.

Dryer, M. (1986). Primary objects, secondary objects, and antidative. *Language, 62*, 808–45.

Everett, D. (1986). Pirahã. In D. C. Derbyshire & G. K. Pullum (Eds.), *Handbook of Amazonian languages* (Vol. I, pp. 200–325). Berlin: Mouton de Gruyter.

Foley, W. A., & Van Valin, R. D., Jr. (1984). *Functional syntax and universal grammar*. Cambridge: Cambridge University Press.

Goldberg, A. (1995). *Constructions: A construction grammar approach to argument structure*. Chicago: University of Chicago Press.

Guerrero, L., & Van Valin, R. D., Jr. (2004). Yaqui and the analysis of primary-object languages. *International Journal of American Linguistics, 70*, 290–319.

Haspelmath, M. (1993). More on the typology of the inchoative/causative verb alternation. In B. Comrie & M. Polinsky (Eds.), *Causatives and transitivity* (pp. 87–120). Amsterdam: John Benjamins.

Holisky, D. A. (1981). Aspect theory and Georgian aspect. In P. Tedeschi & A. Zaenen (Eds.), *Tense and aspect* (Syntax & semantics 14, pp. 127–144). New York: Academic.

Jackendoff, R. (1997). *The architecture of the language faculty*. Cambridge, MA: MIT Press.

Jolly, J. (1991). *Prepositional analysis within the framework of role and reference grammar*. New York: Peter Lang.

Jolly, J. (1993). Preposition assignment in English. In R. D. Van Valin Jr. (Ed.), *Advances in role and reference grammar* (pp. 275–310). Amsterdam: John Benjamins.

Levin, B., & Rappaport Hovav, M. (1994). A preliminary analysis of causative verbs in English. *Lingua, 92*, 35–77.

Mairal, R., & Faber, P. (2002). Functional grammar and lexical templates. In R. Mairal & M. Pérez Quintero (Eds.), *New perspectives on argument structure in functional grammar* (pp. 39–94). Berlin/New York: Mouton de Gruyter.

Michaelis, L., & Ruppenhofer, J. (2001). *Beyond alternations: A constructional model of the German applicative pattern*. Stanford: CSLI.

Payne, D. L., & Payne, T. E. (1989). Yagua. In D. C. Derbyshire & G. K. Pullum (Eds.), *Handbook of Amazonian linguistics* (Vol. 2, pp. 252–474). Berlin: Mouton de Gruyter.

Pinker, S. (1989). *Learnability and cognition*. Cambridge, MA: MIT Press.

Piñón, C. (2001). A finer look at the causative-inchoative alternation. In R. Hastings, B. Jackson, & Z. Zvolenszky (Eds.), *Proceedings of semantics and linguistic theory 11*. Ithaca: CLC Publications/Cornell University.

Pustejovsky, J. (1991). The generative lexicon. *Computational Linguistics, 17*, 409–41.

Pustejovsky, J. (1995). *The generative lexicon*. Cambridge, MA: MIT Press.

Pustejovsky, J. (1998). The semantics of lexical underspecification. *Folia Linguistica, 32*, 323–47.

Rappaport Hovav, M., & Levin, B. (1998). Building verb meanings. In M. Butt & W. Geuder (Eds.), *The projection of arguments: Lexical and computational factors* (pp. 97–134). Stanford: CSLI.

Van Valin, R. D., Jr. (Ed.). (1993). *Advances in role and reference grammar*. Amsterdam/Philadelphia: John Benjamins.

Van Valin, R. D., Jr. (1999). Generalized semantic roles and the syntax-semantics inter- face. In F. Corblin, C. Dobrovie-Sorin, & J.-M. Marandin (Eds.), *Empirical issues in formal syntax and semantics* (Vol. 2, pp. 373–389). The Hague: Thesus [also available on RRG web site].

Van Valin, R. D., Jr. (2006). Semantic macroroles and syntactic processing. In I. Bornkessel & M. Schlesewsky (Eds.), *Semantic role universals and argument linking: Theoretical, typological and psycho-/neurolinguistic perspectives*. Berlin: Mouton de Gruyter.

Van Valin, R. D., Jr. (2004). Semantic macroroles in role and reference grammar. In R. Kailuweit & M. Hummel (Eds.), *Semantische Rollen* (pp. 62–82). Narr: Tübingen.

Van Valin, R. D., Jr. (2005). *Exploring the syntax-semantics interface*. Cambridge: Cambridge University Press.

Van Valin, R. D., Jr., & LaPolla, R. J. (1997). *Syntax: Structure, meaning & function*. Cambridge: Cambridge University Press.

Verkuyl, H. (1972). *On the compositional nature of the aspects*. Dordrecht: Reidel.

Walton, C. (1986). *Sama verbal semantics: Classification, derivation and inflection*. Manila: Linguistic Society of the Philippines.

Watters, J. K. (1988). *Topics in the Tepehua Grammar.* Unpublished Ph.D. dissertation. Berkeley: University of California.

Weber, D. J. (1989). *A grammar of Huallaga (Huanuco) Quechua* (University of California publications in linguistics 112). Berkeley: University of California Press.

Wilkins, D. P. (1989). *Mparntwe Arrernte (Aranda): Studies in the structure and semantics of grammar.* PhD dissertation, Australian National University.

Wunderlich, D. (1997). Cause and the structure of verbs. *Linguistics Inquiry, 28,* 27–68.

Chapter 5
The Telic Relationship in Compounds

Christian Bassac and Pierrette Bouillon

5.1 Introduction

The treatment of nominal compounds raises several problems for NLP. On the one hand the relationship between the head noun and the modifier can be implicit, such as in *petrol gauge*, where the *gauge* is an instrument that measures an amount of fuel. On the other hand this relationship can be ambiguous such as in *release signal* which can either refer to a signal which is activated when the release begins or to a signal that indicates that the release is on its way. It is thus necessary to have a representation language powerful enough to make these various interpretations explicit. The aim of this paper[1] is to use the Generative Lexicon (Pustejovsky 1995) to offer a detailed analysis of the telic relationship in nominal compounds both in French and in Turkish. We first focus on general properties of this kind of compound (taking our examples from French but the explanations provided to account for the general properties here discussed hold for Turkish too) and then we suggest that lexicalization both in French and Turkish directly follows from the aspectual properties of the complement (or the predicate recoverable from it) encoded within the telic and from the position of the argument they instantiate.

---

[1] We thank our Turkish informants, E. Boton, A. Erturk, C. Hakiemez, I. Yildiz, for their help with the Turkish data. This work has also benefited from comments, and valuable suggestions from people to whom we are grateful: A. Birturk, M. Ciçek and A. Göksel. Many thanks too are due to J. Pustejovsky for his advice on a previous version of this paper. We remain responsible for the interpretation of facts given here and for any mistake.

C. Bassac (✉)
Université Michel de Montaigne Bordeaux 3, Pessac, France

CRTT & INRIA, Université de Lyon 2, Lyon, France
e-mail: cbassac@mail.univ-lyon2.fr

P. Bouillon
FTI/TIM/ISSCO, University of Geneva, Geneva, Switzerland
e-mail: pierrette.bouillon@issco.unige.ch

J. Pustejovsky et al. (eds.), *Advances in Generative Lexicon Theory*, Text, Speech and Language Technology 46, DOI 10.1007/978-94-007-5189-7_5,
© Springer Science+Business Media Dordrecht 2013

Fig. 5.1 Embedded structure
of the telic role

$$\begin{bmatrix} \alpha \\ \text{QS} \begin{bmatrix} \text{type-lcp} \\ \text{FM} = \dots \\ \text{TEL} = \begin{bmatrix} \text{FM} = \text{event} \\ \text{AG} = \text{precondition} \end{bmatrix} \\ \text{AG} = \dots \end{bmatrix} \end{bmatrix}$$

5.2 The Telic Relationship

In some nominal compounds the implicit relation is encoded in the telic role (Busa 1996; Fabre 1996; Copestake 2003). This is clear from the comparison between the following pairs in (1) and (2):

(1)   verre de vin
      (glass prep-*de* wine)
      "glass of wine"

(2)   verre à vin
      (glass prep-*à* wine)
      "wine glass"

In these examples of French nominal compounds the prepositions *à* and *de* are indications that the complement specifies relationships which are encoded in two different roles namely the formal role (in which case it follows that the compound refers to a container) or the telic one (in which case nothing is said about the content of the glass; what is focused is the function of the object). This is summarized in (3) and (4):

(3)   verre de vin/pot de confiture/flacon de parfum/etc.
      ⇒ a glass/pot/bottle which contains an amount of wine/jam/perfume, etc.

(4)   verre à vin/pot à confiture/flacon à parfum/etc.
      ⇒ a glass/pot/bottle/into which you pour/put wine/jam/perfume

The saturation of the telic role instead of the formal role leads to various consequences. As Pustejovsky showed, the event encoded in the telic role receives a modal interpretation, which can be accounted for by its embedded structure illustrated in Fig. 5.1 (Pustejovsky 1998; Bouillon 1997; Busa 1996).

A *knife* for instance can be used for the act of cutting as shown by the representation in Fig. 5.2 where the act of cutting is a necessary condition for the result of the event. In other words, a knife cuts something (CUT_RES(ULT)) if somebody makes use of it (USE ∧ CUT_ACT).

As will be seen later on, this complex structure accounts for some important characteristics of this type of nominal compound. We will first show how some empiric phenomena allow us to motivate the distinction between these two types of compounds and then analyse the problems raised by their lexicalization both in French and in Turkish.

Fig. 5.2 Lexical entry
of "knife"

$$
\text{knife} \begin{bmatrix}
\text{ARGSTR} = \begin{bmatrix} \text{ARG1} = x : \text{artifact} \\ \text{D-ARG1} = y : \text{ind} \\ \text{D-ARG2} = z : \text{ind} \end{bmatrix} \\[2em]
\text{EVENSTR} = \begin{bmatrix} \text{D-E1} = e_2 : \text{state} \\ \text{D-E2} = e_1 : \text{event} \\ \text{D-E3} = e_0 : \text{event} \end{bmatrix} \\[2em]
\text{QS} = \begin{bmatrix} \text{artifact-lcp} \\ \text{FM} = x \\ \text{TEL} = \begin{bmatrix} \text{FM} = \text{cut\_res}_2(e,y) \\ \text{AG} = \text{use } 0 (e,z,x) \wedge \text{cut\_act}_1(e,x,y) \end{bmatrix} \end{bmatrix}
\end{bmatrix}
$$

5.3 On Some General Characteristics

At least three characteristics motivate the distinction between the two types of compounds previously mentioned in (1) and (2). As was noticed in Anscombre (1999) and Bassac and Bouillon (2005), they first differ in the grammaticality of anaphoric reference as the following examples show:

(5) le verre de vin$_i$ est sur la table; le vin$_i$/il$_i$ a une belle couleur
   "the glass of wine is on the table; the wine/it has a nice colour"

(6) ??le verre à vin$_i$ est sur la table; le vin$_i$/il$_i$ a une belle couleur
   "??the wine glass is on the table; the wine/it has a nice colour"

The respective qualia structures readily account for these differences. We will consider that the default representation of *verre* ("glass") is as shown in Fig. 5.3. It is something used as a container you pour liquid into.

In composition with a **liquid** PP introduced by the preposition *de* (*de vin* in example *(5))*, the semantics of this type of noun is however modified and *verre* is then coerced to a complex object. In more formal terms, the composition rule introduces a dot object (as described in Pustejovsky 1995 and Asher and Pustejovsky this volume). This rule forces the container reading with the indication *of the presence of wine within it*. The function of the compound is that of the complement i.e. *boire* ("to drink"), as shown in its interpretation in (7):

(7) $\lambda x \exists y \, [verre\text{-}de\text{-}vin(x{:}\text{artifact}.y{:}\text{wine}) \wedge hold_F(x,y) \wedge \Diamond \lambda w \, \lambda e[drink_T (e,w,y) \ldots] \wedge \ldots]$

On the contrary, in *verre à vin* ("wine glass"), *vin* instantiates the argument of the telic of the head noun (**y**), hence the reading of an object that *may be used to contain wine*. V*erre à vin* therefore receives the interpretation in (8).

(8) $\lambda x \, [verre\text{-}\grave{a}\text{-}vin(x) \wedge \text{artifact}(x) \wedge \Diamond \lambda e \, \exists y \, [contain_T(e,x,y{:}\text{wine}) \ldots] \wedge \ldots]$

Fig. 5.3 Lexical entry for
verre (glass)

$$\begin{bmatrix} \text{verre/glass} \\ \begin{bmatrix} \textbf{artifact-lcp} \\ \text{FM} = x : \text{artifact} \\ \text{TEL} = \begin{bmatrix} \text{FM} = \text{contain(E2,x,y:liq)} \\ \text{AG} = \text{use(e0,z,x)} \wedge \text{pour-into\_act(e1,z,y,x)} \end{bmatrix} \\ \text{AG} = ... \end{bmatrix} \end{bmatrix}$$

Here the existence of wine is thus modal and consequently *verre à vin* does *not* presuppose the presence of wine in the glass. From there it follows that the anaphoric reference in the form of *le vin* ("the wine") or *il* ("it") is impossible in (6) as there is reference to an element which is opaque in the representation but is licit in (5) where this element is quantified.

These representations also explain why coercion is variably successful according to the type of compound. In example (9) *verre de vin* can be coerced into 'drink the liquid contained in the glass' as *verre de vin* refers to the object which contains the liquid. In (10) the only element available is the event in the agentive ("make") as *verre à vin* refers only to the artifact.

(9)   Je termine mon verre de vin ⇒ de boire le verre de vin
        "I am finishing my glass of wine" ⇒ drinking the glass of wine

(10)   Je termine le/mon verre à vin ⇒ *de boire le verre vin/de fabriquer le
              verre vin
        "I am finishing the/my wine glass"⇒ *drinking the wine
        glass/making the wine glass

Finally, the same explanation accounts for the different distributional properties of the two types of compounds. In examples (11) and (12), the verb "to drink" selects for a **liquid** object, a constraint that can be satisfied in (12) for the reasons explained below, but not in (11).

(11)   ??je bois mon verre à vin
        "I drink my wine glass"

(12)   je bois mon verre de vin
        "I drink my glass of wine"

Yet, Anscombre (1999) noticed that although in examples (13) and (14) compounds have the forms of those in (2) or (6) namely "N1 à N2", contrary to what could be expected, anaphoric reference is clearly possible:

(13)   mon stylo à bille$_i$ est nouveau mais sa/la bille$_i$ est de mauvaise qualité
        "my ballpoint pen is brand new but its/the ball is of poor quality"

(14)   mes patins à roulettes$_i$ sont sur la table; leurs/les roulettes$_i$ sont usées
        "my roller skates are on the table; their/the rollers are starting to wear"

However, (13) and (14) are not counter examples and can be explained as follows. Despite the apparent similarity in their construction *stylo à bille* ("ball point pen") or *patins à roulettes* ("roller skates") and *verre à vin* ("wine glass") differ in that in the former couples of compounds the complements refer to an actual subpart of the object. This argument is then existentially quantified, as shown in the representation below:

(15) $\lambda x \; \exists w \; [patins\text{-}à\text{-}roulettes(x) \land \text{artifact}(x) \land \text{has\_part}(x,w \text{ :rollers}) \land \Diamond \; \lambda e$
       $[\text{roll}(e,x,w)] \land \dots]$

Patins à roulettes are skates composed of rollers that can be used for rolling. In fact the existence of the ball or that of the rollers is predicted with simple nouns as indicated by the example below and contrary to what happens with the noun *verre* (see example 17).

(16)   mon stylo est nouveau mais sa bille est de mauvaise qualité/mes patins
       sont sur la table; leurs roulettes sont usées
       "my pen is new but its ball is of poor quality»/"my skates are on the
       table but their rollers are starting to wear"

(17)   ??le verre est sur la table mais son eau est froide
       "the glass is on the table but its water is cold"

In what follows we will see how this complex representation of telic compounds explains the range of possible lexicalizations both in French and Turkish.

5.4   Lexicalization in French

5.4.1   Introduction

A predictable consequence of the fact that the telic has a complex structure is that the complement of the compound may instantiate the various arguments available in the telic of the head noun, with connected various lexicalizations and interpretations. As expected, the complement can therefore be an event (in that case, it specifies the event of the resulting telic; see Sect. 5.4.2) or an individual (it will then instantiate one of the arguments of the telic of the head noun, cf. Sect. 5.4.3).

5.4.2   Event Modifier

In French, three different types of compounds should be distinguished depending on the type of event denoted by the complement and the way it composes with the head:

Fig. 5.4 Lexical entry for
fusil de chasse (hunting rifle)

$$\left[\begin{array}{l} \text{fusildechasse/huntingrifle} \\ \text{TEL} = \begin{bmatrix} \text{FM} = \text{hunt}(e_2, x, y) \\ \text{AG} = \text{use}(e_1, x, y\text{: rifle}) \end{bmatrix} \end{array}\right]$$

Fig. 5.5 Lexical entry
for *armée de protection*
(protection army)

$$\left[\begin{array}{l} \text{arméedeprotection/protectnioarmy} \\ \text{TEL} = \begin{bmatrix} \text{FM} = \text{protect\_sre}(e_2, y) \\ \text{AG} = \text{protect\_tac}(e_1, x\text{: army,y}) \end{bmatrix} \end{array}\right]$$

- **"N1 de N2"** with N2 **process:** here the **process** complement noun N2 instantiates the formal within the telic. For instance a *fusil de chasse* ("hunting rifle") is a rifle used in order to go hunting (*chasser*) (Fig. 5.4).
- **"N1 de N2"** with N2 denoting the **result** of an activity that can be caused by N1: in this case, the complement noun N2 is a complex event (**process.state***) whose headed state part instantiates the formal within the telic. For instance *une armée de protection* ("a protection army") is an army whose action leads to actual protection (see also Johnston and Busa 1999) (Fig. 5.5).

The two different instantiations of the roles embedded within the telic in compounds "N1 de N2: **process**" and "N1 de N2: **result nominal**" result from differences in reference connected with these compounds. A *fusil de chasse* ("hunting rifle") is a weapon that actually allows you to go hunting with no other requirement or intermediary step than that of carrying a gun. Things are slightly different with the compound *armée de protection* ("protection army"). Here the dynamic action of the army is a sine qua non condition that will allow and lead to actual protection. It seems that to some extent, a similar opposition is lexicalised in the English affixes "–ion" and "–ing" (Pustejovsky 1995). Thus, "a protecting garment" provides immediate protection against rain or cold, and correlatively, "??a protection garment" is unlikely whereas "a protective garment" seems fine. In "a protection racket" what is expressed is different: the racket is a sine qua non condition, a necessary intermediate step that will lead to protection and correlatively "??a protecting racket" and "??protective racket" are unlikely. In a nutshell, in the former compound N2-"ing" gives protection, in the latter, N2-"ion" leads to protection thanks to the actualization of the event identified by N2.

- **"N1 à V"** with V in the infinitive, denoting a left headed transition: when the complement is in the infinitive form, the event it denotes co-composes with that of the head. It is an indication of the resultative state brought about by the event encoded in the telic of the head noun such as in (18) and (19):

  (18)   fer à repasser
         (iron prep iron)
         "iron"

Fig. 5.6 Lexical entry for *fer à repasser* (iron)

$$\begin{bmatrix} \text{fer à repasser/iron} \\ \text{TEL} = \begin{bmatrix} \text{FM} = \text{ironed\_res}(e_2, y) \\ \text{AG} = \text{give-shape\_act}(e_1, x, y, z : \text{iron}) \end{bmatrix} \end{bmatrix}$$

Fig. 5.7 Lexical entry for *poudre à lessiver* (washing powder)

$$\begin{bmatrix} \text{poudre à lessiver/washing powder} \\ \text{TEL} = \begin{bmatrix} \text{FM} = \text{wash\_res}(e_2, y) \\ \text{AG} = \text{clean\_act}(e_1, x, y, z : \text{powder}) \end{bmatrix} \end{bmatrix}$$

(19)   poudre à lessiver
       (powder prep wash)
       "washing powder"

The telic of these compounds are respectively shown in Figs. 5.6 and 5.7.

Here however the result state has not been achieved. The "iron" and the "powder" in (18) and (19) can be used to reach a state but will not lead to it. Hence the different readings of the two compounds in composition with *ancien* ("former/ancient"). Compare for example *une ancienne armée de protection* (that does not protect any more, "a former protection army") (or *une ancienne procedure de divorce* -> "a former divorce procedure", *un ancien hall d'arrivée* -> "a former arrival hall") and un *ancien fer à repasser* ("old iron") (or *une ancienne table à repasser* -> "old ironing board", etc.) (cf. Bouillon 1997 for an analysis of this type of adjectives).

From these respective representations, it follows that some constraints on the viability and productivity of compounds can readily be accounted for:

- In the latter type of compounds the verb in the infinitive must refer in its event structure to one resultative state. Therefore (20), (21), and (22) are all ruled out since in these examples the verbs refer to processes.

(20)   *fusil à chasser
       (rifle prep hunt)

(21)   *outil à travailler
       (tool prep work)

(22)   *table à masser
       (table prep massage)

- The contrast in the grammaticality of the following pairs (23)/(24) and (25)/(26) results from the fact that in the former pair *fer* ("iron") encapsulates a function with the mention of a resultative state (to give shape to). This is not the case for *table* ("board") whose telic is a process (support, bear the weight of). Therefore, in *fer à repasser* ("iron") or *fer à friser* ("curling tongs") the complement can only specify the resultative state, whereas with *table*, the telic does not contain any resultative state and it can therefore be either a process or a left-headed transition.

(23)   fer à repasser
        (iron prep iron)
        "iron"

(24)   *fer de repassage
        (iron prep ironing)

(25)   table de repassage
        (table prep ironing)
        "ironing board"

(26)   table à repasser
        (table prep iron)

• If the N2 is a result nominal, the compound should have the form "N1 de N2"
  versus "N1 à V" in the infinitive, as shown in the following pairs:

(27)   carte de credit
        *carte à créditer
        (credit card)

(28)   maison de retraite
        (pansioner's home)

(29)   camp de concentration
        *camp à concentrer
        (concentration camp)

5.4.3 Individual Modifier

Mutatis mutandis our treatment of event complements can be applied to individual
complements. There again different interpretations of the individual noun appear
in connection with the nature of the argument that is instantiated. Consider the
following examples discussed at length in Fabre and Sebillot (1994):

(30)   filet à cheveux
        (net prep hair)
        "hair net"

(31)   filet à crevettes
        (net prep shrimps)
        shrimping net"

   Example (30) refers to a net that keeps hair in place, whereas *filet à crevettes*
in (31) refers to a net you catch shrimps with. These two apparent contradictory
interpretations neatly follow from the default telic of *net* whose function is to catch
something and keep it (Fig. 5.8).

Fig. 5.8 Lexical entry
for *filet* (net)

$$\left[\begin{array}{l} \text{filet/net} \\ \text{TEL} = \left[\begin{array}{l} \text{FM} = \text{keep\_res}(e_2, x, y) \\ \text{AG} = \text{catch\_act}(e_1, z, y, x : \text{net}) \end{array}\right] \end{array}\right]$$

Fig. 5.9 Lexical entry for
filet à cheveux (hair net)

$$\left[\begin{array}{l} \text{filetàcheveux/hair net} \\ \text{TEL} = \left[\begin{array}{l} \text{FM} = \text{keep\_res}(e_2, x, y : \text{hair}) \\ \text{AG} = \text{catch\_act}(e_1, z, y, x : \text{net}) \end{array}\right] \end{array}\right]$$

Fig. 5.10 Lexical entry for
filet à crevettes (shrimping
net)

$$\left[\begin{array}{l} \text{filetàcrevettes/shrimpingnet} \\ \text{TEL} = \left[\begin{array}{l} \text{FM} = \text{catch\_act}(e_2, z, y, x : \text{shrimp}) \\ \text{AG} = \text{use}(e_1, z, x : \text{net}) \end{array}\right] \end{array}\right]$$

Given the complex structure of this telic, the N "in filet prep N" can either instantiate the argument of the whole transition or that of the initial process, thereby leading to the following two interpretations in Figs. 5.9 and 5.10.

In *filet à cheveux* (Fig. 5.9) the net refers to a net used to keep hair, i.e. a net which, whenever used in its capacity, keeps hair. In filet à crevettes (Fig. 5.10) the net refers to a net used to catch shrimps. The complex representation of the telic of *moulin* ("mill") similarly explains how *moulin à café* ("coffee mill") refers to a mill for grinding coffee while a *moulin à huile* ("an oil press") is an apparatus for extracting oil. In the Generative Lexicon, a mill can be characterized as something that grinds/presses an object (agentive of the telic) in order to extract its constitutive elements (formal of the telic). In *moulin à café, café* instantiates the argument of the initial process ('to grind'); in *moulin à huile, huile* saturates the argument of the resultative state ('to be extracted'). This is even more striking with *pressoir* ("press") since the two different types of compound are attested (see le Petit Robert for example), as shown in examples (32) and (33).

(32)   pressoir à cidre/pressoir à pommes
        (press prep cider/press prep apples)

(33)   pressoir à huile/pressoir à olives
        (press prep oil/press prep olives)

These interpretations would be very difficult to explain without a complex apparatus like GL. In some way, it motivates and validates the enumerative interpretation rules provided by Fabre and Sébillot (1994), for examples: *if the telic of the head noun is contain + animate, the interpretation of the compound is N1 catch N2; if it is contain + inanimate, it is N1 contain N2.* We will show now that the same conclusion holds for Turkish too and that a complex telic accounts for both the possible lexicalizations and for the various constructions.

5.5   Lexicalization in Turkish

5.5.1   Introduction

In Turkish, nominal compounds display a fairly strict specialization of two affixes in the expression of constitutive and telic roles. Thus an equivalent for "ballpoint pen" (cf. (13)) would be (34) in which –*li* is attached to the non-head noun:

(34)   bilya-lı kalem
        (ballpoint-li pen)
        "ballpoint pen"

whereas an equivalent for "wine glass" (cf. (4)) would be (35) in which –*i* is attached to the head noun:

(35)   şarap bardağ-ı
        (wine glass-i)
        "wine glass"

An interesting characteristic regarding the expression of the telic role, is that it can be expressed by two concurrent morphemes, namely -*i* (with allomorphs/*i/ı/u/ü/*) which is attached to the head noun or -*lik* (with allomorphs/*lik/ l/ık/luk/lük/*) which is attached to the modifier noun (both sets of allomorphs being phonologically conditioned and distributed according to vowel harmony). This situation is represented in (36) and (37) respectively (*(s)* is a connecting consonant in between two vocalic phonemes):

(36)   N2 N1 -(s)-i

(37)   N2-lik N1

(36) can also represent compounds expressing an agentive role such as in (38):

(38)   meyva suyu
        (fruit water-y-i)
        "fruit juice"

and as the expression of the telic role, the affixation of -*i* to the head noun is much more productive than that of -*lik* to the modifier noun. (39) and (40) below are examples of what from now on will be called **telic1** and (41) and (42) are examples of what will be called **telic2**.

(39)   şarap bardağ- ı
        (wine glass- i)
        "wine glass"

(40)   buz paten-i
        (ice skate -i)
        "ice skates"

(41)   alet-lik kutu
       tool -lik box
       "tool box" (but cf. infra)

(42)   mektup-luk kağıt
       (letter -luk paper)
       "writing paper" (but cf. infra)

Constructions such as (36) are definitely compounds[2] but **telic2** constructions such as that of (37) cannot be considered as compounds.[3] Yet, they are relevant in our study in so far as they are concurrent forms of the expression of the telic and the conditions of concurrence between these two forms must be accounted for.

Most constructions in the form of (37) can have an equivalent in the form of (36) but many compounds lack a concurrent construction in the form of (37). For instance (47) and (48) are fine but (49) is ungrammatical:

(47)   mektup kağıd-ı
       (letter paper-i)
       "writing paper"

(48)   çamaşır makine-s-i
       (linen machine-s-i)
       "washing machine"

---

[2]First, internal modification is impossible as shown by (43) and (44):

(43)   *şarap güzel bardağ-ı
       (wine nice glass–i)
       "*wine nice glass"

(44)   güzel şarap bardağ-ı
       (nice wine glass -i)
       "nice wine glass"

and second such constructions receive only one stress (on the head, which is the final word) contrary to syntactic constructions (phrases), in which both words are stressed.

[3]Internal modification is possible as indicated by (45) and (46):

(45)   recel-lik cilek
       jam-lik strawberry
       "strawberries for jam"

(46)   recel-lik tatlı cilek
       jam-lik sweet strawberry
       "sweet strawberries for jam"

and the [N1-lik] part of the construction is a relational adjective.

Fig. 5.11 Lexical entry
for "N2 –lik N1"

$$\begin{bmatrix} \text{N2-lik N1} \\ \text{TEL} = \begin{bmatrix} \text{FM} = \text{N2\_res}(e_2, z) \\ \text{AG} = \text{N2\_act}(e_1, x : \text{spker}, z, y : \text{N1}) \end{bmatrix} \end{bmatrix}$$

(49)   *çamaşır-lık makine
        (linen -lik machine)

The suffix –*lik* is a denominal suffix used to derive nouns (among other uses irrelevant here) which identify objects conceived so as to serve a particular function, or for a precise use, for instance to adapt to weather conditions or to ease a sensory function. (50) and (51) respectively are examples of such nouns:

(50)   yağmur-luk
        rain-luk
        "rain coat"

(51)   göz-lük
        eye-lük
        "spectacles"

This use of this suffix helps understand the raison d'être of **telic2** which is to express either:

• that the object identified by the head noun, is going to be used for a purpose which 1) depends solely on the speaker's will, and 2) may be more or less different from the use this object habitually has or is supposed to have.
• that the object identified by the modifier noun is the result of particular care, dedication from the part of the speaker.

Therefore the meaning of (41) and (42) must be qualified and understood thus: the former as a box, whose planned and habitual use was for instance to contain shoes, which the speaker wants to turn into a tool-box, the latter as a writing paper whose quality, color, shape, etc. will allow the speaker to write a beautiful, adorned letter very likely to be appreciated.

We propose that the qualia structure of 'N2-lik N1' will encode these properties in the following way. Firstly, the user will be restricted to the speaker and secondly the affixation of –*lik* to the modifier is an indication of an event with visible headed state (Fig. 5.11).

Consequently, the adjective *tam* (used to express that something suits a precise purpose, is very appropriate) can be inserted to modify the resultant state, allowing constructions such as (52):

(52)   bu tam aletlik kutu
        (this perfect tool lik box)
        "this perfect tool box (for me)"

Fig. 5.12 Lexical entry
for *sew –lik thread* (sewing
thread)

$$\begin{bmatrix} \text{dikis-lik iplik/sew-lik thread} \\ \text{TEL} = \begin{bmatrix} \text{FM} = \text{sew\_res}(e_2, z) \\ \text{AG} = \text{sew\_act}(e_1, x : \text{spker}, z : \text{garment}, y : \text{thread}) \end{bmatrix} \end{bmatrix}$$

Fig. 5.13 Lexical entry for
sew thread –i (sewing thread)

$$\begin{bmatrix} \text{dikis ipligi/sew thread - i} \\ \text{TEL} = \begin{bmatrix} \text{FM} = \text{sew\_act}(e_2, x, z, y) \\ \text{AG} = \text{use}(e_1, x, y : \text{thread}) \end{bmatrix} \end{bmatrix}$$

5.5.2   Instantiation of the Telic Role

5.5.2.1   Event Modifier

The claim above predicts that **telic2** is licit if the complement is a dotted type **process.state**. This is the case for instance in (53):

(53)   dikiş-lik iplik
       (sew-lik thread)
       "sewing thread"

Here the embedded formal expresses the resultative state as indicated below.

The form taken by **telic1** as expected is *dikiş ipliği* whose lexical representation is.

Following our definitions previously sketched out in 5.1 the difference between **telic1** (Fig. 5.13) and **telic2** (Fig. 5.12) lies both in the quantification of the variable **x** which is generically quantified in **telic1** and in the instantiation of the embedded roles within the **telic**, as the formal here encodes a process.

5.5.2.2   Consequences

As a consequence of our proposal, **telic2** should be ruled out if the telic encodes a process, as no state is available in his case. This is exactly what happens in the following two cases in examples (54) and (55) below:

• the process is morphologically marked by the nominalization morpheme (*nom* in our glosses) whose allomorphs are */-ma/-me/*like in (54):

(54)   bekle-me salon-u
       (wait-nom room –u)
       "waiting room"

but

(55)   *bekle-me-lik salon
       (wait-nom –lik room)

Fig. 5.14 Lexical entry for
hunt rifle –i (hunting rifle)

$$\begin{bmatrix} \text{avtüfeg-i / hunt rifle-i} \\ \text{TEL} = \begin{bmatrix} \text{FM} = \text{hunt\_act}(e_P, x, y) \\ \text{AG} = \text{use}(e_1, x, y : \text{rifle}) \end{bmatrix} \end{bmatrix}$$

- the process is not marked morphologically like in (56):

(56)   av tüfeğ-i
        (hunt rifle -i)
        "hunting rifle"

but

(57)   *av-lik tüfek
        (hunt-lik rifle)

Here the only telic allowed is a **telic1** whose representation is given below (Fig. 5.14).

The same goes for examples (58) and (59):

(58)   spor sahası
        (sport ground-(s)i)
        "sports ground"

(59)   koşu at-ı
        (race horse-I)
        "race horse"

and as expected (60) and (61) below are ruled out:

(60)   *sporluk saha
        (sport-lik ground)

(61)   *koşuluk at
        (race-luk horse)

Another consequence of our proposal is the following:-*mal-me* being the mark of a process, if –*lik* is an indication of the presence of a resultative state, the co-presence of –*mal-me* and –*lik* should be conflicting and give an ungrammatical construction. This is generally so and (63) is a case in point. Whereas (62) is rare but acceptable to refer to a thread used to perform the general activity of sewing, (here *dikiş* = sewing, *et-* = verb stem of do,-*me* = process affix), (63) is ruled out.

(62)   dikis et-me ipliği
        (sewing do-nom thread-i)
        "a thread to do sewing"

Fig. 5.15 Lexical entry
for *letter -luk paper*

$$\left[\begin{array}{l} \text{mektup-luk kagit/letter-luk paper} \\ \text{TEL} = \left[\begin{array}{l} \text{FM} = \text{written\_rse}(e_2, y) \\ \text{AG} = \text{write\_act}(e_1, x:\text{spker}, y:\text{letter}, z:\text{paper}) \end{array}\right] \end{array}\right]$$

Fig. 5.16 Lexical entry
for *letter paper -i*

$$\left[\begin{array}{l} \text{mektupkagidi/letter paper-i} \\ \text{TEL} = \left[\begin{array}{l} \text{FM} = \text{write\_act}(e_2, x, y:\text{letter}, z) \\ \text{AG} = \text{use}(e_1, x, z:\text{paper}) \end{array}\right] \end{array}\right]$$

(63)   *dikis-lik et-me iplik
        (sewing do-nom thread-i)

This is because it displays the presence of two contradictory marks: that of the resultative state (−*lik*) and that of a process (−*me*). The most natural way to express (63) would be (64) in which the verb *dik-* (verb stem of "sew") is used instead of *et-*, and in which *dikiş,* is the internal argument of *dik-*:

(64)   dikiş dik-me ipliği
        (sewing sew-nom thread-i)

5.5.2.3 Individual Modifier

The analysis previously provided for event modifiers is still valid for individual modifiers and consequently **telic2** should be licit if the individual denoted by the modifier is an argument of an implicit event with a resultative state, i.e. an accomplishment. This is the case exemplified in (42) and (47) where *mektup* (letter) is the result of the implicit event "write". The telics for (42) (**telic2**) and (47) (**telic1**) are then respectively (Figs. 5.15 and 5.16).

Moreover, the impossibility for the process affix −*mel-ma* to appear within event modifiers of **telic2** (cf.(62) and (63) supra) still holds with telic objects. This correctly predicts that (65) and (66) are fine:

(65)   balık ağı
        (fish net-i)
        "fishing net"

(66)   balık tutma ağı
        (fish catch-ma agi)
        "net used to catch fish"

whereas only (67) is correct (vs (68)):

(67)   baliklik ağ
        (fish-lik net)

(68)   *baliklik tutma ağ
        (fish -lik catch-ma net)

When the telic encodes an object, given the theorization proposed here, it follows that another pragmatic requirement must be met for **telic2** to be licit. The head noun must refer to an object whose function is not strictly limited to a precise, determined or unique use. Obviously it is very difficult to turn any machine into a machine which can for instance *wash linen*. Contrary to what happens for a box, in which various objects can be put away, a machine is an apparatus which comes with a given use right from its conception and subsequently no other use than that for which it was conceived is possible, hence the ungrammaticality of **telic2** compounds such as (49) in the pair (48), (49) repeated here under (69) and (70):

(69)   çamaşır makine-s-i
        (linen machine-s-i)
        "washing machine"

(70)   *çamaşır-lık makine
        (linen -lik machine)

5.6   Conclusion

In this paper we have focused on one kind of compounds whose complement saturates the telic of the complex expression. We have shown how the proposed representation and more specifically some particularities of the telic relation (modality/opacity) motivate some general properties of this kind of compound regarding anaphoric reference, coercion, and lexicalization in French and in Turkish. From the representations outlined above, it emerges that French and Turkish display a strictly similar construction of the telic relation when the complement noun encodes a process. But they differ in that whereas in French there seems to be no telic in which the embedded agentive is restricted to the speaker (at least there is no specialized or distinct form for such compounds), in Turkish there seems to be no equivalent for French compounds such as *poudre à lessiver* ("washing powder") or *moulin à huile* ("oil press"). It follows that the nearest equivalent in Turkish for *poudre à lessiver* ("washing powder") is (71):

(71)   çamasır tozu
        (linen powder-u)

Contrary to what happens in French, here the construction expresses a process as indicated by the strictly equivalent (72):

(72)   çamasır yıkama toz-u
        (linen wash-nom powder-u)

In some cases the nearest Turkish equivalent for a French compound is a single noun such as in (73):

(73)   ütü
       "iron"
       (the apparatus used for ironing)

In this case, the corresponding verb is constructed with the denominal affix *–le* as shown in (74):

(74)   ütü-le mek
       (iron-verb affix infinitive affix)

Subsequently, the nearest Turkish equivalent for *table à repasser* (ironing table) is (75):

(75)   ütü masası
       (iron table(s)i)

or as expected (76):

(76)   ütü-le-me masası
       (iron-denom affix-nom table-s-i)

which explicitly is a process as indicated by the affix *–me*. The same goes for the nearest Turkish equivalent for *moulin à huile* which is quite explicitly expressed via a process as indicated by (77):

(77)   zeitun presi
       (olive press-i)

We therefore conclude that in Turkish true compounds, **telic1** never expresses a resultative state and that correlatively **telic2** specialises in the expression of a resultative state, which is coherent with the hypothesis put forward as the starting point of our analysis.

This study and the conclusions we reached are interesting from an NLP point of view because it first shows that there are clear motivations for the existence of a class of telic compounds, and that consequently elements of this class must be identified as such. We have also tried to show that the various lexicalizations (via prepositions in French or affixations in Turkish) and the various constraints and interpretations associated can only be accounted for by the complex representations provided by the Qualia structures; subsequently, assigning simple paraphrastic equivalents to these compounds (along the lines suggested for instance by Copestake (2003)) seems very difficult for this class of compounds. Even two constructions via a single preposition like the French preposition *à* in *filet à crevettes* and *filet à cheveux* (or *pressoir à huile* and *pressoir à olives*) receive two completely different paraphrases. In automatic analyses the extraction from corpora of verbs such as *catch, keep* or *hold*, from a noun like *net* is certainly possible (see Claveau and Sébillot, in this volume;

Claveau et al. 2001; Lapatta and Lascarides 2003), but only when the role they instantiate in the Qualia structure is known (Formal or Agentive of the Telic), can a paraphrastic equivalent be adequate. Consequently, a fine-grained representation such as that provided by the Qualia structure is clearly needed, and we have shown that this representation is both powerful enough to account for the lexicalization and viability of both French and Turkish telic compounds, and precise enough to allow the adequate interpretations.

References

Anscombre, J. C. (1999). Le jeu de la prédication dans certains composés nominaux. *Langue Française, 122,* 52–69.
Asher, A., & Pustejovsky, J. (this volume). *A type composition logic for generative lexicon.* The metaphysics of words in context.
Bassac, Ch, & Bouillon, P. (2005, May 19–21). Qualia structure and anaphoric reference in compounds. In *Third international workshop on generative approaches to the lexicon* (pp. 27–35), Geneva Switzerland.
Bouillon, P. (1997). *Polymorphie et sémantique lexicale: le cas des adjectifs.* Lille: Presse du Septentrion.
Busa, F. (1996). *Compositionality and the semantics of nominals,* PhD Thesis, Brandeis University.
Claveau, V., Sébillot, P., Bouillon, P., & Fabre, C. (2001). Acquérir des éléments du lexique génératif: quels résultats et à quels coût? *Traitement Automatique des Langues, 42*(3), 729–754.
Copestake, A. (2003). Compounds revisited. In *Proceedings of the second international workshop on generative approaches to the Lexicon* (pp. 20–30), Geneva, Switzerland.
Fabre, C. (1996). Interpretation of nominal compounds: Combining domain –independent and domain –Specific Information. In *Coling96,* Copenhagen.
Fabre, C., & Sébillot, P. (1994). Interprétation sémantiques des composes nominaux anglais et français sans constituant déverbal. In *Proceedings of the Workshop on Compound Nouns* (pp. 108–124), Geneva, Switzerland.
Johnston, M., & Busa, F. (1999). Qualia structure and the compositional interpretation of compounds. In E. Viegas (Ed.), *Breadth and depth of semantic lexicon.* Dordrecht: Kluwer.
Lapatta, M., & Lascarides, A. (2003). A probabilistic account of logical metonymy. *In Computational Linguistics, 29,* 261–315.
Pustejovsky, J. (1995). *The generative lexicon.* Cambridge: MIT Press.
Pustejovsky, J. (1998). The semantics of lexical Underspecification. *Folia Linguistia, 32*(3–4), 323–347.

Chapter 6
Metonymy and Metaphor: Boundary Cases and the Role of a Generative Lexicon

Sabine Bergler

6.1 Introduction

Recent advances in language technologies in areas such as information extraction (MUC[1]), question answering (TREC[2]), and summarization (DUC[3]) have explored extensively the power of statistical NLP in the age of ready availability of large, annotated datasets. Groundbreaking efforts of organizers of these and other continued shared tasks in the spirit of shared resources drive to make developed tools robust and available to the community. We can rely thus on annotated corpora (LDC),[4] taggers (Brill 1995; Hepple 2000) and parsers (Grinberg et al. 1995; Briscoe et al. 2006), and development environments such as GATE (Cunningham 2002) which comes with extensive word lists for named entity recognition and partial analysis tools, such as date grammars, *etc.* The overall goal is not to understand and represent the meaning of texts in an application-neutral way, but to "get at" bits of information hidden in textual documents and extract as many of them as possible for a particular application, leading to partial analysis methods. While partial "syntactic" analysis (phrase chunking, tagging, *etc.*) has been a mainstay, partial semantic techniques are still in their infancy, with the notable exception of word sense disambiguation (Edmonds and Kilgarriff 2003), annotation and normalization of temporal information (Verhagen et al. 2005), the detection of

---

[1]http://www.itl.nist.gov/iaui/894.02/related_projects/muc/

[2]http://trec.nist.gov/

[3]http://duc.nist.gov/

[4]http://www.ldc.upenn.edu/

S. Bergler (✉)
Computer Science and Software Engineering Department, Concordia University,
Montreal, QC, Canada
e-mail: sabine.bergler@gmail.com

J. Pustejovsky et al. (eds.), *Advances in Generative Lexicon Theory*, Text,
Speech and Language Technology 46, DOI 10.1007/978-94-007-5189-7_6,
© Springer Science+Business Media Dordrecht 2013

textual entailment (Bar-Haim et al. 2006), and sentiment analysis (Andreevskaia et al. 2006). In current, shallow processing the explicit treatment of metonymy and metaphor can be avoided by, for instance, listing the most important ones as synonymous (as happens also, implicitly, for statistical approaches). But with the renewed importance of symbolic approaches to semantic issues such as recognition of textual entailment, the explicit understanding of the additional connotations implied by metonymy and metaphor receives new impetus.

Metaphor is construed as understanding one thing in terms of another, thus requiring a mapping from the source domain to the target domain along certain salient attributes or features (see Lakoff and Johnson 1980). Metonymy is construed as "a trope in which one word is put for another that suggests it" (Porter 1913) usually requiring some contextual or lexical contiguity between the literal and metonymic term.

This paper addresses a particular problem in the processing of phrases that include both, logical metonymy and metaphor. In particular, we consider here metonymy only in the argument position of words or phrases (where it violates the selectional restrictions but is recoverable as a lexical contiguity in the given context) and metaphor only in the position of those words or phrases that do take arguments. In particular, this paper addresses the case where both interpretations are possible yet not compatible.[5]

Computational linguistics has addressed metonymy either through the structure of an enriched lexicon (see Pustejovsky 1995) or by relaxing subcategorization constraints such as to avoid type violations for most common co-occurrence types (see, for instance, Godard and Jayez 1993). These approaches do not touch on metaphor.

The literature on automatic non-literal language resolution, on the other hand, has proposed several architectures for proof-of-concept implementations of a comprehensive treatment of all (non-anomalous) non-literal language, using few lexical entries with features defined expressly for the purpose of each architecture (cf. Fass 1998). This was due in part to the previous unavailability of sufficiently rich lexica, since one of the major reasons behind these approaches was to reduce the proliferation of lexical entries and streamline the reasoning process for non-literal language resolution by stipulating the type of lexical information required to overcome the brittleness of incomplete lexica. Selectional restrictions and literal meaning are usually more narrowly defined for treatments of non-literal language than they are in treatments that do not have an explicit non-literal language resolution mechanism and deal with part of the phenomena using more encompassing definitions or procedures (cf. Godard and Jayez 1993; Pustejovsky and Bouillon 1995). This paper also assumes narrow definitions to demonstrate the type of interactions, which, on different data, have to be taken into account in more "permissive" approaches, as well.

---

[5]In addition, I only consider productive, ad hoc constructions and not idioms or composite expressions in the sense of Geeraerts (2002).

Work on automatic non-literal language resolution acknowledges the importance of lexical semantics[6] and often describes specific properties of the lexical entries that enable the inference processes that resolve non-literal language. However, the entries described to date are incomplete and ad hoc, focusing on few examples and ease of non-literal language processing without concern for the usefulness and compatibility of the described structures for normal, compositional language processing using sizable lexica. This was unavoidable in the absence of lexical semantic theories that cover non-literal language processing. This paper illustrates how these issues can be addressed comprehensively in the framework of the Generative Lexicon.

The *Generative Lexicon* (GL) (Pustejovsky 1991, 1995) provides a framework to express lexical entries of a large lexicon in a way that allows for easy interconnection on two levels: the pre-theoretic packaging of lexical information in pre-specified roles (in particular the four qualia, discussed below) allows a compositional semantics to operate on general grounds, while a meta-lexical structure enables further conceptual clustering for special purposes.

Lexical semantics benefits greatly from statistical and human analysis of large corpora, enriching our knowledge of usage in different styles and media. Together with improved inheritance techniques, these lexica allow us to look for solutions to problems of ambiguity and non-literal language in the lexicon itself. Proposals in that spirit treat violations of restrictions on semantic types using *coercion rules* (Pustejovsky 1991, 1995), violations of lexical attributes (for instance mass/count) using *lexical rules* (Copestake and Briscoe 1992), and metonymy traversing the structures in the lexicon (Pustejovsky 1991; Copestake 1992).

Thus it seems natural to attempt comprehensive treatment of non-literal language based in part on the lexicon structures described, in part on the computational treatment of the distinction and analysis of metonymy, metaphor, and anomaly found in (Fass et al. 1992; Fass 1998). The attempt to combine the enriched lexical semantics of the Generative Lexicon with the procedures designed independently to resolve non-literal language fails, not because the suggested treatments are inherently flawed, but because they were designed to cover impoverished data. In order to achieve a robust analysis system for free text, we need to study carefully which non-literal phenomena occur in different contexts. This paper illustrates a level of text complexity not yet covered by non-literal language treatments and outlines the mediating role a generative lexicon can play to bridge the gap.

---

[6]For a probabilistic account of logical metonymy see (Lapata and Lascarides 2003). This approach does not take context nor metaphor into account and is thus not further considered here.

6.2 The Generative Lexicon Framework

GL offers a rich, highly structured representation language for lexical semantics. The underlying theory of a generative lexicon stresses the importance of providing principled information associated with a word that is required for its proper use, thus as the rich qualia structure (Pustejovsky 1995). At the same time, GL has been designed to be used for practical applications, when lexical entries may only be partially specified and the lexicon develops incrementally. A lexical semantics based on GL theory should be considered as "when available", that is the reasoning outlined in this paper should be considered as desirable when the appropriate entries are available. Our discussion tries to outline exactly what information is required for the entries to make our analysis possible, when these entries are not available, the benefits of the analysis will not be available, either. We argue here that it is a very powerful notion for a theory to provide for underspecified entries to initiate partial semantic analysis.

Consider the well documented example of coercion of an argument to its expected type (Pustejovsky 1991, 1995). The entry given for *journal* (Fr., newspaper) in Bouillon and Busa (2001), for instance, illustrates this and is repeated here as entry for *magazine*.

$$(1) \quad \begin{bmatrix} \text{magazine} \\ \\ \text{ARGSTR} = \begin{bmatrix} \text{ARG1} = x : \text{org} \\ \text{ARG2} = y : \text{info.physobj} \\ \text{D} - \text{ARG1} = x : \text{hum} \\ \text{D} - \text{ARG2} = w : \text{hum} \end{bmatrix} \\ \\ \text{EVENTSTR} = \begin{bmatrix} \text{D} - \text{E1} = e_1 : \text{transition} \\ \text{D} - \text{E2} = e_2 : \text{transition} \end{bmatrix} \\ \\ \text{QS} = \begin{bmatrix} \text{org.info.physobj} - \text{lcp} \\ \text{FORM} = y \\ \text{TEL} = \text{read}(e_2, w, y) \\ \text{AG} = \text{publish}(e_1, x, y) \end{bmatrix} \end{bmatrix}$$

We are particularly interested here in the control of interpretation. If we view the "control structure" of a sentence rigidly as the verb subcategorizing for its arguments, we get a type clash for simple sentences such as

(2)   John enjoyed the magazine.

since enjoy requires an event. The event will be selected from the qualia structure, by default from the TELIC role encoding purpose. Here we find that the TELIC role (TEL) is given as *read,* which provides a proper event as complement for *enjoy.* (3), however, requires another role of magazine, namely its property physical object (physobj), available from the argument structure and FORMAL role (FORM)

(3)   John dropped the magazine.

Thus the lexical definition of *magazine* specifies *read* as the default purpose, licensing coercion. Coercion and co-specification avoid the proliferation of word senses (here the verb sense for *enjoy,* which selects for an event type, holds, as the argument *magazine* is coerced into a lexically associated event.)

6.2.1 Logical Metonymy

Logical metonymy is defined to occur when a logical argument (i.e. subpart) of a semantic type that is selected by some (contextually determined) function, denotes the semantic type itself (Pustejovsky 1991). Thus logical metonymy is based on a relation recoverable from the lexical structures of a generative lexicon, as opposed to conventional metonymy, which relies only on extra-linguistic knowledge to link the description to the target referent.[7]

Logical metonymy can be resolved by *type coercion,* "a semantic operation that converts an argument to the type which is expected by a function, where it would otherwise result in a type error" (Pustejovsky 1991), as described above.

One example of a typical metonymic extension is *synecdoche,* where the whole stands for a part. Consider

(4)   *The Bush administration said it is tightening controls on the export of U.S. products that could be used to manufacturemissiles and chemical weapons.*

Clearly, *the Bush administration* is an abstract entity, a union of the government employees under Bush. *Say,* on the other hand, specifies for a human subject. The metonymic extension in this example is straightforward: a spokesman, official, or otherwise legitimate representative, "speaking for" Bush and his administrators is metonymically replaced by the abstract entity of which he or she is a part. A lexical

---

[7]To what degree logical metonymy is also conventionalized has been shown in Bergler (1991), where the preferences of several reporting verbs for different types of subject metonymy were derived empirically and subsequently gave rise to the identification of necessary *semantic dimensions* in the definition of the semantic field of reporting verbs (Bergler 1993, 1995). Thus in the American newspaper idiom, *the White House* most comfortably co-occurs with the reporting verbs *claim* and *announce,* but almost never co-occurs with *say* or *tell,* only very infrequently with *admit* and *deny.* We will ignore these finer issues in the rest of this paper.

entry for administration would specify the crucial information for this metonymic extension in the CONSTITUTIVE[8] (CONST) role:

(5)   Partial entry for *administration*

$$\begin{bmatrix} \text{administration} \\ \text{QUALIA} = [\text{CONST} \qquad \text{group}(x, y), \text{human}(y)] \end{bmatrix}$$

This type of metonymic extension for the subject of *reporting verbs* (Bergler 1991), such as *announce, report, release, claim, etc.* is frequent while it is in general not possible with other verbs selecting for human subjects; e.g. motion verbs (with the exception of *move* and *go* and metaphoric use); or verbs of contemplation (such as *contemplate, consider, think*) would require a distributive reading, not the singling out of one member.

These latter verbs are closer to a different type of logical metonymy, reported by Copestake (1992). Copestake discusses the lexical structure of group denoting nouns in a Generative Lexicon environment, noting the metonymic extension from the members of a group to the group as a whole, giving rise to seeming violations of agreement in coordination as in

(6)   *The team was formed in 1977 but they were killed in a plane crash the next year.* (Copestake 1992, p. 109)

Again, it is the CONSTITUTIVE role[9] in the lexical entry for team that specifies that team is a group of humans, licensing the metonymic extension (marked by plural agreement).

Two problems remain with this structural treatment of logical metonymy, namely the required completeness and consistency of the lexicon, which we will ignore here, and the co-occurrence and interaction of metonymy with metaphor, where indeed their boundaries get blurred.

6.3   Data

The *Wall Street Journal* is notorious for word plays and the use of current language outside the stock market reports. Consider Fig. 6.1:

(S_1) displays both metonymy and metaphor in *Revenue-desperate magazines are getting cozy with advertisers.* While *getting cozy* can be construed compositionally as *working towards reaching the state of being cozy*, *getting cozy with someone* means (and this meaning is conventionalized[10]) *establishing close relations (often for a goal or benefit).* Thus the metaphoric meaning is not just an extension of the

---

[8]The **constitutive** role contains "has-part" information, including "consists-of".

[9]Called *constituency* in her notation.

[10]Or a semantic island (Sag and Wasow 1995).

`Garbage' Angers Potential Advertisers

(S₁) In this era of frantic competition for ad dollars, a lot of revenue-desperate magazines are getting pretty cozy with advertisers -- fawning over them in articles and offering pages of advertorial space. (S₂) So can a magazine survive by downright thumbing its nose at major advertisers?

(S₃) Garbage magazine, billed as' The Practical Journal for the Environment," is about to find out.

[...]

(S₄) Garbage editors have dumped considerable energy into a whirling rampage through supermarket aisles in a bid to identify corporate America's good guys and bad boys.

Fig. 6.1 Text by Thomas R. King, 11/02/89, *Wall Street Journal*

literal meaning of working to attain a certain state, but rather attaches a purpose to some action that is like 'getting cozy' in its sense of establishing close relations. It is a metaphor[11] that is frequent enough to be considered a phrasal verb in the American idiom. Tight typing would project a human agent from the literal sense, more permissive typing would add (possibly as alternate word senses) companies, institutions, *etc*. The latter case is not problematic here, in the former, metonymy has to be detected and the mechanisms detailed in (1) metonymically extend the FORMAL role of *organization* to the humans specified in D-ARG1, that make up the *organization*.

Automatic non-literal language resolution systems that treat metonymy, metaphor, and anomaly mostly share a standard sequence of steps during resolution. For instance, *met** (Fass 1991) first attempts a literal reading of a sentence. When no literal interpretation can be found, met* tests for the occurrence of metonymy (taking into account chains of metonymic extensions licensed in the lexicon). If metonymy cannot be established, met* looks for metaphor and finally, if that fails, stipulates an anomalous relationship between source and target. This approach is suitable to (S₁), where the selectional restrictions of the literal meaning of the verb lead to the correct metonymic selection of the *institution* reading for magazine due to its being constituted in part of humans.

6.3.1 GL Entry Fragments for (S₁')

Let us consider some simplified, partial lexical entries to illustrate how the resolution for (S₁') might proceed.

---

[11]Frequent conventionalized metaphor is covered in most computational lexica and in statistical recognition techniques, such as word sense disambiguation. Extensive corpus analysis with the methods of Hindle (1990), Pustejovsky et al. (1993), Smadja and McKeown (1990) can identify the most frequent cases. This paper concerns those metaphors that are not represented in the lexicon.

(S$_1$')   *Revenue-desperate magazines are getting cozy with advertisers.*

Revenue-desperate magazines presents a form of *product-producer* metonymy, where the product (the physical entity *magazine*) stands for the producer (the publishing company).

In the entry for *magazine* in (1) we introduced an implicit argument, namely the audience, *w*, and the two major and inextricably linked arguments, the publishing organization, *x*, associated with the AGENTIVE role and the primary word sense as indicated in the FORMAL role, *y*, the physical object (or issue) of the magazine. The fact that both, the organization and the issue reading can be referred to with the string "the magazine" is captured in the *org.info.physobj-lcp*.[12]

(7)   **revenue-desperate**

λy ([FORMAL: org(y)] [TELIC: generate(P, y, revenue)])

This definition of *revenue-desperate* is loosely modeled after Pustejovsky and Boguraev (1993). Note that the particulars of the compositional semantics are not at issue here and different treatments for adjectives are equally tenable. Important here is that *revenue-desperate* adds to the existing TELIC role of the head noun the (momentary) purpose of generating revenue.

Thus the compositional semantics of *revenue-desperate magazines* resolves to

(8)   compositional NP semantics

$$
\begin{bmatrix}
\text{revenue} - \text{desperate magazines} \\[6pt]
\text{ARGSTR} = \begin{bmatrix}
\text{ARG1} = x : \text{org} \\
\text{ARG2} = y : \text{info.physobj} \\
\text{D} - \text{ARG1} = x : \text{hum} \\
\text{D} - \text{ARG2} = w : \text{hum}
\end{bmatrix} \\[24pt]
\text{EVENTSTR} = \begin{bmatrix}
\text{D} - \text{E1} = e_1: \text{transition} \\
\text{D} - \text{E2} = e_2: \text{transition} \\
\text{D} - \text{E3} = e_3: \text{process}
\end{bmatrix} \\[20pt]
\text{QUALIA} = \begin{bmatrix}
\text{org.info.physobj} - \text{lcp} \\
\text{FORM} = x\,(\text{multiple, generic}) \\
\text{TEL} = \text{read}(e_2, w, y), \text{generate}(e_3, x, \text{revenue}) \\
\text{AG} = \text{publish}(e_1, x, y)
\end{bmatrix}
\end{bmatrix}
$$

---

[12]Such a closely related set of word senses are called *facets* in Paradis (2003) after the notion of *facet* in Cruse (1995). Paradis distinguishes between metonymization, facetization, and zone activation (where a part is functionally salient, but the whole stays in the foreground as in *Fill it up!* referring to the whole glass, even though only the cavity can be meant).

Note the plural in the FORMAL role and that the company reading has been highlighted without, however, losing the implicit trace of the interrelationship with the issue/physical object reading. This is a promising mechanism for entailments, since the *company* reading of *a magazine* entails there to have been at least one issue published. Thus the selection of the proper word sense (or facet) of the word magazine results straightforwardly from compositional semantics.

Let us now consider the object NP, *advertisers*. The entry for *advertiser*[13] has a *semantic argument*, namely the (advertised) product. A semantic argument does not have to be realized syntactically but is a semantic slot that has to be filled for the concept underlying the word to make sense. Thus an *advertiser* cannot exist without a product to be advertised, just as an *employee* by definition cannot exist without somebody who in fact employs him or her.[14] Semantic arguments have to be distinguished from incidental variables needed to define an entry, such as the readership for *magazine* expressed with the implicitly defined variable w in (1)[15] or w in (9).

(9)

$$
\begin{bmatrix}
\text{advertiser} \\[2pt]
\text{ARGSTR} = \begin{bmatrix} \text{ARG1} = x : \text{org} \\ \text{ARG2} = y : \text{product} \\ \text{D} - \text{ARG1} = x : \text{hum} \\ \text{D} - \text{ARG2} = w : \text{org} \end{bmatrix} \\[2pt]
\text{EVENTSTR} = \begin{bmatrix} \text{D} - \text{E1} = e_1 : \text{transition} \\ \text{D} - \text{E2} = e_2 : \text{transition} \\ \text{D} - \text{E3} = e_3 : \text{transition} \\ \text{D} - \text{E4} = e_4 : \text{transition} \end{bmatrix} \\[2pt]
\text{QUALIA} = \begin{bmatrix} \text{FORM} = x \\ \text{TEL} = \text{pay}(e_2, x, e_3), \text{advertisement}(e_4, y) \\ \text{AG} = \text{produce}(e_1, x, y), \text{publish}(e_3, w, e_4) \end{bmatrix}
\end{bmatrix}
$$

---

[13]For brevity, (9) and (10) are already instantiated versions of the basic entries.

[14]For more detail on semantic arguments see Bergler (1991).

[15](9) is, of course, an opportunistic sketch of an entry. In order to properly resolve the (potential) relationship between *revenue-desperate magazine* and *advertisers*, namely the potential profit of the cozy relationship, the entry details the exchange of money for the placement of the advertisement in the media. Again, if such a fortuitous entry is not defined in the lexicon used, this particular nuance is missed.

Let us treat the tricky *getting pretty cozy with* here for the purpose of exposition as a single phrasal verb which behaves much like the similarly metaphoric verb *to court*, as in "magazines are courting advertisers". Note that the metaphoric reading is present since the simple metonymic sense extension to "somebody associated with the magazine is getting cozy with somebody associated with advertisers" is blocked for *magazine* through the word sense determining modification *revenue-desperate*.

We advocate here to strongly type the entry for animate arguments, even though a quick survey on the Internet shows that *getting cozy with* occurs half the time with an inanimate object.[16] An argument could thus be made to have a word sense with inanimate object subcategorization or to make the argument underspecified. To underspecify the selectional restrictions removes some of their semantic power. While most current applications do not take advantage of the semantics encoded in subcategorization frames, this is an important indicator for coherence and the extended use of a metaphor across a stretch of discourse, as discussed in Barnden et al. (2004). The extended use of metaphor across a portion of text also argues against proliferating the word senses, since metaphoric coherence would be lost while the difficulty in assigning the correct word sense has increased.

Thus conventionalized metaphor introduced by the verb has been resolved within the generative lexicon using standard assumptions in the GL literature.

6.3.2 Removing the Metonymy Blocking Adjective

Consider a small variation of (S_1').

(S_1'') Magazines are getting cozy with advertisers.

In (S_1''), the word sense determining adjective revenue-desperate is missing, and standard metonymic extension of the subject NP *magazines* to "somebody associated with the magazine" is possible and will in fact succeed. This is a satisfactory interpretation, since we assume that it is indeed some person(s) inside the magazine that is(are) responsible for the events that are described as "getting pretty cozy with advertisers". Note that in this case, the subject does not force the metaphoric interpretation of the predicate (and by an analogous metonymic extension, neither does the object NP *advertisers*.) Sentence (S_1'') resolves with standard GL techniques.

---

[16]Using Google to extract the string "getting cozy with" and analyzing the first 48 unique occurrences, results in 52% animate objects, 48% inanimate objects (23% of the 48 occurrences had businesses in object position). In subject position, animate dominates with 54%, while inanimate subjects occur only in 8% of the data, all of these are businesses. The remaining 37.5% occurrences had an empty subject. Note that the sample is skewed, Google retrieved 52% headlines and shows an implicit bias toward business and arts and entertainment.

6.4   Context and Co-compositionality

(S_2) challenges most treatments of automatic non-literal language processing and shows that the boundary between metonymy and metaphor is important if not always clear.

(S2)   *So can a magazine survive by downright thumbing its nose at major advertisers?*

This sentence exhibits two cases of metaphor, *survive*[17] and *thumbing one's nose at*, which both apply to the organization reading of *magazine*, despite their subcategorization for animate agents in their literal sense. We will limit our attention to *survive*. In contrast to (S_1'), metonymic extension from *magazine* to *somebody associated with the magazine* is not blocked by an adjectival modifier, yet in contrast to (S_1") this reading is clearly not acceptable and we have to first resolve the metaphor in order to block the metonymic extension that resolves *The magazine announced...* to *A spokesperson for the magazine announced...* This resolution of the seeming logical metonymy would now incorrectly resolve *Can a magazine survive...* to *Can (one/several human/s associated with the institution that issues a magazine) survive...*, which does not capture the relevant meaning of (S_2) at all. Thus, metonymy resolution cannot always precede metaphor resolution and indeed any static ordering of resolution mechanisms is bound to fail in certain instances.

Lytinen et al. (1992) reject the model of computing the non-literal meaning only after literal interpretation has failed on the grounds of independent psycholinguistic data. They advocate a model in which both, literal and non-literal interpretations are always both processed in parallel. Disregarding the high cost of producing all "possible" readings, their solution does not address the problem here: the conflict arises within the realm of non-literal interpretation, because the two different non-literal constructions co-specify each other; thus even if all non-literal readings were compiled in parallel, we still need to select the most plausible one.

Most literature on non-literal language does not consider context. While Fass (1998) stresses the importance of context for the interpretation of non-literal

---

[17]A survey of the first 50 unique results from the Google query "survive" shows that only 53% of the occurrences had an explicit subject, for a total of 31% animate subjects and 22% inanimate subjects. For the first 53 unique results for the query "survived", however, we get 85% animate subjects and 15% inanimate subjects and no occurrences of null subjects. While again not representative, this suggests interesting usage data that should be incorporated in a computational lexicon. Query "survive" shows in the object position in 33% an event (literal sense), in 20% a non-event (often a noun that is very readily associated with events) and in 47% no object at all. Query "survived" shows in the object position only 17% events, 57% non-events, and has no explicit object in 26%. Note that omitted arguments are usually readily inferred from the context or common world knowledge. This paper makes no attempt at justifying just how many and which of these usages should be encoded as a separate word sense, attempting rather to illustrate that the full complexity has to be taken into account when considering control mechanisms for non-literal language resolution. In keeping with GL tradition, we prefer fewer word senses.

constructs, his met* procedure does not have a notion of context. Lytinen et al. (1992) discuss in detail the psycholinguistic data that priming with an appropriate context facilitates comprehension of both, literal and non-literal sentences. But again, the proposed method to analyze metaphor is limited to mapping rules between the literal and the non-literal interpretation of individual constructs. Barnden et al. (2004) stresses the importance of context, but only considers the resolution of metaphor and not other non-literal language constructs.

Predefined one-to-one mapping rules ("to go through the roof" → fast positive change in altitude)[18] require the source and target concepts to be described. This works on the lexical level (*The magazine announced...*), but on the phrasal or higher conceptual levels it requires either an ontology of concepts or an ontology of features. Both will not be able to handle novel metaphor that breaks the existing conceptualization patterns, a major function of non-conventionalized metaphor. In order to achieve a comparable processing of conventionalized and novel metaphor we need additional, generative, mechanisms.

6.4.1 Co-compositionality

Let us consider the semantics of *survive* in more detail. In its literal meaning *survive* clearly subcategorizes for an animate subject which continues living beyond some event that could (likely) have caused it to stop being alive. Merriam-Webster OnLine has the following definitions[19]:

survive

intransitive verb

> **1 :** to remain alive or in existence : live on
> **2 :** to continue to function or prosper

transitive verb

> **1 :** to remain alive after the death of <he is *survived* by his wife>
> **2 :** to continue to exist or live after <*survived* the earthquake>
> **3 :** to continue to function or prosper despite : **WITHSTAND** <they *survived* many hardships>

Interestingly, sense 2 in Merriam-Webster covers the metaphor, by clearly relaxing the subcategorization for an animate subject. It seems to presume a subject with a "function" or a capacity to "prosper", which we would gloss in GL as a *functional type* (Pustejovsky 2001). The sense of survive then is that the purpose of

---

[18] Adapted from Lytinen et al. (1992). Omitted is the mapping rule that maps "altitude" to any numerical value, for instance stock market indexes in "The stock market went through the roof."

[19] http://www.m-w.com/dictionary/survive

the subject continues to be served. It is thus a natural opposite of *spoil*, which also selects for a *functional type* in the Complex Type Language of Pustejovsky (2001). Thus (10a) selects for the functional type of *milk* as a potable liquid as licensed by the partial entry for *milk* given in (10b).

(10)　a)　The milk survived the thunderstorm.
　　　b)　[milk [QS: liquid ⊗T drink]]

While in (10) regular coercion mechanisms select the correct interpretation, (11) poses a problem in not violating even the most stringent subcategorizations.

(11)　The secretary survived the restructuring.

Here, the literal sense of *survive* will select the person who is the secretary as subject, not, as intended, the position description and its function. It is in fact the object NP *the restructuring*, which orchestrates the proper reading of the entire sentence, the metaphoric reading of *survive* and the functional type reading of the subject NP *the secretary*. (11) is a prime example of co-compositionality.

Co-compositionality at the sentence level is the process of considering the role of each constituent in the context of other constituents. Thus, while semantic *composition* answers the question what role arguments play in the context of their predicate, semantic *co-composition* answers the question what role any constituent plays in the context of all the other constituents.

In (11), *the restructuring* describes the event that could have, but did not change some functional aspect (the purpose, or job description) of *the secretary*. The lexical entry for restructuring thus needs to encode some selectional restrictions on suitable targets for restructuring (organizations, not humans). We will not give full entries for the mechanism, rather we illustrate the influence of context on co-compositionality in the case of (S2).

6.4.2　Context

In context, the institution reading of *magazine* is already in focus when processing (S₂) ...*can a magazine survive*... *Revenue-desperate magazines* in (S₁') highlighted the institution reading as the textually relevant one (and in fact what we expect in the *Wall Street Journal*. Issues of a magazine are referred to by giving the date or similar discriminating features.)

This observation gives rise to a general heuristic:

(12)　**Contextual Constancy**
　　　A referring expression assumes the interpretation in focus in the
　　　local context.

For a possible definition of *local context* see Allen (1995). Note that this notion of context is narrower than assumed by Asher and Lascarides (2001), who develop a model of how wider discourse context interacts with metaphor comprehension.

We can motivate this constancy requirement with the well-known examples from coordination:

(13)   ? *The magazine costs $3.50 and is laying off 30 people.*

Note that this concerns the referring expression and not a surface string, as example (12) shows, where "the magazine" refers to the printed object and the institution respectively:

(14)   *The magazine costs $3.50 and the magazine's board of directors*
        decided to freeze that price until 1995.

Allowing predicates and arguments to co-specify the interpretation, the preference from the previous sentence for the institution reading of *magazine* selects the metaphoric meaning of *survive* without the need of computing all possible readings (including the confusing "Can magazine employees survive?" reading.) In a Generative Lexicon framework the required "mapping rule" is embodied in a so-called *Lexical Conceptual Paradigm* (a meta-lexical construct that allows lexical entries to inherit schematic behavior, such as alternations) that indicates that Life is a conventional metaphor for Temporally Limited Existence (see Pustejovsky and Boguraev 1993 for details on Lexical Conceptual Paradigms.)

That contextual constancy is merely a heuristic[20] is illustrated by a simple alternative (S_2'):

---

[20]This paper is only concerned with computational feasibility. Gibbs (1984) suggests that the non-literal sense is computed without necessarily activating the literal sense, if sufficient context is provided. Other studies of human non-literal language processing seem to suggest that salient (that is, conventional or frequent) interpretations of non-literal expressions are activated even if they are not primed by the context or required for the proper interpretation and Giora (1997) presents a "graded salience hypothesis" based on these findings. Most compatible with the process outlined here for a computational model is Utsumi (1999), who summarizes his "dynamic view of salience" as follows:

1. When the intended interpretation is more salient than the unintended one at LA level, the intended interpretation is processed first from LA through MC level, whether contextual support is provided or not.
2. When the intended interpretation is less salient than the unintended one at LA level, but sufficient contextual support (e.g., paragraph-length extrasentential context, or one-sentence-length extrasentential context plus intrasentential context) for the intended interpretation is provided, the intended interpretation is processed first at MC level without the unintended meaning being rejected.
3. When the intended interpretation is less salient than the unintended one at LA level and contextual support for the intended interpretation is not enough, the unintended salient meaning is processed first and rejected at MC or DI level so that the intended meaning is interpreted.

(S₂')   *Can a magazine survive being thrown from a helicopter for*
         advertising purposes?

In (S₂'), *a magazine* refers to the physical entity of an issue, despite the fact that the institution reading was in focus. Note, that the indefinite article indicates that we are not necessarily dealing with the same referring expression and thus are licensed to give a new interpretation, which in fact is forced by the stronger (and more "local") context, again imposed by the event that could jeopardize the survival. This counterforce to the contextual constancy heuristic was not present in (S₂), which also contained the indefinite article for *magazine*. Thus even though (S₂) generated the potential for a new referring expression, the contextual focus still crucially prevailed, due to the absence of contrary co-compositionality constraints from the verbal complement. This difference may in part be explained by the fact that (S₂') assumes a literal reading and we assume that the contextual constancy heuristic is not able to introduce a non-literal meaning, whereas in (S₂) we have the case of conflicting non-literal readings (metonymy and metaphor) and the contextual constancy heuristic merely adds a bias to select among them.

Although (S₂') is construed and the sequence ((S₁) (S₂')) does not make for smooth discourse, it shows that co-compositionality involves all constituents of a sentence (and of the local context.) Thus (S₂) shows that the challenge to non-literal sentence resolution is now one of finding the right *control structure* for interpretation of sentences in their context. Flexible mechanisms have to embed the procedures developed for isolated phenomena and orchestrate them. Co-compositionality, inheritance mechanisms, and large computational lexica provide the tools to address these issues. Free text from extensive corpora has to guide this process; newspaper articles provide an especially rich source of complex data such as non-literal language, complex sentence structure, and indirect knowledge sources. The Generative Lexicon paradigm allows to address these complex issues within the larger context of compositional semantics and does not require them to be cast as exceptions that require non-standard procedures.

6.5   Anomalous Metaphor

To illustrate the surprising data found in newspaper text, let us briefly discuss the problem with analyzing (S₄).

(S4)   *Garbage editors have dumped considerable energy into a*
        whirling rampage through supermarket aisles in a bid to
        identify corporate America's good guys and bad boys.

Garbage editors have dumped considerable energy into ... presents us with a puzzling metaphor. The meaning of dump can be summarized in two main senses[21]:

(15)   to dump
        a) to unload or throw down something in a careless manner
        b) to throw away, to ditch

In the *Wall Street Journal* we find these two meanings realized by different sub-categorization frames, namely (b) in a S-V-O construction (as in *Investors dumped shares.*), and (a) with an additional prepositional phrase, using the prepositions *on* and *onto*. The implication is usually, that the "dumped" objects rest at the dumping spot.

A third, metaphoric pattern is "*to dump* (large amounts of) a valuable *into* a project/cause (which is not deemed worthwhile)" as in *He has dumped so much money in that old car, he could have a new one by now!*

This is the metaphor used in (S_4). It is an anomalous metaphor considering the dictionary senses, where the **theme** is the undesirable object and the **location** the more valuable object (consider *He dumped all the work on his assistant!*) This is exactly opposed to the sense employed here. Without an explicit mention in the lexicon, this metaphorical sense cannot be generated from the other senses, especially not its strong derogatory sense. Any hope of resolving this has to come from the very obvious use of overstatements in the sentence, which will trigger the possibility of irony or sarcasm, suggesting a role reversal (good is bad, what is dumped is desirable, what it is dumped into is not worthwhile).

6.6 Conclusions

Literature in lexical semantics and non-literal language comprehension has given us tools to address metonymy and metaphor. Unfortunately, the solutions outlined address only part of the issues involved and as we have demonstrated, will not easily scale up to the complexity of corpus data. In particular, the data presented here illustrate an issue of control of the interpretation process when metonymy and metaphor produce non-compatible readings, which can be addressed through co-compositionality. We illustrated the need for taking the context into account by stipulating the Contextual Constancy Heuristic. These are thus basic requirements for building up a deeper semantic analysis of texts. We propose to integrate these strategies into a systematic analysis of corpus data, because only the rich interactions of data in context demonstrate all interdependencies. The role of a rich lexical semantics is particularly promising when its mechanisms are designed to work even in case of underspecified entries. Additionally, the accommodation of stylistic preferences in the lexicon is a strong feature that can capture some extra-linguistic

---

[21]WordNet lists six word senses.

knowledge. Analysis of metonymy and metaphor has to be based on standard lexica and cannot assume that the appropriate features to establish the proper analogy are represented in all cases. Deriving additional stylistic preferences for different types of text and associating them with standard lexica is one way to address conventionalized metonymy and metaphor. Still, a robust analysis has to allow for underspecified (or, as in the case of (S₄) above, seemingly anomalous) links between source and target constructions. Because metonymy and metaphor are so ubiquitous, complex control structures for their analysis have to rely on lexical structure, meta-lexical mapping rules, and context. It is thus imperative that these procedures are developed in parallel (and close cooperation) with research on computational lexica.

Acknowledgements I am grateful for Dan Fass' comments on an earlier draft and Jona Schuman's suggestion of the direct opposition of *survive* and *spoil*. This work was supported in part by a grant from the Natural Sciences and Engineering Research Council of Canada.

References

Allen, J. (1995). *Natural language understanding* (2nd ed.). Redwood City: The Benjamin/Cummings Publishing Company Inc.

Andreevskaia, A., & Bergler, S. (2006). Mining WordNet for Fuzzy sentiment: Sentiment tag extraction from WordNet Glosses. In *Proceedings of the 11th conference of the European chapter of the Association for Computational Linguistics, EACL 2006*, Trento, Italy.

Asher, N., & Lascarides, A. (2001). Metaphor in discourse. In P. Bouillon & F. Busa (Eds.), *The language of word meaning* (pp. 262–289). New York: Cambridge University Press.

Bar-Haim, R., Dagan, I., Dolan, B., Ferro, L., Giampiccolo, D., Magnini, B., & Szpektor, I. (2006). The second PASCAL recognising textual entailment challenge. In *Proceedings of the second PASCAL challenges workshop on recognising textual entailment*, Venice, Italy.

Barnden, J. A., Glasbey, S. R., Lee, M. G., & Wallington, A. M. (2004). Varieties and directions of inter-domain influence in metaphor. *Metaphor and Symbol, 19*(1), 1–30.

Bergler, S. (1991). The semantics of collocational patterns for reporting verbs. In *Proceedings of the fifth European conference of the Association for Computational Linguistics* (pp. 216–221), Berlin, Germany.

Bergler, S. (1993). Semantic dimensions in the field of reporting verbs. In *Making sense of words. Proceedings of the ninth annual conference of the UW Center for the New OED and Text Research* (pp. 44–56), Oxford, UK.

Bergler, S. (1995). Generative lexicon principles for machine translation: A case for meta-lexical structure. *Journal of Machine Translation, 9*(3).

Bouillon, P., & Busa, F. (2001). Qualia and the structure of verb meaning. In P. Bouillon & F. Busa (Eds.), *The language of word meaning* (pp. 149–167). New York: Cambridge University Press.

Brill, E. (1995). Transformation-based error-driven learning and natural language processing: A case study in part of speech tagging. *Computational Linguistics, 21*(4), 543–565.

Briscoe, E., Carroll, J., & Watson, R. (2006). The second release of the RASP system. In *Proceedings of the COLING/ACL 2006 interactive presentation sessions*, Sydney, Australia.

Copestake, A. (1992). The representation of group denoting nouns in a lexical knowledge base. In P. Saint-Dizier & E. Viegas (Eds.), *Proceedings of the second seminar on computational lexical semantics, IRIT*, Toulouse, France.

Copestake, A., & Briscoe, T. (1992). Lexical operations in a unification-based framework. In J. Pustejovsky & S. Bergler (Eds.), *Lexical semantics and knowledge representation* (pp. 101–119). Berlin: Springer.

Cruse, A. (1995). Polysemy and related phenomena from a cognitive linguistic viewpoint. In St. P. Dizier & E. Viegas (Eds.), *Computational lexical semantics* (pp. 33–49). New York: Cambridge University Press.

Cunningham, H. (2002). GATE, a General Architecture for Text Engineering. *Computers and the Humanities, 36*, 223–254.

Edmonds, P., & Kilgarriff, A. (2002). Introduction to the special issue on evaluating word sense disambiguation systems. *Journal of Natural Language Engineering, 8*(4).

Fass, D. (1991). met*: A method for discriminating metonymy and metaphor by computer. *Computational Linguistics, 17*(1), 49–90.

Fass, D. (1998). *Processing metonymy and metaphor.* Greenwich: Ablex Publishing Co.

Fass, D., Martin, J., & Hinkelman, E. (Eds.). (1992). *Computational Intelligence, 8*(3). Special Issue on Non-Literal Language.

Geeraerts, D. (2002). The interaction of metaphor and metonymy in composite expres-sions. In R. Dirven & R. Pörings (Eds.), *Metaphor and metonymy in comparison and contrast* (pp. 435–465). Berlin: Mouton de Gruyter.

Gibbs, R. (1984). Literal meaning and psychological theory. *Cognitive Science, 8*, 275–304.

Giora, R. (1997). Understanding figurative and literal language: The graded salience hypothesis. *Cognitive Linguistics, 7*(1), 183–206.

Godard, D., & Jayez, J. (1993). Towards a proper treatment of coercion phenomena. In *Proceedings of the sixth conference of the European chapter of the ACL*, Utrecht, The Netherlands.

Grinberg, D., Lafferty, J., & Sleator, D. (1995). A robust parsing algorithm for link grammars. In *Proceedings of the fourth international workshop on Parsing Technologies*, Prague, Czech Republic.

Hepple, M. (2000). Independence and commitment: Assumptions for rapid training and execution of rule-based part-of-speech taggers. In *Proceedings of the 38th annual meeting of the Association for Computational Linguistics (ACL-2000)*, Hong Kong.

Hindle, D. (1990). Noun classification from predicate-argument structures. In *Proceedings of the 28th meeting of the Association for Computational Linguistics*, Pittsburgh, Pennsylvania.

Lakoff, G., & Johnson, M. (1980). *Metaphors we live by.* London: Chicago University Press.

Lapata, M., & Lascarides, A. (2003). A probabilistic account of logical metonymy. *Computational Linguistics, 29*(2), 261–315.

Lytinen, S. L., Burridge, R. R., & Kirtner, J. D. (1992). The role of literal meaning in the comprehension of non-literal constructions. *Computational Intelligence, 8*(3). Special Issue on Non-Literal Language.

Paradis, C. (2003) Where does metonymy stop? Senses, facets and active zones. *The Department of English Working Papers, 3*, Lund University.

Porter, N. (1913). *Webster's revised unabridged dictionary.* Springfield: G & C. Merriam Co.

Pustejovsky, J. (1991). The generative lexicon. *Computational Linguistics, 17*(4).

Pustejovsky, J. (1995). *The generative lexicon: A theory of computational lexical semantics.* Cambridge, MA: MIT Press.

Pustejovsky, J. (2001). Type construction and the logic of concepts. In P. Bouillon & F. Busa (Eds.), *The language of word meaning* (pp. 91–123). Cambridge: Cambridge University Press.

Pustejovsky, J., & Boguraev, B. (1993). Lexical knowledge representation and natural language processing. *Artificial Intelligence, 63*(1–2), 193–223.

Pustejovsky, J., & Bouillon, P. (1995). Aspectual coercion and logical polysemy. *Journal of Semantics, 12*(2), 133–162.

Pustejovsky, J., Bergler, S., & Anick, P. (1993). Lexical semantic techniques for corpus analysis. *Computational Linguistics, 19*(2), 331–358.

Sag, I., & Wasow, T. (1995). Idiom. *Language, 70*.

Smadja, F. A., & McKeown, K. R. (1990) Automatically extracting and representing collocations for language generation. In *Proceedings of the 28th meeting of the Association for Computational Linguistics*, Pittsburgh, Pennsylvania.

Utsumi, A. (1999) *Explaining the time-course of literal and nonliteral comprehension.* Poster presented at the second International Conference on Cognitive Science and the 16th Annual Meeting of the Japanese Cognitive Science Society Joint Conference (ICCS/JCSS99), Tokyo, Japan. Article in Online Proceedings at http://logos.mind.sccs.chukyo-u.ac.jp/jcss/ICCS/99/olp/p2-19/p2-19.htm.

Verhagen, M., Mani, I., Sauri, R., Littman, J., Knippen, R., Jang, S. B., Rumshisky, A., Phillips, J., Pustejovsky, J. (2005) Automating temporal annotation with TARSQI. Short paper. In *Proceedings of the 43rd annual meeting of the ACL.* Ann Arbor, USA.

Chapter 7
Spanish Clitics, Events and Opposition Structure

José M. Castaño

7.1 Introduction

In this paper we will try to elaborate a unified analysis of the Spanish clitic *se*, capturing its polysemy in terms of underspecification of case features. Although a sense enumeration analysis is always possible,[1] it is not clear that the whole range of data can be captured with a reduced set of senses. Such an approach may also require additional senses (or subcategorization) frames for those verbs that allow the corresponding cliticization. From a computational point of view, a sense enumeration model creates lexical ambiguity, which in the case of *se* results in ambiguous syntactic structures. These multiple syntactic trees must be resolved at discourse level. Consequently we will look at the minimal assumptions for a single lexical entry for the Spanish clitic *se*. It is underspecified for the accusative-dative and singular-plural distinction. It is non-first person (allows 3rd person or 2nd person antecedents: *usted*, *ustedes*). Unlike other clitics it is anaphoric. As the least specified clitic, it can be used as impersonal: it is a least informational referring noun phrase.[2]

---

[1]See Pustejovsky (1995) for a critical view of a sense enumeration model, in particular regarding control and light verbs.

[2]This is not an exclusive characteristic of the *se* clitic in Spanish: third person plural forms are similarly used with impersonal interpretation (with or without clitic), second person singular is used in an impersonal generic interpretation and finally the pronoun *uno* is also used in a similar way.

J.M. Castaño (✉)
Departamento de Computación, Facultad de Ciencias Exactas y Naturales, Universidad de Buenos Aires, Buenos Aires, Argentina

Brandeis University, Waltham, MA, USA

J. Pustejovsky et al. (eds.), *Advances in Generative Lexicon Theory*, Text, Speech and Language Technology 46, DOI 10.1007/978-94-007-5189-7_7,
© Springer Science+Business Media Dordrecht 2013

Given these characteristics, co-composition and underspecification in the sense of the Generative Lexicon (Pustejovsky 1995, henceforth GL) play a crucial role. High underspecification and co-composition result in a very complex set of possible combinations.

The general goal of our approach is to provide a unified analysis for the clitic *se*, while also considering the contribution of this analysis to clitics in general. We argue that the system of syntactic features that characterizes the paradigm of Spanish clitics must map systematically, both to the syntax or the related semantic distinctions that they enable.

The specific goal of this paper is to show that the sense enumerative view of different lexical entries for the clitic *se* is not only theoretically undesirable but also empirically inadequate. Rather, the data strongly suggest a unified generative analysis is superior, in that it accounts for the full range of compositional alternatives presented with *se*. In Sect. 7.1.1 we discuss the sense approaches to *se* and their shortcomings. In Sect. 7.1.2 we briefly present the features of Spanish clitics. In Sect. 7.3 we present data that show the occurrence of the clitic *se* in a paradigmatic variation. These data question the different senses for the clitic *se* assumed in the literature. In Sect. 7.4 we present the basics of the framework we are going to use to consider the data. We also discuss some examples concerning dative clitics. In Sect. 7.5 we discuss the *se* data using the machinery we introduced in the previous section. In Sect. 6 we present the conclusions and we discuss some ideas for future work concerning a mapping from arguments to Event Structure in terms of the computation of the Event Persistence Structure (Pustejovsky 2000).

7.1.1 Lack of Unified Analysis in Different Frameworks

It is not possible to review the rich literature addressing the behavior of the Spanish clitic *se* and equivalent forms in other Romance languages here. What remains in this section presupposes the reader has knowledge of some terminology used concerning clitics. Although we are considering only Spanish data, there are many common properties concerning the clitic *se* in Romance Languages, and common assumptions were made in the literature, as will be seen in this section.

7.1.1.1 The Argument/Non-argument Clitic Distinction

The literature typically assumes that there is a distinction between 'argument' and 'non-argument' clitics, (Monachesi 1999; Sportiche 1998; Grimshaw 1981; Borer and Grodzinsky 1986; Cinque 1988; Zubizarreta 1982 and others), whatever the nature of the non-argument clitic might be. There is a tension between a desired or intended generalization which requires a clitic to be related to an 'argument'.

The 'non-argument' clitics emerge as exceptions that cannot be accounted for by any attempt of generalization. In a GB[3] or Minimalist framework this could be stated as:

> ... the clitic ... must be linked to one of the thematic slots available in the head, ...
>
> Borer (1983), p. 39[4]

There is a change in the following statement after the so called non-argument clitics are acknowledged:

> ... pronominal clitics typically satisfy subcategorization requirements of verbs, and as such are in complementary distribution with the syntactic category for which such a verb subcategorizes
>
> Borer (1986)

> ... all clitics, with the sole exception of ethical clitics, must be linked to a thematic role in the theta-grid of the verb.
>
> Jaeggli (1986) p. 28

The canonical and more recalcitrant example of non-argument clitics is the ethical dative, and a very well known example from Spanish is (11a) a variant of which is quoted by Jaeggli (1986).[5] The problem that non-argument clitics pose has been addressed in the following ways:

> a suggestion that seems plausible is to assume that these clitics [ethical datives] are not assigned a theta role by the predicate but rather that they themselves contribute a theta role to the verb ... as with clitics in the inalienable possession construction ...
>
> Jaeggli (1986) p. 24

Masullo (1992) gives an account of several Dative clitic constructions (with different interpretations: possessor, location, etc.) via an Incorporation analysis. He follows the UTAH (Baker (1988)), and consequently the clitics must be generated in a theta-position.

Sportiche (1998) also proposes certain clitics are exceptional:

> French inherent clitic verbs could just as well list a theta-less clitic object, which would then be subject to the normal rules for clitic placement. Likewise, for ethical dative constructions, in which the clitic is not obviously related to the verb, we would have to allow the generation

---

[3]Government and Binding Theory or the Principles and Parameters Theory, the work which was done in the Chomskyan framework in the 1980s.

[4]Similarly, Kayne (1975) states that clitics must be generated in a subcategorized position. For Jaeggli (1982), clitics absorb government; for Zubizarreta (1982) and Aoun (1985), clitics may absorb theta-roles, and, for Sportiche (1998), clitics are associated with an NP argument (via LF movement).

[5]Jaeggli (1986) claims: "... only first- and second-person clitics are perfectly natural in the ethical dative construction, while third-person clitics are either completely unacceptable or highly unnatural."

We don't agree with this claim. The example he quotes:

Este chico no le come! (This kid does not eat for him/her!)
is perfectly fine for us.

Fig. 7.1 Inherent reflexive

$$\begin{bmatrix} \text{HEAD} \begin{bmatrix} verb \\ \text{AGR} \ \boxed{1} \end{bmatrix} \\ \text{VAL} \begin{bmatrix} \text{SUBJ} \langle \text{NP} \rangle \\ \text{COMPS } elist \end{bmatrix} \\ \text{CLTS} \langle \text{NP} [mark\text{-}ss, \text{AGR } \boxed{1}] \rangle \end{bmatrix}$$

of a theta-less XP headed by the dative clitic, which would then be subject to the normal rules of clitic placement. ... Since clitics usually are linked to an argument position, inherent clitics and ethical datives would constitute an exceptional class of clitics.

In a different framework, HPSG, the "argument-hood" requirement for clitics is stated as an alternation between basic verbal forms and verbal forms bearing clitics. For example, in Miller and Sag (1997) the verbal forms with clitics have reduced subcategorization frames or in Abeill'e et al. (1998), clitics must be connected to the ARG-ST list. In Monachesi (1999) the "argument-hood" requirement is stated as a modification in the COMPS value for a verb with a clitic.[6] The exceptions are encoded as particular lexical entries: e.g. the inherent reflexive proposed as non-arguments by Monachesi (1999), p. 113:2, shown in Fig. 7.1.

As a final example, in LFG, (e.g., Grimshaw 1981) non-reflexive clitics are assigned grammatical functions (OBJ and A OBJ). On the other hand, intrinsic clitics:

do not correspond to logical or grammatical arguments of the verb at all

They are only a grammatical marker. Also, reflexive clitics are dealt with using a lexical reflexivization rule. Alsina (1996) claims that reflexive clitics are argument structure binders.

Assuming this division (argument/non-argument clitic), however, proves to be quite problematic: either different lexical entries for the same clitic must be posited or different syntactic operations must be performed by a single item (which are not allowed for other elements of the same class). On the view presented here, both solutions are equivalent and undesirable.

7.1.1.2 Additional Partitions for the Clitic *se*

Regarding the clitic *se*, there are three additional partitions considered in the literature: The nominative/non-nominative *se*, the anaphoric/non-anaphoric *se* and the pronominal/morphological marker. For instance, Burzio (1986), Manzini (1986), Cinque (1988), Masullo (1992) and others, assume a nominative/non-nominative *se*. On the contrary, Dobrovie-Sorin (1998) claims that Romanian does not have

---

[6]Similarly, the Impersonal, Middle, Ergative Lexical rules (IMPSI-LR), (MIDSI-LR), (ERGSI-LR), operate on the argument structure list and valence values.

nominative *se* and her analysis is based on the anaphoric properties of *se*. The distinctions between nominative *se* is grounded in the Italian tradition[7] and it was based in examples like those in (1) where an explicit subject and the clitic *si* cannot occur[8]:

(1) a. Non si è mai contenti.
        not SI is ever satisfied
        'One is never satisfied'

     b. Spesso   si è trattati male.
        frequently SI is treated bad.
        'One is often ill-treated.'

     c. (Prima o poi)   si   scopre sempre il   colpevole.
        (Sooner or later) SI discover always the   culprit
        '(Sooner or later) one always discovers the culprit.'

However, Manzini (1986) acknowledges the following problems to associate the impersonal *si* with the subject position (or nominative case, if it is assigned to the subject position):

> Similarly, the distribution of impersonal *si* is quite different from the distribution of the subject clitics in Northern Italian. The Northern Italian subject clitics, at least in the variety illustrated here with the Modena dialect, appear before the negation particle, like the French subject clitics and unlike impersonal *si*, ... What is more, in Modenese the impersonal element, s(e) can and must co-occur with a subject clitic, to be precise the expletive subject clitic

For instance, the Manzini (1986) and Cinque (1988) argument for the Italian *si* as nominative is based on the fact that it cannot occur in infinitival control clauses[9]:

(2) *E' bello lavarsi volentieri i bambini.
     It is good [one to gladly wash the children].

(3) *E' bello andarsi volentieri.
     It is good [one to glady go].   Manzini (1986)

---

[7] We are not going to address here if the italian *si* is equivalent to the Spanish *se*, a question which is quite beyond the scope of this paper.

[8] These examples are given by Cinque (1988).

[9] However they do not address the issue of possible interactions between, PRO arb and *si*, considering that although the interpretation is similar, it is not exactly the same: PRO arb is not equivalent to pro arb.

But the following examples show that it is possible in Spanish to have an explicit embedded subject in the same type of clauses, although *se* seems not to be possible (as in the Italian examples above)[10]:

(4)   Es bueno resolver **uno** los problemas.

      Is good to-solve one the problems.

      'It is good to solve the problems oneself.'

(5)   Sería bueno para María resolver **ella misma** los problemas.

      Would-be good for Maria to-solve she self the problems.

      'It would be good for Maria to solve the problems herself.'

These data undermine the argument that impersonal *se* cannot be possible in embedded infinitives because nominative case is not assigned by infinitives. On the other hand, the following examples show that the impersonal *se* is possible in embedded control infinitives.

(6)   En caso que quisiera aprobar*se* estas leyes habría que convencer al gobernador.

      In case that would-want to-aprove-SE these laws would-have that convince the governor.

      'If one wants to aprove these laws one should convince the   governor.'

(7)   En caso que quisiera presentar*se* las propuestas después de té rmino, hay que presentar un escrito.

      In case that would-want to-present-SE these proposals after the deadline have that present a written.

      'If you want to present the proposal after the deadline you have to present a written letter.'

We are not going to discuss at length the whole range of issues that the so called impersonal *se* raise, but we want to point out that its distribution is also constrained by tense/mood and discourse factors (see Cinque 1988). There are other partitions proposed in the literature, like the anaphoric/non-anaphoric *se*, which includes some non-argument (e.g. inherent and nominative *se*). Also, it is very common to assume that the 'non-argument' clitic *se* is an aspectual marker (Nishida 1994; Arce-Arenales 1989; De Miguel Aparicio 1992, and others). How these partitions are integrated, distinguished, or consistent is quite problematic and varies from approach to approach. Although not addressed fully in this paper, it will be apparent that our approach considers the argument/non-argument question in a

---

[10]This is not a clear cut judgment. The following sentence is perfectly fine, although the interaction with PRO arb, makes the interpretation a little different, and clearly similar to an ethical dative:

(1)   Es bueno resolverse los problemas.

      Is good to-solve-SE the problems.

      'It is good to solve the problems by yourself.'

Table 7.1 Spanish clitics features

Clitic	Person	Number	Case	Anaphoric	Gender
me	First	Singular	Accus./Dat.		
te	Second	Singular	Accus./Dat.		
nos	First	Plural.	Accus./Dat.		
os	Second	Plural	Accus./Dat.		
lo	Third	Singular	Accusative	No	Masculine
la	Third	Singular	Accusative	No	Feminine
los	Third/Second	Plural	Accusative	No	Masculine
las	Third	Plural	Accusative	No	Feminine
le	Second/Second	Sing/Plu	Dative	No	
les	Third	Plural	Dative	No	
se	Third/Second		Accus./Dat.	Yes	

unified manner. We will continue to use the following mnemonic terms to describe the constructions with se: reflexive/reciprocal, middle, passive, ergative, inherent, impersonal, ethical, possessive, etc. Use of these terms does not acknowledge any theoretical status to them or to the possible partitions that they could entail, as will be apparent immediately. Moreover, a clear-cut distinction is not so easy to draw using labels of this kind.

7.1.2   Spanish Clitic Features

Romance clitics are pronominal elements (Garcia 1975; Everett 1996). Traditional descriptive grammars like Real Academia Española (1998) or even Fernandez Soriano (1999) consider clitics as pronominal elements. We follow Garcia (1975), believing that clitics complete a system together with verbal agreement and pronouns. Clitics can have accusative or dative case. There is no sustained evidence for a nominative case clitic in Spanish. Verbal agreement can be considered the morphological nominative equivalent of the clitics. Table 7.1 has a descriptive purpose and does not intend to present a theory of the pronominal features corresponding to clitics. It is similar to the one presented by the Real Academia Española (1998) or in Fernandez Soriano (1999).[11,12]

---

[11]The data we are going to consider in this paper is based on the Spanish spoken in the Rio de la Plata region (Argentina and Uruguay). The use of clitics in that area seems more unconstrained than the standard Spanish from Spain. For instance, the sentence (10b) below would be hardly accepted by a speaker from Spain. On the contrary, equivalent pairs like those of (21a) are found everywhere in other dialects. However, this more creative behavior seems to be based more on general properties of the Spanish clitics than peculiar idiosyncratic uses.

[12]The anaphoric nature of se can be reduced to the lack of specification of A′-features (see, e.g. Reinhart and Reuland (1993).

Fig. 7.2 Clitics structural
position

Clitics are affix-like entities. They form clusters that have phonological properties and constrain possible clitic cluster combinations (Fig. 7.2).[13]

7.2 Peculiarities: Unmotivated Distinctions

We understand that the classes of *se* mentioned in the first section correspond to unmotivated distinctions. In this section we present pairs or sets of examples where the distinction between the different "classes" of clitics is difficult to justify. These examples in most cases present either a variation of the person or anaphoric properties of the clitic, but not in their case properties (e.g.: 8a–8b, 10a–10b). Variations in some of the arguments are also introduced (e.g., *nene* ('child') versus '*jefe*' ('boss') in 10c–d)

(8) a. María se fue al mercado.   Inherent Reflexive
         María SE went to-the market.   'María went to the market.'
     b. María le fue al mercado.   Ethical
         María cl-3p-Dat went to-the market.
         'María went to the market for him/her.'

In this pair of sentences the two different interpretations should arise from the different features we find in *se* and *le*: the first is either dative or accusative, whereas the second is dative only. The following pair (9a–9b) shows that the clitic *se* in (8) and (9a) can correspond to an accusative clitic, given that the verb *ir* allows an accusative clitic construction in (9b).

(9) a. María se fue.   Inchoative
         María SE went.
         'María left.'

     b. La   fueron   (a María).   Causative
         cl-3p.Ac.femi go-3p.pl   (to María).
         'They made her/María go.'

Considering the sentences in (10), observe that (10a) is a classical example of the so-called ethical Dative. On the other hand, (10b) and (10c) may be considered aspectual or perhaps possessive. But the only difference between (10a)

---

[13]See Bonet (1995) for morphophonological constraints in clitic cluster combinations.

and (10b–10c) corresponds to the fact that *se* is anaphoric (a fact that at least for these two examples is considered indisputable). If we consider (10a) and (10d), probably interpreted as possessive or source, why should this difference arise? The only difference is the subject: *jefe* versus *nene* ('boss' versus 'child'). And finally in (10e), why should this sentence be ambiguous in so many ways? These data demonstrate that there is no sustained evidence to assume different syntactic structures for each possible interpretation.

(10) a. El nene me   comió (la comida).   Ethical
        The baby cl-1pSg eat-past (the food).
        'The baby ate (the food) for me.'

      b. El nene se comió   *(la comida).   Ethical, Aspectual
         The baby cl-1pSg eat-past (the food).
         'The baby ate the food.' (emphatic)

      c. El nene se comió *(los caramelos).   Aspectual, Ethic. or Poss.
         The baby cl-1pSg eat-past *(the candies).
         'The baby ate the candies.'

      d. El jefe me comió *(la comida).   Ethical, Possessor, Source
         The boss cl-1pSg eat-past *(food).
         'The boss ate/the food for me/on me/my food'

      e. Se comió (la comida).
                        Impersonal, Ethical, Aspectual SE eat-past (food).
         'The food was eaten/Someone ate the food/
         (He/she) ate the food for himself/(He/she) ate the food.'

    The following examples present similar properties to the previous ones. The pair (11a) and (11b) presents the question: why should a change in the subject allow for different readings? Are the specifications of the pronominal clitic any different? If we compare (11a, with (11c), it is apparent that there is no problem for the noun phrase *el barco* to be the subject of a "transitive" *hundir*. Indeed it is consistent with the Burzio (1986) generalization.

(11) a. El barco se hundió (solo).   Ergative reading
         The ship SE sank (alone).   'The ship sank by itself'

      b. Juan se hundió (solo).   Reflexive/Ergative reading
         Juan SE sank (alone).   'Juan sank (himself).'

      c. El barco la hundió.   Transitive
         The ship cl-3pSg.Acc.Fem sank.   'The ship sank it/her.'

    More strikingly, (12a) is ambiguous in four ways: Erg-Passive, Impersonal, Ethical and Possessive. If we compare it with (12b–e), we find out that it can be partially disambiguated. Compare first (12a) with (12b): given that *le* is only Dative and it is not anaphoric, there is only one possible interpretation of the clitic *le*: Possessor. In (12c), the combination of a plural subject (cf. singular subject in (12a)) and a singular noun phrase in object position restricts the possible interpretations. There are two readings that are not available anymore: Impersonal and Ergative-passive. However there is a new one available: the reciprocal. In (12d) the presence of another dative clitic, blocks the interpretation of *se* as a dative.[14]

(12)   a. Se hundió el barco.   Erg-passive,Ethical, Possessive, Impersonal
             SE sank-3pSg. the ship.
             The ship sank/(He/she) sank the ship for himself
             (He/she) sank his ship/(Somebody) sank the ship.
        b. Le hundió el barco.   Dative (Possessor)
             cl-3p-Dat sank-3pSg. the ship.   '(He/she) sank his ship'
        c. Se hundieron el barco.   Reciprocal, Possessive, Ethical
             SE sank-3pPl. the ship.
             '(They) sank each other ship./(They) sank their own ship'/
             '(They) sank the ship (not their ship).'
        d. Se le hundió el barco.   Ergative
             SE cl-3p-Dat sank-3pSg. the ship.
             'The ship sank on him'/'Somebody sank his ship',
             '(He/she) sank (his/her) ship.'
        e. Nuestro piloto se hundió el barco.   Ethical, Possessive
             Our pilot SE sank the ship.
             'Our pilot sank the ship for himself.'/'Our pilot sank his ship'.

7.3 Towards a Unified Analysis of the Clitic *se*

The above examples show that there is nothing in the data that prevents us from assuming there is only one *se*, underspecified for the accusative/dative distinction.[15] These are just the minimal assumptions, and we see no grounds for assuming any additional properties or another lexical entry. On this approach, all the interpretative differences (or theta-roles) are merely an epiphenomenon derived from the interaction with other elements in the construction. The clitic *se* imposes only one additional constraint: it is anaphoric, so in either case it must be co-indexed both to the nominative subject and morphological agreement. Spanish is a *pro-drop* language, so if the subject is not specified lexically, it is interpreted according to the information supplied by the verbal inflection, and restricted to

---

[14]The occurrence of dative clitics is constrained by different factors which we will not consider here.

[15]This is not a peculiar characteristic of the clitic *se* in Spanish, the clitics *me, te, nos* and *os* are the same.

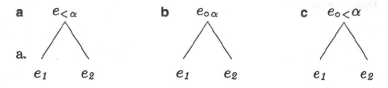

Fig. 7.3 (a) Precedence, (b) Overlapping, and (c) Precedence and partial overlapping

discourse anaphoric relations. Given that the clitic *se* is the least specified (in person and case features), it is quite consistent with its interpretation as impersonal. The referent of the clitic is interpreted as somebody not identified or for which no information is given, and this is highly dependent on whether there is a discourse antecedent for the subject agreement, as we will see later (38a). Our proposal for the analysis of *se* collapses together, on one hand, the ergative, passive, middle and some reflexive/reciprocal (Accusative *se*)[16] and, on the other hand, the so called possessor, ethical, impersonal, and some reciprocal (dative *se*). At the same time, the aspectual effects, which are present in either case, are explained in terms of event structure composition. We flesh out our proposal assuming the Generative Lexicon (GL) framework (Pustejovsky 1995–2000). We propose that Dative clitics in Spanish are capable of introducing an underspecified telic relation. This relation is similar to a telic proto-role, in a sense that will be made more clear later and which differs from the sense of telicity (somehow equivalent to boundedness as an aspectual distinction). This notion of telicity is captured partially by the notion of Opposition Structure (OS) in GL (see Levin (2000) for a discussion on telicity and argument structure relations).

7.3.1 Event and Qualia Structure: Pustejovsky 1988–2000

We assume the notions of Event Structure and Qualia Structure as developed in the Generative Lexicon (henceforth GL) (Pustejovsky 1991, 1995, 2000).

The structure in Fig. 7.3a might be considered an event transition, in other words reflecting a causation relation, somehow equivalent to (13), (cf. Dowty (1979), Levin (2000), and many others):

(13) $e1$[x act]   CAUSE $e2$ [y be/become]

Although this is often the case, we want to adopt a more general alternative, so that we are not committed to a strict causation relation. Instead, Fig. 7.3a may be understood as an abstract version of (13). This can be interpreted as mapping an Opposition Structure (OS) into the event structure in the sense of Pustejovsky (2000), as in:

---

[16]A step which already has been made by Burzio (1986).

Fig. 7.4 Opposition structure

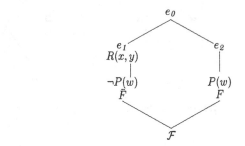

Fig. 7.5 Opposition structure

Fig. 7.6 Transformed
opposition structure

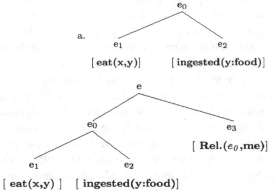

A representation such as the one in Fig. 7.4 enables a higher level of abstraction than the one in (13), in the sense that there is not a causal relation required between the two subevents.

A Qualia Structure in GL is a feature-valued structure, as shown in Fig. 7.7, below. In the following sections we restrict our attention to the interaction of the event structure and the roles in the Qualia structure: FORMAL, AGENTIVE and TELIC.

7.3.2   The Basics of Our Proposal

In a sentence like (10a), El nene me comió (la comida)./'The baby ate (the food) for me.', the presence of the dative clitic triggers the event structure shown in Fig. 7.6 below, as an operation on the event structure shown in Fig. 7.5. Abstractions of temporal relations in Figs. 7.5 and 7.6 can be understood as even more general versions of Fig. 7.3[17] relative to the event structure, where the temporal precedence relations are not specified.

---

[17]We are not considering issues related to tense anchoring nor headedness issues in the event structure. Consequently our event trees will not be annotated with those relations.

$$
\begin{bmatrix}
eat \\
\text{ARGSTR} = \begin{bmatrix} \text{ARG}_1: nene : child \\ \text{ARG}_2: food \\ \text{ARG}_3: me \end{bmatrix} \\
\text{EVENTSTR} = \begin{bmatrix} \text{EVENTSTR} = \text{E}_0: \begin{bmatrix} \text{E}_1 = \ldots \\ \text{E}_2 = \ldots \\ \text{RESTR} = \ldots \end{bmatrix} \\ \text{E}_3 = \ldots \\ \text{RESTR} = \ldots \\ \text{HEAD} = \text{E}_i \end{bmatrix} \\
\text{QUALIA} = \begin{bmatrix} \text{FORMAL} : \textbf{ingested}(e_2, y) \\ \text{AGENTIVE}: \textbf{eat}(e_1, x, y) \\ \text{TELIC} : \textbf{relation}(e_3, e_0, z) \end{bmatrix}
\end{bmatrix}
$$

Fig. 7.7 Feature structure corresponding to the OS in Fig. 7.6

The structure in Fig. 7.6 is equivalent to the following Qualia Structure in Fig. 7.7:

7.3.3 Motivation

The representations in Figs. 7.6 and 7.7 capture the intuition that the entire event e_0 concerns or is related to the argument introduced by the relation in e_3. This is an operation that adds structure on top of already available structure. It follows the same pattern, as the causative alternation, also produced by Spanish clitics as the following examples in (14) show:

(14) a.   Juan corre/sube/baja.
           'Juan runs/goes up/goes down.'

      b.   Lo/la/se   corrieron/subieron/bajaron
           cl-3p-sg-acc   ran-3P.Pl./went-up/went-down.
           'They made him/her/the run/go up/go down.'

For instance, in the verb *correr* (to run), the 'starting point' for the cliticization is not a transition but a process So, in this case, the result is a causativization (examples in (14b) correspond to the event structure in Fig. 7.8b):

Figure 7.9 depicts Fig. 7.8 annotated with the Qualia attributes in the Event tree.[18]

---

[18]We will continue using the event trees instead of the Qualia Structure full specification for expository convenience.

Fig. 7.8 Process-causative
transformation

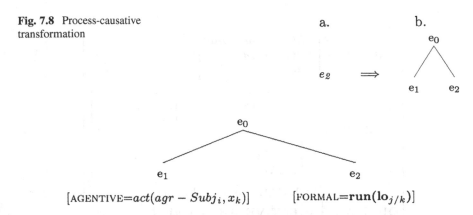

$$[\text{AGENTIVE}=act(agr - Subj_i, x_k)] \qquad [\text{FORMAL}=\mathbf{run(lo}_{j/k})]$$

Fig. 7.9 Causative representation of *correr* (This notation is intended to mean that *x* may be co-referential with *lo* (him, it). If it is co-referential, there is a direct causation, otherwise it is indirect)

This is equivalent to the representation in (15):

(15) $\lambda x\ \lambda e1\ \exists e2$ [act($e1$, they, x) $\wedge$ run($e2$, him/it) $\wedge$ $e1 < e2$]

The event structure depicted in Fig. 7.9 is not an innovation (although the analysis of the corresponding data from (14b) has not been addressed – as far as we know). The contrast between *ir* ('go') – a process – and *irse* ('leave') – an inchoative – supports the analysis presented here. The aspectual properties of sentences with the clitic *se* are a side effect of the corresponding event structure and its opposition structure (as depicted by Fig. 7.4). Furthermore, the following sentences provide additional support to this analysis, i.e.: process verbs like those in (14b) and (16) have the structure depicted in Fig. 7.8 (i.e., a transition event).

(16)   Juan se durmió mirando la tele.
       Juan SE slept watching the TV.   'Juan fell asleep watching TV.'

(17)   # Juan durmió mirando la tele.`
       'Juan slept watching TV.'

In (16) the gerundive phrase *mirando la tele* gives more content to the subevent e_1. On the contrary, the sentence in (17) is deviant because the verbal phrase corresponds to a process, *sleep* (with no OS), and this process is not compatible with watching TV. This contrast shows that the analysis of inchoatives as having the structure depicted in Fig. 7.8b might be superior to one which considers inchoatives as operators as in (Dowty 1979; Jackendoff 1990 and many others). The analysis of (10a) we proposed in Figs. 7.6 and 7.7 is an extension of the same basic mechanism. In Fig. 7.7 a clitic (accusative) which cannot satisfy an argument of the verb produces a change in the event structure. The availability of an underspecified agentive slot in the Qualia Structure enables the corresponding construal and makes possible this composition. On the other hand, the structure shown in Fig. 7.6 (and the

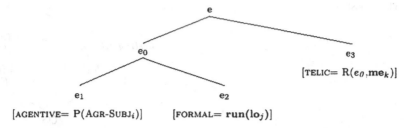

e

e_0

e_3

$[\text{TELIC}= R(e_0,\mathbf{me}_k)]$

e_1

e_2

$[\text{AGENTIVE}= P(\text{AGR-SUBJ}_i)]$ $[\text{FORMAL}= \mathbf{run}(\mathbf{lo}_j)]$

Fig. 7.10 *Correr* (run) with dative and accusative transformation

similar Fig. 7.10 below) is the result of another clitic-verb composition, in this case a dative clitic. This composition produces a change in the event structure given the availability of an underspecified telic slot. It is interesting to note that it is possible to add another clitic to the sentences in (14b) as exemplified in the sentence in (18), and it produces the same effect as in sentence (10a) with the structure shown in Fig. 7.10:

(18)   Me   lo   corrieron.
       cl-1p-sg-dat   cl-3p-sg-acc   ran.
       '(They) made him run/move for/on me.'

There is also some evidence supporting this type of analysis. We consider that the presence of a telic clitic is possible whenever there is a bounded event, and we assume that aspectual properties are captured through the event structure:

(19)   Juan (*se) comió manzanas.
       Juan (*SE) ate-perf apples.   'Juan ate apples.'

(20)   Juan (se) comió una manzana.
       Juan (SE) ate an apple.   'Juan ate an apple.'

In (19) the presence of a bare noun phrase blocks the presence of the clitic *se*. Sanz Yagüe (1996) and Nishida (1994) attribute this to aspectual properties of the clitic *se*.[19] We will not analyze this issue here because the data are much

---

[19]Sanz Yagüe (1996) considers the clitic *se* in these constructions has a + telic feature. The sense of telicity used by Sanz Yagüe (1996) corresponds to the notion of telicity as understood in Tenny (1987), Tenny (1992), Grimshaw (1990), Krifka (1992) and many others. This is totally different from the notion of telic role in the Qualia Structure as we mentioned above. The equivalent of a telic event corresponds here to the notion of transition, or Opposition Structure as presented in the next section.

Fig. 7.11 Opposition
structure

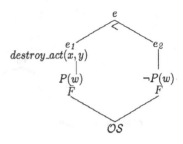

more complex than that considered by Sanz Yagüe and Nishida.[20] This complexity
is due in part to the interaction of opposition structure and event structure.[21]
Although we consider clitics as affix-like syntactic objects, we are not assuming
a lexical argument-changing operation. We understand instead that clitics specify
information that is enabled by the Qualia. The clitics are linked to functions
already present in the Qualia which otherwise might remain underspecified. As a
consequence, the argument structure might be determined co-compositionally by
the predicate and the clitics provided there is a mapping to the Qualia Structure.

7.3.4 Opposition Structures

The operation presented in Figs. 7.8 and 7.9 is equivalent to (and a generalization
of) causativization, where a process is transformed into a transition. As presented
above (see Fig. 7.4), the notion of Opposition Structure (OS) is equivalent to the
notion of transition, in the sense that if there is a transition necessarily there is an
OS.[22] Pustejovsky (2000, p. 458) proposes the notion of OS as a model of change
(and persistence) incorporated into the event structure. For example, in a verb like
destroy, it is represented as in Fig. 7.11.

We propose here that the presence of the clitic also triggers an OS in a structure
like the one in Fig. 7.10 (similar to Fig. 7.12 below). If the argument introduced by
the clitic is affected by the event, there is a change on some property P related to

---

[20]Consider for example the following sentence similar to (28):
(1)   Juan (se) comió   manzanas verdes.
       Juan (SE) ate-pef apples   green   'Juan ate green apples'.
(2)   Juan (se) comía   manzanas a lo loco.
       Juan (SE) ate-imperf apples   as the mad.   'Juan ate/was eating apples as a mad.'

[21]Rigau (1994) (quoted by Sanz Yagüe (1996)) says that the presence of a benefactive *se* produces
the perfective interpretation of the event.

[22]Alternatively, it is not necessarily the presence of an OS that might imply a change. For instance,
change may occur if the OS falls within an 'intensional' domain or a paradigmatic domain.

Fig. 7.12 Opposition
structure for a dative clitic
with locative Interpretation

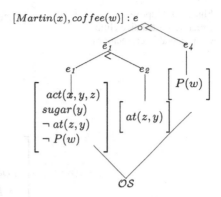

this argument (the clitic). This is illustrated by sentence (21) and the corresponding structure in Fig. 7.12.[23]

(21)   Martín *(le) puso azúcar (al café).   locative
        Martín cl-3pSgDat put sugar (to-the coffee).
        'Martín put sugar into the coffee.'

The role of the argument introduced by the clitic is indirect, so some kind of computation is required to recover the possible relations that are implicitly stated in the Qualia. The OS (and associated Qualia) enable the computation of abduction operations (Hobbs et al. 1993; Ng and Mooney 1990; Charniak and Goldman 1988; and others).

7.3.4.1 Abduction Operations

Hobbs et al. (1993) use abduction as an inference mechanism for sentence interpretation. Given the expression $p(x) \supset q(x)$, and $q(a)$, abduction allows us to conclude $p(a)$. This is not a valid mode of inference, but it is a powerful mechanism that allows us to compute certain interpretations in natural language. These interpretations are usually constrained to reduce the power of the mechanism, and require some minimal consistency checking. In the Dative clitic constructions in Spanish, the clitic can have many different roles (see Castaño (2001) for a discussion) and, in some cases, quite elusive or abstract ones, like the ethical Dative.

We assumed that Dative clitics that are not subcategorized by the verb introduce some relation or property of the clitic argument to the event. This is the minimal assumption (see Figs. 7.6 and 7.10). However there are cases where this relation has some more specific content according to the particular event involved. The computation of abduction operations will allow us to provide more content to the

---

[23]This example, dative clitics and the use of abduction are discussed in Castaño (2001).

Fig. 7.13 Opposition structure for a dative clitic with several interpretations

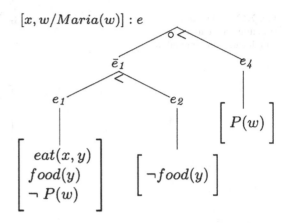

$$[x, w/Maria(w)] : e$$

abstract predicate P whenever it is possible, instead of using a catalog of theta-roles, which are difficult to justify. The use of abduction operations is limited here to predicates already present in the core event structure. In other words, predicates from the OS introduced by the core event are tried first. In this case, the OS [¬at(z, y), **at**(z, y)] encodes the change of location that is required by a verb like *poner* ('put').

Alternatively, the use of abduction can be restricted to predicates that are related to the arguments of those predicates by way of Qualia.

In Fig. 7.12 $P(w)$ is congruent ($\cong$) with **at**(z,y), unifying w with z via Abduction: **at**(w,y) $\cong P(w)$ based on the telic role of *azúcar* (sugar). The structure can be simplified as follows: $e_4 = e_2$, given there is no distinction between both sub-events.

Next, sentence (22) is a variation of the classical ethical dative (10a). The possible operations are the same, either in the interpretation (i) or (ii): $P \cong$ ¬**has_y**. This can be interpreted in two ways. It can be a benefactive, the case in which the argument introduced by the clitic wants the food to be eaten (e.g. (10a)). Otherwise, it is a negatively affected participant, the case in which the argument introduced by the clitic doesn't want the food to be eaten (e.g. one of the possible interpretations of 10d). These are discourse dependent interpretations. We have shown that the paradigm of variations in one or more arguments yields different interpretations. Those interpretations can be computed using the abduction operation constrained by the OS and the Qualia, i.e., it specifies an argument that participates in the OS (Fig. 7.13).

(22)   le comió (la comida) (a María).
        cl-3pSgDat eat-past (food) (to María).
        i) '(he/she) ate (the food) for (he/she) María.'
        ii) '(he/she) ate (the food) from/on María.'

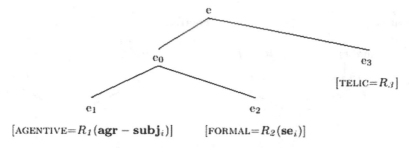

Fig. 7.14 Acusative clitic (*se*) linked to the FORMAL predicate in the Qualia

7.4 Reconsidering the Clitic *se*

Given the clitic *se* is underspecified for Case, the available options are the following, (a) accusative behavior, which corresponds to reflexive, inherent, ergative,[24] inchoative, middle and (b) dative behavior which corresponds to impersonal, ethical, possessive and locative.

7.4.1 Accusative Case: Reflexive, Inherent, Ergative, Inchoative and Middle se

In these cases and if the clitic is not *se*, but an accusative clitic, the verb must be transitive or transitivizable. In the following examples the clitic *se* is linked to the FORMAL predicate in the Qualia.

The structure represented in Fig. 7.14 shows, as a *blueprint*, the general schema that corresponds to the following sentences in (23). The subject (if any, given Spanish is a pro-drop language) and the verbal agreement link to an argument in the Agentive role. The accusative clitic links to an argument in the Formal role. If there is no Dative clitic (the simplest cases we are considering here), no argument is bound to the telic role.

(23)   a. Juan se afeitó.   reflexive
          John SE shaved.   'John shaved himself.'
       b. Se reía.   inherent reflexive
          SE laughed.   'He/she laughed.'
       c. El barco se hundió.   ergative
          The ship SE sank.   'The ship sank'.
       d. Juan se fue/durmió.   inchoative
          Juan SE went/slept.   'Juan left/fell asleep.'
       e. Las manzanas se comen fácilmente.   middle
          The apples SE eat easily.   'Apples are eaten easily.'

---

[24]This interpretation of ergatives is quite similar to the one in Bouchard (1995).

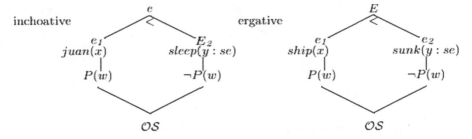

Fig. 7.15 Inchoative and ergative opposition structures

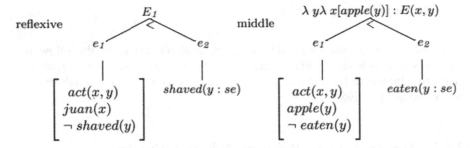

Fig. 7.16 Reflexive and middle opposition structures

We will consider now in detail some of these examples. We will start with the inchoative (23d) and ergative (23c) examples (Fig. 7.15)[25]:

The difference between both sentences is that in the inchoative case (23d) the verb is a process and the core event requires only one argument (in this case the 'sleeper'). The difference between (23c) and a transitive that does not alternate with an ergative construction corresponds to the fact that the core event specifies a sub-event where an action takes place as specified in Fig. 7.16, corresponding to (23a). The middle construction (23e), also represented in Fig. 7.16, contains an unsaturated action sub-event description, which can be interpreted as an event type. It is unsaturated because the *actor* is not specified.

Finally we consider the inherent reflexive as in (23b). The above sentence is similar to (24a) below, and their meaning can barely be distinguished. However, as the contrast between (24b) and (24c) shows, the presence of the clitic produces some differences. This is accounted for if we assume the event structure depicted in Fig. 7.17 is ruled out for sentence (24b) because the phrase *de Pedro* cannot map to a corresponding sub-event in the event structure. The same analysis corresponds to the sentence in (16). This can be seen as an effect of a requirement on mapping

---

[25]The core event associated with the verb, in the sense of Pustejovsky (2000), is capitalized.

Fig. 7.17 Opposition structure for an inherent reflexive

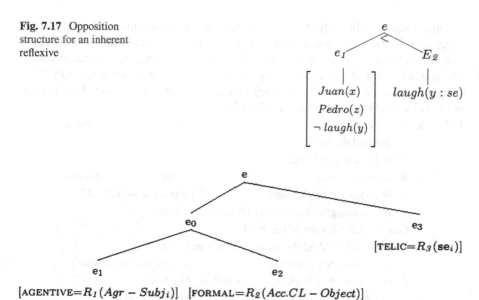

$$
e_1 \qquad\qquad E_2
$$

$$
\begin{bmatrix} Juan(x) \\ Pedro(z) \\ \neg\, laugh(y) \end{bmatrix} \qquad laugh(y : se)
$$

$$
[\text{TELIC}=R_3(\mathbf{se}_i)]
$$

$$
[\text{AGENTIVE}=R_1(Agr - Subj_i)] \quad [\text{FORMAL}=R_2(Acc.CL - Object)]
$$

Fig. 7.18 Dative clitic se

conditions between arguments and event structure.[26] We will discuss this issue in the next section (Fig. 7.18).

(24) a. Juan reía.
        Juan laughed.
      b. *Juan reía de Pedro.
        Juan laughed of-from Pedro.   'Juan laughed at Pedro.'
      c. Juan   se   reía   de   Pedro.
        Juan   SE laughed   of-from Pedro. 'Juan laughed at Pedro.'

7.4.2 Dative Case: Impersonal, Ethical, Possessive and Locative se

In the following examples, the clitic *se* is linked to the telic predicate in the Qualia. This representation makes the interpretation of the impersonal *se* equivalent to

---

[26]For instance, Levin (2000), Rappaport Hovav and Levin (1999) propose the Argument Per Sub-event Condition: there must be at least one argument XP in the syntax per sub-event in the event structure. Under the approach presented here it is a side effect of the computation of the EPS. For more, see Sect. 6.

an ethical dative. The only difference is that the interpretation of the subject as impersonal is due to discourse anaphoric constraints.[27] Unlike the previous case, here the clitic introduces an argument that does not participate in the primary OS; instead it introduces a secondary affected object, i.e. a secondary OS. The interpretation of (25a–b) is the same regardless of the presence of the clitic, except that (25a) may also be interpreted as (25c)[28]:

(25) a. Se robaron el banco.[29]   impersonal with *se*/ethical
          SE robbed the bank.
          'The bank was robbed.'

      b. Robaron el banco.   impersonal without *se*
          robbed-3rd-plural the bank.   'The bank was robbed.'

      c. Nuestros amigos se robaron el banco.   ethical
          Our friends SE robbed the bank.
          'Our friends robbed the bank (for themselves).'

      d. Juan se compró un libro.   benefactive/possesive
          Juan SE bought a book.   'Juan bought a book for himself.'

      e. María se puso el sombrero.   locative/possesive
          María SE put the hat.   'María put the hat on.'

The structure in Fig. 7.19 depicts the impersonal interpretation in (25a). It is equivalent to the ethical interpretation we find in (25c) represented in Fig. 7.20, which we already discussed in (22). The only difference between Figs. 7.19 and 7.20 is the interpretation of the subject (and the clitic *se*), as an unbound argument in Fig. 7.19. This argument is bound at the discourse interpretation level (either as impersonal or as a specific group introduced in the discourse. In both (25a) and (25c) the presence of the clitic is highly redundant, it is not introducing a new argument (it is anaphoric), and it is not introducing a new relation. The content of the abstract relation introduced by the clitic (the OS $[\sim P(w), P(w)]$) is consistent with the relation in the OS:$[\sim has(x,y), has(x,y)]$, given $w = x$. This produces an emphatic contrast between the sentence (25a) and (25b) (either in the impersonal or non-impersonal interpretation). When the clitic is not anaphoric, as in (26) and the corresponding Fig. 7.21, then $w \neq x$. A different role for the clitic argument is

---

[27]This is probably a similar view to the one from Otero (1986) who says that impersonal se allows a definite arbitrary subject (arbitrary pro in GB terminology).

[28]This is the case in the following sentences

i.   Mis amigos lo planearon con cuidado. Ayer se robaron el banco.
      My friends planned it carefully. Yesterday (they) (SE)-robbed the bank

ii.   Juan llegó. Se trajo los libros a la biblioteca.
      Juan arrived. (He) (SE)-brought the books to the library.

[29]See Real Academia Española (1998) page 382 for the use of 3rd person plural as impersonal. Although this example is in plural, equivalent examples are possible in 3rd person singular; see the previous footnote.

Fig. 7.19 Opposition structure with impersonal-posessor-benefactive interpretations

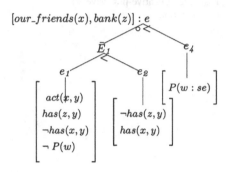

$[\lambda\,x, bank(z)] : e$

$\bar{E}_1$ e_4

e_1 e_2

$$\begin{bmatrix} act(x,y) \\ has(z,y) \\ \neg has(x,y) \\ \neg\,P(x) \end{bmatrix} \quad \begin{bmatrix} \neg has(z,y) \\ has(x,y) \end{bmatrix} \quad \begin{bmatrix} P(w : se) \end{bmatrix}$$

Fig. 7.20 Opposition structure with benefactive interpretation

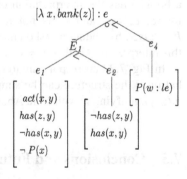

$[our\_friends(x), bank(z)] : e$

$\bar{E}_1$ e_4

e_1 e_2

$$\begin{bmatrix} act(x,y) \\ has(z,y) \\ \neg has(x,y) \\ \neg\,P(w) \end{bmatrix} \quad \begin{bmatrix} \neg has(z,y) \\ has(x,y) \end{bmatrix} \quad \begin{bmatrix} P(w : se) \end{bmatrix}$$

Fig. 7.21 Affected participant opposition structure

$[\lambda\,x, bank(z)] : e$

$\bar{E}_1$ e_4

e_1 e_2

$$\begin{bmatrix} act(x,y) \\ has(z,y) \\ \neg has(x,y) \\ \neg\,P(x) \end{bmatrix} \quad \begin{bmatrix} \neg has(z,y) \\ has(x,y) \end{bmatrix} \quad \begin{bmatrix} P(w : le) \end{bmatrix}$$

required, but the representation of the Event Structure is the same. In this case, the role of *le* is interpreted as the possessor of the bank: *has(w,y)*, given the implication *has_y(w) ⊃ P(w)* and consequently the OS [*has(w,y),~has(w,y)*].

(26) le   robaron   el   banco.
      3pDat   robbed   the   bank.
      His bank was robbed.'

The following examples are similar to the ones we considered before in Sect. 7.3.4. The sentence (25d) above (Juan se compró un libro./'Juan SE bought

Fig. 7.22
Possesor-benefactive
opposition structure

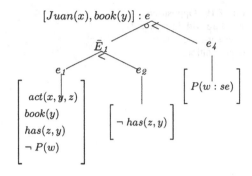

Fig. 7.23 Locative-possesive
interpretation

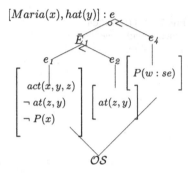

a book.') has the interpretation obtained from the OS in Fig. 7.22: $z \neq w$, $w = x$ by *se*, $e_4 \neq e_2$ and e_4 is not *tense anchored*, so it is an *intensional* domain, $P \cong has\_y$, by abduction (skolemized): $has\_y(w) \supset P(w)$. In this case, what triggers this interpretation is that $w = x$.

In Fig. 7.23 corresponding to (25e), (María se puso el sombrero/'María put the hat on.') the structure can be simplified as follows: $w = x$ by *se*, $e_4 = e_2$, $P(w) \cong at(z, y)$, unifying w with z via Abduction: $at(w, y) \supset P(w)$.

7.5 Conclusions and Future Work

We presented sufficient evidence that supports the view that a sense enumerative view of the clitic *se* is not granted. Crucially, we showed that the claim that it cannot occur in embedded infinitival phrases is not correct, and that it shares properties of other Dative and Accusative clitics, these being the minimal assumptions.

We presented an analysis that provides an account of the full range of data concerning *se* and showed that they can be explained by its underspecified case and anaphoric nature. Given its pronominal nature, its interpretation is context dependent and subject to anaphoric and discourse reference resolution mechanisms.

We used the Generative Lexicon notions of Event Structure, Opposition Structure and Qualia Structure. We also used the mechanism of abduction to compute the interpretations of the so-called non-argument clitics. We showed that Spanish clitics enable the generation of causative constructions and we extended this mechanism to what we called Telic constructions. Although we did not discuss other romance languages, there are enough similarities to suspect that this analysis can be extended to many of them.

There are many other issues we did not address, which are tightly related to the discussion of the mapping from arguments to Event Structures: event composition concerning the Core Event and prepositional and verbal phrases (e.g. causatives). In addidition, a full discussion of the telicity and other aspectual effects is required. Such machinery is necessary for a full discussion of the impersonal *se* and the different interpretations that it enables. Those issues will be addressed in future work. In the remainder of this section we would like to present some ideas that are beyond the data we have been considering, but they are direct generalizations over the analysis we have presented so far.

7.5.1 Mapping from Arguments to Event Structures

The following subsections are highly speculative, and they aim to describe some ideas concerning future work. There are two possible views or aspects of the constraints in the interpretation of the clitic "roles" in the data that we have discussed in this paper. First we consider a mapping procedure from arguments to Qualia Roles, interpreted as structural positions in the Event Structure. Then we consider Argument Linking as a byproduct of the computation of the EPS.

7.5.1.1 Mapping Arguments to Qualia Roles

Implicit in our analysis, there was a straightforward mapping between the Qualia structure and morpho-syntax. In the following two subsections we describe this mapping according to the verb valence.

Intransitive Verbs

The subject maps either to the Formal or the Agentive Quale according to the verb type (so far we have been considering cases where it maps to the Formal). Predicate arity may be modified as follows: if an accusative clitic is present with a unary predicate the subject maps to the Agentive Quale and the Object to the Formal provided the construal is consistent with the predicate properties.

if there is no accusative clitic:

> AGR/Subject ⇒ Formal (or Formal and Agentive Quale)

if there is an accusative clitic:

> AGR/subject ⇒ Agentive Quale
> ACC/OBJECT ⇒ Formal Quale.

Transitive Verbs

The subject maps to the Agentive Quale and the object maps to the Formal Quale. Arity may be modified as follows: We may get the effect of detransitivization (if it is not just reflexive) binding the two arguments in the qualia with an anaphoric clitic, (examples from Sect. 7.4.2). If an extra (Dative) clitic is present then it maps to the Telic Quale (and we get the effect of converting a transitive to a ditransitive verb).

> AGR/subject ⇒ Agentive Quale.
> ACC/OBJECT ⇒ Formal Quale.

if there is a dative clitic:

> DAT ⇒ Telic Quale.

The proposal stated here can be understood as an abstract theory of theta-roles. In a sense similar to the notion of Proto-roles (cf. Dowty (1991)) with the addition of another Proto-role: the Proto-Telic. But we are considering theta roles to be a derivative notion, which must be explained through the syntax of the semantic framework we assume this view is similar to the one in Jackendoff (1990) where theta-roles are reduced to configurations in the Conceptual Structure. We make use of structural configurations with highly underspecified properties which impose very general constraints on the possible construals. The interpretation of a sentence is dependent on the particular expressions involved interacting with the Qualia. We can give, then, a more specific content to the notion of co-composition, which might be considered as the satisfaction of independently stated constraints.

7.5.1.2 Argument Linking as Constraints on the Computation of the EPS

The mapping algorithm sketched above can be understood as a precondition for the computation of the Event Persistence Structure (Pustejovsky 2000):

> We denote the event description assigned to the matrix predicate of the clause, P, as the backbone in the construction of the event persistence structure, that is all additional event predications in the clause are annotations to this core structure.

However, these annotations to the core event cannot be performed unless a mapping from the arguments is given. In GL this mapping is pre-compiled in the

Qualia as Feature Value Sharing from the Argument Structure to the Qualia. We want to present here a general view of argument linking as a mapping from case marked arguments to the Event Structure in the computation of the EPS.

> The goal of the EPS is to represent not only what has changed by virtue of the matrix event description, but to also model secondary effects of the action, if they can be captured, as well as what has stayed the same.
>
>   To this end, I will assume that any predicate, be it verbal, adjectival, or phrasal (PP), is assigned an independent event description δ_i; further, every sortal expression will be assigned an event description.

The consequences of the changes are computed using the event descriptions corresponding to the set Δ of event descriptions in an expression and a gating function (Pustejovsky 2000, p.467):

> GATE: For an event description, $\delta \in \Delta$, in the domain of the matrix predicate P, δ is gated by P only if the property denoted by δ is either initiated or terminated by P.

Argument linking can be seen as a set of constraints on the calculation of the EPS:

The Thematic Argument Constraint

At least the Formal Quale must be specified. (If there is an Opposition Structure, this is clearly the case in which the Formal requires specification). The argument affected by the OS must be specified (Qualia Unified), and the relevant properties gated. This is performed by the accusative case. Otherwise, the Nominative Case arguments can specify the OS. (For instance, if there is no accusative case or the accusative case argument is not gated, but it participates in a relational property of the subject that is gated). The formal quale event must be covered by an argument obligatorily: covering can be made by existential closure of default arguments (e.g., *John already ate*).

The Perspective Argument Constraint

The Agentive Quale specifies the event properties of the initiating conditions of the event. This is performed by the Nominative Case. This may result in underspecified sub-events, i.e. a shadowing effect (unaccusative alternation).

The Telic Role Constraint

Additional participants affected by the event may be introduced. Their role in the event is indirect, so the computation is performed using abduction to recover the possible relations that are implicitly stated in the Qualia and Event Structure.

These constraints can be embedded in the algorithm for computing the EPS, or be a sort of side effect of the algorithm in the computation of the Event Persistent Structure. In this conception, there is no argument structure, but the argument structure is determined compositionally by the predicate and the arguments, given general constraints determined by the particular grammar. For example, Spanish has the clitics, which constrain the quantity of arguments and the mappings in particular ways; other languages have case morphology for noun phrases. Simple or complex predicates (e.g. morphological causatives) will have the same constraints on the argument mapping: the cases available from the grammar constitute a reduced set.

Next, we sketch an algorithm for computing the participant roles. Each expression has its own event variable (or set of event variables associated with it, corresponding to the persistent properties) and the Event Persistence Structure is computed as follows (examples are given in the Appendix).

- If the Core Event Structure has an Opposition Structure, Gating is tested first for the DO/Accusative clitic.

  - If the DO is gated (Case 1), then the subject is assigned the Agentive role.
  - Otherwise gating is tested for Nominative argument (Case 2). If there is only a subject, it must be unified with the Formal.

- If the Core Event Structure has no Opposition Structure:

  - If the DO is Qualia Unified with the Formal, and the Subject is not Qualia Unified with the Formal (Causation), then there is an OS created in the computation of the EPS (Case 5a). In this case the subject is assigned the Agentive role.
  - If both Subject and DO can be Qualia Unified with both Formal and Agentive roles in the core event structure, then both arguments are in an asymmetric relation (Case 5b).
  - If there is no DO, the subject must be unified with the Formal (Case 4).

Acknowledgements I would like to thank James Pustejovsky for his continuous inspiration and discussions on this and related topics. I am grateful to the anonymous reviewers for careful reading and suggestions on how to improve this paper and to the organizers and participants of GL2001 for giving me the opportunity to present my ideas. Finally I would like to thank Jess Littman who helped me to prepare the final version.

Appendix: EPS Computation

A.1 Core Event with OS

Case 1. **Transitives**. If any of the set of properties (events) in the DO are gated, but not the subject (unless the DO is anaphoric) (Fig. 7.24):

(27)   John broke the glass.

Case 2 Unacussativity. If there is no DO then the Subject must be gated: this possibility is constrained in different ways according to the language: e.g. Spanish requires a clitic, so this option is not available with transitive verbs; English doesn't (in the case the Agentive is not the same argument as the Formal) (Fig. 7.25).

Fig. 7.24 Transitives

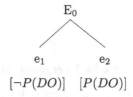

Fig. 7.25 Unacussative

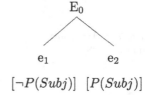

(28) a. The glass broke.
 b. John arrived.

Fig. 7.26 Ditransitive

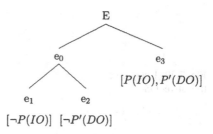

Case 3 Ditransitives. A Dative argument introduces a secondary OS (Fig. 7.26).

(29) John gave a book to Mary.

A.2 Core Event with No OS

If the core event has no Opposition Structure then there is no gating.

Case 4 (Process: Unergatives) (Fig. 7.27):

(30) John walks.

Fig. 7.27 Unergative case
with no OS

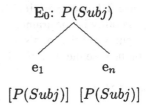

$$E_0:\ P(Subj)$$

$$e_1 \qquad e_n$$

$$[P(Subj)]\ \ [P(Subj)]$$

Case 5a. Unergative-Transitive alternation (Fig. 7.28)

(31) a. Juan se/lo durmió.
Juan SE/3pAc.slept.   'Juan fell asleep.'
b. The lieutenant marched the soldiers for hours.

Fig. 7.28 Unergative
transitive OS

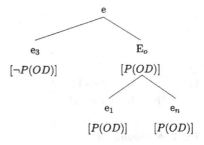

Fig. 7.29 Unergative
transitive- OS

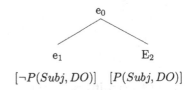

Fig. 7.30 Transitive process
or states

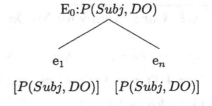

Case 5b. Unergative/Transitive alternation: If no eventualities in the DO are gated, then it is a participant in the OS structure (i.e. it defines the OS of the subject because the gated properties are relational) (Figs. 7.29 and 7.30).

(32) Juan caminó dos kilómetros. 'Juan walked two km.'

Fig. 7.31 Ditransitive process or states

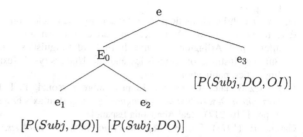

$$[P(Subj, DO, OI)]$$

$$[P(Subj, DO)] \quad [P(Subj, DO)]$$

Case 6. Ditransitive process or States (Fig. 7.31):

(33) Juan le   sabe   la lección (al maestroi).
     Juan 3pDat knows the lesson (to-the teacher).
     Juan knows the lesson for him (the teacher).'

References

Abeill'e, A., Godard, D., & Sag, I. A. (1998). Two kinds of composition in French complex predicates. In E. Hinrichs, A. Kathol, & T. Nakazawa (Eds.), *Complex predicates in nonderivational syntax* (Syntax and semantics, Vol. 30, pp. 1–41). San Diego: Academic.

Alsina, A. (1996). *The role of argument structure in grammar: Evidence from Romance.* Stanford: CSLI Publications.

Aoun, J. (1985). *On the formal nature of anaphoric relations.* Cambridge: MIT Press.

Arce-Arenales, M. (1989). *Semantic structure and syntactic function: The case of Spanish se.* Ph.D. thesis, University of Colorado, Boulder.

Baker, M. (1988). *Incorporation: A theory of grammatical function changing.* Chicago: University of Chicago Press.

Bonet, E. (1995). Feature structure of Romance clitics. *Natural Language and Linguistic Theory, 13,* 607.

Borer, H. (1983). *Parametric syntax.* Dordrecht: Foris Publications.

Borer, H. E. (1986). *The syntax of pronominal clitics* (Syntax and semantics, Vol. 19). New York: Academic.

Borer, H., & Grodzinsky, Y. (1986). Syntactic cliticization and lexical cliticization. The case of Hebrew dative clitics. In H. Borer (Ed.), *The syntax of pronominal clitics* (Syntax and Semantics, Vol. 19, pp. 175–217). Orlando: Academic.

Bouchard, D. (1995). *The semantics of syntax.* Chicago: University of Chicago Press.

Burzio, L. (1986). *Italian syntax.* Dordrecht: D. Reidel Publishing Company.

Castaño, J. M. (2001). Spanish dative clitics: Event and opposition structure. In P. Bouillon & K. Kanzaki (Eds.), *Proceedings of the GL2001* University of Geneva, Switzerland.

Charniak, E., & Goldman, R. (1988). A logic for semantic interpretation. In *Proceedings of the 26th meeting of the ACL*.

Cinque, G. (1988). On si constructions and the theory of arb. *Linguistic Inquiry, 19*, 521–581.

De Miguel Aparicio, E. (1992). *El Aspecto en la Sintaxis del Español: Perfectividad e Impersonalidad*. Madrid: Ediciones de la Universidad Autónoma de Madrid.

Dobrovie-Sorin, C. (1998). Impersonal se constructions in Romance and the passivization of unergatives. *Linguistic Inquiry, 29*, 399–437.

Dowty, D. R. (1979). *Word meaning and Montague grammar*. Dordrecht: D. Reidel Publishing Company.

Dowty, D. (1991). Thematic proto-roles and argument selection. *Language, 67*, 547–619.

Everett, D. L. (1996). Why there are no clitics: An alternative perspective on pronominal allomorphy. Arlington: Summer Institute of Linguistics, University of Texas at Arlington. Summer Institute of Linguistics and the University of Texas at Arlington publications in linguistics, publication 123.

Fernandez Soriano, O. (1999). El pronombre personal. In I. Bosque & V. Demonte (Eds.), *Gramática Descriptiva de la Lengua Española* (Sintaxis básica de las clases de palabras, Vol. 1, pp. 1210–217). Real Academia Española.

Garcia, E. (1975). *The role of theory in linguistic analysis: The Spanish pronoun system*. Amsterdam: North Holland.

Grimshaw, J. (1981). On the lexical representation of Romance reflexive clitics. In J. Bresnan (Ed.), *The mental representation of grammatical relations* (pp. 87–148). Cambridge, MA: MIT Press.

Grimshaw, J. (1990). *Argument structure*. Cambridge: MIT Press.

Hobbs, J., Stickel, M., Martin, P., & Edwards, D. (1993). Interpretation as abduction. *Artificial Intelligence, 63*, 69–142.

Jackendoff, R. (1990). *Semantic structures*. Cambridge: MIT Press.

Jaeggli, O. (1982). *Topics in Romance syntax*. Dordrecht: Foris.

Jaeggli, O. (1986). Three issues in the theory of clitics: Case, doubled NPs, and extraction. In H. Borer (Ed.), *The syntax of pronominal clitics* (Syntax and semantics, Vol. 19, pp. 175–217). Orlando: Academic.

Kayne, R. (1975). *French syntax: The transformational cycle*. Cambridge: MIT Press.

Krifka, M. (1992). Thematic relations as links between nominal reference and temporal constitution. In I. Sag & A. Szabolcsi (Eds.), *Lexical matters*. Stanford: CSLI.

Levin, B. (2000) Aspect, lexical semantic representation, and argument expression. In *Proceedings of the 26th annual meeting of the Berkeley Linguistics Society*.

Manzini, M. R. (1986). On Italian si. In H. Borer (Ed.), *The syntax of pronominal clitics* (Syntax and semantics, Vol. 19, pp. 175–217). San Francisco: Academic.

Masullo, P. J. (1992). *Incorporation and case theory in Spanish: A cross linguistic perspective*. Ph.D. thesis. Seattle: University of Washington.

Miller, P. H., & Sag, I. A. (1997). French clitic movement without clitics or movement. *Natural Language and Linguistic Theory, 15*(3), 573.

Monachesi, P. (1999). *A lexical approach to Italian cliticization* (CSLI lecture notes, No. 84). Stanford: CSLI Publications.

Ng, H., & Mooney, R. (1990). The role of coherence in constructing and evaluating abductive explanations. In *Proceedings of the AAAI spring symposium on automated abduction*.

Nishida, C. (1994). The Spanish reflexive clitic se as an aspectual class marker. *Linguistics, 32*, 425–458.

Otero, C. P. (1986). Arbitrary subjects in finite clasuses. In I. Bordelois et al. (Eds.), *Generative studies in Spanish syntax* (pp. 81–109). Dordrecht: Foris.

Pustejovsky, J. (1991). The syntax of event structure. *Cognition, 41*, 47–81.

Pustejovsky, J. (1995). *The generative lexicon*. Cambridge: MIT Press.

Pustejovsky, J. (2000). Event structure and opposition structure. In C. Tenny & J. Pustejovsky (Eds.), *Events as grammatical objects* (pp. 350–400). Stanford: CSLI Publications.

Rappaport Hovav, M., & Levin, B. (1999). *Two types of compositionally derived events*. Ramat Gan/Evanston: Bar Ilan University/Northwestern University.

Real Academia Española. (1998). *Esbozo de una Nueva Gramática de la Lengua Española*. Espasa Calpe.

Reinhart, T., & Reuland, E. (1993). Reflexivity. *Linguistic Inquiry, 24*, 657–720.

Rigau, G. (1994). *Les propietas dels verbs pronominals. Els Marges 50*. Barcelona: Curial.

Sanz Yagüe, M. M. (1996). *Telicity, objects and the mapping onto predicate types*. Ph.D. thesis. Rochester: University of Rochester.

Sportiche, D. (1998). *Partitions and atoms of clause structure: Subjects, agreement, case, and clitics*. London/New York: Routledge.

Tenny, C. (1987). *Grammaticalizing aspect and affectedness*. Ph.D. thesis. Cambridge, MA: MIT.

Tenny, C. (1992). Aspectual roles and the syntax-semantics interface. In I. Sag & A. Szabolcsi (Eds.), *Lexical matters*. Stanford: CSLI.

Zubizarreta, M. L. (1982). *Levels of representation in the lexicon and in the syntax*. Dordrecht: Foris.

Chapter 8
Adjective-Noun Combinations and the Generative Lexicon

Irena Drašković, James Pustejovsky, and Rob Schreuder

8.1 Introduction

The focus of the present study is on exploring the possibility that the adjectival logical or formal semantic type as outlined in Kamp and Partee (1995) determines the adjectival level of underspecification which affects computational complexity. In addition, computational complexity is affected by the process of conceptual compatibility resolution as proposed in Pustejovsky (1995).

In the theoretical framework proposed by Kamp and Partee (1995), it is suggested that adjectives in general can best be treated as *intensional functions*, that is, as functions mapping the properties of nouns onto the properties of the combinations (see below). The application of this function defines a subset in the noun extension. Adjectives in general can be considered subsective (also called reference- or property-modifying, Siegel 1976). Formally, subsection is expressed as: $||AN|| \subseteq ||N||$, for example: $||skillful \, N|| \subseteq ||N||$ (Kamp and Partee 1995). For an illustration of subsective interpretation, let us consider the combination *skillful surgeon*. The combination refers to that subset of surgeons which are skillful in performing a surgery, (rather than chopping wood skillfully). One consequence of this kind of highly noun-specific mode of adjectival interpretation is that combinations with different nouns, such as *skillful violinist*, will refer to a different set of entities,

I. Drašković (✉)
Department of Primary and Community Care, Radboud University Nijmegen Medical Centre, The Netherlands
e-mail: i.draskovic@elg.umcn.nl

J. Pustejovsky
Department of Computer Science, Brandeis University, Waltham, MA, USA
e-mail: jamesp@cs.brandeis.edu

R. Schreuder
Department of Psychology, Radboud University Nijmegen, The Netherlands

J. Pustejovsky et al. (eds.), *Advances in Generative Lexicon Theory*, Text, Speech and Language Technology 46, DOI 10.1007/978-94-007-5189-7_8, © Springer Science+Business Media Dordrecht 2013

that is, to person(s) skillful in playing a violin. In the semantic interpretation of the combinations *skillful surgeon* and *skillful violinist*, different noun-related properties are used in determining the subset of the noun extension to which the combination refers. Both the intension (set of properties) and the extension (set of entities having those properties) of the adjective *skillful* will be different across different combinations. In other words, the logical type affects both the referential (extensional) and the combinatorial (intensional) part of semantic interpretation.

In addition to the subsective type, Kamp and Partee (1995) identify and describe a subclass of adjectives called *intersective*, which act quite differently. As suggested in Kamp & Partee, this kind of adjective ignores everything about the intension of the noun except the extension it assigns in a given state of affairs. Adjective-noun combinations in which adjectives combine with nouns in an intersective fashion, are also called referent-modifying (Siegel 1976). They refer to the entities in the intersection of the sets denoted by the adjective and the noun (e.g., the adjectives *carnivorous, yellow, long,* etc.). Formally: $||AN|| \cap ||N||$, for example: $||$carnivorous $N|| = ||$carnivorous$|| \cap ||N||$ (in Kamp and Partee 1995). One characteristic of intersective adjectives is that they combine in the same way with different nouns (Kamp and Partee 1995; Sedivy et al. 1999). This characteristic of intersective adjectives can be illustrated by using the adjective *carnivorous*. Compare the meaning of this adjective in the combinations *carnivorous mammal*, and *carnivorous plant*. In both combinations, the meaning of the adjective remains the same (flesh-eating) and the adjective has the capacity to define a set of entities independently of the noun. Generally, to be in the extension of the combination involving an intersective adjective, an entity must be in the extension of both the adjective AND the noun. In contrast, the meaning of the subsective adjective *skillful* is always determined relative to the noun. These differences between the subsective and the intersective adjectives may have implication for cognitive models of combinatorial adjective-noun interpretation. They imply that intersective adjectives are much less underspecified than the subsective ones which renders them much less dependent on the noun than subsective adjectives (see also, Sedivy et al. 1999; Pustejovsky 1995). The first question addressed in the present study is whether we can expect that the above outlined differences between intersective and subsective adjectives affect the process of their semantic interpretation.

Discriminating intersective and subsective adjectives is a non-trivial matter. In the present study, we have used an argument validity test (see, Kamp and Partee 1995) in the selection of the stimuli. According to Kamp and Partee, subsective adjectives typically yield invalid conclusions in the arguments of the type presented in the Example 1 below, while this is generally not the case with intersective adjectives.

(1)   Mary is a skillful surgeon.
       Mary is a violinist.
       _____

       *Therefore, Mary is a skillful violinist. (Kamp and Partee 1995)

From the example above it is clear that in different combinations, the subsective adjective *skillful* selects for different noun properties. In the combination *skillful surgeon* above, a subset of surgeons is defined with respect to the skill of performing a surgery while in the combination *skillful violinist* a subset of violinists is defined with respect to the skill of playing a violin. Substituting an intersective adjective for a subsective one in the same kind of argument yields a valid conclusion, as can be seen from the Example 2, below.

(2)   Mary is a carnivorous surgeon.

Mary is a violinist.

_____

Therefore, Mary is a carnivorous violinist.

Further difference between intersective and subsective adjectives concerns their contrastive function in context. While intersective adjectives may serve the purpose of introducing contrast across different classes of objects (e.g., *blue* vs. *not blue objects*), subsective adjectives seem to contrast within one class, (e.g., *good* vs. *not good chairs*, and not, *good* vs. *not good objects*; the latter seems pragmatically useless). Due to the apparent lack of the capacity to contrast across object classes, subsective adjectives are seldom, if ever, used in sentences requiring referent identification. For an illustration, the sentence *Please hand me the simple, interesting, easy block* sounds odd, to say the least. In this example, further specification of a property which enables considering a block as simple, interesting, or easy is required. In other words, some noun property which renders a subset in its extension as either simple, or interesting, or easy is needed in order to interpret the combination fully (i.e., to complete both combinatorial and referential processing). This kind of noun dependence for subsective adjectives prevents them from being interpreted incrementally. The compensation of adjectival head noun dependence by context, which is observed with intersective adjectives (see, Sedivy et al. 1999), would be very difficult if not impossible for combinations with subsective adjectives.[1] The first question addressed in the present study is whether the above outlined differences between intersective and subsective adjectives affect the process of their semantic interpretation.

In what way can we expect these differences between intersective and subsective adjectives to affect the course of combinatorial processing? We suggest that subsective adjectives lack the referent assignment component in most situations (recall that subsective adjectives are called *reference-* or property-modifying rather than *referent*-modifying; see, Siegel 1976). For intersective adjectives, the incremental character of their semantic interpretation (Sedivy et al. 1999) suggests that they may have a significantly less elaborate combinatorial component because they do not

_____

[1]In Sedivy et al. (1999) it is suggested that "'Incremental processing for subsective adjectives would presumably depend largely on immediate accessibility of information pertaining to the head noun.'" However, this is possible only if the combination referent is already part of the common ground.

require elaborate activation and selection of the noun-related properties. In contrast, semantic interpretation of subsective combinations is assumed to require activation and selection of the noun properties. It can be argued that in this kind of processing the compatibility of the components will affect the complexity of interpretation. For combinations with intersective adjectives, compatibility resolution seems quite straightforward (e.g., *yellow* combines with nouns that denote concrete objects such as the noun *table* rather than abstract entities such as the noun *idea*). These are familiar instances of resolution of selectional restrictions (Katz and Fodor 1963).

Combinations with subsective adjectives, however, appear to be more complex in this respect. More specifically, although a subsective combination may consist of adjective-noun types that are not prohibited by selectional restrictions, the types may still be incompatible in the sense of belonging to different basic concept types (entity, event or quality, (Pustejovsky 1999)). According to the Generative Lexicon theory, the resolution of this kind of incompatibility requires a more complex computational procedure than for the compatible types. For an illustration, although the adjectives *easy*, *fast* and *funny* are all subsective, the former two are considered event modifiers (having strong adverbial usage), unlike the third one (see, Pustejovsky 1999, 2000). Some nouns like *race* and *meeting* denote events. If an event-modifying adjective like *fast* is combined with an event-denoting noun like *race*, the resulting combination involves compatible types of concepts (event - event). In the combination *fast car*, on the other hand, the adjective is an event modifier, while the noun denotes an entity and, although we are not dealing with selectional restrictions here, the phrase as a whole involves incompatible types. Nevertheless, combinations like *fast car* are quite common. In Pustejovsky (1995), it is argued that the interpretation of these kinds of combinations, which consist of incompatible types, makes use of the operation of *type coercion*. Type coercion is "'...a semantic operation that converts an expression, α, to the type expected by a governing function, β" (Pustejovsky 1995). The combination *fast car* can be interpreted through a Telic event of *driving* specifying the built-in function for a car (e.g., *a fast-driving- car*). This kind of interpretation is possible only in those cases in which the noun represents a compatible concept; *natural* type concepts, such as *rock*, do not have a built-in function or purpose (Pustejovsky 1999).

A phenomenon associated with application of type coercion in the interpretation of subsective incompatible combinations is that adjectival modification of the noun actually becomes adverbial modification of the noun-related event. Apparently, type coercion in adjective-noun combination changes one type of semantic structure into another. It seems plausible to expect that the kind of semantic 'restructuring' associated with type coercion will increase the level of computational complexity in subsective interpretation. The findings in the Piñango et al. (1999) study suggest that these kinds of semantic operations are complex and time-consuming. Piñango et al. (1999) argued that in interpreting sentences like *The girl jumped until dawn*, additional information, termed "repetition function", is called for in order "... to achieve compatibility between the head of the verb phrase *jump* and its aspectual modifier, the prepositional phrase *until dawn*" (Piñango et al. 1999, p. 397). The authors suggest that in these kinds of sentences, the incompatibility of a point-action activity (i.e., an activity with an intrinsic beginning and an end such as 'jumped') with any kind of additional temporal boundary ('until dawn') is resolved by using aspectual coercion. This semantic operation is assumed to introduce a repetition function in order to achieve aspectual compatibility between the verbal head and its temporal modifier (see also, McElree et al. 2001). Piñango et al. (1999) found that sentences requiring the application of *aspectual coercion* took significantly longer to process than the non-coercion sentences. Similar processing time costs will be assumed to be involved in resolution of type coercion for the subjective incompatible combinations in the present study. One way to identify subsective incompatible adjectives is through their capability to form bases for adverbial formation. Adjectives in the subsective incompatible category will be selected from the Celex list of adjectives with adverbial usage (e.g., slow - slowly).

To summarize, with respect to differences in the level of computational complexity of semantic interpretation, the following three types of adjective-noun combinations are distinguished: (1) low complex, intersective (e.g. *yellow car*), (2) intermediate, subsective compatible (e.g. *interesting car*), and (3) highly complex, subsective incompatible (e.g. *fast car*). The hypothesis tested in the present study is that, due to a low level of adjectival noun dependence, combinatorial semantic interpretation of intersective combinations will be the least computationally complex, as it requires only a relatively straightforward selectional restriction type of compatibility resolution, and no selection of the noun properties. Semantic interpretation of the two subsective types of combinations can be expected to be progressively more complex. Subsective compatible combinations require establishing of the function-argument dependency relation between the constituents (Kamp and Partee 1995), compatibility resolution and selection of noun properties (e.g., the combination *nice boy* activates/selects boy-properties and becomes *nice-* LOOKING-*boy*). Subsective incompatible combinations require the same amount of operations as the subsective compatible ones plus the application of the operation of type coercion. The more complex types of combinatorial interpretation are assumed to include the operations of the simpler ones and to involve one or more additional operations. Hence, the processing time prediction tested in Experiment 1 is that differences in computational complexity between the three types of adjective-noun combinations will produce reaction time differences on a task requiring semantic interpretation. Intersective combinations are expected to be the least complex, requiring the least time to interpret, followed by subsective compatible and subsective incompatible combinations. Furthermore, the assumed differences in computational complexity were expected to result in differences in error rates between the three types of combinations. Computational complexity was expected to be positively correlated with error rates. The theoretical framework outlined above also predicts differences in content of semantic interpretation between the three types of adjective-noun combinations. Intersective combinations, not involving activation and selection of the noun properties, can be expected to yield plain paraphrases (e.g., *a yellow table* is *a table that is yellow*). The subsective compatible and the subsective incompatible combinations should both contain a mapped noun property or event, respectively (e.g., the compatible combination *an interesting book* can be paraphrased as *a book with an interesting plot*, and the incompatible combination *a fast car as a fast-driving car*). Note that both mapped concepts (plot, driving) originate from the noun and not from the adjective. In order to score the participants' responses, the criteria for their classification were specified (see below). For each combination type, responses were to be classified in four categories: intersective, subsective property mapping, subsective event mapping, and idiosyncratic (other). This issue was addressed in Experiment 2.

8.2 Experiments 1 and 2

In this chapter we will give only a brief summary of the experimental methods used In Experiments 1 and 2. Details of methodology and statistical analyses can be found in Appendix B alongside with a brief statistical introduction.

In Experiment 1, the hypothesis is tested that the degree of complexity of the three types of adjective-noun combinations (intersective, subsective compatible, and subsective incompatible) will be reflected in the length of response times on a task involving semantic interpretation. In order to test this hypothesis, Speeded Semantic Classification task (SSC) was used, which has been proved to elicit semantic processing. In this task, adjective-noun combinations are briefly presented on a computer screen. Participants are instructed to read the combinations carefully, and to decide as quickly as possible if these are meaningful or meaningless. They can respond by pressing one of the two buttons in front of them. One of the buttons is marked as 'YES' ('I find this combination meaningful') and another as 'NO' ('I find this combination meaningless'). Dependent variables are *reaction time* (RT; time between the appearance of a word on the screen and execution of a response by pressing a 'yes' or a 'no' button), and *percentage of no-responses* (classifying combinations as meaningless). Main prediction is that the three types of combinations will differ significantly on RTs for the yes-responses (meaningful). Reaction times for the intersective combinations are expected to be the shortest followed by the two subsective types. In addition, incompatible combinations are expected to take longer to respond to than the compatible ones. At the same time, more complex combinations were expected to yield higher percentages of 'meaningless' classifications. In Experiment 2, the hypothesis is tested that the assumed differences in complexity between the three types of adjective-noun combinations will also be expressed in differences in the kind of content of their semantic interpretation.

8.2.1 Main Findings

Most important finding in Experiment 1 is that Intersective combinations were responded to significantly faster than both kinds of subsective combinations. This finding supports the hypothesis of lower computational complexity for the former than for the latter two types of combinations. The hypothesis that subsective incompatible combinations are the most complex is not supported in the analysis of RTs. This finding will be discussed in the context of the analysis of percentages of no-responses. Although the differences in percentages of no-responses are significant in the analysis by participants but not in the analysis by items (perhaps due to too few items), a high percentage of no-responses (28%) obtained in the subsective incompatible condition suggests that these combinations were difficult to interpret on-line (approximately 50% of items had 20% or more no-responses in this condition). Considering that the combinations in this condition can be easily interpreted off-line (low percentage of idiosyncratic responses) this is a somewhat unexpected finding. It can be argued that the participants might have used deadline processing strategies for this category of combinations. Assuming that semantic interpretation of the subsective incompatible combinations is the most demanding in terms of the complexity of cognitive operations, and taking into consideration the relatively fast pace of the experiment, it is possible that the participants adopted a deadline processing strategy of terminating the most lengthy interpretations, i.e., those using type coercion, at a preset deadline.

In addition to the differences in processing time, the theoretical framework outlined in the introductory section predicts differences in the nature (content) of semantic interpretation for the three types of adjective-noun combinations. This issue was addressed in Experiment 2. Our prediction that the responses on the paraphrase task would vary in complexity and in type of content across the three types of combinations has been confirmed for the intersective and subsective incompatible combinations. A problematic finding is the relatively low percentage of subsective non-event responses in the subsective compatible condition (39%). An equal percentage of responses in this condition involved event mapping. This suggests that some adjectives in this condition, such as interesting and nice, appear to be less constrained with respect to the type of noun-related concept they select than expected. For instance, interesting book can be interpreted as a non-event (e.g., having an interesting plot), as well as event mapping (e.g., interesting to read). The reason why we included these combinations in the subsective property group is that, in our view, some of the constitutive elements of a book concerning its informational content must be found interesting in order to qualify it as being interesting to read. Although the 'interesting-to-read' kinds of event-related interpretations can eventually be arrived at in situations in which the processing time is not limited, property-related interpretations should logically occur prior to event-related interpretations in combinations with adjectives like interesting. However, the paraphrase task is not sensitive enough to trace inferential processing in semantic interpretation of adjective-noun combinations.

8.3   General Discussion

The present study addressed the question whether, in adjective-noun combinations, the complexity of the combinatorial part of semantic interpretation is dependent on the level of noun related processing namely, activation and selection of the noun properties. The first factor assumed to affect the complexity of semantic interpretation was the adjectival logical type. Adjectives characterized as intersective were assumed to represent clear-cut properties (see, Sedivy et al. 1999). This makes them less dependent on the noun compared to the underspecified subsective adjectives. The second factor was conceptual compatibility of the constituents in the combination. Incompatible types involving an event-selecting adjective and an entity-denoting noun (e.g., *fast car*) make use of semantic operation of type coercion in combinatorial interpretation (Pustejovsky 1995). The use of these kinds of semantic operations has been demonstrated to increase the computational complexity in semantic interpretation (McElree et al. 2001; Piñango et al. 1999).

Three types of adjective-noun combinations were distinguished: low-complex intersective combinations, medium-complex subsective compatible, and high-complex subsective incompatible combinations. In Experiment 1, the prediction was that the assumed differences in the level of computational complexity of combinatorial semantic interpretation will be reflected in the time required for their semantic interpretation. To test this prediction, (speeded) semantic classification task was used. The latencies (RTs) obtained in Experiment 1 were significantly longer for the two subsective types of combinations than for the intersective one. This finding supports the hypothesis that the logical type differences are reflected in differences in the complexity of semantic interpretation. The predicted processing time differences between the compatible (property-mapping) and the incompatible (event-mapping) subsective combinations did not show in the analysis of latencies. However, the highest percentage of 'meaningless' classifications (28%) was obtained in the subsective incompatible condition. Nevertheless, the combinations in this condition were easily interpreted off-line, and they consistently involved event mappings (see Experiment 2). Also, the percentage of idiosyncratic responses for these combinations was comparable to the other two conditions. Thus, the higher percentage of meaningless responses in Experiment 1 cannot be attributed to a possible low interpretability of these combinations. Our explanation is that participants may have used a deadline processing strategy. The strategy consists in terminating the interpretations that take too long (in this experiment – the event-mapping ones) at a preset deadline, and in classifying these combinations as meaningless.

Involving the same principle of coercion as investigated in Piñango et al. (1999), our event-mapping combinations require a type mismatch resolution, whereby a noun of the type *entity* is coerced to the type *event* required by the adjective (Pustejovsky 1995). For instance, in combinations like *fast poison*, the noun does not denote any kind of action by itself. Nevertheless, these kinds of combinations are fairly easily interpreted and, as the results of our Experiment 2 show, they consistently involve mapping of noun-related events (the event of *poisoning* in the example above). However, unlike Piñango et al. (1999), we have not found a processing time effect for the combinations involving coercion. What could be the reason for this discrepancy? In Experiment 2 of the present study, subsective compatible combinations showed larger variety in types of interpretation than expected: there were as much event-related interpretations as non-event related. It is possible that in on-line interpretation in Experiment 1 the participants also interpreted a large number of subsective non-event combinations as event-related ones in which case no differences in RTs between the two conditions could be expected. Alternatively, unlike the subsective compatible combinations, interpretations of the subsective incompatible combinations showed high consistency (a high percentage of event-related interpretations) in Experiment 2. This suggests a higher level of underspecification for the former than for the latter type of adjectives. Adjectives in the incompatible, event-related combinations seem to be underspecified with respect to exactly which noun event should be selected. However, they clearly require an event and not some other type of noun property. This can be characterized as partial underspecification. The processing consequences of partial underspecification may be that, although the coercion operation for these combinations is computationally complex, processing time can be won by immediately narrowing down the set of possible types of noun properties to event representations. At the same time, in subsective compatible combinations, adjectives seem to be underspecified not only with respect to the exact property but also to the type of property they select. This can be characterized as full underspecification. For the compatible combinations, there is no narrowing down of the set of possible properties, which may make the selection process more difficult. In sum, it is possible that although the subsective compatible combinations generally do not involve coercion, they can not be interpreted faster than the incompatible ones due to a higher uncertainty with respect to the type of property that should be selected in their interpretation. It seems that the relation between semantic underspecification, noun dependence and computational complexity is not a completely straightforward one, because underspecification may concern different aspects or levels of meaning representation. Further experiments need to be conducted in order to gain more insight into processing consequences of adjective-noun type mismatches.

In Experiment 2, differences in the content of semantic interpretation of the three types of adjective-noun combinations were investigated. To that aim, the written paraphrases of the combinations were classified as indicating one of the following three types of semantic interpretation: intersective, subsective property mapping, subsective event mapping. The highest percentage of responses congruent with the combination type was obtained for the intersective and the subsective incompatible combinations (see Figure 8.1). In the subsective compatible condition, most of the responses indicated subsective interpretation. However, half of these responses were event mappings. In retrospect, this divergence from our classification is not so surprising, since a number of adjectives in this group (e.g., *interesting* and *nice*) are fairly unconstrained with respect to the kind of noun-related concepts they select. For instance, in Experiment 2, *interesting book* was interpreted as property-mapping, *having an interesting plot*, and as event mapping in *interesting to read*. However, the order of sub-events in the event of reading suggests that in order to conclude that a book is *interesting to read* it has to be established that some property of its informational content is interesting, for example, its plot or theme. The paraphrase task, however, is not suitable for tracking inferences in semantic interpretation.

In addition, a consequence of the observed diverging opinions about the subsective compatible class of adjectives should lead to the proposition of new linguistic defining criteria of these three classes. Clearly, adjective-noun combinations where noun is a so called 'exocentric dotted type' (according to GL terminology) are problematic, as soon as one of the types is bound to a TELIC event: such *as book, sonata, newspaper*. This could explain controversial answers about the classification of *nice sonata* or *interesting book*. At the opposite, the classification of the combinations when noun is of simple concrete type is more straightforward. This suggests that cognitive experiments can lead to revisions of theoretical linguistic hypotheses (Bouillon personal communication).

8.4   Concluding Remarks

It is questionable whether the representational formats proposed by the standard models, such as prototype-denoting schemata (Smith et al. 1988) or theory-embedded schemata (Murphy 1988, 1990), can accommodate the kind(s) of combinatorial interpretation proposed in the present study. A problem with the standard formats is that they do not incorporate structures representing information on the type of dependency relation between the adjective and the noun investigated in the present study, namely a predicate conjunction relation for the intersective combinations, and a function-argument relation for the subsective combinations (Kamp and Partee 1995). The type of dependency relation may be very important for the configuration of combinatorial interpretative processes. One representational format that seems to allow for both types of combinatorial interpretation is the generative lexicon format (Pustejovsky 1995, see also Bouillon and Busa 2001; Godard and Jayez 1993). With its different levels of representation of linguistic information in the lexicon (argument structure, event structure, and qualia structure), the generative lexicon format seems to be well suited to accommodate logical type processing as well as fast and accurate compatibility resolution and property selection in conceptual combination.

In conclusion, this study suggests that an effort to use knowledge accumulated in linguistic and computational linguistic theories to build cognitive models of semantic interpretation, and vice versa, may be fruitful (Piñango et al. 1999, present study).

Appendices

Appendix A

A.1 Materials Used in Experiments 1 and 2

Table 8.1 List of Test Combinations Used in Experiments 1 and 2

Combination type		
Nr. Intersective	Subsective compatible	Subsective incompatible
1. bejaarde tandarts (elderly dentist)	ervaren tandarts (skilled dentist)	trage tandarts (slow dentist)
2. dodelijk gif (deadly poison)	sterk gif (strong poison)	snel gif (fast poison)
3. *kapotte pen (broken pen)	goede pen (good pen)	vlotte pen (easy pen)
4. versleten machin (worn out machine)	dome machine (stupid machine)	precieze machine (precise machine)
5. kleine brief (small letter)	komische brief (comic letter)	urgente brief (urgent letter)
6. *moderne roman (modern novel)	interessante roman (interesting novel)	korte roman (short novel)
7. groene gesp (green clasp)	bijzondere gesp (peculiar clasp)	makkelijke gesp (easy clasp)
8. *nieuwe sonate (new sonata)	leuke sonate (nice sonata)	lange sonate (long sonata)
9. bolle lens (convex lens)	zwakke lens (weak lens)	moeilijke lens (difficult lens)
10. verloren opstel missing essay	simple opstel (simple essey)	slordig opstel (sloppy essey)
11. houten schip (wooden ship)	veilig ship (safe ship)	langzaam schip (sluggish ship)
12. dik boek (thik book)	slecht book (bad book)	consequent boek (consequent book)
13. rode trein (red train)	comfortabele trein (comfortable train)	vroege trein (early train)
14. verdwaalde kapitein (lost captain)	bekende kapitein (renowned captain)	voorzichtige kapitein (careful captain)
15. nederlandse acteur (dutch actor)	betrouwbare acteur (reliable actor)	briljante acteur (brilliant actor)

Note. Combinations marked with an asterisk were excluded from the analysis of RTs in Experiment 1

Filler Stimuli Used in Experiment 1

Filler type 1: Additional intersective combinations. (1) metalen lepel (metal spoon), (2) groot hotel (big hotel), (3) gestolen jas (stolen jacket), (4) rijpe appel (ripe apple), (5) hete soep (hot soup).

Filler type 2: Highly familiar (specialized) combinations. (1) lekke band (flat tire), (2) eerste hulp (first aid), (3) gouden medaille (golden medal), (4) tamme kastanjes (tame maroon), (5) witte haai (white shark).

Filler type 3: Meaningless combinations. (1) wrede deur (savage door), (2) spontaan gebit (spontaneous denture), (3) tochtig bier (draughty beer), (4) machtige spons (mighty sponge), (5) zachte vliegtuig (soft airplane), (6) dwaze drop (silly licorice), (7) pezig riool (tendony sewage), (8) brave folder ('nice behaving' folder), (9) dreigende veter (threatening bootlace), (10) brutale steen (brutal stone), (11) roerige bril (restless spectacles), (12) duizelige klok (dizzy watch), (13) blauwe klacht (blue complaint), 14. stille kam (quiet comb), 15. sluwe cadeau (sly present), 16. zoete mouw (sweet sleeve), 17. boze reis (angry journey), 18. slanke storm (slender storm), 19. lenige pap (lithe porridge), 20. zwoele sprong (sultry jump), 21. gespannen zon (tense sun), 22. blonde receptie (blonde reception), 23. rauw hemd (row shirt), 24. serieuze schaar (serious scissors), 25. luchtig stoplicht (airy stoplight).

Appendix B

B.1 Analysis of Variance (ANOVA)

General Comments

Although ANOVA is an extension of the two group comparison embodied in the *t*-test, understanding ANOVA requires some shift in logic. In the *t*-test, if we wanted to know if there was a significant difference between two groups we merely subtracted the two means from each other and divided by the measure of random error (standard error). But when it comes to comparing three or more means, it is not clear which means we should subtract from which other means.

For example, with five means, we could compare Mean 1 against Mean 2, or against Mean 3, or against Mean 4, or against Mean 5. We could also compare Mean 2 against Mean 3 or against Mean 4, or against Mean 5. We could also compare Mean 3 against Mean 4, or against Mean 5. Finally, we could compare Mean 4 against Mean 5. This gives a total of 10 possible two-group comparisons. Obviously, the logic used for the *t*-test cannot immediately be transferred to ANOVA. Instead, ANOVA uses some simple logic of comparing variances (hence the name 'Analysis of Variance'). If the variance amongst the five means is significantly greater than our measure of random error variance, then our means must be more spread out than we would expect due to chance alone.

Table 8.2 Example 5 means

Mean 1	Mean 2	Mean 3	Mean 4	Mean 5
7.0	6.9	11.0	13.4	12.0

$$F = \frac{\text{variance among sample means}}{\text{variance expected from sampling error}}$$

If the variance amongst our sample means is the same as the error variance, then you would expect an $F = 1.00$. If the variance amongst our sample means is greater than the error variance, you would get $F > 1.00$. What we need therefore is a way of deciding when the variance amongst our sample means is *significantly* greater than 1.00. (An $F < 1.00$ indicates that error-term variance is higher than the variance among sample means; it is always non-significant). This is achieved by means of the distribution of the *F-ratio*. F distributions depend on the degrees of freedom associated with the numerator in the ratio and the degrees of freedom associated with the denominator.

(From: http://www.une.edu.au/WebStat/unit_materials/c7_anova/).

Brief Explanation of Statistical Terms

F-Ratio

The statistic calculated by Analysis of Variance, which reveals the significance of the hypothesis that Y depends on X. It comprises the ratio of two mean-squares: MS[X]/MS[e]. The mean-square, MS, is the average sum of squares, in other words the sum of squared deviations from the mean X or e (as defined above) divided by the appropriate degrees of freedom. This is why the F-ratio is always presented with two degrees of freedom, one used to create the numerator MS[X], and one the denominator, MS[e]. The F-ratio tells us precisely how much more of the variation in Y is explained by X (MS[X]) than is due to random, unexplained, variation (MS[e]). A large proportion indicates a significant effect of X. In fact, the observed F-ratio is connected by a very complicated equation to the exact probability of a true null hypothesis, i.e. that the ratio equals unity, but you can use standard tables to find out whether the observed F-ratio indicates a significant relationship.

Significance

This is the probability of mistakenly rejecting a null hypothesis that is actually true. In the biological sciences a critical value $P = 0.05$ is generally taken as marking an acceptable boundary of significance. A large F-ratio signifies a small probability that the null hypothesis is true. Thus finding a significant nationality effect: $F(3,23) = 3.10$, $P < 0.05$ means that the variation in weight between the samples from four nations is 3.10 times greater than the variation within samples, and that tables of the F-distribution tell us we can have greater than 95% (i.e. $>[1-0.05] \times 100$) confidence in an effect of nationality on weight (i.e. less than 5% confidence in the null hypothesis of no effect).

(From: http://www.soton.ac.uk/~cpd/term.html).

Table 8.3 Examples of the tree types of adjective-noun combinations used in the present study.

Complexity		
Low complex: intersective	Intermediate: subsective compatible	High complex: subsective incompatible
Yellow car	*Interesting car*	*Fast car*

Experiment 1

Participants. 45 students of the Nijmegen University participated in this experiment.

Materials and Design. The set of stimuli consisted of 45 adjective-noun combinations (see Appendix A). The combinations were formed by pairing 15 nouns with three adjectives each, thus representing the three experimental conditions as presented in Table 8.3, below.

The stimuli in the three conditions were assumed to differ with respect to the level of computational complexity in their semantic interpretation. A within-items design was used. The noun was kept constant, while different conditions were formed by replacing adjectives (*yellow car, interesting car, fast car*). In order to be able to ascribe possible effects to the manipulated variable Complexity and not the other variables which may also produce effects in the same direction, adjective-noun combinations were matched for length and (written) word frequency of the adjectives (nouns were the same). The mean lengths of the adjectives in the Intersective, Subsective Compatible and Subsective Incompatible conditions are 6.9, 7.4, and 7.5 letters respectively [$F < 1$; no significant differences], and mean log-frequencies (based on the Celex corpus of 42 million tokens (Baayen et al. 1993) are 3.4, 3.5, and 3.5 respectively [$F < 1$; no significant differences]. In addition, two rating studies were conducted in order to match the stimuli in the three conditions on the variables salience of the adjectival property in the semantic representation of the noun, and typicality of the combination referent for the category of entities denoted by the noun (e.g., typicality of *red apple* for the category apple is higher than the typicality of *brown apple*). This kind of matching is important because salience and typicality may produce effects in the same direction as the factor Complexity manipulated in our experiment (see, e.g., Hampton 1997a; Murphy 1988, 1990). Both rating studies were performed in the same way. The 45 combinations were divided into three lists containing 15 combinations each. On each list, each condition was represented by five combinations. In addition filler combinations of high and low salience/typicality (15 and 10, respectively) were added to the lists. Five practice items were added to each list. In the salience rating study, noun -dimension[1] pairs (e.g., LEAF – green) were printed together with a

---

[1]This format is based on the frame or schemata format introduced by Minsky (1977) and Rumelhart (1980), respectively. This format is widely accepted in psycholinguistic theories of word meaning. We adopt a different representational format. However, since the present study is largely

Table 8.4 Examples of usage of an argument validity test as a diagnostic tool to discriminate between de intersective and the subsective combinations

TYPE OF COMBINATION		
Intersective	Subsective compatible	Subsective incompatible
Jan is an *elderly dentist*	Jan is an *skilled dentist*	Jan is a *slow dentist*
Jan is a *swimmer*	Jan is a *swimmer*	Jan is a *swimmer*
Jan is an *elderly swimmer*	*Jan is an *skilled swimmer*	*Jan is a *slow swimmer*

7-point rating scales. In the typicality rating study, adjective-noun combinations (e.g., *brown soil*) were printed together with a 7-point rating scale. Participants (typicality: N = 15, salience: N = 15) were instructed to rate the stimuli for their salience/typicality. In both rating studies the mean scores in the three experimental conditions did not differ significantly. Mean scores for salience (on a 7-point scale in the intersective, subsective compatible and subsective incompatible condition are 4.0, 3.9, 3.7 respectively (all F < 1). Mean scores for Typicality (on a 7-point scale in the same three conditions are 4.4, 4.3, 3.8 respectively (all F < 1). In addition to typicality and salience, familiarity with the combinations is another possible covariate. As an indirect measure of familiarity, the co-occurrence frequency of the constituents of the combinations was used. To that aim we have used corpus data from a (written) corpus based on the Dutch daily newspaper 'Trouw', editions from 1993/1994; approximately 163000 tokens. Two out of 45 test combinations appeared in the corpus. The combination *dik boek* (thick book) appeared 6 times (of which three times in plural form, and 1 time as *dik boekwerk* where the noun *boekwerk* is a close synonym of *thick book*). The combination *Nederlandse acteur* (Dutch actor) appeared once. This low co-occurrence frequency implies low familiarity of all test combinations.

The argument validity test. In order to differentiate between the intersective and subsective types of combinations, the argument validity test for subjectivity was used (see Table 8.4). For all 45 adjective-noun combinations, arguments with two premises and a conclusion were formed. In this test, valid conclusions indicate that the combination in the first premise is intersective, while invalid conclusions indicate that the combination in the first premise is subsective. Although this test does not differentiate between the subsective compatible and subsective incompatible combinations, it is important to establish that both are indeed subsective. Adjectives in the subsective incompatible condition were selected from the Celex

---

exploratory we do have to match our stimulus materials according to the prevailing frame-based models in order to be able to draw valid conclusions from our results. In other words, matching the stimuli the way we did ensures that our effect can be ascribed to the factors manipulated in the present study and not to other factors such as salience of the adjectival dimensions in the representation of the noun. Term 'dimension' is used in frame-based theories to refer to meaning components. Capitals are used for the noun in order to make it easier for the participants to perform the task at hand.

list of adjectives with adverbial usage (e.g., slow - slowly) which renders them event modifiers. The 45 items (arguments) containing our experimental combinations (see Table 8.4) were divided in three lists according to a Latin-square design.

Each list contained 20 items (arguments): five arguments formed with intersective combinations, ten arguments with subsective combinations (five compatible, and five incompatible), and five additional intersective combinations which were added to each list in order to balance the proportion of intersective and subsective combinations. Nine judges were presented booklets containing an instruction and a list of 20 arguments. They were naive with respect to the relation between the argument validity and adjectival type. Their task was to decide, for each argument, whether the conclusion was valid i.e., whether the conclusion followed *necessarily* from the premises. The judges fulfilled the task individually, at their own pace. A 'yes' response classifies the conclusions as valid, indicating that the combination in the first premise is intersective, whereas a 'no' response classifies the conclusion as 'invalid', indicating that the combination is subsective. The percentage of agreement amongst judges was calculated for each combination. Combinations with minimally 67% agreement were entered into the experimental stimulus set. The combinations with less than 67% agreement were replaced by new ones which were also subjected to the argument test and for which the criteria for inclusion in the experimental set were the same as for the initial set. In this way, 15 triplets of adjective-noun combinations were selected and were used in the two experiments reported below.

Semantic classification experiment. Fifteen participants were randomly assigned to each list. Each participant was presented with 50 adjective-noun combinations: 15 experimental combinations (five in each condition), five intersective filler combinations, five specialized filler combinations (e.g., *gold medal*, expected to yield fast YES-responses because of high familiarity). Twenty-five meaningless filler combinations (e.g., *sensitive folder*) were added in order to yield NO-responses in the Semantic Classification task. There was no adjective or noun repetition on any of the three lists. The three sets of five adjective-noun combinations on each list were matched for length and log-frequency of adjectives. There were no significant main effects of list or condition [length: all $F < 1$, frequency: all $F < 1$], and no interaction effect [length: $F < 1$, frequency: $F < 1$].

Procedure. Participants were tested individually, in noise-attenuating booths. Stimuli were presented on a CRT connected to an 80486DX2/66 personal computer which controlled the presentation of the stimuli and the registration of responses. Stimuli (adjective-noun combinations) were presented at the center of the computer screen. Each trial started with the presentation of the fixation mark (*) for 800 ms. After a blank screen for 150 ms, adjective-noun combinations, printed in lower-case letters, were presented for 650 ms. Time-out was set to 1,750 ms after target-offset. Inter-trial interval was 1,500 ms. Participants were instructed to read carefully the adjective-noun combinations appearing on the screen, and to decide as quickly and as accurately as possible whether the combinations were meaningful

Table 8.5 Mean latencies (in milliseconds), and percentages of 'No' responses (in parentheses) obtained in Experiment 1

	Complexity of the combinations		
	Low complex intersective	Medium complex subsective compatible	Highly complex subsective incompatible
	794 (10%)	851 (16%)	855 (28%)

or meaningless. They were instructed to push the yes-button if they found a combination meaningful; otherwise they had to push the no-button. Both right- and left-handed participants gave yes-responses using their dominant hand. When an error was made on a trial immediately preceding an experimental combination, a dummy item was inserted in between the two in order to attenuate the effects of erroneous responding on the subsequent processing of an experimental item. A set of 28 practice items was presented prior to the experimental session, 4 of which were buffer items at the beginning of the experimental series. The set of practice items had characteristics similar to the experimental set. The whole session lasted about 15 min.

Results

Two items were excluded from the analysis of Reaction times (RTs) in all conditions, because the results of Experiment 2 reported below clearly showed that one of the combinations, *vlotte pen* (facile pen), involved an idiomatic reading (*talented writer*); the other combination elicited more than 70% responses in a different category in two conditions. Latencies for the no-responses ($M = 18.8\%$; based on the remaining 13 items) were excluded from the analysis of reaction times (RTs). Outliers were determined on the basis of items (per list, condition) and participants (per list, condition) statistics (2SD). No outliers were found. Analysis of RTs were conducted with complexity as a within-participants and within-items factor. Overall, the effect of complexity was significant [$F_1(2,88) = 6.09$, Mse $= 8,534$, $p < .005$, $F_2(2,24) = 3.41$, MSe $= 6,501$, $p = .05$]. Planned comparisons confirmed our prediction regarding differences in latencies between the intersective and both subsective combinations (see Table 8.5). Latencies for the intersective combinations are significantly shorter than those for either the subsective compatible [$F_1(1,44) = 14.60$, MSe $= 5,016$, $p < .001$, $F_2(1,12) = 7.38$, MSe $= 2,374$, $p < .05$], or the subsective incompatible combinations [$F_1(1,44) = 6.67$, MSe $= 12,368$, $p < .05$, $F_2(1,12) = 5.02$, MSe $= 8,610$, $p = .05$]. However, latencies in the latter two conditions did not differ significantly [$F_1 < 1$, $F_2 < 1$]. The finding of significant differences between the intersective and both subsective conditions supports the hypothesis of lower computational complexity for the former than for the latter two types of combinations. The hypothesis that subsective incompatible combinations are the most complex is not supported in the analysis of RTs.

The analysis of percentages of no-responses was conducted with all items ($N = 15$). (The removal of the same two items as in the analysis of RTs did not affect the outcomes of the analyses). Mean percentages of 'no' responses per condition are presented in Table 8.5. The three conditions differed from each other only in the analysis by participants: intersective vs. subsective compatible – [$F_1(1,44) = 4.60$, $MSe = 189.29$, $p < .05$, $F_2 < 1$]; intersective vs. subsective incompatible – [$F_1(1,44) = 28.54$, $MSe = 262.02$, $p < .001$, $F_2(1,14) = 4.16$, $MSe = 598.31$, $p > .05$]; subsective compatible vs. subsective incompatible [$F_1(1,44) = 18.37$, $MSe = 176.36$, $p < .001$, $F_2(1,14) = 2.43$, $MSe = 445.08$, $p > .10$].

Experiment 2

Method

Participants. The same 45 participants as in the Experiment 1 took part in the present experiment. All were paid for their participation.

Materials and Design. In this experiment, the same materials were used as in the Experiment 1, with the exception of the 'meaningless' filler combinations used only in Experiment 1. Forty-five experimental combinations were divided in three lists, so that each list contained 15 combinations: five in each of the three conditions. In addition, each list was supplemented with five filler intersective combinations (in order to counterbalance the number of intersective and subsective combinations), and five practice combinations. For each list, three different randomizations were made. The lists were counterbalanced across the two experiments. This way, participants responded to different sets of stimuli in each part of the study.

Procedure. The participants were tested individually. They received a booklet containing an instruction to perform a paraphrase task, and a list of 25 combinations, 5 of which were practice combinations at the beginning of each list. They were instructed to write down paraphrases for the combinations, reflecting as precisely as possible how they interpreted them. They were told that the combinations may vary with respect to how easily they can be interpretated. After reading the instruction, they performed the task at their own pace. The whole session lasted approximately 10 min. Participants performed this task after taking part in Experiment 1. They had a short break between the two experiments.

Criteria for the Classification of the Paraphrase Task Responses

1. *Intersective*. Responses are simple paraphrases of the combinations. No additional noun-related concepts are present. Adjectives and nouns may be substituted by their synonyms. In Example 1 below, the response is a simple paraphrase with no additional noun-related concepts inserted. In Example 2, there is a substitution such that the synonymous *more than 70 years old* is substituted for the adjective *elderly*.

1. *groene gesp* : Een gesp die groen is.
    green clasp: A clasp that green is.
    (A clasp which is green.)

2. *bejaarde tandarts* : Tandarts van meer dan 70 jaar oud.
    elderly dentist : Dentist of more than 70 years old.
    (A dentist who is more than 70 years old.)

2. *Subsective compatible*. Paraphrases contain one or more simple (non-event) noun properties which define a nominal subset. In Example 3 below, *strong poison* is interpreted as *very concentrated poison*. In Example 4 *interesting novel}* is interpreted as *a novel with an interesting plot*. In both cases, the interpretations involve knowledge related to the nouns and not the adjectives, This is suggested by the fact that changing the noun (or at least the noun class) automatically results in a different insertion (e.g., *a strong horse* would not be *a very concentrated horse*, similarly *an interesting car* would not be *a car with an interesting plot*).

3. *sterk gif* : Gif dat zeer geconcentreerd is.
    strong poison: Poison that very concentrated is.
    (A very concentrated poison.)

4. *interessante roman* : Een roman die een interessant verhaal heeft.
    interesting novel: A novel that an interesting plot has.
    (A novel with an interesting plot.)

3. *Subsective incompatible* (event mapping). Paraphrases of the event-mapping combinations contain one or more noun-related events. In Example 5 below, *slow dentist* is interpreted as *a dentist which works slowly*, that is, the event *to work* associated with the noun *dentist* is modified. In Example 6, *urgent letter* is interpreted as *a letter which has to be delivered urgently*. In both cases, adjectival modification became adverbial modification (or manner PPs), modifying the events of *working* and of *delivering*, respectively.

5. *trage tandarts* : Een tandarts die langzaam werkt.
    slow dentist: A dentist who slowly works.
    (A dentist who works slowly.)

6. *urgente brief* : Een brief die met spoed moet worden bezorgd.
    urgent letter: A letter that with urgency must be delivered.
    (A letter that must be delivered urgently.)

4. *Idiosyncratic*. Either it is not clear from the paraphrase what the meaning of the combination should be, or no agreement amongst the judges can be reached regarding the classification of a response (e.g., for the combination *versleten*

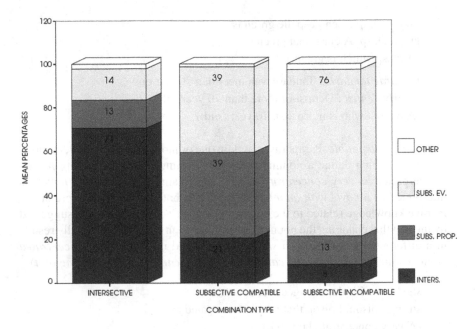

Fig. 8.1 Mean response type percentages per combination type in experiment 2

machine (*worn-out machine*) the paraphrase classified as idiosyncratic was *a machine which should be replaced*). This is an inference based on knowledge of the world, rather than a representation of the content of the semantic interpretation of the combination.

Results

On the basis of the criteria outlined above, the responses were scored by two judges (experimenters), independently of each other, as indicating one of the three types of semantic interpretation, namely intersective, subsective compatible, or subsective incompatible (event mapping). The final scoring involved reaching consensus amongst judges. Responses for which no consensus could be obtained were placed in the category idiosyncratic, together with the responses that were idiosyncratic by consensus. In each condition responses were classified in four categories, namely intersective, subsective property mapping, subsective event mapping, and idiosyncratic. For each condition, one of the response types is congruent with the combination type while the others are incongruent. For instance, in the condition intersective, a response classified as indicating an intersective kind of interpretation is congruent while all other responses are incongruent.

In general, the results are convergent with those obtained in Experiment 1 (see Fig. 8.1 below). The results were analyzed using the non-parametric Friedman test (Friedman ANOVA) and involving factor response type. We looked at differences between the conditions in percentages of congruent responses. Overall, the percentage of idiosyncratic responses was very low (M = 2.1%) with 2.22% in the intersective condition, 1.33% in the subsective compatible condition, and 2.67% in the subsective incompatible condition. The three types of combinations did not differ significantly with respect to percentages of idiosyncratic responses [$\chi^2_{(2)} < 1$, p = .92]. The highest percentage of responses congruent with the combination type was obtained in the conditions intersective (71%), and subsective incompatible (76%). The lowest percentage of congruent responses was obtained in the subsective compatible condition (39%). However, in this condition half (39%) of the subsective kind of responses involved event mappings. Although these interpretations are also subsective, contrary to our expectation, they involved noun related events. In addition, the three conditions differed significantly in percentages of each of the three response types (except the idiosyncratic). The differences were in the expected directions. Intersective – [$\chi^2_{(2)} = 65.34$, p < .001]; subsective property mapping – [$\chi^2_{(2)} = 32.08$, p < .001]; and subsective event mapping – [$\chi^2_{(2)} = 63.33$, p < .001]. These findings are being discussed in the main text, above.

References

Baayen, R., Piepenbrock, R., & van Rijn, H. (1993). *The CELEX lexical database (CD-ROM)*. Philadelphia: Linguistic Data Consortium.

Bouillon, P., & Busa, F. (Eds.). (2001). *The language of word meaning*. Cambridge: CUP.

Godard, D., & Jayez, J. (1993). Towards a proper treatment of coercion phenomena. In *Proceedings of the 31st annual meeting of the Association for Computational Linguistics* (pp. 168–177), Columbus, OH.

Hampton, J. A. (1997a). Conceptual combination. In K. Lamberts & D. Shanks (Eds.), *Knowledge, concepts and categories* (pp. 133–159). Cambridge, MA: MIT Press.

Hampton, J. A. (1997b). Conceptual combination: Conjunction and negation of natural concepts. *Memory & Cognition, 25*(6), 888–909.

Kamp, H., & Partee, B. (1995). Prototype theory and compositionality. *Cognition, 57*, 129–191.

Katz, J., & Fodor, J. (1963). The structure of a semantic theory. *Language, 39*, 170–210.

Lapata, M., & Lascarides, A. (2003). A probabilistic account of logical metonymy. *Computational Linguistics, 29*(2), 261–315.

McElree, B., Traxler, M. J., Pickering, M. J., Seely, R. E., & Jackendoff, R. (2001). Reading time evidence for enriched composition. *Cognition, 78*, B17–B25.

Minsky, M. (1977). Frame theory. In P. Johnson-Laird & P. Wason (Eds.), *Thinking: Readings in cognitive science*. Cambridge: Cambridge University Press.

Murphy, G. L. (1988). Comprehending complex concepts. *Cognitive Science, 12*, 529–562.

Murphy, G. L. (1990). Noun phrase interpretation and conceptual combination. *Journal of Memory and Language, 29*, 259–288.

Piñango, M. M., Zurif, E., & Jackendoff, R. (1999). Real-time processing implications of enriched composition at the syntax-semantics interface. *Journal of Psycholinguistic Research, 28*(4), 395–414.

Pustejovsky, J. (1995). *The generative lexicon*. Cambridge, MA: MIT Press.

Pustejovsky, J. (1999). Type construction and the logic of concepts. In P. Bouillon & F. Busa (Eds.), *The language of word meaning*. Cambridge: Cambridge University Press.

Pustejovsky, J. (2000). Syntagmatic processes. In D. Cruse (Ed.), *Handbook of lexicography*. Berlin: Mouton De Gruyter.

Rumelhart, D. E. (1980). Schemata: The building blocks of cognition. In R. J. Spiro, B. Bruce, & W. F. Brewer (Eds.), *Theoretical issues in reading and comprehension*. Hillsdale: Erlbaum.

Sedivy, J. C., Tanenhaus, M. K., Chambers, C. G., & Carlson, G. N. (1999). Achieving incremental semantic interpretation through contextual representation. *Cognition, 71*, 109–147.

Siegel, M. (1976). Capturing the Russian adjective. In B. Partee (Ed.), *Montague grammar* (pp. 293–309). New York: Academic.

Smith, E., Osherson, D., Rips, L., & Keane, M. (1988). Combining prototypes: A selective modification model. *Cognitive Science, 12*, 485–527.

Chapter 9
Combination of the Verb Ha- 'Do' and Entity Type Nouns in Korean: A Generative Lexicon Approach

Seohyun Im and Chungmin Lee

9.1 Introduction

The verb *ha-*'do' is known as a typical light verb in Korean like *suru* 'do' in Japanese. Since Grimshaw and Mester (1988), there has been much research on the light verb construction in Korean and Japanese. The verb *ha-*'do' usually combines with verbal nouns that denote events as in (1):

(1) a. Jane-un i pangbep-uro <u>pap-cis-ki</u> -rul   ha-ess-ta
        J-TOP   this way-in   meal-making-ACC do-PAST-DEC
        '(lit.) Jane did making a meal in this way'

    b. Jane-un <u>tarimi-cil</u> -ul   ha-ko iss-ta
        J-TOP   ironing-ACC   do-PROG-DEC
        'Jane is doing ironing'

    c. haksayngtul-i <u>siwui</u> -rul   ha-ko iss-ta
        students-NOM   demonstration-ACC do-PROG-DEC
        'Students are demonstrating'

    d. Sue-ka <u>swuhak kongpwu</u> -rul   ha-ess-ta
        S-NOM   mathematics study-ACC   do-PAST-DEC
        'Sue did the study of mathematics'

In (1), *pap-cis-ki* 'meal-making', *tarimi-cil* 'ironing', *siwui* 'demonstration', *kongpwu* 'study' are all event type arguments. The interrogative sentence in (2) shows the semantic selection restriction of the verb *ha-* 'do'.

S. Im (✉)
Department of Computer Science, Brandeis University, Waltham, MA, USA

C. Lee
Seoul National University, Seoul, South Korea

J. Pustejovsky et al. (eds.), *Advances in Generative Lexicon Theory*, Text,
Speech and Language Technology 46, DOI 10.1007/978-94-007-5189-7_9,
© Springer Science+Business Media Dordrecht 2013

(2)   A: John, ne   mwue-ha-ni?
           John you what-do-INT
           'John, what are you doing?'
      B: chengso/*yenphil/*chayksang
           'Cleaning/*pencil/*desk'

The answer to the question 'what are you doing' is limited to the event
type argument. The entity type noun *yenphil* 'pencil' and *chayksang* 'desk' is
inappropriate as an answer to the question in (2). This means that the verb *ha-* 'do'
typically takes an event type complement. Because the interrogative *what* is neutral
in terms of which type of information it requires, the answer to *what*-question
depends on the argument type of a predicate in the interrogative sentence. In other
words, the answer to *what*-question can be either a substantial or an abstract entity
(e.g. What did you make, yesterday? I made a <u>doll</u>), or an event (e.g. what are you
doing? I'm doing <u>cleaning</u> my room). The conversation in (2) shows that *ha-*'do'
prefers an event argument as its complement.

The sentence with a dot object noun (Pustejvosky 1995) and *ha-* 'do' shows
that the verb *ha-* 'do' takes an event type argument (Im and Lee 2002). The noun
ppallay 'laundry' is a typical dot object and its meaning in a context is chosen by its
governing predicate.

(3)   a.   Sue-nun ppallay-rul   ha-ko iss-ta
           S-TOP   laundry-ACC do-ing-DEC
           'Sue is washing'
      b.   ppallay-ka   mwul-ey   cec-ese   nemwu mwugep-ta
           laundry-NOM water-particle wet-particle too   heavy-DEC
           'since the wash is wet, it is too heavy'

The verb *ha-* 'do' selects the event meaning of *ppallay* 'laundry' and therefore
ppallay 'laundry' in (3a) is interpreted as a washing act. However, the adjective
mwugep- 'heavy' chooses *ppallay* 'laundry' as a physical object. *Ppallay* 'laundry'
is an event type noun in (3a) and an entity type noun in (3b). Semantic selection of
the predicates in (3) implies that the verb *ha-* takes an event type argument as its
complement.

However, special groups of entity nouns are allowed as complement arguments
of the verb *ha-*'do'. Consider:

(4)   a.   John-un piano-rul   ha - n-ta
           J-TOP   piano-ACC do-PRES-DEC[1]
           'John plays the piano as a profession/major.'
      b.   John-un piano yencwu-lul   (cikepcek-ulo/cenkong-ulo)   ha-n-ta.
           J-TOP piano performance-ACC (as an occupation/as a major) do
           'John does piano performance as an occupation/major.'

---

[1]TOP: topic marker, NOM: nominative case marker, ACC: accusative case marker, LOC: locative
case marker, PRES: present tense, PAST: past tense, PROG: progressive aspect marker, DEC:
declarative sentence marker, INT: interrogative sentence marker

The sentence in (4a) is interpreted as the sentence in (4b) in its individual level predication reading. The understanding of the sentence in (4a) requires some ellipsed information like playing or performing. Because this construction presupposes recoverable information ellipsis, we can assume that the combination like the sentence in (4a) is not a canonical form of *ha-* 'do' construction. Therefore, we note a superficial type conflict in the construction of entity type nouns with *ha-* 'do'. We can see this phenomenon, however, in many languages as in (5):

(5)   a.   John <u>did the chocolate cake</u> for my birthday.
      b.   Tell her to go and <u>do her hair and nails</u>.
      c.   Susan-wa <u>sukapu-o   si-ta</u>
           S-TOP   scarf-ACC do-PAST
           '(lit.) Susan did a scarf'
           'Susan wore a scarf'
      d.   Susan <u>fait une maison</u>
           '(lit.) Susan did a house'
           'Susan built a house'
      e.   Susan <u>fait le chamber</u>.
           '(lit.) Susan did the room'
           'Susan cleaned the room'

The verb *do* in English, *suru* 'do' in Japanese, and *faire* 'do' all mean do and take verbal nouns denoting events as their arguments naturally. In the above examples, they take some part of entity type nouns as their complements as *ha-* 'do' does in Korean. This phenomenon seems to be a type conflict outwardly.

This paper aims to account for direct combination of special entity type nouns with *ha-* 'do' in Korean. We, basically, argue that the combination is possible via the nature of the verb and the qualia of the relevant noun through the operation of coercion or co-composition, based on Generative Lexicon Theory (henceforth, GL, Pustejovsky 1995). The combination is possible only in the case that we can derive eclipsed predicate information from the qualia of the entity type nouns. J.-S. Jun (2001) also argues the combination of the verb *ha-* 'do' and entity type nouns in Korean. According to him, the combination is interpreted by a generative mechanism based on the qualia of the entity type nouns, not by simple pragmatic inference. The combination of entity type nouns and the Korean verb *ha-* 'do' is interpreted by the generative mechanism like type coercion or co-composition and by the qualia of the entity type nouns (Lee and Im 2003).

In Sect. 9.2, we show that the verb *ha-* 'do' typically takes an event type argument. When there is superficial type error in the combination of an entity type noun and *ha-* 'do', the verb *ha-* 'do' coerces type shifting of the entity type noun.

In Sect. 9.3, we argue that qualia structure has to have limited information necessary to explain the lexical meaning relation of words and co-occurrence constraint. In addition, the entity type nouns are classified as natural type, functional type, and complex type nouns following Pustejovsky (2001). In Sect. 9.4, we argue that qualia have to be extended to explain linguistic phenomena such as thematic role alternation or constraints on type coercion. A telic quale has to be subdivided into a direct telic, an indirect telic, and an engagement telic. An agentive quale also can be divided into 1st and 2nd agentive quale and so on.

9.2 Deep Semantic Type and Type Coercion

Some verbs allow several semantic types of arguments in deep semantic structure. Other verbs take only a semantic type of its argument but allow syntactic polymorphism of the argument (Pustejovsky 1995, 2001). The verb *cohaha*- 'like' in Korean takes any type of argument as *like* does in English. The sentences in (6) show different type arguments of the verb *cohaha*- 'like'.

(6)   a.   Verbal Noun Phrase Construction
              Sue-nun scarf chakyong-ul cohaha-ess-ta
              S-TOP   scarf wearing-ACC like-PAST-DEC
              'Sue liked wearing a scarf'
       b.   Entity Type Noun Construction
              Sue-nun scarf-rul   cohaha-n-ta
              S-TOP scarf-ACC like-PRES-DEC
              'Sue likes a scarf'
       c.   '-ki' Nominalization Construction
              Sue-nun scarf chakyongha-ki-rul   cohaha-n-ta
              S-TOP scarf wear-nominalizer-ACC like-PRES-DEC
              'Sue likes wearing a scarf'
       d.   'kes' Nominalization Construction
              (Same Subjects, Present-tense-relative clause)
              Sue-nun scarf-rul chakyongha-nun kes-ul   cohaha-n-ta
              S-TOP   scarf-ACC wear-REL[2]   kes-ACC like-PRES-DEC
              'Sue likes wearing a scarf'

---

[2]REL: relative clause marker

In (6a, c), the verb *cohaha-* 'like' takes event type arguments and takes a proposition type argument in (6d). Specially, the verb in (6b) takes a simple entity type noun as its argument. More important point is that the interpretation of the sentence in (6b) does not need some recoverable predicate information because the verb *cohaha-* 'like' takes entity type arguments. However, the semantic selection of the verb *ha-* 'do' is different from that of the verb *cohaha-* 'like'.

(7) a. Verbal Noun Construction
         Jane-un scarf chakyong-ul   ha-ess-ta
         J-TOP   scarf wearing-ACC do-PAST-DEC
         '(lit.) Jane did wearing a scarf'
         'Jane wears a scarf'
     b. Entity Type Noun Construction
         Jane-un *scarf* -rul   ha-n-ta
         J-TOP scarf-ACC do-PRES-DEC
         '(lit.) Jane does a scarf'
         'Jane wears a scarf'
     c. '-ki' Nominalization Construction
         ?Jane-un scarf chakyongha-ki-rul   ha-n-ta
         J-TOP   scarf wear-nominalizer-ACC do-PRES-DEC
         'Jane does wearing a scarf'
     d. 'kes' Nominalization Construction
         *Jane-un *scarf-rul   chakyongha-nun kes* -ul   ha-n-ta
         J-TOP   scarf-ACC wear-REL   kes-ACC   do-PRES-DEC
         'Jane does that she wears a scarf'

The verb naturally takes a verbal noun phrase that denotes an accomplishment event – wearing a scarf (7a). Unlike *cohaha-* 'like', the verb *ha-* 'do' does not allow proposition type arguments. It is necessary because *ha-*'do' takes an event type noun as its complement. We need to take note on the difference between *cohaha-* 'like' and *ha-* 'do' in (7b). The interpretation of *scarf* in (7b) is not a scarf but wearing a scarf. The VP *scarf-rul ha-* 'scarf-ACC do' cannot be interpreted only by simple composition of *scarf* and *ha-* 'do'. We extract some implicit predicate denoting wearing from *scarf* to interpret the sentence in (7b) for *ha-* 'do' requires an event type argument. The information extraction depends on the qualia of the noun *scarf*. The verb *ha-* 'do' takes an event type noun and can take the entity type noun whose type *ha-* 'do' can coerce. Thus, type coercion explains its superficial type conflict in our first approximation, as done for the verb *enjoy* in English. We now show a tentative specific type coercion of the VP *scarf-rul ha-* '(lit.) do a scarf'. Consider:

(8)   *scarf* 'scarf'

$$\begin{bmatrix} \text{Scarf 'scarf'} \\ \begin{bmatrix} \text{ARGSTR} = & \text{Arg} = \text{x: apparel} \end{bmatrix} \\ \begin{bmatrix} \text{QUALIA} = & \text{FORMAL} = \text{x} \\ & \text{CONST} = \dots \\ & \text{TELIC} = \text{Direct\_telic} = \text{wear (x)} \\ & \text{AGENTIVE} = \text{make(x)} \end{bmatrix} \end{bmatrix}$$

A scarf is a kind of apparel that people wear. Wearing is a direct telic of scarf. We explain direct telic (Pustejovsky 1995) and our extended qualia in more detail in Sect. 9.4. The verb *ha-* 'do', requiring an event type argument, coerces the type shifting of the entity type noun *scarf* 'scarf' on the basis of the qualia of the noun, as in (9):

(9)

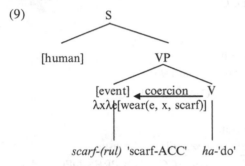

scarf-*(rul)* 'scarf-ACC'   *ha-*'do'

Type coercion of *scarf-rul ha-* 'scarf-ACC do' is based on the predicate information of the telic quale of the noun *scarf* 'scarf'. The qualia of the entity type noun are important in type coercion of the entity type noun to an event type one by the governing verb *ha-* 'do'. In Sect. 9.2, we showed type coercion of the verb *ha-* 'do' simply based on telic quale of its complement noun. Type coercion of the verb *ha-* 'do' is likely to rely on telic quale of its argument in the case that its argument denotes artifacts. While, it is inclined to make an event interpretation based on agentive quale of its argument in the case that its argument denotes a natural object. We discuss this tendency in more detail in Sect. 9.5. Before we show classification of the entity type noun and the verb *ha-* 'do' construction and its type coercion more specifically, we explore the qualia and extension of qualia.

9.3   Qualia of Entity Type Nouns in Korean

9.3.1   Construction of Qualia

It is one of important issues what the contents of qualia are. GL argues that lexical semantic structure has to have substructures and inferential relations among lexical items, arguing against the Lexical Atomism (Fodor and Lepore 1998). However, GL also does not agree with some cognitive linguists' view that linguistic knowledge – dictionary meaning is not distinguished from world knowledge – encyclopedia meaning. Pustejovsky (2001) points out that research in GL points to a view of the mental lexicon that is neither that of a classical dictionary nor that of a warehouse of data within an information processing system. This means that lexical semantic structure has to explain the creative use of language but need not to include all the possible information. Therefore, lexical semantic structure, especially qualia structure has to include limited information. Let us see *coffee* for example;

(10) *coffee* [American Heritage Dictionary]

    a.   Any of various tropical African shrubs or trees of the genus coffee, especially C. arabica, widely cultivated in the tropics for their seeds that are dried, roasted, and ground to prepare a stimulating aromatic drink.

    b.   The beanlike seeds of this plant, enclosed within a pulpy fruit.

    c.   The beverage prepared from the seeds of this plant.

(11) *coffee* [Columbia Encyclopedia]

Dictionary definition and Coffee plant cultivation, preparation and types of coffee, coffee in commerce, classification of the coffee plant, etc.

Although encyclopedia includes much more information of the word *coffee* than a dictionary does, linguistic meaning of *coffee* does not need to include all of the information it has. Lexical semantic structure has to have information as much as it can explain linguistic phenomena related with the word including syntax and semantics. Therefore, we suggest the two principles with which we describe qualia as in (12):

(12) a.   qualia of a word have to explain the inferential relation between that and other words like antonym, synonym, hypernym, hyponym, etc.

    b.   qualia of a word have to explain the co-occurrence constraint, that is, semantic selection restriction.

First, let us explore the qualia in terms of the inferential relation of a word in ontology. The inferential relation of lexical items consists of a lexical meaning type lattice or a lexical concept lattice. For example, to know the meaning of *beer* is to know that a beer is a kind of alcoholic beverage but not a wine or whisky. A word inherits meaning elements from hypernym but it has distinguished meanings from the other words. In other words, the lexical meaning has to satisfy the two conditions: "∼is∼" and "∼is not∼". Both beer and wine are alcoholic beverages but their materials and making ways are different from each other. We describe the qualia of *beer* and *wine*:

(13)   *beer*

$$
\begin{bmatrix}
\textit{beer} \\
\begin{array}{l}
\text{ARGSTR} = \quad \text{Arg} = \text{x: alcoholic\_beverage} \\[1em]
\begin{array}{ll}
\text{QUALIA} = & \text{FORMAL} = \text{x} \\
& \text{CONST} = \text{material(malt\&hops, x)} \\
& \qquad\qquad \text{element (alcohol, x)} \\
& \text{TELIC} = \text{Direct\_telic} = \text{drinking (e2, x)} \\
& \text{AGENTIVE} = \text{fermentation (e1,x)}
\end{array}
\end{array}
\end{bmatrix}
$$

(14)   *wine*

$$
\begin{bmatrix}
\textit{wine} \\
\begin{array}{l}
\text{ARGSTR} = \quad \text{Arg} = \text{x: alcoholic\_beverage} \\[1em]
\begin{array}{ll}
\text{QUALIA} = & \text{FORMAL} = \text{x} \\
& \text{CONST} = \text{material(grape, x)} \\
& \qquad\qquad \text{element (alcohol, x)} \\
& \text{TELIC} = \text{Direct\_telic} = \text{drinking (e2, x)} \\
& \text{AGENTIVE} = \text{fermentation (e1,x)}
\end{array}
\end{array}
\end{bmatrix}
$$

Although beer and wine are alcoholic beverages, beer is not wine. The meaning difference of *beer* and *wine* comes from different materials. Beer is made from malt and hops but wine is made from grape. Therefore, constitutive and agentive quale makes it possible to distinguish the two words. Although *beer* and *wine* inherit information common with each other from hypernym 'alcoholic beverage', they have different meanings based on different qualia information.

Secondly, qualia have to have enough information to explain co-occurrence constraint. We show example sentences in which *beer* is used.

(15)   a.   I want to drink/gulp/*chew a beer
       b.   I want to drink a glass of/*a piece of beer
       c.   The man liked beer
       d.   Let's have a glass of beer.

The co-occurring predicates or words are related to the qualia of the word *beer*. Because beer is a kind of liquid, we can only drink or gulp it but cannot chew it. The information is formal quale. In addition, that shows the constraint on classifiers used with *beer*. In (15c), the verb *like* has the entity type noun *beer* as its argument. It can take almost all types of arguments. We argue that the verb *ha-* 'do' can co-occur with the entity type noun *beer* by type coercion as in (15d).

In sum, qualia have to have limited information necessary to explain the relation of a word with other words including antonym, synonym, hypernym and hyponym and co-occurrence constraint. Now, we classify the Korean entity type nouns following Pustejovsky (1995, 2001).

9.3.2   Type System and Korean Entity Type Nouns

We think that generative type system suggested by Pustejovsky (2001) is a good device to describe lexical meanings of words. The architecture of the upper semantic type lattice is structured into three domains: entities, qualities, and events. Each domain is itself structured by a type ordering relation, from simpler to more complex types. The simple types in each domain are natural types. Functional types are unified types that combine qualia-based information from AGENTIVE and TELIC modes of explanation with a simple type. Complex types are even richer in structure and are formed by the application of a type constructor, creating a type that is the reification of a specific relation between two types (Pustejovsky 2001). We show the types in (16):

(16)   a.   Natural Type (simple type): meaning description by FORMAL and
            CONSTITUTIVE quale.
        b.   Functional Type (unified type): meaning description by TELIC and
            AGENTIVE quale
        c.   Complex Type: Cartesian type by construction of dot objects.

For example, the word *rock* in English is natural type word whose meaning is described by only formal and constitutive qualia. It is not an artifact and has no function. On the other hand, the noun *knife* is a functional type one because it is used for cutting and made by someone. A typical complex type word in English is *book*. It is a physical object but has information (Pustejovsky 1995).

We show entity type nouns that belong to the three types in Korean.

(17)   *nuktay* 'wolf' – simple type

$$
\begin{bmatrix}
nuktay \text{ 'wolf'} \\
\text{ARGSTR} = \begin{bmatrix} \text{Arg} = \text{x: mammal} \end{bmatrix} \\
\text{QUALIA} = \begin{bmatrix} \text{FORMAL} = \text{x} \\ \text{CONST} = ... \\ \text{TELIC} = \varnothing \\ \text{AGENTIVE} = \varnothing \end{bmatrix}
\end{bmatrix}
$$

The noun *nuktay* 'wolf' denotes a carnivorous mammal of the family Canidae following taxonomic classification. Because we do not eat or raise it for food, wolf is not a foodstuff unlike pig or cow. Therefore, *nuktay* 'wolf' in Korean or *wolf* in English belongs to natural type words. However, *toayci* 'pig' is different from *nuktay* 'wolf' in that it is used as foodstuff and raised for human's use, although it is a kind of mammals like *nuktay* 'wolf'. The noun *toayci* 'pig' is a unified functional type word.

(18)   *toayci* 'pig'

$$
\begin{bmatrix}
\textit{toayci} \ '\text{pig}' \\
\begin{bmatrix} \text{ARGSTR} = & \text{Arg} = \text{x: mammal\_livestock\_foodstuff} \end{bmatrix} \\
\begin{bmatrix}
\text{QUALIA} = & \text{FORMAL} = \text{x} \\
& \text{CONST} = ... \\
& \text{TELIC} = \text{eat (x)} \\
& \text{AGENTIVE} = \text{raise (x)}
\end{bmatrix}
\end{bmatrix}
$$

Alternation of animals and foodstuffs has been one of important issues in computational linguistics and lexical semantics. In English, they use *beef* in substitute for *cow* and *pork* for *pig* in the case that they mean foodstuff. On the other hand, we, Korean, add *koki* that means meat to the animal name like *toayci-koki* 'pig-meat' and *so-koki* 'cow-meat'. In any case, there is alternation between the two meanings. Although Copestake and Briscoe (1996) explain the alternation by a lexical rule, we think that functional type in Pustejovsky (2001) would be better in that it shows that the words have taxonomic meaning based on formal and constitutive qualia even in the case that the animals denoted by the words are used as foodstuff. The noun *toayci* 'pig' is a unified functional type. Now, let us see an instance of complex type.

(19)   *ppallay* 'laundry'

$$
\begin{bmatrix}
\textit{Ppallay} \ '\text{laundry}' \\
\begin{bmatrix} \text{ARGSTR} = & \text{Arg} = \text{x} \bullet \text{y: [laundry\_stuff]} \bullet \text{[laundry\_activity]} \end{bmatrix} \\
\begin{bmatrix}
\text{QUALIA} = & \text{FORMAL} = \text{x} \bullet \text{y} \\
& \text{CONST} = ... \\
& \text{TELIC} = \text{direct\_telic} = \text{y(x)} \\
& \text{AGENTIVE} = \text{make(z, x)}
\end{bmatrix}
\end{bmatrix}
$$

The noun *ppallay* 'laundry' is a complex type noun. We showed the example sentences that choose appropriate interpretation out of two meanings of *ppallay* 'laundry' in (3). One of its types is laundry stuffs as physical objects. The other is an activity of washing the laundry stuffs. Different predicates choose one of the two meanings. In sum, a lexical concept lattice is composed of entities, events, and qualities. Each domain is structured of simple natural type, unified functional type, and complex type. In the next section, we show the extended qualia and necessity of the extension.

9.4   Extended Qualia

Pustejovsky (1995) suggested that a telic role can be divided into a direct telic and a purpose telic and the division reflects syntactic distribution. A direct telic represents a predicate taking the noun as its direct object. The qualia of *toayci* 'pig' have only a direct telic quale as in (20):

(20)   *icecream* 'icecream'

$$
\begin{bmatrix}
\text{icecream} \\
\quad \begin{bmatrix} \text{ARGSTR} = & \text{Arg} = \text{x: [food]} \end{bmatrix} \\
\quad \begin{bmatrix} \text{QUALIA} = & \text{FORMAL} = \text{x} \\ & \text{CONST} = \dots \\ & \text{TELIC} = \text{direct\_telic} = \text{eat (x)} \end{bmatrix}
\end{bmatrix}
$$

The expression *icecream* has only a direct telic quale - eating. On the other hand, a purpose telic quale is used to explain thematic role alternation of nouns denoting an instrument such as *hammer*. We present an example of alternation as in (21):

(21)   a.   John broke the window with a hammer.
       b.   The hammer broke the window.   (Pustejovksy 1995)

The noun *hammer* in (21b) is a subject of the sentence but that in (21a) is an object of the preposition *with*. When John broke the window with a hammer, John did some action that caused a hammer to break the window. It is a hammer to have broken the window. The nouns that belong to instrument class show the same alternation as *hammer*. Therefore, the hammer's role is more active than stative. The nouns need the expression *-cil* which denotes repetition of some action when they are combined with the verb *ha-* 'do'.

(22)   a.   <u>instruments</u>

           kawi 'scissors', *kalkhwi* 'rake', *keley* 'duster or mop', *koayngi* 'hoe', *tarimi* 'iron', *thop* 'saw', etc.
       b.   <u>action with instruments</u>

           kaw-icil 'scissoring', *kalkhwi-cil* 'raking', *keley-cil* 'scrubbing or mopping', *koayngi-cil* 'hoeing', *tarimi-cil* 'ironing', *thop-cil* 'sawing', etc.

The above nouns show agent and instrument thematic role alternation. Another example of syntactic alternation is the noun *bus* as a means of traffic.

(23)   a.   John-i bus-ro cip-ey ka-ess-ta
           J-NOM bus-by home-to go-PAST-DEC
           'John went home by bus'
       b.   Bus-ka sunggayktul-ul swusongha-n-ta
           bus-NOM passengers-ACC transport-PRES-DEC
           'A bus transports passengers'

The words denoting vehicles also can have an agent thematic role. Although a person drives the vehicle, it is the vehicle that transports passengers. Thus, it is more agentive. The next example sentence shows alternation.

(24)   a. seyra-ka seythakki-ro ppallay-rul   ha-ko-iss-ta
            S-NOM washer-with   laundry-ACC do-PROG-DEC
            'Seyra is washing with washer'
        b. seythakki-ka ppallay-rul ha-ko-iss-ta
            S-NOM   laundry-ACC do-PROG-DEC
            'A washer is doing washing'

A washing machine also belongs to an instrument class broadly. Objects denoted by the above class of nouns have more active role.

However, there is a class of entity type nouns without alternation. The class of nouns denotes artifacts with a telic because they are used for some human activity but do not show alternation syntactically. For example, a *chayksang* 'desk' is used for studying or other activities but the noun *chayksang* 'desk' does not show syntactic alternation. Let us show the following nouns as examples that do not allow thematic role alternation.

(25)   a. John-un chayksang-ey chayk-ul   noh-ass-ta.
            J-TOP desk-on   book-ACC put-PAST-DEC
            'John put a book on the table'
        b. Sue-ka kangphan-ey tanggun-ul   kal-ko-iss-ta
            S-NOM grater-on   carrot-ACC grate-PROG-DEC
            'Sue is grating a carrot'
        c. Sue-nun pakwuni-ey sakwa-rul   tam-ass-ta
            S-TOP   basket-in   apple-ACC put-PAST-DEC
            'Sue put apples in the basket'
        d. John-un ku congi-ey kurim-ul   kuri-ess-ta
            J-TOP the paper-on picture-ACC draw-PAST-DEC
            'John drew a picture on the paper'
        e. Sue-nun kancang-uro   kan-ul   matchwu-ess-ta.
            S-TOP   soy souce-with saltiness-ACC adjust-PAST-DEC
            'Sue adjusted saltiness with soy source'

The nouns like *chayksang* 'desk', *kangphan* 'grater', *pakwuni* 'basket', *congi* 'paper', and *kancang* 'soy source' do not show thematic role alternation. They do not take any active roles to cause the result of the entire event. Therefore, we can say they are passive and stative. In other words, they are engaged in the entire event but do not do anything. They are just used for some purpose. We showed the two different groups of nouns out of the words with purpose telic quale. We suggest that a purpose telic quale should be divided into at least two telic qualia. We name those as indirect telic quale and engagement telic quale instead of a purpose telic quale. Therefore, we argue that a telic quale has to be divided into 3 different telic qualia. Those are a direct telic, an indirect telic, and an engagement telic quale.

(26)   TELIC QUALE

    a. Direct Telic
       A lexical item has a direct telic quale when the object denoted by the
       word is a direct object of the event or activity the predicate in its telic
       quale denotes.
       (a typical instance is the object argument of the predicate in its telic
       quale)
    b. Indirect Telic
       A lexical item has indirect telic quale when the use of an object
       denoted by the word give an effect to other objects. It takes more
       active role in the entire event that the telic of the word denotes.
       (nouns with thematic role alternation between instrument and agent)
    c. Engagement Telic
       A lexical item has an engagement telic quale when an object denoted by
       the word has some use but does not show thematic role alternation. It
       takes no active role in the entire event that the telic of the word denotes.
       It is only used for some activity related with itself.
       (the nouns denoting artifacts except for the words in (b))

More specific distinction of telic quale explains some linguistic phenomena like type coercion we argue in this paper. In Sect. 9.6, we show the constraints on type coercion of the Korean verb *ha-* 'do' that depend on the telic quale of the entity type nouns combined with *ha-* 'do'. Now, let us consider the qualia of the noun *seythakki* 'washer' and *chayksang* 'desk' based on our extended qualia. We assume that *seythakki* 'washer' has an indirect telic because it undergoes thematic role alternation as in (24).[3] However, we do not assume a direct telic because it has no predicate denoting a specific activity which influences a washer other than the verb *sayongha-* 'use' or the verb *mantul-* 'make' in agentive telic quale. We present the qualia of *seythakki* 'washer' as in (27):

(27)   *seythakki* 'washer'

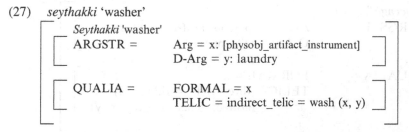

The noun *seythakki* 'washer' has only an indirect telic quale. On the other hand, *chayksang* 'desk' denotes a table used for studying or reading. Although *chayksang* 'desk' denotes an artifact with some use, it is not a direct object of an activity or

---

[3]Thematic role alternation between agent and instrument in Korean is not as much natural as that of English. In Korean, thematic role alternation like (24) tends to be possible through personification of instrument.

an event. Therefore, *chayksang* 'desk' has no direct telic quale. Moreover, because *chayksang* 'desk' does not show a thematic role alternation, it does not have an indirect telic. *Chayksang* 'desk' has only an engagement telic quale as in (28):

(28)   *chayksang* 'desk'

$$
\begin{bmatrix}
\textit{chayksang}\text{ 'desk'} \\[4pt]
\text{ARGSTR} = \begin{bmatrix} \text{Arg} = \text{x: [physobj\_artifact\_instrument]} \\ \text{D-Arg} = \text{y:[human]} \end{bmatrix} \\[8pt]
\text{QUALIA} = \begin{bmatrix} \text{FORMAL} = \text{x} \\ \text{TELIC} = \text{engagement\_telic} = \\ \text{use\_for\_reading\_or\_some\_activities(y, x)} \end{bmatrix}
\end{bmatrix}
$$

The word *mokkeli* 'necklace' has only a direct telic and an engagement telic with exception of an indirect telic because it does not show an alternation.

(29)   *mokkeli* 'necklace'

$$
\begin{bmatrix}
\textit{mokkeli}\text{ 'necklace'} \\[4pt]
\text{ARGSTR} = \begin{bmatrix} \text{Arg} = \text{x: [physobj\_artifact\_accessories]} \\ \text{D-Arg} = \text{y: [human]} \end{bmatrix} \\[8pt]
\text{QUALIA} = \begin{bmatrix} \text{FORMAL} = \text{x} \\ \text{TELIC} = \text{ direct\_telic= wear (y, x)} \\ \text{engagement\_telic=use\_for\_adornment(y, x)} \end{bmatrix}
\end{bmatrix}
$$

The noun *mokkeli* 'necklace' is an object of wearing act but is used for personal adornment. Therefore, *mokkeli* 'necklace' has a direct telic quale and an engagement telic. Some words such as *cacenge* 'bicycle' have direct telic and indirect telic.

(30)   *cacenge* 'bicycle'

$$
\begin{bmatrix}
\textit{cacenge}\text{ 'bicycle'} \\[4pt]
\text{ARGSTR} = \begin{bmatrix} \text{Arg} = \text{x: [physobj\_artifact\_traffic-means]} \\ \text{D-Arg} = \text{y:[human]} \end{bmatrix} \\[8pt]
\text{QUALIA} = \begin{bmatrix} \text{FORMAL} = \text{x} \\ \text{TELIC} = \text{direct\_telic} = \text{ride (y, x)} \\ \text{Indirect\_telic} = \text{convey (x, y)} \end{bmatrix}
\end{bmatrix}
$$

People ride a bicycle and move to their destination. Therefore, *cacenge* 'bicycle' has direct telic and indirect telic. It shows thematic role alternation. The noun *thayksi* 'taxi' has all of the three telic quales. First, a taxi-driver drives a taxi and passengers ride on a taxi to move to their destination. The word *thayksi* 'taxi' has direct_telic qualia: driving and riding. A taxi-driver conveys his passengers by driving his taxi.

Moreover, it is a taxi that transports the passengers to their destination. Therefore, *thayksi* 'taxi' has an indirect telic quale: conveying. A more interesting point is that a taxi was made originally for business unlike other vehicles such as a bicycle that has use of transportation. We suggest the engagement telic quale as in (35). In other words, a taxi not used for business is not a taxi but a car in terms that it has lost an original aim of existence. To include this information, we assume an engagement telic quale in the qualia of *thayksi* 'taxi'.

(31) *thayksi* 'taxi'

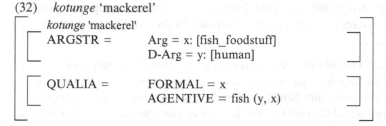

Now we argue that agentive qualia also should be extended. First, a noun class like *kotunge* 'mackerel' does not need to have extended agentive qualia. It is originally a kind of natural kind things but is reified as a unified functional type noun. Kotunge, a fish, is caught by fishing. We present only a specific agentive quale – fishing – for *kotunge* 'mackerel'. *kotunge* 'mackerel' has an undivided agentive quale as in (32):

(32) *kotunge* 'mackerel'

```
┌─ kotunge 'mackerel'
│  ┌─ ARGSTR =       Arg = x: [fish_foodstuff]          ─┐
│  └─                D-Arg = y: [human]                  ─┘
│  ┌─ QUALIA =       FORMAL = x                          ─┐
│  └─                AGENTIVE = fish (y, x)              ─┘
└─
```

In the above, we present only agentive quale of *kotunge* 'mackerel'. It represents a fish caught by fishing. Thus, it has one agentive quale. Of course, it has telic quale: eating as a functional type word.

However, some complex type nouns require more than two agentive qualia. For example, *tampay* 'cigarette' denotes an artifact and a plant. Therefore, we have to describe enough information to show both of the two meanings.

(33)   *tampay* 'cigarette'

$$
\begin{bmatrix}
\textit{tampay} \text{ 'cigarette'} \\
\text{ARGSTR} = \begin{bmatrix} \text{Arg} = x\bullet y: [\text{plant}]\bullet[\text{artifact}] \\ \text{D-Arg1} = z: [\text{human}] \\ \text{D-Arg2} = w: [\text{human}] \end{bmatrix} \\[3mm]
\text{QUALIA} = \begin{bmatrix} \text{FORMAL} = x \\ \text{AGENTIVE} = 1^{st}\_\text{agentive} = \text{grow}\,(z, x) \\ \qquad\qquad\quad 2^{nd}\_\text{agentive} = \text{process}\,(w, x) \end{bmatrix}
\end{bmatrix}
$$

The noun *tampay* 'cigarette' originally denotes a plant and is reified as a material of cigarette we smoke. At the same time, it denotes an artifact we buy and smoke. Hence, it is a complex type noun. For us to smoke a cigarette, we have to grow a tobacco plant and dry its leaf and then process the material. In order to include all of the information, we suggest that an agentive quale has to be subdivided into 1st and 2nd agentive quale.[4] Until now, we argued the extended qualia are necessary for explanation of linguistic phenomena related to lexical semantics and syntax. We presented a direct, indirect, and engagement telic and argued that agentive qualia can be subdivided.

(34)   Extended Qualia

    A.   TELIC quale
        a. Direct Telic
        b. Indirect Telic
        c. Engagement Telic

    B.   AGENTIVE quale
        Agentive qualia can be subdivided into several items depending on the events in which the object denoted by the word comes into the world.

Extended qualia in (34) make it possible for us to define the meaning of a lexical item and explain linguistic phenomena such as a thematic role alternation or a semantic selection constraint better. Especially, extended qualia are so helpful to explain type coercion of the verb *ha-* 'do' in Korean. Now, we explore type coercion of the verb *ha-* 'do' based on extended qualia.

9.5   Type Coercion of the Verb *Ha-* 'Do'

In Sect. 9.2, we argued that the verb *ha-* 'do' in Korean takes an event type argument as its object and coerces type shifting of the object noun when there is a type error.

---

[4]We do not exclude the possibility that agentive qualia are subdivided into more than two types.

In this section, we show more specific type coercion process of the verb *ha-* 'do'. Let us see the sentences in (35):

(35)   John-uy apeci-nun   thayksi-rul ha-si-pnita.
        J-POSS father-TOP taxi-ACC   do-Honorific-PRES.
        '(lit.) John's father does taxi'
        'John's father is a taxi driver.'

The sentence in (35) means that John's father is a taxi driver. That is, the sentence implies that the job of John's father is taxi driving as an individual predication. What derives the meaning from the sentences in (35)? Our argument is this; since the verb *ha-* typically takes an event type argument, *ha-* 'do' coerces type shifting of the entity type noun *thayksi* 'taxi' to an event type one so that it has the meaning of taxi driving. The type coercion is based on the qualia information of *thayksi* 'taxi'. The noun *thayksi* 'taxi' has three kinds of telic qualia. We showed the qualia of *thayksi* 'taxi' in (31). Type coercion by the verb *ha-* 'do' requires its direct_telic and engagement_telic so that *thayksi-rul ha-* 'taxi-ACC do' is interpreted as *thayksi-wuncen-ul ha-* 'do taxi-driving (to earn money as a profession)' as an individual level predication.

(36)

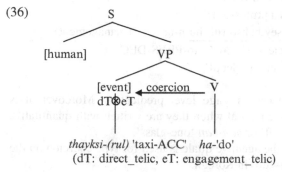

thayksi-(rul) 'taxi-ACC'   *ha-*'do'
(dT: direct_telic, eT: engagement_telic)

As in (36), the verb *ha-* 'do' coerces the entity type noun *thayksi* 'taxi' into event interpretation using direct and engagement telic qualia of *thayksi* 'taxi'. In the same way, *piano-rul ha-* 'piano-ACC do' can be interpreted as a professional activity and individual predication.

Type coercion on the entity type nouns by the verb *ha-* 'do' in Korean is not based only on a telic quale of the nouns but also its agentive quale. We present the kinds of nouns based on each quale. First, there are examples of type coercion based on telic quale.

(37) a. Jane-un onul   <u>scarf-rul   ha</u>-ess-ta   (wearing)
          J-TOP   today   scarf-ACC do-PAST-DEC
          'Jane wears a scarf today'

      b. Jane-un onul   <u>maskhara-rul   ha</u>-ess-ta   (applying)
          J-TOP   today   mascara-ACC do-PAST-DEC
          'Today, Jane applied mascara.'

      c. John-un <u>tampay-rul   han-tay   ha</u>-ess-ta.   (smoking)
          J-TOP   cigarette-ACC one-whiff do-PAST-DEC
          'John had a smoke'

      d. John,   <u>swul   han-can   ha</u>-ca   (drinking)
          J-VOC⁵   alcoholic beverage one-glass do
          'John, let's have a drink'

      e. Jane-un <u>piano-rul   ha</u>-n-ta   (playing)
          J-TOP   piano-ACC do-PRES-DEC
          'John plays the piano (as a profession)'

      f. John-un <u>thayksi-rul ha</u>-n-ta   (driving)
          J-TOP   taxi-ACC do-PRES-DEC
          'John drives a taxi (as a profession)'

      g. John-un Seoul-eyse <u>seythakso-rul ha</u>-n-ta   (management)
          J-TOP   Seoul-LOC cleaner's-ACC do-PRES-DEC
          'John manages a cleaner's in Seoul'

Type   coercion in (37 a–d) causes stage level predication. Moreover, it is
interesting that (37 c, d) are more natural when they are written with quantitative
expressions like *han-tay* 'one whiff' or *han-can* 'one-glass'.

The sentences in (38) shows the agentive quale is used for type coercion on the
entity type nouns by the verb *ha-* 'do' in Korean.

(38) a. wuri maul-un   <u>sakwa-rul   ha</u>-n-ta   (growing)
          we   village-TOP apple-ACC do-PRES-DEC
          'our village people grow apples'

      b. Jane-un <u>pap-ul   ha</u>-n-ta   (making)
          J-TOP   rice-ACC do-PRES-DEC
          'Jane boils rice (to prepare for a meal)'

      c. John-un <u>namwu-rul   ha</u>-re   ka-ess-ta.   (gathering)
          J-TOP   wood-ACC   do-ending go-PAST-DEC
          'John went the mountain to gather firewood'

The above examples in (38) undergo type shifting based on an agentive quale.

---

⁵VOC: vocative case

Until now, we showed type shifting of object nouns coerced by *ha-* 'do' based on either telic quale or agentive quale. However, composition of a subject noun phrase with the verb phrase can change the meaning of the verb phrase type-coerced by *ha-* 'do'. In (39a), the sentence means only that Sue is cooking noodles, but the sentence in (39b) means that this restaurant cooks and sells noodles.

(39)   a.   <u>Sue-ka</u>   wudong-ul   ha-n-ta
            S-NOM   noodle-ACC do-PRES-DEC
            'Sue is cooking noodles'

       b.   i siktang-un   wudong-ul   ha-n-ta
            this restaurant-TOP   noodles-ACC do-PRES-DEC
            'This restaurant sells noodles'

The telic quale of the noun *siktang* 'restaurant' in (39b) adds the information of selling noodles to the meaning of *wudong-ul ha-* 'cooking noodles', because the qualia of *siktang* 'restaurant' has the telic quale – cooking and selling of foods. In this way, the meaning of the entire sentence is composed through the process in which the qualia information of the subject NP choose appropriate meaning of the VP after type coercion on the entity type object argument by the governing verb *ha-* 'do'. In the next section, we explore constraints of type coercion in *ha-* 'do' construction with entity type nouns more specifically.

9.6   Constraints on Type Coercion

We explained combination of the verb *ha-* 'do' with some entity type nouns by type coercion. However, it is not applied to all entity type nouns in Korean. We show that a generative mechanism such as type coercion – especially type coercion by the verb *ha-* 'do' on entity type nouns in Korean – has some constraints.

(40)   a.   John-un kang-ul   cohaha-n-ta
            J-TOP   river-ACC like-PRES-DEC
            'John likes a river'

       b.   ??John-un kang-ul   ha-n-ta
            J-TOP   river-ACC do-PRES-DEC
            'John does a river'

The verb *cohaha-* 'like' can take the natural type noun *kang* 'river' as its argument, because it can have arguments of almost all types. However, since the verb *ha-* 'do' coerces type shifting of the argument to an event type, the noun has to satisfy the condition for type coercion. First, type coercion by *ha-* 'do' requires that the noun must be a functional type noun. Natural type nouns such as *kang* 'river' without its telic or agentive quale cannot undergo type coercion.

Secondly, entity type nouns without a direct telic cannot shift the types of themselves via type coercion as we can see in (41):

(41)   a.   ??John-un seythakki-rul ha-ess-ta
              J-TOP washer-ACC do-PAST-DEC
              '(lit.) John did a washer'
        b.   ??John-un chayksang-ul ha-ess-ta
              J-TOP   desk-ACC   do-PAST-DEC
              '(lit.) John did a desk'

In (41), *seythakki* 'washer' and *chayksang* 'desk' do not have a direct telic quale. The noun *seythakki* 'washer' has only indirect and engagement telic qualia. Moreover, *chayksang* 'desk' has only an engagement telic quale. Although the predicate in indirect or engagement telic quale denotes a typical activity related to denotation of the noun, the verb *ha-* 'do' cannot combine with the nouns. It is because the nouns have no direct telic quale predicate that takes the noun as its object argument. However, *culki-* 'enjoy' can combine with the nouns because the verb has wider range of type coercion. That is, *culki-* 'enjoy' allows event interpretation related to the noun without specific description of events and thus it can combine with more functional nouns than the verb *ha-* 'do' does. Pustejovsky (2001) calls this kind of type coercion by *enjoy* in English Natural Coercion.[6]

Thirdly, when there is an aspectual conflict between a governing verb such as *ha-* 'do' and a telic or agentive predicate of the noun, type coercion is not allowed. However, the verb *ha-* 'do' has no aspectual constraints.

(42)   a.   John-un caknyen-ey piano-rul   sicakha-ess-ta
              J-TOP   last year   piano-ACC begin-PAST-DEC
              'John began the piano last year'
        b.   Sue-nun caknyen-ey kwikeli-rul   sicakha-ess-ta
              S-TOP   last year   earring-ACC begin-PAST-DEC
              'Sue began the earring last year'
        c.   ??Jane-un 1pwun cen-ey mokkeli-rul   sicakha-ess-ta
              J-TOP   1minute before necklace-ACC begin-PAST-DEC
              'Jane began the necklace one minute before'

The verb *sicakha-* 'begin' is a kind of aspectual verbs that takes the expression denoting an accomplishment or an activity event. Therefore, *piano* in (42a) can combine with *sicakha-* 'begin' because the telic quale predicate *yencwu* 'play' is an activity verb. On the other hand, the noun *mokkeli* 'necklace' in (42c) cannot be

---

[6]Pustejovsky (2001) suggests the four kinds of type coercion. Those are Subtyping, Evaluative Predicates, Natural Coercion, and Imposed Telic. If we follow Pustejovsky (2001), type coercion by the verb *ha-* 'do' is a kind of Imposed Telic like *begin* in English because *ha-* coerces type shifting of an entity type noun based on telic quale of the noun. However, we should consider type coercion based on agentive quale of the noun.

used together with *sicakha-* 'begin' because the telic predicate *chakyong* 'wearing' is an achievement verb. However, it is interesting that *kwikeli* 'earring' in (42b) can undergo type coercion by the aspectual verb *sicakha-* 'begin', although the telic predicate of *kwikeli* 'earring' is *chakyong* 'wearing' as the case of *mokkeli* 'necklace'. Where the difference is from? The sentence in (42b) is interpreted as an habitual activity. *Kwikeli chakyong* 'wearing earring' is Sue's habit or long-term activity. That is, the sentence in (42b) means that Sue began wearing an earring as her habit or something from last year. Although the telic quale predicate of a noun is an achievement verb, type coercion by *sicakha-* 'begin' is possible, in the case that the entire event is interpreted as a habitual activity. Let us see the aspectual verb *kkutnay-* 'finish'.

(43) a. ??John-un olhay   piano-rul kkutnay-ess-ta
         J-TOP   this year piano-ACC finish-PAST-DEC
         'John finished the piano this year'
      b. ??Jane-un pangkum kwikeli-rul   kkutnay-ess-ta
         J-TOP   just now   earring-ACC finish-PAST-DEC
         'Jane has finished the earring just now'
      c. Sue-nun ecey   chayk han-kwon-ul   kkutnay-ess-ta
         S-TOP   yesterday book one-volume-ACC finish-PAST-DEC
         'Sue finished one book yesterday'

The aspectual verb *kkutnay-* 'finish' can combine only the expression denoting an accomplishment event. Since the event denoted by *piano* is individual level predication, *kkutnay-* 'finish' cannot coerce type shifting of the noun *piano*. In addition, the telic predicate *chakyong* 'wearing' is an achievement verb that cannot combine with *kkutnay-* 'finish'. Therefore, the sentence in (43b) is difficult to be interpreted. Even though the telic quale predicate *ilk-* 'read' is an activity verb, the quantization expression *han-kwon* 'a volume' changes the aspectual property of the telic predicate to be an accomplishment predicate. It makes it possible to combine with *kkutnay-* 'finish'.

On the other hand, type coercion by *ha-* 'do' on the entity type nouns does not have an aspectual constraint.

(44) a. John-un piano-rul   ha-n-ta
         J-TOP piano-ACC do-PRES-DEC
         'John does the piano'
      b. Jane-un mokkeli-rul   ha-ess-ta
         J-TOP necklace-ACC do-PAST-DEC
         'Jane did a necklace'
      c. Sue-ka pap-ul   ha-ess-ta
         S-NOM rice-ACC do-PAST-DEC
         'Sue did the rice'

Telic quale predicates *yencwu* 'play', *chakyong* 'wearing', and *ciski* 'making' are respectively activity, achievement, and accomplishment predicate. All of the nouns with the telic quale predicates can combine with the verb *ha-* 'do'. In sum, the verb *ha-* 'do' has no aspectual constraint.

We argued that type coercion by *ha-* 'do' is possible only on the functional type nouns. The nouns without a direct telic quale cannot combine with *ha-* 'do'. On the other hand, the verb *ha-* 'do' does not have a constraint on type coercion regarding aspect. Until now, we have explored type coercion by the governing verb *ha-* 'do' on the entity type complement.

9.7   An Alternative Explanation: Co-composition

We explained the combination of the verb *ha-* 'do' with some entity type nouns by type coercion. However, the vague property of the verb *ha-* 'do' in Korean makes it possible for us to consider an alternative way to explain the combination. If we think the verb *ha-* 'do' as a kind of generic verbs that replace other more specific verbs, we can consider the possibility of explanation by co-composition. The verb *ha-* 'do' shows some different aspects from typical type coercion verbs such as *begin* or *enjoy*.

(45)   a.   John-un piano-rul   sicakha-ess-ta
             J-TOP   piano-ACC begin-PAST-DEC
             'John began the piano'
       b.   John-un piano-rul   yencwuha-ess-ta
             J-TOP   piano-ACC play-PAST-DEC
             'John played the piano'

The verb *sicakha-* 'begin' cannot be replaced by the verb *yencwuha-* 'play'. The sentence in (45a) does not have the same meaning as the sentence in (45b). However, *ha-* 'do' construction shows different aspect from type coercion of the verb *sicakha-* 'begin' in (45).

(46)   a.   John-un piano-rul   ha-ess-ta
             J-TOP   piano-ACC do-PAST-DEC
             'John played the piano'
       b.   John-un piano-rul   yencwuha-ess-ta
             J-TOP   piano-ACC play-PAST-DEC
             'John played the piano'

The sentences in (46) both have the same meaning as each other. The verb *ha-* 'do' can be replaced by *yencwuha-* 'play'. Therefore, we can consider the following structure of the verbs in Korean.

(47)

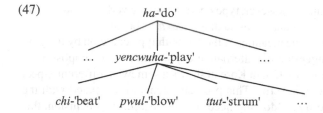

The predicates related to musical instruments have the above hierarchical lattice. The higher-level predicate is more abstract than lower-level predicates. If so, we can consider co-composition as an alternative explanation, as in the case of the verb *use* in English. Especially, the nouns denoting artifacts based on agentive telic makes the possibility more persuasive. The underspecified verb *ha-* 'do' is interpreted as a verb with a specific meaning via the specification process of its meaning by co-composition based on the qualia of the entity type nouns. However, the explanation by co-composition has a weak point in that it makes us to consider *ha-* 'do' combined with the event type noun like a predicative noun and this *ha-* 'do' as homonym. In addition, it is difficult to explain by co-composition that only some entity type nouns, not all, can combine with the verb *ha-* 'do'. Moreover, other languages have more constraints on combination of the verb class and entity type nouns. Both of the two explanations have technical merits and weak points. Which is right depends on the property of the verb *ha-* 'do'.

9.8 Conclusion

Qualia of entity-type nouns bring about direct combination of nouns with the Korean verb *ha-* 'do'. In that construction, elided information is derived from the qualia of the entity-type noun. In the end, composition of words derives a new additional meaning by using the lexical semantic structure of the words such as qualia, not simple contextual inferences. Hence, the combination has some generative principles and constraints as we show above.

Since qualia are important for explanation of syntactic or lexical semantic phenomena such as type coercion, we tried to analyze qualia more specifically. We argued that qualia have necessary information to explain the lexical semantic relation between lexicon and co-occurrence constraint. What is more, we extended the qualia: a telic quale into a direct telic, indirect telic, engagement telic and an agentive quale into the 1st agentive and 2nd agentive quale. Especially, we introduced the concept of an engagement telic quale. In addition, we described the Korean entity type nouns using the lexical meaning type lattice (Pustejovsky 2001). It consists of natural type, functional type, and complex type.

Type coercion by *ha-* 'do' has some constraints. First, natural type nouns cannot undergo type coercion. Secondly, the verb *ha-* 'do' cannot coerce type shifting of nouns without direct telic quale. However, type coercion by the verb *ha-* 'do' has no aspectual constraint unlike aspectual verbs such as *sicakha-* 'begin'.

The subject NP also affects the meaning of the VP with type coercion by the governing verb. Finally, we suggested the alternative explanation – co-composition – because the verb *ha-* 'do' construction in Korean shows a somewhat different aspect from other typical type coercion verbs. This problem seems to be related with the essential property of the verb *ha-* 'do' and need more research. In conclusion, this research shows the nature of *ha-* 'do' in Korean in its combinability with entity-type nouns, not event-type nouns and the property of qualia of entity type nouns.

References

Copestake, A., & Briscoe, T. (1996). Semi-productive polysemy and sense extension. In J. Pustejovsky & B. Boguraev (Eds.), *Lexical semantics: The polysemy of polysemy*. Oxford: Clarendon.

Fodor, J. A., & Lepore, E. (1998). The emptiness of the lexicon: Critical reflections on J. Pustejovsky's "the generative lexicon". *Linguistic Inquiry, 29–2.*

Grimshaw, J., & Mester, A. (1988). Light verbs and theta-marking. *Linguistic Inquiry, 19–2.*

Im, S-H., & Lee, C-M. (2002). Type construction of nouns with the Verb *ha-* 'do'. In *Proceedings of the 16th Pacific Asia conference on language information and computation*, Jeju, Korea.

Jun, J.-S. (2001). Semantic co-composition of the Korean substantival nouns-ha(ta) construction: Evidence for the generative lexicon. In N. Akatsuka & S. Strauss (Eds.), *Japanese/Korean linguistics 10*. Stanford: CSLI.

Lee, C.-M., & Im, S.-H. (2003). How to combine the verb ha- 'do' with an entity type nouns in Korean – Its cross-linguistic implications. In *Proceedings of the 2nd international workshop on generative approaches to the lexicon*, Geneva, Switzerland.

Pustejovsky, J. (1995). *The generative lexicon*. Cambridge, MA: MIT Press.

Pustejovsky, J. (2001). Type construction and the logic of concepts. In P. Bouillon & F. Busa (Eds.), *The language of word meaning*. Cambridge: Cambridge University Press.

Chapter 10
Generative Lexicon Approach to Derived Inchoative Verbs in Korean

Yoon-shin Kim and Chungmin Lee

10.1 Introduction

Since Vendler (1967), the event structure and the verbal aspect have been one of the controversial issues in verbal semantics. These issues result from the fact that all the verbs, which belong to each aspectual class, do not behave in the same way within each class. Among four aspectual classes suggested by Vendler (1967), achievement verbs show various behaviors and the subclasses of achievement verbs can be classified according to several patterns based on the similarity and difference between the various behaviors of achievement verbs. As some semanticists have suggested, some of them are called *degree achievement*.

In particular, we can observe the pattern of the change, which the verbal events show, because achievement and accomplishment events involve the changing event and their core events are also changes. According to Smith (1999), *telicity* is the important property for characterizing achievement and accomplishment situations and differentiating them from state and activity situations. A telic event implicates the heterogeneity and the complex event. This indicates that a telic event should denote the changing event. Therefore, exploiting the verbal semantics in terms of the changing event is one way of solving the long-discussed but unsolved problems related to Vendler's aspectual classes in Lexical Semantics.

We thank an anonymous reviewer for his/her helpful comments on our paper, Pierrette Bouillon for her constant editorial support and the second GL workshop audiences for questions and comments on our presentation. Also, we are grateful to Michael Kline for his kind reading of our paper for improvement of style. However, we are solely responsible for all errors in this paper.

Y.-s. Kim
Department of Korean Language Education, Silla University, Busan, South Korea

C. Lee (✉)
Department of Linguistics, Seoul National University, Seoul, South Korea
e-mail: clee@snu.ac.kr

J. Pustejovsky et al. (eds.), *Advances in Generative Lexicon Theory*, Text,
Speech and Language Technology 46, DOI 10.1007/978-94-007-5189-7_10,
© Springer Science+Business Media Dordrecht 2013

The *inchoative* aspect is another term for the achievement aspect focused on the beginning of a process or state that is the moment of a change.[1] In Korean, there are many inchoative verbs, which are composed of adjectival/verbal stems and $(-e)$-$ci(-ta)$.[2] The form $(-e)$-$ci(-ta)$ is an auxiliary formative, which denotes a change of state like *become* in English and can be attached to intransitive verbs and transitive verbs as well as the Korean adjectives,[3] that is, state verbs. It is a limitlessly productive device for creating morphologically-derived verbs. The noticeable phenomenon is that the derived inchoative verbs in Korean denote a variety of aspectual meanings and different argument structure, depending on their stem adjectives/verbs. In other words, the lexico-semantic structure of the derived inchoative verbs in Korean is based on the semantics of their stem adjectives/verbs.

This paper aims to explain the lexico-semantic structure of the derived inchoative verbs in Korean, focusing on $(-e)$-$ci(-ta)$ class, by means of the Generative Lexicon approach. This paper uses the extended concepts and formalisms of the Generative Lexicon Theory (Pustejovsky 1995, 2000), especially Pustejovsky's (2000) opposition structure. The semantic structure of the Generative Lexicon Theory has three substructures: Event Structure (EVENTSTR), Argument Structure (ARGSTR), and Qualia Structure (QUALIA).[4] Also, the anlaysis on the Korean inchoative verbs is based on Y.-s. Kim et al. (1999) and Y.-s. Kim et al. (2003). Although our main interest is the Korean case, our study can be extended to other languages, such as English, Japanese, French, and so on.

The organization of this paper is as follows: In Sect. 10.2, we observe the distribution and the interpretation of the Korean derivational inchoative verbs. We try to classify three types of them based on the stem verbs. In Sect. 10.3, we analyze the argument structure based on the distribution. In Sect. 10.4, we examine the event

---

[1] Instead of *achievement*, we use the term *inchoative* for the achievement verbs having the *change-of-state* meaning, because we will analyze these verbs focusing on the change.

[2] In Korean, some single stems can occasionally function as either an adjective or a verb, as in *palk-ta* 'bright'/'become bright,' the verb meaning of which is equivalent to *palk-a ci-ta* 'become bright' (the present tense –*nun*- can be attached), and subject to all the constraints discussed here. There are still two more types of change-of-state verbs: one has the form composed of a verb/adjective stem + *key* (or a predicate noun + NOM) and an auxiliary but unbound verb *toy-ta* 'become'. The other type is with a causative/passive meaning derived from a verbal stem with a causative/passive morpheme, such as -*i*-, -*hi*-, -*li*-, -*ki*-, forming the causative/passive category as well as the inchoative. In this paper, we aim to explain the lexico-semantic structure of the derived inchoative verbs by the bound morpheme $(-e)$-$ci(-ta)$ 'become' in Korean based on the property of their adjective/verb stems and focusing on the aspect of the changing events which the inchoatives denote. In this sense, $(-e)$-$ci(-ta)$ class shows a relatively pure change-of-state event and our analysis excludes other types of verbs.

[3] In Korean grammar, adjectives (*hyengyongsa* in Korean) are a kind of predicate similar to verbs rather unlike in English grammar Here we call Korean adjectives *state* verbs tentatively but adjectives with $(-e)$-$ci(-ta)$ become real verbs. There are few ambiguous stems. In (2a), the stem.*nuc*- is ambiguous between an adjective 'late' and a verb 'get delayed'.

[4] But C. Lee et al. (1998) develops the semantic structure to describe the lexical semantics of Korean predicates and adds one extra substructure, the so-called "**Case Structure (CASESTR),**" which illustrates case realization patterns of core arguments of predicates in Korean.

structure of each type by means of the opposition structure suggested by Pustejovsky (2000) and suggest the qualia structure of $(-e)$-$ci(-ta)$ inchoatives. In Sect. 10.5, we explain the variety of the argument realization by the generative mechanism *type coercion*.

10.2 Distribution, Interpretation and Types

10.2.1 Distribution and Interpretation

As we noted in Sect. 10.1, $(-e)$-$ci(-ta)$ is a very productive morpheme which results in inchoative verbs. It can be attached to any kind of predicate, but the derived inchoative verbs behave differently according to which kind of verb is their stem. So the distribution of the Korean $(-e)$-$ci(-ta)$ inchoative verbs is unrestricted, but their interpretations are various depending on their stem's meaning. Consider the following examples;

(1) (a) i   wulthali-ka   noph-a-ci-ess-ta.
          This   fence-Nom   become higher-Past-Dec
          Lit. 'This fence became higher.'
     (b) pang-uy   onto-ka   nac-a-ci-n-ta.
          roon-Gen   temperature-Nom become lower-Present-Dec
          Lit. 'The temperature of the room becomes lower.'
(2) (a) kicha-uy   chwulpal-i   nuc-e-ci-ess-ta.
          train-Gen   departure-Nom   become late-Past-Dec
          Lit. 'The train's departure became delayed.'
     (b) sikthak-i   kkaykkusha-e-ci-ess-ta.
          Table-Nom   become clean-Past-Dec
          Lit. 'The table became clean.'
(3) (a) John-i   eps-e-ci-essta.
          John-Nom   become-not exist-Past-Dec
          Lit. 'John disappeared.'
     (b) chospwul-i   kku-e-ci-ess-ta.
          the candle-light-Nom   become extinguished-Past-Dec
          Lit. 'The candle-light became extinguished.'

In (1), *noph-a-ci-ta* (to become higher) and *nac-a-ci-ta* (to become lower) are interpreted as *the change of degree*, while (2) and (3) means *the change of state* which happens to their subjects. In the case of (1), the stem verbs are gradable state verbs, *noph-ta* (to be high) and *nuc-ta* (to be delayed). *Pang-uy onto* (The temperature of the room), the subject in (1b), is a typical degree noun. *Nuc-e-cita* (to become delayed) and *kkaykkusha-e-cita* (to become clean) in (2) are considered as the change of state about an event at a certain criterion, although they are related to some scale. That event is related to the theme argument of the sentence. However, *eps-e-cita* (to disappear) and *kku-e-cita* (to become extinguished) in (3) are derived from non-gradable verbs, *eps-ta* (not to be) and *kku-ta* (to extinguish), respectively. Thus, the sentences in (3) denote the typical change of state and achievement event.

10.2.1.1   Time Adverbials and Comparative Phrases

As Dowty (1979) and many other have mentioned, one of the classical tests for the aspectual classes is the test by means of the time adverbials, such as *in an hour*, *for an hour*, and *at one o'clock*. Many previous studies explained that the frame adverbials, such as *in an hour*, can co-occur with accomplishments and achievements, but the durative adverbials, such as *for an hour*, can modify activities and accomplishments. The point adverbials, such as *at one o'clock*, appear with the verbs denoting the culminating point, such as achievements and accomplishments. We can also observe the distribution of the comparative phrases related to the progression of the whole event denoted by the verb. Now we will examine these adverbials one by one.

First, the point adverbials, such as *twu-si-ey* (at two o'clock), can occur with *noph-a-ci-ta* because its event implicates the changing event and has the culminating point, as we see in (4a). However, *noph-a-ci-ta* does not guarantee the definite resultant state. In (4c), this adverbial can also occur with *kku-e-cita* because of the prominent resultant state involved. On the other hand, *nuc-e-ci-ta* with a point adverbial is somewhat anomalous in (4b). Observe the following examples:

(4)   (a)   onto-ka   twu-si-ey   noph-a-ci-ess-ta.
            temperature-Nom two o'clock-Loc   become higher-Pat-Dec
            Lit. 'The temperature rose at two o'clock.'
      (b)   ??kicha-uy   chwulpal-i twu-si-ey   nuc-e-ci-ess-ta.
            train-Gen departure-Nom two o'clock-Loc become late-Past-Dec
            Lit. 'The train's departure became delayed at two o'clock.'
      (c)   chospwul-i twu-si-ey   kku-e-ci-ess-ta.
            candle-Nom   two o'clock-Loc become extinguished-Past-Dec
            Lit. 'The candle was extinguished at two o'clock.'

Second, we can make sure that the event structure of *noph-a-ci-ta* and *kkaekkusha-e-ci-ta* can have a prominent process, considering the combining relation with durative adverbials, such as *kyeysok* (continuously), and frame (or time span) adverbials, such as *samsippwun-tongan* (30 min). Observe the following examples:

(5)   (a)   onto-ka   kyeysok   noph-e-ci-ess-ta.
            temperature-Nom continuously become higher-Pat-Dec
            Lit. 'The temperature rose continuously.'
      (b)   sikthak-i   kyeysok   kkaykkusha-e-ci-ess-ta.
            table-Nom   continuously become clean-Past-Dec
            Lit. 'The table became clean continuously.'
      (c)   haksayng-tul-i kyeysok   eps-e-ci-ess-ta.
            Student-pl.-Nom continuously disappear-Past-Dec
            Lit. 'Students disappeared continuously.'

(6)   (a)   onto-ka   samsippwun-tongan noph-a-ci-ess-ta.
            temperature-Nom for thirty minutes become higher-Pat-Dec
            Lit. 'The temperature rose for thirty minutes.'
      (b)   sikthak-i   samsippwun-tongan kkaykkusha-e-ci-ess-ta.
            table-Nom   for thirty minutes become clean-Past-Dec
            Lit. 'The table became clean for thirty minutes.'
      (c)   haksayng-tul-i   samsippwun-tongan eps-e-ci-ess-ta.
            student-tul-Nom   for thirty minutes disappear-Past-Dec
            Lit. '?*Students disappeared for thirty minutes.'

The sentences in (5a-b) and (6a-b) mean that their processes keep on going, but
the sentences in (5c) and (6c) have two meanings: the continuation of the result
state, or the reiteration of the whole event. As Dowty (1979) and others have
said, the former examples, (5a-b) and (6a-b), reflect the ambiguity of the degree
achievements.

Third, the comparative phrase, such as *pothong-pota* (more than normal state)
or *cen-pota* (than the degree of dimension at a specific time of e_1), can occur with
noph-a-ci-ta and *nuc-e-ci-ta*, instead of the point adverbials, because their events
implicate the degree changing events compared with another value, that is, the
criterion. But, *kku-e-cita* does not appear with the comparative phrase because the
criterion is not necessary to judge the change. Consider the following examples:

(7)   (a)   onto-ka   pothong-pota   noph-a-ci-ess-ta.
            temperature-Nom normal-COMP[5]   become higher-Pat-Dec
            Lit. 'The temperature rose more than normal state.'
      (b)   kicha-uy   chwulpal-i   pothong-pota   nuc-e-ci-ess-ta.
            train-Gen departure-Nom normal-COMP become late-Past-Dec
            Lit. 'The train's departure became more delayed than normal time.'
      (c)   *chospwul-i   pothong-pota kku-e-ci-ess-ta.
            candle-Nom   normal-COMP become extinguished-Past-Dec
            Lit. '*The candle was more extinguished than normal time.'

---

[5]COMP = comparative

10.2.1.2 V-*ko iss-ta* and V-*e iss-ta*

Generally, 'V-*ko iss-ta*' is considered as the corresponding construction of '*be – ing*,' while 'V-*e iss-ta*' is thought of as that of '*have –en*.' So, 'V-*ko iss-ta*' means the progressive meaning, i.e., the continuing process, and 'V-*e iss-ta*' denotes the perfective, i.e., the resultant state. In Korean, however, 'V-*ko iss-ta*' has another aspectual meaning: the resultant state and the iteration of the whole event. Look at the examples in (8) and (9).

(8)   (a)   onto-ka   noph-a-ci-ko   iss-ta.
            temperature-Nom become higher-Asp be-Dec
            Lit. 'The temperature is rising.'
      (b)   sikthak-i   kkaykkusha-e-ci-ko iss-ta.
            table-Nom become clean-Asp be-Dec
            Lit. '?*The table is getting cleaned.'
      (c)   ?*haksayng-tul-i   eps-e-ci-ko   iss-ta.
            Student-pl.-Nom   disappear-Asp be-Dec
            Lit. '?*Students are disappearing.'

(9)   (a)   onto-ka   noph-a-ci-e   iss-ta.
            temperature-Nom become higher-Asp   be-Dec
            Lit. 'The temperature has risen.'
      (b)   sikthak-i kkaykkusha-e-ci-e   iss-ta.
            table-Nom   become clean-ASP   be-Dec
            Lit. 'The table became clean.'
      (c)   haksayng-tul-i   eps-e-ci-e   iss-ta.
            student-tul-Nom   disappear-Asp   be-Dec
            Lit. 'Students have gone.'

As we can see in (8), *noph-a-ci-ta* and *kkaekkusha-e-ci-ta* appear in the 'V-*ko iss-ta*' construction, which denotes a continuous process, while *eps-e-ci-ta* does not. If (8c) is possible, it means the iteration of the whole event. In the cases of *noph-a-ci-ta* and *kkaekkusha-e-ci-ta*, the aspectual meanings of the 'V-*ko iss-ta*' constructions are the same as those of the activity verbs. *Noph-a-ci-ta* and *kkaekkusha-e-ci-ta* are degree achievements, but *eps-e-ci-ta* belongs to the typical achievements. On the other hand, all of these verbs, such as in (9), can occur with the 'V-*e iss-ta*' construction, which denotes the continuation of a result state.

10.2.2   Three Types

According to the distribution and interpretation as in (1)–(9), we can suggest three types of (−*e*)-*ci*(−*ta*) inchoative verbs in Korean as follows:

(10)   (a)   Type-I: *Gradable inchoatives*
           noph-a-ci-ta[6] ('to become higher'),
           nac-a-ci-ta ('to become lower'),
           nelp-e-ci-ta ('to become wider'),
           cop-a-ci-ta ('to become narrower'),
           . . .
       (b)   Type-II: *Semi-gradable inchoatives*
           nuc-e-ci-ta ('to become delayed'),
           kkaykkusha-e-ci-ta ('to become clean'),
           . . .
       (c)   Type-III: *Ungradable inchoatives*
           eps-e-ci-ta ('to become non-existent, to disappear'),
           kku-e-ci-ta ('to become extinguished'),
           . . .

The first verbal type is derived from stem verbs with a scalar dimension, the second is from stem verbs with a scalar dimension and a criterion for the change, and the third is derived from the stem verb without such a dimension or a criterion.[7] Based on this observation, we call Type-I *gradable inchoatives*, Type-II *semi-gradable inchoatives*, and Type-III *ungradable inchoatives*, respectively.[8] In particular, we can infer that semi-gradable inchoatives are related to a certain scale but restricted to the culmination point.

In the following sections, we continue to discuss the argument, qualia structure, and event structure of three types of derived inchoatives. We will also talk about type coercion, which is one of the generative mechanisms in Generative Lexicon.

10.3   Argument Structure

Above all, we will examine the argument structure. Basically, each argument of each type is a theme in terms of theta-role, because it has no volition. We can recognize that in the following examples:

---

[6] '*-a-cita*' is a vowel harmony phonetic variant of '*-e-ci-ta*.'

[7] We will discuss the nature of the criterion in Sect. 10.3.

[8] Instead of *gradable*, the term *scalar* can be used. Generally, however, this is used for the scales of different predicate items, while that is for the difference of the degree in the same predicates. Therefore, we adopt the term **gradable**.

(11)   (a) *i wulthali-ka ilpwure   noph-a-ci-ess-ta.
           This fence-Nom intentionally become higher-Past-Dec
           Lit. '*This fence became higher intentionally.'
       (b) *kicha-ka ilpwule   nuc-e-ci-ess-ta.
           train-Gen intentionally become late-Past-Dec
           Lit. '?*The train became delayed intentionally.'
       (c) *chospul-i   ilpwule   kku-e-ci-ess-ta.
           candle-Nom   intentionally become extinguished-Past-Dec
           Lit. '*The candle became extinguished intentionally.'

(12)   (a) *i wulthali-ka   cosimsulepkey   noph-a-ci-ess-ta.
           This fence-Nom carefully become higher-Past-Dec
           Lit. '*This fence became higher carefully.'
       (b) *kicha-ka cosimsulepkey   nuc-e-ci-ess-ta.
           train-Gen carefully   become late-Past-Dec
           Lit. '?*The train became delayed carefully.'
       (c) *chospul-i   cosimsulepkey   kku-e-ci-ess-ta.
           candle-Nom   carefully become extinguished-Past-Dec
           Lit. '*The candle was extinguished intentionally.'

The adverb *ilpwule* (intentionally) denotes the volition of a subject. Thus, *ilpwule* does not appear with all the verbs in (11). Also, the adverb *cosimsulepke* (carefully) cannot present itself with these inchoative verbs, as in (12).

The most outstanding point is that the arguments of gradable inchoatives and semi-gradable inchoatives have a unique property. Consider the following examples:

(13)   (a) i wulthali-ka   noph-a-ci-ess-ta.
           This fence-Nom   become higher-Past-Dec
           Lit. 'This fence became higher.'
       (b) i   wulthali-uy nophi-ka   noph-a-ci-ess-ta.
           This fence-Gen   height-Nom become higher-Past-Dec
           Lit. 'The height of this fence became higher.'
       (c) i   wulthali-ka nophi-ka noph-a-ci-ess-ta.
           This fence-Nom height-Nom become higher-Past-Dec
           Lit. 'The height of this fence became higher.'

(14)   (a) onto-ka   noph-a-ci-ess-ta.
           temperature-Nom   become higher-Asp-Dec
           Lit. 'The temperature rose.'

     (b) i   pang-uy onto-ka   noph-a-ci-ess-ta.
        this room-Gen temperature-Nom become higher-Asp-Dec
        Lit. 'The temperature of this room rose.'
     (c) i   pang-i   onto-ka   noph-a-ci-ess-ta.
        This room-Nom temperature-Nom become higher-Asp-Dec
        Lit. 'The temperature of this room rose.'

(15) (a) kicha-ka   nuc-e-ci-ess-ta.
        train-Gen become late-Past-Dec
        Lit. 'The train became delayed.'
      (b) kicha-uy   chwulpal/tochak-i   nuc-e-ci-ess-ta.
        train-Gen departure/arrival-Nom   become late-Past-Dec
        Lit. 'The train's departure/arrival became delayed.'
      (c) kicha-ka   chwulpal/tochak-i   nuc-e-ci-ess-ta.
        train-Nom departure/arrival -Nom   become late-Past-Dec
        Lit. 'The train's departure/arrival became delayed.'

(16) (a) chospwul-i   kku-e-ci-ess-ta.
        the candle-light-Nom   become extinguished-Past-Dec
        Lit. 'The candle-light became extinguished.'
      (b) *chospwul-uy   palkki/khyeki-ka   kku-e-ci-ess-ta.
        the candle-light-Gen brilliance/lighting-Nom become
        extinguished-Past-Dec
        Lit. 'The brilliance of the candle/Lighting the candle
        became extinguished.'
      (c) *chospwul-i   palkki/khyeki-ka   kku-e-ci-ess-ta.
        the candle-light-Nom brilliance/lighting-Nom become
        extinguished-Past-Dec
        Lit. 'The brilliance of the candle/Lighting the candle became
        extinguished.'

Nophi (height) in (13b) and (13c) and *onto* (temperature) in (14) denote a certain dimension, or scale. In the case of gradable inchoatives, the change does not appear directly on a theme argument, but reflects indirectly by the change of degree. Actually, the noun *onto* itself means the degree of *hotness*. So the argument of gradable inchoatives is *dimensional noun* which is related to a scale or dimension. As in (13b), dimensional nouns, such as *nophi*, can occur as only argument, like *onto* in (14b), when they are modified with the nouns with the genitive case –*uy* (of). In other related sentences like (13c) and (14c), the genitive modifiers, such as *i wulthali-uy* or *i pang-uy*, are replaced with the subject arguments with nominative markers, such as *i wulthali-ka* or *i pang-i*. These dimensional expressions, however, are not allowed to occur with semi-gradable or ungradable inchoatives. In (15a), *kicha* (train) does not express just the vehicle as a physical object, but the event related to the train, the departure or arrival, depending on the context, as in (15b). That is, *kicha* is forced to have the eventual argument's interpretation. Although the event nouns are not dimensional nouns, the sentences including them denote accessing the criterion point, the culmination point. The event nouns can offer a kind of dimension *indirectly* and semi-gradable inchoatives like (15) have the somewhat weak scalar property, because the theme argument itself is not affected and what undergoes the actual change is the subevent related to it. In other words, the degree of the event's access to the culmination point has the scalar property. Thus, semi-gradable inchoatives take the event noun as their true argument. On the other hand, ungradable inchoatives like (16b) and (16c) are not associated with the scale of any domain. As in (16a), the affected theme is *chospwul*, and the event like *khyeki* or degree noun like *palkki* is not allowed, as we see in (16b) and (16c).

In the argument structure, there is a difference between the three types of $(-e)$-$ci(-ta)$ inchoative verbs. Gradable inchoatives are a dimensional noun as a true argument. Semi-gradable inchoatives, however, take an event argument, while ungradable inchoatives have the typically affected theme argument. Each inchoative verb has a different kind of argument from each other. But, the arguments of all these inchoatives are not volitional and these verbs can be characterized as unaccusatives.

10.4   Opposition Structure, Event Structure, and Qualia Structure

In this section, we discuss the event structure and qualia structure of three types of inchoatives, considering their opposition structures suggested by Pustejovsky (2000). Lee (1973) suggests that $(-e)$-$ci(-ta)$ is an inchoative auxiliary formative and the most productive construction for forming the change-of-state construction. In particular, if $(-e)$-$ci(-ta)$ is attached to a state verb's stem, which denotes a pure state, it adds a certain changing process to a pure state. The inchoative verb, however, expresses an instantaneous change, not a gradual one, and it is usually accepted that an inchoative verb is an achievement verb. So the added process is relatively short and instantaneous.

Generally, we can assume three basic event types (Vendler 1967; Dowty 1979): state, process and transition. Pustejovsky (1991) suggests that state and process are homogeneous events but, that transition is not. Transition is composed of at least two subevents. The inchoative sentence should presuppose the negative state before the change of state, which the verb stem denotes (Lee 1973; Pustejovsky 1991). In this vein, Pustejovsky (2000) indicates that the event implying a certain change has the opposition structure. Let us observe the following examples:

(17)   (a) The window broke.

          (b) [become([broken(the-window)])]

In (17a), *broke* is a typical inchoative verb and (17b) is its lexical conceptual structure (LCS). (17a) presupposes the unbroken state of the window. After the instantaneous change happens, the resultant state of (17a) is the broken window. Pustejovsky (1991) describes the event structure and its related qualia structure of the inchoative (=achievement) verb and the accomplishment verb as follows:

(18)   *inchoative* (=achievement)

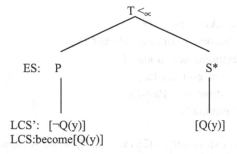

(19)   *accomplishment*

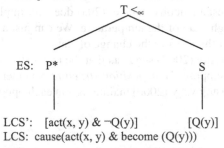

But, all the event structures and qualia structures of the $(-e)$-$ci(-ta)$ inchoative verbs are not similar to (18). Gradable inchoatives do not denote instantaneous changes, but gradual ones, and have no presupposition of their negative states. Dowty (1979) called these kinds of achievement verbs, *degree achievements*. He and other scholars also have mentioned that the degree achievements denote telic or atelic events depending on the argument or the adjunct, like activity verbs. Observe the following examples:

(20)   (a) onto-ka   cemcem   noph-a-ci-ess-ta.
            temperature-Nom gradually become higher-Past-Dec
            Lit. 'The temperature rose gradually.'
       (b) catongcha-uy sokto-ka cemcem   nuc-e-ci-n-ta.
            car-Gen   speed-Nom gradually become slower-Present-Dec
            Lit. 'The car's speed became slower and slower gradually.'

(21)   (a) kicha-uy chwulpal-i cemcem   nuc-e-ci-ess-ta.
           train-Gen departure-Nom   gradually become late-Past-Dec
           Lit. 'The train's departure became delayed gradually.'
       (b) sikthak-i   cemcem   kkaykkusha-e-ci-ess-ta.
           table-Nom   gradually become clean-Past-Dec
           Lit. 'The table became clean gradually.'

(22)   (a) ?*chospwul-i   cemcem kku-e-ci-ess-ta.
           candle-Nom gradually become extinguished-Past-Dec
           Lit. '*The candle was extinguished gradually.'
       (b) ?*John-i   cemcem   eps-e-ci-ess-ta.
           John-Nom   gradually disappear-Past-Dec
           Lit. '*John disappeared gradually.'

The adverb *cemcem* (gradually) can occur in (20) and (21), while it cannot in (22). That is because *cemcem* modifies only the process and cannot be an adjunct of achievement verbs. So, gradable inchoatives express a gradual change, while ungradable inchoatives denote an instantaneous change. (20a) does not imply that the resultant state is the absolute high state of the temperature. We can just assume that the temperature becomes higher than before the change of state.

As we mentioned above, Pustejovsky (2000) suggests that the event structure of the change of state verb should presuppose *the opposition structure*, whether it is a *binary* opposition or a *polar* one. Pustejovsky (2000) maintains that each opposition has the property as follows:

(23)   Binary Property
       (a) $<\sigma_1, \sigma_2, \tau, \sqcup, \sqsubseteq>$ *realizes* a binary predicate P, where τ is a local top
           type for this sortal array, such that $\sigma_1, \sigma_2 \sqsubseteq \tau$, and $\neg\exists\, \sigma\, [\sigma \neq \sigma_1 \vee$
           $\sigma \neq \sigma_2]$. That is, σ_1 and σ_2 exhaustively partition τ.
       (b)

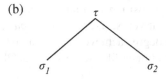

       (c) $<P, \neg P>, <P,Q>, <\neg Q, Q>$

(24)   Polar Property
       (a) $<\Sigma,\tau,\sqcup,<,\sqsubseteq>$ *realizes* a polar predicate P, where Σ is a sortal array of
           types, τ is a local top for this sortal array, such that $\sigma_1, \ldots, \sigma_n \sqsubseteq \in \Sigma$
           for $\sigma_i \sqsubseteq \tau$, and $\sigma_i < \sigma_{i+1}$, and there are two poles σ_1, and σ_n, that are
           distinguished sorts.

(b)

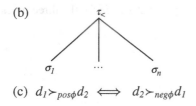

(c) $d_1 \succ_{pos\phi} d_2 \iff d_2 \succ_{neg\phi} d_1$

In our analysis, gradable inchoatives have the *polar* property, while ungradable inchoatives have the *binary* property. In the case of gradable inchoatives, when the change denotes increasing degrees gradually on a scale, the scale should have just one end expressing the lowest degree. In this vein, in (20a) and (20b), we cannot guess the end point of its process because the scale of *temperature* or *speed* is open-ended.

However, the sentences in (22) have the presupposition of the negative state. Therefore, the adverb *cemcem* (gradually) can occur in (20a) and (20b), while it cannot in (22a) and (22b). In the case of ungradable inchoatives, two end points are contradictory and incompatible. On the other hand, two end points of gradable inchoatives are contrary and it is possible that there is something belonging to neither endpoint.

Semi-gradable inchoatives, as in (21), seem to be problematic. They are ambiguous, because they behave as gradable or ungradable inchoatives depending on the context. But this problem can be solved simply by using the opposition property, binary or polar. Thus, it can be inferred that semi-gradable inchoatives have both binary and polar property, because they appear as two contrastive inchoatives, scalar or non-scalar.[9]

Accepting Pustejovsky's (2000) opposition structure, we can assign the binary or polar property to each inchoative type as follows and differentiate theme from each other:

(25)   Binary/Polar Property and Three Types of Inchoatives

	Binary	Polar
Gradable inchoatives	−	+
Semi-gradable inchoatives	+	+
Non-gradable inchoatives	+	−

The distribution of the opposition in (25) suggests that the changing aspects of the three types of inchoatives are different and these different aspects are reflected in the lexico-semantic structure of each type's inchoatives. According to Pustejovsky (2000), the opposition structure is related to a *gating function*, which introduces the new resultant state or removes or changes the initial state. The binary or polar property make a verb denote the changing event.

---

[9]This can be treated as the underspecification of the property. In this case, however, we should underspecify the value of two properties, binary and polar. Generally, it is possible to underspecify only one property's value.

Now we can suppose each event structure and qualia structure for the three types of inchoatives as follows:

(26)   *Gradable inchoatives*

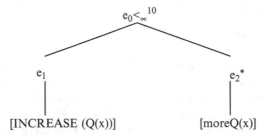

$$e_0 <_\infty {}^{10}$$

$$e_1 \qquad\qquad e_2{}^*$$

[INCREASE (Q(x))]   [moreQ(x)]

(27)   *Semi-gradable inchoatives*

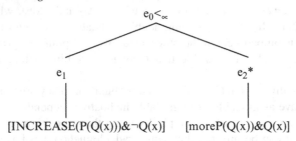

$$e_0 <_\infty$$

$$e_1 \qquad\qquad e_2{}^*$$

[INCREASE(P(Q(x)))&¬Q(x)]   [moreP(Q(x))&Q(x)]

(28)   *Ungradable inchoatives*

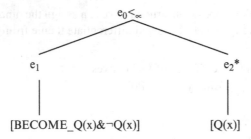

$$e_0 <_\infty$$

$$e_1 \qquad\qquad e_2{}^*$$

[BECOME_Q(x)&¬Q(x)]   [Q(x)]

The asterisks show the headedness of the event structure. According to Pustejovsky (1995), headedness is assigned to the most prominent subevent in the event structure of a predicate and is very important to link the surface structure. All the event structures of derived inchoatives in (26)–(28) assign the headedness to the resultant state and there is no negative presupposition. This means that all of these inchoatives belong to achievement verbs.

---

[10] According to Y-S. Kim (2002), scalar inchoatives are typical degree achievements and the subevents are overlapping each other partially. In this paper, however, we will not discuss the overlapping subevents in detail, because the opposition structure is the focus of this paper.

In Hay et al. (1999), the event of degree achievement is represented as follows:

(29)   (a) INCREASE(Q(x))(d)
     (b) DECREASE(Q(x))(d)

As Rothstein (2004) indicated, Hay et al.'s (1999) event structure of degree achievement is a non-complex event, that is, a single event, 'INCREASE.' Here, 'x' is the property of change, 'Q' is a function changing 'x' to the property related to the verb, and 'd' denotes the difference value. If a degree achievement verb occurs with an adjunct related to a difference value, the event of that verb is telic. However, Rothstein (2004) maintained that the extent of an event is not determined by the relation between the event and an argument, but that it should be defined by the event structure itself. She offered an example in this connection: "My mother-in-law shortened the sleeves of my jacket 5 cm in only half an hour." According to her, the culmination of the particular event described in this sentence is determined by the canonical endpoint of that process, not the extent of the difference variable such as "5 cm." In this paper, we do not adopt this difference variable 'd' either; basically it is not a lexical property. The difference of a change is determined by context.

In their qualia structures, there are obvious differences between them. As for inchoatives with scalar property, the predicate INCREASE, denoting changed degree, appears in the initial subevent and the predicate moreQ or moreP in the terminus subevent. The latter expresses the resultant state of changing degree. In particular, the event denoted by a verb should be telic if it is quantized by means of adverbials and contexts.

As we see in (26), the qualia structure for gradable inchoatives only has INCREASE(Q(x)) in the initial subevent and moreQ(x) in the terminus subevent. This means that these inchoatives have the scalar property. On the other hand, the qualia structure for semi-gradable inchoatives as in (27) includes INCREASE(P(Q(x))) and $\neg$Q(x) as its conjunct in the initial subevent, while it has moreP(Q(x)) and its conjunct Q(x) in the terminus subevent. As we have mentioned in Sect. 10.3, semi-gradable inchoatives take an event argument, such as *tochak* (arrival) or *chwulpal* (departure), so Q(x) inside P implies an event argument. Thus, INCREASE(P(Q(x))) means that the theme argument itself is not affected and the degree of the related subevent changes. MoreP(Q(x)) denotes the resultant state of the event changing degree. $\neg$Q(x) in the initial subevent and Q(x) in the terminus subevent contrast each other in the opposition structure. In the case of semi-gradable inchoatives, the qualia structure has the scalar property and the binary property at the same time. In (27) and (28), the second conjunct of e_1 is a presuppositional meaning, so its precise representation should be [INCREASE(P(Q(x)))&presupp:$\neg$Q(x)] and [BECOME_Q(x)&presupp: $\neg$Q(x)], respectively.

The aspectual meanings similar to activities, which appear with gradable inchoatives and semi-gradable inchoatives, as in (6), (7) and (8), result from the interaction of the polar property and INCREASE predicate. The ending point is not fixed because of the polarity and INCREASE predicate can applied endlessly. So their events seem to be extended without restriction and behave like activities. There is, however, no such predicate in the event structure of ungradable inchoatives. In terms of the event structure, ungradable inchoatives are typical achievements.

Considering the characteristics of these inchoatives and using the frame of the Generative Lexicon, we can suggest the following lexico-semantic structure:

(30)
$$
\left[
\begin{array}{l}
\textit{Gradable Inchoatives} \\[2ex]
\text{EVENTSTR} \quad = \left[
\begin{array}{l}
E_1 = e_1: \text{process} \\
E_2 = e_2: \text{state} \\
\text{RESTR} = < \\
\text{HEAD} = e_2
\end{array}
\right] \\[6ex]
\text{ARGSTR} \qquad = \left[\text{ARG}_1 = x : \text{dimension} \right] \\[4ex]
\text{QUALIA} \qquad = \left[
\begin{array}{l}
\textit{state\_change\_lcp} \\
\text{FORMAL} = \text{moreQ}(e_2, x) \\
\text{AGENTIVE} = \text{increase}(e_1, Q(x))
\end{array}
\right]
\end{array}
\right]
$$

(31)
$$
\left[
\begin{array}{l}
\textit{Semi-gradable Inchoatives} \\[2ex]
\text{EVENTSTR} \quad = \left[
\begin{array}{l}
E_1 = e_1: \text{process} \\
E_2 = e_2: \text{state} \\
\text{RESTR} = < \\
\text{HEAD} = e_2
\end{array}
\right] \\[6ex]
\text{ARGSTR} \qquad = \left[\text{ARG}_1 = x : \text{event} \right] \\[4ex]
\text{QUALIA} \qquad = \left[
\begin{array}{l}
\textit{state\_change\_lcp} \\
\text{FORMAL} = \text{moreP}(e_2, Q(x)) \& Q(e_2, x) \\
\text{AGENTIVE} = \text{increase}(e_1, P(Q(x)))
\end{array}
\right]
\end{array}
\right]
$$

(32)
$$
\left[
\begin{array}{l}
\textit{Ungradable Inchoatives} \\[2ex]
\text{EVENTSTR} \quad = \left[
\begin{array}{l}
E_1 = e_1: \text{process} \\
E_2 = e_2: \text{state} \\
\text{RESTR} = < \\
\text{HEAD} = e_2
\end{array}
\right] \\[6ex]
\text{ARGSTR} \qquad = \left[\text{ARG}_1 = x : \text{physical\_obj} \right] \\[4ex]
\text{QUALIA} \qquad = \left[
\begin{array}{l}
\textit{state\_change\_lcp} \\
\text{FORMAL} = Q(e_2, x) \\
\text{AGENTIVE} = \text{become\_}Q(e_1, x)
\end{array}
\right]
\end{array}
\right]
$$

10.5   Generative Aspects of Derived Inchoatives

We mentioned the various surface syntactic forms in Sect. 10.3. Now, we consider
the polymorphic realization of the argument structure in gradable inchoatives and
semi-gradable inchoatives and look at the following examples again:

(33)   (a) i wulthali-ka noph-a-ci-ess-ta.
            This fence-Nom become higher-Past-Dec
            Lit. 'This fence became higher.'
       (b) i wulthali-ka   nophi-ka noph-a-ci-ess-ta.
            This fence-Nom height-Nom become higher-Past-Dec
            Lit. 'The height of this fence became higher.'
       (c) i wulthali-uy   nophi-ka noph-a-ci-ess-ta.
            This fence-Gen   height-Nom become higher-Past-Dec
            Lit. 'The height of this fence became higher.'

(34)   (a) kicha-ka   nuc-e-ci-ess-ta.
            train-Gen become late-Past-Dec
            Lit. '?*The train became delayed.'
       (b) kicha-uy   chwulpal/tochak-i   nuc-e-ci-ess-ta.
            train-Gen departure/arrival-Nom   become late-Past-Dec
            Lit. 'The train's departure/arrival became delayed.'
       (c) kicha-ka   chwulpal/tochak -i   nuc-e-ci-ess-ta.
            train-Nom departure/arrival -Nom   become late-Past-Dec
            Lit. 'The train's departure/arrival became delayed.'

As we noted in Sects. 10.3 and 10.4, gradable inchoatives take a dimensional
noun as their true argument and semi-gradable inchoatives take an event noun.
However, (33a) and (34a) are not compatible with their lexico-semantic structures
and we predicted that their arguments should be interpreted as a dimensional or
an event noun, respectively. To explain this polymorphic phenomenon, we must
examine the semantics of the argument noun. Then, we will try to explain the
generative mechanism for this polymorphism.

First, we examine the argument noun of gradable inchoatives in (33a). This
noun denotes just a physical object; we have to infer how this physical object can
be interpreted into a dimensional noun. But, all the nouns meaning the physical
object have the size, weight, and other properties, by which they are characterized
in the perceptual aspect. Thus, it is necessary that the lexico-semantic structure
of the physical object noun should include the information of these properties.
In this point, we must decide which role these properties are assigned in the
qualia structure. The abstract properties of the physical object, including the
dimensional properties, can belong to the elements of the physical object. So the
CONSTITUTIVE role covers the predicate related to the dimensional properties.

But, if the number of the predicate in the CONSTITUTIVE is more than two, how can we express them? In this case, the properties in CONSTITUTIVE are unique and they are independent of the context. Therefore, each predicate related to each property conjuncts to another predicate and the dimensional property is also one of the conjunct in CONSTITUTIVE role. We can represent this as follows:

(35)

$$
\begin{bmatrix}
\textit{wulthali} \text{ (fence)} \\[2mm]
\text{ARGSTR} \quad = \quad
\begin{bmatrix}
\text{ARG}_1=x : \text{physical\_obj} \\
\text{D\_ARG}_1=y: \text{human} \\
\text{D\_ARG}_2=z: \text{material} \\
\text{D\_ARG}_3=w: \text{dimension}
\end{bmatrix} \\[10mm]
\text{QUALIA} \quad = \quad
\begin{bmatrix}
\text{FORMAL}=x \\
\text{CONSTITUTIVE}=\text{material\_of}(e^T,z,x)\& \\
\qquad \text{dimension\_of}(e^T,w,x) \\
\text{TELIC}=R(e^P,y,x) \\
\text{AGENTIVE}=\text{make}(e^T,v,x)
\end{bmatrix}
\end{bmatrix}
$$

When the noun *wulthali* (fence) is the theme argument of gradable inchoatives, type coercion operates, such as in (36), and the argument must be interpreted as the dimensional noun.[11] In other words, gradable inchoatives coerce the argument NP type as the dimensional noun.

(36)

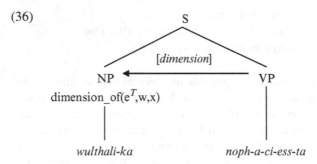

Then, we look into the case of semi-gradable inchoatives. In that case, the theme argument is also a physical object and artefact alike. So its TELIC role is outstanding, but depends on the context. If the number of the predicate is more than

---

[11] A reviewer indicated that this analysis looks more like a case of selective binding. We think that selective binding is a device for solving the polysemy of adjectives which we can find in examples such as *a fast boat*, *a fast typist*, or *a fast driver*. In the case that we treat here, the meaning of a verb is fixed, while its noun complement can be interpreted variously. Therefore, we can infer this case as a kind of type coercion.

two, we can disjoint each predicate in TELIC role. The representation of the noun *kicha* (train) is as follows:

(37)

$$
\begin{bmatrix}
\text{\textit{kicha} (train)} \\[4pt]
\text{ARGSTR} \quad = \quad
\begin{bmatrix}
\text{ARG}_1 = x : \text{vehicle} \\
\text{D\_ARG}_1 = y : \text{human} \\
\text{D\_ARG}_2 = z : \text{material} \\
\text{D\_ARG}_3 = w : \text{dimension}
\end{bmatrix} \\[24pt]
\text{QUALIA} \quad = \quad
\begin{bmatrix}
\text{FORMAL} = x \\
\text{CONSTITUTIVE} = \text{material\_of}(e^T, z, x) \,\& \\
\qquad\qquad \text{dimension\_of}(e^T, w, x) \\
\text{TELIC} = \text{move\_by}(e^P, y, x) \vee \\
\qquad \underline{\text{depart\_by}(e^T, y, x)} \vee \\
\qquad \underline{\text{arrive\_by}(e^T, y, x)} \vee \\
\qquad \cdots \\
\text{AGENTIVE} = \underline{\text{make}(e^T, v, x)}
\end{bmatrix}
\end{bmatrix}
$$

When the noun *kicha* (train) is the theme argument of semi-gradable inchoatives, type coercion operates, such as in (38), and the argument must be interpreted as the event noun. That is, semi-gradable inchoatives coerce the argument NP type as the event noun. The event interpretation also results from TELIC role or AGENTIVE role depending on the context.

(38)

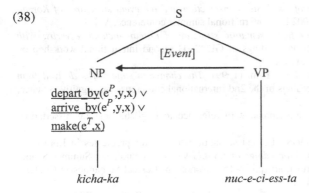

$$
\begin{array}{c}
S \\
\diagup \quad [\textit{Event}] \quad \diagdown \\
\text{NP} \longleftarrow \qquad\qquad \text{VP} \\
\underline{\text{depart\_by}(e^P, y, x)} \vee \\
\underline{\text{arrive\_by}(e^P, y, x)} \vee \\
\underline{\text{make}(e^T, x)} \\
\mid \qquad\qquad\qquad\qquad \mid \\
\textit{kicha-ka} \qquad\qquad \textit{nuc-e-ci-ess-ta}
\end{array}
$$

10.6 Conclusion

In this paper, we have analyzed three types of derived inchoative verbs and their lexico-semantic structures in Korean, based on Generative Lexicon Theory. The proposed typology and the lexico-semantic structures of derived inchoatives, the (−e)-ci-(ta) verbs, are just a starting point for further study of a comprehensive class of inchoative verbs; this typology can be easily extended to the description of various kinds of other change-of-state verbs, which are related to inchoatives, such as *nem-e-ci-ta* (to fall down), *cwuk-ta* (to die), and *palk-ta* (to become brighter). The last intransitive verb, *palk-ta,* forms a class of such verbs that are identical to their original adjective forms, such as *palk-ta* (bright). But, we predict that their lexico-semantic structures are basically identical to their *verbal stem* $+ (-e)-ci-(ta)$ counterparts. We may be able to consider the possibility of having both the adjective meaning and the inchoative intransitive meaning in one AVM lexical representation, as done for transitive and intransitive verbs such as *break* in English by Pustejovsky (1995), although its plausibility is a different matter.

Also, this observation shows that the stem verbs of the $(-e)-ci-(ta)$ class inchoatives can be classified into three groups: the gradable, the semi-gradable and the ungradable. This paper also identifies various types of change-of-state verbs in Korean with semantic structures unlike those in Pustejovsky (1995). In addition, we suggest that gradable and semi-gradable inchoatives show the generativity of the lexicon by type coercion.

References

Dowty, D. R. (1979). *Word meaning and Montague grammar.* Dordrecht: Reidel.

Hay, J., Kennedy, C., & Levin, B. (1999). *Scalar structure underlies telicity in degree achievements.* SALT 9.

Kim, Y-s. (2002). *The ambiguity of '-ko issta' construction and the event structures of Korean verbs.* In Proceedings of the 2002 LSK international summer conference, Vol. 1.

Kim, Y-s., & Lee, C. (2003). *The lexico-semantic structure of Korean inchoative verbs: With reference to '-e-ci-ta' class.* In Proceedings of GL '2003 second international workshop on generative approaches to the Lexicon.

Kim, Y-s., Lee, C., Nam, S., & Kang. B-m. (1999). *The change-of-state verbs derived from adjectives in Korean.* In Proceedings of the 2nd international conference on cognitive science, Tokyo.

Lee, C. (1973). Abstract syntax and Korean with reference to English. Doctoral dissertation, Indiana University.

Lee, C., Nam, S., & Kang, B. (1998). Lexical semantic structure for predicates in Korean. In J. Boas & P. Buitelaar (Eds.), *Proceedings of ESSLLI-98* (Tenth European Summer School in Logic, Language and Information) (pp. 1–15). Workshop: Lexical Semantics in Context-Corpus, Inference and Discourse.

Pustejovsky, J. (1991). The syntax of event structure. In B. Levin & P. Steven (Eds.), *Lexical & conceptual semantics.* Cambridge/Oxford: Blackwell.

Pustejovsky, J. (1995). *The generative lexicon.* Cambridge, MA: The MIT Press.

Pustejovsky, J. (2000). Events and the semantics of opposition. In C. L. Tenny & J. Pustejovsky (Eds.), *Events as grammatical objects.* Stanford: CSLI.

Rothstein, S. (2004). *Structuring events: A study in the semantics of lexical aspect.* Cambridge/Oxford: Blackwell.

Smith, C. (1999). Activities: States or events? *Linguistics and Philosophy, 22,* 479–508.

Vendler, Z. (1967). *Linguistics in philosophy.* Ithaca: Cornell University Press.

Chapter 11
Degree vs. Manner *Well*: A Case Study in Selective Binding

Louise McNally and Christopher Kennedy

11.1 Introduction

Among the various strategies natural languages employ for expressing intensification of degree is the use of expressions that are demonstrably manner adverbs, including *well* and its negative counterparts *poorly* and *badly*, as illustrated in (1).[1]

(1)   a. well/poorly acquainted with the facts
      b. a well/badly paid position

However, a degree reading for *well*, etc., is not always available, and, as will be shown below, its distribution is not random. Kennedy and McNally (1999) observe that *well* allows both a degree reading and a "quality" reading in examples like those in (2), but only a quality reading cases like those in (3).

(2)   a. a well loaded packing box
      b. a well documented case
      c. a well understood phenomenon

---

[1]Combining forms such as *over-*, *under-* and *ill-*, as in *overloaded*, *underpaid* and *ill-nourished* show a similar distribution and pattern of behavior, and are thus likely to be amenable to a similar analysis, but since their syntax and semantics is slightly different from that of manner adverbs, we will not discuss them here. See Katz (2005) on the use of other manner adverbs such as *surprisingly* in degree modification contexts.

L. McNally (✉)
Department of Translation and Language Sciences, Universitat Pompeu Fabra, Barcelona, Spain
e-mail: louise.mcnally@upf.edu

C. Kennedy
Department of Linguistics, University of Chicago, Chicago, IL, USA

J. Pustejovsky et al. (eds.), *Advances in Generative Lexicon Theory*, Text,
Speech and Language Technology 46, DOI 10.1007/978-94-007-5189-7_11,
© Springer Science+Business Media Dordrecht 2013

(3)   a. well loaded hay
      b. a well written paper
      c. a well cut suit

Kennedy and McNally (1999) account for this contrast by treating *well* as ambiguous between a degree reading and a quality reading and by placing constraints on its use as a degree modifier which exclude a degree reading in cases like (3). However, positing an ambiguous *well* is ad hoc, and unsatisfactory for two reasons. First, as Bolinger (1972:29) aptly noted, at times the two readings are difficult to distinguish, and, at least in combination with past participles, the degree reading appears in a proper subset of the contexts in which the manner reading appears. This suggests that *well* is not ambiguous but rather merely vague, and that the degree reading simply corresponds to one of the ways this vagueness can be resolved. Second, positing lexical ambiguities when they can be avoided is computationally undesirable, at least for parsing, as the multiplication of lexical entries can greatly (and unnecessarily) increase the number of parses that have to be considered in the analysis of any given sentence.

In this paper, we defend and then formalize Bolinger's intuition that the two senses of *well* are deeply related. Specifically, we show how the attested readings are in fact predicted when a simple and well-motivated representation for past participles in the Generative Lexicon framework (hereafter, GL; see Pustejovsky 1995) is combined with an equally simple and unambiguous analysis of *well* via Selective Binding as used in certain GL analyses of adjectival modification (e.g. Pustejovsky 1995; Bouillon 1999; Badia and Saurí 1999). Moreover, the specific semantics we adopt for adjectives and extend to the participles under study here entails that Selective Binding, understood specifically as the possibility of acting on a variable in the telic or agentive qualia of an adjective (as opposed to the formal quale) is not merely an attractive option for capturing polysemy; it is, in fact, the only option for *well* in the cases we discuss.[2]

The structure of the paper is as follows. In Sect. 11.2, we present the core facts concerning *well*: first, evidence that, even on the degree reading, *well* does not belong to the category of degree modifiers such as *very*; second, a description of the constraints on the availability of the degree and manner readings. We develop the GL analysis of *well* in combination with past participles in Sect. 11.3. Section 11.4 presents our conclusions.

---

[2]Throughout, we will refer to past participles as such; however, see Kennedy and McNally (2005) for a variety of arguments that at least those participles which interest us here behave like adjectives on a series of morphological and syntactic tests.

11.2   The Data

11.2.1   The Syntax of **Well** vs. Degree Morphology

In addition to constituting the null hypothesis, the effort to reduce *well*'s degree reading to a version of its manner reading is motivated by the fact that *well* has crucially different distributional properties from other degree modifiers, such as *very*. These differences are exactly what we would expect if *well* belongs to the category of manner adverbs, while degree modifiers form a special category of their own (Jackendoff 1977). In order to make these differences clear, we first briefly present our assumptions about the syntax and semantics of gradable adjectives, which follow the analysis defended in Kennedy (1999).[3]

Kennedy argues that adjectives denote measure functions: functions from individuals to degrees on a scale. It is the job of degree morphology (which includes comparative and superlative morphemes, measure terms such as *5 ft*, intensifiers such as *very*, and a null morpheme *pos* in the unmarked 'positive' form) to convert this measure function into a property of individuals. This property expresses a relation between two degrees: one derived by applying the measure function expressed by the adjective to the subject, and one provided by the degree morphology. Degree morphemes differ both in the nature of the degree that they introduce and in the type of ordering relation they encode, but as a class they translate into logical expressions that match the template in (4), where **R** is an ordering relation and **d** is a degree.

(4)   T(DegP): $\lambda G_{<e,d>} \lambda x . G(x) \textbf{ R d}$

The derivation of (5a) illustrates. (5b) provides a translation for the adjective alone; (5c), the measure phrase; (5d), the combination of the two, which denotes the property of having a (positive) degree of height that is at least as great as the degree corresponding to '6 ft'. This property can then be combined with the copula (assumed here to be semantically empty) and applied to the subject, with the result in (5e): *Sandra is 6 ft tall* is true just in case Sandra's degree of height is at least as great as 6 ft.[4]

---

[3]These assumptions are not crucial; our central claims can be just as well implemented in a more standard semantic analysis of gradable adjectives in terms of relations between degrees and individuals. Under these assumptions, degree morphemes are expressions that saturate the degree argument of the adjective, and *well* remains a function from adjective meanings to adjective meanings.

[4]The denotations of some other common degree terms are listed in (i): the *pos* morpheme in (ia), where **stnd** is a function that returns an appropriate standard of comparison given an adjective denotation G and a contextually supplied property C (a 'comparison class'; see Klein 1980);

(5)   a. Sandra is 6 ft tall.
      b. T(tall): **tall** (type $<e,d>$)
      c. T(6 ft): $\lambda G_{<e,d>}\lambda x.G(x) \geq$ **6-ft**
      d. T(6 ft tall): $\lambda x.\textbf{tall}(x) \geq$ **6-ft**
      e. T(Sandra is 6 ft tall): **tall**(s) $\geq$ **6-ft**

Among the facts that this analysis of adjectives accounts for is the impossibility of multiple degree modification of a single adjective, as shown in (6).[5] Multiple modification is ruled out because the application of the first degree modifier produces an expression which is not of the appropriate type to serve as input to a subsequent degree modifier.

(6)   a. *Spade was less very happy about the fact than I was.
      b. *Sally was very quite pleased with the results.

The behavior of *well* contrasts crucially with degree modifiers in this respect, as the output of *well* modification *can* be the input to degree morphology. We can be sure that the degree morpheme affects the *well* + participle combination and not just *well* by itself in an example like (7a) because this sentence entails that Spade was well acquainted with the facts, and not simply acquainted with them, as in (7b).

(7)   a. Spade was less well acquainted with the facts than his assistant was.
      b. Spade was less acquainted with the facts than his assistant was.

Likewise, (8a) entails that my brother was well prepared, an entailment that does not hold when *well* alone is first modified by a degree modifier, as in (8b). Here the suppletive *better* serves as the comparative form of *well*, which then combines with the participle:

(8)   a. My brother was more well prepared for the events than the rest of us were.
      b. My brother was better prepared for the events than the rest of us were.

We thus conclude that *well* is not a true degree morpheme even when it has an intensifying interpretation, and posit instead that it functions syntactically and semantically on this reading essentially as it does on its manner reading.

---

very in (ib), which fixes the comparison class to be just those objects that the positive form is true of (Wheeler 1972); and comparatives of superiority in (ic), where d_c is the denotation of the comparative clause.

(i)   a. $T(pos) = \lambda G_{<e,d>}\lambda x.G(x) \geq \textbf{stnd}(G)(C_{<e,t>})$
      b. $T(very) = \lambda G_{<e,d>}\lambda x.G(x) \geq \textbf{stnd}(G)(\lambda y.pos(G)(y))$
      c. $T(more\ than\ d_c) = \lambda G_{<e,d>}\lambda x.G(x) > d_c$

[5] Of course, sequences of degree modifiers do occur, as in *very very afraid*, but in these cases one degree modifier combines first with the other, and then the result combines with the adjective (Kennedy and McNally 2005).

11.2.2 The Distribution of the Degree and Manner Readings

Since our analysis of *well* ultimately involves deriving its polysemy from the interaction of its lexical semantics with the lexical semantics of the expressions it modifies, it is necessary to describe briefly exactly when modification by *well* is possible, and when the degree and manner readings are available. In this section, we consider only cases involving past participles, leaving the facts concerning *well* with other categories for Sect. 11.4.

As discussed in Kennedy and McNally (1999, 2005), *well* modification in general is possible only with participles that meet two semantic requirements: (1) they must denote gradable properties, and so must be associated with *scales* as part of their semantics, and (2) those scales must be *closed* on both ends (i.e. have minimum and maximum values). Closed-scale participles can be distinguished from open-scale ones in that only the former permit modification by proportional degree modifiers such as *partially* or *fully*:

(9) a. The truck was partially/fully loaded.

   b. The truck was well loaded.

As shown in (10), participles associated with open-scales, such as *worried*, do not permit modification by proportional modifiers, nor do they permit modification by *well*:

(10) a. ??Marge was partially/fully worried when she saw the flying pig.

   b. ??Marge was well worried when she saw the flying pig.

For those participles that accept *well* modification, the possibility of a degree reading is conditioned by a third feature: the nature of the participle's *standard of comparison* – the value on a scale that determines whether or not the positive form truthfully holds of an entity (see note 4). Specifically, the standard cannot be the maximum value on the scale. This condition follows from the central semantic effect of the degree reading of *well*: it "boosts" the standard for the attribute with which it combines.

Consider for example the participle *acquainted* (*with*). The standard of comparison for *acquainted* is demonstrably a minimum value on the "acquaintedness" scale: x counts as acquainted with y as long as x has some minimal (non-zero) degree of acquaintance with y. (Correspondingly, the negation x *is not acquainted with* y entails that x has a zero degree of acquaintance with y; see Kennedy and McNally 2005 for detailed discussion.) Such a standard can in principle be raised, and this is what we see with *well* modification: holding all potentially variable factors constant, the degree of acquaintedness which must be reached for an entity to be considered well acquainted with y in any given situation is considerably higher than that required for it to qualify as simply acquainted with y.

Now consider for example the participle *written*. In order for an object x to count as written, it must be the case that x has a maximal degree of "writtenness": it must be completely written. (Thus *x is not written* entails only that *x* is not fully written, not that it is not written at all.). Since the standard is already a maximum, it cannot be further raised, with the result that a degree interpretation of *well* is unavailable. A well-written novel is therefore a novel that is written in a good manner, not one that (necessarily) contains a lot of writing.

Given these observations, we may hypothesize that a degree reading of *well* is always in principle available, but that this interpretation is neutralized whenever the standard of comparison for the modified expression is a maximum value on a scale. But while this hypothesis gets the facts right, it raises a more general question: how do we know when the standard for some gradable property corresponds to a minimum or a maximum value on the relevant scale?

To answer this question, we first need to step back and see how participial scales are derived in the first place. Kennedy and McNally (2005) show that the scales associated with participles can be homomorphically related to (and, ultimately, derived from) aspects of their event structures, and that a given participle may be associated with more than one scale, depending on the type of measurement it describes.

For illustration, consider the case of participles derived from so-called *spray/load* verbs (we will focus on *load* for the sake of illustration). A (maximal) loading event involving a container *x* and contents *y* can be divided into temporally and incrementally ordered subevents of loading *x* with amounts of *y*. The temporal endpoints of each of these subevents can be mapped onto an ordered set of degrees on the "loadedness" scale. The endpoint of the first subevent of loading of the smallest amount of *x* onto *y* corresponds to the minimal non-zero degree on the scale for both *x* and *y* (the zero element represents not having participated in an event of loading at all).

However, what constitutes the maximum value on the scale depends on the participle's argument structure, since argument structure affects the nature of the event described by the participle (see e.g. Dowty 1991; Levin and Rappaport-Hovav 1999). The endpoint of the last subevent of loading of the last bit of *x* onto *y* corresponds to the maximum on a scale when *x* is being described, i.e., when the participle is *loaded-on*. In contrast, the endpoint of the subevent of loading the last bit of *x* that fits onto *y* corresponds to the maximum on a scale when *y* is being described; i.e., when the participle *loaded-with*. In other words, *loaded-on* measures *x* relative to how much of it is on *y*; *loaded-with* measures *y* relative to how much of it is filled with (amounts of) *x*.

The result is that the participle *loaded* always involves measurement with respect to a closed scale whose structure is based on the event structure of the verb, but the type of the measurement differs depending on the semantic role of the argument, so the scales themselves differ. This is illustrated by the fact that the two arguments are not commensurable: while it is possible to compare the loadedness of two containers (11a) or of two types of cargo (11b), it is not possible to compare the loadedness of a container with that of some cargo (11c).

(11)   a. More of the truck is loaded than the van.
     b. More of the hay is loaded than the oats.
     c. ??More of the hay is loaded than the truck.

What is relevant to us here is that this distinction also determines whether the standard of comparison is a maximum or minimum value. If the argument is a classic incremental theme (see Dowty 1991), the sort that Ramchand (1997) calls "Pat$_=$" as in the case of the cargo argument of *loaded*, the standard is the maximal value on the scale. This is so because the conditions for truthful application of the participle are not met unless all of the incremental theme has undergone the event in question. Thus (12a) is not true of the hay unless 100% of it has undergone loading, as illustrated by the anomaly of the continuation in (12b) (where *it* refers to the hay).

(12)   a. The hay is loaded on the truck.
     b. ??But it's only half loaded.

The proportional modifier *half* explicitly indicates that the argument of the participle is mapped to the midpoint of the scale, which is incompatible with it having a maximum degree of the relevant property. (Thus *half loaded on* entails *not loaded on*; see Kennedy and McNally 2005 for further discussion.)

In the case of non-incremental theme argument (including e.g. arguments bearing Ramchand's "Pat$_{+/-}$" role), the participle is assigned a minimum standard. We can see this by examining the container argument of *loaded*, where the argument as a whole is involved in each subevent of loading, but where one of its properties, namely the degree to which its volume is occupied, changes incrementally. Thus (13a) can be true as soon as the truck has undergone a minimal loading event of some amount of cargo; it is not necessary for its entire volume to be occupied. This is illustrated by the felicity of the continuation in (13b) (where *it* refers to the truck).

(13)   a. The truck is loaded with the hay.
     b. But it is (still) only half loaded.

In sum, the standard of comparison for a closed-scale participle is a maximum value when it applies to a true incremental theme argument, and a minimum when it applies to other arguments. Returning to *well* modification, we can now refine our generalization about the possibility of a degree reading: such an interpretation is possible only if the argument of the modified participle is a non-incremental theme argument of the source verb. (The participle must also have a closed-scale to begin with; this is an independent requirement of *well*, as discussed above.) This generalization is illustrated by the examples in (14).

(14)   a. That is well loaded hay.
     b. That is a well loaded truck.
     c. Those are well loaded boxes.

(14a) with an incremental theme argument has only a manner interpretation, while (14b) with a non-incremental theme argument allows a degree interpretation as well. (14c) is clearly ambiguous, but this is because boxes can be construed either as containers (non-incremental theme) or as cargo (incremental theme); only the former construal allows a degree reading.

11.3   A GL Analysis of *Well* with Past Participles

11.3.1   Basic Assumptions

We now present a GL analysis of *well* modification which accounts in a unified way for *well*'s manner and degree readings and their distribution as observed in the previous section. We assume basic familiarity with the GL framework and only mention here those details which are specific to our analysis. For explicitness, we integrate our GL representations into a version of Head-Driven Phrase Structure Grammar (HPSG, see e.g. Pollard and Sag 1994) as follows. Semantic representations in HPSG appear under the content (CONT) feature, and include information about the referential index of an expression, when it has one (the INDEX feature), and about the expression's descriptive content (the REST(riction) feature).[6] We follow Badia and Saurí (2000, 2013) in making sets of qualia the values of the REST feature, though we diverge from them on other details. We also subsume GL's event structure (EVENTSTR) under the CONT feature, and to it we add another element: *scale structure* (SCLSTR), which identifies the type of scale associated with an expression. In contrast, the standard value associated with the scale (STD, whose value is a degree), will be introduced independently as the relation denoted by certain kinds of degree expressions. The specification of SCLSTR includes, on the one hand, a description of the scale in question via the SCLNAME feature (e.g. dimension, temperature, or properties such as goodness or "loadedness") and, on the other, information about whether the scale is open or closed (the OP/CL feature).[7]

The remaining basic GL structure, namely argument structure (ARGSTR), is treated as in HPSG as a category (CAT) feature, alongside subcategorization information (the (VAL)ence feature) and HEAD features. A crucial HEAD feature is MOD, which controls the selection between modifiers (such as adjectives or adverbs) and heads (via ARG), and which manages the internal and external semantics of modifiers (via ICONT and ECONT, respectively; see Kasper 1997), so as to provide for a proper analysis of modifiers of modifiers (such as *well*). This overall syntactic-semantic architecture is shown in Fig. 11.1.

---

[6]For the purposes of this paper we ignore the other standardly-posited element of the CONT feature, the CONTEXT feature.

[7]The exact configuration we have given to scale structure is not crucial for the analysis, so for reasons of space we will not justify it here. We use (0,1) to represent an open scale and [0,1] for closed scales; partially closed scales (0,1] and [0,1) are also possible though we will not discuss such examples here.

Fig. 11.1 Basic
syntactic/semantic
architecture

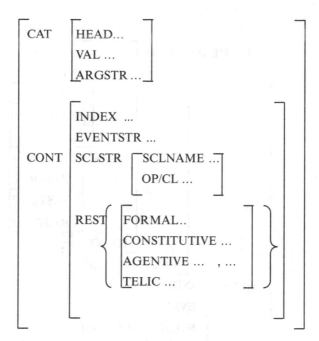

11.3.2 **Well** *and Past Participles*

Our representation for *well* appears in Fig. 11.2.[8] This representation encodes, on
the one hand, information about the expressions *well* combines with and, on the
other, information about its semantics, including specifically the semantics of the
well + participle result. As mentioned in the previous section, we follow Kasper's
(1997) extension of Pollard and Sag's (1994) treatment of adjective premodifiers
to handle multiple premodification. *Well* is treated as an intersective modifier of
participles; the participle is the head of the resulting expression, which in turn will
be a modifier of a noun. The semantics of the *well* + participle phrase (represented
in the ECONT feature) will thus be inherited almost entirely from the semantics of
the participle, with the sole addition of the condition contributed by *well*.

The fundamental assumption we make about the semantics of *well* is that it
denotes a measure function on events. This should not be surprising. If we combine
a Davidsonian semantics for manner adverbs (treated as properties of events), with
a Kennedy-style account of their gradability characteristics, all gradable manner
adverbs, and not just *well*, will denote measure functions on events. Although
we will not attempt here to unify *well's* verb-modifying uses with its participle-
modifying uses, adopting an event-oriented denotation for the latter is a step towards
such a unification.

---

[8]Our analysis will ignore those details which do not bear directly on the issue of how both the
degree and non-degree reading of *well* can be derived from an unambiguous *well*.

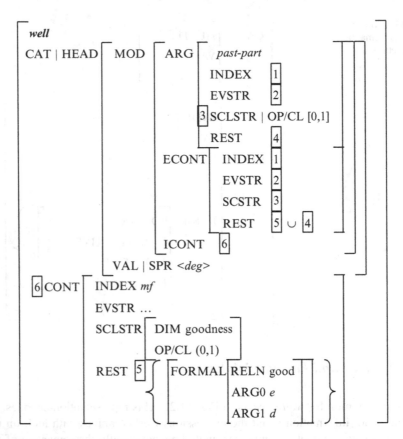

Fig. 11.2 Lexical representation for *well*

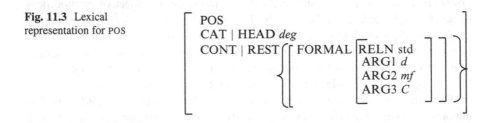

Fig. 11.3 Lexical representation for POS

We encode the denotation of *well* in its restriction as a relation between an event and a degree. We posit that the measure function denoted by *well* is the same as that denoted by the adjective *good*: it maps an event onto a(n open) scale of goodness. Note that the denotation for *well* does not contain any information about the standard for what counts as good. This information, we posit, is provided by degree morphology, which is selected for as a specifier (SPR) by *well*, following the suggested analysis of the syntax of degree modifiers in Pollard and Sag (1994). For example the null morpheme POS is represented in Fig. 11.3; it provides an

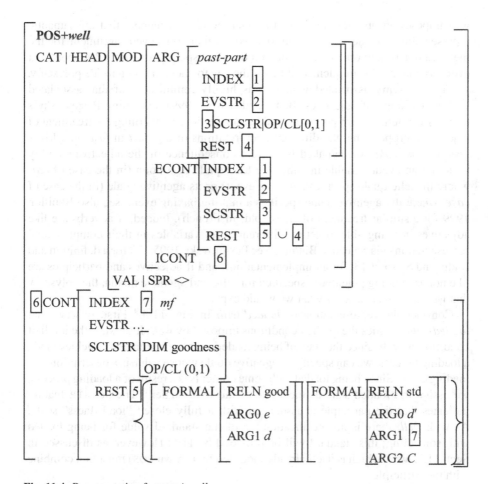

Fig. 11.4 Representation for POS+*well*

additional, conjunctive condition on the semantics of adjective phrases which
established the standard value relation between a degree d, a measure function
(*mf*, contributed by the expression POS combines with), and a comparison class C.
When the expression with which POS combines is associated with an open scale,
this comparison class will have to be determined by the context; however, when the
scale is closed, we will assume that the comparison class variable will default to the
minimal or maximal value on the scale.

The combination of POS + *well* appears in Fig. 11.4. Note that the SPR list is now
empty – we now have a syntactically and semantically complete phrase which can
combine with the participle.

Let us first consider the conditions that *well* imposes on its participial argument.
The ARG feature specifies the one condition that is explicitly imposed: the modified
participle's scale must be closed. However, in addition to this explicit condition,

well imposes an obvious and crucial implicit condition, namely that the semantic representation for the participle must make available an event argument for the measure function to operate on, though it does not specify anything else about that event argument. This implicit condition is the key to understanding *well*'s polysemy.

The polysemy associated with *well* is highly reminiscent of that associated with many kinds of adjectives. Badia and Saurí (1999), extending Pustejovsky's (1995) treatment of verb polysemy and his suggestions concerning the treatment of adjectives, propose that the different interpretations of e.g. *fast* in *fast car* (drives fast) vs. *fast cake* (made/baked fast) are a consequence of the adjective's ability to act on an event variable in either the telic quale of a noun (in the case of *car*, where the telic quale specifies a driving event) or its agentive quale (in the case of *cake*, where the agentive quale specifies a making/baking event; see also Bouillon 1999 for a similar treatment of *vieux* 'old' in French). Indeed, if adverbs are like adjectives in being able to act on different event variables in their complements' representations via Selective Binding (see Pustejovsky 1995:129 for a definition and Badia and Saurí 2013, for an implementation), and if adjectives and participles are like nouns in being potentially specified for telic and agentive qualia, the polysemy that *well* exhibits is exactly what we would expect.

Consider the representation of *loaded-with* in Fig. 11.5.[9] First, observe that *loaded-with* satisfies the explicit conditions imposed by *well*. It satisfies the implicit condition as well: since the state of being loaded with some contents is achieved via a loading process, we can specify an agentive quale whose value is a description of a loading event. Since being loaded with some contents is a result of a loading process, we assign the loaded state as the value of the telic quale.[10] The SCLSTR feature indicates that the participle is associated with a fully closed "loadedness" scale. As with *well*, there is no specification yet of the standard value for being loaded with something; this standard will be provided by POS. However, as discussed in Sect. 11.2, *well* (which is itself already modified by its own POS) must first combine with the participle.

The combination of POS + *well* will form a phrase with *loaded-with* in an HPSG head-modifier structure. In such structures, according to the Semantics Principle,[11]

---

[9]Although we assign *loaded* two different lexical entries corresponding to its two argument structures, these two entries are highly redundant and could be partially unified in a hierarchical lexicon (see e.g. Koenig 1999). To save space we have represented the values of the qualia as simple formulae, rather than as feature-structures.

[10]Here our treatment of result states differs from Pustejovsky's (1995), resembling instead the analysis developed independently by Lautenbacher (2001).

[11]We adopt the version of the Semantics Principle for head-modifier structures proposed in Kasper (1997, (31)):

(a) For a head-adjunct phrase, the semantic content (CONT) is token-identical with the MOD|ECONT value of the adjunct daughter, and the MOD|ICONT value of the adjunct daughter is token identical with the adjunct daughter's CONT.

(b) For all other types of headed phrase, the CONT is token-identical with the CONT of the head daughter.

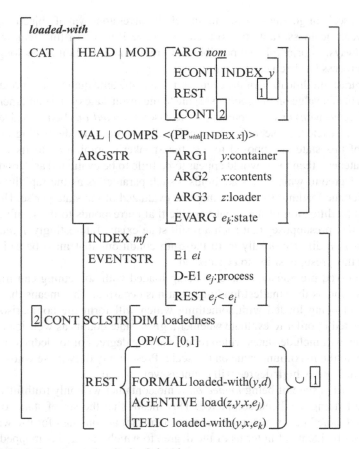

Fig. 11.5 Lexical representation for *loaded-with*

the modifier determines the way in which the respective restrictions of the head and modifier combine[12]; however, all remaining aspects of the semantics will be inherited from the head daughter. The analysis of *loaded-on* will be identical, except that the container and contents arguments will be crucially interchanged: the measure function denoted by *loaded-with* applies to the container argument, while that denoted by *loaded-on* applies to the contents.

What happens when *well* combines with these representations? The formal quale of the participle does not provide any event variable for *well* to act on. Thus, there remain only the event variable in the agentive quale or that in the telic quale. Modification of the event variable in the agentive quale via Selective Binding corresponds to a manner/quality reading of *well*: the loading process is assigned a

---

[12]This is to allow for the fact that some modifiers are not intersective and thus cannot be subject to a general rule according to which the REST of a phrase is the union of the REST values of its daughter phrases.

value on a scale of goodness which intuitively involves approval of objective aspects of the event: neatness, rapidity, skill, etc. Selective Binding of this agentive quale should always, in principle, be possible and pragmatically felicitous as long as the loading process has been carried out to some degree.

In contrast, modification of the event variable in the telic quale corresponds to the assignment of a value on the goodness scale to the result state of the container (in the case of *loaded-with*) or the contents (in the case of *loaded-on*) being loaded. If the adverb is restricted, as seems to be empirically the case, to describing objective aspects of this state as opposed to e.g. the speaker's opinion as to its utility or appropriateness, then there would appear to be little to be evaluated as "good" other than the degree to which the state holds – such parameters as the rapidity or skill with which the loading was done cannot be evaluated of the state per se. However, felicitous modification of the event variable that corresponds to the result state of being loaded presupposes that such a result state exists. Interestingly, *loaded-with* and *loaded-on* differ crucially as to the truth conditions that must be satisfied in order for this presupposition to be satisfied.

As observed previously, a state of being loaded with something can truthfully obtain as soon as the smallest loading event has occurred. This means that the set of states of being loaded with something which will form the comparison class that is needed in order to evaluate whether a given state counts as well-loaded with something, will include states which reflect varying degrees of loadedness from the minimum to the maximum value on the scale. Presumably only those whose values are of a sufficiently high degree will count as well loaded.

In contrast, a state of being *loaded on* some container will only truthfully obtain when the loading has been completed. This means that the set of states of being loaded on (something) which might constitute a comparison class for use with *well* will always be identical in terms of the degree to which the state is mapped on the loadedness scale. If all such states are identical in degree, it will make little sense to try to qualify any of them as better than any other, and thus modification by *well* will not be felicitous. Only the option of a manner reading via Selective Binding of the agentive quale will remain.

11.4   Conclusions

We have sketched an account of *well*'s polysemy in combination with participles which avoids the undesirable ambiguity posited in Kennedy and McNally 1999. While we maintain two lexical entries for the participle exemplified, this ambiguity is independently motivated on argument structure grounds and has been claimed to have semantic consequences (by e.g. Dowty 1991). Moreover, maintaining an ambiguity in the participle turns out to correctly predict that the phenomenon illustrated in (2)–(3) occurs only with participles for which multiple semantic representations can be independently motivated.

The fact that existing analyses of adjectival modification can be adapted so straightforwardly to this case of adverbial polysemy lends further support to the selective binding approach in general. In the case studied here, the option of using selective binding obviates the need to assign *well* to two semantic types: that of a measure function on events for its verb modifier use, and that of a function from measure functions to measure functions for its adjective modifier use. However, it comes at a price: in the case of adjective-noun modification on the traditional analysis (or analyses such as that in Larson 1998), Selective Binding captured a simpler relationship between modifier and modified: the adjectival property could be said to apply to an entity in virtue of the entity's participation in an event. The distance between modifier and modified is rather greater in the case of *well*: a measure function on events applies to a measure function on individuals in virtue of the fact that the measure function on individuals is related to an event. The question is how complex can such indirect modification relations be?

There are two paths to follow in pursuit of an answer to this question. One is to ask what kinds of constraints should be put on Selective Binding or its implementational equivalent if it is to tell us something interesting about natural language modification. The other is to begin integrating the long tradition on the scalar semantics of adjectives into the treatments of adjectives from the perspective of event semantics, in the hopes of eventually reducing or rationalizing the complexity of the modification relation instantiated by *well*. In making a first attempt to integrate scale structure into GL, we hope to have taken a first step on this latter path.

Acknowledgments We are grateful to audiences at the First International Workshop on Generative Approaches to the Lexicon and at Universitat Pompeu Fabra for comments, and to Tom Rozario for assistance with data collection. All errors are our own. This paper is based upon work supported by the National Science Foundation under Grant No. 0094263, and by the Department of Universities, Research, and Information Society of the Generalitat de Catalunya.

References

Badia, T., & Saurí, R. (1999). Semantic disambiguation of adjectives in local context: A generative approach. In P. Bouillon & E. Viegas (Eds.), *Proceedings of TALN 99* (pp. 163–180). Cargèse: Corsica.

Badia, T., & Saurí, R. (2000). Enlarging HPSG with lexical semantics. In A. Gelbukh (Ed.), *Proceedings of CICLing 2000* (pp. 101–122). Mexico City: Computer Research Center, National Polytechnic Institute.

Badia, T., & Saurí, R. (2013). Developing a generative lexicon within HPSG. In J. Pustejovsky (Ed.), *Advances in generative lexicon theory* (Text, speech and language technology). Dordrecht: Springer.

Bolinger, D. (1972). *Degree words*. The Hague: Mouton.

Bouillon, P. (1999). The adjective 'vieux': The point of view of 'generative lexicon'. In E. Viegas (Ed.), *Breadth and depth of semantic lexicons* (pp. 148–166). Dordrecht: Kluwer.

Dowty, D. R. (1991). Thematic proto-roles and argument selection. *Language, 67*, 547–619.

Jackendoff, R. (1977). *X-bar syntax*. Cambridge, MA: MIT Press.

Kasper, R.T. (1997). *The semantics of recursive modication*. Ms., Ohio State University.

Katz, G. (2005). Attitudes towards degrees. In E. Maier, C. Bary, & J. Huitink (Eds.), *Proceedings of SuB9* (pp. 183–196). Nijmegen: NCS.

Kennedy, C. (1999). *Projecting the adjective: The syntax and semantics of gradability and comparison*. New York: Garland.

Kennedy, C., & McNally, L. (1999). From event structure to scale structure: Degree modification in deverbal adjectives. In T. Matthews & D. Strolovitch (Eds.), *Proceedings of SALT IX* (pp. 163–180). Ithaca: CLC Publications.

Kennedy, C., & McNally, L. (2005). Scale structure, degree modification, and the semantics of gradable predicates. *Language, 81*, 345–381.

Klein, E. (1980). A semantics for positive and comparative adjectives. *Linguistics and Philosophy, 4*(1), 1–45.

Koenig, J.-P. (1999). *Lexical relations*. Stanford: CSLI Publications.

Larson, R. (1998). Events and modification in nominals. In D. Strolovitch & A. Lawson (Eds.), *Proceedings of SALT VIII* (pp. 145–168). Ithaca: CLC Publications.

Lautenbacher, O.-P. (2001). What is formal and what is telic in a predicate? An alternative vision of the Generative Lexicon's qualia. In P. Bouillon & K. Kanzaki (Eds.), *Proceedings of the First International Workshop on Generative Approaches to the Lexicon*. Geneva: Switzerland.

Levin, B., & Rappaport-Hovav, M. (1999). Two structures for compositionally derived events. In T. Matthews & D. Strolovitch (Eds.), *Proceedings from SALT IX* (pp. 199–223). Ithaca: CLC Publications.

Pustejovsky, J. (1995). *The generative lexicon*. Cambridge, MA: MIT Press.

Pollard, C., & Sag, I. (1994). *Head-Driven Phrase Structure Grammar*. Chicago: CSLI.

Ramchand, G. C. (1997). *Aspect and predication*. Oxford: Clarendon.

Wheeler, S. (1972). Attributives and their modifiers. *Noûs, 6*(4), 310–334.

Chapter 12
V-Concatenation in Japanese

Kentaro Nakatani

12.1 Introduction

In this paper I examine the semantic properties of what I call the *V-te V predicates* in Japanese, a type of complex predicate composed of two verbs, which I label V_1 and V_2 according to their linear order, and a conjunctive morpheme, *-te*. Some examples are shown below:

(1) Taroo-ga ofisu-ni   syasin-o   **mot**-te **ki**-ta.
    Taro-NOM office-DAT photo-ACC **hold**-TE **come**-PAST
    'Taro brought the photo to the office.'

(2) Taroo-ga hon-o   **kat**-te **kure**-ta.
    Taro-NOM book-ACC **buy**-TE **give**-PAST
    'Taro bought the book for me.'

Note that a phrase headed by *-te* (*te*P) is usually an adjunct floating around in a sentence (like English gerunds); however, when V-*te* is adjacent to a verb from a certain set of verbs, they jointly form a single complex predicate. The status of a [V-*te* V] string as a complex predicate (rather than two separate predicates) is clear when the semantics of V_2 is significantly lightened, but even if the lightening effect is not very clear, its status as a single predicate can be verified through various linguistic tests including a Negative Polarity Item test (NPI test), as discussed in previous studies (Matsumoto 1996; McCawley and Momoi 1986; Miyagawa 1987). Below are some examples illustrating this point. As seen in (3), *te*P can be adjoined to a sentence-initial position; in such a case, the *te*P is an adjunct and thus an NPI in the *te*P cannot be licensed by NEG attached to the matrix predicate, as shown in (4).

K. Nakatani (✉)
Department of English and American Literature and Language, Konan University, Kobe, Japan

J. Pustejovsky et al. (eds.), *Advances in Generative Lexicon Theory*, Text,
Speech and Language Technology 46, DOI 10.1007/978-94-007-5189-7_12,
© Springer Science+Business Media Dordrecht 2013

However, the same does not apply in (5), where V-*te* is adjacent to the matrix verb; this probably shows that the two verbs are now restructured as, or *concatenated into*, a single predicate. (6) and (7) further show that not all verbs can be concatenated.

(3) [syasin-o   mot-te]   Taroo-ga   ki-ta.
    [photo-ACC hold-TE]   Taro-NOM   come-PAST
    'Taro came holding the photo.'

(4) *[*nanimo*   mot-te]   Taroo-ga   ko-*nakat*-ta.
    [*anything* hold-TE]   Taro-NOM   come-NEG-PAST

(5) Taroo-ga   *nanimo*   [mot-te   ko] -*nakat*-ta.
    Taro-NOM *anything* [hold-TE   come] -NEG-PAST
    'Taro did not bring anything.'

(6) Taroo-ga   [syasin-o   mot-te]   tootyakusi-ta.
    Taro-NOM [photo-ACC hold-TE]   arrive-PAST
    'Taro arrived at the office holding the photo.'

(7) *Taroo-ga   [*nanimo*   mot-te]   tootyakusi-*nakat*-ta.
    Taro-NOM [*anything* hold-TE]   arrive-NEG-PAST

In this type of complex predicate, V_2 is usually semantically "light" and thus is often labeled "auxiliary verb" (Aux) in the literature (Yoshikawa 1973; Martin 1975; Morita 1977; Teramura 1984, among others). In such a traditional approach, the instances of "Aux" V_2 are usually studied independently of their main verb (henceforth, MV) counterparts, treated as separate entities. However, the research in this vein fails to account for the fact that similar constructions composed of similar verbs are found in many languages that are not historically related. For example, one may be surprised to find that, say, West African Kwa languages such as Yoruba exhibit the same instances of V-complexes corresponding to Japanese (1) and (2), as shown in (8) and (9) below (cited from Bamgbos•e 1974 and Ekundayo and Akinnaso 1983, respectively):

(8) ó   **mú** ìwé   **wá**.
    He **take** book **come**
    'He brought the book.'

(9) ó   **ra** isu **fún** mi.
    He **buy** yam **give** me
    'He bought a yam for me.'

Such crosslinguistic similarities indicate that the generation of V-complexes is governed by universal principles that have certain biological bases. In other words, it is likely that the human language capacity has a built-in mechanism that drives the formation of such V-complexes. In the present paper, I will show a few pieces of evidence for a generative approach and present an analysis based on the Generative Lexicon (GL) framework (Pustejovsky 1995).

12.2   Why Not the Aux Hypothesis?

Let us see in more detail why it is inadequate to simply label V_2 in the V_1-*te* V_2 predicate an auxiliary verb (Aux) and to analyze them independently of their main verb (MV) counterparts. I call such a simplistic approach the "Aux Hypothesis". Note that the present paper is not arguing against the view that V_2 in the V_1-*te* V_2 predicate has properties similar to auxiliary verbs, nor is it rejecting the possibility of concrete instances of V_2 being stored as separate entries in the adult mental lexicon. What is argued here is that we need an association theory that accounts for the systematic connection between the Aux-like V_2s and their MV counterparts.

12.2.1   Crosslinguistic Similarities

One reason for the inadequacy of the Aux Hypothesis has already been pointed out earlier: a simple Aux Hypothesis cannot account for the striking crosslinguistic similarities. An adequate linguistic theory needs to account for why such similarities emerge across languages, that is, why certain verb combinations transform into verbal complexes in a similar manner in historically unrelated languages. A simplistic Aux Hypothesis is unable to give a reasonable answer to such a question.

12.2.2   Phonological and Morphosyntactic Properties

There are a number of language-internal reasons to believe that the associations between the "Aux" V_2s of the V-*te* V predicate and their MV counterparts are synchronically real.

First of all, in the V-*te* V predicate, *all* of the attested "Aux" V_2s have phonologically indistinguishable MV counterparts, and none of these MVs is obsolete; in actuality, the MV usage of these "Aux" V_2s is highly frequent. It is crosslinguistically common that main verbs are grammaticalized into Aux's, losing their MV usage, but in the case of the V-*te* V predicate in Japanese (as well as similar V-complexes in serializing languages), both versions (i.e., the MV and "Aux" versions) co-exist, pointing to the non-accidental synchronic associations between the two.

Second, there is a general fact that auxiliary verbs are often different from main verbs in terms of syntactic distribution (e.g., English modals often require the verb that follows to be in its bare infinitival form, while English main verbs usually (if not always) require the *to*-infinitivals); however, the "Aux" Vs in the V-*te* V predicate do not show any peculiar external syntactic properties distinct from those of main verbs in general.

Third, no conjugational differences are found between the "Aux" Vs of the V-*te* V predicate and their MV counterparts. Even *ku* 'to come', one of the few truly irregular verbs in Japanese, retains its full conjugational paradigm when used as V_2 of the V-*te* V predicate. It is unlikely that the "Aux" *ku* and the MV *ku*, both of which show the same irregular conjugational patterns, are totally unrelated in our lexical knowledge.

12.2.3 Semantic Parallelism

Because we find no phonological or morphosyntactic grounds for separating the "Aux" V_2s of the V-*te* V predicate from their MV counterparts, the only motivation for isolating the two sides, if any, should lie in their semantics. It is true that the "Aux" V_2s of the V-*te* V predicate are often, if not always, significantly lighter in semantics than their MV counterparts. However, a closer examination will reveal close semantic links between the "Aux" V_2s and their MV counterparts. Most notably, it can be easily observed that distinctive contrasts found in certain minimal pairs or triplets of the MVs are retained in the corresponding "Aux" V_2s. For example, the directional contrast between two directional verbs, *ku* 'to come' and *ik* 'to go', can be found in their "Aux" versions, even when the "Aux" semantics is significantly lightened:

(10)   Taroo-wa hon-o   **wasure**-te **ki**-ta
        Taro-TOP book-ACC   **forget**-TE **come**-PAST
        'Taro left his book (somewhere other than here).'

(11)   Taroo-wa hon-o   **wasure**-te   **it**-ta
        Taro-TOP book-ACC   **forget**-TE   **go**-PAST
        'Taro left his book (here).'

The directional contrasts between the three verbs of giving, *kure* 'to give (to the speaker or somebody psychologically close to the speaker)', *age* 'to give (to a non-speaker)', and *moraw* 'to be given', are also observable in the corresponding "Aux" triplet[1]:

(12)   Taroo-ga hon-o   **yon**-de **kure** / **age**-ta
        Taro-NOM book-ACC   **read**-TE **give** / **give**-PAST
        'Taro read the book for me / for somebody.'

(13)   Taroo-ga hon-o   **yon**-de   **morat**-ta
        Taro-NOM book-ACC   **read**-TE **be_given**-PAST
        'Somebody read Taro the book.'

---

[1]The first segment of -*te* is systematically voiced under certain morphophonological conditions, the details of which are irrelevant to the goal of the present paper.

The same is observed in more abstract cases where the semantics of the "Aux" V$_2$s is more drastically lightened, in such cases as the contrast between *ok* 'to put' and *simaw* 'to put away' (to which we will get back later) and the contrast between *mi* 'to see' and *mise* 'to show'. Again, one might argue in defense of the Aux Hypothesis that the observed correspondences are merely traces of historical changes. However, given the straightforward nature of the semantic correspondences and the indistinguishable phonological and morphosyntactic properties, it would be surprising if no synchronic connections were present between these Aux Vs and their MV counterparts in native speakers' minds.

12.2.4 Honorific Variants

Finally, one of the most straightforward pieces of evidence for the synchronic association between the Aux Vs of the V-*te* V predicate and their MV versions comes from the fact about honorific forms. In Japanese, honorific forms can be productively made up with honorific morpheme -*rare* or complex morphological template *o-V-ni nar*, but at the same time, many of the frequently used verbs have their own lexicalized, non-productive honorific variants. For example, the honorific form of *ku* 'to come' can be made up with productive -*rare* (as in *ko-rare*), but *ku* also has its own lexicalized honorific forms such as *irassyar* or *o-ide-ni nar*, which are phonologically unrelated to *ku*. For *mi* 'to see', there is *goran-ni nar*; for *kure* 'to give (to the speaker)', there is *kudasar*; for *age* 'to give (to a non-speaker)', there is *sasiage*; for *moraw* 'to be given', there is *itadak*, and for *i* 'to exist', there is *irassyar* (which is homophonous to *irassyar* as an honorific form of *ku* 'to come'). *All* of these forms are found in the "Aux" V$_2$ position in the V-*te* V predicate. This shows that simply sweeping the "Aux" V$_2$s under the "auxiliary" category is inadequate. An adequate theory should capture the Aux-MV associations. One possible approach, which I will take in the rest of the paper, is a derivational approach, which assumes a process of deriving the syntax and semantics of the V-*te* V predicate from those of its parts, namely, two Vs and -*te*.

12.3   Semantic Interaction Between V$_1$ and V$_2$

In this section, I will closely examine the semantic and syntactic properties of the V-*te ku* ('come') predicate. It will be revealed that a derivational approach is appropriate for accounting for the observed facts.

12.3.1 Degree of Bleaching

It is known that the lightness of the semantics of V_2 in the V_1-*te* V_2 predicate may vary: in some cases, the semantics of V_2 is concrete and close to the MV semantics, while in many other cases, it is abstract and seems distant from the original MV semantics. Such variation is particularly observable when the verbs of coming and going, *ku* and *ik*, are used as V_2. For example, in the following, *ku* 'to come' denotes a concrete physical movement in (14), and some highly abstract sense in (16); (15) is an intermediate case:

(14)   Taroo-wa itiba-ni   kani-o   **mot**-te   **ki**-ta.
         Taro-TOP market-DAT crab-ACC **hold**-TE **come**-PAST
         'Taro brought a crab to the market.'
(15)   Taroo-ga boku-ni denwa-o   **kake**-te **ki**-ta.
         Taro-NOM I-DAT   telephone-ACC **use**-TE   **come**-PAST
         'Taro came (here) after calling me.'
         or 'Taro called me.' (Not implying Taro came.)
(16)   boku-wa kanasiku **nat**-te   **ki**-ta.
         I-TOP   sad   **become**-TE **come**-PAST
         'I am getting sad.'

In (14), the physical movement of Taro to the market is involved, and V_2 *ku* (*ki*) is fully responsible for this denotation of the movement event (because V_1*mot* does not entail such a movement). It thus can be concluded that V_2 in (14) retains its original semantics to a considerable extent. (15) is ambiguous, being interpreted as either involving or not involving the physical movement of Taro to the location of the speaker. In the former reading, V_2 retains its original semantics, whereas in the latter reading, the original semantics of V_2 is somewhat bleached, only giving a metaphorical flavor of Taro's action rather than Taro himself being directed toward the speaker. V_2 in (16) has undergone even more drastic abstraction: there is nobody taking an action even in a metaphorical sense, and what is "coming" here is the state depicted in the rest of the sentence. The point here is that the degree of the semantic bleaching of V_2 is not arbitrarily determined: rather, the degree of semantic bleaching is determined interactively with the semantic content of V_1 (more precisely, VP_1). This is not surprising in a sense generation theory like the GL theory, under which semantic modification may interact with syntactic structure building (e.g., type-coercion, selective binding, etc.).

12.3.2 Argument of V_2

Furthermore, there is another type of evidence that shows the influence of the V_1 semantics on the V_2 semantics. This evidence is related to the acceptability of a potential argument associated with V_2: the argument-taking capability of V_2 sometimes depends on the semantics of VP_1. This is notable, again, when V_2 is a verb of coming or going. We find that a potential dative argument associated with *ku* or *ik* is impossible when semantic bleaching takes place, like in (16) above, and this is no surprise considering the possibility that semantic bleaching alters the argument structure of V_2 when it wipes out the entailment of the physical movement of the agent. What is surprising, however, is the fact that such a dative argument of V_2 is not always allowed even when V_2 retains its original meaning of physical movement. For example[2]:

(17) Taroo-ga ofisu-ni   e-o   katui-de   ki-ta.
       Taro-NOM office-DAT picture-ACC shoulder-TE   come-PAST
       'Taro shouldered the picture all the way to the office.'
(18) Taroo-ga (??ofisu-ni)   e-o   mi-te   ki-ta.
       Taro-NOM (??office-DAT) picture-ACC see-TE   come-PAST
       'Taro saw the picture and came (??to the office).'

In both of the above examples of the V-*te* V predicate, V_2 retains its original semantics of physical movement of the agent, Taro, and thus it is expected that V_2 can license a dative argument. In actuality, however, the dative argument is acceptable in (17) while not in (18). Note that there is no pragmatic reason why the dative argument is unacceptable in (18), as confirmed in the non-concatenated example (19) below, where the concatenation is interfered by *ofisu-ni*:

(19) Taroo-ga [e-o   mi-te] ofisu-ni   ki-ta.
       Taro-NOM [picture-ACC see-TE] office-DAT come-PAST
       'Taro saw the picture and came to the office.'

These data show that when concatenation takes place, the argument-taking capability of V_2 may be affected, depending on what kind of V_1 V_2 is concatenated with. This supports a derivational approach to the V-*te* V predicate, under which the semantic properties of the V-*te* V predicate is dynamically determined depending on the semantics of its parts.

---

[2]In (18) and other examples, verb *mi* is glossed as 'to see'. However, this may be problematic. In Japanese, there is no lexical distinction comparable to English *see* vs. *watch* vs. *look at*. This issue should not be treated lightly in a semantic theory; I nevertheless stick to the gloss 'see' in the examples and in the semantic representations, to avoid unnecessary complications.

12.4   The Mechanism of V-Concatenation

Now let us consider what effects the concatenation process has on the semantic representations. I propose that predicate concatenation in the semantic component is fundamentally a process of collapsing two separate qualia structures (Pustejovsky 1995) into one qualia structure (COLLAPSE), optionally followed by manipulations on variables (VARIABLE SHIFT), which is constrained by a well-formedness condition, the PRINCIPLE OF CAUSATION FLOW (PCF). Furthermore, a theme argument is often eventified (THEME EVENTIFICATION). I assume that *-te* is a relative past tense marker (Nakatani 2003a, 2004, see also Kuno 1973; Matsuo 1936; Ogihara 1998; Yoshikawa 1973), which I argue plays a role in determining how two qualia are collapsed.

12.4.1   Collapse

One of the main issues regarding predicate concatenation in the semantic component is how two semantic representations can be contracted preserving the qualia schema. In the case of sentential complementation, there arises no such problem, because when representation R_α is selected by representation R_β, there is a slot reserved in R_β for R_α to sit in. However, in the case of V-concatenation, there is often a conflict between the two qualia structures. An operation that resolves the potential conflict and contracts the two into a single well-formed qualia structure is thus called for. I call this operation COLLAPSE. I do not assume that COLLAPSE is an operation that has the same effects on all the instances of V-complex formation in general. Rather, I assume that COLLAPSE is simply an underspecified operation. The actual effects of COLLAPSE on the output representation vary depending on various factors such as the syntactic properties of the complex predicate, the functional projections involved, and the general aspectual properties of qualia structure.

Let us first consider a regular non-collapsing adjunction process. For two clauses CL_1, whose qualia structure is QS_1, and CL_2, whose qualia structure is QS_2, suppose CL_1 is adjoined to CL_2. The question is what happens to QS_1 and QS_2 when CL_1 is adjoined to CL_2. I simplistically assume that nothing drastic happens: QS_1 and QS_2 are simply juxtaposed in the semantic representation of the adjunction structure. I also tentatively assume that the representation of an adjunction structure has a single event structure and a single argument structure. Note that V-concatenation in Japanese generally does not allow a phrase to intervene between the two Vs (Matsumoto 1996; Miyagawa 1987). Thus the following examples are instances of simple adjunction constructions.

(20)   kare-wa   e-o   mi-te   ofisu-ni   ki-ta.
       hi-TOP   picture-ACC see-TE   office-DAT come-PAST
       'He saw the picture and then came to the office.'

(21)   kare-wa e-o   katui-de   ofisu-ni   ki-ta.
       hi-TOP   picture-ACC shoulder(verb)-TE office-DAT come-PAST
       'He shouldered the picture and then came to the office.'

Under the assumption that adjunction does not affect qualia structures, the GL representation of the matrix VP[3] in (20) would look like the following[4,5]:

(22)   ADJOINED:

$$
\begin{bmatrix}
\textbf{[e-o mi-te] ofisu-ni ku} \\
\textbf{'[picture-ACC see-TE] office-DAT come'} \\[4pt]
\text{EVENTSTR} = \begin{bmatrix} \boxed{4} \; {<}^o_\alpha \, \boxed{5} \\ e_2 \; {<}^o_\alpha \; e_3 \end{bmatrix} \\[12pt]
\text{ARGSTR} = \begin{bmatrix} \text{ARG1} = \boxed{1}\,[\ \textbf{human}\ ] \\ \text{ARG2} = \boxed{2} = \textbf{the\_picture} \\ \text{ARG3} = \boxed{3} = \textbf{the office} \end{bmatrix} \\[16pt]
\text{QUALIA1} = \boxed{4}\Big[\ \text{AGENTIVE} = \textbf{see}(e_1,\ \boxed{1},\ \boxed{2})\ \Big] \\[8pt]
\text{QUALIA2} = \boxed{5}\begin{bmatrix} \text{FORMAL} = \textbf{to\_at}(e_3,\ \boxed{1},\ \boxed{2}) \\ \text{AGENTIVE} = \textbf{move\_act}(e_2,\ \boxed{1}) \end{bmatrix}
\end{bmatrix}
$$

In the above, two qualia structures are simply juxtaposed, showing that this is an adjunction structure, with no unified qualia characteristics. The temporal relation between the two qualia structures is determined by the function of -*te*, which is a sequencer (Nakatani 2003a, 2004).

---

[3]Or *v*P. Throughout this paper, I do not make the distinction between *v*P and VP to simplify the discussions, and keep using VP even if *v*P may be theoretically more appropriate.

[4]Type specifications for event variables are omitted in order to make the representation shorter. This applies to the representations that follow.

[5]I tentatively assume that *ku* 'to come' and *ik* 'to go', which seem to show properties of both unaccusatives and unergatives, are "unheaded", with no event prominence specified. They do behave differently from strongly right-headed predicates like *moraw* 'to be given'.

Now let us eliminate the intervening dative phrase *ofisu-ni* 'to the office' so that
V_1-*te* can concatenate with V_2:

(23) kare-wa e-o   mi-te ki-ta.
      he-TOP   picture-ACC see-TE come-PAST
      'He saw the picture and came here.'
(24) kare-wa **nanimo** [mi-te ko]-**nakat**-ta.
      he-TOP **anything** [see-TE come]-**NEG**-PAST
      'He didn't see anything before he came here.'
(25) ?*kare-wa **nanimo** mi-te ofisu-ni   ko-**nakat**-ta.
      he-TOP   **anything** see-TE office-DAT come-**NEG**-PAST

Although the concatenation status of (23) is not clear from its translation, the
concatenation can be confirmed by the NPI licensing test (see (24) vs. (25)).
I assume that in a concatenated case, the two qualia structures like in (22) are
collapsed into one.

However, in an attempt to collapse the two qualia structures in (22), we find
a potential problem: there is a conflict between them. Specifically, there exists a
conflict between the two AGENTIVEs. From a more general perspective, we can
expect that such a conflict is generally more serious when two predicators of the
same syntactic category are concatenated; on the other hand, when two different
categories are concatenated, qualia structures may be easily collapsed: for example,
when a verb and a PP are concatenated, a clear division of labor is likely, in such
a way that the V contributes an AGENTIVE and the PP a FORMAL. The question is,
when there is a conflict between the two qualia structures that are being collapsed,
which is often the case when two Vs are collapsed, the conflict should be resolved
somehow.

In order to deal with this issue, we must consider the role of the conjunctive
morpheme -*te* in the V-*te* V predicate. I assume that the function of -*te* as a relative
past tense marker that sequences events affects the way COLLAPSE works in the V-*te*
V predicate. Because of this sequencing function, the event e_1 denoted by the V_1
projection is interpreted such that e_1 starts prior to the point the event e_2 denoted
by V_2 starts ($e_1 < e_2$ or $e_1 < e_2$). Having this in mind, let us consider the aspectual
properties of the qualia. According to Pustejovsky (1995), the qualia structure of
a linguistic entity x consists of four eventive roles: AGENTIVE (how x came into
being), FORMAL (what x is; extensional), TELIC (how x ends up; intensional), and
CONSTITUTIVE (what x is made of). Because it is not entirely clear what role
CONSTITUTIVE plays in predicative semantics, I exclude this from the discussion in

this paper, which is a tentative decision that needs closer examination. Our current goal is to figure out how two independent qualia structures can fit into a single qualia structure, in which there are three available slots, AGENTIVE, FORMAL, and TELIC. Note that TELIC introduces intensionality into the picture; this means that if the TELIC slot is used when collapsing two qualia structures into one, an extra semantic operation must be assumed, which brings in a considerable complication in the collapsing procedure. In fact, intentionality plays a significant role when considering the semantics of certain types of the V-*te* V predicate such as V-*te* i(−ru) and V-*te* hosi(−i). These cases are beyond the scope of the present paper, so I will focus on the cases in which only the AGENTIVE and FORMAL slots are utilized in collapsing two qualia structures.

Now, let us return to the question of how the function of -*te* as an event sequencer affects the procedure of collapsing two input qualia structures, assuming that the AGENTIVE and FORMAL slots in the output qualia structure are used. Let QL_1 be the qualia structure of V_1 and QL_2 be the qualia structure of V_2 in the V_1-*te* V_2 predicate. How QL_1 and QL_2 fit in a single qualia structure in which the AGENTIVE and FORMAL slots are available? As mentioned earlier, the FORMAL of x characterizes what x is, whereas the AGENTIVE of x characterizes how x came into being, by definition; therefore, temporally speaking, it follows that the AGENTIVE event never follows the FORMAL event. Considering that -*te* in the V_1-*te* V_2 predicate is an event sequencer, the denotation of V_1 would never temporally follows V_2. The conclusion drawn from this consideration is, the unmarked collapsing procedure in the V-*te* V predicate should be to put QL_1 in the AGENTIVE slot of the output qualia structure and QL_2 in the FORMAL slot. This is illustrated below:

(26)   ADJOINED: COLLAPSED:

$$
\begin{bmatrix}
[\mathbf{V_1\text{-}te}]\ \mathbf{V_2} \\
QL_1 = [\cdots] \\
QL_2 = [\cdots]
\end{bmatrix}
\rightarrow
\begin{bmatrix}
[\mathbf{V_1\text{-}te\text{-}V_2}] \\
QL = \begin{bmatrix} \text{FORMAL} = QL_1 \\ \text{AGENTIVE} = QL_2 \end{bmatrix}
\end{bmatrix}
$$

The representation of the V-*te* V predicate in (23), thus, should look like the following:

(27)   COLLAPSED:

$$
\begin{bmatrix}
\textbf{e-o [mi-te ku]} \quad \text{'picture-ACC [see-TE come]'} \\[4pt]
\text{EVENTSTR} =
\begin{bmatrix}
\mathbf{e_1}^* <_\alpha \boxed{1} \\
\mathbf{e_2} <\!o_\alpha \mathbf{e_3}
\end{bmatrix} \\[14pt]
\text{ARGSTR} =
\begin{bmatrix}
\text{ARG1} = \textbf{x:human} \\
\text{ARG2} = \textbf{y} = \textbf{the\_picture} \\
\text{D-ARG1} = \textbf{z: speaker-location}
\end{bmatrix} \\[20pt]
\text{QUALIA} =
\begin{bmatrix}
\text{FORMAL} = \boxed{1}
\begin{bmatrix}
\text{FORMAL} = \textbf{to\_at(e}_3\textbf{, x, z)} \\
\text{AGENTIVE} = \textbf{move\_act(e}_2\textbf{, x)}
\end{bmatrix} \\[14pt]
\text{AGENTIVE} = \textbf{see(e}_1\textbf{, x, y)}
\end{bmatrix}
\end{bmatrix}
$$

(17), repeated below as (28), is derived in the same manner.

(28)   Taroo-ga ofisu-ni   e-o   katui-de   ki-ta.
        Taro-NOM office-DAT picture-ACC shoulder-TE   come-PAST
        'Taro shouldered the picture all the way to the office.'

(29)   ADJOINED:

$$
\begin{bmatrix}
\textbf{ofisu-ni [e-o katui-de] ku} \\
\textbf{'office-DAT [picture-ACC shoulder-TE] come'} \\[4pt]
\text{EVENTSTR} =
\begin{bmatrix}
\boxed{5} <_\alpha \boxed{6} \\
\mathbf{e_1}^* <_\alpha \mathbf{e_2} \\
\mathbf{e_3} <_\alpha \mathbf{e_4}
\end{bmatrix} \\[18pt]
\text{ARGSTR} =
\begin{bmatrix}
\text{ARG1} = \boxed{1}[\ \textbf{human}\ ] \\
\text{ARG2} = \boxed{2} = \textbf{the\_picture} \\
\text{ARG3} = \boxed{3} = \textbf{the\_office} \\[10pt]
\text{D-ARG1} = \boxed{4}
\begin{bmatrix}
\textbf{body\_part} \\
\text{CONST} = \textbf{is\_shoulder\_of(e}_7\textbf{, } \boxed{4}\textbf{, } \boxed{1}\textbf{)} \\
\text{FORM} = \boxed{4}
\end{bmatrix}
\end{bmatrix} \\[20pt]
\text{QUALIA1} = \boxed{5}
\begin{bmatrix}
\text{FORMAL} = \textbf{on(e}_2\textbf{, } \boxed{2}\textbf{, } \boxed{4}\textbf{)} \\
\text{AGENTIVE} = \textbf{lift(e}_1\textbf{, } \boxed{1}\textbf{, } \boxed{2}\textbf{)}
\end{bmatrix} \\[14pt]
\text{QUALIA2} = \boxed{6}
\begin{bmatrix}
\text{FORMAL} = \textbf{to\_at(e}_4\textbf{, } \boxed{1}\textbf{, } \boxed{3}\textbf{)} \\
\text{AGENTIVE} = \textbf{move\_act(e}_3\textbf{, } \boxed{1}\textbf{)}
\end{bmatrix}
\end{bmatrix}
$$

(30)   COLLAPSED:

$$
\begin{bmatrix}
\textbf{ofisu-ni e-o [katui-de ku]} \\
\textbf{'office-DAT [picture-ACC shoulder-TE] come'} \\[2mm]
\text{EVENTSTR} = \begin{bmatrix}
\boxed{5} <_\alpha \boxed{6} \\
e_1{*} <_\alpha e_2 \\
e_3 <_\alpha e_4
\end{bmatrix} \\[6mm]
\text{ARGSTR} = \begin{bmatrix}
\text{ARG1} = \boxed{1}\,[\ \textbf{human}\ ] \\
\text{ARG2} = \boxed{2} = \textbf{the\_picture} \\
\text{ARG3} = \boxed{3} = \textbf{the\_office} \\[2mm]
\text{D-ARG1} = \boxed{4} \begin{bmatrix}
\textbf{body\_part} \\
\text{CONST} = \textbf{is\_shoulder\_of}(e_7, \boxed{4}, \boxed{1}) \\
\text{FORM} = \boxed{4}
\end{bmatrix}
\end{bmatrix} \\[10mm]
\text{QUALIA} = \begin{bmatrix}
\text{FORMAL} = \boxed{6} \begin{bmatrix}
\text{FORMAL} = \textbf{to\_at}(e_4, \boxed{1}, \boxed{3}) \\
\text{AGENTIVE} = \textbf{move\_act}(e_3, \boxed{1})
\end{bmatrix} \\[4mm]
\text{AGENTIVE} = \boxed{5} \begin{bmatrix}
\text{FORMAL} = \textbf{on}(e_2, \boxed{2}, \boxed{4}) \\
\text{AGENTIVE} = \textbf{lift}(e_1, \boxed{1}, \boxed{2})
\end{bmatrix}
\end{bmatrix}
\end{bmatrix}
$$

This roughly reads: $\boxed{1}$ lifts $\boxed{2}$ (='the picture') so that $\boxed{2}$ is on $\boxed{1}$'s shoulder and then $\boxed{1}$ moves to $\boxed{3}$ (='the office'). The only difference between (29) and (30) is whether the representation contains of one or two qualia structures. This difference may appear trivial at this point; in fact, it is native speakers' intuition that there is no great semantic effect of concatenation in this case. One detectable effect of concatenation is the possibility of NPI-licensing:

(31)   Taroo-ga   ofisu-ni   **nanimo**   [katui-de   ko]-**nakat**-ta.
        Taro-NOM   office-DAT **anything** [shoulder-TE come]-NEG-PAST
        'He came to the office without shouldering anything.'

(32)   ?*Taroo-ga [**nanimo**   katui-de]   ofisu-ni   ko-**nakat**-ta.
        Taro-TOP   [**anything**   shoulder-TE] office-DAT   come-NEG-PAST

This contrast can be explained in terms of the difference in the semantic representations: the qualia structures are unified in concatenated cases, making it possible for the negation attached to V_2 to license an NPI argument for V_1. However, this can also be accounted for in terms of the changes in syntactic structure

(McCawley and Momoi 1986; Miyagawa 1987). In the rest of the present paper, I will further examine the V-*te* V predicate and discuss the effects of concatenation that cannot be reduced to syntactic structural changes.

12.4.2   Principle of Causation Flow

Operation COLLAPSE by itself does not explain why a dative argument for V_2 sounds awkward in some cases depending on the semantics of V_1, as observed in (17–18) above, repeated below as (33–34).

(33)   Taroo-ga   ofisu-ni   e-o   katui-de   ki-ta.
       Taro-NOM office-DAT picture-ACC shoulder-TE come-PAST
       'Taro shouldered the picture all the way to the office.'
(34)   Taroo-ga   (??ofisu-ni)   e-o   mi-te ki-ta.
       Taro-NOM (??office-DAT) picture-ACC see-TE come-PAST
       'Taro saw the picture and came (??to the office).'

Let us first consider why (34) is bad with an overt dative. COLLAPSE generates a representation like the following:

(35)   COLLAPSED:

$$
\begin{bmatrix}
\text{\textbf{??ofisu-ni e-o [mi-te ku]}} \\
\text{\textbf{??'office-DAT picture-ACC [see-TE come]'}} \\[6pt]
\text{EVENTSTR} = \begin{bmatrix} e_1{}^* <_\propto \boxed{1} \\ e_2 <^o{}_\propto e_3 \end{bmatrix} \\[12pt]
\text{ARGSTR} = \begin{bmatrix} \text{ARG1} = \textbf{x:human} \\ \text{ARG2} = y = \textbf{the\_picture} \\ \text{ARG3} = z = \textbf{the\_office} \end{bmatrix} \\[18pt]
\text{QUALIA} = \begin{bmatrix} \text{FORMAL} = \boxed{1} \begin{bmatrix} \text{FORMAL} = \textbf{to\_at}(e_3, x, z) \\ \text{AGENTIVE} = \textbf{move\_act}(e_2, x) \end{bmatrix} \\ \text{AGENTIVE} = \textbf{see}(e_1, x, y) \end{bmatrix}
\end{bmatrix}
$$

Why does this representation lead to awkwardness? The only difference between acceptable (27) and awkward (35) is whether or not the goal location is specified. It should be noted that the issue is *not* whether the goal argument is *present*; it is always present in the semantic representation.

I assume that the awkwardness stems from a bad flow in the sequence of the matrix[6] AGENTIVE and FORMAL events: although the sequence of the event of x's seeing y and the event of x's coming to z is common in the real world, the sequence does not represent a most natural-sounding causal flow from the cognitive perspective. In a more natural-sounding flow, if the preceding event starts as x's acting on y, then the following event should depict what happens to y, rather than what happens to x. Such a principle is quite well known in the literature, and has been implicitly and explicitly formulated in various ways (e.g., Argument Coherence and Default Causative Paradigm (DCP) in Pustejovsky and Busa 1995 and Pustejovsky 1995; Direct Object Restriction in Levin and Rappaport Hovav 1995; etc.) The basic idea is stated below:

(36) PRINCIPLE OF CAUSATION FLOW (PCF) (preliminary version):
      If the causing event involves a patient, then the resulting event must
             specify the state of the patient, rather than the agent (i.e., Pustejovsky's
             DCP must be respected).

(37) DEFAULT CAUSATIVE PARADIGM (Pustejovsky 1995)
      a. DCP (direct causation):

$$\left[\text{QUALIA} = \begin{bmatrix} \text{FORMAL} = \alpha_{\text{result}}(e_2, y) \\ \text{AGENTIVE} = \alpha_{\text{act}}(e_1, x, y) \end{bmatrix} \right]$$

      b. DCP (indirect causation):
          (Where y consists of or constitutes w)

$$\left[\text{QUALIA} = \begin{bmatrix} \text{FORMAL} = \alpha_{\text{result}}(e_2, y) \\ \text{AGENTIVE} = \alpha_{\text{act}}(e_1, x, w) \end{bmatrix} \right]$$

Now the awkwardness of (34) with an overt dative argument is captured as the violation of PCF: it is awkward because the FORMAL specifies the result of the agent rather than the patient.

Then why is (34) acceptable without an overt dative? It should be noted that, as mentioned earlier, we cannot eliminate the goal argument for V_1 from the semantic representation even if it is absent in syntax, because the goal is always implied in *ku* 'to come'; thus, the meaning will change if *ku* 'to come' in the V-*te* V predicate

---

[6]I call the topmost qualia in the representation the matrix qualia.

is replaced with *ik* 'to go', even when no goal argument is syntactically present. Because of this, the qualia structure in (27) is essentially identical to the qualia in (35). This means that the qualia structure in (27) violates PCF just like (35). Still, the two yield different degrees of acceptability: (27) leads to perfect acceptability, while (35) yields awkwardness.

I assume that the reason why (27) sounds acceptable despite its apparent PCF violation is that in (27), the goal argument is syntactically hidden, which in turn makes the FORMAL quale less prominent, or *shadowed*. This is stated below[7]:

(38)   EVENT SHADOWING:

Event e_i in EVENTSTR is *shadowed* if

a. e_i is not headed (is a headless event); and
b. All the individual arguments of e_i that are syntactically overt are shared with the headed event e_j.

Returning now to (27), the FORMAL is not a headed event, while the AGENTIVE is. Although the FORMAL has one independent argument $\boxed{1}$ (=Goal) that is not shared with the headed AGENTIVE, this unshared independent argument is not syntactically realized. Therefore, the FORMAL in (27) is *shadowed*. I assume that if the FORMAL is shadowed, DCP (37) may not be strictly respected: by having either the cause event or the result event syntactically hidden, the constraint on the causal relationship becomes weaker. On the other hand, in (35), the FORMAL is not shadowed, because the goal argument of this FORMAL is syntactically represented as a dative argument *and* is not shared with the headed AGENTIVE quale. In such a case, both the AGENTIVE and the FORMAL are said to be *syntactically explicit*.

(39)   SYNTACTIC EXPLICITNESS:

Event *e* in EVENTSTR is *syntactically explicit* if *e* is not shadowed.

---

[7]It should be noted that the definitions of shadowing and headlessness in the present analysis is a little different from Pustejovsky's (1995). For Pustejovsky (1995: 191ff), "shadowed event" is essentially synonymous to "headless (un-headed) event", because by definition, a headless event has no syntactically overt argument other than the arguments shared with the headed event. This means that ditransitive verbs should be double-headed under Pustejovsky's (1995) framework. This in turn means that ditransitive verbs are neither left-headed or right-headed (because they are double-headed). However, in Japanese, ditransitive verbs may exhibit a left- vs. right-headedness dichotomy. The contrast between *kure/age* 'to give' and *moraw* 'to be given/obtain' is such a case: both are ditransitive verbs (licensing accusative and dative), yet the former should be left-headed (i.e., the giving event is the head), while the latter should be right-headed (i.e., the receiving event is the head). In order to capture the headedness contrast in ditransitive verbs, I believe that it is necessary to distinguish the concept of headlessness from the concept of event shadowing, so that a headless event may have a syntactically linked argument on its own.

Then PCF is redefined as follows:

(40) PRINCIPLE OF CAUSATION FLOW (PCF):

If the AGENTIVE and the FORMAL are both syntactically explicit, and
if the AGENTIVE involves a patient, then DCP must be respected.

Now the fact that the acceptability of (34) varies depending on the pres-
ence/absence of the syntactic dative argument for V_2 is accounted for: when the
dative argument in question is absent in syntax, the FORMAL will be shadowed,
making the qualia structure exempt from PCF.

12.4.3 Variable Shift

However, the combination of COLLAPSE and PCF wrongly predicts that an overt
goal argument is also unacceptable in (28), the semantic representation of which is
given in (30). (30) should be ruled out by PCF because (i) the matrix AGENTIVE
involves a patient $\boxed{2}$, (ii) both the matrix AGENTIVE and the matrix FORMAL are
syntactically explicit (each quale involves at least one syntactically overt argument
that is not shared by the other), and (iii) the matrix FORMAL does not represent the
effects on the patient in the matrix AGENTIVE (i.e., DCP is not respected). Contrary
to this prediction, (30) is perfectly acceptable, unlike (35).

Intuitively, there is one crucial difference between acceptable (30) and unacceptable (35): in the former, the theme ('the picture') accompanies the agent to the
goal, while there is no such implication in the latter. That is to say, it is possible
to pragmatically infer from (30) that the picture reaches the goal ('office') as
well. I assume that in such a case, a specific occurrence of $\boxed{1}$ (=the subject) in
the FORMAL in (30) can be *shifted* into $\boxed{2}$ (='the picture'). I call this operation
VARIABLE SHIFT.

(41) VARIABLE SHIFT:

A specific occurrence of variable x in a lexical representation *LR* can
be shifted to another variable y in *LR* if the outcome of the shift is
compatible with the pragmatic inference obtained from *LR*.

$\boxed{1}$ in the FORMAL in (30) can be shifted to y (='the picture'), because of the
"accompaniment" inference. Then the representation will look like the following:

(42)   V-SHIFTED:

$$
\begin{bmatrix}
\textbf{ofisu-ni e-o [katui-de ku]} \\
\text{'office-DAT picture-ACC [shoulder-TE come]'} \\[2mm]
\text{EVENTSTR} = \begin{bmatrix} \boxed{5} <_\alpha \boxed{6} \\ e_1{}^* <_\alpha e_2 \\ e_3 <_\alpha e_4 \end{bmatrix} \\[6mm]
\text{ARGSTR} = \begin{bmatrix}
\text{ARG1} = \boxed{1}[\ \textbf{human}\ ] \\
\text{ARG2} = \boxed{2} = \textbf{the\_picture} \\
\text{ARG3} = \boxed{3} = \textbf{the\_office} \\
\text{D-ARG1} = \boxed{4} \begin{bmatrix} \textbf{body\_part} \\ \text{CONST} = \textbf{is\_shoulder\_of}(e_7, \boxed{4}, \boxed{1}) \\ \text{FORM} = \boxed{4} \end{bmatrix}
\end{bmatrix} \\[10mm]
\text{QUALIA} = \begin{bmatrix}
\text{FORMAL} = \boxed{6} \begin{bmatrix} \text{FORMAL} = \textbf{to\_at}(e_4, \boxed{2}, \boxed{3}) \\ \text{AGENTIVE} = \textbf{move\_act}(e_3, \boxed{1}) \end{bmatrix} \\
\text{AGENTIVE} = \boxed{5} \begin{bmatrix} \text{FORMAL} = \textbf{on}(e_2, \boxed{2}, \boxed{4}) \\ \text{AGENTIVE} = \textbf{lift}(e_1, \boxed{1}, \boxed{2}) \end{bmatrix}
\end{bmatrix}
\end{bmatrix}
$$

(42) reads: $\boxed{1}$ lifts $\boxed{2}$ and put it on $\boxed{1}$'s shoulder; then $\boxed{1}$ moves and as a result, $\boxed{2}$ reaches $\boxed{3}$. Ultimately, this qualia structure specifies the effect on the patient, conforming to PCF.

12.4.4   Acceptable Violations of PCF

I have argued that syntactically explicit qualia must follow the prototypical causation schema in order to sound natural (PCF: PRINCIPLE OF CAUSATION FLOW). The reason for this stricter condition on syntactically explicit events is probably because (i) when two matrix qualia are syntactically explicit, an explicit logical relationship between the two is expected by the speaker/hearer, (ii) there is no overt logical marker bridging the two qualia because -te is a T, not a real conjunction, and therefore (iii) the default causative paradigm (DCP) must be respected to ensure the establishment of a logical relationship in the absence of a real conjunction. However, if there are other clues for the establishment of the connection between the two syntactically explicit qualia, such as discourse contextual support, then the prediction is that the violation of PCF can be circumvented. This actually seems to be the case. For example, the *mi-te ku* ('see-and-come') predicate may be acceptable with an overt dative if an appropriate contextual support is present: e.g., (43b) shown below sounds acceptable given a context like (43a)[8]:

(43) a. In the last class, students were asked by a teacher to look at paintings
      by Picasso, Van Gogh, and Cezanne at a museum, before they come
      to class today. However, Taro, one of the students, only looked at
      Picasso's.
   b. Taroo-wa kurasu-ni Pikaso-no   e-sika   mi-te
      Taro-TOP class-DAT Picasso-GEN picture-only$_{NPI}$ see-TE
      ko-nakat-ta.
      come-NEG-PAST
      'Taro came to class having looked at only Picasso's paintings.'

The qualia structure of (43b) violates PCF, which should thus leave the logical relationship between the matrix AGENTIVE (Taro's appreciating Picasso's painting) and the matrix FORMAL (Taro's coming to class) uninterpretable. However, with the contextual support given in (43a), the connection between the two matrix qualia is provided extralinguistically: it is known from the context that the students had been asked to look at several famous paintings before coming to class, probably because the paintings were going to be discussed in class; thus, it can be inferred that the AGENTIVE event (looking at paintings) should have a non-trivial effect on the FORMAL state (being in class). In other words, even though nothing physical is to be brought to the classroom, the result of the AGENTIVE must be metaphorically "brought" there. In such a case, PCF violation is permissible.

The contrast in the following pair is suggestive in the same way:

(44)   a. ?? boku-wa tyuusyazyoo-ni   nanimo tabe-te ika-nakat-ta.
         I-TOP   garage-DAT   anything eat-TE go-NEG-PAST
         (Intended: 'I went to the garage without eating anything.')
   b. boku-wa gakkoo-ni   nanimo   tabe-te ika-nakat-ta.
         I-TOP   school-DAT anything eat-TE go-NEG-PAST
         'I went to school without having eaten anything.'

These minimally different sentences both violate PCF, but (44b) sounds acceptable. The reason is that in (44b), it is easily imaginable what consequence having not eaten anything before going to school would lead to with regard to the state of being in school.[9]

---

[8]I am indebted to Susumu Kuno for bringing up this example.

[9]Interestingly, many of the awkward/unacceptable sentences due to PCF violation would sound good if the dative goal phrase were replaced with *gakkoo-ni* 'school-DAT' —probably because so many things can be interpreted as requirements when it comes to school.

On the other hand, when PCF is respected, no such contextual support is needed:

(45)   a. boku-wa tyuusyazyoo-ni nanimo katui-de   ika-nakat-ta.
           I-TOP   garage-DAT   anything shoulder-TE go-NEG-PAST
           'I went to the garage without shouldering anything.'
       b. boku-wa gakkoo-ni nanimo katui-de   ika-nakat-ta.
           I-TOP   school-DAT anything shoulder-TE go-NEG-PAST
           'I went to school without shouldering anything.'

The above two sentences are equally acceptable. The reason is that they represent a default causative paradigm (DCP) through VARIABLE SHIFT, conforming to PCF.

12.4.5 Theme Eventification

It is typical in the V-*te* V predicate that V_2 undergoes drastic semantic changes. For example:

(46)   Taroo-ga boku-ni tegami-o   okut-te   ki-ta.
         Taro-NOM I-DAT   letter-ACC send-TE come-PAST
         'Taro sent a letter to me and came here'
         or 'Taro sent a letter to me.'
(47)   Taroo-ga boku-ni   denwa-o   kake-te ki-ta.   (=15)
         Taro-NOM I-DAT   telephone-ACC use-TE come-PAST
         'Taro gave me a call and then came here.'
         or 'Taro gave me a call.'

These examples are ambiguous between the reading under which Taro physically moves towards the goal and the one under which Taro does not. In the latter reading, the sentences are almost synonymous to the following sentences, where no -*te ku* is attached:

(48)   Taroo-ga boku-ni tegami-o   okut-ta.
         Taro-NOM I-DAT   letter-ACC send-PAST
         'Taro sent a letter to me.'
(49)   Taroo-ga boku-ni denwa-o   kake-ta.
         Taro-NOM I-DAT   telephone-ACC use-past
         'Taro gave me a call.'

The difference between the second readings of (46)–(47) and the interpretations of (48)–(49) is subtle, but we could say that the former bear a sense of emphasis on the directionality of Taro's action: in other words, the former put a slightly more emphasis than the latter on the fact that Taro took the action toward the speaker. We can thus assume that what metaphorically "comes" toward the speaker-associated location in the second readings of (46)–(47) is Taro's activity of sending or calling. Some more examples:

(50)   sora-ga   kumot-te   ki-ta.
       sky-NOM get_cloudy-TE come-PAST
       'It was (is) getting cloudy. (*lit.* The sky is getting cloudy.)'

(51)   onaka-ga   sui-te   ki-ta.
       stomach-NOM get_empty-TE come-PAST
       'I am getting hungry. (*lit.* My stomach is getting empty.)'

Neither (50) nor (51) involves any physical movement of grammatical arguments (i.e., neither 'sky' or 'stomach' moves). What 'comes' toward the speaker-location is the state of the sky being cloudy or of the stomach being empty. I assume that such a lightening effect on V_2 is caused by a modification on the properties of V_2's arguments, especially on the theme argument: the semantics of V_2 seems to be lightened because its theme argument, which was originally a physical object, is changed into an eventive entity. I call such a semantic change THEME EVENTIFICATION. The present subsection discusses how this effect is formalized under the present framework.

Let us consider the semantic derivation of (47). Below is a simplified representation of the predicate in (47) after COLLAPSE is applied:

(52)   COLLAPSED:

$$
\begin{bmatrix}
\textbf{boku-ni denwa-o kake-te ku} \\
\textbf{'I-DAT telephone-ACC use-TE come'} \\[4pt]
\text{EVENTSTR} = \begin{bmatrix} \boxed{1}\,* <_{\propto} \boxed{2} \\ \cdots \end{bmatrix} \\[6pt]
\text{ARGSTR} = \begin{bmatrix} \text{ARG1} = \textbf{x:human} \\ \text{ARG2} = \textbf{y} = \textbf{telephone} \\ \text{ARG3} = \textbf{z} = \textbf{I} \\ \text{D-ARG1} = \textbf{w: speaker-location} \end{bmatrix} \\[10pt]
\text{QUALIA} = \begin{bmatrix} \text{FORMAL} = \boxed{2}\begin{bmatrix} \text{FORMAL} = \textbf{to\_at}(\textbf{e}_4, \textbf{v}, \textbf{w}) \\ \text{AGENTIVE} = \textbf{move\_act}(\textbf{e}_3, \textbf{v}) \end{bmatrix} \\[8pt] \text{AGENTIVE} = \boxed{1}\begin{bmatrix} \text{TELIC} = \textbf{reach}(\textbf{e}_2, \textbf{y}, \textbf{z}) \\ \text{AGENTIVE} = \textbf{use}(\textbf{e}_1, \textbf{x}, \textbf{y}) \end{bmatrix} \end{bmatrix}
\end{bmatrix}
$$

This represents the first reading: x uses y (telephone) so that y reaches z,[10] and then x comes to the speaker-location. For the second reading, I assume a special version of VARIABLE SHIFT as defined in the following[11]:

(53)   THEME EVENTIFICATION

    A specific occurrence of a theme variable in a non-headed (headless) quale
    may be replaced with the AGENTIVE event.

In the case of (52), the theme argument ($=x$ in the FORMAL) can be eventified. The outcome will then be like the following, where the eventified theme is underscored:

(54)   THEME EVENTIFIED:

$$
\begin{bmatrix}
\textbf{boku-ni denwa-o kake-te ku} \\
\textbf{'I-DAT telephone-ACC use-TE come'} \\[4pt]
\text{EVENTSTR} = \begin{bmatrix} \boxed{1}^* <_{\propto} \boxed{2} \\ \cdots \end{bmatrix} \\[10pt]
\text{ARGSTR} = \begin{bmatrix}
\text{ARG1} = \textbf{x:human} \\
\text{ARG2} = \textbf{y} = \textbf{telephone} \\
\text{ARG3} = \textbf{z} = \textbf{I} \\
\text{D-ARG1} = \textbf{v} = \boxed{1} \\
\text{D-ARG2} = \textbf{w: speaker-location}
\end{bmatrix} \\[10pt]
\text{QUALIA} = \begin{bmatrix}
\text{FORMAL} = \boxed{2} \begin{bmatrix} \text{FORMAL} = \textbf{to\_at}(e_4, \textbf{v}, \textbf{w}) \\ \text{AGENTIVE} = \textbf{move\_act}(e_3, \textbf{v}) \end{bmatrix} \\[8pt]
\text{AGENTIVE} = \boxed{1} \begin{bmatrix} \text{TELIC} = \textbf{reach}(e_2, \textbf{y}, \textbf{z}) \\ \text{AGENTIVE} = \textbf{use}(e_1, \textbf{x}, \textbf{y}) \end{bmatrix}
\end{bmatrix}
\end{bmatrix}
$$

This denotes an event that is initiated by the activity $\boxed{1}$ of x calling z, with $\boxed{1}$ directed towards the speaker location, which should somehow be associated with

---

[10]This is an oversimplification: what reaches z is a transmission from the telephone (i.e., a telephone call), not the telephone itself. Thus, strictly speaking, the representation of V_1 should involve a hidden argument, a transmission from y created by x's use of y. I did not include such a detail in (52) in order to keep the representation simple.

[11]The condition under which this special operation may be triggered is not clear at this point and will be left open.

z. By THEME EVENTIFICATION, the physical movement of *x* disappears, while the directionality of *x*'s action is emphasized.

In THEME EVENTIFICATION in the V-*te* V predicate, it is always the arguments of V_2, not the arguments of V_1, that are eventified. Although this is stipulated in the definition of THEME EVENTIFICATION given in (53), this may follow from various independent factors. I argue that the interaction between the syntactic structure and its semantic interpretation is one such factor. I assume that syntactic cycles play some role in mapping syntactic structures onto semantics (Nakatani 2003b; cf. Chomsky 1966, 1973, 1981, 2000, 2001). I do not go into the details of the theory of cyclicity, but for the present purpose, I loosely follow the traditional assumption on cyclicity that a cyclic domain is propositional in nature, like a clausal category. I assume that -*te* is a T (tense marker), and thus it (or *v* under T) introduces a clausal category: that is, V_1-*te* constitutes a clausal or semi-clausal category along with its arguments. Prior to the point when V_1-*te* is concatenated with V_2, V_1-*te* and its arguments are semantically interpreted as a fixed chunk because they constitute a syntactic cycle by themselves. Because of this derivational process, the interpretation of V_1 remains intact even after concatenation. After V_1-*te* and its arguments are attached to V_2, concatenation takes place, and the qualia structures are collapsed. Because the semantic interpretation of the V_1 projection has already been fixed, the operation COLLAPSE does not alter the semantic representation corresponding to the V_1 projection; semantic changes are made on the semantic representation of V_2. I conjecture that this is the reason why V_2 is light in the V-*te* V predicate, and also the reason why it is usually "higher verbs", not the lower verbs, that are auxiliarized in many languages.

The theory of THEME EVENTIFICATION straightforwardly accounts for the semantics of various instances of the V-*te* V predicate. An extensive discussion on this is beyond the scope of the present paper, so here I limit the discussion to the two verbs of putting, *ok* 'to put (onto)' and *simaw* 'to put away/stow (into)', both of which can trigger concatenation with V_1-*te*. When concatenated, they are semantically bleached, losing much of the original semantics. Thus, it is often difficult to find proper English translations of these predicates. For example, if we compare the base sentence (55) below with the versions to which *ok* and *simaw* are added ((56) and (57)), there is no eventive difference between the three examples. Traditional Japanese linguists have thus labeled these V_2s as aspectual auxiliary verbs or auxiliary verbs of "attitude" or "planning" (see Takahashi 1969).

(55)   Taroo-wa syukudai-o   yat-ta.
       Taro-TOP homework-ACC do-PAST
       'Taro did the homework

(56)   Taroo-wa syukudai-o   yat-te oi-ta.
       Taro-TOP homework-ACC do-TE put-PAST
       'Taro did the homework. (Emphasizing that Taro is ready for the next move; for example, Taro can now submit the finished homework anytime he is asked to do so.)'

(57)   Taroo-wa syukudai-o   yat-te simat-ta.
        Taro-TOP homework-ACC do-TE put_away-PAST
        'Taro did the homework. (Emphasizing the completion of the activity.)'

However, if we take a closer look at the original semantics of these V_2s, it is revealed that such subtle semantics clearly stem from the original main-verb semantics. *ok* 'to put (on)' as a main verb is for moving a thing into an open space so that the thing is accessible; on the other hand, *simaw* 'to put away' as a main verb is a verb of moving something into a closed place that is usually hard to access. For example, to describe the situation where one puts money on the table, *ok* should be used, and for the situation where one puts money into the safe, *simaw* should be used. In this sense, these verbs are semantically in complementary distribution. This is illustrated below, where the representational contrast between the two is highlighted by boxes[12]:

(58)

$$
\begin{bmatrix}
\textbf{ok} \quad \textbf{'put'} \\[4pt]
\text{EVENTSTR} = \begin{bmatrix} e_1{}^* \ <_{\circ}{}_{\propto} \ \boxed{2} \\ \textbf{...} \end{bmatrix} \\[10pt]
\text{ARGSTR} = \begin{bmatrix}
\text{ARG1} = \textbf{x:human} \\
\text{ARG2} = \textbf{y:phys\_obj} \\
\text{D-ARG1} = \boxed{1} \begin{bmatrix}
\text{ARGSTR} = \begin{bmatrix} \text{ARG1} = \boxed{1} \end{bmatrix} \\
\text{QUALIA} = \begin{bmatrix} \textbf{location} \\ \text{FORM} = \neg\textbf{enclosed}(\boxed{1}) \end{bmatrix}
\end{bmatrix}
\end{bmatrix} \\[14pt]
\text{QUALIA} = \begin{bmatrix}
\text{FORMAL} = \boxed{2} \begin{bmatrix} \text{FORM} = \textbf{to\_in}(e_3, \textbf{y}, \boxed{1}) \\ \text{AGENT} = \textbf{move}(e_2, \textbf{y}) \end{bmatrix} \\
\text{AGENTIVE} = \textbf{act\_on}(e_1, \textbf{x}, \textbf{y})
\end{bmatrix}
\end{bmatrix}
$$

---

[12]An anonymous reviewer pointed out to me that the contrast between *ok* and *simaw* might be better captured as the absence vs. the presence of the sense of removal. This certainly is a legitimate way of capturing the contrast, but we still cannot do away with the goal specifications. If one wants to *remove* the/a newspaper from a table, she can simply throw it away in a trashcan, but if one wants to *simaw* the newspaper, she cannot throw it away, nor can she put it on the floor: she must stow them into some secure place. Because the goal specification is lexically necessary anyway, and the sense of removal is probably pragmatically derivable from the goal specification, I conclude that the goal specification approach is better in characterizing the lexical semantics of the two verbs.

(59)

$$
\begin{bmatrix}
\textbf{simaw}\quad \textbf{'put away / stow'} \\[4pt]
\text{EVENTSTR} = \begin{bmatrix} e_1{}^* & <o_\propto & \boxed{2} \\ \cdots \end{bmatrix} \\[10pt]
\text{ARGSTR} = \begin{bmatrix}
\text{ARG1} = \textbf{x:human} \\
\text{ARG2} = \textbf{y:phys\_obj} \\
\text{D-ARG1} = \boxed{1}\begin{bmatrix}
\text{ARGSTR} = \begin{bmatrix} \text{ARG1} = \boxed{1} \end{bmatrix} \\
\text{QUALIA} = \begin{bmatrix} \textbf{location} \\ \text{FORM} = \textbf{enclosed}(\boxed{1}) \end{bmatrix}
\end{bmatrix}
\end{bmatrix} \\[10pt]
\text{QUALIA} = \begin{bmatrix}
\text{FORMAL} = \boxed{2}\begin{bmatrix} \text{FORM} = \textbf{to\_in}(e_3, y, \boxed{1}) \\ \text{AGENT} = \textbf{move}(e_2, y) \end{bmatrix} \\
\text{AGENTIVE} = \textbf{act\_on}(e_1, x, y)
\end{bmatrix}
\end{bmatrix}
$$

This crucial contrast between the two verbs remains intact when concatenated. The following representations, with the application of THEME EVENTIFICATION, illustrate this point (where the eventified theme is underscored and the representational contrast is hi-lighted by boxes):

(60)   COLLAPSED AND THEME EVENTIFIED:

$$
\begin{bmatrix}
\textbf{syukudai-o yat-te ok}\quad \textbf{'homework-ACC do-TE put'} \\[4pt]
\text{EVENTSTR} = \begin{bmatrix} e_1{}^* & <o_\propto & \boxed{2} \\ \cdots \end{bmatrix} \\[10pt]
\text{ARGSTR} = \begin{bmatrix}
\text{ARG1} = \textbf{x:human} \\
\text{ARG2} = \textbf{y:homework} \\
\underline{\text{D-ARG1} = z = e_1} \\
\text{D-ARG2} = \boxed{1}\begin{bmatrix}
\text{ARGSTR} = \begin{bmatrix} \text{ARG1} = \boxed{1} \end{bmatrix} \\
\text{QUALIA} = \begin{bmatrix} \textbf{location} \\ \text{FORM} = \neg\textbf{enclosed}(\boxed{1}) \end{bmatrix}
\end{bmatrix}
\end{bmatrix} \\[10pt]
\text{QUALIA} = \begin{bmatrix}
\text{FORMAL} = \boxed{2}\begin{bmatrix} \text{FORM} = \textbf{to\_in}(e_3, z, \boxed{1}) \\ \text{AGENT} = \textbf{act\_on}(e_2, x, z) \end{bmatrix} \\
\text{AGENTIVE} = \textbf{do}(e_1, x, y)
\end{bmatrix}
\end{bmatrix}
$$

(61)   COLLAPSED AND THEME EVENTIFIED:

$$
\left[
\begin{array}{l}
\textbf{syukudai-o yat-te simaw}\quad\text{'homework-ACC do-TE put\_away'}\\[4pt]
\text{EVENTSTR} = \left[\begin{array}{l} \underset{\cdots}{\underline{e}_1^{*}}\ \ <\!\!\circ_\alpha\ \boxed{2} \end{array}\right]\\[10pt]
\text{ARGSTR} = \left[\begin{array}{l}
\text{ARG1} = \textbf{x:human}\\
\text{ARG2} = \textbf{y:homework}\\
\underline{\text{D-ARG1} = \textbf{z} = \textbf{e}_1}\\
\text{D-ARG2} = \boxed{1}\ \left[\begin{array}{l}
\text{ARGSTR} = \left[\text{ARG1} = \boxed{1}\right]\\
\text{QUALIA} = \left[\begin{array}{l}\textbf{location}\\ \boxed{\text{FORM} = \textbf{enclosed}(\boxed{1})}\end{array}\right]
\end{array}\right]
\end{array}\right]\\[10pt]
\text{QUALIA} = \left[\begin{array}{l}
\text{FORMAL} = \boxed{2}\ \left[\begin{array}{l}\text{FORM} = \textbf{to\_in}(e_3, z, \boxed{1})\\ \text{AGENT} = \textbf{act\_on}(e_2, x, z)\end{array}\right]\\
\text{AGENTIVE} = \textbf{do}\,(e_1, x, y)
\end{array}\right]
\end{array}\right]
$$

(60) represents an event that is initiated by x's activity e_1 of doing the homework, the result[13] of which ends up being metaphorically placed in an open space, which is usually easy to access. This semantics eventually leads to the nuance of 'having the homework done so that it can be submitted anytime', because it is metaphorically put into an accessible place. On the other hand, (61) denotes an event that is initiated by x's activity e_1 of doing the homework, the result of which ends up being metaphorically placed into a closed space not easy to access. Because of this FORMAL component of the predicate ('y being in a closed, hard-to-access space'), the completion of the AGENTIVE event is emphasized, implying that the trouble (=homework) is gone and Taro does not have to worry about it any longer.

It is also worth noting that *simaw* in the V-*te simaw* predicate can yield a regretful nuance as well, if the AGENTIVE denotes an undesirable event. For example:

(62)   Taroo-wa kabin-o   wat-te   simat-ta.
        Taro-TOP vase-ACC break-TE put_away-PAST
        'Taro broke the vase (which is bad news).'

In (62), the event of Taro having broken the vase has gone into an inaccessible space, emphasizing that the event cannot be undone. Because breaking a vase does

---

[13]I assume that the "result" reading emerges through the function of -*te*, an event sequencer. More specifically, the sequential order $e_1 < e_2$ is determined by -*te*, and because of this, the interpretation of e_1 as an argument of e_2 is adjusted (by a mechanism that is not made explicit in the present proposal) so that it denotes the result state of e_1 rather than e_1 itself.

not sound like a desirable thing to do, (62) yields a regretful reading, unlike in (57). The present analysis straightforwardly predicts that if the completion of the AGENTIVE in the V-*te simaw* (put away) predicate is regarded as undesirable, the regretful nuance emerges, because it is not good that it cannot be undone; on the other hand, if the completion is regarded as desirable (as in (57)), the "emphasized completion" reading emerges, because it is good to not have to worry about the required task any longer. These two subtly different senses of V-*te simaw* are generated interactively with the semantics of VP_1. The first language learner does not have to "learn" these two senses, because the two readings are automatically generated. Such a sense generation phenomenon cannot be adequately explained (nor can it be adequately described) by a non-generative approach to the semantics of the V-*te* V predicate. Thus the above discussion should be considered strong evidence for a derivational, sense-generative theory such as the one explored in the present study.

12.5   Conclusion

In this paper, I have argued for the necessity of developing a generative theory that dynamically derives instances of the V-*te* V predicate from the original semantics of the two Vs and -*te*. I have proposed three semantic operations, COLLAPSE, VARIABLE SHIFT and THEME EVENTIFICATION, along with one constraint, the PRINCIPLE OF CAUSATION FLOW (PCF). I have shown that the proposal naturally accounts for the semantic interactions between V_1 and V_2 in the V-*te* V predicate. It should be noted that the current theory is not a production theory; it is a theory of linguistic knowledge.

It is not surprising if some or many of the frequently used V_2s are actually stored in the brain separately from their main verb versions, so that these items are easily retrievable. I conjecture that such a process of "lexical shortcut" plays an important role in acquiring a language and in making language processing and production effective. It should be emphasized that such an idea does not contradict the present proposal. The point made in the present paper is that even if the "Aux" V_2s are eventually stored as independent entries in the adult lexicon, a generative theory is still crucial in accounting for the proper acquisition of their syntax, semantics, and morphology.

References

Bamgbos•e, A. (1974). On serial verbs and verbal status. *Journal of West African Languages, 9,* 17–48.

Chomsky, N. (1966). *Topics in the theory of generative grammar.* The Hague: Mouton.

Chomsky, N. (1973). Conditions on transformations. In S. Anderson & P. Kiparsky (Eds.), *A festschrift for Morris Halle* (pp. 232–286). New York: Holt, Rinehart and Winston.

Chomsky, N. (1981). *Lectures on government and binding*. Dordrecht: Foris.

Chomsky, N. (2000). Minimalist inquiries: The framework. In R. Martin, D. Michaels, & J. Uriagereka (Eds.), *Step by step: Essays on minimalist syntax in honor of Howard Lasnik* (pp. 89–155). Cambridge, MA: MIT Press.

Chomsky, N. (2001). Derivation by phase. In M. Kenstowicz (Ed.), *Ken Hale: A life in language* (pp. 1–52). Cambridge, MA: MIT Press.

Ekundayo, S. A., & Akinnaso, F. N. (1983). Yoruba serial verb string commutability constraints. *Lingua, 60*, 115–133.

Kuno, S. (1973). *The structure of the Japanese language*. Cambridge, MA: MIT Press.

Levin, B., & Rappaport Hovav, M. (1995). *Unaccusativity: At the syntax-lexical semantics interface*. Cambridge, MA: MIT Press.

Martin, S. E. (1975). *A reference grammar of Japanese*. New Haven: Yale University Press.

Matsumoto, Y. (1996). *Complex predicates in Japanese: A syntactic and semantic study of the notion 'word'*. Stanford: CSLI Publications.

Matsuo, S. (1936). *Kokugohoo Ronkoo* [Considerations on Japanese Grammar]. Tokyo: Hakuteisha.

McCawley, J. D., & Momoi, K. (1986). The constituent of *-te* complements. *Papers in Japanese Linguistics, 11*, 1–60.

Miyagawa, S. (1987). Restructuring in Japanese. In T. Imai & M. Saito (Eds.), *Issues in Japanese linguistics* (pp. 273–300). Dordrecht: Foris.

Morita, Y. (1977). *Kiso Nihongo* [Basic Japanese]. Tokyo: Kadokawa.

Nakatani, K. (2003a). Analyzing *-te*. In W. McClure (Ed.), *Japanese/Korean linguistics 12* (pp. 377–387). Stanford: CSLI Publications.

Nakatani, K. (2003b). Cyclic interpretation in verbal complexes in Japanese, Harvard Working Papers in Linguistics Volume 9: Papers from the GSAS/Dudley House Workshop on Light Verbs, pp. 95–121.

Nakatani, K. (2004) *Predicate concatenation: A study of the V-te-V predicate in Japanese*. PhD thesis, Harvard, Cambridge, MA.

Ogihara, T. (1998). The ambiguity of the *Te Iru* form in Japanese. *Journal of East Asian Linguistics, 7*, 87–120.

Pustejovsky, J. (1995). *The generative lexicon*. Cambridge, MA: MIT Press.

Pustejovsky, J., & Busa, F. (1995). Unaccusativity and event composition. In P. M. Bertinetto, V. Bianchi, & J. Higginbotham (Eds.), *Temporal reference: Aspect and actionality, Vol. 1: Semantic and syntactic perspectives* (pp. 159–177). Torino: Rosenberg and Sellier.

Takahashi, T. (1969). *Sugata to mokuromi* [Aspect and Intention], Textbook for Kyooiku-Kagaku Kenkyuukai Bunpoo Kooza. (Reprinted in Kindaichi, 1976, pp. 117–153.)

Teramura, H. (1984). *Nihongo no Shintakusu to Imi, II* [The Syntax and Semantics of Japanese II]. Tokyo: Kurosio.

Yoshikawa, T. (1973). *Gendai nihongo no asupekuto no kenkyuu* [A Study of Aspect in Modern Japanese], *Linguistic Communications* (Monash University) 9. (Reprinted in Kindaichi, 1976, pages 117–153.)

Chapter 13
Change of Location and Change of State

Chungmin Lee

13.1 Introduction

This paper discusses possible parallels between change of location and change of state, involved in locomotive (=motion), change of state, and creation/removal verbs, examining cross-linguistic typological variation in lexical patterning and syntactic behaviors.[1]

Spatial uses of prepositions are closely connected with temporal uses, although the latter are more abstract and limited because of directionality and dimensionality (Bennett 1975).

Change of state (qualities) is structurally associated with change of location, with its Source and Goal. Change always means a shift from ≠P to P in state as well as in location in time. But the change of state (quality) is more abstract.

When change of state becomes psychological, it becomes even more abstract. As seen in build tension or its Korean (K) equivalent kincangkam-ul coseng-ha-ta, indirect constitutive causation changes to experienced (direct) causation and does not need any part of the object such as 'material' (from a default argument). This is 'derived unaccusativity' (Pustejovsky and Busa 1995). This allows for modification by the degree adverbial maywu 'very' in K. Imperfective paradox disappears because there is no telicity involved any more.

---

[1]I am most grateful to Pustejovsky for his comments on this paper, which appears at the end as Review. I also thank anonymous reviewers of the GL Workshop in Geneva for their comments and the participants for their questions and comments. I benefited from our project on Semantic Structures of Korean Predicates (from 1997 to 2000 with Beommo Kang and Seungho Nam). This was partially supported by the KRF 074-AM1534 grant and the NRF 100-20090049 grant.

C. Lee (✉)
Department of Linguistics, Seoul National University, Seoul, South Korea
e-mail: clee@snu.ac.kr

J. Pustejovsky et al. (eds.), *Advances in Generative Lexicon Theory*, Text, Speech and Language Technology 46, DOI 10.1007/978-94-007-5189-7_13, © Springer Science+Business Media Dordrecht 2013

13.2   Temporal Expressions

13.2.1   Typology of Motion Expressions

Typologically, in verb-framed languages (Talmy 2000) such as K/J, Hindi, Romance, Semitics, Bantu and Polynesian languages, an existential stative location post-/pre- position such as –ey (K), -ni (J), à (F), -meN (Hindi) is further used only for directed motion verbs but not for mannerVs (Lee 1999, 2006).

(1)   hakkyo-ey iss-ta/ka-ass-ta
      school-LOC be-DEC go-PAST-DEC
      '(She) is in/went to school.'

(2)   *hakkyo-ey(K)/gakko-ni(J) talli–ess-ta
                                 ran

(3)   *LaD.kaa kamre-meN dauD.aa (Hindi)
      boy –NOM room-LOC ran
      Lit. 'The boy ran in the room.' (in the sense of 'to') (Narasimhan 1998)

(4)   El hombre {ha corrido/corrió} hasta/*a la casa
      the man ran up to/*at the house
      Lit. 'The man ran up to/*at the house.' (in the sense of 'to')

In satellite-framed languages like English, a stative locative preposition in/at/on is separate from a Path (Goal) preposition to and to is applied to manner verbs such as run and walk in addition to basic directed motion verbs such as go and come but not arrive. In verb-framed languages, however, a correspondent such as –ey in K of the stative locative preposition basically functions as a stative and additionally is used as Goal postposition for directed motion verbs of go and come, the Goal-oriented achievement verb arrive and further for transitive motion verbs in (23).

13.2.2   Temporal Expressions Examined

Time expresses the orientation anterior and posterior by before and after (in K and J as well), as in spatial contexts. Events and periods/points of time metaphorically have a front and a back like objects in space. The front is the leading end/side (time moving past the stationary observer), or the side the observer first reaches (time stationary, with the observer moving through it). The other side is the back. Consider:

(5) Mary finished the book before she died/her death.
      [−V-ki **cen**-ey -]'before - V-'
(6) Mary died after she finished the book.
      [−V-un **twi**-ey -] '—after (in the back of) - V-'
(7) Mary died before she finished the book.
      [V-ki **cen**-ey —] '—before- V-'

Unlike in (5), before in (7) is counterfactive (Fillmore 1971) and licenses NPIs in various languages such as K, Greek and English (and J to a certain extent). The future is expressed by the location orientation of 'front' in K. The same period of time may be referred to by the coming months or the months ahead in English (Fillmore 1971).

The unidimensionality of time limits necessary temporal relation terms to a very small class, whereas space, being three-dimensional, shows the relation between two objects variously by over/above/under and at/to the right/left of in addition to at/on/in and in front of/behind. No zigzag Path is allowed for time.

13.3 Alternation Patterns Between Goal and Derived Theme

In case alternations in transitive motion verbs, a Goal expression changes to a derived Theme (C. Lee 1997) ('globally affected') as Incremental one (Dowty 1991) in quantization (Krifka 1998) and tends to exhibit change of state, as in (8), (10) and (12) below in English and in K. However, alternation patterns in English and in K/J are typologically different from each other. The class of verbs corresponding to such verbs as 'load,' 'pile,' and 'spray' are non- alternating in K/J, unlike in English, as (9), (11) & (13) show. Consider:

(8)   a. Yumi loaded hay onto **the truck** (for two hours/*in two
              hours/for a day/all day long).
      b. Yumi loaded **the truck** with hay (in an hour/?for an hour).
              (derived Theme) (change of state)
      c. Yumi loaded **two trucks** with hay in an hour.
      d. Yumi loaded **the truck** with two tons of hay.

(9)   a. Yumi-nun kkol -ul truck-ey   sil-ess-ta (K)/tsumi-kon-da (J)
              Y-TOP hay -ACC   -LOC *ni*-J load-PAST-DEC/load-insert
              'Yumi loaded hay onto the truck.'
      b. *Yumi-nun truck-ul   kkol-lo   sil-ess-ta (K)/tsumi-kon-da (J)
              Y-TOP truck-ACC hay-with loaded/load-insert-PAST
              Lit. 'Yumi loaded [K/J] the truck with hay.' INSTR *de* (J)

(10)   a. Yumi piled books on the table.
       b. Yumi piled the table with books.

(11)   a. Yumi-nun chayk-ul table-ey ssah-ass-ta (K)/tsumi-age-ta (J)
          Y-TOP book -ACC table-on pile -PAST-DEC/pile-raise-PAST
          'Yumi piled books on the table.'
       b. *Yumi-nun table-ul chayk-uro ssah-ass-ta (K)
          Lit. 'Yumi piled [K] the table with books.'

(12)   a. Yumi sprayed oil colors on the wall.
       b. Yumi sprayed the wall with oil colors.

(13)   a. Yumi-nun mulkkam-ul pyek-ey ppuri-ess-ta
          Y-TOP colors-ACC wall-on spray-PAST-DEC=(12a)
       b. *Yumi-nun pyek-ul mulkkam-uro ppuri-ess-ta
          'Yumi sprayed [K/J] the wall with oil colors.'

In the Goal PP (a) sentences, either the initial process event (e1) is headed (e1*) or the second state event is headed (e2*) and the durative adverbial 'for 2 h in (8a) can be ambiguous, modifying either the process or possibly the state, unlike in other typical accomplishments of creation such as *build a house*, of which the initial process subevent is headed. However, *all day long* can only modify the process in (8a). One way of treating the ambiguity in these verbs may be **underspecification of headedness**. Because the headed process interpretation is possible, this type is distinct from the achievement type, in which a headed process reading is impossible; **I-process** to be discussed is involved.

Although we do not perceive 'affected' or parts for the Goal *the truck* or the moving object Figure *hay* in (8a), we do perceive that the incremental objects in (8b,c,d) undergo certain change in their external parts and can say they are 'affected' (Lakoff 1970) as well as quantized. Therefore, we can possibly represent [*load the truck with hay*](*pile/spray* —) as a **change-of-state lcp** with FORMAL = (globally) **affected** (e2, <2>)(or Figure affecting Ground), AGENTIVE = (e1, **move_act** (e1, <1>, <3>, (<2>)). Typically consumption verbs involve the kind of internally 'affected' incremental Themes (cf. Tenny 1987; Dowty 1991) and those location change alternation verbs involve externally 'affected' derived Themes as their direct objects, not just positional variants. As in (8d), a backgrounded moving object *2 t of hay*, with the oblique Instr case, does not seem to contribute to the concept of 'affected,' although it very weakly retains quantization and contributes to quantizing *the truck* more specifically and blocking the durative adverbial modification (**for an hour* (for some), but other people judge it as ??*for an hour*). Here, 'quantized' is defined by proper part relation (Krifka 1998); we are concerned with the globally viewed external state of the truck in the object position. Note that *two trucks* in the object position in (8c) as a derived Theme is quantized but the same NP in the PP in (8a) as a Goal is not. In particular, consider the Figure of numeral measure expression in the PP:

(14)   ?*Mary loaded trucks with two tons of hay in an hour.

This is contrasted with Jackendoff's claim that 'the theme (our Figure) can *always* measure out the event, regardless of its syntactic position.' (14), above, is bad because *trucks* is not quantized, although the Figure in the PP has a numeral measure expression. If we say *Mary loaded 2 t of hay onto the truck in an hour*, the object *2 t of hay* (or *the hay*), differently from the indefinite nonspecific *hay* in (8a), has parts and is quantized but not 'affected.' Pustejovsky (1995) does not provide any mechanism to represent this quantization effect on Figure. If we put the durative adverbial *for an hour* instead of *in an hour*, then the imperfective reading of, say, doing it to pass time is hesitantly obtained. In Krifka's *The army crossed the river in an hour*, the subject *the army* may have relevant parts and be quantized but is not affected.

The verb class of 'paint,' 'smear,' 'stuff,' 'pack,' 'wrap' show alternation cross-linguistically, whereas the 'pour'-class in all languages (most concrete and dynamic with Pattern 1) are non-alternating (Lee et al. 1999; Kim et al. 1999). The Figure object such as 'paint' or 'butter' for the verbs moves to the Goal and if the Goal gains weight and is regarded as globally 'affected' it becomes a derived Theme (12b).

A very interesting kind of verb is 'fill' and its counterparts in K/J. A Figure/Ground case alternation typology must explain why the alternation in (15) in K/J is possible, unlike in adult English:

(15)   a. Yumi-nun swul-ul   pyeng-ey chay-wu-ess-ta (K)/mitasi-da (J)
           Y-TOP wine-ACC   bottle-in get full-CAUS-PAST-DEC
           Lit. 'Yumi filled wine **into** the bottle.' (impossible in adult English)
        b. Yumi-nun pyeng-ul mwul-lo chay-wu-ess-ta (K)/mitasi-da (J)
           Y-TOP bottle-ACC water-with get full-CAUS- PAST-DEC
           'Yumi filled the bottle with wine.'
        c. mwul-i   pyeng-ul   chay-wu-ess-ta
           water-NOM bottle-ACC filled
           'Water filled the bottle.'
        d. *pyeng-i mwul-ul chay-wu-ess-ta
           bottle-NOM water-ACC filled
           'The bottle filled water.'

In (15a) the process subevent regarding the Figure 'wine' wins, whereas in (15b) the result state subevent regarding the Ground or rather a derived Theme 'bottle' wins. We may be tempted to make use of the underspecification of headedness, somehow showing the 'globally affected' change of state, which is not entailed but (conventionally) implicated. However, the denotation of (**e2**) in (15a) is satisfied by the Figure's mere contact with the Ground, whereas the interpretation of (15b) requires the derived Theme's being 'globally affected.' This **change of state** may better be represented by **co-composition** of the verb with the artifact container Theme, e.g., for load in (8b), on the basis of the identical AGENTIVE quale. In spite of its motion process, 'fill' or chae-wu- seems to be more state-oriented. But in Thai, the verb term 'fill' has a non-alternating Ground PP pattern (Kim et al. 1999). It is heavily manner-oriented. It shows language- specific parameterization.

Lexically the verb is associated with full. In K, the verb chae-wu is the combination of the inchoative/unaccusative verb cha- 'become full' and the causative morpheme –wu- 'CAUSE.' As in (15d), the Container subject-ka(NOM) is a Theme in the <u>unaccusative</u> construction and it is <u>natural</u> for it to be an object in the causative pattern, not being able to surface as a subject in the causative pattern   of   (21) Pattern 4 below. Numerous transitive motion verbs in K belong to this type of chay-wu 'fill.'

Another type (B) of verbs such as tam-'put_into' allow for Case Patterns 1 and 4 but not 2 and 3.

(16)   Yumi-ka sakwa-lul pakwuni –ey
        Y-NOM apple-ACC basket-LOC
        tam-ass-ta (put-Past-Dec)
        'Yumi put apples into a basket.'

The Ground/container is overwhelming over the Figure for Type B, whereas <u>the Figure is overwhelming over the Ground for Type C</u> (and Type D). For each type, the following specifications hold:

(17)   a. Type B (*tam*- 'put (into)'): FORMAL = R' (e2, z, y)
        b. Type C (*chay-wu*- 'fill'): FORMAL = R (e2, y, z)

The R' of Type B verbs can be understood as something like "contain" or "have in." The R for Type C verbs can be viewed as "be/exist in/at/on," of which the essential minimal concept is 'contact.' This contact is realized as an endpoint of change of location involved in all the different types of verbs under discussion.

The final problem is the one regarding Case Pattern 2, [x-Nom y-Inst z-Acc]. This pattern is possible only for Types C and D verbs (*chay-wu*- 'fill') of Goal Thematization but not for Type B verbs (*tam*- 'put_into'). Here y (Figure) is assigned the case INST because it is conceptualized as being causally related to the agentive causation. However, the adult English verb *fill* cannot have case Pattern 1:

(18)   *Mary filled water into the bottle.
        (Reported to occur in child English, cf. Gropen, Pinker, et al. 1992)

The headed Goal is directly associated with the verb to become a derived Theme to show the change of state of the container with respect to Figure. This fact about the verb *fill* in English suggests that e1 (agentive process) has weight in child English just as in the manner-oriented verb *pour* and then it comes to lose its weight as the speaker grows up (Lee 1997).

English verbs such as *put* and *pour* behave like Type A verbs, *keep* and *store* like Type B verbs, and *fill* and *hit* like type C verbs, respectively.

But there are some interesting differences. For instance, the verb *load* in English shows Goal Thematization, showing Case Pattern 2, whereas its equivalent verb *sit-*

'load' in K does not. In consequence, the K verb *sit-* 'load' belongs to Type B, while the English verb may belong to Type C. Indeed, our classification can predict correct case alternation patterns. Consider:

(19)   *The truck loaded the hay.
       cf. Store-rooms store things and containers contain things.
          –type B [Pattern 4]

(20)   thurek-i   capcho-rul sil-ess-ta (loaded) (type B in Korean) [P4]
       truck-NOM hay-ACC
       Lit. 'The truck loaded the hay.'

This important difference shows that the English verb *load* gives weight to the agentive act of e1, whereas the K counterpart gives weight to the e2-related Goal, and the Goal (container) in K gets salient to become the subject of the same verb in an alternation (like *store* in English). In English, the Goal is Thematized, being globally affected. The so-called 'swarm' verbs show case alternations analogous to the alternation between Pattern 1 and Pattern 2 above both in English and K, unlike in Hindi, though Hindi shows other commonalities with K. Three different verbs are employed for 'float into' in Korean (*hule-tule-ka-* 'go by entering by flowing'). Therefore, it is striking to see the general alternation patterns in transitive motion Vs.[2]

Patterns of case alternations and types for transitive motion verbs in K can be summarized as:

(21)   Patterns of Case Alternations
       [Nom = N, Acc = A, Loc = L, Inst = I]
       P(attern) 1: x-ka[N] y-lul[A] z-ey[L] V
       P2:   x-ka[N] z-lul[L] y-lo[I] V
       P3:   y-ka[N] z-lul[A] V
       P4:   z-ka[N] y-lul[A] V

(22)   Types

	Type A noh-	Type B tam-	Type C chaywu-	Type D puthi-
P1	o	o	o	o
P2	x	x	o	o
P3	x	x	o	x/$^?$o
P4	x	$^{(?)}$o	x	x

---

[2]In V-framed languages like Korean, V + V verbal compounds like this rather than V + preposition expressions are used and categories *in* (containment) and *on* (support) are differently categorized and instead the verb *kki-ta* 'fit in tightly' for most of the two categories are acquired by 2-year-old Korean children, according to Choi (2003).

Instances of each type are:

(23)   Types of Verbs
        Type A: *neh*- 'put (into)', twu- 'put', noh-'put (on)', pus- 'pour', olmki-
               'move', ...
        Type B: *tam*- 'put (into)', sit- 'load (onto)', pokwanha- 'store',
               cecangha- 'store' ...
        Type C: *chaywu*- 'fill', machchhwu- 'hit', teph- 'cover', ssa- cover',
               mukk- 'tie', ...
        Type D: *puthi*- 'attach, paste', palu- 'paste', chilha- 'paint', sekk- 'mix', ..
                                                          (see Lee et al. 1999).

The transitive motion verbs in question can be decomposed as having two subevents (process and state) and three arguments (Agent, Figure and Ground) with the qualia already discussed (QUALIA = FORMAL = R(e2, y, z)).

The basic representation must be like it for Types A, C, and D but for Type B because of the relative saliency order between Goal and Figure, as in (20a), the FORMAL must be different, i.e., R'(e2, z, y). For the type of verbs that can have Goal Thematization both in K and English, we can consider applying the operation of co-composition of the basic verb with the affected direct object.

13.4   Enter/Exit Verbs and Unaccusativity

Path verbs of 'enter' and 'exit' in K/J, i.e., *tul-ta* and *na-ta* (K)/*hairu* and *deru* (J) show interesting developments. As pure Path verbs they hardly show any explicit motion/process meaning part in modern K but in J they are freely used in the Path reading, as in (26), whereas in modern K their use is very limited, although in Middle K they were freely used just as in J (Lee 2008, cf. Lim 2001). Consider:

(24)   Taro-ga heya-ni   hait-ta/de -ta
        T-NOM   room-at entered/exited
        'Taro entered/exited the room.'

This is impossible in K without deictic motion verbs *ka*- 'go' and *o*- 'come' attached. The verb *na*- 'exit' is not used in the Path interpretation at all and the use of *tul*- 'enter' is limited to contexts of entering a hotel/bed and its progressive use is disallowed, as in (25):

(25)   a. Inswu-ka   cumak/camcari-ey tul –ess-ta /*tul-ko iss-ta
           I-NOM hotel/bed   -at enter-PAST-DEC/enter-PROG-DEC
           'Inswu entered/*is entering/put up at a hotel/bed.'
        b. Yumi-ka puek-ul   tul-lak -na-l-lak-ha-n-ta
           Y-NOM kitchen-ACC keep entering and exiting
           'Yumi keeps going in and out of the kitchen.'

The simple verb *tul-* 'enter' in (25a) is still different from the complex form with the directed motion verb *tul –e ka-* 'enter-go' in that the former shows an event for the Goal enclosure nominal's telic quale, i.e., 'to stay' for a hotel and 'to sleep' for a bed, while the complex verb with 'go' just shows a physical motion and freely takes the progressive form, denoting motion explicitly. The verbs *tul-* and *na-* still maintain a physical motion interpretation only in frozen expressions of repetition in (25b) and *tu-na-tul-* 'go in and out often.' The verbs in frozen expressions can take the progressive form. In (25a), a durative adverbial modification such as *sahul tongan* 'for 3 days' is quite possible because the result state is salient in connection with TELIC of the Goal nominal. The event of 'entering a hotel' with the verb *tul-* in K is understood to be instantaneously achieved at a telic point. Then, the lexical semantic representation of the verb *tul-* 'enter' must have **e1: I-process** and **e2: state** but **e2** is headed and **e1** is not headed and is implicit. The verb's FORMAL role must show FORMAL = **be inside of** (e2, x, y). The complex verb with the directed motion verb *ka-*, i.e., *tul –e ka-* 'enter-go,' 'go into' may be represented by (co-)composing with that verb, with E1 headed. That is why the progressive becomes possible.

For the J *hairu* 'enter' and *deru* 'exit' pair, Kita (1999) argues that they lack semantic encoding of motion and therefore discrete change of state must be posited in the set of primitives in addition to motion and location in spatial semantics. But Tsujimura (2002) argues against Kita's claim that the pair of verbs lacks 'motion,' saying that they pattern with motion verbs in J. The controversy is rather natural because the motion part exists physically but not cognitively. Also in J, when the pair of verbs appear in the *-te iru* form, they are normally not associated with the progressive interpretation, as in (26), according to Kita, but they can give a progressive reading if they have a Source role and a time adverbial reinforcing the action-in-progress, as in (27), according to Tsujimura.

(26)   uma-ga   saku –no naka-ni hai -te iru[5]
       horse-NOM   fence-GEN inside-into enter
       'A horse has been in/*is entering the fence-enclosure.'

(27)   uma-ga ima umagoya-kara de -te   iru (–no o mitegoaran)
       horse-NOM now barn-from exit COMP   ACC   look
       '(Look at) the horse that is exiting from the barn right now'

In the K correspondents, neither (26) nor (27) is possible in its progressive reading. It is interesting to see that the J counterparts are still widely used in physically motional contexts, though their progressive is extremely limited. In both languages, they are combined (co-composed) with the deictic directed motion verbs *ka-* 'go' and *o-* 'come' to be freely associated with the progressive form. Therefore, these verbs, without directed motion verbs attached, are felt to denote the change of 'outside' state to 'inside' state or vice versa. The two opposite states may be felt to be discrete. Location change develops into state

change, still maintaining the flavor of the former. I see this as <u>unaccusativization.
When they become completely unaccusative, they denote abstract change of state
productively.</u> On the other hand, they can take a causative morpheme to produce
causative transitive verbs both in K and J.

We can notice a similar unaccusativity tendency in verbs such as *ttu-* 'float,'
oru- 'rise,' *nayri-* 'fall, get down,' *huru-* 'flow,' (and *sos-* 'soar,' *ci-*'set,' 'fall') and
they have causative counterparts with causative morphemes (*nayri-* having the same
form). In the case of *ttu-* 'float,' there seems to be a slight upward motion because
of buoyancy but that part may or may not be linguistically encoded and we can
represent its event structure simply as **e1: = state**. Its stage-level is expressed by
the resultative form *ttu-e iss-* 'is floating.' We feel less motion Path in the manner
verb *ttu-* 'float,' exhibiting no exertion of force (or being out of control), than in the
verbs *oru-* 'rise,' *nayri-* 'fall, get down.' There are subtly different degrees of motion
perceived but the latter two also show more explicit motion when composed with
directed motion verbs of 'go' and 'come.' Therefore, I propose that we distinguish
the two different types of processes or initial events:

$E1 = \textbf{e1:I}(\text{mplicit})\text{-}\textbf{Process}$ and
$E1 = \textbf{e1:E}(\text{xplicit})\text{-}\textbf{process}$.

Then, **e1:I-process** applies to those verbs of unaccusative/achievement type such
as *tul-* 'enter' and *na-* 'exit' and other verbs that behave similarly. This uniformly
explains why achievements are rather incompatible with progressive. Pustejovsky's
headedness differentiation is not sufficient because of transitive motion Vs we dealt
with.

More contexts of their use are <u>abstract</u> unaccusative verbs. They must co-occur
with deictic motion verbs *ka-* 'go' and *o-* 'come' to be used freely in the physical
motional Path interpretation in K and J. Because of the near lack of process sense,
they came to be extended and used for abstract change of state rather easily and
productively. Observe:

(28)   a. Yumi-nun chel-i   tul-ess-ta
           Y –TOP sense-NOM entered
           'Yumi became sensible'
        b. Yumi-ka cengshin-i na-ss-ta vs. na-ka-ss-ta
           Y –NOM spirit-NOM exited vs.   out-went
           'Yumi became sober' vs. 'got crazy'
        c. na-nun Yumi-ka maum-ey tu-n-ta
           I-TOP Y-NOM heart-at   enter
           'I am satisfied (happy) with Yumi.'

Mental state changes are expressed by (28a,b) and a psychological state by (28c).
These new meanings are generated by co-composition of the verb with mental or
psychological nominals, constituting an **I-process.state-lcp**. The formal quale of
the second argument of (28) must be **mental/psychological** or **abstract**. In (28a),
the Experiencer Topic (the original Goal) undergoes the change or process of mental

state from being not sensible to being sensible. The co-composed predicate *chel-i tul-* 'become sensible' is a result-salient one as an individual-level predicate and the past form in this case entails the present relevance. In contrast, *cengshin-i na-* 'become sober' in (28b) is a stage-level predicate. Here, *na-* means 'come out,' 'come into being,' 'be generated' but *na-ka-* with its motion verb *ka-*'go' means 'go out of.' Therefore, when the former combines with *cengshin* 'spirit,' 'mind' it means 'become sober instantly' but when the latter combines with the mental nominal it means 'go crazy.' In (28c), because of the psychological nominal *maum* 'heart' the composed predicate becomes a pure psychological predicate, being subject to subjectivity constraint (permitting only the first person Experiencer in the present form). Here, *maum* is the Experiencer's and it retains the original Loc/Goal marker *ey-* 'in,' 'at.' This composed predicate is largely a stage-level one.

Therefore, we can posit an implicit or void initial event (e1) and a result state event (e2) with the head on the second event for the pair of verbs *tul-* and *na-* (K)/*hairu* and *deru* (J) and other similar unaccusative verbs to block the progressive.

Various psychologically extended uses of motion verbs are witnessed in K. They show an ambivalent behavior in case realization between the original (Goal) Dative case (29a) and the new Stimulus NOM case (29b), which co-occurs with psychological verbs, constituting derived psychological verbs. Observe:

(29) a. na –nun Yumi –eke maum-i kkul-i-n-ta/ka-n-ta
       I-TOP   Y   -to   mind –NOM attract-PASS-PRES-DEC/go
      b. na –nun Yumi –ka maum-i   kkul-i-n-ta/ka-n-ta
       I-TOP   -NOM mind -NOM attract-PASS-PRES-DEC/go
       'I am attracted by Yumi.'

13.5 Relation to Change of State

13.5.1 Parallels

Change of state parallels change of location to a certain degree. They are represented similarly. Consider:

(30) a. Two pages yellowed.
      b. 'Going TO' a state of being yellow (Jackendoff 1983)
         or [x BECOME [x BE AT –STATE]].
                        (Generative Semantics and Levin and Hovav 1991).

Change of state can be ['GO/COME (=MOVE) TO' a state] in general. It is a change or moving from a state of being not yellow to a state of being yellow. All kinds of change of state can be conceptualized this way. The only difference is that some **abstract (metaphorical) motion** is involved in change of state, with little exertion of force felt. In English, a satellite-framed language, Path particles get abstract (Talmy 2000), their correspondents being verbs in verb-framed languages (31).

(31)   a. The ball rolled in [Path]
                cf. (kule) ture-o- '(roll)-enter-come'
        b. They talked on [Aspect]
                cf. kyeysok-ha- 'continue'
        c. The candle blew out. [state change]
                cf. kkeci 'get extinguished'

When associated with the intransitive verb 'change,' the target Goal is expressed by –*uro* 'toward' in K, whereas it is expressed by –*ni* 'at,' 'to' in J. It is telic in both languages, although –*uro* 'toward' itself in K is originally directional and atelic; it changes to telic when it co-occurs with final-state salient verbs by the telicity strength (weight) of the verbs or by conventional implicature based on the verbs.

(32)   mul-i erum-uro pyen-hay-ss-ta
        water-NOM ice-to(ward) changed

(33)   mizu-ga koori-ni kawat-ta
        water-NOM ice -at   changed
        (32–33) 'Water changed to ice.'

The change involved in (32) and (33) may be gradual but telic and can be modified by a time span adverbial ($---$-*man-ey* 'in'). The change has the abstract (state) Source of 'being water' (not ice) and the abstract (state) Goal of 'being ice' and the stative Goal marker –*ni* 'at' indeed shows up in J (33). When the directional marker –*uro* 'toward' is attached to the virtual Goal nominal in K (32), the abstract Goal interpretation of it is conventionally unmistakable with those verbs like *pyen-ha-* 'change' and its causative *pyenhwa-shikhi-* 'change (Vt).' There are several motion verbs that take -*uro* 'toward' to virtually denote Goal, unlike in J, where –*ni* 'at' is regularly used.

Accomplishments such as *build a house* and *write a letter* have endpoints of events, i.e., the complete house and the end of a letter. Now let us see how telicity is defined.

(34)   A predicate *P* is *quantized* iff no entity that is *P* can be a subpart of another
        entity that is *P* (see Krifka 1998) (Kennedy 2002)

(35)   An event description *R* is *telic* iff it applies to events *e* such that all parts of
        e that fall under *R* are initial and final parts of *e* (see Krifka 1998)
        (Kennedy 2002)

Kennedy (2002) argues that certain degree achievements such as *lengthen the icicle for an hour* cannot be solved with (35) because an atelic reading is possible even when the object argument is quantized. Thus, he proposes that the aspectual behavior of these verbs can be explained in terms of underlying scalar properties of

the source verbs, particularly, the structure of "degree of change," *d*. He posits a
degree "increase" function for both positive (such as *long*) and negative (such as
short), having open-scale and closed-scale for respective default atelic and telic
interpretations for deadjectival Vs.

Krifka (1998) uses the notion of **movement in space** for change of state
representation. The state of $\neq P$ is the Source and a telic degree the Goal.

(36)   Mary baked the lobster till half done (in an hour/*for an hour).
        λeEz [BAKE(M. L, z, e) $^\wedge$ SOURCE(z, RAW, e) $^\wedge$ GOAL(z,
            HALF DONE, e)]

Here *till* is a Goal marker and the Source state of the lobster's being RAW is
presupposed. Degrees are proportional for telic events up to *complete*.

K and J, as numeral classifier languages, express quantization in terms of numeral
classifiers. Otherwise their nominals remain underspecified, unlike in English. The
quantization of Figure object for motion also needs elaboration.

13.6 Metonymic Variation in Change/Creation and Polysemy

Creation verbs involve a (change of state) process subevent and a created artifact as
their objects. Typical creation verbs are verbs such as *mantul-* 'make' and *cis-* 'build
or construct.' These verbs take only resulting entities (artifacts) and not material
objects as their direct arguments. In contrast, there are a great deal of creation verbs
that come from change of state verbs, showing polysemy between change of state
and creation, exhibiting Material/Product alternation. Verbs such as *kwup-* 'bake,'
kkulh-i- 'boil', *thuyki-* 'fry', *el-li-* 'freeze' form the first class of such polysemous
verbs, which can take either artifacts or raw material objects as direct arguments and
thus can be interpreted in two ways (37).

(37)   a. Mary-ka (han sikan -tongan) muwl -ul kkulh-i -ess -ta.
           M-NOM (one hour for)   water-ACC boil-CAUS-PAST -DEC
           'Mary boiled water (for one hour).' (change of state)
        b. Mary-ka (han sikan -maney) miyek-uro kuk -ul kkulh-i -ess -ta.
           'Mary made/cooked soup with seaweed (in an hour).' (creation)
           cf. *simmer* (not *boil*) stew

(38)   a. o   -yu   -o   wakasu (J)
           HON-hot water-ACC   boil
           'make hot-water'
        b. ?*mizu-o   wakasu
           water-ACC boil
           'boil water'(Intended)
           cf. mizu-o futoo-saseru 'boil water'

Verbs of the second class such as *chari-* 'set,' *tha-* 'mix,' *kakkwu-* 'grow,' *kkwuri-* 'and *ssah-* 'pile' behave like *kkulh-i-* 'boil', though with a heavier manner sense involving some sense of motion. Unlike their counterparts in English, these verbs in K show Figure = Material/Product alternation.

The third set of verbs *kkakk-* 'cut,' *pic-* 'shape (dough)' *mal-* 'roll (into),' *kko-* 'twist,' *yekk-* 'weave' can apply alternatively to the Material object or the Product object. The Product object generates the creation reading. They behave like the English *carve* (Levin and Rappaport 1993a), even though the K verb *kkakk-* 'carve' with the Material object does not show the resultative Product part *into a toy* in one sentence (see Lee and Kim 2000). The co-composed predicate forms a **creation-lcp** with its formal quale becoming [**exist**(e2, y(artifact)), with an Agent argument and the backgrounded Default Arg1 = z [**material**, formal = **mass**], which in turn is linked to the constitutive = z of arg2 = y. Our case structure = case frame1 = x_-*ka*(NOM)_ z_-*ro*(INST)_y_-*rul*(ACC). Another group consists of *ttulh-* 'bore' and *pha-* 'dig.' Unlike *bore* in English, *ttuwlh-* 'bore' can also take either a Location argument or an artifact such as 'hole' as its direct object. If *ttulh-* is composed with an artifact, of which the predicate is like (*pyek-ey*) *kumeng-ul ttwulh-ess-ta* Lit. 'bored a hole (in the wall),' it constitutes a creation-lcp. The relationship between the two internal arguments (artifact *kumeng* and Location *pyek*) is not PART-OF, differently from that in *kkulhi-*. Rather the Location seems to contain the artifact. Therefore, we can encode this semantic relation in FORMAL, not in CONST of the artifact nominal. The default argument for this class interpreted as a kind of container of the artifact is syntactically realized as a Loc –*ey* argument instead of an Instr –*uro* (not manageable). If the verb *ttwulh-* 'bore' takes a Location object, its event may be a process. This is clearer with the verb *pha-* 'dig'; the event is a process when the object is a Location (Ground) and is a creation when the object is a functional entity such as a 'well.' An aspectual shift is necessitated by polysemous creation verbs in K. The shift is proposed to be done by means of co-composition of verbs with their associated result artifact nominals or 'effected objects' (Levin 1993). All the creation verb polysemy occurs when the resultant Product/artifact completed via motion/process is directly employed as Theme metonymically.

Despite variation in argument realization, all kinds of atypical creation verbs taking an artifact nominal as an object via metonymy share a semantic property of accomplishment event structure, which is characteristic of typical creation verbs.

It is also interesting to investigate what kinds of substantive nominals the general action verb 'do' (*ha-* in K and *suru* in J) in various languages can take for what kinds of predicate meanings. (see Im and Lee 2012 in this volume and Lee and Im 2001). Artifact/functional nominals are permissible as objects and natural kind nominals are blocked from combination.

13.7 Removal

Let us turn to locative removal verbs. This class of verbs shows the characteristics of the salient encoding of the non-presence of the Figure involved at the Source from which it moved. The removal verb *chiu-* 'remove, clear' shows the Figure object and the Source Ground/Theme object alternation. Consider:

(39)   Yumi-ka cepsi-rul table-eyse (thong-uro) chiwu-ess-ta (katazuke-ta)
       Y-NOM dish-ACC -from basket-toward remove-PAST-DEC
       'Yumi removed dishes from the table (into the basket).'

(40)   Yumi-ka table-ul (*cepsi- ro/(???cepsi-rul) chiwu-ess-ta
       Y-NOM dish-ACC dish-ACC/INSTR clean-PAST-DEC
       'Yumi cleared the table.'

(41)   a. ttal –ul   chiwu-ess-ta (J. musume-o katazuke-ta)
          daughter-ACC clear-PAST-DEC
          'got rid of (married) the daughter.'
       b. *cip-ul   chiwu-ess-ta (K)
          *ie-o   katazuke-ta (J)
          house-ACC cleared
          'cleared the house' in the marrying interpretation

When the removal verb has its spatial interpretation, the Source and the directive can occur, as in (39). However, if the Source is Thematized (being affected) and becomes the object, as in (40), the Figure argument cannot co-occur with it. In English the Figure can be realized as *of dishes*. Moreover, there are clearer cases of argument reduction, e.g., an abstract metaphorical instance of removal, as shown in (41); the Source cannot appear (41a) and cannot function as the object (no Thematization). The Ground/Theme object cannot co-occur with the Figure expression and as the meaning becomes more abstract the number of arguments decreases in general (Lee 1993). The change of location interpretation changes to its change of state interpretation, becoming more abstract; state is property. In this line of thinking, <u>Thematization can be viewed as one kind of abstraction</u>, causing limited syntactic behavior. Including other locative removal verbs such as *chiwu-* 'clear,' verbs like *eps-ay-* 'cause become not existent' tend to lean toward change of state, showing no Goal and often no Source expressed. This type tends to be more abstract. Naturally, when Source Thematization occurs it involves change of state (may not be internal quality change). By the process the result such that the Figure (in Vi/Vt) is not at the Source or $\neq P$ becomes salient. This is in contrast with Goal-oriented motion (change of location) verbs in which the result such that the Figure is at the Goal or the shifted P is salient.

A crucial point about the removal type of verbs is that the non-presence of the Figure at the Source is salient and therefore this type tends to be negatively oriented, as witnessed in *ciwu-ta* 'erase' and *turn off* or its equivalent *kku-ta* in K. These verbs involve both process and negatively oriented state change and behave as weakly (implicature canceling) negative (though not downward-entailing) predicates (Joe and Lee 2002) and even tend to license weak NPIs. When they become psychological, they get more abstract and limited syntactically, as seen by *kiek-eyse yengyeng ciwu-ta* 'erase from memory ever,' *maum-ul yengyeng kku-ta* 'turn off the mind ever.'

13.8 Degree Modification

Change of state, involved in all atelic and telic events, can have degree/scale representation theoretically in some respect (cf. Kennedy 2002) In E, only gradable adjectives with "nontrivial standards" are modified by *very*. But different languages show different ranges of modification by a degree adverb corresponding to 'very,' i.e., *maywu* (K) and *totemo* (J). In K it modifies gradable adjectives, a wide range of intransitive verbs of emission (47), psychological state change and change of state (49) and certain transitive verbs of similar nature. The range is far more extensive than in J (cf. Tsujimura 2001). 'Partial' (existential) predicates such as *dirty, fill, wet, different* (Yoon 1996) can be modified by *maywu* 'very' in their change of state (de-adjectival) verbal forms in K (48). Observe:

(42)   a. pyel-i maywu pitna-n-ta/panccak-i-n-ta
        star- NOM very shine/twinkle
        Lit. 'Stars shined very.'

       b. hosi-ga totemo hika-t-ta (*hika-te iru*)
        star –NOM very shine   (J)
        Lit. 'The star very shined.' (Tsujimura 2001)

(43)   a. swugen-i   maewu cec-ess-ta
        towel -NOM very get wet-PAST-DEC
        Lit. 'The clothes got-wet very.'

       b. [wet: $\lambda x \exists y [y \subseteq x \wedge \text{WET}(y)]$ ($\subseteq$ denotes part relation)]

(44)   maywu nol-ass-ta/kekceng-hay-ssta/hwanyeng-hay-ss-ta
       very got surprised/worried//welcomed

(45)   nay cheycwung-i   maywu nur-ess-ta/cwur-ess-ta
       my weight -NOM very increased/decreased
       Lit. 'My weight very increased/decreased.'

(46)   ?maywu ttam-ul   huli-n-ta (K)
       very   sweat-ACC make-flow
       '(She) is sweating a lot'

(47)   maywu kincangkam-ul   coseng-ha-n-ta
       very   tension   -ACC build –do-PRES-DEC
       Lit. '(She) is very building tension.'

Regarding (47), if *Yumi's presence is building tension* then *Yumi's presence has built tension* – no imperfective paradox.

Partial predicates (a class not identified by Kennedy) are optimally modified by 'very' over total predicates such as *clean, close, empty, dry* and *same* also in their adjectival forms in K. Such expressions with partial predicates as *not entirely sick* are bad. Observe:

(48)   a. i kes -kwa ce- kes-un maywu   taru-ta
          this thing and that-TOP very diff't-DEC
          'This and that are very different.'
       b. ??i kes -kwa ce- kes-un maywu kath-ta
          this thing-and that-TOP very same-D
          'This and that are very same.'

Although 'same' is stative, because of the comparison sense involved there occurs a sense of reaching the terminal or complete point of sameness and the degree modification is infelicitous. On the other hand, if we replace *maywu* 'very' by *keuy* 'almost' in (48), then the situation changes: (a) becomes unacceptable and (b) becomes quite all right. 'Almost' requires a telic aspect and 'same' involves something like a telic interpretation (as in 'become the same') just like 'dead' in English (as in 'die'). Because of this, 'very dead' is bad. For telic verbs of achievement and accomplishment in various languages, degree modification is hardly possible, although changed result state expressions (with *–te iru* in J for instance) may barely be modified by degree adverbs. All the adjectives such as *taru-* 'different' become intransitive verbs when an inchoative suffix morpheme *-e–ci-ta* is attached and these de-adjectival verbs can also be modified by the degree adverb *maywu* 'very.' Attitudinally (in evaluation) negative state/event is modified by a sort of NPI-like *yeng* 'impossibly' (as in **yeng**theli-ess-e 'It got wrong irrevocably') and negative removal by the NPI *yengyeng* '(for)ever' (as in **yengyeng**saraci-ess-ta 'disappeared forever').

In contrast, telic events of (creation) accomplishment, in which process is headed, and activity, the process (rather than state) is modified by *well* and its equivalent *cal*, as in *well-built* and *cal cie-ci-n* 'well-built.'

13.9 Interface with Syntactic Position

In K and probably in J as well, locative/dative inversion occurs with existential
and other unaccusative verbs and this tendency is also witnessed in English. The
locative/dative in its original position has a more physical interpretation (location)
than in its inverted order (possession, etc.). Observe:

(49)   She signed the letter at the end. [spatial/locational]
(50)   At the end, she signed the letter. [temporal]

(51)   engine-i   i cha-ey   iss   -ta
        -NOM this car on   exist –DEC
        'The engine is in this car.'   [locational]

(52)   i cha-ey engine-i iss-ta [whole-part]
        this car-on engine-NOM exist-DEC
        'This car has an engine.'

Inverted elements are familiar and topical. They are 'greater' than the rest in the
abstract sense of the term. This kind of construction is pervasive in K and is similar
to existential *there* and locative inversion constructions in English in the sense that
some familiar stuff is inverted but is different in that the latter is normally for stage-
level unaccusative(–like) verbs. The English existential construction is similar to
the Chinese existential construction in (53):

(53)   chu -li   you ni de   yaoshi   (Tham 2002)
        cupboard-in   were you POSS keys
        'In the cupboard were your keys.'

We have tried to see parallels or relations between location change and state
change in languages including K/J, revealing significant cross-linguistic variation.
The generative lexicon theory must show how to specify the quantization of
nominals.

13.10 Conclusion

We could see various phases and degrees of abstraction between location change and
other changes such as temporal change, state change and telic (transitional) events
of accomplishment involving creation or removal. Even within location change, we
could see case alternation causing a turn to more abstract state change and Path-
involving *enter/exit* verbs in K/J becoming unaccusative-like. My proposed implicit
I-Process is involved here. Abstraction involves argument reduction and change in
syntactic behavior.

We also distinguished between modification of state-oriented event expressions by the degree modifier *very* and its equivalents in K/J (despite vast cross-linguistic variation in the range) and modification of process-oriented event expressions by the quality modifier *well* and its equivalents in other languages. We also identified negatively oriented predicates and modifiers.

References

Bennett, D. C. (1975). *Spatial and temporal uses of English prepositions*. London: Longman.
Choi, S. (2003). A spatial semantics and cognition in infancy and adulthood. In P. Clancy (Ed.), *Japanese-Korean linguistics conference 11*. Stanford: CSLI.
Dowty, D. (1991). Thematic proto-roles and argument selection. *Language, 67*, 547–619.
Fillmore, C. (1971). Lectures on 'Space, Time and Deixis'. Delivered in Copenhagen.
Im, S.-C. (2001). *Typological patterns of motion verbs in Korean*. Ph. D. dissertation. SUNY Buffalo. New York.
Im, S., & Lee, C. (2012). Combination of the verb Ha- 'Do' and entity 2 type nouns in Korean: A generative lexicon 3 approach. In J. Pustejovsky, P. Bouillon, K. Kanzaki, & C. Lee (Eds.). *Advances in generative lexicon theory*. Dordrecht: Springer.
Joe, J., & Lee, C. (2002). A 'Removal' type of negative predicates. In N. Akatsuka et al. (Eds.), *Japanese/Korean linguistics 10*. Stanford: CSLI.
Kennedy, C. (2002). M.A. lectures titled 'Telicity corresponds to degree of change.' UCLA.
Kim, H., Lee, C., & Nam, S. (1999). *Korean creation verbs and lexical – semantic structure*. In Proceedings of the Korean Society for Cognitive Science Spring Conference.
Kita, S. (1999). Japanese enter/exit verbs without motion semantics. *Studies in Language, 23*, 307–330.
Krifka, M. (1998). The origins of telicity. In S. Rothstein (Ed.), *Events and grammar*. Dordrecht: Kluwer.
Lee, C. (1993). Frozen expressions and semantic representation. *Language Research, 29*, 3.
Lee, C. (1997). Argument structure and the role of theme. In *Proceedings of Cognitive Science Society Conference 1997*, Stanford.
Lee, C. (2006). Change of location: With reference to change of state, creation/removal, degree and telicity. In S. Haraguchi, O. Fujimura, & B. Palek (Eds.), *LP 2002: Studies in language, speech and communication* (Vol. I, II, pp. 487–521). Prague: The Karolinum Press.
Lee, C. (2008). Motion and state: verbs tul-/na- (K) and hairu/deru (J) 'enter'/'exit'. In M. E. Hudson, S-A Jun, P. Sells, P. M. Clancy, S. Iwasaki, & S.-O. Sohn (Eds.). *Japanese/Korean Linguistics* 13(2003), 293–307. Stanford: CSLI.
Lee, C. (1999). A GL Approach to '-ey' and '-eyse' (in Korean). In H. Lee et al. (Eds.) *To where modern linguistics goes* (in Korean). Seoul: Hanshin.
Lee, C., & Kim, H. (2000). Telicity and scale-boundedness of change-of-state/creation verbs in Korean. Web Journal of Cognitive Approach to Verb Semantics, Kazan State University, Russia.
Lee, C., Kang, B., Nam, S., & Kim, Y. (1999). Underspecification in transitive motion verbs in Korean, at the Texas Linguistic Society Workshop on Argument Structure.
Lee, C., & Im, S. (2001). Type-shifting of the Korean substantival nouns with the verb ha-ta 'do'". In *Proceedings the 3rd international conference on cognitive science*. Peijing: Press of University of Science and Technology of China.
Levin, B. (1993). *English verb classes and alternation: A preliminary investigation*. Chicago: The University of Chicago Press.
Levin, B., & Hovav, M. R. (1991). Wiping the slate clean: A lexical semantic exploration. *Cognition, 41*, 123–151.
Levin, B., & Pinker, S. (Eds.) (1991). *Lexical and conceptual semantics*. Oxford: Blackwell.

Narasimhan B. (1998). *The encoding of complex events in Hindi and English.* Ph.D. dissertation. Boston University.

Pustejovsky, J. (1995). *The generative lexicon.* Cambridge, MA: MIT Press.

Pustejovsky, J., & Busa, F. (1995). Unaccusativity and event composition. In P. M. Bertinetto, V. Binach, J. Higginbotham, & M. Squartini (Eds.), *Temporal reference: Aspect and actionality.* Turin: Rosenberg and Sellier.

Talmy, L. (2000). *Toward a cognitive semantics* (Vols. I and II). Cambridge, MA: MIT Press.

Tenny, C. (1987). *Grammaticalizing aspect and affectedness.* MIT Dissertation, Cambridge, MA.

Tham, S. W. (2002). Extended postposing and focus structure in mandarin locatives. In D. Beaver et al. (Eds.), *The construction of meaning* (pp. 190–217). Stanford: CSLI.

Tsujimura, N. (2001). Degree words and scalar structure in Japanese. *Lingua, 111,* 29–52.

Tsujimura, N. (2002). Japanese enter/exit verbs revisited. *Studies in Language, 23,* 165–180.

Yoon, Y. (1996). Total and partial predicates and the weak and strong interpretations. *Natural Language Semantics, 4*(3), 217–236.

Chapter 14
Event Structure and the Japanese Indirect Passive

Naoyuki Ono

14.1 Introduction

There is a consensus among researchers working on causation and causative constructions that the causal relation encoded in the meaning of a verb is decomposed into two events e_1 and e_2, such that e_2 is temporally and causally dependent on e_1 (Shibatani 1976; Dowty 1979; Pustejovsky 1991, among many others). Within the generative lexicon theory (Pustejovsky 1995), the causative verb *break* is assumed to exhibit the event structure and qualia structure as shown in (1).

(1) break

$$\begin{aligned} \text{EVENTSTR} = \quad & E_1 = e_1 \text{: process } (x, y) \\ & E_2 = e_2 \text{: state } (y) \\ \text{QUALIA} = \quad & \text{AGENTIVE} = break\_act \ (e_1, x, y) \\ & \text{FORMAL} = broken\_state \ (e_2, y) \end{aligned}$$

The event structure, composed of two subevents, e_1 and e_2, is mapped onto the qualia structure, which provides more detailed information about the components of event structure. The causing event e_1 corresponds to the AGENTIVE quale and the resulting event e_2, the FORMAL quale.

The causative event structure is assumed to be encoded not only in the lexical causatives as in (1) but also in the resultative sentences in (2):

(2) a. John hammered the metal flat.

  b. The dog barked the neighbors awake.

N. Ono (✉)
Graduate School of International Cultural Studies, Tohoku University, Sendai, Japan
e-mail: nono@intcul.tohoku.ac.jp

J. Pustejovsky et al. (eds.), *Advances in Generative Lexicon Theory*, Text, Speech and Language Technology 46, DOI 10.1007/978-94-007-5189-7_14, © Springer Science+Business Media Dordrecht 2013

In the resultative construction, noncausative verbs are causativized by specifying the resultant state. Many researchers assign resultatives the same semantic structure as lexical causatives (e.g. Dowty *op. cit.* among others). For example, in (2a), the verb *hammer* is not a lexical causative verb but in combination with the result phrase *flat*, the sentence compositionally denotes a causative situation consisting of the following event structure and qualia structure in (3b):

(3)   a. John hammered the metal flat.
       b. EVENTSTR $=$ E1 $= e_1$: (John, the metal)
                         E2 $= e_2$: (the metal)

       QUALIA $=$ FORMAL $= flat\_result$ (e_2, the metal)
                       AGENTIVE $= hammer\_act$ (e_1, John, the metal)

Thus, the causative event structure, which is lexically encoded in a verb's entry, can be encoded constructionally or compositionally in a sentence.

On the other hand, we do not normally regard an event denoted by a passive sentence as the "passive event" consisting of multiple-subevent structure because a passive sentence usually denote a single event which could be described by the corresponding active sentence. The active sentence in (4a) and the passive sentence in (4b) are assumed to denote the same situation.

(4)   a. The assassin killed the senator.
       b. The senator was killed by the assassin.

We normally think that the passive and the causative constructions are used to describe rather different situations.

The situation described by the English active and passive sentences in (4) can be expressed as an active sentence and its passive counterpart in Japanese as shown below:

(5)   a. Ansatusha-ga giin-o korosita.
           assassin-Nom senator-Acc kill-past
           ($=$(4a))
       b. Giin-ga ansatusha-ni koros-are-ta.
           senator-Nom assassin-by kill-pass.-past
           ($=$(4b))

Both of the active and passive sentences denote the same single event. This type of passive sentences are called direct passives.

Japanese has yet another type of passive sentences, called indirect passives, that can be formed on the basis of either transitive or intransitive verbs, as shown in the following examples.

(6)   a.   Kodomo-ga nai-ta.
           child-Nom cry-past
           "The child cried."
      b.   Taroo-ga kodomo-ni nak-are-ta
           Taro-Nom child-by cry-pass.-past
           "Taro was adversely affected by the child's crying."

(7)   a.   Gakusei-ga piano o asa made hiita.
           student-Nom piano-Acc morning-until played
           "The student played the piano until morning."
      b.   Hanako-ga gakusei-ni piano-o asa-made hik-are-ta.
           Hanako-Nom student-by piano-Acc morning-until play-pass.-past
           "Hanako was adversely affected by the student's playing the piano until
           morning."

The intransitive verb *nak* (cry) can be passivized as shown in (6b). In (7b) the object
of the transitive verb *hik* (play) remains in the passive. The passive subject *Hanako*
is not an original argument of the verb but added in the passive construction. Note
that the active and passive pairs in (6) and (7) denote different situations, where a
new participant (the syntactic subject) is added to the event denoted by the base
verb.

Indirect passives are often called adversative passives because it is often the case
that the new subject (e.g. *Taro* in (6b) or *Hanako* in (7b)) is adversely affected by
the event denoted by the active counterpart.

The idea that is widely accepted among researches is that the adversative
interpretation of indirect passive sentence is dependent on how the entity associated
with the passive subject is related with the event denoted by the passive verb. Kuno
(1983) calls this relation "involvement"; Washio (1993) calls the same relation
"inclusion (and exclusion)". According to Washio's claim, the passive sentence has
an adversative reading if the passive subject is "excluded" from the event; whereas,
the interpretation is "neutral", i.e. non-adversative, if it is included in the event. As
shown in (6) and (7), passives of exclusion, i.e. adversative passives, can be formed
from either transitive or intransitive verbs.

I would like to show that the indirect passive exhibits the event structure
and qualia structure which follow from the causative lexical conceptual paradigm
proposed within the model of generative lexicon (Pustejovsky 1995). Focusing on
two types of passives in Japanese, I will suggest that a mapping condition between
event structure and syntax explains the syntactic realization of arguments, and that
an elaboration of the agentive qualia role is needed to account for the selection of
verbs in the passive.

Given the proposed account of the distinct types of passive constructions in
Japanese, we will show that the following two generalizations observed in the
previous works in Japanese linguistics will be accounted for in a principled way.

- **Obligatory adjuncts**: Generally, the agentive phrase in direct passives may or may not be present in syntax; however, it is obligatory in indirect passives (Miyagawa 1989).
- **The unaccusative restriction**: Unaccusative verbs are in general excluded from indirect passives (Kageyama 1993).

The present chapter is organized as follows. In the following section, I will show that there are two types of the composition of events into a causative event structure, which, following Pustejovsky (1995), are referred to as *argument coherence* and *event coherence*. Then, an account of passives in Japanese in terms of event structure and qualia structure is proposed. In Sect. 14.3 inclusion and exclusion are reanalyzed in terms of coherence in event structure. Section 14.4 deals with obligatory adjuncts in the passive. Section 14.5 is concerned with the unaccusative restriction. I will propose that the AGENTIVE quale in the qualia structure of passives involves a causal chain. The final section is a summary and conclusion.

14.2 Event Integration

14.2.1 Default Causative Paradigm

A fundamental aspect of the theory developed in the present paper is the assumption that events denoted by verbs or constructions are developed from conceptual cores of our event construal, which we call "event schemas". Event schemas provide bases on which linguistic meanings of lexical items and grammatical constructions are specified. Of particular relevance to our discussion here is the schematic causative structure that embodies the simplest causal relation between two subevents. The causative event schema we are assuming here is what Pustejovsky (1995: 187) refers to as the *Default Causative Paradigm* in (8).

(8) $\lambda y \lambda x \lambda e_1 \lambda e_2 \exists P \exists R [a: \text{AGENTIVE} = [R(e_1, x, y)] \wedge$
        $\text{FORMAL} = [P(e_2, y)] \wedge e_1 <_\alpha e_2]$

The DCP can be realized as various causal relations that are lexicalized as causative verbs, and causative constructions such as the one discussed above.

If two events (e_1 and e_2) are integrated into a single causative event structure in terms of the DCP, they must be "coherent" in some way. Following the basic idea of Pustejovsky (1995), we assume here two types of coherence between events: *argument coherence* and *event coherence*.

As suggested by Pustejovsky (1995: 186), the causal relation encoded in a lexical causative verb such as *break* must obey the condition on argument coherence. Argument coherence holds for the relation between the causing event and the resulting event if the two subevents make reference to at least one event participant in common. This is illustrated in (9).

(9)   Argument Coherence

e_1: process (x, y)

e_2: state (y)

Break in (1) exhibits argument coherence on the affected object. The idea underlying this linguistic constraint is that a lexical item is predicated of the same individual over at least two consecutive events.

Notice that, unlike the lexically encoded causal relation, in the causative event represented as a syntactic causative, there is no argument coherence. Because of their constructional nature, syntactic causatives differ from lexical causatives. As noted by Pustejovsky (1995: 220), within the interpretation of a syntactic causative, argument coherence is not required. Rather, it exhibits event coherence denoted by the event as a whole. In (10) we have two instances of event coherence, where e_1 and e_2 do not share any arguments in common.

(10)   Event Coherence

a. e_1: process (e_1, x)

e_2: state (e_2, y)

b. e_1: process (e_1, x, y)

e_2: state(e_2, z)

Unlike the lexicalized causal relations in (9), the subevents of the composed event structure do not make reference to any individuals in common.

Argument coherence and event coherence differ in the interpretation of causal relations represented in the event structure. When the two events in a causal relation exhibit argument coherence, they form a direct causation. In contrast, event coherence yields a situation where the causal relation is underspecified in some way. Thus, some factors such as lexically specified causative morphemes or the pragmatics of the discourse or extralinguistic context are needed in order to supplement missing information and coerce a causal interpretation.

Given the proposed account of event integration into the causative event structure, we find that those two distinct modes of event integration are observed in resultatives. As noted in previous works (Simpson 1983; Carrier and Randall 1992; Goldberg 1995; Rappaport Hovav and Levin 2001), resultatives fall into several syntactic classes, depending on the verb that heads the construction. Notice that resultatives based on transitive verbs such as the one in (11) exhibit argument coherence since *the metal* is referred to in both of the subevents.

(11)   a. John hammered the metal flat.

b. EVENTSTR $=$ E1 $= e_1$: (John, the metal)

E2 $= e_2$: (the metal)

QUALIA $=$ FORMAL $= flat\_result$ $(e_2,$ the metal)

AGENTIVE $= hammer\_act$ $(e_1,$ John, the metal)

On the other hand, resultatives based on intransitive verbs such as the one in (12) (Rappaport Hovav and Levin 2001) do not exhibit argument coherence.

(12)   a. They drank the pub dry.
        b. EVENTSTR = $E1 = e_1$: (they)
                         $E2 = e_2$: (the pub)
            QUALIA =   FORMAL = dry_result (e_2, the pub)
                         AGENTIVE = drink_act (e_1, they)

Along with Rappaport Hovav and Levin, we assume that the causal relation between
the two events is formed on pragmatic grounds. Because the causal relation is not
lexically specified, it must be identified through pragmatic inference. As noted by
Rappaport Hovav and Levin, that is where the adversity interpretation comes about.
"[(12a)] is understood to imply a situation where the subject's action adversely
affects the pub (789)". A similar point is made by Goldberg (1995: 195–197).

14.2.2 Passives

Within the Generative Lexicon model (Pustejovsky 1995), the passive is assumed to
shift the headedness of event structures associated with active verbs. The headedness
in the event structure determines the syntactic realization of event participants,
or arguments of verbs. Complex events, which are composed of a process and
a state, can express left-headed events (accomplishments), right-headed events
(achievements), and headless events (causative/inchoative alternation), depending
on the position of head. The passive in general gives rise to a right-headed event
structure (Pustejovsky 1995: 104). For a lexically left-headed event such as *break*,
this has the effect of shadowing the agent, and allowing expression of this argument
only by adjunction.

(13)   a.

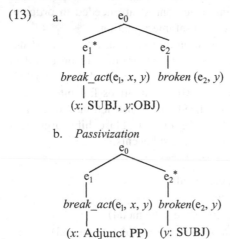

e_0

e_1^* e_2

break_act(e_1, x, y)   *broken* (e_2, y)

(x: SUBJ, y:OBJ)

        b. *Passivization*

e_0

e_1 e_2^*

break_act(e_1, x, y)   *broken*(e_2, y)

(x: Adjunct PP)   (y: SUBJ)

Normally, passivization results in the change of the headedness in event structure and it does not introduce any extra events with respect to the active. The agent argument is projected to the adjunct PP in the derived passive.

The description of the passive in terms of event-headedness in (13) applies to the direct passive in Japanese; however, it does not apply to the indirect passive. In contrast with the direct passive construction, the indirect passive construction has an extra argument that is not involved in the event denoted by the active verb.

I would like to propose that a Japanese indirect passive sentence describes a complex event consisting of two subevents, the causing event represented by the verb and the resulting event represented constructionally by the passive subject and the passive morpheme. The indirect passive sentence in (14) describes an event of the child's crying and a state of Taroo's being annoyed.

(14)   Taroo-ga kodomo-ni nak-are-ta.   (=(6b))
        Taro-Nom child-by cry-pass.-past
        "Taro was adversely affected by the child's crying."

   The event structure of this sentence is represented below:

(15)

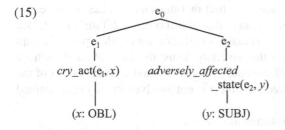

These two subevents map onto the AGENTIVE and FORMAL qualia roles, as illustrated below.

(16)   QUALIA =   AGENTIVE = $cry\_act(e_1, x)$
                    FORMAL = $adversely\_affected\_state(e_2, y)$

Notice that the event structure in (15) and the qualia structure in (16) are formed under the event coherence. This means that inherently underspecified causal relation between the two events must be supplemented by some extralexical factors.

Contrary to what its name implies, the causal relation denoted by the indirect passive construction is that of direct causation, in that there is no intervening event implied in the causal chain between the causing event and the resulting event. For example, (17)(=7b) cannot be used to describe a situation in which the student's playing the piano at night caused Hanako's baby's cry which in turn gave rise to her mental state in the next morning.

(17)   Hanako-ga gakusei-ni piano-o asa-made hik-are-ta.
        Hanako-Nom student-by piano-Acc morning-until play-pass.-past
        "Hanako was adversely affected by the student's playing the piano until
        morning."

14.3   Inclusion and Exclusion

It should be noted that indirect passives do not always impose an adversative
interpretation on the affected subject. Under a natural interpretation of the indirect
passive sentence in (18), we do not detect any adversative interpretation.

(18)   Taroo-ga Hanako-ni kodomo-o home-rare-ta.
        Taro-nom Hanako-By child-acc praise-pass-pst
        "Taro was affected by his child's being praised by Hanako."

However, a closer look at this sentence reveals that it is in fact ambiguous.
If we understand the direct object of the verb (child) as Taroo's child (the most
natural interpretation of the sentence), we find that the sentence has no adversity
implication, in other words, it simply says that Hanako praised Taro's child. But
if the direct object is understood as Hanako's child (or some other person's than
Taro's), the same sentence implies the adversity. Thus, the indirect passives have
the sense of adversity when the affected subject is not related with the object of the
verb; in other words, when the affected subject is not involved in the event denoted
by the active verb.

This point is schematically illustrated as follows:

(19)   Taro $_i$Event[Hanako$_j$ his$_i$/her$_j$ child V]

As noted, Washio (1993) generalizes the situation in terms of the notion *inclusion*
and *exclusion*. Taro is said to be included in the event denoted by the verb if it is
coreferential with the argument of the verb. On the other hand, Taro is excluded if
it is not. The adversative reading is imposed on the exclusion situation. We have
suggested that the indirect passive has a multiple event structure and the adversity
is a compositionally derived meaning of the construction. We must explain why
the indirect passive fails to have an adversative interpretation when the subject is
included in the event.

14.3.1   Inclusion and Argument Coherence

Consider what happens if the relationship between e_1 and e_2 is made explicit by
making reference to the noun associated with them. In the inclusion passive, the

passive subject is associated with the object of the verb through a possession relation between them. In (20), *Taroo* is said to be included in the event.

(20)   Taroo-ga Hanako-ni kodomo-o home-rare-ta.. (Neutral)
       Taro-nom Hanako-By child-acc praise-pass-pst
       "Taro was affected by his child's being praised by Hanako."

(21)   EVENTSTR= $E_1 = e_1$: process
                   $E_2 = e_2$: state
       QUALIA =   AGENTIVE *home_act*(e_1, *h*, *k*)
                   FORMAL *state*(e_2, *t*)

We may call a situation in (21) "partial inclusion" because it is different from the situation where the two subevents have the same argument in common.

Under the argument coherence, no extra means is necessary to ensure the causal relation between the events. The event structure directly instantiates the default causative paradigm; hence, no strong implication of adversity is involved. Thus, this type of indirect passives is said to be "neutral" in the literature.

14.3.2   Exclusion and Event Coherence

Recall that the complex event structure of indirect passives is formed under the condition of event coherence. This means that the subevents of composed event structure do not make reference to any individuals in common. Thus, we do not normally expect any connection between arguments separated in the two subevents. In (22) the event denoted by the intransitive verb *nak* (cry) is conflated with the event denoted by the passive. *Taroo* is not the argument of the verb. In other words, as shown in (23) the argument mapped onto the passive subject is excluded because it is independent of the causing event.

(22)   Taroo-ga kodomo-ni nak-are-ta
       Taro-Nom child-by cry-pass.-past
       "Taro was adversely affected by the child's crying."

(23)   EVENTSTR= $E_1 = e_1$: process
                   $E_2 = e_2$: state
       QUALIA =   AGENTIVE = *nak_act*(e_1, kodomo)
                   FORMAL = *adversely_affected_state*(e_2, taro)

The FORMAL quale of the indirect passive construction provides the adversative interpretation when it is composed with the event structure of the verb. This is also the case in the exclusion passive based on transitive verbs. As shown in (24) *Taroo*, the affected subject, is excluded because it is not associated with any participants in the verb's event.

(24)   Taroo-ga Hanako-ni kodomo-o home-rare-ta.. (Adversative)
        Taro-nom Hanako-By child-acc praise-pass-pst
        "Taro was affected by his child's being praised by Hanako."

(25)   EVENTSTR= $E_1 = e_1$: process
                     $E_2 = e_2$: state
        QUALIA =   AGENTIVE *home_act*(e_1, h, k)
                     FORMAL *adversely_affected_state*(e_2, t)

Under the event coherence, the interpretation of event structure is not fully specified. Thus, the causal relation should be coerced on pragmatic grounds. That is why we obtain the adversative interpretation in indirect passives. Recall that, as we discussed in (12), English resultatives with intransitive verbs exhibit a causal relation induced by pragmatic inference. Adversity is the primary instantiation of pragmatically-induced causal relation. Thus, under certain conditions, an adversative effect on the referent of the post-verbal NP is implicated in order to ensure a causal relation between the causing event and the resultant event.

14.4 Obligatory Adjuncts

What we have discussed in the previous section explains why the agentive phrase is obligatorily present in indirect passives while it may be deleted in direct passives. Another property noted with respect to the indirect passive construction (Miyagawa 1989).

We propose that there is a well-formedness condition on the mapping from event structure to syntax stated in (26):

(26)   **Argument-per-subevent condition**:
        There must be at least one argument XP in the syntax per subevent in the event structure.

(26) is drawn from Rappaport Hovav and Levin (2001: 779). A similar idea is proposed by Grimshaw and Vikner (1993: 144).

This condition says that each event participant involved in subevents must be realized as an argument of the predicate. As we have seen in the previous section, lexical causative verbs such as *break* have an event structure composed of two coherent subevents shown in (14b):

(27)   a. The vase was broken.
        b. EVENTSTR = $E_1 = e_1$: process (x, y)
                       $E_2 = e_2$: state (y)

The logical subject (agent) of the passive verb is mapped onto the *by* adjunct phrase in English, which is in general optional. The event structure formed under the argument coherence condition allows one participant to be optional since there is another argument the causing and result subevents have in common. Thus, x may or may not be present in the passive.

The well-formedness condition in (26) accounts for why the *by* adjunct phrase is obligatory when verbs of creation such as *build* in (28) are passivized, as pointed out by Grimshaw and Vikner (1993). They call this class of causative verbs "constructional accomplishments". We assume that the verbs in this class must obey the mapping condition on argument coherence but the event structure of *build* is slightly different from that of *break*. Compare (28b) with (27b).

(28)   a. *The house was built
       b. EVENTSTR = $E_1 = e_1$: process (x)
                            $E_2 = e_2$: state (x, y)

The Argument-per-subevent Condition requires that the argument *x* in the causing subevent be realized as an adjunct phrase in the syntax.

The logical subject of the passive verb in Japanese occurs with the oblique case *ni*. The *ni* phrase is optional in the direct passive, as shown in the following example.

(29)   Giin-ga koros-are-ta. (cf. (5b))
       senator-Nom kill-pass.-past
       "The senator was killed."

But the same phrase must be present in indirect passives.

(30)   *Taroo-ga nak-are-ta. (cf. (6b))
       Taro-Nom cry-pass.-past
       "Taro was adversely affected by someone's crying."
(31)   *Hanako-ga piano-o asa-made hik-are-ta. (cf. (7b))
       Hanako-Nom piano-Acc morning-until play-pass.-past
       "Hanako was adversely affected by someone's playing the piano until morning."

As the contrast suggests, indirect passives require the presence of *ni* phrases.

Given the complex event analysis of indirect passives we have proposed above, the obligatoriness of the oblique NP in question follows from (26). The argument coherence condition is not imposed on an indirect passive event because the event participants are 'separated' into subevents as illustrated in the following event structures. (32a) is the event representation of (30) and (32b) is that of (31).

(32)   a. EVENTSTR = $E_1 = e_1$: cry_act (x)
                            $E_2 = e_2$: state (y)
       b. EVENTSTR = $E_1 = e_1$: play_act (x, y)
                            $E_2 = e_2$: state(z)

Thus, together with the condition in (26), the proposed event structure of indirect passives must give rise to sentences where every participant is syntactically present.

14.5   Unaccusative Restriction

It is often argued (e.g. Kageyama 1993 among others) that the indirect passive construction is sensitive to the distinction between unaccusative and unergative intransitive verbs. In general, unergative verbs can appear in the construction while unaccusative verbs cannot. The legitimate examples of the indirect passive below include unergative verbs, *nak* (cry) in (33a) and *aruk* (walk) in (33b).

(33)   a. Taroo-ga kodomo-ni nak-are-ta.
           Taro-Nom child-by cry-pass.-past
           "Taro was adversely affected by the child's crying."
       b. Kyooju-ga jugyoochuu gakusei-ni aruk-are-ta.
           professor-Nom in-class student-By walk-pass.-past
           "The professor was annoyed by some students' walking during his lecture."

In contrast, the ill-formed sentences in (34) are based on unaccusative verbs.

(34)   a. *Nooka-ga shuukakumaeni ringo-ni otir-are-ta.
           farmers-Nom preharvest apples-By drop-pass.-past.
           "Farmers are adversely affected by the preharvest drop of apples."
       b. *Untenshu-ga yuki-ni koor-are-ta node unten-ni kuroo-sita.
           the driver-Nom snow-By freeze-pass.-past driving have-trouble-past
           "The driver had trouble driving on frozen snow."

Otir (drop) and *koor* (freeze) are unaccusative verbs; hence, they do not occur in indirect passive construction.[1]

This generalization holds also for intransitive verbs that have corresponding transitive forms, i.e. verbs that undergo the causaltive/inchoative alternation. (35) shows a causative/inchoative alternation verb pair, *kowas/koware* (break).

(35)   a. Kodomo-ga kabin-o kowasita.
           child-Nom vase-Acc break-past
           "The child broke the vase."
       b. Kabin-ga kowareta.
           vase-Nom broke
           "The vase broke."

---

[1] Verbs that allow the indirect passive are unergative verbs implying a volitional instigator of action, such as *hasir* (run), *sawag* (romp), *utau* (sing). Unaccusative verbs such as *tir* (fall), *otir* (drop), *suber* (slip), *okor* (happen) do not turn up in the indirect passive construction. However, it should be noted that the unergative/unaccusative distinction is not always clear-cut: *sin* (die), for example, is assumed to be a typical unaccusative verb in the literature but it can occur in the indirect passive. I argue below that the simple classification of verbs does not explain what is called "the unaccusative restriction" on the indirect passive formation.

The transitive causative version of the verb can appear in the indirect passive as shown in (36a), but the unaccusative intransitive version of the same verb cannot, as shown in (36b).

(36) a. Taroo-ga kodomo-ni kabin-o kowas-are-ta.
          Taro-Nom child-By vase-Acc break-pass.-past.
          "Taro was adversely affected by the child's breaking the vase."
      b. *Taroo-ga kabin-ni koware-are-ta.
          Taro-Nom vase-By break-pass.-past
          "Taro was adversely affected by the vase's breaking."

The same is true for another causative/inchoative alternation verb, *taos/taore* (fall). The unaccusative version does not occur in the indirect passive ((37b)).

(37) a. Taroo-ga Ziroo-ni isu-o taos-are-ta.
          Taro-Nom Ziro-By chair-Acc let-fall-pass.-past
          "Taro was adversely affected by Ziro's letting the chair fall."
      b. *Taroo-ga isu-ni taore-rare-ta.
          Taro-Nom chair-By fall-pass.-past
          "Taro was adversely affected by the fall of the chair."

An explanation is needed for why unaccusative verbs do not co-occur with the indirect passive construction.

Furthermore, the problem seems more complicated when we see that the same verbs can be used in the indirect passives as in (38). (38a) and (38b) show that *taore* (fall) and *koware* (break) can be used in the indirect passive. In light of the observation presented above (see (36b) and (37b)), they seem to be apparent exceptions (see Takami and Kuno 2002: 238 for more examples).

(38) a. Taroo-ga tuma-ni taore-rare-ta.
          Taro-Nom wife-By fall-pass.-past
          "Taro was in trouble because his wife got sick in bed."
      b. Taroo-ga pasokon-ni koware-rare-ta.
          Taro-Nom computer-By break-pass.-past
          "Taro was in trouble because his computer broke down."
      c. Taroo-ga ame-ni hur-are-ta.
          Taro-Nom rain-By fall-pass.-past
          "Taro was rained on."

Notice that animacy is not solely responsible for this matter because an artifact like a computer in (38b) or a natural kind like rain in (38c) can cause events denoted by indirect passives.

I want to propose an elaboration of the AGENTIVE quale embodied in the semantic representation of the indirect passive construction. According to Pustejovsky (1995: 86), the AGENTIVE role represents factors involved in the origin or "bringing about" of an object, or an event. One of the values that the AGENTIVE quale assumes is a causal chain, a notion first proposed by Talmy (1985: 78–85). The causal chain represented in an event structure is essentially a representation of the event as a series of force-dynamic relations with distinct participants as initiator and endpoint (Croft 1991). In the following causative verb, *John* is the initiator and *the boulder*, the endpoint.[2]

(39)   John broke the boulder with a hammer.

     John   hand   hammer   boulder (boulder) (boulder)

     • -------- • -------- • -------- • -------- • -------- •

         Vol   Grasp Contact Change   Result

A closer look at the data in (36)–(38) reveals that what is crucially relevant to the grammaticality of the indirect passive is the initiator of the causal chain associated with the causing event. The unaccusative verbs in (36b) and (37b) are ungrammatical because the segment of the causal chain associated with the causing event does not include the initiator of the event. There is an indirect participant (i.e. a remote causer) that initiates the event denoted by the verb because the vase does not break or the chair does not fall spontaneously in a normal situation. Thus, the initiator of the event is represented as an external causer as in the following causal chain.

(40)   a. koware (break)/taore (fall)

        EVENTSTR = $E_1 = e_1$: process (x)

                   $E_2 = e_2$: state (y)

     b. causer   vase   Taro   Taro

        x -------- y -------- z -------- z

        CAUSE CHANGE RESULT

The starting point of the causal chain is not specified by the argument realized in the sentence. This means that the adversity Taro experiences in this situation cannot be attributed to the responsibility of the causer of the event.

In contrast, computers tend to break or people get sick without an external cause. Thus, the subjects in (41) can be the initiator of the causal chain.

---

[2]The causal chain in (39) represents a typical scenario of the "breaking" event, which involves a volitional instigator (Vol) who uses an instrument (Grasp) which contacts an object (Contact). The object in turn undergoes a change (Change) and results in a certain state (Result). See Talmy (1985: 78–85) and Croft (1991: 176–182) for details.

(41)   a. Taroo-ga tuma-ni taore-rare-ta.
           Taro-Nom wife-By fall-pass.-past
           "Taro was in trouble because his wife got sick in bed."
       b. Taroo-ga pasokon-ni koware-rare-ta.
           Taro-Nom computer-By break-pass.-past
           "Taro was in trouble because his computer broke down."

This means that the primary causer of the event is mapped onto the *ni* phrase in the passive.

(42)   a. koware (break)
           computer   Taro   Taro
           y -------- z -------- z
           CHANGE RESULT
       b. taore (fall)
           wife   Taro   Taro
           y -------- z -------- z
           CHANGE RESULT

In the indirect passive, the initiator and the endpoint of the causal chain must be realized as arguments.

The external causer of the event must be realized as the *ni* phrase. In (38), the external cause is realized as the adjunct (instrumental) phrase.

(43)   *Taroo-ga kaze-de kabin-ni koware-are-ta.
        Taro-Nom wind-Inst. vase-By break-pass.-past
        "Taro was adversely affected by the fact that the vase was broken by the wind."

The indirect passive is the construction which requires the initial point and the endpoint of a causal chain is realized as the *ni* phrase and the subject respectively.

14.6   Conclusion

In this chapter we have proposed an event structure account of indirect passives in Japanese within the generative lexicon model. I have suggested that a mapping condition between event structure and syntax explains the argument realization in the indirect passive. I have presented a problem of verb selection in indirect passives and proposed a solution that the agentive qualia role must be elaborated in terms of the notion of causal chain.

References

Carrier, J., & Randall, J. H. (1992). The argument structure and syntactic structure of resultatives. *Linguistic Inquiry, 23*, 173–234.

Croft, W. (1991). *Syntactic categories and grammatical relations*. Chicago: The Chicago University Press.

Dowty, D. R. (1979). *Word meaning and Montague grammar: The semantics of verbs and times in generative semantics and in Montague's PTQ*. Dordrecht: Reidel.

Goldberg, A. E. (1995). *Constructions: A construction grammar approach to argument structure*. Chicago: The University of Chicago Press.

Grimshaw, J., & Vikner, S. (1993). Obligatory adjuncts and the structure of events. In E. Reuland & W. Abraham (Eds.), *Knowledge and language* (Lexical and conceptual structure, Vol. II, pp. 143–155). Boston: Kluwer Academic.

Kageyama, T. (1993). *Bunpoo to gokeisei [Grammar and word formation]*. Tokyo: Hituji Shobo.

Kuno, S. (1983). *Shin nihonnbunpo kenkyu [New studies in Japanese grammar]*. Tokyo: Taishukan.

Miyagawa, S. (1989). *Structure and case marking in Japanese*. San Diego: Academic.

Pustejovsky, J. (1991). The syntax of event structure. *Cognition, 41*, 47–81.

Pustejovsky, J. (1995). *The generative lexicon*. Cambridge, MA: MIT Press.

Rappaport Hovav, M., & Levin, B. (2001). An event structure account of English resultatives. *Language, 77*, 766–797.

Shibatani, M. (1976). The grammar of causative construction: A conspectus. In M. Shibatani (Ed.), *Syntax and semantics 6: The grammar of causative constructions* (pp. 1–40). New York: Academic.

Simpson, J. (1983). Resultatives. In L. Levin, M. Rappaport, & A. Zaenen (Eds.), *Papers in lexical-functional grammar* (pp. 143–157). Bloomington: Indiana University Linguistics Club.

Takami, K., & Kuno, S. (2002). *Nitieigo no jidoosikoobun [A functional analysis of intransitive constructions in English and Japanese]*. Tokyo: Kenkyusha.

Talmy, L. (1985). Lexicalization patterns: Semantic structure in lexical forms. In T. Shopen (Ed.), *Language typology and syntactic description 3: Grammatical categories and the lexicon* (pp. 57–149). Cambridge: Cambridge University Press.

Washio, R. (1993). When causatives mean passive: A cross-linguistic perspective. *Journal of East Asian Linguistics, 2*, 45–90.

Chapter 15
Developing a Generative Lexicon Within HPSG

Toni Badia and Roser Saurí

15.1 Introduction

Traditionally NLP systems are syntactically centered and tend to use semantics as a complement to syntactic analyses in cases that cannot be handled by syntax alone. It is true that most theoretically oriented approaches to syntax in NLP introduce an abstract level of representation which they label as semantic. This level, however, can hardly be called semantic, if the information that is represented in it is carefully considered. There are basically two aspects that are dealt with under this heading: predicate-argument structure (which also includes modification relations) and quantification. Although quantification is an essential element in semantic analysis, we are not going to be concerned with it here, since it is not a matter of lexical semantics (but rather belongs to the structural component of semantics). Let us just mention in passing that in many cases quantification is treated only to the extent that the problems it brings about can be really avoided in parsing sentences.

Argument structure and modification, however, are both essential to syntactic analysis and central to any approach to lexical semantics. In this paper we are interested in showing that these two perspectives can be integrated into a single approach and that the resulting system behaves better than traditional approaches. We will focus on HPSG because it has become one of the standards for NLP applications, and there are now many projects that use HPSG (or HPSG-like)

T. Badia (✉)
Translation and Language Sciences Department, Pompeu Fabra University, Barcelona, Catalonia, Spain
e-mail: toni.badia@upf.edu

R. Saurí
Voice and Language Group, Barcelona Media, Barcelona, Catalonia, Spain
e-mail: roser.sauri@barcelonamedia.org

J. Pustejovsky et al. (eds.), *Advances in Generative Lexicon Theory*, Text, Speech and Language Technology 46, DOI 10.1007/978-94-007-5189-7_15,
© Springer Science+Business Media Dordrecht 2013

grammars for the syntactic processing of texts.[1] We are convinced however that
nothing essential hinges on these choices: that is to say the basic ideas contained
in this paper could be implemented with other syntactic theories. Our working
language is Catalan, but the analyses can be extended easily to other languages.

In the next section, we start by considering the traditional approach to both
argument structure and modification in HPSG, and seeing its limitations. This is
done in the light of data that cannot be dealt with by following older versions
of HPSG. We develop our proposed revision of the HPSG semantic treatment in
Sect. 15.3, and apply it to the cases previously introduced (Sect. 15.4). The last
section is devoted to show how the semantic representation that has been provided
for lexical entries can be the basis for the generative capability of words in context,
within the framework of an effective computational environment.

15.2   Semantic Phenomena with Impact to Syntax

In standard linguistic practice, the relation between heads and their complements
is governed by syntax and is generally accounted for by syntactic principles
and relations. In HPSG, the valence and head principles account for the well-
formedness of syntactic constructs. It is true that phrasal signs have also to conform
to the semantics principle, but semantic information is only complementary to the
syntactic structure and relations, and helps overcome the inadequacies of a purely
surfacy approach to head-complement relations. Thus, the distinction between
subcategorisation and argument structure within HPSG signs allows the encoding
of general grammatical relations to overcome some of the most well-known form-
function mismatches. For example, control relations are expressed by means of the
coindexing of argument values in the CONTENT, so that a single element in the
VALENCE lists provides the content to two distinct argument positions. And passive
is treated as a change in the correlation between elements in the VALENCE lists and
elements in the corresponding CONTENT.

In the last versions of HPSG, a further step has been taken towards facilitating
the semantic calculation. The different treatment of semantic information for nouns
and verbs, traditional in HPSG for many years, has been superseded in more recent
works. To list but a few, Badia and Colominas (1998), Sag and Wasow (1999),
Asudeh and Crouch (2002), and the MRS work (see, e.g., Copestake et al. 2005),
provide a cross-category treatment of semantic representation. In all these works,
it is assumed that both nominal and verbal expressions introduce an existential
variable, over individuals or events, as the case may be.[2] By this means, noun

---

[1] Some relevant references are Van Eynde and Schmidt (1998), Kay et al. (1994), and http://lingo.
stanford.edu.

[2] The proposal that events introduce an existential variable comes from Davidson (1967).

arguments and verb modifiers can be easily integrated into equivalent semantic representations, thus providing a consistent typing among all complement classes (arguments and modifiers), irrespective of their syntactic head.

In the following two subsections, however, we point to linguistic data showing that this move is not sufficient to satisfactorily account for head-complement relations. In particular, the data show that lexical semantic information has to be taken into account. We consider first cases concerning argument structure, and then move to cases of modification.

15.2.1 Argument Structure

Generally, only two basic kinds of complements are distinguished: those that are strictly subcategorised by the head (also referred to as "arguments") and those that are not required for by their head – that is, modifiers. However, as it has often been noted, this distinction is not sufficient. Firstly, it cannot account for complement optionality in a satisfactory way, forcing most syntactically-based systems to list distinct lexical entries of verbs in order to encode their multiple realisations. Secondly, it cannot represent those complements that are optional but still semantically selected by their heads, as it is the case with most noun complements. And finally, it does not allow for an adequate treatment of complements that are semantically implied but cannot be expressed at the surface.

Complements to verbs are often optional, but their optionality can be of different sorts. In some cases, distinguishing between two (or more) lexical entries for the same verb might be justified. But very often this is not the case, since the presence or absence of the complement is due to syntactic and semantic properties of the sentence, which have nothing to do with the lexical semantics of the verb. This is so, for example, with direct object elision in generic sentences (1) and object deletion structures (2):

(1) La meva germana compra a plaça   cada dissabte.
     The my   sister   buys   in farmer's market each Saturday

(2) Aquest noi menja molt de pressa.
     this   boy eats   very of hurry

In addition, Pustejovsky (1995) points out the existence of complements that are clearly optional but whose relation to the head is controlled by the semantics of the verb. This is the case of the so-called *default* (*D-arg*) and *shadow arguments* (*S-arg*). The former are defined as those arguments that participate in the predicate semantics but which do not need to be syntactically expressed (3), whereas the latter are conceived as semantic content that can only be expressed at the surface under specific semantic conditions (cf. the anormality of 4 if the modifier *expensive* would not appear: ??*Mary buttered her toast* **with butter**):

(3)   *D-Arg*: John built the house **out of bricks**

(4)   *S-Arg*: Mary buttered her toast **with an expensive butter**

Noun complements are even more optional than verbal ones. As a matter of fact almost every nominal complement can be omitted in some circumstance, as shown here:

(5)   a. Aquesta tarda   un grup de nens   jugava a la plaça
           This   afternoon a group of children played in the square
       b. El   grup l'   ha acceptat molt bé
           The group him/he has accepted very well

(6)   a. Compraré   dos fulls de cartolina
           will-buy(1st-sing) two sheets of paperboard
       b. Escriu -ho en un full
           write   -it on a sheet

For noun complements, the strategy of listing every subcategorisation option as a different lexical entry is not very convincing, as there is almost no grammatical cue that may help to choose a particular lexical entry over another. This is even more problematic in languages like Catalan or Spanish, in which the great majority of complements to nouns are introduced by the preposition *de*. Furthermore, choosing between the objective and subjective interpretation of complements of transitive deverbal nouns is very often not possible on simple syntactic grounds. Examples (7–8) illustrate that this choice strictly depends on the complement's semantic value, since their syntactic structure is exactly the same.

(7)   l' estudi de les plantes   (*the study of plants*)

(8)   l' avaluació dels inspectors   (*the evaluation of the inspectors*)

Further arguments in favor of a semantically-oriented treatment of VP and NP optional complements can be derived from examples like those in (9–10). They illustrate that discourse elements can influence the interpretation of complements. Complements that are not explicitly present may serve as antecedent of an anaphoric relation or of a discourse inference. Thus, the use of the definite determiners *el seu* ('her') in (9), and *l'* ('the') in (10), marked in bold face, is licensed by the omitted complements of *mare* ('mother') and *amanir* ('to dress'), respectively.

(9)   Avui ha vingut una mare. Venia   a dir que **el seu** fill no
       podrà   venir a l' excursió
       today has come a   mother. came(3rd-sg) to say that the her son not
       will-be-able come to the excursion

(10)   Hem   amanit l' enciam però l' hem   llençat
       perquè l' oli era ranci
       have(1st-pl) dressed the salad   but it have(1st-pl) thrown-away
       because the oil was rancid

Finally, there are arguments that cannot appear at the surface as complements, although they are implied by their predicates. Redescription predicates like *copiar* ('copy'), *analitzar* ('analyse'), or *traduir* ('translate') are an interesting class of predicates in this sense. Semantically, they introduce at least three different entities: the agent (expressed by the subject), the entity that undergoes the process denoted by the verb (expressed by the object), and the entity resulting from the process. The latter one cannot be expressed as a syntactic complement, and yet its identification is relevant for interpreting phrases in which those predicates appear. This is at least relevant in two contexts: when it is denoted by the corresponding verbal nominalisation (11), and when it can be referred to anaphorically after the appearance of the predicate ((12) and (13)) (as pointed out in Badia and Saurí 1998).

(11) He   llegit la traducció de Hamlet que em vas deixar
      have(1st-sg) read the translation of Hamlet that me lent(2nd-sg)

(12) Traduir   aquest pamflet m' ha costat molt però al   final
      crec   que ha quedat molt natural
      to-translate this   pamphlet me has cost   a-lot but in-the end
      think(1st-sg) that has resulted very natural

(13) La decoració del   pont ens ha portat molt de temps, però ha
      quedat   tan bonica!
      the decoration of-the bridge us   has taken much of time, but   has
      resulted so beautiful!

Example (11) shows that the nominalisation *traducció* ('translation') can denote the entity resulting from the process. The verb involved (*llegir,*'to read') causes the nominal to be interpreted as an individual (and not as an event). This individual is not the one undergoing the translation process, but the one resulting from it. Sentences (12–13) exemplify the fact that anaphors can be based on the entity resulting from the process denoted by the predicate, even if this cannot be expressed by any argument of the verb. In the first clause, the redescription predicates (*traduir* and *decoració*) express the process reading, whereas in the second clause they are referred to as denoting the object resulting from the process. Data like that above justify then a more sophisticated approach to lexical semantics.

Redescription predicates present yet another feature that shows the limitations of a standard approach to argument structure, hence pointing to the need of an improved treatment along the lines we are claiming.

(14) a. En Joan va copiar l'aquarel·la (*Joan copied the watercolour*)
      b. En Joan va copiar molt l'aquarel·la (*Joan copied a lot the watercolour*)

(15) a. És una aquarel·la molt copiada (*It's a very copied watercolour*)
      b. És una aquarel·la copiada (*It's a copied watercolour*)

In (14a) the denotation of the theme (an original watercolour) undergoes a transformation (that of being copied) and a new object is created after the process is finished (a new watercolour, which is a copy of the original one). As shown in (14b) the process can be quantified. The quantification does no affect the degree of the transformation of the theme, but it is a real event quantification (a lot of different copies have been painted out of this original watercolour). This interpretation is also available from the participle *copiada* (with the quantifier *molt* ('very')) when used as a noun modifier (15a). Note however that when the participle is not quantified the meaning of the phrase is different: in (15b) the modifier *copiada* indicates that the entity denoted by the whole NP is a watercolour which is not original, but a copy. These two last examples show that passive participles of redescription verbs may relate to either of the two entities involved in the process denoted by the predicate: the theme or the created object. The created object interpretation is usually the preferred one, unless there is some particular specification in the context.

(16)   a. És una novel·la traduïda   (*It's a translated novel*)
       b. És una novel·la traduïda del basc

                                            (*It's a novel translated from Basque*)
       c. És una novel·la traduïda al basc

                                            (*It's a novel translated into Basque*)

Sentences above offer additional examples of contextually determined sense variation: the participle interpretation in (16a) (i.e., without modification) is equivalent to the one in (16b); that is, they both relate to the created object. It is only when the goal complement appears (16c) that the participle relates to the theme of the verb (i.e., to the original object being translated). This behaviour asks for a rich semantic treatment capable of both representing the different entities introduced as participants, and accounting for the sense alternations observed here.

15.2.2   Modification Relations

Modifiers can also be difficult to integrate by means of standard approaches. Particularly, non-intersective modifiers are problematic with regard to their interpretation. Most adjectives, for instance, denote differently depending on the context in which they appear. Adjectives in (17) and (18) allow an intersective (let's say, "literal") interpretation, or a non-intersective (or "figurative") one, depending on the noun they modify.

(17)   a. un plàstic dur   (*a hard plastic*)
       b. una feina dura   (*a hard job*)

(18)   a. una biga llarga   (*a long beam*)
       b. una llarga tradició   (*a long tradition*)

Of course, the difference here concerns the distinction between intersective and non-intersective interpretations of the adjective. But there is sense variation among cases of non-intersective use as well. Consider the adjective *ràpid* ('fast'): it usually modifies events, and yet it can appear in expressions like those in (19) where it predicates of individuals –thus resulting in a non-intersective use. In these examples, *ràpid* ('fast') denotes differently ('who types fast', 'who drives fast', 'that can be driven fast') depending on the noun with which it is combining (Bartsch 1985).

(19)   a.   un mecanògraf ràpid   (*a fast typist*)
       b.   un conductor ràpid   (*a fast driver*)
       c.   un cotxe ràpid   (*a fast car*)

Furthermore, some adjectives can express different properties at the very same local context, hence allowing for both an intersective and a non-intersective interpretation. Example (20) refers to either a red-coloured pencil or a pencil that colours red –being the latter sense the most prominent. Similarly, *trencat* ('broken') in (21) can apply over the whole entity or just over a part of it, which is the preferred reading.

(20)   un llapis vermell   (*a red pencil*)

(21)   un braç trencat   (*a broken arm*)

To deal with cases like all those above, in the next section we modify and enrich the content description level of HPSG by integrating a component of lexical semantics information along the lines of GL (Pustejovsky 1995).

15.3   Proposed Treatment

15.3.1   *The Organisation of Semantic Information*

Data in the previous section have shown the need for a new view of HPSG content structure with richer and more semantically-oriented information. This new approach should aim at overcoming two issues in formal and computational semantics: the integration of treatments for verbal and nominal adjuncts, and the representation of nominal predicate structure. Older versions of HPSG were not able to deal with these two problems because of their category-oriented treatment of semantics. On the one hand, the reasonably established approach to nominal adjuncts could not be extended to verbal modifiers because the semantic structure for verbs did not introduce any INDEX attribute to which the possible adjuncts could be linked. On the other, nominal signs had no level where to express their predicate-argument structure, in contrast to verbs. In more recent versions of HPSG, however, these problems have been addressed, and a homogeneous treatment across the different major syntactic categories is proposed. Based on work pioneered by Davidson (1967), in HPSG-related work this has been introduced in Badia and Colominas (1998) and Sag and Wasow (1999), among others. It is also customary in Minimal Recursion Semantics (MRS), the computational semantics framework

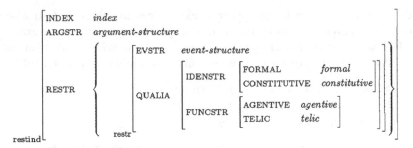

Fig. 15.1 Basic Sign for the content level

developed by A. Copestake (Copestake et al. 2001, 2005; Flickinger and Bender 2003), and in the large grammars development project LinGO (Copestake and Flickinger 2000). The Glue Semantics approach to interpretation within the HPSG framework also opts for a move along similar lines (Asudeh and Crouch 2002).

Our work aims at integrating lexical semantics representations within the HPSG framework, so we start by stating the basic semantic structure for linguistic signs. Based on the proposals just mentioned, we posit a unique semantic structure for all major syntactic categories. As a result, the representation of the CONTENT level of linguistic units is as follows (Fig. 15.1):

The CONTENT level integrates the INDEX and RESTRICTION (RESTR) attributes used in the description of the semantics of nominals, together with ARGUMENT-STRUCTURE (ARGSTR), which would correspond to NUCLEUS, the attribute that introduces the predicate-argument information of verbal signs in standard HPSG. We adopt here the term ARGSTR from GL since, in contrast to NUCLEUS, ARGSTR classifies the arguments according to the distinction among true-, default- and shadow-arguments (cf. examples (3–4)). Some proposals in HPSG introduce an argument structure feature (named arg-st) as attribute at the lexical-sign type (e.g., Davis and Koenig 1999; Koenig and Davis 2003; Ginzburg and Sag 2000). Although it is limited to the description of lexical entries, its functionality can be seen as equivalent to our argstr in that it also manages the correlation between the entities satisfying predicate argument positions and the elements fullfiling the subcategorisation restrictions of a phrasal head.

Given that now predicates introduce an INDEX attribute in the same way as referential categories such as nouns do, an enlargement of the *index* type hierarchy is needed. Thus, the standard divison of the *index* type into *expletive* (*it* and *there*) and *referential* subtypes, is complemented with the distinction among *entity* (*individual* and *eventuality*) and *degree* indexes. The type *individual* subsumes the cases treated by the standard *referential* type; that is, non-predicative nouns. The type *eventuality* is adequate for verbal predicates, adjectives and predicative nouns in general. Finally *degree* is used for quantifiers and certain kind of adverbs. We distinguish here between the types *degree* and *entity* because there are modifiers that select heads that are either individuals or eventualities, such as *in Chicago*. This way, the type *entity* (that includes both individuals and eventualities, but excludes degrees) provides the

Fig. 15.2 Index type
hierarchy

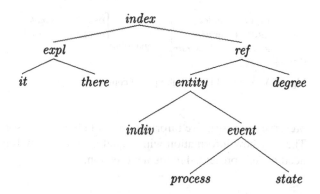

appropriate subspecification that is needed for a neat account of these modifiers.[3]
The partial hierarchy for the *index* type is as shown here (Fig. 15.2):

The third attribute in CONTENT, RESTR, is also modified from standard HPSG
in order to introduce a component of lexical semantics information. Now it is not
a set of *psoas* but a set of *restr* structures, each of them composed of two different
information levels: event structure (EVSTR), and qualia structure (QUALIA), which
is further subdivided into identity structure (IDENSTR) and functional structure
(FUNCSTR). Thus, the semantic restrictions that the denoted entity has to satisfy
are not constituted of a single relation or property (one per *psoa*); instead, each
description level in the restriction introduces at least one relation that concerns a
particular aspect of the word meaning.

Let us now turn to the specific information in the qualia structure. The two
attributes represented, IDENSTR and FUNCSTR, group into two levels the four
classic qualia roles: FORMAL and CONSTITUTIVE on the one hand, and AGENTIVE
and TELIC on the other. We thus incorporate the four specific dimensions that
are customary in GL: the properties that classify a given entity within the class
it belongs to (the FORMAL role), its constitutive structure (CONSTITUTIVE), its
originating process (AGENTIVE), and its purpose (TELIC). The dual distinction
within QUALIASTR is based on the lines drawn by the work in GL where special
attention is given to the functional qualia levels (Pustejovsky 1998, 1999). The
particular formalisation that we adopt here is argued for in Sect. 15.4.6.

Note also that we include the EVSTR level in the *restr* type, at the same level as
the qualia structure. In GL, EVSTR is an independent semantic level that represents
information of the eventuality expressed by the entity. Here we include EVSTR
within the *restr* structure, which is the type appropriate for the RESTR value,
because for most kinds of predicative expressions it conveys semantically relevant
information that restricts the entity pointed at by the index and that has to be

---

[3]Note in addition that if the type hierarchy of Bender, Sag and Wasow (2003) were used, the partial
hierarchy of index would differ considerably, since in this new version of Sag and Wasow (1999)
it and *there* have *none* as value of the feature INDEX.

Fig. 15.3 Assumed HPSG subtypes of content

preserved as restrictive information through the processes of phrasal composition.[4] The way how information within qualia structures will be projected to the phrasal head node is presented in the next section.

15.3.2 Basic Semantic Types and Composition of Semantic Information

In order to preserve the cross-category approach to basic lexical meaning, we modify the subtypes of *content* in Pollard and Sag (1994). We restate them taking *restind* as the structure appropriate for the semantic representation of every major part of speech. First, the *restind* type as represented in Fig. 15.3 substitutes *nom_obj*. Secondly, it is established as the value for the RESTIND attribute in the *quantifier* semantic structure as well. And finally, it is also adopted to express the nuclear information in *psoa*, the semantic structure for the description of predicates. We therefore adopt the new *restind* type as the value for the NUCLEUS attribute, which from now on will be renamed RESTIND. Regarding quantification, we follow the treatment given in Pollard and Sag (1994). The three subtypes of *content* in Pollard and Sag (1994) are respectively transformed as shown in Fig. 15.3.[5]

Following Sag and Wasow (1999) in assuring a 'head-driven' character to semantic composition in a parallel way with the syntactic processing, we restate the Semantics Principle in order to adequately account for the composition of semantic information[6]:

---

[4]Note that if EVSTR were an attribute of the *restind* type, alongside INDEX, ARGSTR, and RESTR, the event structure information obtained from the different constituents during the compositional process would be unified. On the other hand, keeping it in the *restr* type allows for composing the EVSTR of the different constituents by an operation of union (as ruled by the Semantics Principle, to be restated in the following section) which, in contrast to unification, is preserving by nature.

[5]For practical reasons, from now on we will use the *restind* type to represent not only the semantic structure of non-quantified nominal expressions, but also both quantified and predicative expressions, omitting the other attributes in the *quantifier* and *psoa* types.

[6]Since we have not discussed the HPSG treatment of quantification, we assume that the part of the Semantics Principle that concerns quantification remains unaltered.

In a headed phrase:

1. the RETRIEVED value is as in Pollard and Sag (1994:323); and
2. the INDEX and ARGSTR attributes of the CONTENT value are identical to those of the head daughter, whereas the RESTR set value is composed of the union of each daughter's RESTR set.

15.4 Analysis of the Data

15.4.1 Optional Complements

We will first try to account for optional complements of verbal and nominal predicates, partially following the proposal developed in Badia and Saurí (1998). Given their optionality, the standard HPSG treatment of obligatory complements by means of valence lists is not adequate, because it does not allow a phrase to combine with a head if it is not fully saturated. Treating optional complements as free adjuncts does not work either, since in many cases their semantics is integrated into that of the main predicate, and may be referred to by anaphors even if they are not present. On the other hand, listing lexical entries would result in an undesired increase of lexical items and the missing of fairly productive regularities throughout the lexicon.[7] Thus, we need a treatment that (i) accounts for complement optionality (i.e., that phrases can be saturated even if some complements are not present), (ii) guarantees that, if they are present, their semantics integrates with that of the other elements in the construction (in the same way as obligatory complements do), and (iii) allows the non present complements to be referred to by anaphors, because they are essential components of the meaning of the predicate in which they are involved.

At the moment we know of two possible accounts for optional complements within HPSG. As part of the development of the English Resource Grammar (ERG), a proposal has been put forward (Götz and Meurers 1997; De Kuthy and Meurers 2003) which deals with the optionality of complements without having to resource to the listing of each option in a different lexical entry. Roughly stated, their proposal amounts to allowing for a specific marking of complements indicating whether they are obligatory or optional. The Subcategorisation Principle is then modified so that phrases are saturated if there are no obligatory complements left in the valence lists. This treatment directly complies with conditions (i) and (ii) above.

The second proposal we know for optional complements is Sanfilippo's (1997). For independent reasons he proposes that some complements can be treated as actual adjuncts from a syntactic point of view, even if they are thematically bound to the relation denoted by the head. This complies with the three requirements above, but it has the drawback that complements that can never appear in long-distance contexts

---

[7] A nominalisation of a simple transitive verb would have 4 distinct lexical entries: with the two complements, with either of the complements, or without any complement.

(like complements to nouns) are classed at the NONLOC level of information within the linguistic sign. Given that standard HPSG considers members at NONLOC level of obligatory retrieval, in a similar way that those elements in valence lists, Sanfilippo's proposal guarantees the optional retrieval of such complements by partitioning the sort appropriate for nonlocal set members (*local*) into a sort appropriate for structures of obligatory retrieval (*gap*, which becomes the sort for extracted phrases) and a sort for structures of optional realisation (named θ-*adjuncts*, which becomes the sort adequate for thematic adjuncts).

In Badia and Saurí (1998, 2000), we adopt this mechanism and represent optional complements (D- and S-Args) as thematically bound adjuncts, introduced as set members at the nonlocal (NONLOC) information level. In this paper, however, we adopt a more conservative approach to complement optionality. We follow the suggestion in Sag and Wasow (1999) and Flickinger (2000), and tag optional complements with a specific feature. At the same time, we assume that the ARGSTR list contains information about the specific semantics of the complement that allows for maintaining its semantic information even if it is absent in the surface string.

In order to illustrate how this proposal is applied, consider first the creation verb *construir* ('build'), from which an ordinary process-result nominalisation can be derived (*construcció*'building'). As stated in Pustejovsky (1995), this verb subcategorises for two obligatory complements (the agent and the theme resulting of the building process, as usual in creation verbs) and a third argument that expresses the material out of which the resulting entity is built. This third argument is considered a D-Arg because it is syntactically optional but participates in the logical expression of the event (cf. example (3)). Figure 15.4 shows the coexistence of obligatory and optional complements in the syntactic part of the sign: both complements are declared in the VALENCE lists, but optional complements are declared between brackets. Recall that these, in addition, are identified as *default arguments* (D-Args) at the ARGSTR.[8]

In the deverbal nominalisation of *construir*, which is *construcció* ('building'), it is not only the'material' argument but also the agent and result arguments that are optional. Hence all three arguments are considered D-Args and are represented as optional complements in the VALENCE lists. Figure 15.5 represents the process reading of *construcció*.

This treatment is also applicable to the verbs *menjar* ('eat') and *amanir* ('dress (a salad)') in examples (2) and (10) above. Similarly, the treatment also applies to transformation verbs, as shown in Fig. 15.6: it represents the process of *subratllar* ('underline'), referred by the *e1*, which is detailed in the AGENTIVE structure as a process with two participants from ARGSTR: the agent and the theme of the process (the entity being transformed, which corresponds to the complement of the verb).

[8]In this and the following figures, the *index* subtypes for each entity involved in the semantics of the word being represented will be indicated within boxes and using the following code: *t* for *entity* indices, *d* for *degree*, *i* for *individuals*, and *e* for *eventualities*, which in addition can be split into *s* and *p* (for *states* and *processes*, respectively). Also, the IDENSTR and FUNCSTR attributes within the qualia structure will not be represented unless they are relevant for the discussion.

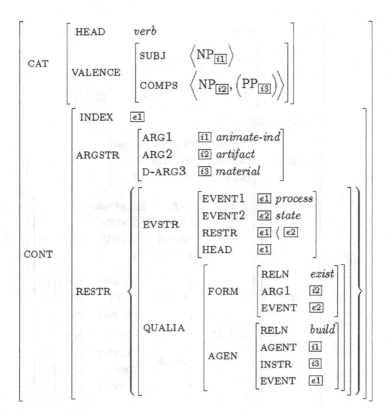

Fig. 15.4 construir ('build')

The process leads to a resulting state $e2$, expressed in the FORMAL role as usual in the GL treatment for accomplishment verbs (Pustejovsky 1995; Johnston 1996). In particular, it denotes the state of being modified of the theme. This is different from creation verbs (Fig. 15.4), in which the theme expresses the newly created object and it is thus introduced by the *exist* relation.[9]

15.4.2 Selectional Constraints on Predicate Arguments

Other types of nouns with semantically implied (optional) complements can be similarly treated. For example, non-deverbal nouns expressing a relation with another entity, like nouns denoting sets or partitions (*grup* 'group' in (5) and *full* 'sheet' in (6)) or relational nouns (*mare* 'mother' in (9)). In the lexical entry for

---

[9] As noted in Pustejovsky (1995:122ff), there are certain verbs that can contextually alternate between a transformation and a creation interpretation (such as 'bake' in 'bake a potato' or in 'bake a cake'). We will address this issue in Sect. 15.5.3.3.

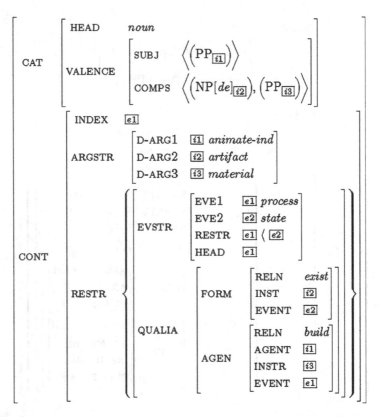

Fig. 15.5 construcció (process reading)

mare'mother' in Fig. 15.7, the ARGSTR represents the optional argument required by the noun, which is coindexed with the content part of the complement expressed as optional in the VALENCE attribute, while the relationship between the individual referred to by the noun and its complement is expressed in the formal role of the qualia structure).

The complement of *mare*, although optional, is of sort *shadow argument*. Examples (22–24) show that it cannot be realised at the syntactic surface unless it is more specific than the semantic restrictions provided by the nominal head.

(22) *Ha   vingut el   pare d' un   fill
       Has   come   the father of a   son

(23) Ha   vingut el   pare d' un nen   canadenc
       Has   come   the father of a   boy   Canadian

(24) Ha   vingut el   pare de   la   Joana
       Has   come   the father of   the Joana

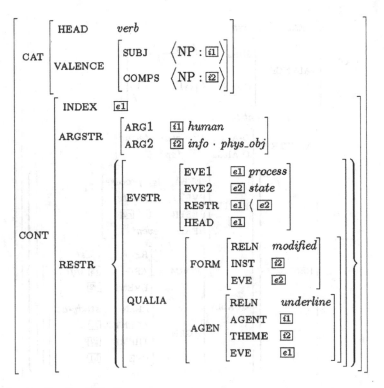

Fig. 15.6 subratllar ('underline')

$$
\left[
\begin{array}{ll}
\text{CAT} & \left[
\begin{array}{ll}
\text{HEAD} & noun \\
\text{VALENCE} & \left[\text{COMPS} \quad \left\langle \left(\text{NP}_{s\boxed{i2}} \right) \right\rangle \right]
\end{array}
\right] \\
\text{CONT} & \left[
\begin{array}{ll}
\text{INDEX} & \boxed{i1} \\
\text{ARGSTR} & \left[\text{D-ARG1} \quad \boxed{i2} \; animate\text{-}ind \right] \\
\text{RESTR} & \left\{ \left[\text{QUALIA} \mid \text{FORM} \left[
\begin{array}{ll}
\text{RELN} & mother\text{-}of \\
\text{ARG1} & \boxed{i1} \\
\text{ARG2} & \boxed{i2}
\end{array}
\right] \right] \right\}
\end{array}
\right]
\end{array}
\right]
$$

Fig. 15.7 mare ('mother')

In order for the representation of S-Args to be appropriate, a constraint has to be formulated upon the semantics of the optional complement: namely, that it be more specific than the semantic implication.

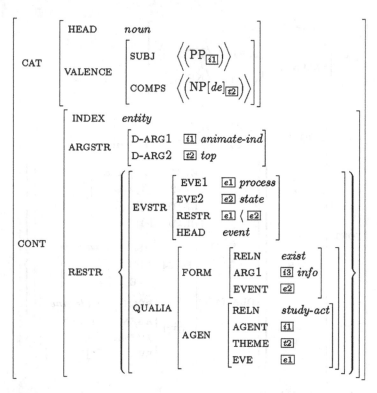

Fig. 15.8 estudi ('study')

In addition to the benefits seen above, the rich semantic information we use also allows for coping with the distinction between subjective and objective complements shown in (7–8). The representation structure in Fig. 15.8 adequately blocks the false ambiguity of example (7) by avoiding an entity like *plantes* ('plants') be the agent of *estudi* ('study') –it has to be an animate individual. Furthermore, the underspecification of the *index* value allows for having just one lexical entry for the two interpretations of *estudi*: as the process, with an index value of type *eventuality*, or as the resulting object, thus bearing an *individual* index.

15.4.3 Hidden Arguments

In order to see that other types of verbal and nominal predicates can also be treated in this way, consider for instance redescription predicates such as *traduir* ('translate') and *copiar* ('copy'). As seen above, they involve at least three different entities: the agent (realised by the subject), the entity that undergoes the process denoted by the verb (expressed by the object), and the entity resulting from the process (which cannot be expressed as a syntactic complement of the predicate). When

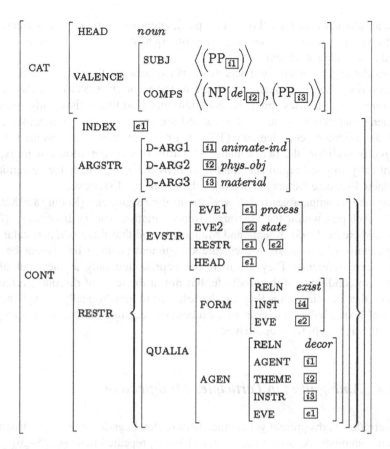

Fig. 15.9 decoració (process reading)

viewed in this way, redescription predicates share some characteristics with both transformation and creation predicates. The object of transformation predicates like *subratllar*, ('underline', in Fig. 15.6) denotes the entity that undergoes the transformation –as with redescription predicates. And creation predicates (like *construir*,'build', in Fig. 15.4) imply the appearance of a new entity (as with redescription predicates), the difference being that with the former the resulting entity is expressed by the object, whereas with the latter it cannot appear in the surface as a complement. Similarly, the process reading of the nominalisations of these verbs cannot syntactically express the argument denoted by the result nominalisation, in contrast with the process reading of creation nominalisations.

However, as seen in examples (12–13) above, there are discourse factors that ask for the possibility of referring to the result arguments of this and similar predicates, even if it cannot be syntactically realised. We therefore assume that redescription predicates introduce the relation of existing a new object in the FORMAL quale, the level that represents the state resulting from the decoration process, in the same way creation predicates do. As shown in Fig. 15.9, the reference to the result is allowed by the argument of the formal role. This participant is not bound by any element in the ARGSTR just because it can never be syntactically realised as an argument: it is treated as a hidden argument.

Thus the argument structure acts as interface between the rich semantic representation (i.e., the set of qualia structures in the value of RESTR) and the surface mechanism that licenses predicate complements (VALENCE list): only semantic arguments that may be syntactically realised are present in the argument structure, either as obligatory complements (T-Args) or as optional complements (D- and S-Args). In addition, the rich semantic structure of the sign allows us to express semantically implied arguments, and thus provides a treatment for semantically motivated discourse factors like the ones shown in (12–13) above.

This take is comparable to other work on implicit arguments (Koenig and Mauner 1999) developed within the Discourse Representation Theory framework (DRT, Kamp and Reyle 1993). Koenig and Mauner defend that there is a particular type of arguments which satisfy a predicate's argument position but cannot be used as discourse referents. They are therefore represented only at the level of the predicative conditions of the predicate, but not at the level of discourse referents. The fact that in some cases they can be referred to anaphorically is explained by means of lexically-based devices or a process of accommodation, in an analogous way to the treatment we propose here.

15.4.4 Ambiguities in Participles Modification

Redescription verbs present yet another feature that begs for an accurate treatment of their semantics. As seen in examples (15–16), repeated here as (25–26), when they appear in the passive participle form and thus behave as modifiers, the entity they modify can be interpreted as either one of the two entities involved in the process denoted by the verb: the theme or the created object. The meaning related to the created object is the preferred one (25a, 26a), unless there is a contextual specification that triggers the one related with the theme (25b, 26c).

(25)   a. És una aquarel·la copiada (*It's a copied watercolour*)
       b. És una aquarel·la molt copiada (*It's a very copied watercolour*)

(26)   a. És una novel·la traduïda (*It's a translated novel*)
       b. És una novel·la traduïda del basc
                                    (*It's a novel translated from Basque*)
       c. És una novel·la traduïda al basc
                                    (*It's a novel translated into Basque*)

Particular specifications that promote sense alternations are: modifying the participle by some quantification adverb, such as *molt* ('very') (25b), or the presence of the predicate goal complement (26c). Both elements force the participle form to relate to the predicate theme (i.e., the object undergoing the process) instead of relating to the resulting object, as is the case in (25a) and (26a-b). Compare now those examples with the sentences in (27a) and (28a), in which *molt* appears modifying a transformation and creation predicate, respectively.

(27) a. En Joan subratlla molt el llibre   (*Joan underlines the book a lot*)
      b. És un text subratllat   (*It's an underlined text*)
      c. És un text molt subratllat   (*It's a very underlined text*)

As a transformation predicate, *subratllar* can be quantified by an adverb such as *molt* ('very') in example (27a). Transformation predicates can be quantified, and there is a correlation between the quantification of the process they denote and the degree of the transformation of the entity denoted by the object (Dowty's'1991 incremental theme). (27b-c) show how passive participles can be used to express that the entity denoted by the head noun has been transformed, and that this transformation can be measured. As is the case with passive participle forms, the verb here denotes the resulting state.

(28) a. *En Joan construeix molt la casa   (*Joan builds the house a lot*)
      b. ??És una casa construïda   (*It's a built house*)
      c. *És una casa molt construïda   (*It's a very built house*)

By contrast, creation predicates (and their corresponding resulting states) cannot be quantified (28), and this is certainly related to the fact that there is no degree applicable to the extent to which the object has been created (that is, a house has to be completely built in order to exist; otherwise it is not a house).[10] As said redescription predicates share with creation verbs the obtention of a new entity as a result of the denoted process. When both kinds of predicates are used in their active form, this new entity realises as the object only in the case of creation verbs (29), but when creation and redescription predicates are used as passive participles, the resulting entity realises as the nominal that both of them modify (30).

(29) a. Maria copia l'aquarel·la.   (*Maria copies the watercolour*).
      b. Maria construeix una casa.   (*Maria builds a house*).

(30) a. una aquarel·la copiada   (*a copied watercolour*)
      b. una casa construïda amb totxana vermella
          (*a house built out of red bricks*)

Creation and redescription predicates however mainly differ in that, whereas the former class does not accept quantification, the latter do, given that their

---

[10]The ?? in (28b) show that a creation participle can only be used to modify a head noun under certain circumstances. Here its use is somewhat awkward because it is not informative enough: all houses are objects that have been built. A default argument such as *amb totxana vermella* ('with red bricks') appears here obligatory in order to make the sentence pragmatically acceptable. See Goldberg and Ackerman (2001) for a detailed analysis of similar data.

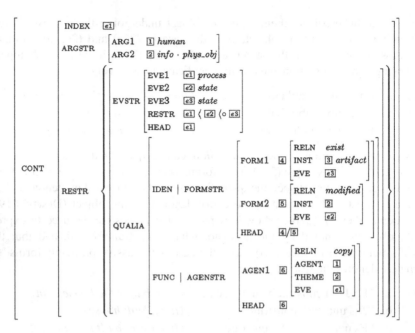

Fig. 15.10 copiar ('copy')

elements express not only a creation process but also a transformation one, and thus quantification can apply to this last process. Quantification of redescription predicates active forms is straightforward because the object refers to the entity being transformed by the process (31a). It is not the case, however, with their passive participle forms since, as creation predicates, they express the process of creating a new object (30a). Thus in this case the introduction of a quantifier such as *molt* ('very') triggers a sense alternation; that is, instead of denoting the default reading for redescription participle forms (the creation process), they denote the transformation process (31b).

(31)   a. Maria copia molt l'aquarel·la   (*Maria copies the watercolour a lot*)
       b. una aquarel·la molt copiada   (*a very copied watercolour*)

We therefore put forward the introduction of an additional relation in the FORMAL role: one expressing a relation of transformation over the theme of the process. From now on, redescription predicates will be characterised by presenting a complex formal structure (FORMSTR), constitued of two FORMAL relations: a first one, stating the existence of a new entity, and a second one, denoting the state of being modified of the original object. Figure 15.10 for the redescription verb *copiar* ('copy') illustrates this modification.

The two states in FORMSTR are related by the restrictions over eventualities expressed at the EVSTR. In addition, the attribute HEAD in the *formstr* type expresses which one of them corresponds to the head of the structure. This is necessary for representating redescription predicates when denoting the resulting state, as happens when the verb is used in its passive participle form (25–26). Since participles of redescription verbs relate to either the theme (25b) or the resulting object (25a) of the process described, depending on the contextual information, the head of FORMSTR in the representation for *copiar* in (25a) corresponds to the *exist* relation (index 5). By contrast it corresponds to the *modified* relation (index 4) when the participle relates to the theme (as in 25b). The selection of one value or the other is determined by the restrictions that the adverb *molt* imposes on its head.

Indeed, the introduction of a complex formal structure also applies to predicates with a single formal relation (Figs. 15.4 and 15.6), though they will only instantiate one of the possible *formal* types. Similarly, the complexity of the formal structure will be also reproduced in the other qualia roles, for cases where it may be necessary more than one agentive or telic relations.

15.4.5 A General Treatment for Modifiers

The modification of the HPSG content structure also has positive effects on the treatment of modifiers. We start by considering pure intersective adjectives like *inacabat* ('unfinished') and *eficaç* ('effective') in examples (32) and (33):

(32)   a.   un poema inacabat   (*an unfinished poem*)
       b.   *un roc inacabat   (*an unfinished stone*)

(33)   a.   un ganivet molt eficaç   (*a very effective knife*)
       b.   una postura eficaç contra la ciàtica
                                    (*a position effective against sciatica*)

The enlargement of the semantic structure benefits the treatment of adjuncts. They now can precisely select for their head, thus accounting for differences of acceptance such as the one in (32). As can be seen in Fig. 15.11, *inacabat* ('unfinished') is an adjective modifying the process in the agentive quale of its nominal head, which in turn must express some kind of creation process in its agentive structure (that is, it must be an artifact). This is the case of *poema* ('poem') in (32a), in contrast to *roc* ('stone') in (32b), which is a natural object.

Conversely, the adjective *eficaç* ('effective') asks for a telic event. Note that it is naturally interpreted when combining with an instrumental noun such as *knife* (33a). But when it modifies a noun with an empty telic structure (as is the case with *position*, in (33b), mainly featured by its formal and agentive role), or a noun in which the information it contains does not unify with the requirements of the adjective, an explicit complement has to be added to the resulting NP (or an appropriate context has to be given) in order to know the event that the adjective is modifying (33b). Thus, an effective knife is commonly understood as a 'knife that cuts well', but an effective position or an effective sneeze can be useful

348

T. Badia and R. Saurí

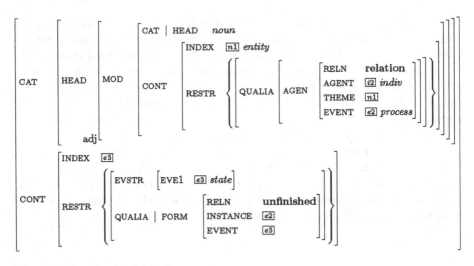

Fig. 15.11 inacabat ('unfinished')

for different purposes not inherent to the noun denotation. In example (33b), for instance, position is effective against sciatica, whereas in appropriate contexts a sneeze can be effective to frighten an annoying fly away.

The rich semantic structure proposed for the treatment of all major categories contributes further benefits to adjuncts. As with nouns and verbs, it enables to deal with their potential argument structure and their capability of being modified. The use of *eficaç* ('effective') in (33) is an example of an adjective presenting argument structure. Other adjectives behaving in a similar way are: *aliè (a)* ('foreign (to)'), *assequible (a/per)* ('attainable (to)'), *apte (per)* ('suitable (for)'), *coetani (de)* ('contemporary (with)'), *conseqüent (amb)* ('consistent (with)'), *ample (de)* ('wide/broad'), etc. With the introduction of ARGSTR as an essential level in the semantic structure of all major categories, the use of *eficaç* ('effective') in (33) is represented as follows (Fig. 15.12)[11]:

The information concerning the argument structure of *eficaç* is displayed at the ARGSTR attribute. It introduces the two arguments of the adjectival predicate: the indexes *i1* and *e2*, respectively referring to the entity denoted by the modified noun, and the state introduced by the complement PP. In addition, VALENCE introduces the information relative to the subcategorised PP complement. Since this PP can be headed by the prepositions *for* and *against*, the qualia role adequate to represent the denoted state is TELIC, which is shared with the TELIC role of the adjective.

Of course, this structure represents a subsidiary use of *eficaç*. Namely, the one that is triggered when the nominal head lacks the telic information that is

---

[11]The same consideration is applicable to adverbs introducing complements, as *independentment (de)*, ('independently (of)'), *paral·lelament (a)* ('in a parallel way (to)'), and similar deadjectival adverbs.

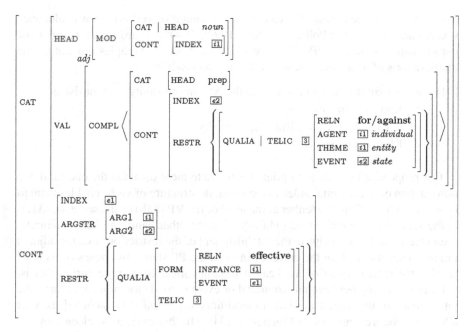

Fig. 15.12 eficaç ('effective')

required by the adjective. There are other possible uses of *eficaç*: combining with a pure instrumental-denoting noun with the information in telic compatible with the adjective requirements (as in (33a)); similarly, modifying an instrumental noun but in a context where additional telic information is required, as in *a knife effective for slicing cured ham*.[12] The treatment for *eficaç* in all these uses, in addition to the relation it maintains with the use represented above, will be illustrated in Sect. 15.5, when addressing the linguistic mechanisms.

The proposed semantic treatment brings about a final remarkable change in the content structure of modifiers and predicates in general: they now introduce an index attribute, in the same way referential categories such as nouns do. Intersective adjectives already introduced it in the HPSG standard treatment, although in that case the index value was coindexed with the index introduced by its nominal head, and therefore it expressed the referent denoted by the noun instead of the state denoted by the adjective. As already mentioned, that strategy caused undesirable consequences: it forced modifiers of adjectives (as for instance the adverb *molt* ('very') in example (33a)) to also bear a nominal index. In that same treatment, verbs did not bear any index attribute, thus being impossible to relate any adjunct to them. As a consequence,'polymorphic' adjuncts required different lexical entries in order

---

[12]As we will see in Sect. 15.5, this case corresponds to what Pustejovsky (1995) identifies as shadow arguments. See also Sect. 15.2.2 above.

to combine with their possible heads (either nominal or verbal). That inadequacy was already observed in Pollard and Sag (1994:57) with regard to the treatment of phrasal adjuncts such as PPs. We repeat here their set of examples illustrating the multiple sorts of heads the phrase *in Chicago* can modify:

(34) a. A man in Chicago claims that the Axiom of Infinity is inconsistent.
      b. Kim slept in Chicago.
      c. In Chicago (at last), Kim slept soundly.
      d. Kim is in Chicago.

Our proposal allows an appropriate treatment to these data. On the one hand, the introduction of a referential index to the semantic structure of verbs enables them to be modified by *in Chicago* (either at the level of the VP (34b) or the sentence (34c)) in the same way a noun can be (34a). And on the other hand, the *index* hierarchy presented in Sect. 15.1 helps in the establishment of the restrictions that the adjunct imposes over its head. In the current example, the PP states, by means of its head *in*, that the INDEX value of the head it modifies must be of type *entity* (that is, without specifying between an individual or eventuality denotation). Similarly, the introduction of the INDEX attribute to modifiers in general (PPs included) is what allows for the treatment of *in Chicago* in (34d). In this case, it is selected by the copula, which requires as attribute an item presenting an INDEX value of type *state*.

Other'polymorphic' adjuncts that illustrate the phenomena we are dealing with are degree adverbs such as *molt* ('very'). As shown below, they can modify either an adjective, an adverb, or a verb.

(35) És   un llibre molt bonic.
      Is$_{3S}$ a   book very nice.

(36) Miràvem   molt detalladament totes les coses.
      Looked$_{1P}$ very in-detail   all   the things.

(37) En   Bernat corre molt.
      The Bernat runs a-lot.

In the standard treatment molt would require two lexical entries: a first one bearing a nominal index in order to combine with a noun-modifying adjective, and a second one, free of any index attribute and combining (how?) with adverbial and verbal heads.

Nevertheless, thanks to the introduction of an INDEX attribute to predicates and modifiers in general, it is possible to provide a uniform treatment for *molt* and other degree adverbs. Figure 15.13 illustrates the lexical entry for this adverb.

Note that, as a degree modifier, its *index* value is of type *degree*. In addition, it requires a head with an index of type *event*. This allows the filtering of both adjectives, adverbs and verbs, but rejects other linguistic units that can present eventive information, such as predicative nouns. Finally, *molt* also asks for a

$$
\begin{bmatrix}
\text{CAT} & \begin{bmatrix} \text{HEAD} & \begin{bmatrix} \text{MOD} \mid \text{CONT} & \begin{bmatrix} \text{INDEX} & \boxed{e} \\ \text{RESTR} & \left\{ \begin{bmatrix} \text{QUALIA} \mid \text{FORM} & \begin{bmatrix} \text{RELN} & scalar \\ \text{EVE} & \boxed{e} \end{bmatrix} \end{bmatrix} \right\} \end{bmatrix} \\ \text{adv} \end{bmatrix} \end{bmatrix} \\
\text{CONT} & \begin{bmatrix} \text{INDEX} & \boxed{d} \\ \text{RESTR} & \left\{ \begin{bmatrix} \text{QUALIA} & \mid \text{FORM} & \begin{bmatrix} \text{RELN} & molt \\ \text{ARG1} & \boxed{e} \\ \text{EVE} & \boxed{d} \end{bmatrix} \end{bmatrix} \right\} \end{bmatrix}
\end{bmatrix}
$$

Fig. 15.13 molt ('very')

gradable head, which is precisely what accounts for the sense alternation of redescription participle forms (cf. example (25)). Recall that on a regular basis the nouns modified by those participles are interpreted as the entity being created. However, when *molt* and similar adverbs modify these sort of predicates, they happen to be interpreted as denoting the state of an object of being transformed because, from the two relations in the FORMSTR, only the *modified* one satisfies the requirement of the adverb of being marked as a gradable event.[13] In this case, then, the noun modified by the participle is interpreted as the original entity that has undergone the transformation process.[14]

15.4.6   Non-intersective Modification

We now turn to non-intersective, nominal modifiers, which, as pointed out, also demand a revision of the standard HPSG semantic treatment. The problems illustrated by the adjective *ràpid* ('fast') in (19) above are two. On the one hand, the adjective presents a non-intersective interpretation: it is generally an eventuality predicate but here it modifies individual-denoting nouns. On the other hand, it denotes differently ('who types fast', 'who drives fast', 'that can be driven fast') depending on the noun it combines with, although there is indeed a semantic core that is common to all three instances of *ràpid* –that is, the property of being fast of a given event.

Larson (1998) explains similar non-intersective cases by adapting Davidson's event analysis, originally developed for adverbs, into the semantic structure of the nominal expressions. His proposal, particularly focussed on agentive nouns like

---

[13]This can be obtained by having a hierarchy of *scalar* values, where *modified* belongs to.

[14]Such an approach goes pretty much along the lines of McNally and Kennedy (this volume) for the treatment of 'well' and its effects in the interpretation of 'load'-like verbs.

dancer or *typist*, provides good insight into the problem but leaves some aspects unresolved, such as the pervasivity of event modification in nominals. Interestingly, however, Pustejovsky's GL approach offers an adequate and systematic treatment of these facts. If we assume that *ràpid* ('fast') is an event predicate, then we can argue it triggers an event interpretation for the noun it modifies. This can be done by applying the selective-binding mechanism, which forces the adjective to predicate over the qualia level that is adequate to its selectional restrictions (i.e., an event), instead of predicating over the whole entity. Thus, when modifying *mecanògraf* ('typist'), *ràpid* predicates about the process of typing, the event encoded at the telic level of the semantic structure of the noun, whereas with *conductor* ('driver'), *ràpid* predicates about the 'driving' event.

GL therefore provides an elegant treatment of the non-intersective use of adjectives that predicate over events. It is also general enough to explain their apparent sense variation depending on the noun they appear with. These advantages are mainly due to two elements. First, the distinction between individual- or eventuality-modifying adjectives. Second, the introduction of a structured multi-layered semantic level to describe the content of nominals (and other categories). However, there is still one unsolved issue: there are at least two event values in the qualia structure of all nouns (at the agentive and telic level), and it is not clear how event-selecting adjectives manage to choose between them. The adjective *ràpid* ('fast') provides examples of this:

(38)   a.   un mecanògraf ràpid   (*a fast typist*)
           b.   un cotxe ràpid   (*a fast car*)
(39)   a.   un pastís ràpid   (*a quick cake*)
           b.   una construcció ràpida   (*a fast building*)

Ràpid selects the telic quale of the noun when modifying *mecanògraf* ('typist') or *cotxe* ('car') (38); that is, it selects the information about the goal of the denoted entity. But when combining with *pastís* ('cake') or *construcció* ('building'), *ràpid* selects the agentive level (39), which conveys information concerning the genesis of the entity.

It is our intuition that not all nominal entries have their qualia structured in the same way. That is to say, every nominal class has a particular quale role more prominent than the others. For instance, instrumental and agentive nouns (such as *knife* and *typist*, respectively) are characterised by the prominence in their telic quale; whereas in result nominalisations (such as *building*) and nouns like *statue* the most prominent event level is the agentive quale. We will not discuss this issue any further here, but see Badia and Saurí (1999) for detail. What mainly interests us is how to indicate what particular quale role in the qualia structure of nominals is the prominent one in each case. As an example, Fig. 15.14 shows the entry for *ganivet* ('knife'), a noun highlighting the telic role[15]:

---

[15]For reasons of space, from now on we only show the relevant levels.

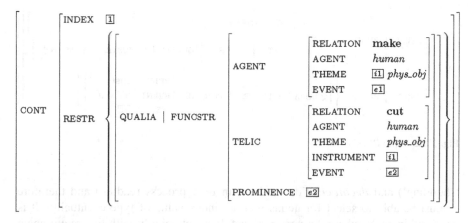

Fig. 15.14 ganivet ('knife')

Prominence highlights a particular piece of the noun semantic information. The four GL qualia roles are subject to tensions and oppositions among them, which are manifested through analogous pieces of information: between the formal and the constitutive qualia, on the one hand, as the roles that express properties relevant for the identity of entities; and between the agentive and telic information, on the other hand, as eventuality-referring levels. Although for reasons of space this account is very roughly sketched here, this fact is what grounds the division into two pairs of the four classic GL qualia roles: one named *identity structure*, which concerns the identity of the entity referred to by the noun, and a second one which concerns its functionality (*functional structure*). Within this picture, prominence is, then, the feature that expresses the strongest role within each of these two basic relations.

The notion of prominence turns out to be necessary in adjective-noun composition processes; particularly in those cases where the adjective (individual- or eventuality-modifying) is underspecified as to the qualia role that it selects for. The adjective then predicates about the prominent quale in the noun.[16] Take Fig. 15.15 as an example. The requirements imposed by a simple eventuality-modifying adjective like *ràpid* ('fast') on non-predicative nouns (such as *cotxe*'car', and *pastís*'cake') would be expressed basically as shown there.

The adjective content level states that *ràpid* predicates the property of being fast of an eventuality, which in turn corresponds to the prominent eventuality in the FUNCSTR of the modified noun. This structure represents the information that *ràpid* should contain in order to allow for a non-intersective use (as in examples (19)). But *ràpid* is actually a modifier of eventuality-denoting nouns (such as *construcció*

---

[16]The fact that nouns present two different prominent qualia (one in IDENSTR and the other in FUNCSTR) is not a problem. The former is established among individual-type indices, whereas the latter is chosen from eventualities.

$$\left[\text{LOC} \begin{bmatrix} \text{CAT} \mid \text{HEAD} \mid \text{MOD} \begin{bmatrix} \text{CAT} & \begin{bmatrix} \text{HEAD} & noun \end{bmatrix} \\ \text{CONT} \mid \text{RESTR} & \left\{ \begin{bmatrix} \text{QUALIA} \mid \text{FUNCSTR} & \begin{bmatrix} \text{PROM} & \boxed{e2} \end{bmatrix} \end{bmatrix} \right\} \end{bmatrix} \\ \text{CONT} \mid \text{RESTR} \left\{ \begin{bmatrix} \text{QUALIA} \mid \text{IDENSTR} \mid \text{FORMAL} & \begin{bmatrix} \text{RELN} & \text{fast} \\ \text{EVENT} & \boxed{e1} \ state \\ \text{INST} & \boxed{e2} \end{bmatrix} \end{bmatrix} \right\} \end{bmatrix} \right]$$

Fig. 15.15 ràpid ('fast')

('building') and *decoració* ('decoration') in their process reading) and therefore it must be able to select for nouns with an index value of type eventuality. It is precisely in cases where the nominal head does not comply with this requirement that a non-intersective interpretation of the adjective is allowed by means of the selective-binding mechanism. The issue arising at this point is how to implement, within a real typed feature system, the selective-binding mechanism used to explain the non-intersective use of certain adjectives. In what follows, we focus on the treatment of this GL mechanism, as well as the other two; namely, co-composition and type coercion.

15.5 Putting the Lexicon at Work

15.5.1 How to Exploit the Semantic Creativity of Words in Context

So far we have extended the semantic information level in HPSG with the representational apparatus of GL, and we have shown how the resulting lexical representation can perfectly undergo the semantic compositional process provided that some changes are introduced in the HPSG grammatical system. The resulting framework has been proved necessary in order to deal with some linguistic data that cannot be accounted for from standard approaches. We have developed the lexical entries for some of those cases by using typed feature structures (in fact, as in HPSG 1994 book), so that they can be effectively implemented in a unification-based system and take advantage of some of the devices provided by such systems to manage linguistic data: underspecification, multiple inheritance, overwriting, etc.

In this section we address how lexical entries like those introduced above can account for polysemy, and thus be sensitive to the context in which they appear. GL deals with lexical creativity by means of three generative mechanisms: *Co-composition*, *Selective Binding* and *Type Coercion* (Pustejovsky 1995:ch.7). They are general devices that cope with polysemy throughout the compositional process, and an elegant solution for lexical resources given that lexical entries can be maintained simple and, in most cases, monosemous. Let us briefly illustrate this with a couple of cases from Pustejovsky (1995), which have also been introduced in the current article.

A first example is provided by adjectives like *ràpid* ('fast'): although they are event-modifying adjuncts, they can also modify individual-denoting nouns such as 'boy', 'car', or 'food'. In addition, they are interpreted differently depending on the noun they modify. In GL, the *Selective Binding* mechanism is the one that allows for maintaining such adjectives monosemous while accounting for their ability to modify both eventualities and individuals.

A second example are transformation verbs (like 'bake' and 'paint'), which present two possible meanings depending on the noun they subcategorise for. Pustejovsky (1995) deals with their sense alternations by using the *Co-composition* mechanism, a process in which not only the syntactic head semantically specifies its argument, but also the argument has an effect over its head, provided that this argument presents an agentive qualia identical to the one in the head. The operation results in a change of the verbal meaning, and thus allows verbs belonging to that class to have only one lexical entry.

The generative capability of the system is therefore essential in order to reduce the number of lexical entries and, consequently, potential parsing ambiguities. In what follows, we will see how the three generative mechanisms put forward in GL can be implemented in the model introduced so far, in order to provide our lexicon with real contextual-based generativity.

15.5.2 The Framework

The enrichment of the HPSG semantic machinery with the GL treatment of the meaning of linguistic expressions is not new. An integration of GL semantic representation and HPSG syntax was initially proposed in the mid 1990s (Copestake 1993; Copestake and Briscoe 1996; Johnston 1996), and more explicitly in Badia and Saurí (1998, 1999, 2000), so that a reasonably straightforward interaction between syntax and semantics become available. Furthermore, a simplified version of the standard GL representation has been used in two EU-funded projects: Acquilex and SIMPLE.[17] However, common to these approaches is the fact that they do not implement the generative dimension of GL, but merely use its representational structure. In recent years the interest for semantics mechanisms from a lexicalist perspective has increased significantly. See, for instance, the work on MRS and Glue Semantics in the HPSG framework (Copestake et al. 2005; Asudeh and Crouch 2002).

---

[17]The Acquilex project references are Esprit-BRA 3030 and Esprit-BRA 7315. SIMPLE is funded by EU's DG-XIII, within the LE programme (LE4-8346).

In GL implementation proposals, the generative mechanisms are generally less used than the representational structure of GL, probably because they are not easy to implement. For example, the LKB used to implement the Acquilex proposals (Copestake 1993) was not powerful enough to introduce the generative mechanisms. We claim, however, that there are currently actual ways of implementing the generative capacity of the lexicon: basically, what is needed is a proper type system with multiple inheritance and enough inference capacity. If these requirements are met, either with subspecification (Markantonatou and Sadler 1998) or default inheritance (Copestake and Briscoe 1992), or with both (Lascarides and Copestake 1999), most of the devices originally contemplated in GL (and a few others) can be implemented.

For our implementation we use the LKB system (Copestake 1998, 2002), a grammar and lexicon development environment which is specifically designed for the use of typed feature structures with underspecification and multiple default inheritance. Such a flexible and robust platform allows us to implement the GL generative mechanisms by simply exploiting the expressiveness of the type system, instead of having to view them as extra processes that apply to the lexicon. In particular, we take benefit of YADU ('Yet Another Default Unification'), the default representation proposal by Lascarides and Copestake (1999) which is effectively integrated in LKB

In YADU, types are represented by means of bipartite structures (typed default feature structures (TDFSs)) of the form *Indefeasibe/Tail*: *Indefeasible* is a simple typed feature structure that expresses what is indefeasible, whereas *Tail*, which specifies the defeasible information, consists of a set of pairs where the first member of the pair is an atomic feature structure (a single path or equivalence) and the second one is a type.

15.5.3 Implementing GL Mechanisms

15.5.3.1 Selective Binding

We will start by looking at the Selective Binding mechanism since it is the generative mechanism we have been considering in more detail so far. In Pustejovsky (1995:129) it is technically defined as follows:

SELECTIVE BINDING:
If α is of type $< a, a>$, β is of type b, and the qualia structure of β, QS_β has quale, q of type a, then $\alpha\beta$ is of type b, where $||\alpha\beta|| = \beta \cap \alpha(q_\beta)$.

Roughly speaking, the Selective Binding mechanism consists of an operation that allows a predicate to apply to one of the qualia levels of its argument, in case that the semantic type of the argument does not coincide with the one required by the predicate, but the semantic type of the qualia does. The archetypical case here is the eventuality-modifying adjective *fast*. As seen before, when the noun it modifies does not denote an entity of type *event*, it predicates over the eventuality of one of the noun's functional qualia (telic or agentive). The resulting interpretation corresponds then to the non-intersective use of the adjective.

The lexical entry for *fast* needs then to have available the information concerning both its intersective and non-intersective use. By means of YADU, the implementation of this case of selective binding in our lexicon is as follows: given that non-intersective uses of adjectives are secondary to the common intersective ones, we establish a partial hierarchy for eventuality-modifying adjectives. It consists of a first general type (*event_modifier_adj*), which represents the intersective use of adjectives, and a subtype of it (*subevent_modifier_adj*) representing the non-intersective one. Since part of the information of both types is incompatible (basically, the CONTENT attribute of the modified noun) we need some overwriting mechanism.

The partial YADU hierarchy needed to account for both intersective and non-intersective uses of eventuality-modifying adjectives is as shown in Fig. 15.16.[18] The indefeasible information stated in the general supertype is completely subsumed by the subtype. The difference between both TDFSs is in the Tail, where the supertype asks for an eventuality-denoting noun, whereas its subtype selects for the prominent eventuality in the functional structure of the noun –the other attribute in CONTENT where eventuality-typed indexes are stated. Note that the information in the subtype TDFS basically corresponds to that stated in Fig. 15.15. Lexical entries inherit from the appropriate type in the hierarchy and specify the particular relation introduced by the adjective as the value of RELN in the formal qualia.

Other classes of adjectives require a similar treatment; for instance, concrete entities modifiers. We exemplify it with color-denoting adjectives. They typically modify individuals (40). When the entity denoted by the noun is constituted of several parts, one of which being neatly delimited as the most external or visible one, this is taken to represent the whole entity (thus giving rise to a case of metonimy). The adjective then predicates on the part instead of the whole entity (41).

(40) a. un paper vermell   (*a red piece of paper*)
      b. un pètal vermell   (*a red petal*)

(41) a. una poma vermella   (*a red apple*)
      b. una casa vermella   (*a red house*)

Furthermore, some nouns introduce additional participants in their functional qualia structures, which can be modified by a colour adjective. If this functional qualia is the prominent one, an ambiguous interpretation is triggered. That is the

---

[18]Due to space limitations, we will not represent the first members of each pair in the tail set as an atomic feature structure. Instead, we integrate all of them in a unique, non-atomic feature structure – this is why there is just one pair in both tails. In addition, we have abbreviated some of the (already abbreviated) attribute names: C | H | M stands for CAT | HEAD | MOD, whereas R stands for RESTR.

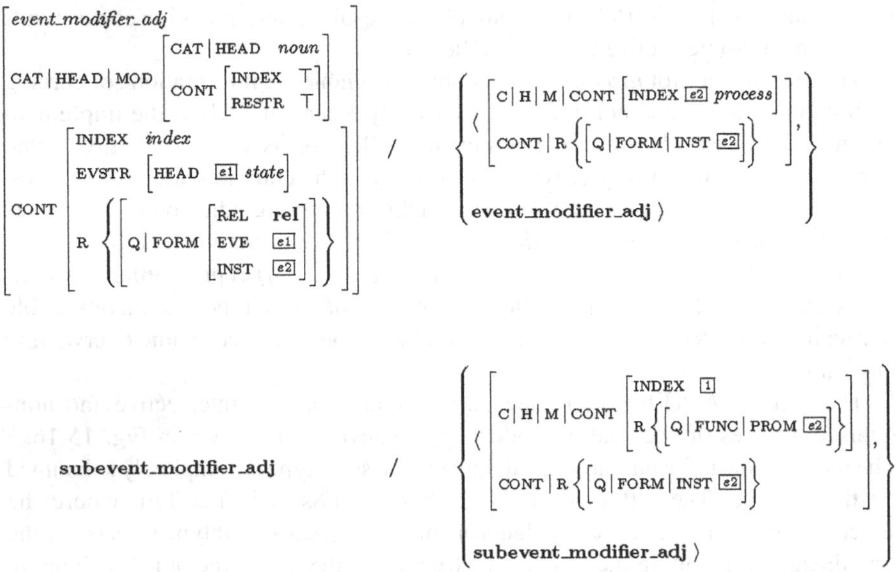

$$
\begin{bmatrix}
\textit{event\_modifier\_adj} \\
\text{CAT} \mid \text{HEAD} \mid \text{MOD}
\begin{bmatrix}
\text{CAT} \mid \text{HEAD} \quad \textit{noun} \\
\text{CONT}
\begin{bmatrix}
\text{INDEX} \quad \top \\
\text{RESTR} \quad \top
\end{bmatrix}
\end{bmatrix} \\
\text{CONT}
\begin{bmatrix}
\text{INDEX} \quad \textit{index} \\
\text{EVSTR} \quad \begin{bmatrix} \text{HEAD} \quad \boxed{e1} \ \textit{state} \end{bmatrix} \\
\text{R} \left\{ \begin{bmatrix} \text{Q} \mid \text{FORM} \begin{bmatrix} \text{REL} & \textbf{rel} \\ \text{EVE} & \boxed{e1} \\ \text{INST} & \boxed{e2} \end{bmatrix} \end{bmatrix} \right\}
\end{bmatrix}
\end{bmatrix}
\Bigg/
\left\{
\left\langle
\begin{bmatrix}
\text{C} \mid \text{H} \mid \text{M} \mid \text{CONT} \begin{bmatrix} \text{INDEX} \ \boxed{e2} \ \textit{process} \end{bmatrix} \\
\text{CONT} \mid \text{R} \left\{ \begin{bmatrix} \text{Q} \mid \text{FORM} \mid \text{INST} \ \boxed{e2} \end{bmatrix} \right\}
\end{bmatrix}
\right\rangle,
\ \textbf{event\_modifier\_adj} \right\rangle
\right\}
$$

$$
\textbf{subevent\_modifier\_adj} \Bigg/
\left\{
\left\langle
\begin{bmatrix}
\text{C} \mid \text{H} \mid \text{M} \mid \text{CONT} \begin{bmatrix} \text{INDEX} \ \boxed{1} \\ \text{R} \left\{ \begin{bmatrix} \text{Q} \mid \text{FUNC} \mid \text{PROM} \ \boxed{e2} \end{bmatrix} \right\} \end{bmatrix} \\
\text{CONT} \mid \text{R} \left\{ \begin{bmatrix} \text{Q} \mid \text{FORM} \mid \text{INST} \ \boxed{e2} \end{bmatrix} \right\}
\end{bmatrix}
\right\rangle,
\ \textbf{subevent\_modifier\_adj} \right\rangle
\right\}
$$

Fig. 15.16 Partial type hierarchy for fast-like adjectives

reason why the expression in (42a) can be interpreted as a'red-colored pencil' or a'pencil that colours red' and why, similarly, the phrase in (42b) can denote a'red-colored bulb' or a'bulb that emits red light'.

(42) a.   un llapis vermell   (*a red pencil*)
      b.   una bombeta vermella   (*a red bulb*)

The appropriate representation for colour-denoting adjectives would be similar to that for eventuality-modifying adjectives in Fig. 15.16 above. The main difference being that the former would consist of a partial hierarchy of three types (instead of the two types for eventuality-modifying adjectives): a first one for the intersective interpretation (corresponding to the examples in 40), and its two subtypes, one for the non-intersective use that triggers the metonymical interpretation of the noun (41) and the other one, for the use in which the adjective predicates on participants of the prominent functional quale (42).

Other interesting examples of noun-modifier relations show no correspondence between the selectional restrictions imposed by the predicate and the semantic information of its participant which cannot be repaired by selecting a deeper layer in the semantics structure of the participant. Common to these examples is that the argument participating in the predication does not present enough semantic information. An extra argument introduces then the information needed by the predicate.

This behaviour is characteristic of the whole group of instrument-modifying adjectives, such as *eficaç* ('effective'), *adequat* ('adequate','appropriate'), *útil* ('useful'), etc. When they combine with an instrument-denoting noun, they modify the relation stated at the telic quale of that noun. For instance, in example (43a) the adjective modifies the relation of 'cutting' that *ganivet* specifies in its telic role.

(43)   a.   un ganivet molt eficaç (*a very effective knife*)
       b.   un ganivet molt eficaç per tallar carn congelada
            (*a very effective knife to cut frozen meat*)

However, when instrument-modifying adjectives appear with nouns that have no particular telicity, a PP introduced by the prepositions *per* ('for','to') or *contra* ('against') is required in order to supply the telic information missing in the noun (44). Indeed, this complement is also allowed in contexts like (43a) if we want to express a purpose different from the one specified at the telic level of the noun head (43b).

(44)   a.   ??un esternut eficaç   (*an effective sneeze*)
       b.   un esternut eficaç per espantar la mosca que tenies sobre el nas
            (*a snezee effective for causing the fly over your nose to fly away*)

Examples like (44) illustrate that, based on semantic grounds, complements traditionally taken as optional may be obligatory in certain contexts. In (44a), the use of *eficaç* modifying a non-telic noun without a PP conveying purpose, like the one present in (44b), causes a semantic anomaly. Purpose complements appear therefore as obligatory complements of non-telic nouns when modified by adjectives that predicate over the telic role of their head.[19]

To wrap up, instrument modifying adjectives can be realised in three different contexts: a general one in which they attribute a property to the telic event expressed by the noun they modify (43a); a second one in which the property does not apply to the inherent telicity of the instrument but to an additional eventity introduced by the adjective complement (43b); and a third one, in which the adjective is not modifying an instrument denoting noun and therefore it necessarily relies on the

---

[19]This need for additional structure in order to meet predicate restrictions is in fact significantly pervasive. For instance, it seems to regulate the use of shadow arguments – those that are only semantically adequate if specific semantic conditions are given. Example (i) is from Pustejovsky (1995); example (ii) is ours:

(i)   a.   ??Mary buttered the toast with butter.
       b.   Mary buttered the toast with an expensive butter.
(ii)   a.   ??This is an effective knife to cut.
       b.   This is an effective knife to cut frozen meat.

The oddness of both (i.a) and (ii.a) is due to redundancy of the PP complements *with butter* and *to cut*, respectively. In (i.a), the PP is redundant with the semantics of just one lexical item, the verbal predicate *butter*, whereas in (ii.a) it is redundant with the semantics resulting from the composition of a noun and its modifier (*effective knife*). However, both cases are similar in that the acceptance of a presumably optional argument is only possible if this argument is further specified.

existence of an extra argument (44b). Lexical entries for this kind of adjectives can thus be represented as a triplet of types (or partial hierarchy) along the lines we have already introduced for other adjectives.

15.5.3.2 Type Coercion

Type Coercion is generally defined as "a semantic operation that converts an argument to the type which is expected by a funtion, where it would otherwise result in a type error" (Pustejovsky 1995:111). GL considers two main modes of coercion: Subtype Coercion and True Complement Coercion. The first one consists on the semantic shifting of a type *t1* when the predicate that selects it requires an argument of type *t2*, which is a supertype of *t1* in the hierarchy. Thus for the adequate interpretation of sentence (45a) (from Pustejovsky 1995:113) it is necessary to ensure that, although *drive* selects an argument of type *vehicle*, the actual occurrence *Honda* is also acceptable. In fact, such a process is frequent among predicate-argument relations, given that the restrictions imposed by predicates over their arguments are generally less specific than the types of the arguments themselves. In (45b), for instance, *eats* only requires an edible entity as a type of its complement NP.

(45)   a. Mary drives a Honda to work.
        b. Tom always eats a banana for lunch.

The implementation of the Subtype Coercion is fairly simple in a system like LKB, which controls the information by means of a hierarchy of types. In such a framework, all the types inherit the properties defined at their supertypes. It is then just by means of this inheritance relation that a Honda is recognised as the vehicle required by the predicate, in the same way a banana satisfies the requirement of being an edible entity.

Let us now turn to the treatment of True Complement Coercion. One of the paradigmatic examples of this operation are verbs of polymorphic syntactic nature; that is, verbs that can subcategorise for complements of different syntactic category, though there exists a semantic relation between these complements. The following example is extracted from Pustejovsky (1995:115):

(46)   a. Mary enjoyed the movie.
        b. Mary enjoyed watching the movie.

Supposedly, *enjoy* requires a complement of type eventuality. The phrase *watching the movie* in (46b) satisfies this requirement, contrary to what happens with *the movie* in (46a), which denotes an individual. And yet example (46a) is acceptable.

GL deals with this systematic subcategorisation alternation by using the true complement type coercion as an alternative to type shifting (Partee and Rooth 1983, Klein and Sag 1985, Pustejovsky 1993; among others) or meaning postulates

(Dowty 1985). The type coercion operation promotes a change of the complement semantic type without modifying its syntactic category, allowing then for the semantic equality between the two sentences in (46) and similar cases. As explained in Pustejovsky (1995:116), the coercion is only successful if the complement has an alternative appropriate type, which in cases like (46a) can be recovered from the qualia of the NP.

From our implementation point of view, however, the operation applied to those verbal complements is of similar nature to the selective binding mechanism. That is, verbs like *enjoy* select for a complement of a specific semantic type, and when it does not correspond to the type of the actual complement, an operation is applied which recovers an entity of the needed type from the appropriate attribute in the complement qualia structure. For example, *enjoy*-like verbs can accept a clausal (46b) or NP (46a) complement provided that it satisfies their semantic requirement, which can be met directly (as in *watching the movie*) or applying a selective binding-like operation (as in *the movie*). Indeed, such an analysis avoids analysing *enjoy*-like verbs as syntactically polymorphic.

The lexical representation for this sort of verbs is pretty similar to the one for *fast*: it is constituted of a first type, which specifies the subcategorisation of a complement denoting an eventuality, and a second one, stating that this eventuality type can be found in the argument's prominent functional quale (Fig. 15.17).[20]

From this perspective, true complement coercion is a relation of the same nature as non-intersective modification. The former is held between predicates and their arguments. The latter, between nominal heads and their modifiers. Both of them however are caused by an initial mismatch between the selectional preferences imposed by the predicate to its argument, and the semantic type of that argument. And also in both cases the selective binding mechanism is the generative device carrying on the compositional interpretation when the default interpretation is not allowed.

15.5.3.3 Co-composition

We finally turn to the Co-composition mechanism. In Pustejovsky (1995:61) it is formally described as an operation "where multiple elements within a phrase behave as functors, generating new non-lexicalised senses for the words in composition." In other words, it is a relation between two predicative elements, one of which happens to undergo a semantic change; specifically, in its eventive properties.

---

[20] Actually, the information required to the noun is more constrained, since *enjoy* does not accept to co-occur with every eventuality-denoting noun (e.g., **John enjoyed the building*). Pustejovsky and Bouillon (1995) analyze these data proposing the existence of aspectual constraints on the type of the coerced complement; i.e., that it must denote a transition. We fully assume this, although for the sake of clarity we do not introduce the information in the figure.

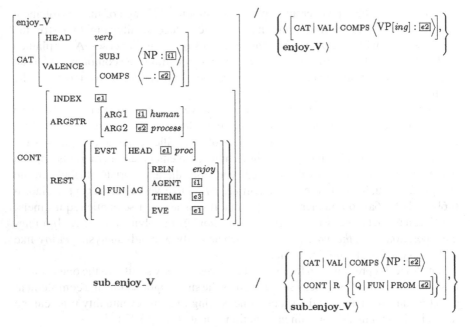

Fig. 15.17 Partial type hierarchy for *enjoy*-like verbs

Consider first verbs like *float*, which alternate between denoting a manner or a process of movement, depending on the context. So for instance, *floating in the cave* allows only the manner of movement interpretation (which is stative), whereas the PP headed by the preposition *into,* in *floating into the cave,* triggers the process of movement interpretation. Other examples of co-composition are the well-known cases of process-denoting verbs like *wipe* or *hammer*, which can also denote transitions if a resultative adjective is modifying them (*wipe the table clean* or *hammer the metal flat*).

The lexical semantics literature accounts for these alternations by considering the different meanings as separate (though somehow related) lexical entries in the lexicon. However, GL co-composition operation allows to have only one basic sense for *float-* and *wipe*-like verbs: given the semantics of the prepositional or adjectival predicates accompanying them in the examples above, the co-composition operation contextualises the verb basic sense in order to bring about the movement process (in the former cases) or stative interpretation (in the latter).

Co-composition is then an operation that builds up phrasal meaning from the meaning of the phrase's predicative constituents. And such a process can be easily assimilated within our framework since it offers an adequate way of composing the semantics in a parallel way with the syntactic process. In Figs. 15.18, 15.19 and 15.20 we illustrate how the co-composition mechanism for the phrase *float into the cave* works within the framework we have developed. Such a treatment is very close to the one that accounts for the sense alternation in *wipe*-like verbs.

$$
\begin{bmatrix}
\text{CONT} & \begin{bmatrix}
\text{INDEX} & \boxed{e}\ state \\
\text{ARGSTR} & [\ \text{ARG1}\ \boxed{i}\ ] \\
\text{RESTR} & \left\{ \begin{bmatrix}
\text{EVSTR} [\text{EVE1}\ \boxed{e}\ ] \\
\text{QUALIA} \mid \text{FUNC} \mid \text{AGEN} \begin{bmatrix}
\text{RELN} & float \\
\text{THEME} & \boxed{i} \\
\text{EVE} & \boxed{e}
\end{bmatrix}
\end{bmatrix} \right\}
\end{bmatrix}
\end{bmatrix}
$$

Fig. 15.18 float

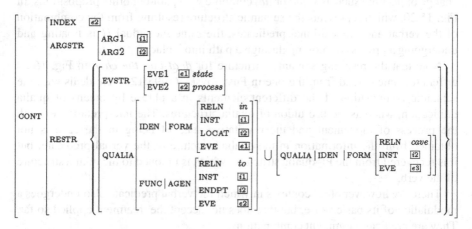

Fig. 15.19 into the cave

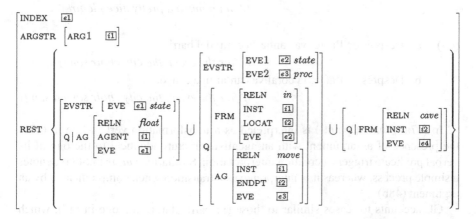

Fig. 15.20 float into the cave

Figure 15.18 corresponds to the lexical entry for *float* denoting the state of floating in its agentive quale. Figure 15.19 shows the representation of the PP *into the cave*. In an analogous way, the preposition *into* denotes the process of going through a path (at the agentive level, applied to the individual pointed by *i1*) and ending at the state of being in a particular place (*i2*, as shown at the formal level). The partition of the preposition semantics into two different predicates (or functions) goes along the lines of Jackendoff (1990, 2002), and offers a general explanation of the stative component shared by *into the cave* and *in the cave*. In addition, it goes along the lines of Verspoor (1997) in adopting the LOCATION and ENDPOINT attributes to account for paths and places. The piece of information in the agentive quale is important in order to prevent that other verbs of movement (e.g., verbs of change of position such as *stand* or *lie*) combine with path-denoting prepositions. In Fig. 15.20, which represents the semantic structure resulting from the combination of the verbal and prepositional predicates, the same individual *i1* is floating and undergoing a process of moving through a path into a place.

Note that the resulting semantic structure for *float into the cave* in Fig. 15.20 differs to some extend from the one in Pustejovsky (1995:126). He deals with the semantic composition of the different elements in a phrase by means of qualia unification, whereas we use union of qualia structures. The interpretation of both the process of movement and the resultative state of being in the cave is not obtained from the information in the qualia structure of the verbal predicate, but it is recovered from the PP qualia structure, which is unioned to the qualia structure of the verb.

There are however other contexts in which the verbal predicate also undergoes a modulation of its basic sense, but that does not accept the treatment applied so far. They are predicate-argument combinations:

(47)   a. En Joan va pintar la paret.   (*John painted the wall*)
       b. En Joan va pintar un quadre força bonic
                                (*John painted a pretty nice picture*)

(48)   a. Després de l'acte, va cantar la coral del barri.
                                (*After the event, the city choir sang*)
       b. Després de l'acte, la coral va cantar una cançó.
                                (*After the event, the city choir sang a song*)

In (47a) *pintar* ('paint') is interpreted as a transformation verb, while in (47b) the presence of an argument with an agentive structure identical to the one of its verbal predicate triggers a creation interpretation. Similarly, *cantar* in (48a) denotes a simple process, whereas it is interpreted as a transition when complemented by an argument (48b).

GL accounts for cases similar to those (in particular, to the one in (47), which behaves in the same way as *bake* verbs (Pustejovsky 1995:123ff.)) by means of Co-composition. However, it is not clear how the operation of qualia unification, as put

$$
\left[
\begin{array}{l}
\text{CONT}
\left[
\begin{array}{ll}
\text{INDEX} & \boxed{e1} \\[4pt]
\text{ARGSTR} &
\left[
\begin{array}{ll}
\text{ARG1} & \boxed{i1}\ human \\
\text{D-ARG2} & \boxed{i2}
\end{array}
\right] \\[16pt]
\text{RESTR} &
\left\{
\left[
\begin{array}{l}
\text{EVSTR}\left[\text{EVE}\quad \boxed{e1}\ process\right] \\[8pt]
\text{QUALIA}\ |\ \text{AGEN}
\left[
\begin{array}{ll}
\text{RELN} & sing \\
\text{AGENT} & \boxed{i1} \\
\text{EVE} & \boxed{e1}
\end{array}
\right]
\end{array}
\right]
\cup
\left[
\text{QUALIA}\ |\ \text{FORM}
\left[
\begin{array}{ll}
\text{RELN} & song \\
\text{INST} & \boxed{i2} \\
\text{EVE} & \boxed{e2}
\end{array}
\right]
\right]
\right\}
\end{array}
\right]
\end{array}
\right]
$$

Fig. 15.21 cantar una cançó ('to sing a song')

forward in Pustejovsky (1995), works in cases like those, where the information at the formal role of the argument is of different nature from that expressed in the formal role of the verbal predicate.[21] Contrary to previous cases of co-predication, the present examples are constituted of an object of predicative sort and another one, denoted by the argument, which is of referential type and thus cannot change the semantic properties of the predicate. Our treatment based on unioning the qualia of the predicates cannot account either for the sense alternation. Unioning the qualia of the argument and the verbal predicate in *cantar una cançó* ('to sing a song') (48b) would result in the structure of Fig. 15.21, which does not account for the desired transition interpretation because there is no formal structure depicting a resultative state.

These facts beg for a different treatment of verbal semantic alternations induced by the verb's internal arguments. Given that the differences in the interpretation are contextually guided, we will make use of the composition device –as it has been done in all other treatments developed in the current section. In addition, we will rely on the expressivity of the type system and the operations allowed for in LKB. In order to account for the different interpretations of transformation (47) or process-denoting verbs (48), we state the possible senses in the same verbal lexical entry. Once again, we do it by taking advantage of the expressive capability of YADU; in particular, its overwriting mechanisms. Figure 15.22 represents the lexical type for transformation verbs like *pintar* ('paint'). It is a partial hierarchy constituted of a first type, denoting the transformation sense, and a second one, which denotes a creation act for cases when its agentive quale coincides with that of its argument.

In a similar way, *cantar*-like verbs are represented by means of a partial hierarchy constituted of a first type for the intransitive, process-denoting use, and a second one for their transition interpretation.

Note that adapting HPSG in order to allow for an adequate semantics compositionality allows to rethink the co-composition operation. Cases of co-predication can now be easily explained by means of the semantic representational and

---

[21]Recall that the formal quale of nominal predicates expresses the kind of the entity pointed at (instrument, mother_of, song, building, etc.). By contrast, the formal quale of verbs conveys the state resulting from the process denoted by the verb.

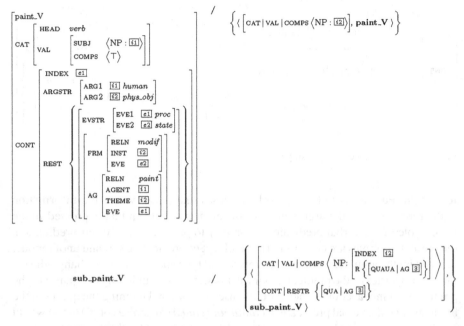

Fig. 15.22 Partial type hierarchy for paint-like verbs

compositional devices provided by our framework. But a particular treatment has to be developed for cases of meaning alternation in predicate-argument combinations, which consists of representing lexical types as conveying different meaning realisations.

15.5.4 Final Remarks

According to what we have introduced so far, the three GL generative devices have been reduced to just one, the Selective Binding mechanism. Co-composition has been integrated within the general process of structure composition. And the cases analysed by standard GL as undergoing either (True Complement) Type Coercion or Selective Binding have been shown to respond to the same linguistic behaviour:

- All of them are relations between a predicative head (be it an adjectival adjunct or a verbal predicate) and its participants (the modified noun or the arguments of the event denoted by the verb),
- They present a general identical problem (the non-satisfaction of the selection restrictions that the predicate imposes onto its participants), which is solved in the very same way: selecting a deeper layer in the semantics structure of the participant.

We consider the Selective Binding mechanism (as understood here) as an abstraction of a general linguistic operation that takes place in the process of meaning composition whenever the selectional restrictions are not satisfied, and that gives rise to the non-intersective interpretation of adjectives or the complement coercion of certain verbs. We have also looked at a completely opposed linguistic operation, consisting on the generation of new structure based also on semantic grounds. Such an operation accounts for the obligatory nature of certain complements traditionally considered as optional. Both the Selective Binding mechanism and this operation of structure generation have been implemented taking benefit of the hierarchic organisation of the lexicon, and the overwriting mechanisms that the last version of LKB provides.

In our implementation, these two wide operations are not general principles applying over the entire lexicon, as it is theoretically proposed in GL regarding the Selective Binding mechanism. Instead, they are expressed as an integral part of lexical types. In spite of their general nature, they adopt specific forms according to the features of the items involved. For instance, the alternative content attribute selected by the Selective Binding operation when an eventuality-modifying adjective is modifying a noun that does not denote an event (as in *fast typist*) is different from the alternative level in the case of colour-denoting adjectives (*red apple*). Hence, in building a real lexicon dealing with contextually-based semantic alternations, the generative mechanisms are implemented tailored to the lexical types.

Of course, it may appear that such an approach does not account for lexical creativity in its purest essence, since all possible word meanings have to be encoded as part of the lexical entries. We are facing here the dichotomy between unrestricted creativity, with its subsequent non-desired overgeneration, and controlled word meaning generation, limited to the regular cases of contextually-induced sense alternation. Our implementation of GL generative mechanisms follows this last direction.

15.6   Conclusions

In this paper we have shown that a syntactically oriented approach is inadequate to deal with both verbal and nominal complement optionality, and modification in general. A basic requirement is having a semantic representation level that, although connected, is independent from the syntactic information. This content level should be based on a rich and robust conception of semantics, allowing to address several issues in a natural way: the implication of participants and events that take part in the denotation of lexical items but are not syntactically expressable, the selection restrictions imposed by predicates to their arguments, and the non-intersective use of adjectives.

Following the latest trends in the HPSG literature, we have introduced several modifications in the standard HPSG content level by adopting a cross-category approach to semantics. Our basic semantic model has been GL, by means of which we addressed several cases of sense creativity. In particular, we have dealt with the generative capability of the lexicon by means of three different information levels:

1. The semantic structure of words, which accounts for:

   - Lexical semantics information, composed of different layers (i.e., eventive, argument and qualia structures).
   - The multiplicity of lexical senses, conveyed in lexical types (by means of the YADU overwriting mechanisms).

2. The compositional process. Our formulation of HPSG allows for a parallel syntactic and semantic computation. This enables implementing the co-composition mechanism in a straightforward way.
3. Two general generative operations: Selective Binding (which now subsumes the two other GL generative mechanisms: Selective Binding and True Complement Coercion), and an operation of structure generation. We have shown several examples of implementing this mechanisms in a proper type system (the LKB system), with multiple inheritance and default unification.

References

Asudeh, A., & Crouch, R. (2002). Glue semantics for HPSG. In F. Van Eynde, L. Hellan, & D. Beermann (Eds.), *Proceedings of the 8th. International HPSG conference*. Stanford: CSLI Publications.

Badia, T., & Colominas, C. (1998). Predicate-argument structure. In F. Van Eynde & P. Schmidt (Eds.), *Linguistic specifications for typed feature structure formalisms*. Studies in machine translation and natural language processing, Vol. 10 Luxembourg: European Communities.

Badia, T., & Saurí, R. (1998). The representation of syntactically unexpressed complements to nouns. In *COLING-ACL'98* (pp. 1–10). Workshop on the Computational Treatment of Nominals, Montréal, Québec.

Badia, T., & Saurí, R. (1999). Semantic disambiguation of adjectives in local context: A generative approach. In P. Bouillon & E. Viegas (Eds.), Description des Adjectifs pour les Traitements Informatiques. Workshop. TALN'99, Corsica.

Badia, T., & Saurí, R. (2000). Enlarging HPSG with lexical semantics. In *Proceedings of the International Conference on Intelligent text processing and Computational Linguistics* (CICLing-2000), Mexico City, Mexico, pp. 101–122.

Bartsch, R. (1985). The structure of words meanings: Polysemy, metaphor, metonimy. In F. Landman & F. Veltman (Eds.), *Varieties of formal semantics*. Dordrecht: Foris.

Bender, E. M., Sag, I., & Wasow, T. (2003). *Syntactic theory: A formal introduction. Instructor's manual* (2 ed.). Stanford: CSLI.

Copestake, A. (1993). The compleat LKB. Acquilex-II deliverable, 3.1. ms. CCL.

Copestake, A. (1998). *The (New) LKB system*. http://hypatia.stanford.edu/aac/lkb.html

Copestake, A. (2002). *Implementing typed feature structure grammars*. Stanford: CSLI Publications.

Copestake, A., & Briscoe, T. (1992). Lexical operations in a unification-based framework. In J. Pustejovsky & S. Bergler (Eds.), *Lexical semantics and knowledge representation. Proceedings of the ACL SIGLEX workshop on lexical semantics and knowledge representation, Berkeley* (pp. 109–119). Berlin: Springler.

Copestake, A., & Briscoe, T. (1996). Semi-productive polysemy and sense extension. In J. Pustejovsky & B. Boguraev (Eds.), *Lexical semantics. The problem of polysemy.* Oxford: Oxford University Press.

Copestake, A., & Flickinger, D. (2000). *An open-source grammar development environment and broad-coverage English grammar using HPSG.* In Proceedings of the second conference on Language Resources and Evaluation (LREC-2000), Athens, Greece.

Copestake, A., Flickinger, D., Pollard, C., Sag. I. A. (2005). Minimal recursion semantics: An introduction. *Research on Language and Computation, 3,* 281–332.

Copestake, A., Lascarides, A., & Flickinger, D. (2001). *An algebra for semantic construction in constraint-based grammars.* In Proceedings of the 39th annual meeting of the Association for Computational Linguistics (ACL 2001), Toulouse, France.

Davidson, D. (1967). The logical form of action sentences. In N. Rescher (Ed.), *The logic of decision and action* (pp. 81–120). Pittsburgh: University of Pittsburgh Press.

Davis, A., & Koenig, J.-P. (1999). Linking as constraints on word classes. *Language, 76,* 56–91.

De Kuthy, K., & Meurers, W. D. (2003). Dealing with optional complements in HPSG-based grammar implementations. In S. Müller (Ed.), *Proceedings of the HPSG-2003 conference, Michigan State University, East Lansing* (pp. 88–96). Stanford: CSLI Publications.

Flickinger, D., & Bender, E. M. (2003). Compositional demantics in a multilingual grammar resource. In *Proceedings of the Workshop on Ideas and Strategies for Multilingual Grammar Development, ESSLLI 2003* (pp. 33–42), Vienna, Austria

Dowty, D. R. (1985). On some recent analyses of control. *Linguistics and Philosophy, 8,* 1–41.

Dowty, D. R. (1991). Thematic proto-roles and argument selection. *Language 67,* 547–619.

Flickinger, D. (2000). On building a more efficient grammar by exploiting types. *Natural Language Engineering, 6*(1), 15–28.

Ginzburg, J., & Sag, I. A. (2000). *Interrogative investigations. The form, meaning, and use of English interrogatives.* Stanford: CSLI Publications.

Goldberg, A. E., & Ackerman, F. (2001). The pragmatics of obligatory adjuncts. *Language, 77*(4), 798–814.

Götz, T., & Meurers, W. D. (1997). Interleaving universal principles and relational constraints over typed feature logic. *ACL, 1997,* 1–8.

Jackendoff, R. (1990). *Semantic structures* (Current studies in linguistics). Cambridge, MA: MIT Press.

Jackendoff, R. (2002). *Foundations of language.* Cambridge, MA: MIT Press.

Johnston, M. (1996). *Semantic underspecification in lexical types: Capturing polysemy without lexical rules.* Acquilex Workshop on Lexical Rules, 1995, Cambridge.

Kamp, H., & Reyle, U. (1993). *From discourse to logic. Introduction to model-theoretic semantics of natural language, formal logic and discourse representation theory* (Vols. 2). Dordrecht: Kluwer.

Kay, M., Gawron, J. M., & Norvig, P. (Eds.). (1994). *Verbmobil, a translation system for face-to-face dialog.* Stanford: CSLI Publications.

Klein, E., & Sag, I. (1985). Type-driven translation. *Linguistics and Philosophy, 8,* 163–202.

Koenig, J.-P., & Davis, A. (2003). Semantically transparent linking in HPSG. In S. Müller (Ed.), *Proceedings of the HPSG03 conference.* Stanford: CSLI Publications.

Koenig, J.-P., & Mauner, G. (1999). A-definites and the discourse status of implicit argument. *Journal of Semantics, 16,* 207–236.

Larson, R. K. (1998). *Events and modification in nominals.* In Proceedings of the Semantics and Linguistics Theory.

Lascarides, A., & Copestake, A. (1999). Default representation in constraint-based frameworks. *Computational Linguistics, 25*(1), 55–105.

Markantonatou, S., & Sadler, L. (1998). Lexical generalisations. In F. Van Eynde & P. Schmidt (Eds.), *Linguistic specifications for typed feature structure formalisms.* Studies in machine translation and natural language processing, Vol. 10. Luxembourg: European Communities.

Partee, B., & Rooth, M. (1983). Generalized conjunction and type ambiguity. In: S. Bäuerle, & A. von Stechow (Eds.). *Meaning, use, and interpretation of language.* Berlin: Walter de Gruyter.

Pollard, C., & Sag, I. (1994). *Head-driven phrase structure grammar*. Stanford: CSLI Publications.

Pustejovsky, J. (1993). Type coercion and lexical selection. In J. Pustejovsky (Ed.). *Semantics and the lexicon*. Dordrecht: Kluwer Academic.

Pustejovsky, J. (1995). *The generative lexicon*. Cambridge, MA: The MIT Press.

Pustejovsky, J. (1998). *The semantics of lexical underspecification. ms.* Computer Science Department, Brandeis University, Waltham.

Pustejovsky, J. (1999). *Type construction and the logic of concepts. ms.* Computer Science Department, Brandeis University, Waltham.

Pustejovsky, J., & Bouillon, P. (1995). Logical polysemy and aspectual coertion. *Journal of Semantics, 12,* 133–162.

Sag, I., & Wasow, T. (1999). *Syntactic theory: A formal introduction*. Stanford: CSLI.

Sanfilippo, A. (1997). Thematically bound adjuncts. In S. Balari & L. Dini (Eds.), *Romance in HPSG*. Stanford: CSLI.

Van Eynde, F., & Schmidt, P. (Eds.). (1998). *Linguistic specifications for typed feature structure formalisms*. Luxembourg: European Communities.

Verspoor, C. M. (1997) *Contextually-dependent lexical semantics*. Ph.D. thesis. University of Edinburgh, Edinburgh.

Chapter 16
Purpose Verbs

Christiane Fellbaum

16.1 Introduction

Work on ontologies and lexical semantics has long been aware of different subsumption relations among concepts that are lexically encoded as nouns (Gangemi et
al. 2001, 2002; Guarino and Welty 2001). An important distinction is that between
TYPES and ROLES (Guarino and Welty 2002; Pustejovsky 1995). For example,
poodle and *Welsh corgi* are TYPES of *dog*, while *pet*, *hunting dog*, *guard dog*,
and *working dog* are ROLES associated with *dogs*. This distinction has important
consequences for the structure of an ontology, its potential for reasoning, and its
usefulness in AI and NLP applications.

The Generative Lexicon observes the difference between types and roles,
labeling the latter Functional Types. Functional Types have a telic role associated
with them (perhaps companionship for pet) and an intentionality that is introduced
by an Agent.

While this distinction among entities, lexicalized as nouns, is fairly established,
little work has been done on events, lexicalized as verbs. The Generative Lexicon
distinguishes Functional Events, which are characterized by a telic and/or an
agentive role in the qualia structure of their arguments.

We examine the distinction between the two different event types from the
perspective of WordNet, where verbs like run and speak are distinguished from
verbs like exercise and greet. We argue for a classification into "manner" and
"purpose" verbs; purpose verbs overlap only partially with the Functional Events
of the Generative Lexicon.

Section 16.2 discussed the polysemy of the manner relation as it is coded in
WordNet (Miller 1995; Fellbaum 1998). In Sect. 16.3, we argue that manner is far

C. Fellbaum (✉)
Department of Computer Science, Princeton University, Princeton, NJ, USA
e-mail: fellbaum@princeton.edu

J. Pustejovsky et al. (eds.), *Advances in Generative Lexicon Theory*, Text,
Speech and Language Technology 46, DOI 10.1007/978-94-007-5189-7_16,
© Springer Science+Business Media Dordrecht 2013

too broad a label, hiding in fact at least two distinct relations. This section motivates the distinction drawn in Sect. 16.4, which introduces purpose verbs and examines their property as distinct from other, established verb classes. In Sect. 16.5, purpose verbs are compared to Functional Events in the Generative Lexicon. Section 16.6 is concerned with the representation of manner vs. purpose verbs, and Sect. 16.7 discusses the distribution of purpose verbs in the lexicon.

16.2 Verbs in Wordnet

WordNet's approach to the structure of the lexicon is to view it as a large network where each word is linked via one or more semantic relations to other words. The most important relation among linking verbs in WordNet is the manner relation (Fellbaum 1990, 1998).

MANNER is frequently taken to be a semantic primitive that defies further analysis (Wierzbicka 1996). In the lexical-conceptual structures of many verbs a MANNER component is assumed whose presence may have syntactic consequences (Rappaport Hovav and Levin 1998; Hale and Keyser 1993; Krifka 1999; Jackendoff 1990; Talmy 1985; Fellbaum and Kegl 1989), inter alia. Yet the exact nature of MANNER has never been made explicit.

At the same time, MANNER clearly plays an important role in verb meaning and structuring the lexicon. The WordNet experiment has shown that an intuitive notion of MANNER allows one to distinguish verbs and arrange them into tree-like hierarchies, with verbs denoting events that are increasingly semantically specified as one descends the hierarchy (Fellbaum 1990, 1998). WordNet makes use of a MANNER relation that constitutes a kind of counterpart to the ISA relation among nouns in WordNet and to subtyping in the Generative Lexicon.

One verb can be said to be subordinate of another verb when it denotes an event with an additional manner component that is missing in the less elaborate superordinate (Levin and Rapoport 1988). For example, *stammer*, *lisp*, and *whisper* are among the many manner subordinates of *speak*, as the statement "to stammer/lisp/whisper is to speak in some manner" shows. Manners of *walking* include *ambling*, *slouching*; *splinter*, *crumble*, and *crush* are among the verbs elaborating specific manners of *break*. And so forth.

Similarly to subtyping in the noun lexicon, it turns out that the manner relation is quite well suited to relate verb meanings to one another. WordNet has over 13,500 verb synonym sets; the vast majority are manner elaborations of some 500 basic verbs.

Fellbaum (1998) points out that MANNER, as it is used in WordNet's hierarchical structures, is highly underspecified. Depending on the semantic domain, the differentiae distinguishing a base verb and a more elaborate subordinate may be dimensions like SPEED (*walk-run*), DIRECTION (*move-rise*), VOLUME (*talk-scream*), INTENSITY (*persuade-brainwash*), etc.

But Fellbaum (2002a, b) noted that WordNet's verb hierarchies ignore a more fundamental distinction among the concepts expressed by verbs.

16.3 Two Types of Manner Relations

Two apparently different relations can be found among verbs and their semantically elaborated manner subordinates. The distinction between the relations reveals a difference among types of verbs and the associated concepts, and parallels the distinction between type and roles in the noun lexicon drawn in the Generative Lexicon.

Consider the verb *exercise* on the one hand and verbs like *jog*, *swim*, and *bike*, on the other hand. *Jog*, *swim*, and *bike* refer to manners of *exercising*, but they are clearly also manners of *moving/travelling*. Both the following statements are true:

(1)   To jog/swim/bike is to exercise in some manner.

(2)   To jog/swim/bike is to move in some manner.

But clearly, there is a difference. The relation between *jog*, *swim*, *bike* and *exercise* is defeasible: Not every jogging/swimming/biking event is necessarily an exercising event. By contrast, every jogging/swimming/biking event is necessarily a moving event:

(3)   She jogged/swam/biked but did not exercise.
(4)   *She jogged/swam/biked but did not move.

The concept "exercise" is definable only by means of subordinates like *swim*, *jog*, and *bike* that are shared with another subordinate, *move*. But *move* has many subordinates that are not shared with *exercise*, such as *fly* and *drive*.

The relation of *jog*, *swim* and *bike* to their superordinates *move* and *exercise* is similar to that between, e.g., *dog*, *cat*, and *goldfish* to *animal* on the one hand and to *pet* on the other hand:

(5)   A dog/cat/goldfish is a kind of pet.

(6)   A dog/cat/goldfish is a kind of animal.

(7)   That's a dog/cat/goldfish, but it is not a pet.

(8)   *That's a dog/cat/goldfish, but it is not an animal.

Just as one can recognize dogs, cats, and goldfish as animals, but not (necessarily) as pets (Guarino 1998), so one can recognize instances of biking, swimming, jogging as moving events, but not (necessarily) as exercising events. Unlike moving, the exercise component of biking, swimming, and jogging does not supply an identity criterion and is notionally dependent. Moving, but not exercising, is a necessary component of a biking/swimming/jogging event. So verbs like *exercise* seem similar to role nouns like *pet*, and verbs like *move* seem similar to type nouns like *animal*.

A random search in WordNet shows up a fair number of defeasible subsumption cases. One example is *treat*. A medical practitioner can treat a patient by massaging, injecting, bleeding, etc. But none of these necessarily constitute a treatment. A statement like "massaging (someone) is a manner or treating (him)" is not necessarily true, whereas the statement "massaging (someone) is manually manipulating (his body)" is necessarily true. So massaging is necessarily a manner of manipulating, but not necessarily a manner of treating.

16.4 Purpose Verbs

What kind of concepts are encoded by verbs like *exercise*, *control*, *help*, and *treat*, which may be, but are not necessarily, part of the network of verbs that can be constructed around MANNER? Unlike the non-defeasible superordinates of verbs like *swim* and *massage*, verbs like *exercise* etc. do not contribute a MANNER component to the meanings of their subordinate verbs. Instead, such verbs seem to express concepts that encode a kind of telicity or goal or purpose: One exercises, helps, treats, cheats, etc. with some goal or purpose in mind, and this goal or purpose is generally intended by the agent of the event.

We will refer to verbs like *exercise*, *treat*, *cheat*, *control* and *help* as PURPOSE VERBS, and we assume that their lexical-semantic structure includes a meaning component that could be labeled PURPOSE.

16.4.1   Purpose, Manner, and Change-of-State Verbs

A common distinction among verb classes is that between manner and change-of-state (COS) verbs (Rappaport Hovav and Levin 1998), inter alia. We propose that purpose verbs constitute a third, distinct class.

16.4.2   Purpose and Manner

Rappaport Hovav and Levin (1998) observe that English verbs encode either a RESULT or a MANNER, but not both.

Similarly, we could not identify verbs that encode both a MANNER and a PURPOSE component as necessary parts of their lexical make-up, although we saw that manner verbs can be subordinates of purpose verbs in appropriate contexts.

Manner verbs do not say anything about a result that may ensue from the activity denoted by the verb. Resultant end states may be encoded by secondary predicates:

(9)   Tim wiped the table clean.

(10)   Kim shouted herself hoarse.

(11)   The couples waltzed themselves tired.

By contrast, purpose verbs do not admit resultatives, even though many denote activities, an aspectual class that in principle admits resultatives:

(12)   *I exercised myself strong.

(13)   *The doctor treated me healthy.

(14)   *The company cheated their stockholders poor.

(15)   *Paul helped Sue safe.

(16)   *The police controlled the crowd frightened.

The fact that purpose verbs do not pattern with manner verbs further indicates that they do not contain a MANNER component.

16.4.3   Purpose and Change-of-State

COS verbs, like purpose verbs, do not refer to MANNER. There are many ways of breaking a vase or of opening a door, and the manner in which a COS was effected may be stated in an adjunct phrase. Because the resultant state is expressed in the verb, no further resultative phrase is admitted:

(17)   *Tim destroyed the painting ruined.

(18)   *Kim shredded the document illegible.

Note that PP resultatives may be admissible, as in "Kim shredded the documents into small pieces". Fong et al. (2001) distinguish several types of resultatives and their compatibility with different verb classes. Following their distinction, a verb like *shred* denotes a TRANSFORMATION, rather than a COS.

But purpose verbs are distinct from COS verbs in some important ways. First of all, purpose verbs may be activities, whereas COS verbs are always accomplishment or achievements, as the standard tests (Vendler 1967) show:

(19)   He exercised for hours.

(20)   *He exercised in two hours.

(21)   The doctor treated me for years with the wrong medicine.

(22)   *The doctor treated me in minutes with the wrong medicine.

(23)   *He broke the vase for hours.

(24)   He broke the vase in seconds.

(25)   *She shredded the letter for days.

(26)   She shredded the letter in minutes.

Second, COS verbs are causatives and have corresponding intransitives:

(27)   Tim opened the door.

(28)   The door opened.

(29)   Kim broke the vase.

(30)   The vase broke.

Transitive purpose verbs do not share this syntactic alternation:

(31)   The doctor treated the patient.

(32)   *The patient treated.

(33)   The police controlled the crowd.

(34)   *The crowd controlled.

Neither are intransitive purpose verbs unaccusatives, as their aspectual properties show, as in (19).

However, transitive purpose verbs freely enter into middle constructions:

(35)   The lawn mower controls easily.

(36)   Naive customers cheat easily.

The subject in middle verbs is commonly referred to as "affected" (Keyser and Roeper 1984; Fellbaum 1985; Fagan 1988), inter alia. Affectedness is commonly treated as an unanalyzable primitive and has not received a precise semantic characterization. In particular, it is unclear how it contrasts with the notion "change of state." Whatever the exact semantics of these concepts may be, purpose and COS verbs indicate that that there is a real difference between them. While COS verbs change the state of the Theme, purpose verbs merely affect them.

16.4.4 Purpose Verbs and Adverbs

The PURPOSE component of verbs like *exercise* and *treat* has an effect on the selection and interpretation of adverbs that co-occur with these verbs.

Pustejovsky (1995) offers a Generative Lexicon account for the polysemy of adjectives. He notes that the telic role of nouns binds selectively with adjectives modifying the nouns, and that this process accounts for the appropriate reading of polysemous adjectives. For example, a "fast car" is a car that drives fast: the adjective is interpreted with respect to the telic role of the noun, which is "drive". A different reading of the adjective obtains in the phrase *fast typist*, where the adjective is interpreted with respect to the telic role of typist, namely "type".

Similarly, the purpose component of a verb appears to interact with certain adverbial modifiers. First, only purpose verbs select adverbs like *(un)successfully*, *(in)effectively*, *fruitlessly*, and *with(out) result* that modify the outcome of the event:

(37)   John exercised with good results.

(38)   Peter cheated successfully.

(39)   Mary treated the patient effectively.

Such adverbs cannot be interpreted with manner verbs whose meanings lack a goal or purpose:

(40)   ? John limped (un)successfully.

(41)   ? Mary murmured fruitlessly.

(42)   ? Kim scribbled effectively

Second, polysemous verbs with distinct manner and purpose readings are disambiguated by adverbs like *(un)successfully*. In the examples below, two different readings of *run* are accessed. Example (43) refers to a motion event, modified by a manner adverb. The event in the second sentence is interpreted as a competition or political race; *run* here is easily assigned the meaning "run for office", i.e., a purpose verb.

(43)   John ran fast.

(44)   John ran (un)successfully.

The adverb may force a verb reading that assumes a purpose or goal:

(45)   John spoke successfully.

Although *speak* does not have an inherent purpose, (45) can be interpreted as a speaking event for a political purpose or a debate. Such a reading appears impossible for verbs that have a strong manner component:

(46)   ? John stammered/stumbled/limped successfully.

While verbs like *speak* and *run* can be coerced into a purpose verb reading in the presence of adverbs like successfully, COS verbs cannot receive a purpose reading even when modified by such adverbs:

(47)   ? She opened the door with good results.

(48)   ? He cracked the box successfully.

16.5   Functional Events in the Generative Lexicon

The Generative Lexicon (Pustejovsky 1995, 2001) classifies some verbs as Functional Events. Examples given in Pustejovsky (2001) are *eat*, *feed*, *greet*, and *spoil*. Functional events are characterized by telic and/or agentive roles in the qualia of the verbs' arguments, i.e., the semantics of the verb arise from those of its arguments. *Eating*, *feeding*, and *running* are classified as Functional Events because they require agentivity and intention (Asher and Pustejovsky 2006, this volume). Similarly, a statement such as the food spoiled can be made only by an entity capable of judging the spoiled food's state with respect to its telic role (presumably, "nourishment").

The telic role here that defines the event as functional is that of the verb's argument (*food*). By contrast, the purpose or goal that defines a purpose verb resides in the event and not in the telic role of the arguments. For example, the purpose of a *greeting* event is to acknowledge someone's presence, show recognition or kindness, etc. A purpose or goal presupposes an agentivity and intention, but not the telic roles of the participants.

Functional Events are defined intuitively rather than rigorously in Pustejovsky (2001). And intuitively, there is some overlap between Functional Events and purpose verbs. Functional Events include purpose verbs, but the broad definition of Functional Events further encompasses verbs that are not purpose verbs. Beyond the agentivity and intentionality for Functional Events like eat cited by Pustejovsky (2001), purpose verbs imply a purpose or telicity of the event that the Agent has in mind. A Functional Event like *eat* does not clearly express such a purpose, although the Agent involved in an eating event acts intentionally. By contrast, a purpose verb like *greet*, which is also classified by Pustejovsky (2001) and Asher and Pustejovsky (2006) as a Functional Event, qualifies as a purpose verb under the distinction proposed here.

To clarify the distinction, recall that a purpose verb like *greet* does not encode a manner: one can greet someone by nodding, waving, or pronouncing a greeting formula. Rather, *greet* expresses the purpose of a nodding, waving, or speaking event.

Another difference is that the Generative Lexicon's Functional Events, such as *eating* and *running*, are always recognizable as such, independent of the situational context. But labeling an event with a purpose verb like *greet* may depend on a subjective interpretation of that event. A nodding or waving event is not necessarily a greeting event, while a running event will be recognized and labeled as such by every observer.

There is a further difference between verbs like *eat* and *run* on the one hand, and verbs like *greet* on the other hand, which indicates that including them all in the category of Functional Events is too broad. In the case of verbs like *eat* and *run*, their relation to more specified manner verbs like *munch* and *jog* is not defeasible:

(49)   *She munches but does not eat.

(50)   *They jog but don't run.

But the relation of manner-of-greeting verbs like *nod* or *wave* to the base verb *greet* is defeasible:

(51)   His waving/nodding is not a greeting.

The distinction among verbs like *munch* and *jog* on the one hand, and *greet* on the other hand, is erased in the Generative Lexicon, where all these verbs are subsumed under the category of Functional Events. We argue that *munch* and *jog* are manner verbs, distinct from purpose verbs like *greet*.

In conclusion, we argued that Functional Events, as characterized by Pustejovsky (2001) and Asher and Pustejovsky (2006), include purpose verbs as well as other verbs that are not purpose verbs. Like Functional Events, purpose verbs presuppose intention and volition and hence agentivity. But these are merely necessary, not sufficient, meaning components.

16.6   Representation

How can one represent the distinct meanings of verbs with both "manner" and "purpose" readings in a semantic network like WordNet?

16.6.1   Regular Polysemy?

One possibility is to posit two senses for verbs like *swim*, *bike* and *jog*, each with a different superordinate, here *move* and *exercise*. Some traditional dictionaries take this route; for example, *jog* is represented in the American Heritage Dictionary as having distinct running and exercising senses. But this solution has two undesirable effects. One is that it increases polysemy and suggests, falsely, that the two readings are unrelated. Moreover, there are likely to be contexts allowing only for an underspecified reading.

More seriously, positing two distinct senses misses the fact that every instance of jogging-as-exercise is necessarily also an instance of moving.

One might ask whether the "manner/purpose" readings of verbs like *jog* reflect a kind of systematic polysemy that can be accounted for by means of productive rules, similar to those found in the noun lexicon (Apresyan 1973). However, we could find no patterns of manner/purpose polysemy in the verb lexicon. Moreover, verbs denoting events that can be manners of treating, controlling, or helping can be semantically heterogeneous and do not seem to admit of any regularity that can be captured by means of regular polysemy rules.

Instead, the readings of many verbs as events with a purpose appear to be construed in an ad-hoc fashion from context. We will examine this point in more detail later.

16.6.2 *Multiple Inheritance?*

Verbs like *jog* and *bike* could be related via the same labeled MANNER pointer to two superordinate parent concepts, one link being necessary and another defeasible. However, the resultant "tangled hierarchy" is clearly unsatisfactory, as it implies that every jogging/swimming/biking event is both an exercising and a moving event, when in fact only the latter is true.

A better way to capture the relevant semantic facts is to introduce two distinct kinds of relation linking a single verb to two superordinate concepts. In addition to strict hyponymy, there would be a "parallel" hyponymy relation with the appropriate properties.

16.6.3 *Para-Relations*

Cruse (1986), in discussing the TYPE-ROLE distinction among nouns, proposes a relation dubbed para-hyponymy for organizing nouns like *dog* and *pet* hierarchically. Like regular hyponymy, para-hyponymy admits the formula Xs and other Ys, where X is the subordinate and Y the superordinate: Both statements, "dogs and other canines" (type) and "dogs and other pets" (role) are good. This formula can easily be adopted for verbs, and fits both strict hyponymy and para-hyponymy:

(52)   Biking/swimming/jogging and other manners of moving/travelling

(53)   Biking/swimming/jogging and other manners of exercising

The "but not"-test for nouns (Cruse 1986) that shows defeasibility, can be readily applied to verbs:

(54)   It's a walking/jogging/biking event but it's not an exercising event.

16.6.4 Expectation

Cruse (1986) characterizes para-hyponymy among nouns not in terms of logical necessity but "expectation." Thus, there seems to be an "expectation" that a jogging event is an exercising event, even though jogging is not necessarily exercising. While intuitively convincing, the notion of "expectation" immediately raises several questions, in particular if one wants to co-opt it to represent verbs and the events they denote. How can expectation be characterized? Can it be quantified? How can verb pairs related by para-hyponymy be identified in the lexicon? And how do we know whether, say, a verb token *jog* in a text or utterance refers to an exercising event or (merely) to a running event?

To begin with, expectation often appears to be context-dependent rather than inherent in the concept. In some contexts, a given verb's interpretation as a para-hyponym is more salient, whereas in other context, its reading as a strict manner hyponym of another superordinate is more appropriate.

For example, the verb's interpretations as a manner of moving is more salient in (55–57), whereas in (58), the events are readily interpreted as exercise:

(55) The boat capsized and we had to swim to the shore.

(56) My car is in the repair shop so I'll bike to work.

(57) It started to rain heavily so she ran into the library.

(58) He swims/bikes/runs 3 miles every morning before work.

Some contexts seem to favor an underspecified reading:

(59) He jogged to the store.

Second, the degree of expectation may differ across verbs independently of specific contexts, but be part of their lexical make-up. For some verbs, the para-relation is stronger than the strict relation, and the reverse may be true for other verbs. For example, *jog* intuitively is more strongly associated with its defeasible superordinate *exercise* than with its logical superordinate *run*. This is reflected in the fact that some dictionaries have distinct running and exercising senses for *jog*, as noted earlier. Conversely, *walk* seems be more strongly associated with *move* that with *exercise*. *Walk* seems like a less canonical form of exercise than *jog*, and thus exhibits a weaker association with its defeasible hypernym and a correspondingly stronger link to its strict superordinate.

The relative frequency of one reading as compared to another presumably influences expectation. Just as, say, "hawks as pets" may be more conventional in certain cultures than in others, there are probably cultures where jogging and running are not done for exercise but, say, for pursuing game in a hunt.

16.7 Purpose Verbs and Para-Hyponymy in the Lexicon

This paper has cited only a handful of examples for purpose verbs and para-relations. At this point, we don't know how many such verbs there are in the English lexicon. If we think of the lexicon as a structured ontology, e.g., a large semantic network, one might ask whether such verbs are distributed randomly or in a systematic fashion. Another open question is whether the kinds of concepts expressed by purpose verbs are universally lexicalized and to what extent.

Almost any verb that is a hyponym of move could be made a para-hyponym of *exercise*, just as a "pet" reading can be coerced for many animals. If one wants to code para-relations in a lexicon, it is important to avoid flooding it with links that reflect readings with very low expectancy. It would therefore be desirable to firm up intuitions about the relative strength or weakness of the (para)hyponymy relation with the aid of corpus data.

16.7.1 Finding Para-Relations

Fellbaum (2002b) discusses ways of finding cases of para-relations among verbs from corpus data, and cites examples of attested data found on the web by means of characteristic pattern searches. These patterns are frames such as

(60)   ..and other ways of (Y-ing)

(61)   to (X) is to (Y)

(62)   to (X) is not to (Y)

These searches overgenerate, as the frames turn up cases of hyponymy involving both manner and purpose. Manual sorting leaves us with examples such as these:

(63)   Befriending, listening and other ways of helping....
            (www.britishcouncil.org/sudan/science/)

(64)   Walking and other exercise use many muscles.
            (www.lungusa.org/diseases/exercise.html)

(65)   Swimming, running, biking, walking and other exercise that are at a time
            length of over 20 minutes.
            (www.pmssolutions.com/Hiddentruth.html)

(66)   ... shake hands, using the right hand, and explain that this is a way of
            greeting one another. Pair up children and allow them to practice
            shaking hands.
            (www.atozkidsstuff.com/math.html)

(67)   Tipping, leaving a gratuity, is a way of thanking people for their service.
        (www.istudentcity.com/stages/)

These examples show that targeted corpus searches can reveal the semantic relations among verbs (see (Hearst 1998) for a discussion of patterns to find other semantic relations).

16.8   Summary and Conclusions

We have identified a class of "purpose" verbs that includes *exercise, cheat, help*, and *treat*. Such verbs encode neither MANNER nor RESULT, but encode an event with telicity. Unlike in the case of Functional Event in the Generative Lexicon, the telicity of purpose verbs is inherent in the event rather than in an argument of the verb expressing that event. Purpose verbs differ in several other respects from Functional Events in the Generative Lexicon. Functional Events are rather intuitively defined, and no test for distinguishing them from other event types has been given. By contrast, purpose verb can be clearly distinguished from manner and COS verbs and are incompatible with secondary predicates expressing results. Purpose verbs can be clearly distinguished from manner verbs, as the relations to their superordinate is defeasible. Finally, we showed that certain adverbs bind with the purpose component of these verbs for an appropriate interpretation.

Several open questions remain. How many purpose verbs are there in the English verb lexicon, and where in the lexicon are they? Do purpose verbs follow specific lexicalization patterns, similar to manner verbs? Fellbaum (2002a) discusses ways of collecting naturally attested cases of this relation from corpora.

Semantic relations that are not based on logical necessity but on expectations grounded in pragmatics or world knowledge are an important area for lexical and ontological research. But we need to know more about how expected readings are generated from contexts.

Acknowledgment This work was supported in part by the Alexander-von-Humboldt Foundation through the Zukunftsinvestitionsprogramm and ARDA (Advanced Research and Development Agency). I am grateful to the editors of this volume and to the reviewers of earlier drafts for many valuable comments. Special thanks go to Benjamin Haskell, without whose help this paper would not have materialized.

References

Apresyan, Y. (1973). Regular polysemy. *Linguistics, 147*, 5–32.
Asher, N., & Pustejovsky, J. (2006). A type composition logic for generative lexicon. *Journal of Cognitive Science, 6*, 1–38.
Cruse, A. (1986). *Lexical semantics*. Cambridge: Cambridge University Press.

Fagan, S. (1988). The English middle. *Linguistic Inquiry, 19*, 181–203.

Fellbaum, C. (1985). Adverbs in agentless actives and passives. In *Papers from the parasession on causatives and agentivity* (Vol. 21, pp. 21–31). Chicago: University of Chicago Press.

Fellbaum, C. (1990). The English verb lexicon as a semantic Net. *International Journal of Lexicography, 3*(4), 278–301.

Fellbaum, C. (Ed.). (1998). *WordNet: An electronic lexical database*. Cambridge, MA: MIT Press.

Fellbaum, C. (2002a). On the semantics of troponymy. In R. Green, S. Myang, & C. Bean (Eds.), *Relations* (pp. 23–34). Dordrecht: Kluwer.

Fellbaum, C. (2002b). Parallel hierarchies in the verb lexicon. In K. Simov (Ed.), *Proceedings of the Ontolex02 workshop on ontologies and lexical knowledge bases* (pp. 27–31). Paris: ELRA.

Fellbaum, C., & Kegl, J. (1989). Taxonomic structure and object deletion in the English verbal system. In K. deJong & Y. No (Eds.), *Proceedings of the sixth eastern states conference on linguistics* (pp. 94–103). Columbus: Ohio State University Press.

Fong, S., Fellbaum, C., & Lebeaux, D. (2001). Ghosts, shadows, and resultatives: The lexical representation of verbs. *Traitement Automatique de Langues, 42*, 755–784.

Gangemi, A., Guarino, N., & Oltramari, A. (2001). Conceptual analysis of lexical taxonomies. In *Proceedings of FOIS* (pp. 285–296). Ogunquit: ACM.

Gangemi, A., Guarino, N., Oltromari, A., & Borgo, S. (2002). Cleaning up WordNet's top level. In U. N. Singh (Ed.), *Proceedings of the first global WordNet conference* (pp. 109–121). Mysore: Center for Indian Languages.

Guarino, N. (1998). Some ontological principles for designing upper level lexical resources. In *Proceedings of the first international conference of language resources and evaluation* (pp. 527–534). Paris: ELRA.

Guarino, N., & Welty, C. (2001). *Identity and subsumption*. Padua: LADSEP-CNR Internal Report.

Guarino, N., & Welty, C. (2002). Evaluating ontological decisions with ontoclean. *Communications of the ACM, 45*(2), 61–65.

Hale, K., & Keyser, S. (1993). On argument structure and the lexical expression of syntactic relations. In K. Hale & S. Keyser (Eds.), *The view from building twenty* (pp. 53–109). Cambridge, MA: MIT Press.

Hearst, M. A. (1998). Automatic discovery of WordNet relations. In C. Fellbaum (Ed.), *WordNet: An electronic lexical database* (pp. 131–151). Cambridge, MA: MIT Press.

Jackendoff, R. (1990). *Semantic structures*. Cambridge, MA: MIT Press.

Keyser, S., & Roeper, T. (1984). On the middle and ergative constructions in English. *Linguistic Inquiry, 15*, 381–416.

Krifka, M. (1999). Manner in dative alternation. In *Proceedings of the 18th west coast conference on formal linguistics*. Cornell: Cascadilla Press.

Levin, B., & Rapoport, T. (1988). Lexical subordination. In *Proceedings of the Chicago linguistic society* (pp. 275–289). Chicago: University of Chicago Press.

Miller, G. A. (1995). WordNet: A lexical database for English. *Communications of the ACM, 38*(11), 39–41.

Pustejovsky, J. (1995). *The generative lexicon*. Cambridge, MA: MIT Press.

Pustejovsky, J. (2001). Type construction and the logic of concepts. In P. Bouillon & F. Busa (Eds.), *The syntax of word meaning*. Cambridge: Cambridge University Press.

Rappaport Hovav, M., & Levin, B. (1998). Building word meanings. In M. Butt & W. Geuder (Eds.), *The projection of arguments: Lexical and compositional factors* (pp. 97–174). Stanford: CSLI Publications.

Talmy, L. (1985). Lexicalization patterns: Semantic structure in lexical forms. In T. Shopen (Ed.), *Language typology and semantic description* (pp. 57–149). Cambridge: Cambridge University Press.

Vendler, Z. (1967). *Linguistics in philosophy*. Ithaca: Cornell University Press.

Wierzbicka, A. (1996). *Semantics, primes, and universals*. Oxford: Oxford University Press.

Chapter 17
Word Formation Rules and the Generative Lexicon: Representing Noun-to-Verb Versus Verb-to-Noun Conversion in French

Fiammetta Namer and Evelyne Jacquey

17.1 Introduction

The issues we address in this paper focus on the interface between lexical semantics and morphology. Just as lexical semantics can be viewed from a compositional point of view, morphology (that is, morpho-semantics) can be understood as a compositional semantics-constrained mechanism according to Corbin's approach (Corbin 1987, 2001). These two levels of description give us distinct types of intrinsic information on the semantic content of derived words. One way to establish links between the two levels of description is to choose a common formalism for their representation.

Basing our work on the study of the prefixation by M. Aurnague and M. Plénat (1996, 1997), limited to the popular prefix é- in French, we (Jacquey and Namer 2003; Namer and Jacquey 2003) have suggested modelising the semantic role of this prefix within the framework of the Generative Lexicon Theory (Pustejovsky 1995). In this paper, we further this approach to modelisation of word formation mechanisms and apply this modelisation to account for another word formation (WF) process type in French, namely the NtoV versus VtoN conversion. Our reasons for focusing on the phenomenon of conversion are threefold.

First, it consists in a non-conventional mechanism because of the absence of any affix. The absence of such morphological mark is crucial as far as conversion orientation is concerned. On the basis of the pairs $dance_N/dance_V$ and $butter_N/butter_V$ for example, what has to be decided is whether the (output) verb is converted from the (input) noun or vice-versa. This decision will allow us to draw the definition of the output with respect to that of the input.

F. Namer (✉) • E. Jacquey
UMR 7118 ATILF CNRS & Université de Lorraine, Nancy, France

J. Pustejovsky et al. (eds.), *Advances in Generative Lexicon Theory*, Text,
Speech and Language Technology 46, DOI 10.1007/978-94-007-5189-7_17,
© Springer Science+Business Media Dordrecht 2013

Second, verb and noun pairs related by the conversion process is of interest not only for WF research, but also for the lexical semantics. For instance, Goverment and Binding-oriented literature sometimes refers to it as to *noun incorporation* phenomenon (Hale and Keyser 1993), while Generative Lexicon Theory proposes to characterise their structure with the so-called *shadow argument* (Pustejovsky 1996).

Finally, this WF process is a multilingual phenomenon. It is both productive and frequent, and found at least in French and English.

Focusing on the French language, our formalisation proposal aims to account for the following aspects, as it will be discussed in this chapter: (1) a corpus-based analysis producing 2,500 homograph Noun/Verb pairs; (2) a ranking of these pairs according to semantic criteria; (3) a modelisation proposal stemming from the analysis of the most frequent and productive classes.

The rest of the chapter is structured as follows: Sect. 17.2 summarises briefly why and how we propose to modelise WF processes within the Generative Lexicon Theory; Sects. 17.3 and 17.4 focus on the conversion process itself. Section 17.3 compares hypotheses coming from linguistic theoretical studies with empirical results obtained by means of the corpus-based analysis mentioned above. Section 17.3 ends by a synthetic table which ranks conversion classes as a result of this comparison. According to these classes, Sect. 17.4 finally suggests two formal models for NtoV and VtoN conversion processes, respectively.

17.2 Word Formation Modelisation Within GL: MS-CS

This section focuses on modelisation backgrounds. First, Sect. 17.2.1 gives the linguistic theoretical background WF on which processes rely. Section 17.2.2 deals with the motivation for modelisation itself.

17.2.1 Theoretical Background: Corbin's Approach to Word Formation

Among WF theories, research initiated for French in Corbin (1987) provides descriptions that put semantics in the forefront. More precisely, her WF theory is based on three statements:

1. Morphology is autonomous. In other words, the lexicon of the morphologically constructed words is generated by domain specific rules: WF rules and their outputs are independent of e.g. syntactic information. This statement agrees with e.g. (Aronoff 1976);
2. Morphology is regular, i.e. the morphologically constructed words lexicon is regular. Surface exceptions can always be given some explanation whether semantic, phonetic, diachronic, etc..;

3. WF rules associate several kinds of constraints, phonetic, semantic and categorial ones being the most important. It has been established that categorial conditions for WF can be derived from semantics (Corbin 2001; Dal 1997).[1]

Consequently, Corbin's theory foresees that part of the lexical meaning of a morphologically constructed word, called "lexical constructed meaning", is built together with its constructed form.

Considering WF rules from this theoretical point of view clarifies the relationship between lexical semantics and morphology which rules WF, since a morphologically constructed word is above all a matter of semantic constraints. Constraints are exerted both on the **base** (called here **input**) and on the **derived word** (called here the **output**), through WF processes, which can be suffixation, prefixation, conversion or compounding processes. The lexical meaning of both the input and output are opposed to the meaning of the WF process itself, which can be seen as a computational (or instructional) device. In contrast with an input or an output, a WF process does not "mean" anything, but provides a guideline for the output meaning.

As stated in Sect. 17.1, in order to enable WF rules to be displayed as lexical semantics constraints, one way to proceed is to choose a common formalism of representation. The chosen formalism must be able to express semantic constraints at distinct levels, especially at syntactic and semantic levels, for any WF process. In addition, a given WF process may select only specific aspects of its input meaning, in order to build the meaning of the corresponding output.

The expressivity of the Generative Lexicon Theory (GL) makes it suitable to represent the just mentioned constraints. More precisely, GL is modular enough to integrate a level of morphological description and it is rich enough to constrain both input and output of a given WF process. The next section summarises how the GL-based WF mechanism has been set.

17.2.2 Formal Background: Our Approach to WF Modelisation

To achieve the goal of modeling WF in French, two basic approaches can be considered: (a) encoding the affixes themselves or (b) setting up abstract parametrised lexical units describing the outputs. One argument for the first choice would be the fact that affixes can be considered as some type of predicates operating on and controlling both the input and the output, from structural, categorial and semantic points of view. The first approach though is inadequate for two main reasons:

1. Encoding affixes to model WF would mean reducing WF to affix-based processes, and would consequently exclude both compounding and conversion. Keep in

---

[1] Phonetics blocks semantics if one is competing with the other. This phenomenon will not be addressed in this paper, since we focus only on WF semantic constraints: for a detailed description, see Plénat and Roché (2004).

mind that the latter consists, loosely speaking, in building new words by means of a simple part of speech (POS) change[2];

2. The very nature of affixes is another counterargument. According to the morphological theory our study is based on, an affix does not belong to any of the major POS categories. In addition, it bears no referential meaning: consequently, it does not seem logical to modelise its semantic content since it has no proper semantic content.

Thus, in previous studies (Jacquey and Namer 2003; Namer and Jacquey 2003), we turned to the second approach: namely, designing an abstract model which is intended to define the common properties shared by the **outputs** of a given WF process,[3] whatever the involved morphological process. This **abstract lexical unit** (ALU) is instantiated through the **input** content of the WF process, which provides thus the abstract output with distinctive, specific properties.

In order to constrain the combination of an ALU with and only with licensed inputs, we have decided to add a new attribute-value pair at the most ALU embedding level: this pair, encoding the required semantic features of the WF inputs, is referred to as the **morphological structure** (MS).

Finally, in order to instantiate a well-formed constructed word content from the ALU, we assumed one unification mechanism: the **morphological structure composition schema** (MS-CS).[4] Through MS-CS, only the candidate inputs with the appropriate features matching the MS content of the ALU are selected for the formation of well-formed ouputs. This unification procedure also entails the instanciation of the right features on the output.

Based on the unification principle, the morphological structure composition schema (MS-CS) in (Fig. 17.1) governs the composition between a given abstract lexical unit and an actual input, in order to build the meaning of a well-formed output. In our conception, MS-CS is meant to be WF process-independent: among its arguments, ALUs are thus likely to represent any WF process, and actual words (both input and output) can belong to any major POS categories.

The MS-CS behavior is twofold. First, when the ALU morphological structure (MS) unifies with the actual input, the success of this unification, noted by the $\boxed{ms}$ index,[5] means that this input satisfies the constraints required by the ALU MS. As a first consequence, relevant features are propagated into the appropriate ALU structures, namely the argumental structure $\boxed{as}$, the event structure $\boxed{es}$ and the qualia structure $\boxed{qs}$. Second, the MS-CS schema ensures the propagation of the updated features from the ALU to the output in order to provide the latter with a well-formed semantic content.

---

[2]See Sect. 17.3 for a more accurate definition of conversion.

[3]i.e. an underspecified referential lexical unit.

[4]For a detailed description of the model, see Jacquey and Namer (2003) and Namer and Jacquey (2003).

[5]As is well-known in the framework of typed feature structures, indices are used to ensure value unification (Shieber 1986).

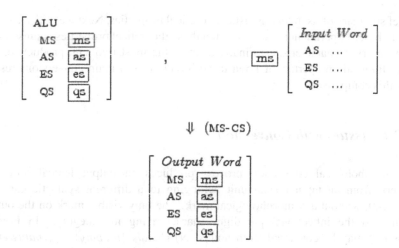

Fig. 17.1 Composition Schema (MS-CS)

The role played by our morphological device, in which MS-CS interact with an abstract lexical unit, can be viewed as a lexical semantics-driven modelisation of the so-called 'word-based' model in morphological theory. The choice of such a model (Bybee 1988; Koenig 1999; Fradin 2003) is opposed to 'morpheme-based' model (Selkirk 1982; Di Sciullo and Williams 1987; Lieber 1992). Unlike the latter, the word-based model is suitable for the description of non-concatenative word formation processes. In word-based models, the relationship between complex words is captured by formulating **word-schemas** which represent the common features of sets for morphologically related words. According to (Haspelmath 2002:47), "a word-schema is like a lexical entry in that it contains information on pronunciation, syntactic properties and meaning, but it may contain variables. In this way, it abstracts away from the differences between the related words and just expresses the common features". A word-schema **subsumes** a set of words, that in turn **match** given schemas. Morphological relationships are therefore represented by correspondences between word-schemas. Word pairs that match correspondent schemas are thus related by a particular morphological relationship.

Hence it can be easily seen that ALUs formalise word-schemas and MS-CS represents morphological correspondences between schemas, which inputs and outputs have to match in order to instantiate actual morphologically related word pairs.

17.3 Data and Linguistic Description

Our aim is to reuse the MS-CS approach just discussed, in order, this time, to formalise the so-called conversion morphological process in French. This section covers the arguments for choosing this particular word formation type, together with a brief summary of its main linguistic theoretical properties. Next we will see how a corpus-based experiment is used to match these theoretical properties against large-scale observed characteristics. Finally a set of the most frequent, productive, and stable linguistic properties of noun to verb and verb to noun conversions results from this comparison.

17.3.1   Issues with Conversion

The morphological conversion process produces an output lexical unit (the convert) from an input lexical unit belonging to a different syntactic category (the base), without any morphological mark. The only visible mark on the output belongs to the inflectional paradigm characterizing its category.[6] In French, verbs (V) may be converted from nouns (N) ($balai_N$ [$broom_N$]$\rightarrow_{conv}balay(er)_V$[7] [$sweep_V$]), or from adjectives (A) ($vide_A$ [$empty_A$]$\rightarrow_{conv}vid(er)_V$ [$empty_V$]); N may be converted from verbs ($vol(er)_V$ [fly_V]$\rightarrow_{conv}vol_N$ [$flight_N$]) or from adjectives ($portable_A$ [$portable_A$]$\rightarrow_{conv}portable_N$ [$laptop_N$]), the opposite rarely being true ($orange_N\rightarrow_{conv}orange_A$). Being unmarked,[8] this type of word formation entails the issue of the process orientation[9] i.e. there is no formal way to decide which one of N or V is the conversion output in e.g. *balai*, *balay(er)*, *vol* and *vol(er)*. Within the chosen WF theoretical approach, answering the orientation question amounts into making semantically driven decisions. In other words, detecting e.g. the **NtoV** versus **VtoN** conversion orientation means classifying Noun/Verb (quasi)homograph pairs according to a semantic relation.

17.3.2   NtoV Versus VtoN

The choice of focusing on the Noun/Verb pairs has been motivated by the presence of a large amount of such pairs, and by the high interest they gather within the

---

[6]Some authors, especially those who belong to the Government and Binding tradition, call conversion by means of the term *zero affixation*.

[7]We choose to represent verbs by means of their infinitive form: the inflection ending marking the V infinitive *–er* is put between brackets. Some phonological variations, such as here $/\varepsilon/\rightarrow/\varepsilon j/$, graphically realized by the [ai] $\rightarrow$ [ay] alternation, may occur within the conjugation paradigm.

[8]Inflectional endings, such as infinitive *–er*, are surface marks which have nothing to do with word formation.

[9]When conversion involves morphologically complex lexical units, orientation may be decided from the input and output internal structure. For instance, the suffix *–ure*, building deverbal nouns, appears in the pair $hachure_N/hachur(er)_V$ [*hatching, zebra marking$_N$/hatchy*], forcing the N $\rightarrow_{conv}$ V orientation. In fact, the other orientation would imply the output noun be formed both by conversion, from *hachur(er)*, and by suffixation, from *hach(er)* [*chop, cut, mince$_V$*], which is not possible since *hachure* is not polysemous. See Namer (2003), which follows Corbin (1987), for a conversion typology according to input/output morphological complexity.

linguistic community. In fact, according to Corbin (2004), there are no cases of V →$_{conv}$ A in French. Moreover the N →$_{conv}$ A type is limited to the production of chromatic adjectives derived from nouns referring to fruits or flowers (*rose, orange...*), and to the production of behavior adjectives converted from nouns referring to stereotypical animals (*bête [beast$_N$], cochon [pig$_N$]* ...). Conversely, both N →$_{conv}$ V and V →$_{conv}$ N have been observed, in French as in other languages, even though morphology researchers (at least, the authors whose results are briefly reported below) do not often agree as far as conversion orientation is concerned.

A second argument, directly related to the first one justifying our choice is the semantic heterogeneity of verbs and nouns involved in conversion processes. Regardless, for the time being, of their possible role of input or output in the conversion process, let us notice that nouns may denote concrete (*sucre$_N$/sucr(er)$_V$ [sugar$_{N/V}$]*), animate (*singe$_N$/sing(er)$_V$ [monkey$_N$/mimic$_V$]*), human (*guide$_N$/guid(er)$_V$ [guide$_{N/V}$]*), or abstract entities (*nage$_N$/nag(er)$_V$ [swimming$_N$/swim$_V$]*); that verbs may describe instrumental (*hache$_N$/hach(er)$_V$ [axe$_N$/chop$_V$]*), dissociative (*plume$_N$/plum(er)$_V$ [feather$_N$/pluck$_V$]*), or locative (*coffre$_N$/coffr(er)$_V$ [chest$_N$/throw inside$_V$]*) processes; and that they may belong to all kinds of eventualities: activities (*crayon$_N$/crayonn(er)$_V$ [pencil$_N$/scribble$_V$]*), transitions (*transport$_N$/transport(er)$_V$ [transport$_N$/carry$_V$]*), etc.

Last but not least, our interest in the Noun/Verb pairs is related to the fact that their linguistic description bridges together word formation and lexical semantics. Given that the Noun/Verb orientation is exclusively a matter of semantics, deciding for N→$_{conv}$ V or for V→$_{conv}$ N amounts to detecting the semantic properties on V and/or on N. This is in order (1) to check which of V or N is obtained from the other one, and, consequently, (2) to determine the semantic relationship holding N and V. This second point amounts to draw the definition of the output word by means of the input meaning. From these results, a (first attempt of a) semantic-based typology of NtoV and VtoN conversion should emerge, as we shall see below.

17.3.3 Theoretical Assumptions

Apart from the attempt of orienting NtoV from VtoN conversion according to **phonological marks** (see e.g. Katamba 1993[10]), literature regarding Noun/Verb conversion tries to give semantic motivations to their classification proposals. For Aronoff *and alii* (1984), the orientation has to do with **thematic roles attached to V**, and to which role N may, or may not play. For Mel'cuk (1996, 1997), some VtoN conversions are what he calls empty categorial conversions, which may occur between an input lexical unit and an output lexical unit with **stronger distributional constraints** than those of the input. On the other hand, non-empty categorial

---

[10]His approach, that follows e.g. Marchand (1969), Adams (1973), Kiparsky (1982) is not applicable for French. Also it is not useful for providing outputs with a definition involving their input.

conversions are generally oriented according to the **semantic inclusion relation** between the involved lexical units X and Y: if the meaning of X is included in that of Y, then X→Y. Moreover, he proposes, following (Corbin 1987), a **paradigmatic orientation**[11] of Noun/Verb conversion: it is oriented in the same way as affixation with the same semantic relation. For instance, since –*eur* in French basically builds agents (*nag(er)*$_V$ →$_{-eur}$*nageur*$_N$ [*swim*$_V$/*swimmer*$_N$]), and no other affix involves agents, all Noun/Verb pairs exhibiting an "agent" semantic relation should belong to that paradigm, and thus, for instance *guid(er)*$_V$→$_{conv}$*guide*$_N$.

Among the assumptions briefly reported above, the **paradigmatic orientation** hypothesis seems to be the most promising: in fact, Aronoff's relying on **thematic roles** would require a clear, stable and homogeneous definition of them, which is unfortunately not the case. As for Mel'cuk, he is neither able to define formally **distributional constraints** (which rules empty VtoN categorial constraint) nor **semantic inclusion** (which rules non-empty NtoV conversion).

However, paradigmatic orientation hypothesis is not a completely satisfactory solution. First, it does not account for pairs such as *babouin*$_N$/*babouiner*$_V$ [*baboon*$_N$/*act as a baboon*$_V$], in which **imitation verbs** depict the referent of the agent as acting in the same way as the referent of the base noun they are morphologically constructed from. Second, it leads to contradictory situations, e.g. when nouns refer to instruments. According to the paradigm, the conversion relation of Noun/Verb pairs should be V →$_{conv}$ N oriented when N denotes an instrument, since the only affixation process dealing with instruments in French are suffixes –*oir* and– *eur*, which both form deverbal nouns. Therefore, for –*oir*, we have for instance *hach(er)*$_V$ →$_{-oir}$*hachoir*$_N$[*chop*$_V$/*chopper*$_N$]. But for the same input, we notice that we also have *hach(er)*$_V$ →$_{conv}$*hache*$_N$, [*axe*$_N$] bearing (apparently) the same semantic relation. This is also the case with other N/N-*oir* or N/N-*eur* pairs: *drain*$_N$/*draineur*$_N$ [*drain*$_N$/*drainer*$_N$], *gril*$_N$/*grilloir*$_N$ [*gril*$_N$/*griller*$_N$]. The meaning variation between the compared nouns may indicate that Noun/Verb and N-*oir*/V or N-*eur*/V do not belong exactly to the same paradigm. A clear example of this is the case of the the verb *agraf(er)*$_V$ [*staple*$_V$]: the noun *agrafe*$_N$ [*staple*$_N$] refers to the concrete entity that performs the process itself; and the noun *agrafeuse*$_N$[12] [*stapler*$_N$], the instrument which must be used so that these staples can do their job. If the instrumental paradigm cannot always be clearly stated, then there is no longer much evidence for the V →$_{conv}$ N orientation, when N is an instrument. Furthermore, D. Corbin partially reconsiders in later papers the overall paradigmatic hypothesis (Corbin 1997, 2004), mentioning instruments and instrumental verbs (*scie*$_N$/*sci(er)*$_V$ [*saw*$_{N/V}$]) as NtoV conversion cases.

---

[11]also called 'overt analogue' principle (Sanders 1988).

[12]Actually, -*eur*/-*euse* are nothing but two gender variations of the same affix: -*euse* is a possible feminine form corresponding to -*eur*. We assume that gender variation has to do with inflection, and thus is not a matter of WF, at least for nouns referring to inanimate entities, see (Corbett 1991) for an accurate discussion on this issue.

Be that as it may, we shall keep this paradigmatic assumption as a starting point. In addition to the NtoV WF processes, this hypothesis has also been the theoretical foundation for VtoN descriptions and analyses. One of the main contributors to these studies for French is F. Kerleroux: a very detailed analysis of converted deverbal nouns' properties has been carried out by Kerleroux (1996a, b, 1997, 1999). Furthermore, Kerleroux (2004), Fradin and Kerleroux (2003a, b) redefine the notion of a lexeme. Consequently, they draw a set of conditions constraining VtoN conversion, using the differences these authors record between conversion and apocope, from both distributional and semantic points of view. VtoN conversion is also the object of study in Meinschäfer (2003); J. Meinschäfer proposes a set of criteria predicting the deverbal noun argument structure, with respect to that of the input verb. More precisely, she shows that deverbal nouns share with their input verb their aspectual and argumental properties, provided that the verb is not a causative event: *Max recule la chaise [Max moves back the chair]* → **Le recul de la chaise (par Max) [(Max's) moving back of the chair]*. However, she observes that causative and non-causative readings always alternate, thus allowing conversion: *Max recule [Max is going back]*→ *le recul de Max [Max's backward movement]*.

To sum up Noun/Verb conversion orientation possibilities, we can make the following assumptions:

- N →$_{conv}$ V holds when (a) N is itself morphologically constructed (*hachure [hatching$_N$]*), (b) N is an instrument/substance used to perform the process described by V (*scie [saw$_N$], sucre [sugar$_N$]*), (c) N is the place where the process is performed (*coffre [chest$_N$]*), (d) N is the stereotypical agent of the process (*singe [monkey$_N$]*);
- V →$_{conv}$ N holds, basically, when N is abstract; so N describes the process, its result or its product (*transport*); besides, N may denote the process agent (*guide*).

With this first classification in mind, let us now turn to the corpus analysis. We have collected a set of Noun/Verb homographs pairs, in order to (a) try to classify them according to the above criteria, (b) if (a) is not possible, to define new classes.

17.3.4   Corpus

To check the validity of the linguistic hypotheses performed above, we have collected the set of quasi-homograph verbal and nominal lexical units from a large-scale machine readable dictionary, mainly the TLFnome[13] word list. Lexical units

---

[13] *TLFnome* is a lexicon of inflected forms developed at the INaLF based on the nomenclature of the *Trésor de la Langue Française*, a general language multi-volumes dictionary. It currently contains 63,000 lemmas, 390,000 forms and 500,000 entries. It is in the course of being supplemented by 36,400 additional lemmas from the *TLF* index.

are labeled with the appropriate part-of-speech, and have at worst different endings, and allomorphic variants (e.g., changing thematic vowel aperture, graphically marked by a diacritic, e.g. with /B/→/ɛ/in $relev(er)_V/relève_N$ [pick $up_V/relief_N$], or by doubling consonant e.g. with /T/→/Cn/in $collision_N/collisionn(er)_V$ [collision_N/collide_V]).[14] A set of 2,500 Noun/Verb pairs have thus been gathered, half of which have been manually verified. The verification objectives are the following:

- checking whether the paired elements are actually linked by conversion;
- deciding for the conversion orientation, according to: (1) the theoretical assumptions given in Sects. 17.3.3 and 17.2 definitions and etymologies provided within dictionaries;
- if needed, proposing new classes, or constraining the existing ones.

The conclusions of this large-scale verification are summed up in Sect. 17.3.5, from both a qualitative (ranking Noun/Verb pairs with respect to semantic classes) and quantitative (classifying Noun/Verb pairs according to their frequency) point of view.

17.3.5   Synthesis

Tables 17.1 and 17.2 below summarize the observations resulting from corpus data analysis. First, as far as **VtoN** conversion conditions are concerned (Table 17.2), the results are all in all in conformity with the hypotheses made in the previous section. Nouns massively refer to abstract entities (class -2-), although semantic derivations are sometimes observed: for instance, the process noun $applique$ ([$application_N$]) converted from $appliquer$ ([$apply_V$]) has a specialised meaning which leads this noun to refer to (concrete) entities, "whose function is to be fixed/mounted/hung (onto the wall)" namely $wall$ $lamps$.

Concerning **NtoV** (Table 17.1), there are discrepancies between theoretical assumptions and corpus analysis results, which makes the definition of new classes. For instance, similarity verbs are not only met with respect to the agent ($singer_V$), but also with respect to the theme, which is affected by the change-of-state transition process described by the verb: $marbr(er)_V$ [$marble_V$] (class -8-). The property acquired by the theme is a shape, a color, etc. described by the referent of the input noun. In addition to class -2-, grouping artefactual instruments/substance-based verbs, another set of rather similar verbs, has been collected in the so-called class -2'-: the input noun, referring to a part of the body

---

[14]Due to the technique we used to collect our corpus, N/V pairs exhibiting strong allomorphy or suppletive variations are not included in our study (e.g. $pleuv-oir_V/pluie_N[rain_{V/N}]$). A manual checking should be necessary to confirm their behaviour to be in conformity with the obtained conclusions (Sect. 17.3.5, Table 17.1).

Table 17.1 NtoV conversion classes

Class	N → V	Nb	%[a]
		789	73.6
1	N is a morphologically constructed lexical unit: *hach/hachurer* [*hatching/hatch*] N = "*action of V*"	86	8.02
2	N refers to either a typical instrument (*drain/drain(er)*) or to the substance (*sucre/sucr(er)*) implied as a mean to realise the process described by V: $V(N_{theme})$ = "*do smthing to N_{theme} using N*"	372	34.73
2′	N refers to either a part of human body or a human characteristics (*cil/cill(er), raison/raisonn(er)*) $N_{agent}V$ = "*Use N, which (is part of/characterizes) $N_{agent[+hum]}$*"	14	1.3
3	N refers to a stereotypical agent of the process: *singe/sing(er)* V = "*(do what N would do|behave as N)*"	69	6.44
4	N refers to the place or temporal interval in which the process takes place: *coffre/coffr(er)* $V(N_{theme})$ = "*do or put N_{theme} (with)in/during N*"	50	4.66
5	N is a meteorogical phenomenon: *neige$_N$/neig(er)$_V$* [*snow$_{N/V}$*] (V is impersonal) V = "*It does N*"	5	0.46
6	N refers to the product obtained by dissociating via V the entity referred to by the V theme: *plume/plum(er)* $V N_{theme}$ = "*produce N by dissociating N from N_{theme}*"	34	3.17
7	N refers to a sound, a noise, a (speech) act (*belote/belot(er), laïus/laïuss(er), peste/pester*) N and V may be borrowings (*crash(er)/crash*) or onomatopoeias lexical units (*blablat(er)/blabla*) V = "*do/say/have N*"	92	8.59
8	Either N, or some of its metonymic derived entities (N_{mtny}) is what N_{theme} looks like at the end of the process described by V (*marbr(er)*) $V(N_{theme})$ = "*provide N_{theme} with either N or N_{mtny} characteristics or appearance*"	67	6.25

[a] Among the 1,250 collected Noun/Verb pairs, 1,071 are truly related through conversion. The 179 other ones often correspond to homonymy cases, such as *griffon$_N$/griffonner$_V$* [*scribble$_V$*]. Total and percentages are calculated on the basis of these actual 1,071 conversion pairs

Table 17.2 VtoN conversion classes

Class	V → N	Nb	%
		282	26.4[14]
1	N refers to the verb agent: *guid(er)/guide* N = "*the one who V*"	10	0.93
2	N refers to the process described by V, or its result, or its product: *vol(er)/vol, recul(er)/recul* N = "*action | result of V*"	272	25.39

(*cil*$_N$ [*eyelash*$_N$]) or a human characteristic (*raison*$_N$ [*reason*$_N$]) is namely used as an instrument (*cill(er)*$_V$ [*blink*$_V$], *raisonn(er)*$_V$ [*reason*$_V$]). Finally, a 'default', heterogeneous class has been drawn, grouping together Noun/Verb pairs in which N may refer to speech acts (*laïus*$_N$ vs *laïuss(er)*$_V$ [*long winded speech*$_N$/*expatiate*$_V$]), to noise or sounds (*vacarme*$_N$ vs *vacarmer*$_V$ [*uproar*$_N$/*make an uproar*$_V$], *clic*$_N$ vs *cliquer*$_V$ [*click*$_{N/V}$]), to concrete action results (*sieste*$_N$ vs *siester*$_V$ [*nap*$_N$/*have a nap*$_V$], *balafre*$_N$ vs *balafrer*$_V$ [*cut, slash, gash*$_{N/V}$]). This class, labeled with -7-, is defined by means of a shallow link: $V =$ "*do/say/have N*". Within this class are also listed N/V pairs where V denotes delocutive acts: *choucou*$_N$ vs *chouchouter*$_V$ ([*darling*$_N$/*pet*$_V$]), *peste*$_N$ vs *pester*$_V$ ([*heavens!*$_N$/*curse*$_V$]). The 'delocutive derivation', originally introduced in Benveniste (1966) has been investigated in Cornulier (1976) and Anscombre (1979). Delocutive denominal verbs can be glossed by "*To say « N »* ". Recently, an historical review of this notion has been described in Larcher (2003).

Moreover, a productive class has been isolated, namely that of borrowings (*crash(er)*$_V$/*crash*$_N$) and onomatopoeias (*blablat(er)*$_V$/*blabla*$_N$ [*waffle on*$_V$/*waffle*]). As nouns belonging to these N/V pairs denote concrete entities (sounds and (speech) acts), they have been included in class -7-.

In addition to both the initial linguistic assumptions and the newly discovered classes, Tables 17.1 and 17.2 also includes both new columns with quantitative results obtained from the dictionaries corpus analysis, and new cells, corresponding to the new discovered semantic classes just described.

Whereas VtoN conversion appears to be a stable WF process, leading to the formation of almost only abstract nouns, characterising NtoV types is a much less straightforward task. In fact, for this purpose, we have examined input N (formal, semantic, etymologic) features only. To refine this classification, a next step will be to compare these criteria with output verbs properties.

According to these (though perfectible) results, we can model the most frequent and seemingly productive conversion classes. With this choice, classes -2'-, -5- and -6- in Table 17.1, together with class -1- in Table 17.2, are excluded. Furthermore, we have chosen to disregard heterogeneous cases (i.e. classes -7- and -8- in Table 17.1) at the time being, the linguistic content of this set of nouns and verbs having in fact to be further examined; in particular, in Sect. 17.4.1.3, we come back to the reasons why Noun/Verb pairs which are members of class -8- are not accounted for in this chapter. Finally, the last excluded class is class -1-, Table 17.1, since NtoV orientation is in this group purely structure-driven. These decisions amount to design two ALUs, the former constraining and producing denominal converted verbs, the latter defining the basic structure of deverbal converted nouns. In Sect. 17.4, we shall see which of the input properties can be encoded within ALUs, which ones fall within the competence of the actual input, and how the MS-CS mechanism is able to build the right output representations, whatever the requested Noun/Verb class.

17.4 Modeling

As announced in Sect. 17.2, the formal representation we wish to obtain combines the following requirements: (1) MS-CS is taken as an input to output unification mechanism, (2), a unique **NtoV** unified $[X_N]_V$ ALU records the linguistic constraints common to classes -2-, -3- and -4- in Table 17.1, while a unique **VtoN** $[X_V]_N$ ALU does the same for the representation of class -2- in Table 17.2 (see Sect. 17.3.5). Behind the idea of accounting for regular, productive and frequently represented conversion classes, the goal is to predict the characteristics of the most likely Noun/Verb conversion producted neologisms.

17.4.1 Noun-to-Verb

Examining Table 17.1, Sect. 17.3.5, and excluding class -8-, three **NtoV** classes are very productive: class -2- (V = "*do something using N*"), class -3- (V = "*(do what N would do|behave as N)*") and class -4- (V = "*do or put something (with)in/during N*"). As we shall see in the Sect. 17.4.1.1, all output verbs are based on a unique ALU called $[X_N]_V$. Section 17.4.1.2 focuses on some examples for each of the classes which has been taken into account.

17.4.1.1 $[X_N]_V$ Abstract Lexical Unit for Noun-to-Verb Conversion

The following ALU in (Fig. 17.2) accounts for the way output verbs inherit properties from the appropriate input nouns:

- They inherit relevant argumental properties from their input noun, namely only those parameters which are used in input noun qualia roles $\boxed{2}$ and which are inherited by the verb. These parameters are encoded by $\boxed{a_i}$ variables;
- They inherit relevant aspectual and event structure parameters from their input noun, namely only those parameters which are used in the input noun qualia roles $\boxed{2}$ and which are inherited by the verb. These parameters are encoded by $\boxed{e_j}$ variables;
- They inherit only a part of the semantic content of their input noun, represented here by a part of the noun qualia. Mutual disjunctions (⊕) rule out overlapping between classes which have been accounted for:
  - **if** the input noun denotes an artefact (class -2-) or a location (class -4-), **then** the qualia of the output verb consists only in the telic value of the input qualia $\boxed{4}$,
  - **if** the input noun denotes a natural entity (class -3-), **then** the output verb inherits only the agentive value in the formal quale QS|FORM|AG of the input

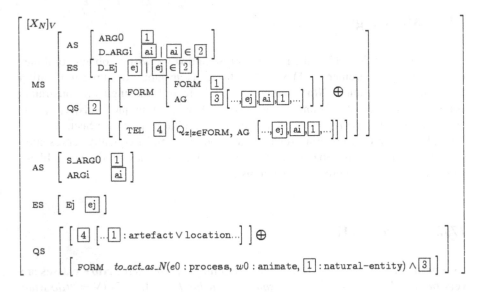

Fig. 17.2 $[X_N]_V$ ALU

$\boxed{3}$, and as a consequence, the qualia of the output verb consists in this case in a formal role whose value is the conjunction of the predicate ***to_act_as_N*** and the QS|FORM|AG value, if any.

17.4.1.2 Some Examples

As we shall see with the examples below, *$[X_N]_V$* combined with the appropriate input noun enables the representation, via MS-CS, of each sort of output verbs from the following **NtoV** conversion classes: class -3-, with imitation verbs like *sing(er)*, class -2-, with instrumental verbs like *drain(er)*, *crayonn(er)*, *dynamit(er)* [*dynamite*$_V$] and class -4-, with locative verbs like *usin(er)* [*manufacture*$_V$], *coffr(er)*. Examples from each class are meant to illustrate various cases of inherited aspectual properties.

Imitation Verbs

As said before, class -3- imitation verbs are built from nouns which denote natural entities, e.g. *singe*. Let us see how the output verb *sing(er)* is produced from its nominal input *singe* (Fig. 17.3). First, we may notice that the input noun qualia structure indicates that *singe* is an animal $\boxed{5}$ bearing a prototypical behavior i.e. imitating a model $\boxed{6}$. This behavior is propagated through $\boxed{6}$ and via *$[X_N]_V$* onto the constructed verb FORMAL role. Therefore, the MS-CS-driven combination

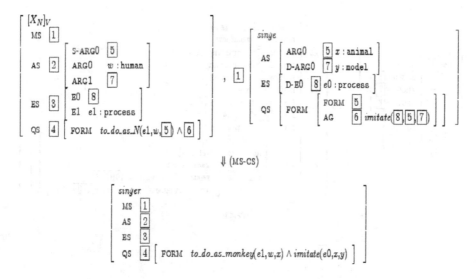

Fig. 17.3 Conversion class -3-: $singe_N \rightarrow_{conv} sing(er)_V$

between $[X_N]_V$ and the lexical properties of the input noun entails the output verb to be provided with a qualia structure that can be paraphrased by: X $sing(er)$ $Y =$ "X acts as a N_monkey AND monkeys imitate Y".

Instrumental Verbs

Prototypically, instrumental verbs are morphologically constructed from input nouns referring to artefacts. Let us consider for instance, the example of $drain_N/drain(er)_V$ pair (Fig. 17.4). The output verb $drain(er)$ inherits the TELIC role from its input noun $drain$, because of the artefactual nature of the noun referent. This TELIC value is a complex structure which is characterised by the qualia label transitition_lcp and which consequently contains the specific features for transitions. Since $drain(er)$ describes an instrumental predicate, its meaning, carried through index $\boxed{4}$, can be expressed through the following gloss: X $drain(er)$ $Y =$ "X uses N_drain to extract Y from Z AND Y is extracted from Z".

In addition, the inheritance of argumental and aspectual properties follows the general principles of noun and verb descriptions in GL. Except for the denoted entity $\boxed{1}$, input nouns argumental parameters are always encoded as default arguments (MS|AS|D_ARGi), whereas they are inherited as true arguments in the output verb argumental structure (AS|ARGi). In the same way, the default evenemential parameters in MS|ES|D_Ej are inherited as true parameters in output ES|Ej.

Following the lexical shadowing principle, the argumental parameter $\boxed{1}$ which encodes the entity denoted by the input noun is displayed as a shadow argument (S_ARG0) in the output verb AS.

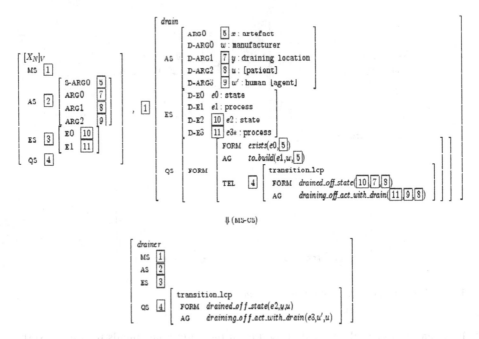

Fig. 17.4 Conversion class -2-: $drain_N \rightarrow_{conv} drain(er)_V$

The same mechanism is at play with verbs *crayonn(er)* and *dynamit(er)* excepted that here the TELIC role of the input noun *crayon* (resp. *dynamite*) encodes an activity (resp. an achievement). This TELIC value is reflected within the inherited qualia structure of each corresponding output verb: *crayonn(er)* denotes an activity whereas *dynamit(er)* describes an achievement.

Locative Verbs

As shown in Fig. 17.5, the fact that the input noun *coffre* refers to a place $\boxed{5}$ leads to the morphological formation of the locative verb *coffr(er)*. The meaning of *coffr(er)* can be paraphrased by *X coffr(er) Y = "X locks up Y in N_chest AND Y is locked up in N_chest"*. This verb inherits the relevant part from the input noun qualia (i.e. $\boxed{4}$, its TELIC value), and those appropriate argumental and evenemential parameters which are linked within this inherited qualia part (the state $\boxed{9}$ and the process $\boxed{10}$; the agent $\boxed{8}$, the patient $\boxed{7}$ and the location $\boxed{5}$). The input noun TELIC value being of type transition_lcp, this label is propagated in order to characterize the output verb qualia structure.

The same is at play with the Noun/Verb pair *usine_N/usin(er)_V* excepted for the kind of event which is denoted in the TELIC value of the input noun *usine*. This value is of type activity_lcp, and it also characterises the qualia structure of the output verb.

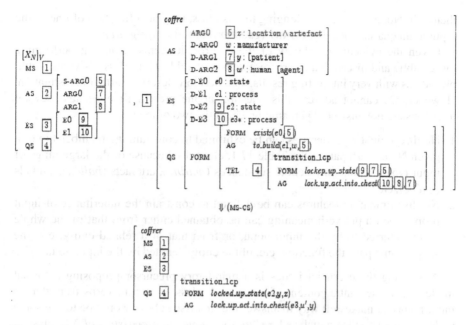

Fig. 17.5 Conversion class -4-: *coffre*$_N$ →$_{conv}$ *coffr(er)*$_V$

17.4.1.3 Conclusion

This section was devoted to NtoV conversion WF process. We have seen that a unique ALU called *[X$_N$]$_V$* combined with the appropriate input noun through MS-CS schema is sufficient to build well-formed output verb meanings in a systematic way with respect to the ontological type of input nouns. Three kinds of output verbs are built in this way: imitation verbs like *sing(er)* from input nouns which denote natural entities; instrumental verbs like *drain(er)* from input nouns which denote artefacts; locative verbs like *coffr(er)* from input nouns denoting places or time intervals. As said above, these three kinds of output verbs correspond to three classes of Noun/Verb pairs, respectively class -3- (V = *"(do what N would do|behave as N)"*), class -2- (V = *"do something to N$_{theme}$ using N"*) and class -4- (V = *"do or put N$_{theme}$(with)in/during N"*).

Let us come back to the reasons Table 17.1, class -8- has not been taken into account here. Observing this class, we may notice that a change of state is exerted by the output verb on its theme either with respect to the input noun itself (*marbre*$_N$ →$_{conv}$ *marbr(er)*$_V$X$_{Theme}$: *"X$_{Theme}$ looks like marble"*), or with respect to its shape (*ballon*$_N$ [balloon] →$_{conv}$ *ballonn(er)*$_V$X$_{Theme}$: *"X$_{Theme}$ is round as a balloon"*), or with respect to one of its parts (*guêpe*$_N$ [wasp] →$_{conv}$ *guêp(er)*$_V$X$_{Theme}$: *"X$_{Theme}$ has a wasp waist"*), or with respect to its function (*frégate*$_N$ [frigate] →$_{conv}$ *frégat(er)*$_V$X$_{Theme}$: *"X$_{Theme}$ is such that its speed is that of a frigate"*). In other words, the very meaning within the change of state affecting the referent of the verb theme, in Noun/Verb pairs belonging to this class, may be a function of one of the input noun qualia roles: e.g. CONST (*guêp(er)*) or TELIC (*frégat(er)*).

Given the evident complexity of these verbs, it seems clear that performing more subtle and discriminating representation of Table 17.1, class -8- verbs would provide us with very interesting results, and therefore deserves further investigation. However, we cannot address this question at the present time because several questions are not answered yet, among which the two of them:

1. No discriminating properties can be exhibited to constrain the membership of a given Noun/Verb pair to the Table 17.1, class -8-, because of the large range of input types: inputs may denote substances (*marbre*), artefacts (*ballon*), animals (*guêpe*), etc.;
2. No discriminating features can be defined to constrain the inheritance of input properties: output verb meaning can be obtained either from that of the whole entity referred to by the input noun, or from that of a related entity: e.g. the shape, some part, the function, etc. of the entity denoted by the input noun.

Answering these crucial issues is a mandatory precursor proposing a formal model for the semantic content of Table 17.1, class -8- output verbs from that of input nouns. A makeshift way to answer the first issue above would be to use some underspecified predicate such as $V = $ "*to_give_some_characteristics_of_N*", but such a controversial solution would not solve the second question. As a consequence, we prefer not to account for Noun/Verb pairs of Table 17.1, class -8- as long as points 1 and 2 remain unanswered issues.

17.4.2   Verb-to-Noun

As it emerges throughout the section devoted to linguistic descriptions, and according to the quantitative corpus-based values reported on the Table 17.2, Sect. 17.3.5, most deverbal converted nouns (i.e. those labelled by class -2-) describe either the verbal process or its result.[15] A third reading consists in a conceptual or propositional one.[16]

These interpretations are all possible. Some nouns may realise all of them, for instance *marche* [*march*$_N$/*walk(ing)*$_N$]: (processive) *la marche durera environ une heure* [*the walk/march will last one hour long*], (result) *la marche des Américaines a été un succès* [*The American women's march has been a success*], (concept) *la marche est une discipline olympique* [*walking is an olympic sport*]; some other

---

[15]VtoN conversion class -1-, Table 17.2 in which N denotes the agent (*guide, garde*) gathers a non-representative amount of Noun/Verb pairs; therefore we have chosen not to take them into account in our model.

[16]See Pustejovsky (1995:175) for an illustration of this type of denotation with the ambiguous noun *belief*.

nouns have only two interpretations. So *chant* [*song$_N$/singing$_N$*] is only either resultative *le chant des sirènes a ensorcelé Ulysse* [*The mermaid's song bewitched Ulysses*] or conceptual *le chant est un art* [*singing is an art*]. The MS-CS output lexical unit does not try to guess which of the readings is actually realised by the noun, it just provides nouns with the three possibilities.

17.4.2.1 V and N Minimal Required Features

Gathering the main properties accounted for by various authors (Corbin, Kerleroux, Fradin, Meinschäfer) and mentioned in Sects. 17.3.3, 17.3.4, and 17.3.5, we obtain the following list of minimal requirements the VtoN ALU, noted *[X$_V$]$_N$*, must satisfy in order to properly constrain the abstract semantic structure of deverbal converted nouns:

1. Its MS – collecting the characteristics all input candidate verbs must share – is as follows:

   - causative readings of input verbs being excluded, the verb qualia label should exclude any potential causative interpretation;
   - the event structure should not be that of a simple state;
   - the argument structure is unconstrained: actually, candidate verbs may or may not be transitive;

2. The description of the noun itself denotes an abstract entity with three possible readings: processive, resultative, or conceptual,

   - in its evenemential (processive or resultative) readings, the output noun inherits all the verbal aspectual and argumental properties, following (Meinschäfer 2003);
   - in its conceptual reading, the output noun refers a priori to a so-called proposition entity. So, this denotation, noted *prop*, must be part of the ouput qualia label.

Finally, in contrast to what happens for denominal verbs, described in Sect. 17.4.1, and to what Pustejovsky (1996) assumes, input verbs do not carry the output noun index as shadow argument (S_ARG). We have to remember that Pustejovsky (1996) proposes the S_ARG value to be instantiated for verbs as *dance*$_V$ or *butter*$_V$ by means of what could be considered as an incorporated noun: we agree with this assumption as far as *butter* is concerned: the entity is a logical part of the predicate, but not for *dance*, at least in French. Actually, as for any input verb of a VtoN conversion process, allowing for an S_ARG value in *dance*AS would amount allowing for a circular definition of V and N: the output noun would namely be, at the same time, both morphologically obtained from the verb, and semantically integrated in the verb definition.

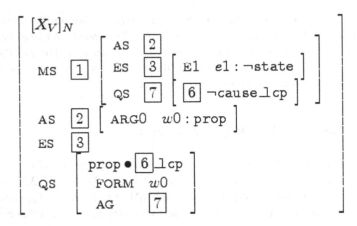

Fig. 17.6 *[X$_V$]$_N$*ALU for VtoN conversion

17.4.2.2 *[X$_V$]$_N$* Abstract Lexical Unit

Figure 17.6 below formalizes the set of constraints just recalled in the *[X$_V$]$_N$*ALU.

For readibility sake, input verb AS (resp. ES) is directly coindexed through $\boxed{2}$ (resp. through $\boxed{3}$) with ALU AS (resp. ES). All the nominal arguments (excepted AS|ARG0 value) are inherited as default arguments, and value sharing would have required a slighly more complex representation.

In the ALU qualia (QS), a new parameter **w0** is used in the FORM value to ensure the existence of a conceptual interpretation of the expected output noun. The MS QUALIA value, characterising the potential input verb, is shared with that of the output noun QS|AGENT'S value through index $\boxed{7}$, as soon as this shared value meets the type constraint exerted on the input verb. Recall (Sect. 17.3.3) that, following (Meinschäfer 2003) this type constraint says that V should not have a causative reading, that is identified by the label ¬cause_lcp. The input verb type, represented by the LCP label, and indexed with $\boxed{6}$, becomes one component of the output noun qualia label. Given that none of the three potential interpretations of the output noun cooperates in any context, the LCP of this output noun is identified by an exocentric dotted type.[17] This complex type is composed of two simple types: the input verb type indexed with $\boxed{6}$ and the prop type. Therefore, deverbal converted nouns' LCPs are identified with: prop • $\boxed{6}$_lcp, where $\boxed{6}$ stands for any aspectual type, but cause.

---

[17]Following Pustejovsky (1996), the distinction between endocentric and exocentric dotted types is based on the acceptability of the contextual cooperation between the two readings of a logical polysemic word, these readings being accounted for by two corresponding types which are embedded in the dotted type. The readings of a word associated to an exocentric dotted type do not cooperate, while the two readings of a word associated to an endocentric dotted type do. The exocentric/endocentric distinction seems to be close to that of Cruse (1986) between cooperative versus non cooperative readings of word.

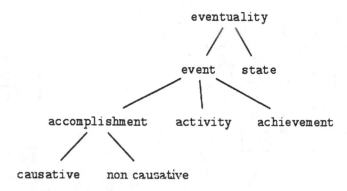

Fig. 17.7 Usual type hierarchy of eventualities

Furthermore, ⟨3⟩ indicates that the type of the first ES event, i.e. E1, cannot be a state. Still according to Meinschäfer (2003), cf. Sect. 17.3.3, this second constraint filters out stative verbs. In other words, deverbal converted nouns denote basically abstract entities, and their AGENTIVE role (in fact, their origin) is the meaning of the verb they are converted from.

As for type accommodation between input verbs and the $[X_V]_N$ALU constraints, according to the usually adopted type hierarchy, given in (Fig. 17.7), ¬cause is equivalent to the entirety of the event subtypes, but cause. Now, cause being an accomplishment subtype, a ¬cause_lcp marked verb may express any non-causative accomplishments, activities or achievements.

In the case of a candidate input verb which includes a causal reading and is of an exocentric dotted type, filtering out by unification ⟨6⟩ the verb cause component amounts to keep only its non causative interpretation, by means of those QUALIA role predicates the remaining component type can access. And, consequently, only those evenemential and argument variables used in the accessed predicates are kept in the respective structures.

The whole word formation mechanism, made up with the $[X_V]_N$ALU, the candidate input verb **X1**, the MS-CS system and the nominal output noun $[X1_V]_N$ is given in (Fig. 17.8).

1. the $[X_V]_N$ALU subsumes the common properties of all converted deverbal noun, by defining the minimal requirements on the expected input verb;
2. the potential input verb **X1** has to unify with the ALU MS, in order to activate MS-CS;
3. the actual deverbal noun $[X1_V]_N$ results from MS-CS unification process, instanciating $[X_V]_N$ by means of appropriate **X1** features. Examples of VtoN conversions involving non causative verbs or non causative verb readings, presented in Sect. 17.4.2.3, illustrate this mechanism.

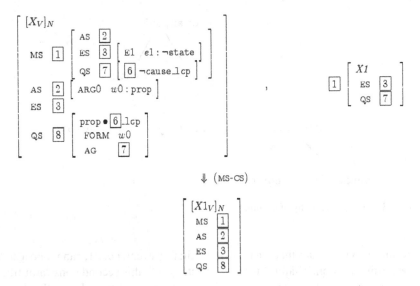

$\Downarrow$ (MS-CS)

Fig. 17.8 MS-CS with VtoN conversion

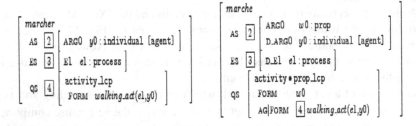

Fig. 17.9 VtoN conversion: *march(er)*$_V$ $\rightarrow$$_{conv}$*marche*$_N$

17.4.2.3 Examples

In the following section we illustrate the various verbal lexical types which can unify with MS in *[X$_V$]$_N$*ALU. The section starts with non causative verb types, i.e. the case of an activity input verb (*march(er)* [*walk*$_V$]), followed by the case of a non-causative accomplishment (*transport(er)* [*carry*$_V$]). Then, the last two examples are meant to indicate how the mechanism works in order to deal with input verbs which bear a causative interpretation (*recul(er)*, *angoiss(er)* [*distress*$_V$]).

Activities

In simple activity (non telic) qualia structures, such as in *march(er)* (or *dans(er)* [*dance*$_V$] or *chant(er)* [*sing*$_V$] . . .), only the FORMAL role is defined, as shown on the lefthand side of Fig. 17.9. The successful MS-CS output deverbal noun appears

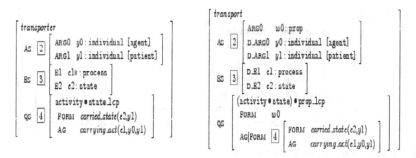

Fig. 17.10 VtoN conversion: *transport(er)*$_V$ →$_{conv}$ *transport*$_N$

on its righthand side. As indicated in Fig. 17.8, both input argument structure (MS|AS) and event structure (MS|ES) are inherited by the output noun, through, respectively, indices $\boxed{2}$ and $\boxed{3}$. As for the input qualia structure (index $\boxed{7}$ in Fig. 17.8, and $\boxed{4}$ in Fig. 17.9), it matches against the noun AGENTIVE qualia value, according to *[X$_N$]$_V$* recommendations. *[X$_N$]$_V$* also imposes to the output noun an exocentric dotted type labelled with activity• proposition_lcp. This type results (1) from the successful unification of *march(er)* lexical entry with the *[X$_N$]$_V$*MS value (Fig. 17.8, index $\boxed{1}$), which means: (a) event types compatibility (*march(er)* does not designate a state), and (b) LCP compatibility (activity is a case of ¬cause); and (2) from the successful verb LCP propagation into the nominal LCP labelling (Fig. 17.8, index $\boxed{6}$). MS value $\boxed{1}$ is propagated onto the output noun structure, though this is not represented in (Fig. 17.9). As shown by its QS, the exocentric dotted typed noun *marche* holds two readings: the first refers to a process *la marche des soldats sur la ville* [*The soldiers' march on the city*] or to its result: *trois longues marches en forêt* [*three long walks in the forest*] (depending on the agent **y0** realisation) and the second to a concept *la marche est une discipline olympique,* [*race walk is an Olympic sport*] activating only the QS|FORM value.

Accomplishments

With *transport(er)*, we intend to illustrate (Fig. 17.10) a case of non-causative accomplishment. The input verb's event structure, headed by the process, is propagated into the output noun $\boxed{3}$, together with its argument structure $\boxed{2}$. The MS-CS unification principle works in the same way as for *marche,* and gives raise to the definition of an exocentric dotted typed qualia structure composed with two mutually exclusive types: (prop) *un transport nécessite toujours un transporteur* [*transports always require conveyors*], and accomplishment, with type activity• state. Accomplishments can be realised, as nominal lexical units, either through the QS|AG|AG activity value: *le transport, lundi prochain, de la marchandise par le premier convoi* [*Goods conveying, next Monday, by the first train*], or through

$$
\begin{bmatrix}
reculer \\
\text{AS} \quad \boxed{2} \quad \begin{bmatrix} \text{ARG0} \quad y0: \text{individual} \\ \text{ARG1} \quad y1: \text{individual} \end{bmatrix} \\
\text{ES} \quad \boxed{3} \quad \begin{bmatrix} \text{E1} \quad e1: \text{cause} \\ \text{E2} \quad e2: \text{process} \end{bmatrix} \\
\text{QS} \quad \boxed{4} \quad \begin{bmatrix} \text{cause} \bullet \text{activity\_lcp} \\ \text{FORM} \quad movement\_act(e2, y1\,[\text{agent}]) \\ \text{AG} \quad movement\_cause(e1, y0\,[\text{agent}], y1\,[\text{patient}]) \end{bmatrix}
\end{bmatrix}
$$

Fig. 17.11 Lexical entry of *recul(er)*$_V$

the QS|AG|FORM resultative (state) value: *Tous les transports sont annulés jusqu'à lundi prochain*[18] [*all transports are cancelled until next Monday*].

Causatives

Let us now turn to more complex verb types or so it seems. The verbs *recul(er)* and *angoiss(er)* illustrate the case of causative predicates, that are mainly movement or psychological predicates. In *Max recule la chaise* [*Max moves back the chair*], the agent *Max* voluntarily causes the chair movement, and in *Le film a angoissé Max* [*The movie distressed Max*], the movie content entails Max psychological state of anxiety. These verbs generally carry a second resulting and intransitive reading. The subsequent movement for verb types like *recul(er)*: *Les ennemis reculent* [*Enemies are going back*], and the caused state for verb types like *angoiss(er)*: *Max angoisse* [*Max is worried sick*]. As J. Meinshäfer pointed out, only the non causative reading is an available candidate input for VtoN conversion: **le recul de la chaise par Max* [*Max's moving back of the chair*], versus *le recul de Max* [*Max's backward movement*], **l'angoisse de Max par le film* [*The movie distress of Max*], versus *l'angoisse de Max* [*Max's distress*].

From a formal point of view, these distinct, and non-overlaping verb interpretations are represented by exocentric dotted typed structures. As illustrated by (Fig. 17.11) *recul(er)* and by (Fig. 17.12) *angoiss(er)*, the activation of causative readings (AGENTIVE role) and that of resultative readings (FORMAL role) are therefore mutually exclusive.

Unifying *recul(er)*, as illustrated above, with the *[X$_N$]$_V$*ALU MS (see Fig. 17.6) is above all in this case a matter of QUALIA types unification. In fact, the cause component within the cause• activity_lcp labelled verbal exocentric dotted type is neutralised through unification with the ¬cause_lcp required input verb. As this

---

[18]Since nouns carry only default event parameters, there is no headedness involved in their event structure, so, for accomplishments such as *transport*, both process and state can be realized. And since deverbal nouns inherit input verb argument structure content only as default arguments, noun arguments are always optional.

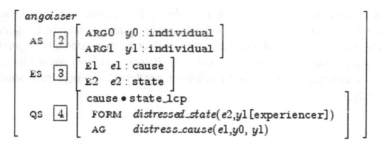

$$\begin{bmatrix} angoisser \\ \text{AS} \quad \boxed{2} \quad \begin{bmatrix} \text{ARG0} \quad y0 : \texttt{individual} \\ \text{ARG1} \quad y1 : \texttt{individual} \end{bmatrix} \\ \text{ES} \quad \boxed{3} \quad \begin{bmatrix} \text{E1} \quad e1 : \texttt{cause} \\ \text{E2} \quad e2 : \texttt{state} \end{bmatrix} \\ \text{QS} \quad \boxed{4} \quad \begin{bmatrix} \texttt{cause} \bullet \texttt{state\_lcp} \\ \text{FORM} \quad distressed\_state(e2, y1[\texttt{experiencer}]) \\ \text{AG} \quad distress\_cause(e1, y0, y1) \end{bmatrix} \end{bmatrix}$$

Fig. 17.12 Lexical entry of *angoiss(er)*$_V$

$$\begin{bmatrix} recul \\ \text{AS} \quad \boxed{2} \quad \begin{bmatrix} \text{ARG0} \quad w0 : \texttt{prop} \\ \text{D\_ARG1} \quad y1 : \texttt{individual} \end{bmatrix} \\ \text{ES} \quad \boxed{3} \quad \begin{bmatrix} \text{D\_E1} \quad e2 : \texttt{process} \end{bmatrix} \\ \text{QS} \quad \boxed{4} \quad \begin{bmatrix} \texttt{prop} \bullet \texttt{activity\_lcp} \\ \text{FORM} \quad w0 \\ \text{AG|FORM} \quad \boxed{4} \; movement\_act(e2, y1[\texttt{agent}]) \end{bmatrix} \end{bmatrix}$$

Fig. 17.13 VtoN conversion output *recul*$_N$

$$\begin{bmatrix} angoisse \\ \text{AS} \quad \boxed{2} \quad \begin{bmatrix} \text{ARG0} \quad w0 : \texttt{prop} \\ \text{ARG1} \quad y1 : \texttt{individual} \end{bmatrix} \\ \text{ES} \quad \boxed{3} \quad \begin{bmatrix} \text{D\_E2} \quad e2 : \texttt{state} \end{bmatrix} \\ \text{QS} \quad \boxed{4} \quad \begin{bmatrix} \texttt{prop} \bullet \texttt{state\_lcp} \\ \text{FORM} \quad w0 \\ \text{AG|FORM} \quad \boxed{4} \; distressed\_state(e2, y1[\texttt{experiencer}]) \end{bmatrix} \end{bmatrix}$$

Fig. 17.14 VtoN conversion output *angoisse*$_N$

component is filtered out, so are the corresponding qualia roles, together with their event and argument parameters. The unification effect is that of selecting only the verb resultative reading. The same occurs for *angoiss(er)*: through unification with ALU MS, the causative interpretation is rejected, whereas the resultative static predicate is kept as the actual VtoN conversion input.

Once the correct reading has been selected, the remaining WF mechanism works on in a straighforward way: (1) the appropriate qualia label fulfills the missing slot on the output noun LCP (providing thus *recul* with proposition• activity_lcp, and *angoisse* with proposition• state_lcp), (2) the qualia structure defining the resultative predicate is inherited by the noun AGENTIVE value, while its FORMAL value is the prop typed index **w0**. Output nouns *recul [backward movement$_N$/retreat$_N$]* and *angoisse [distress$_N$]* are displayed respectively in Figs. 17.13 and 17.14. It can be noticed that (1) *recul* may denote an agentive intransitive movement process (*le recul de l'armée [The army's retreat]*), or the movement result (*les reculs sont* *inévitables* [*Backward movements are unavoidable*]), or a concept (*le recul s'oppose à l'avancée* [*Backward movements are opposed to advancements*]); (2) similarly, *angoisse* is a static nominal, that may or not affect an experiencer (*l'angoisse (de Max) a été provoquée par un stress* [*(Max's) distress has been caused by stress*]) or depict a concept (*l'angoisse est étudiée en psychanalyse* [*Anguish is studied in psychology*]).

17.5 Conclusion and Perspectives

In this paper, we have described a GL-based model designed for Word Formation. This model includes a composition schema called MS-CS and several abstract lexical units, each of which simulating a Word Formation process. This device has first been used to represent noun to verb *é*-prefixation in French (Jacquey and Namer to appear; Namer and Jacquey 2003). The robustness of the chosen approach has been confirmed when applied in the conversion framework presented here. The success of this approach is due to the fact that it combines linguistic hypotheses from a well-established morphological theory (inspired from D. Corbin work), as well as a lexical semantics formalism, namely GL (Generative Lexicon).

Moreover, coupling Word Formation theory with lexical semantics, through this method, has two additional effects:

- It makes obvious differences between seemingly identical phenomena. This paper has illustrated the structure distinctions for verbs such as *walk* and *dance*, or *drain* and *butter*, whereas they were analyzed in the same way in Pustejovsky (1996),[19] although they belong to opposite Word Formation families according to the morphological theory we rely on.
- It draws out similarities concealed behind apparent differences. Hence this paper has shown that verbs *drain(er)* and *sing(er)* result from a single WF rule, via $[X_N]_V$ALU. Each time, only one mechanism is at play, their corresponding input nouns being responsible for the differences in verbal meanings.

Both similarities and differences are detected and analyzed within morphological theory; GL collects, ranks and formally expresses all of these linguistic hypotheses. In addition to this new collaboration between these two linguistic fields, the model also seems to provide new future prospects in Natural Language Processing. In fact, formalizing both NtoV and VtoN conversion, on the basis of a corpus analysis, can be viewed as an empirical checking of linguistic predictions about neologisms. In this regard, this experiment has confirmed the productivity of verb-to-noun (VtoN) conversion leading to processive nouns, or that of noun-to-verb (NtoV) conversion process leading to instrumental, locative or stereotypical agentive verbs. On the

---

[19] Actually, only *dance* and *butter* are mentioned in Pustejovsky (1996): we assume that *walk* and *drain* would be represented in the same way.

other hand, it has also allowed to detect the emergence of new, quantitatively important classes: nominal verbs denoting a change-of-state (*marbr(er), guêp(er)*), borrowings and onomatopoeias Noun/Verb pairs denoting (speech) acts or sounds (*patch/patch(er), blabla/blablat(er), glouglou/glouglout(er)*).

Identifying the most creative conversion types, predicting their semantic constraints exerted on both input and output, and drawing their input-to-output semantic relationships, through the choice of the right conversion orientation are results which could be used further in NLP systems in order to enrich lexical contents.

References

Adams, V. (1973). *An introduction to modern English word-formation*. London: Longman Group Limited.

Anscombre, J.-C. (1979). Délocutivité benvenistienne, délocutivité généralisée et performativité. *Langue Française, 42*, 69–84, Paris.

Aronoff, M. (1976). *Word formation in generative grammar*. Cambridge, MA: MIT Press.

Aronoff, M., Oehrle, R., Kelley, F., & Stephens, B. W. (Eds.). (1984). *Language sound and structure*. Cambridge, MA: MIT Press.

Aurnague, M., & Plénat, M. (1996). La préfixation en é- et la relation de partie à tout. In D. Genthial et al. (Eds.), *Seminaire Lexique. Représentations et outils pour les bases lexicales. Morphologie robuste* (pp. 43–52). Grenoble: CLIPS-IMAG, Université de Grenoble.

Aurnague, M., & Plénat, M. (1997). Manifestations morphologiques de la relation d'attachement habituel. In D. Corbin, G. Dal, B. Fradin, B. Habert, F. Kerleroux, M. Plénat, & M. Roché (Eds.), *Silexicales 1: Mots possibles, mots existants* (pp. 15–24). Villeneuve d'Ascq: Presses de l'Université de Lille III.

Benveniste, E. (1966). *Problèmes de linguistique générale*. Paris: Gallimard.

Bybee, J. (1988). Morphology as lexical organization. In M. Hammond & M. Noonan (Eds.), *Theoretical morphology* (pp. 119–141). San Diego: Academic.

Corbett, G. (1991). *Gender*. Cambridge: Cambridge University Press.

Corbin, D. (1987). *Morphologie dérivationnelle et structuration du lexique* (2 Vols.). Max Niemeyer Verlag, Tübingen (2nd ed.). Villeneuve d'Ascq: Presses Universitaires de Lille.

Corbin, D. (2001). Préfixes et suffixes: du sens aux catégories. *Faits de langue, 15*, 41–69, Ophrys, Paris.

Corbin, D. (2004). French (Indo-European: Romance). In G. Booij, C. Lehmann, & J. Mugdan (Eds.), *Morphology. An international handbook on inflection and word formation* (Vol. 1). New York: Walter de Gruyter, art. 121.

Cornulier, B. d. (1976). La notion de dérivation délocutive. *Revue de linguistique romane, 40*, 116–144, Champion, Paris.

Cruse, D. A. (1986). *Lexical semantics*. London: Cambridge University Press.

Dal, G. (1997). Du principe d'unicité catégorielle au principe d'unicité sémantique: incidence sur la formalisation du lexique construit morphologiquement. In P. Greenfield, H. Madec, P.-A. Buvet, & S. Cardey (Eds.), *Actes de Fractal'97, BULAG numéro spécial* (pp. 105–115). Besançon: Presses universitaires de Franche-Comté.

Di Sciullo, A.-M., & Williams, E. (1987). *On the definition of word*. Cambridge: MIT Press.

Fradin, B. (2003). *Nouvelles approches en morphologie*. Paris: Presses Universitaires de France.

Fradin, B., & Kerleroux, F. (2003a). Quelles bases pour les procédés de la morphologie constructionnelle ? In B. Fradin, G. Dal, N. Hathout, F. Kerleroux, M. Plénat, & M. Roché (Eds.), *Silexicales 3: Les unités morphologiques* (pp. 76–84). Villeneuve d'Ascq: SILEX: CNRS & Université de Lille 3.

Fradin, B., & Kerleroux, F. (2003b). Troubles with lexemes. In G. Booij, J. De Cesaris, A. Ralli, & S. Scalise (Eds.), *Topics in morphology. Selected papers from the third mediterranean morphology meeting* (pp. 177–196). Barcelona: Institut Universitari de lingüistica aplicada, Univertat Pompeu Fabra.

Hale, K., & Kayser, S. J. (1993). On argument structure and the lexical representation of syntactic relations. In K. Hale & S. J. Kayser (Eds.), *The view from building 20: Essays in linguistics in honor of Sylvain Bromberger* (pp. 53–110). Cambridge, MA/Cambridge, UK: MIT Press.

Haspelmath, M. (2002). *Understanding morphology*. London: Arnold.

Jacquey, E., & Namer, F. (2003). Morphosémantique et modélisation: les verbes dénominaux préfixés par é-,in: Actes de la seconde conférence "Représentation du sens linguistique", Montréal.

Katamba, F. (1993). *Morphology*. Houndmills, Basingstoke: Palgrave Macmillan.

Kerleroux, F. (1996a). *La coupure invisible: études de syntaxe et de morphologie*. Villeneuve d'Ascq: Presses universitaires du Septentrion.

Kerleroux, F. (1996b). Représentations de l'absence de suffixe dans les noms déverbaux processifs du français. In *Travaux linguistiques du CERLICO, n°9* (pp. 141–170). Rennes: Presses Universitaires de Rennes.

Kerleroux, F. (1997). De la limitation de l'homonymie entre noms déverbaux convertis et apocopes de noms déverbaux suffixés. In D. Corbin, G. Dal, B. Fradin, B. Habert, F. Kerleroux, M. Plénat, & M. Roché (Eds.), *Silexicales 1: Mots possibles, mots existants* (pp. 163–172). Villeneuve d'Ascq: Presses de l'Université de Lille III.

Kerleroux, F. (1999). Identification d'un procédé morphologique: la conversion. *Faits de langues, 14*, 89–100. Ophrys, Paris.

Kerleroux, F. (2004). Sur quels objets portent les opérations morphologiques de construction ? In *Lexique 16* (pp. 85–124). Villeneuve d'Ascq: Presses universitaires du Septentrion.

Kiparsky, P. (1982). Lexical phonology and morphology. In I.-S. Yang (Ed.), *Linguistics in the morning calm* (pp. 3–91). Seoul: Hanshin.

Koenig, J.-P. (1999). *Lexical relations*. Stanford: CSLI publications.

Larcher, P. (2003). La dérivation délocutive: Histoire d'une notion méconnue. *Historiographia Linguistica, 30*(3), 389–406(8), John Benjamins Publishing Company, Amsterdam.

Lieber, R. (1992). *Deconstructing morphology*. Chicago: University of Chicago Press.

Marchand, H. (1969). *The categories and types of present-day English word-formation*. Munich: C.H. Beck Verlagsbuchhandlung.

Meinschäfer, J. (2003). Remarques sur l'interprétation des déverbaux sans affixe en français. In B. Fradin, G. Dal, F. Kerleroux, N. Hathout, M. Plénat, & M. Roché (Eds.), *Silexicales 3: Les unités morphologiques* (pp. 118–125). Villeneuve d'Ascq: Presses universitaires de Lille.

Mel'cuk, I. (1996). *Cours de morphologie générale* (Vol. 3). Montréal/Paris: Presses de l'université de Montréal -CNRS.

Mel'cuk, I. (1997). *Cours de morphologie générale* (Vol. 4). Montréal/Paris: Presses de l'université de Montréal -CNRS.

Namer, F. (2003). Automatiser l'analyse morpho-sémantique non affixale: le système DériF. In *Cahiers de Grammaire 28* (pp. 31–48). Toulouse: Presses universitaires du Mirail.

Namer, F., & Jacquey, E. (2003). Lexical semantics and derivational morphology: The case of the popular 'é-' prefixation in French. *Proceedings of the Second Workshop on Generative Approaches to the Lexicon, Geneva*, pp. 115–122.

Plénat, M., & Roché, M. (2004). Prosodic constraints on suffixation in French. In G. Booij, J. De Cesaris, A. Ralli, & S. Scalise (Eds.), *Topics in morphology. Selected papers from the third Mediterranean morphology meeting* (pp. 285–299). Barcelona: Institut Universitari de lingüistica aplicada, Univertat Pompeu Fabra.

Pustejovsky, J. (1995). *The generative lexicon*. Cambridge, MA: MIT Press.

Pustejovsky, J. (1996). *Lexical shadowing and argument closure, ms*. Boston: Brandeis University.

Sanders, G. (1988). Zero derivation and the overt analogue criterion. In M. Hammond & M. Noonan (Eds.), *Theoretical morphology: Approaches in modern linguistics* (pp. 155–175). San Diego: Academic.

Selkirk, E. (1982). *The syntax of words, Linguistic Inquiry Monograph.* Cambridge, MA: MIT Press.

Shieber, S. M. (1986). *An introduction to unification-based approaches to grammar* (CSLI Lecture Notes Series, Vol. 4). Stanford: Center for the Study of Language and Information.

Chapter 18
Boosting Lexical Resources for the Semantic Web: Generative Lexicon and Lexicon Interoperability

Nicoletta Calzolari, Francesca Bertagna, Alessandro Lenci,
and Monica Monachini

18.1 Introduction

Computational lexicons can play a key role in the Semantic Web: aiming at making word content machine-understandable, they intend to provide an explicit representation of word meaning, so that it can be directly accessed and used by computational agents, such as large-coverage parsers, modules for intelligent Information Retrieval or Information Extraction. In all these cases, semantic information is necessary to enhance the performance of Natural Language Processing (NLP) tools, and to achieve a real understanding of text content. Moreover, in multilingual computational lexicons we find the linguistic (morphosyntactic/semantic) information necessary to establish links among words of different languages, information of great importance for systems performing multilingual text processing, such as Machine Translation, Cross-lingual Information Retrieval.

If we look at the past, in the last decade many activities have contributed to substantially advance knowledge and capability of how to represent, create, maintain, acquire, access large lexical repositories. These repositories are rich in linguistic knowledge, and based on best practices and standards that have been consensually agreed on or have been submitted to the international community as *de facto* standards. Core – or even large – lexical repositories have been and are being built for many languages. Besides WordNet (Fellbaum 1998), important examples are EuroWordNet (Vossen 1998), PAROLE (Ruimy et al. 1998), SIMPLE (Lenci et al. 2000a) in Europe, ComLex (Grishman et al. 1994), FrameNet (Fillmore et al. 2001)

N. Calzolari (✉) • F. Bertagna • M. Monachini
Istituto di Linguistica Computazionale – CNR, Pisa, Italy
e-mail: glottolo@ilc.cnr.it; monica.monachini@ilc.cnr.it

F. Bertagna • A. Lenci
Università di Pisa, Pisa, Italy
e-mail: alessandro.lenci@ling.unipi.it

J. Pustejovsky et al. (eds.), *Advances in Generative Lexicon Theory*, Text,
Speech and Language Technology 46, DOI 10.1007/978-94-007-5189-7_18,
© Springer Science+Business Media Dordrecht 2013

in the US, among many others. Many came into existence in European projects, and continued in National Projects (cf. e.g. Ruimy et al. 2002), thus creating the necessary platform for a future European lexical infrastructure.

Looking at the future, a further step and radical change of perspective is now needed in order to facilitate the integration of the linguistic information resulting from all these initiatives, to bridge the differences between various perspectives on language structure and linguistic content, to put an infrastructure into place for content description at the European level, and beyond. A natural convergence exists between some of the core activities in the field of Human Language Technology (HLT) and the Semantic Web long-term goals.

18.2   Resources in the Semantic Web Vision

The vision of Semantic Web (thought up by Berners-Lee) is the attempt to efficiently represent data on the Web, in such a way that they can be easily processable by machines on a global scale (Fensel et al. 2003). If the Web is a huge bulk of data that become information when interpreted by humans, the aim of the Semantic Web is make this information directly understandable by computational agents. To achieve this goal, The Semantic Web needs explicit semantics to allow interoperability, system and database integration to be used in tasks such as semantic search, content/knowledge management, agent communication and collaboration, creation of smart documents, etc. (Benjamins et al. 2002). In this context, a crucial role is obviously played by multilingual semantic processing, which lies at the heart of NLP and Language Engineering (LE) research and technological development, since no effective text understanding can be envisaged without the proper identification and representation of the semantic content of documents encoded in different languages.

Lexicons will undoubtedly form an essential component and a building block of great impact to make the vision of a European pervasive Information Infrastructure and of the Semantic Web a reality. Language – and lexicons – are the gateway to knowledge. Lexicons – especially within a multilingual dimension – are at the base of bridging the knowledge gap in a multilingual society such as Europe: only through them can we tackle the twofold challenge of digital content availability and multilinguality. Semantic Web developers will need repositories of words and terms – and knowledge about their relations within language use and ontological classification. The cost of adding this structured and machine-understandable lexical information can be one of the factors that delays its full deployment. But linguists alone will not be able to solve this. Like with the Web (where many contribute), we have to get many people involved to make steps forward. This unavoidable shift in the lexical paradigm – whereby many participants add linguistic content descriptions in an *open distributed lexical framework* – is required and proposed to make lexical resources usable within the emerging Semantic Web scenario.

Moreover, computational lexicons should be conceived as *dynamic systems*, whose development needs to be complemented with the automatic acquisition of semantic information from texts. Gaining insights into the deep interrelation between representation and acquisition issues is likely to have significant reper- cussions on the way linguistic resources will be designed, developed and used for applications in the years to come. As the two aspects of knowledge representation and acquisition are profoundly interrelated, progress on both fronts can only be achieved through a full appreciation of this deep interdependency.

These objectives can only be met when working in the direction of an integrated open and distributed lexical infrastructure, which is able to simultaneously tackle the following aspects:

– the design of advanced architectures for the representation of lexical content;
– the development of new methods and techniques for the automatic acquisition of semantic knowledge from texts and for the customization and update of lexical resources;
– the standardization of various aspects of the lexicon, up to content interoperabil- ity standards.

Some of the prerequisites of this new lexical framework are:

– open framework, where everyone must be able to access, put new information, get parts of the lexicons;
– multilingual, multimodal, multimedial, dynamic, i.e. comprising tools for acquir- ing information from texts (e.g. the web);
– integrative, allowing the integration into different environments and enabling a bidirectional interaction between corpus and lexicon;
– knowledge intensive, allowing representation of rich semantic information, and bootstrapping new semantic information starting from the available one.

18.3 Meaning, Lexicons and Ontologies: The Challenge of Generative Lexicon

In the vision of the Semantic Web, by which the Web is turned into a machine- understandable knowledge-base, it is necessary to tackle two aspects, content and multilinguality, i.e. the information crucial to be represented is semantic information in a multilingual environment. In the Semantic Web ontologies are the key components for applications to manage knowledge and content based systems. In HLT semantic description is committed to computational lexicons, which are the critical resource for most systems and constitute a precondition to deal with the full complexity of multilingual text processing.

There are some close similarities between ontologies and computational lexi- cons. An ontology carves out the shape of a particular portion of semantic space, by individuating the relevant basic elements and the topology of relations holding among them. Lexicons actually provide the interface between text/documents (i.e. knowledge realised in written, spoken, image form) and ontologies, bridging the gap between conceptual/domain nodes and how they are realised in language (in written, spoken, image form). Furthermore, in semantic lexicons, ontologies are used to represent the lexical content of words and play a very important role in lexicon design: the meaning of an item is defined by the position of the concept it expresses in the ontology.[1]

Commonalities should however not overshadow the differences between ontologies and computational lexicons, nor blur the specific character of the challenge set by lexical meaning description. This the reason why semantic lexicons should not be considered strictly speaking as ontologies (Hirst 2004).[2] Differences mainly reside in the peculiar character of lexical knowledge, which computational lexicons purport to describe. Some of the main features of the latter can be described as follows:

1. Lexical knowledge is inherently *heterogeneous* and *implicitly structured*. For instance, describing the semantic content of words like *element, material, link*, etc. necessarily implies to refer to their inherent relational and functional nature (Busa et al. 2001b). Verbs also require specific representational solutions, often quite different from the ones adopted for nouns. In fact, the specification of the number and types of participants to the event expressed by the verb or the temporal properties of the event itself are crucial conditions for a satisfactory description of its meaning. Moreover, word meaning is always the product of complex dynamics: what appears in a computational lexicon must be regarded as the result of an abstraction process from the concrete and multifaceted behavior of words in texts, which in turn keeps on re-shaping its organization.

2. *Polysemy* is a widespread and pervasive feature affecting the organization of the lexicon. The different senses of a word are only rarely separate and well-distinguished conceptual units. In a much more common situation, words have multiple meanings that are in turn deeply interwoven, and can also be simultaneously activated in the same context.

3. Ontology design must be firmly grounded on a solid methodology of formal analysis, in order to avoid inconsistent concept descriptions and to allow the ontology to become the basis of a sound inferential system. Computational lexicons can truly benefit from current work in formal ontology design (cf. for instance Oltramari et al. 2002), but at the same time natural language semantic systems must be flexible enough to account for the complexity of perspectives that spring out of language data. Word senses are *multidimensional entities* that can barely be analyzed in terms of unique assignments to points in a system of concepts. A suitable type system for lexical representation must be provided with an unprecedented complexity of architectural design, exactly to take into account the protean nature of lexicon and its multifaceted behavior.

---

[1] This is the case of the EuroWordNet Top Ontology (Rodriguez et al. 1998) which is used to describe the basic concepts and the SIMPLE Core Ontology (Lenci et al. 2000b) which provides the core type system to classify word-senses.

[2] Although the term (*linguistic*) *ontology* is often used to refer to WordNet or other lexical resources.

As a direct consequence of these issues, although "shallow" semantic representations can be profitably exploited in various NLP tasks such as "semantic tagging"
or Information Extraction, the need to account for the multidimensional nature
of linguistic data and to get at a deeper understanding of text content requires
the development of richer systems of semantic types, where the conceptualization
expressed by word meanings must be analyzed along various orthogonal dimensions. The relational aspects of lexical items, the argument structures of predicative
expressions, and the complex interplay of syntactic and semantic conditions must
therefore find a proper place within lexical architectures. Besides, the notion itself
of lexical unit is not without problems, given the pervasive presence of *non-
compositional aspects* in the lexicon, such as collocations, multiword expressions,
idioms, etc. As a result, a suitable lexical architecture must provide a "hybrid
environment", where the semantic content is represented through a careful and
variously weighted combination of different types of lexical information.

The theory that mainly and convincingly tries to address the issues of complexity
and multidimensionality is the *Generative Lexicon* (GL) (Pustejovsky 1995). The
main characteristic of GL is to allow expressive and uniform lexical semantic
representations of meanings of heterogeneous complexity. The sense is viewed as a
complex bundle of information consisting of orthogonal dimensions which cannot
be captured in terms of mere subtype relations: the most important component
for representing all of the meaning dimensions is the *Qualia Structure*, which
consists of four qualia roles. Each Qualia role can be considered as an independent
element or dimension of the vocabulary for semantic description. The GL theory
enables a uniform representation of lexical meanings of heterogeneous complexity.
Pustejovsky defines in fact the semantics of a lexical item as a structure involving
different components. One of these, *qualia structure*, is a rich and structured
representation of the relational force of a lexical item. It enables one to express
different or orthogonal aspects of word sense, whereas one-dimensional (or even
multiple) inheritance can only capture standard hypernymic relations.

18.3.1 SIMPLE: A GL-Based Computational Lexicon

The approach adopted in the SIMPLE model (Lenci et al. 2000b; Ruimy et al.
2000) tries to meet the above issues and give its own answer to the problems
of semantic type-system design for the lexicon. The SIMPLE project was aimed
at building wide-coverage, multipurpose and harmonised computational semantic
lexicons linked to the morphological and syntactic ones which were elaborated for
12 European languages,[3] during the PAROLE project. The general, all-purpose NLP
lexicons built in the framework of PAROLE and SIMPLE are well harmonised: all

---

[3]Catalan, Danish, Dutch, English, Finnish, French, German, Greek, Italian, Portuguese, Spanish
and Swedish.

over the three description levels they share a theoretical and representational model (EAGLES/GENELEX/PAROLE/SIMPLE), a working methodology, a Document Type Definition (DTD), the XML output format, as well as a core of lexical entries. The theoretical linguistic background on which the SIMPLE model is based is an extended version of Generative Lexicon (Busa et al. 2001b).[4]

SIMPLE provides a system of semantic types where multidimensionality is explicitly taken into account. The idea of this structure is an important contribution from the Generative Lexicon which constitutes the answer to the limitations of conventional type systems structured in a purely taxonomic way (Busa et al. 2001a). The validity of the principle of Qualia Structure in designing top-level ontologies based on an orthogonal architecture of semantic types was already been proven (Pustejovsky and Boguraev 1993). The SIMPLE ontology enriches the conventional architecture by organizing the semantic types along multiple dimensions, provided by the Qualia Structure. It has been elaborated combining both top-down and bottom-up approaches, in such a way as to permit an exhaustive characterization of different levels of complexity of lexical meanings and to capture, besides the essence of a word sense, additional meaning components that are crucial to a thorough lexical description.

18.3.1.1 The SIMPLE Ontology

The SIMPLE semantic type system, whose top types can be mapped on the EuroWordNet ontology, consists of a set of 153 language-independent semantic types, which are of two different kinds:

- *simple types* (i.e. one-dimensional), which can be fully characterized in terms of a hyperonymic relation, e.g.: the semantic type EARTH_ANIMAL is a subtype of ANIMAL, which, in its turn, is a subtype of LIVING_ENTITY;
- *unified types* (i.e. multi-dimensional), which can only be identified through the combination of a subtyping relation and the reference to orthogonal (telic or agentive) dimensions of meanings, e.g.: ARTIFACT is a unified type which inherits not only the properties of its supertype CONCRETE_ENTITY but also agentive and telic dimensions of meaning as well.

The SIMPLE ontology also allows for a variable degree of granularity of semantic description. The *Core Ontology* consists of the hierarchy of upper and general types, i.e. those that meet a large consensus across languages and provide the most essential information for describing word senses, whereas the so-called *Recommended Ontology* includes the hierarchy of lower and specific types that clearly provide more granular information about word meaning. Language/application-specific semantic types may also be designed in order to allow for a more refined

---

[4]SIMPLE is also grounded on the recommendations which emerged from the EAGLES project as well as on the results of the EuroWordNet, AQUILEX and DELIS EC Semantic Projects.

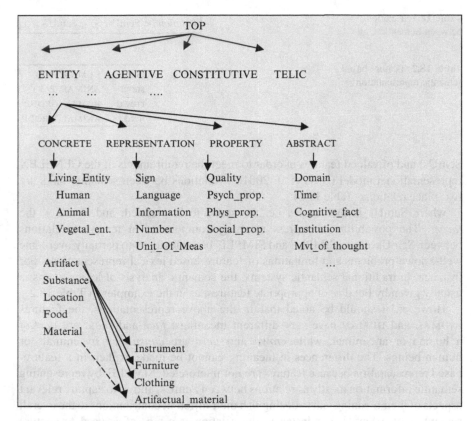

Fig. 18.1 A section of the SIMPLE ontology

description level. Dominating the type system hierarchy are the generic semantic type ENTITY and three other types, named after the qualia roles since they were designed to encode units definable only in terms of qualia dimensions (Fig. 18.1). The CONSTITUTIVE type, which encodes word meanings such as *ingrediente* (ingredient), that are intrinsically constitutive, subsumes the types PART, GROUP and AMOUNT. Besides prototypical lexical units indicating a quantity, the AMOUNT type encodes also the content reading of container denoting nouns, i.e. *un cucchiaio di sale* (a spoonful of salt). The AGENTIVE type encodes word senses such as *causa* (cause), which lexically instantiate the agentive quale, while the TELIC type encodes very underspecified nouns, not easy to formalize from a taxonomic point of view, such as *scopo* (aim), which only convey a bare telic dimension.

18.3.1.2 The Extended Qualia Structure

In SIMPLE, qualia structure has been modified, in the sense that qualia roles have been implemented in terms of relations between semantic units (henceforth,

Table 18.1 Relation
between Semantic Units

$$\boxed{Relation\ (<\ SemU\ _1\ >,\ <\ SemU\ _2\ >\ )}$$

Table 18.2 Feature-based
semantic representation

face	HUMAN, PART
snout	ANIMAL, PART
crowd	HUMAN, GROUP
herd	ANIMAL, GROUP

SemUs) and of valued features in order to meet the requirements of the GENELEX representational model (Busa et al. 2001b). Relations between semantic units are two-place relations (Table 18.1):

where SemU$_1$ is the *source*, i.e. the sense to be defined, and SemU $_2$ the *target*. The possibility to express meaning components in terms of relations between SemUs allows SIMPLE and SIMPLE-based lexicons to partially overcome well-known problems and limitations of feature-based lexical representations. For instance, in traditional semantic systems, the semantic analysis of lexical items is usually given by bundles of appropriate features, as in the examples in Table 18.2.

However, it should be noted that in the above representations, the features ANIMAL and HUMAN have very different meanings: *face* and *snout* are *part_of* a human or an animal, while *crowd* and *herd* are *constituted by* animals or human beings. The differences in meaning cannot be made explicit in a feature-based representation because features are not interpreted. SIMPLE, by representing semantic information mostly as relations between SemUs, allows to capture relevant aspects of their meaning and to distinguish their different contributions to the overall semantics of a SemU. For instance, the relation *is_a_part_of* is used to capture meronymic relations, and the relation *has_as_member* to represent the collective dimension of an entity (for more examples, cf. Ruimy et al. 2002).

In this extended framework, information is also provided in terms of valued features, when, as a rule of thumb, they express attributes of entities with a closed set of values, e.g. *Sex, Age, Dimension, etc.*

The novelty of SIMPLE is that semantic relations are not only used for the representation of information traditionally referred to by relations, as meronymy, *part_of (finger, hand)*, and its inverse relation holonymy, *has_as_part (carburettor, car)*, or antonymy, with its various types of opposite relations (*true, false*); (*hot, cold*), but it is also extended along the four Qualia roles. Relations are organized along taxonomically structured hierarchies within each quale, specifying for each of them its extended qualia set, i.e. defining for each role more specific subtypes of a given relation that provide a far more refined information, consistent with its interpretation (Busa et al. 2001b). For instance, *indirect_telic* is one of the most general subtypes of *telic*, subsuming, e.g., *instrumental* which, on its turn, subsumes *used_for, used_as, used_by, used_against*. This hierarchical structure allows for two opposite kind of operations, underspecification, as well as the representation of fine-grained meaning distinctions (Ruimy et al. 2002). This new expressive means enables qualia to capture more subtle linguistic differences holding within the same meaning component: *used_for* (leather, manufacture), *used_as* (leather, material), *used_by* (lancet, surgeon), *used_against* (antibiotic, infection).

In the *Extended Qualia structure* the relevance of a relation is marked with a different weight, for each of its actual uses in a type definition. The weight indicates whether the relation is type defining, i.e. encoding an information that intrinsically characterizes a semantic type, as the telic relation '*is_the_activity_of*' for members of the type PROFESSION, or whether it conveys 'optional' – mainly world-knowledge – information, i.e. a property not really crucial to the definition of a semantic type but that provides additional knowledge about specific lexical units, as e.g. the constitutive relation '*made_of*' for artifact-typed lexical items. Relations are used, hence, to capture multiple aspects of word meaning, ranging from functionality, to mode of creation, internal constitution, etc. and connect a semantic unit to other SemU in such a way that these interconnections can be computationally managed and made understandable by an automatic system.

The use of relations between semantic units has also been extended to deal with other types of information: derivational information – *beauty, beautiful*; *mixer, mix* – and regular polysemous classes – ANIMAL, FOOD (*lamb_1, lamb_2*); SUBSTANCE, COLOR (*amethyst_1, amethyst_2*); PRODUCER, PRODUCT: *lemon_1, lemon_2*.

18.3.1.3 The SIMPLE Templates

Templates are part of the formal entities of the SIMPLE model. The template structure is built like a schema that works as interface between lexicon and ontology: each semantic type has a corresponding *template type*, which reflects well-formedness conditions and provides constraints for lexical items belonging to that type. In the lexicon building phase, a template-driven encoding methodology was adopted: once the adequate semantic type was identified, the corresponding template type supplied the lexicographer with relevant language-independent information to be instantiated in the language (Table 18.3).

Encoding semantic units by means of template*s* ensures intra- and inter-language encoding uniformity and consistency, and eases the reusability of data. Templates constrain in fact the clustering of semantic entries according to the properties of the underlying semantic types. The lexicon uniformity is therefore guaranteed from the theoretical standpoint by the semantic types and from the practical one by templates. The template provides the specification for the representation and encoding of the information which is intended to allow identifying a word sense and discriminating it from the other senses of the same lexical unit.

It is worth noticing that the SIMPLE model covers a great range of information. Moreover, its model and architecture offer the opportunity to deal with natural language complexity by providing a highly expressive and versatile way for language content description.

Table 18.3 Template for container

SemU:	<u>1</u>: *identifier of a SemU*
SynU:	*id. of the SynU which the SemU is linked to*
BC number:	*N° of the corresponding Base Concept in EWN*
Template_Type:	[Container]
Unification_path:	[Concrete_entity | Artifact$_{Agentive}$ | Telic]
Domain:	General
Semantic Class	Container
Gloss:	*lexicographic definition*
Pred_Rep.:	Lex_pred (<arg0> (Head_quantifier))
	predicate pointed to the SemU its argument structure
Selection. Restr.:	arg0 = [ENTITY]
Derivation:	*derivational relation between SemUs*
Formal:	*isa* (<u>1</u>, <container> *or* <hyperonym>)
Agentive:	*created_by* (<u>1</u>, <Usem>: [CREATION])//def//
Constitutive:	*made_of* (<u>1</u>, <Usem>)//opt//
	has_as_part (<u>1</u>, <Usem>)//opt//
	contains (<u>1</u>, <Usem>)//opt//,
Telic:	*used_for (1,* <contain>*)*//def//
	used_for (1, <measure>*)*//opt//
Synonymy:	*Synonyms of the SemU*//opt//
Collocates:	*Collocates* (<Usem1>,...,<Usemn>)//opt//
Logical polysem.	[AMOUNT] [CONTAINER]

18.4 Standardization as a Way Towards Lexicon Interoperability

The design of a common and standardized framework for lexicon and knowledge resources which may ensure the encoding of linguistic information in such a way to grant its reusability by different applications and in different tasks, can lead to the optimization of the whole process of production and sharing of resources: their creation, maintenance, and (also automatic) extension. Standards are, hence, critical to achieve the interoperability needed for effective integration, being a precondition for a qualitative improvement in multilingual content processing technologies.

The standardization initiative promoted by the ISLE Computational Lexicon Working Group (CLWG) is directly connected to this vision. The ISLE[5] (*International Standards for Language Engineering*) project is a continuation of the long standing EAGLES initiative (Calzolari et al. 1996).[6] ISLE is carried out in

---

[5]ISLE Web Site URL: lingue.ilc.cnr.it/EAGLES96/isle/ISLE_Home_Page.htm

[6]EAGLES stands for *Expert Advisory Group for Language Engineering Standards* and was launched within EC Directorate General XIII's Linguistic Research and Engineering programme in 1993, continued under the Language Engineering programme, and then under the Human Language Technology (HLT) programme as ISLE, since January 2000.

collaboration between American and European groups in the framework of the EU-US International Research Co-operation, supported by NSF and EC. EAGLES work towards *de facto* standards has already allowed the field of Language Resources (LR) to establish broad consensus on critical issues for some well-established areas, providing thus a key opportunity for further consolidation. Existing EAGLES results in the lexicon and corpus areas are currently adopted by a number of European – and also National (Ruimy et al. 2002, 2003) – projects (e.g. LE-PAROLE and LE SIMPLE), thus becoming "the *de-facto* standard" for LR in Europe.

The ISLE Computational Lexicon Working Group (CLWG) has consensually defined a standardized infrastructure to develop multilingual resources for HLT applications, with particular attention to the needs of Machine Translation (MT) and Crosslingual Information Retrieval (CLIR) systems. Compared with other standardization initiatives active in this field (e.g. OLIF-2, Lieske et al. 2001), the original character of ISLE resided in its specifically focusing on the *grey area* of HLT where well-assessed language technology meets more advanced levels and forms of linguistic description. In particular, various aspects of lexical semantics, although still part of ongoing research, are nevertheless regarded by industrials and developers as the "next-step" in new generation multilingual applications. Standard definition in this area thus means to lay a first bridge between research in multilingual resource development and its exploitation in advanced technological systems. With this respect, the ISLE CLWG adhered to the leading methodological principle that the process of standardization, although by its own nature not intrinsically innovative, must – and actually does – proceed shoulder to shoulder with the most advanced research. Consistently, the ISLE standardization process has pursued a twofold objective:

- defining standards both at the content and at the representational level for those aspects of computational lexicons which are widely used by applications;
- proposing recommendations for the areas of computational lexical semantics which are still in the "front line" of on-going research, but also appear to be ready for their applicative exploitation and are most required by HLT systems to achieve new technological leap forward.

The process of standard definition undertaken by CLWG, and by the ISLE enterprise in general, on one side has provided an essential interface between advanced research in the field of multilingual lexical semantics, and the practical task of developing resources for HLT systems and applications. It is through this interface that the crucial trade-off between research practice and applicative needs will actually be achieved.

On the other side ISLE results have paved the way to a needed cooperation between until now separate communities, such as HLT and other actors and groups specifically involved with 'content' and knowledge (ontologies, semantic web, content providers, etc.), enabling future common efforts and resource sharing. Finally, one of the targets of standardization, and actually one of the main aims of the CLWG activities, was to create a common parlance among the various actors (both of the scientific and of the industrial R&D community) not only in the field of computational lexical semantics and multilingual lexicons, but also in the areas e.g. of ontologies and the emerging semantic web, so that synergies will be enhanced, commonalties strengthened, and resources and findings usefully shared.

18.4.1   ISLE Result: The MILE

The ISLE CLWG has pursued these goals by designing the MILE (*Multilingual ISLE Lexical Entry*), a general schema for the encoding of lexical information for multilingual linking (Calzolari et al. 2002). This has to be intended as a meta-entry, acting as a common representational layer for multilingual lexical resources.[7] The ISLE intention was to exploit the EAGLES bulk of work and to extend the results in a multilingual perspective, trying to make a synthesis of all the information that is relevant to build a multilingual lexical entry (a MILE) starting from a monolingual description. One of the first objectives of the CLWG was to discover and list the (maximal) set of (granular) basic notions needed to describe the multilingual level. For the expressiveness of its lexical model, SIMPLE has played a crucial role in the design of the MILE: the wealth of semantic information encoded in the SIMPLE lexicon has been taken as the monolingual basis for the analysis carried out in ISLE, re-examined, integrated and all wrapped up in view of the MILE.

While the basic notions for the morphological, syntactic and semantic levels come directly from the previous EAGLES-PAROLE-SIMPLE experience, the information connected to the description of the multilingual entry (such as the operations useful in the bilingual transfer or in the interlingua environment) has fallen within the ISLE CLWG activity: earlier linguistic analysis (previous EAGLES work, essentially monolingual) was revisited to see what had to be changed/added or what could be reused for the multilingual layer. The EAGLES guidelines have been examined with the aim of proposing a broad format for multilingual lexical entries which is of general utility to the community.

The basic notions, selected for their lexicographic relevance or because consensually agreed on represent *de facto* standards in the NLP community, constitute a first attempt to provide a multidimensional, orthogonal, yet in some ways redundant representation of the lexical meaning, Examples of basic notions are the concepts of (ontological) semantic type or the device represented by the semantic relations.

18.4.1.1   The MILE Lexical Model

The MILE Lexical Model (MLM) is intended to provide the common representational environment needed to implement such an approach to multilingual resource

---

[7]Different possible lexical entries can be designed as instances of the schema provided by the MILE. Instances of entries might differ for the type of information they include and the depth of lexical description.

```
<SynU mlc:ID="SYNUamareV">
<example>Gianni ama Maria</example>
<hasSyntacticFrame> <SyntacticFrame mlc:ID="amare-SyntFrame">
   <hasSelf> <Self mlc:ID="amare-Self">
    <headedBy> <Phrase mlc:ID="VAUXavere">
        <hasSynFeature> <SynFeature>
            <hasSynFeatureName mlc:value="aux"/>
            <hasSynFeatureValue mlc:value="avere"/>
        </SynFeature> </hasSynFeature> </Phrase> </headedBy>
    </Self> </hasSelf>
   <hasConstruction> <Construction mlc:ID="amare-Constr">
    <slot> <SlotRealization mlc:ID="NPsubj">
        <hasFunction mlc:value="Subj"/>
        <filledBy mlc:value="NP"/>
      </SlotRealization> </slot>
    <slot> <SlotRealization mlc:ID="NPobj">
        <hasFunction mlc:value="Obj"/>
        <filledBy mlc:value="NP"/>
      </SlotRealization>
    </slot> </Construction>
```

Fig. 18.2 RDF instantiation of a MILE-conformant lexical entry

development, with the goal of maximizing the reuse, integration and extension of existing monolingual computational lexicons. The main objective is to provide computational lexicon developers with a formal framework to encode MILE-conformant lexical entries. MILE is based on the experience derived from existing computational lexicons (e.g. LE-PAROLE, SIMPLE, WordNet, EuroWordNet, etc.). It is structured according to the entity-relationship (ER) schema and based on a distributed architecture and open to various types of users.

The MILE Lexical Model (MLM) includes three types of components:

- the MILE Lexical Classes (MLC) represent the main building blocks which formalize the basic lexical notions. The MLM provides a definition of the classes, i.e. their attributes and the way they relate to each other. Classes represent notions like syntactic features, syntactic phrase, predicate, semantic relation, synset, etc. (Fig. 18.2 provides an RDF instantiation of lexical classes in a MILE-conformant syntactic entry).
- The instances of MLC are the MILE Data Categories (MDC). NP and VP are data category instances of the class <Phrase> and SUBJ and OBJ are data category instances of the class <Function>. Each MDC is identified by a URI and can be either "user defined" or belong to "shared repositories" (In Fig. 18.2 some syntactic Data Categories are instantiated).
- lexical operations which are special lexical entities allowing the user to define multilingual *conditions* and perform *operations* on lexical entries.

The MILE Lexical Entry is an ideal structure to render in Resource Definition Framework (RDF) (Brickley and Guha 2000). An RDF schema defines classes of objects and their relations to other objects: it consists of a hierarchy of lexical objects that are built up by combining data categories via clearly defined relations. RDF may be used to instantiate lexical objects at various levels of granularity, which can be used and reused to create lexical entries within a single lexicon as well as across lexicons.

Users will be able to define new instances of lexical objects for their lexicon or language specific needs. This way, both at the monolingual and multilingual level (but with particular emphasis on the latter), ISLE has intended to start up the incremental definition of a more object oriented architecture for lexicon design. Developers will be able to develop their own lexicon project either by selecting some of the MILE Shared Lexical Objects or by defining new MILE conformant objects, which in turn might then enrich the common core if they reach a certain amount of consensus in the field. Lexical objects will be identified by a URI and will act as common resources for lexical representation, to be in turn described by RDF metadata.

18.5   Concluding Remarks

Semantic content processing lies at the heart of the Semantic Web vision, and requires to squarely address the complexity of natural language. Existing experience in language resource development proves that such a challenge can be tackled only by pursuing a truly interdisciplinary approach, and by establishing a highly advanced environment for the representation and acquisition of lexical information, open to the reuse and interchange of lexical data.

With MILE, the basis for the realization of a common platform for interoperability between different fields of linguistic activity – such as lexicology, lexicography, terminology – and Semantic Web development has been set. The platform will provide a flexible common environment not only for linguists, terminologists and ontologists, but also for content providers and content management software vendors, for development and communication. This will enable users to share lexicons and collaborate on parts of it. The lexicons may be distributed, i.e. different building blocks may reside at different locations on the web and linked by URLs. This appears strictly related to the Semantic Web standards (e.g. RDF metadata to describe lexicon data categories). Overall, lexicons will perform the bridging function between documents and conceptual categorization. The common conceptual model within the envisaged architecture will ensure content interoperability between texts, lexicons and ontologies.

The multidimensional perspective is one of the peculiar features of the ISLE activities, and contributes to its added value with respect to other current standardization initiatives. This way, ISLE intends, on the one hand, to answer to the need of fostering the reuse and interchange of existing lexical resources and, on the other hand, to enhance the technological transfer from advanced research to applications. It also prepares the ground for a "new generation" of "knowledge resources".

Coming from the experience gathered in developing advanced lexicon models such as the SIMPLE one, and along the lines pursued by the ISLE standardization process, a new generation of lexical resources can be envisaged. GL represents an important framework with which rich lexical descriptions can be achieved, to tackle the challenges of semantic complexities. These resources will crucially provide the semantic information to allow for effective content processing. On the other hand, they will in turn benefit from the Semantic Web itself. Thus, it is possible to state the existence of a bi-directional relation between the Semantic Web enterprise and computational lexicon design and construction. In fact, the Semantic Web is going to crucially determine the shape of the language resources of the future. Semantic Web emerging standards, such as ontologies, RDF, etc., allow for a new approach to language resource development and maintenance, which is consistent with the vision of an open space of sharable knowledge available on the Web for processing.

References

Benjamins, V. R., Contreras, J., Corcho, O., & Gómez-Pérez, A. (2002, April 19–20). Six challenges for the semantic web. In *Proceedings of SemWeb@KR2002 Workshop*, Toulose.

Brickley, D., & Guha R. V. (2000). Resource Description Framework (RDF) Schema specification. W3C Proposed Recommendation.

Busa, F., Calzolari, N., & Lenci, A. (2001a). Generative lexicon and the SIMPLE model: Developing semantic resources for NLP. In P. Bouillon & F. Busa (Eds.), *The language of word meaning* (pp. 333–349). Cambridge: Cambridge University Press.

Busa, F., Calzolari, N., Lenci, A., & Pustejovsky, J. (2001b). Building a semantic lexicon: Structuring and generating concepts. In H. Bunt, R. Muskens, & E. Thijsse (Eds.), *Computing meaning* (Vol. II, pp. 29–51). Dordrecht: Kluwer.

Calzolari, N., McNaught, J., & Zampolli, A. (1996). EAGLES Final Report: EAGLES Editors' Introduction. EAG-EB-EI, Pisa.

Calzolari, N., Bertagna, F., Lenci, A., & Monachini, M. (Eds.). (2002). Standards and best practice for multilingual computational Lexicons. MILE (the Multilingual ISLE Lexical Entries), ISLE Deliverable 2.2 &2.3 CLWG, Pisa.

Fellbaum, C. (Ed.). (1998). *WordNet. An electronic lexical database*. Cambridge: The MIT Press.

Fensel, D., Hendler, J., Lieberman, H., & Wahlster, W. (Eds.). (2003). *Spinning the semantic web*. Cambridge: The MIT Press.

Fillmore, C. J., Wooters, C., & Baker, C. F. (2001). Building a large lexical databank which provides deep semantics. In *Proceedings of the Pacific Asian Conference on Language, Information and Computation*, Hong Kong.

Grishman, R., Macleod, C., & Meyers, A. (1994). COMLEX syntax: Building a computational Lexicon. In *Proceedings of COLING-1994*, Kyoto.

Hirst, G. (2004). Ontology and the lexion. In S. Staab & R. Studer (Eds.), *Handbook on ontologies* (pp. 209–229). Berlin: Springer.

Lenci, A., Bel, N., Busa, F., Calzolari, N., Gola, E., Monachini, M., Ogonowsky, A., Peters, I., Peters, W., Ruimy, N., Villegas, M., & Zampolli, A. (2000a). SIMPLE: A general framework for the development of multilingual Lexicons. *International Journal of Lexicography, 13*(4), 249–263.

Lenci, A., Busa, F., Ruimy, N., Gola, E., Monachini, M., Calzolari, N., Zampolli, A., Guimier, E., Recourcé, G., Humphreys, L., Von Rekovsky, U., Ogonowski, A., McCauley, C., Peters, W., Peters, Y., Gaizauskas, R., & Villegas, M. (2000b). *SIMPLE Work Package 2 – Final Linguistic Specifications*, D2.2 – WP2, LE-SIMPLE (LE4-8346).

Lieske, C., McCormick, S., & Thurmair, G. (2001). The open lexicon interchange format (OLIF) comes of age. In *Proceedings of the MT Summit VIII*, Santiago de Compostela, Spain.

Oltramari, A., Gangemi, A., Guarino, N., Masolo, C. (2002). Restructuring WordNet's top-level the OntoClean approach. In *Proceedings of LREC2002 (OntoLex workshop)*, Las Palmas, Spain.

Pustejovsky, J. (1995). *The generative Lexicon*. Cambridge: The MIT Press.

Pustejovsky, J., & Boguraev, B. (1993). Lexical knowledge representation and natural language processing. *Artificial Intelligence, 63*, 193–223.

Rodriguez, H., Climent, S., Vossen, P., Bloksma, L., Peters, W., Alonge, A., Bertagna, F., & Roventini, A. (1998). The top-down strategy for building EuroWordNet: Vocabulary coverage, base concepts and top ontology. *Computers and the Humanities, 32*, 117–152.

Ruimy, N., Corazzari, O., Gola, E., Spanu, A., Calzolari, N., & Zampolli, A. (1998). The European LE-PAROLE Project: The Italian Syntactic Lexicon. In *Proceedings of the LREC1998*, Granada, Spain, pp. 241–248.

Ruimy N., Del Fiorentino, M. C., Monachini, M., & Ulivieri, M. (2000). SIMPLE – Lexicon Documentation for Italian. SIMPLE–WP3.9, Final Deliverable, D3.9.2, Pisa.

Ruimy, N., Monachini, M., Distante, R., Guazzini, E., Molino, S., Ulivieri, M., Calzolari, N., & Zampolli, A. (2002). CLIPS, a multi-level Italian computational lexicon: A glimpse to data. In *Proceeding of the LREC2002* (pp. 792–799). Spain: Las Palmas de Gran Canaria.

Ruimy, N., Monachini, M., Gola, E., Calzolari, N., Ulivieri, M., Del Fiorentino, M. C., Ulivieri, M., Rossi, S. (2003). A computational semantic lexicon of Italian: SIMPLE. In Linguistica Computazionale, Pisa, Giardini Editori.

Vossen, P. (1998). Introduction to EuroWordNet. *Computers and the Humanities, 32*, 73–89.

Chapter 19
Automatic Acquisition of GL Resources, Using an Explanatory, Symbolic Technique

Vincent Claveau and Pascale Sébillot

19.1 Introduction

The Generative Lexicon (GL) theory (Pustejovsky 1995) has proved its usefulness in the analysis of numerous linguistic phenomena across languages. Moreover, elements from Generative Lexicons have been shown to be relevant in several natural language processing (NLP) applications (*e.g.* information retrieval, *etc.*). For instance, the qualia structure gives access to relational information, crucial for such applications. In particular, the qualia roles (namely the telic, agentive, constitutive and formal roles) express, in terms of predicative formulae, the basic features of the semantics of nouns. In a GL model, the noun is linked not only to other nouns via traditional lexical relations (such as meronymy and hyperonymy) but also to verbs. For example, the noun *book* is linked to the verbal predicate *read* via its telic role and to the predicate *write* via its agentive role. Hereafter, a noun(N)-verb(V) pair in which V expresses one of the qualia roles of N (like *book-read* or *book-write*) is called a *qualia pair*. Previous work by Fabre and Sébillot (1999) has demonstrated that these N-V relations provide lexical resources that are found to be useful for information retrieval systems. Different studies (Grefenstette 1997; Pustejovsky et al. 1997, *inter alia*) also show that N-V pairs can feed indexes that help a user to select the most interesting occurrences of a given noun in a text. Moreover, a short survey (Vandenbroucke 2000) at the documentation center of the Banque Bruxelles Lambert (Brussels) shows that verbs that express a qualia relation seem to be more relevant than others for a document retrieval task; indeed, in this

V. Claveau (✉) • P. Sébillot
IRISA – CNRS, Rennes, France
e-mail: vincent.claveau@irisa.fr; pascale.sebillot@irisa.fr

J. Pustejovsky et al. (eds.), *Advances in Generative Lexicon Theory*, Text, Speech and Language Technology 46, DOI 10.1007/978-94-007-5189-7_19, © Springer Science+Business Media Dordrecht 2013

study, no non-qualia N-V pairs were considered as interesting by the documentalists. Furthermore, the global relevance of qualia verbs for the interpretation of binominal sequences (Fabre 1996) gives access to various interesting applications in the domain of term variations.

Thus, possessing such GL resources is fundamental for many NLP applications. However, there are two main difficulties to handle:

1. the lack of Generative Lexicons or lexical resources containing those qualia pairs;
2. and the fact that verbs in those pairs may vary considerably from one domain to another (especially in technical domains).

A corpus-based method to acquire such N-V qualia resources has to be found, which would eventually lead to an automatic way to populate Generative Lexicons. This is the precise focus of this chapter, in which we propose and describe such a technique.

This chapter is divided in four parts: we first position our acquisition method within the wide domain of corpus-based acquisition techniques for lexical semantic relations, and differentiate it from other attempts to automatically fill in Generative Lexicons. Our approach relies on a symbolic machine-learning method that infers morpho-syntactic and semantic patterns from examples and counter-examples of N-V qualia pairs in context. These patterns distinguish the examples from the counterexamples and then can be applied on a corpus in order to retrieve new N-V qualia pairs. The second part of the text is dedicated to the presentation of our symbolic learning tool, named ASARES, and the description of the corpus on which it has been trained and evaluated. One of the interests for choosing a symbolic method is to obtain explicative patterns, *i.e.* patterns that explain the concept of qualia role as it is expressed in the studied corpus. The third section presents the inferred patterns, and discusses their linguistic relevance. Finally, a complete evaluation of ASARES is provided in terms of correct N-V qualia pair extraction, and we compare its acquisition performances to those of standard statistical and syntactical approaches. The linguistic discussions in those two last parts of the text are based on a work jointly realized with P. Bouillon (ISSCO, Geneva, Switzerland) and C. Fabre (ERSS, Toulouse, France).

19.2 Automatic Acquisition of Semantic Relations

Numerous studies have been dedicated to the corpus-based acquisition of semantic relations. Grefenstette (1994) and Pichon and Sébillot (1997) provide some states-of-the-art of the domain, and Manning and Schütze (1999) describe a large panel of statistical methods that have been used for that purpose. Rather than an exhaustive description of all the elaborated techniques, we present here a reading of the domain, structured by the type of global approach that they can choose. We then give some arguments explaining our choice of a symbolic technique to acquire N-V qualia pairs, and conclude this section by an overview of the (few) studies that have already been realized about Generative Lexicon filling.

19.2.1   Overview of Possible Methods

One relevant way to structure the domain of lexical relation acquisition from corpora is to oppose numerical *versus* symbolic approaches. Numerical approaches of acquisition exploit the frequential aspect of data while symbolic approaches exploit the structural aspect of data, and use symbolic information. Note that no assumption is made about the actual technique manipulating symbolic or numerical information; a statistical technique can be used to acquire lexical relations on the basis of symbolic information, and conversely, a symbolic technique can make the most of numerical information.

Within the numerical approach, relations between lexical units can be acquired by studying word co-occurrences in a text window (or specific syntactic structures). The strength of the association is usually evaluated with the help of a statistical score (association coefficient) that detects words appearing together in a statistically significant way. For example, Church and Hanks's work (1989) is based on such a statistical co-occurrence method. Following the linguistic principles of Harris (1989), numerical distributional analysis methods respect a 3-step approach: extraction of the cooccurrents of one word (within a text window or a syntactic context), evaluation of proximity/distance between two terms, based on their shared or not shared cooccurrents (various measures are defined), clustering into classes (*e.g.* following different data analysis or graph techniques). For example, Bouaud et al. (1997) and Grefenstette (1994) follow this kind of technique to discover paradigmatic relations.

The symbolic approach of acquisition groups into two strategies: symbolic linguistic approach, and machine-learning (ML) approach. In the first one, operational definitions of the elements to acquire are manually established by linguists, usually in the form of morpho-lexical patterns that carry the relations that are studied, or by a list of linguistic clues (*e.g.* see Oueslati 1999). However, when such patterns or clues are unknown, but examples of elements respecting the target relation are known, ML can be used to automatically extract patterns from the descriptions of those examples. The technique is based on a 5-step methodology initiated by Hearst (1992):

1. select one target relation R;
2. gather a list of pairs following relation R;
3. find the sentences that contain those pairs; keep their lexical and syntactic contexts;
4. detect common points between those contexts; suppose that they form a pattern for R;
5. apply the patterns to get new pairs and go back to 3.

ML (inductive logic programming, grammatical inference, *etc.*) (Mitchell 1997) offers a framework to automate step 4, and aims at automatically producing unknown morpho-lexical patterns that carry the target relation.

Both approaches present advantages and drawbacks. Numerical approaches are usually portable and automatic but produce non-interpretable results; the detection is realized at the corpus level: thus, the detection of one specific occurrence cannot be explained. Symbolic approaches need *a priori* knowledge (patterns or examples), but produce interpretable results; detection is done at the occurrence level.

19.2.2 Arguments to Choose a Symbolic ML Technique

Let us have a look at each kind of methods listed above and examine its relevance for a corpus-based acquisition of N-V qualia pairs.

First, a N-V qualia pair can be considered as a special kind of co-occurrence, and a statistical approach that extracts N-V pairs related in a statistically significant way can be chosen. We have however proved that this type of methods is not accurate enough to extract precise relations, *i.e.* N-V pairs linked by a qualia relation *versus* other pairs in our case (see Sect. 19.5.3).

Another possibility is to use a symbolic linguistic approach and to extract the N-V pairs by spotting a set of syntactic structures related to qualia roles. In this last case, the advantage is that such patterns can be very precise, but the major problem is that the patterns that carry N-V qualia pairs in a given corpus are mainly unknown; they have to be defined, and adapted to every new text and corpus.

In our case, we have no *a priori* knowledge concerning the structures that are likely to convey qualia roles in a corpus, but we are able to (manually) find some examples of N-V qualia pairs in a text to feed an automatic technique. Thus, we have developed and applied a supervised symbolic machine-learning method. This method automatically produces general rules that explain what, in terms of surrounding context (part-of-speech and semantic tags; see Sect. 19.3) in a text, differentiate examples of N-V qualia pairs from non-qualia ones in a given corpus. The rules produced this way—morpho-syntactic and semantic patterns—are then applied to the corpus to detects unseen qualia N-V pairs. Therefore, with this system, we aim at combining the precision of linguistic rules (or patterns) in extraction tasks and the flexibility of an automated method. Unlike most statistical methods that only provide a predictor (this N-V pair is qualia, this one is not), our symbolic ML method infers general rules able to explain the examples, that is, bring relevant and linguistically interpretable elements about the predicted qualia relations in the studied corpus.

19.2.3 Related Work

Only a few projects have been undertaken to automatically construct qualia structures. Among them, Pustejovsky et al. (1993) propose to acquire elements of these structures from a syntactically-tagged corpus by the means of a co-occurrence-based statistical extraction technique coupled with a set of heuristics, *i.e.* syntactic patterns. However, no precise evaluation of the performances of this work is given and this study makes strong assumptions on the structures conveying the qualia relations and heavily relies on the good results of syntactic parsers, not available for most of the languages.

Using qualia verbs of nouns to define a framework for logical metonymy interpretation, Lapata and Lascarides (2003) also present an acquisition method for N-V qualia pairs. This technique relies on a probabilistic learning based on Naive Bayes (Mitchell 1997), and uses a syntactic parser to establish the necessary joint appearance probabilities. More than on the extraction task itself, the evaluation of this work mostly focuses on the possibilities of acquired N-V pairs to interpret metonymies. As the previous one, this study also uses a syntactic parser, and detects potential N-V qualia pairs only if the two elements are syntactically related. If the members of some qualia pairs can obviously be syntactically bound, all syntactically related pairs are not qualia pairs and, conversely, no theoretical or experimental clue ensures that qualia pairs have to be syntactically bound. Indeed, those hypotheses are partially invalidated by results of an experiment described in Sect. 19.5.4.

19.3   Symbolic Acquisition of Qualia Elements

This section is devoted to the description of ASARES, a symbolic acquisition tool used to extract qualia pairs from corpora. It follows the previously seen 5-step approach proposed by Hearst, but its originality lies in the fact that the fourth step (detecting the common points in the examples) is considered as a machine-learning task. In order to manage this task, ASARES makes the most of a powerful symbolic machine learning technique: Inductive Logic Programming (ILP). ILP is adapted to our qualia extraction task in order to produce relevant contextual patterns (that is, from a "machine-learning" point of view, to infer rules) from examples and counter-examples of qualia pairs in the corpus.

First, the corpus used in our experiments and its several steps of tagging is presented in the next sub-section. Then, the whole machine learning process is described, including a discussion about the use of ILP for this task, the selection and the encoding of the examples, and an overview of the learning process itself.

19.3.1   Corpus and Tagging

This sub-section is devoted to the presentation of the corpus used in our experiments. First, the choice of this corpus is described in the next sub-section. Then, Sects. 19.3.1.2 and 19.3.1.3 respectively present the Part-of-Speech and semantic taggings, whose information is used as a basis for the extraction patterns.

19.3.1.1 The MATRA-CCR Corpus

The French corpus used in this project is a 700 kbytes handbook of helicopter maintenance, given to us by MATRA-CCR Aérospatiale, which contains more than 104,000 word occurrences. It has some specific characteristics that are especially well suited for our task: it is coherent, that is, its vocabulary and syntactic structures are homogeneous; it contains many concrete terms (screw, door, *etc.*) that are frequently used in sentences together with verbs indicating their telic ("screws must be tightened", *etc.*) or agentive roles.

19.3.1.2 Part-of-Speech Tagging

This corpus has been tagged with Part-of-Speech (PoS) information with the help of annotation tools developed in the Multext project (Armstrong 1996). Thus, sentences and words are first segmented with MTSEG; words are analyzed and lemmatized with MMORPH (Petitpierre and Russel 1998; Bouillon et al. 1998). Finally, words having more than one possible PoS tag are disambiguated by the TATOO tool, a Hidden Markov Model (HMM) tagger (Armstrong et al. 1995), which can be trained directly on a non-disambiguated part of the corpus. Each word (eventually) receives a single tag that indicates its PoS as well as inflection information (gender, number or conjugation where it applies). Finally, the accuracy of this tagging, evaluated with a 4,000 word hand-tagged part of the corpus, is very good: only 2% of the words are detected as wrongly tagged.

19.3.1.3 Semantic Tagging

A semantic tagging has also been performed on the corpus, following the work of Bouillon et al. (2000). It aims at providing some general semantic information about words (*e.g.* this word designates a human, this one an action verb, *etc.*).

The main hypotheses guiding the method of semantic tagging are that:

- morpho-syntatic information can help to distinguish meanings of words that are polyfunctional, such as *règle* in French which can be the indicative of the verb to regulate and the noun rule (see also (Wilks and Stevenson 1996; Yarowsky 1992; Ceusters et al. 1996)),
- morpho-syntactic analysis can be done by a probabilistic (HMM) tagger and,
- more daringly, remaining semantic ambiguity can also be solved (*mutatis mutandis*) by an HMM tagger.

These hypotheses are not new, but here, we describe the way we have implemented them, and we evaluate our method with the MATRA-CCR corpus.

After the PoS-tagging and disambiguation of the corpus previously explained, one or more semantic tags are associated with each word of the corpus. The TATOO HMM tagger, applying a model trained on the ambiguous semantic tags, resolves the remaining semantic ambiguities. As we are in a restricted domain, homonyms are very rare; what need to be disambiguated here are mostly polysemes whose senses are related in a systematic way (Pustejovsky 1995). These polysemes are particularly suitable for this kind of method since, by definition, the correct sense can be identified by the context around the word and their disambiguation does not require pragmatic disambiguation.

Thus, the first step is to choose a set of semantic tags for each category of a word. In order to classify the nouns, the most generic classes of WordNet (Fellbaum 1998) are used. However, they are modified and refined in two ways: irrelevant classes (*i.e.* classes not used in the corpus; *e.g.* abstraction) have been withdrawn; for large classes, a more precise granularity has been chosen, in order to distinguish and characterize their elements (*e.g.* the concrete object class). This has led to 33 classes. Figure 19.1 presents a part of their hierarchical organization as defined in WordNet.

Concerning verbs, WordNet classification was judged too specific and divided into too many classes for our corpus. A minimal partition into five classes has been chosen: cognitive activity, physical activity, state, modality and temporality. *Ad hoc* tagsets have also been defined for all other categories of word. To sum up, here is some numerical information about the file gathering all the possible semantic tags for each word of the corpus. It contains 1,489 different nouns, 129 (8.7%) of them being ambiguous (*i.e.* that can be classified in more than one class and thus receive more than one semantic tag). Most of these ambiguities correspond to complementary polysemy, in particular classical semantic alternations (for example, *enfoncement* (hollow) can both indicate a process or its result) or contextual variants (for example, *bout* (end) can be temporal or locative). The file also contains 8 different acronyms, one of them being ambiguous; 567 different verbs, 6 of them being ambiguous; 68 adjectives, 4 of them being ambiguous; 53 prepositions, 9 of them being ambiguous; about 15 determiners and 30 pronouns, none of them being ambiguous.

Each occurrence in the corpus is given all its possible tags according to this file. Then, the HMM-based disambiguation training is done just as for the PoS-tagging. However, since the ambiguities are very limited, this training has been done with a set of interesting sentences. For the evaluation, a subset of about 6,000 words of the MATRA-CCR corpus has been manually tagged and compared with the output of the tagger. In this subset, 455 words were ambiguous (7.78%). The application of the semantic tagging method has led to a score of 1.18% of remaining errors, that is, (when compared with to the 7.78% of ambiguous words) 85% of good disambiguation.

More than one third of the remaining errors are due to prepositions. The errors concerning nouns and verbs, which are the key elements of the qualia structures we are willing to extract, are therefore relatively rare in the disambiguated corpus.

Finally, after these PoS and semantic tagging processes, a sentence such as "*L'opérateur utilise les tournevis pour visser . . .*" ("The operator uses the screw-drivers to screw . . .") appears in the following format:

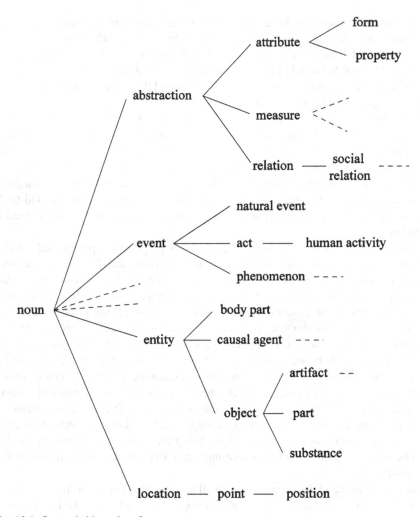

Fig. 19.1 Semantic hierarchy of nouns

m151	L'	le	det_masc_sg	–
m152	opérateur	opérateur	noun_masc_sg	human
m153	utilise	utiliser	verb_ind_3_sg	phys_action
m154	les	le	det_masc_pl	–
m155	tournevis	tournevis	noun_masc_pl	artifact
m156	pour	pour	prep	goal_prep
m157	visser	visser	verb_inf	phys_action
	...			

The first column gives a unique identifier to each word of the corpus, the second and third ones respectively contain the words as they appear and the corresponding lemmas, the fourth column gives the PoS information and the last one the semantic information.

19.3.2 Inferring Extraction Patterns with ILP

All those PoS and semantic tags in the MATRA-CCR corpus are the contextual key information used by ASARES to extract qualia pairs with the help of an inductive method called inductive logic programming (ILP). The choice of this symbolic learning method is explained in the next sub-section. Since ILP is a supervised ML technique, we need examples; the way they are obtained and their representations are described in Sect. 19.3.2.2; and the learning step, which infers the extraction patterns from the examples, is finally presented in Sect. 19.3.2.3.

19.3.2.1 About the Use of ILP

Our selection of a learning method is guided by the fact that this method must not only provide a predictor (this N-V pair is qualia, this one is not), like most statistical methods, but must also infer general rules able to explain the examples, that is, give rise to linguistically interpretable elements which predict qualia relations. This essential explanatory characteristic has motivated our choice of the ILP framework (Muggleton and De Raedt 1994) in which programs that are inferred from a set of facts (examples and counter-examples of the concept to be learned) and background knowledge, are logic programs, that is, sets of Horn clauses. Indeed, ILP's relational nature can provide a powerful expressiveness for the still unknown linguistic patterns expressing qualia relations in a given corpus. Moreover, errors inherent in the automatic PoS and semantic tagging process previously described make the choice of an error-tolerant learning method essential. The relative ease with which ILP handles noisy data guarantees this robustness.

Most ILP systems provide a way to deal more or less with the form of the generated rules but only some of them enable a total control of this form. Moreover, the particular hierarchical structure of our PoS and semantic information makes it essential to use a relational background knowledge processing capable ILP system. For these reasons, we have chosen ALEPH (a state-of-art Prolog implementation freely available at http://web.comlab.ox.ac.uk/oucl/research/areas/machlearn/Aleph/). This ILP implementation has already proved to be well suited to deal with a large amount of data in multiple domains (mutagenesis, drug structure . . .) and allows us to precisely customize all the settings of the learning task.

19.3.2.2 Example Construction

As explained above, ILP algorithms generate rules explaining what distinguishes
examples of the concept to be learned from counter-examples. In our case, we want
to discriminate qualia N-V pairs from non-qualia ones according to their PoS and
semantic context in the MATRA-CCR corpus. Therefore, our first task consists in
building the sets of examples and counter-examples (hereafter, respectively E+ and
E−), that is, in describing the sentences where qualia N-V pairs and non-qualia
ones occur in terms of PoS and semantic information. It is well worth noting that no
distinction is made between the different qualia roles (it is not considered as relevant
for our information retrieval application of the acquired N-V pairs (Claveau and
Sébillot 2004b)); thus, every telic, agentive or formal N-V pair may be considered
as an example. Here is our methodology for their construction.

   Given a subset of N-V pairs of our corpus, every occurrence in the text of
each pair of this subset is manually annotated as relevant or irrelevant according
to Generative Lexicon's qualia structure principles. The considered occurrence is
then added to the E+ set if it is annotated as relevant, to the E− one otherwise,
and the contextual information of this occurrence is added to the background
knowledge. The examples and counter-examples therefore contain clauses of the
form is_qualia(noun identifier, verb identifier) where noun identifier and verb
identifier are the unique identifier of the considered N-V pair occurrence. The
contextual information is stored as background knowledge in the form of the
following clauses:

tags(w1 identifier, PoS-tag, semantic-tag).
tags(w2 identifier, PoS-tag, semantic-tag).
pred(w2 identifier, w1 identifier).
tags(w3 identifier, PoS-tag, semantic-tag).
pred(w3 identifier, w2 identifier).
tags(w4 identifier, PoS-tag, semantic-tag).
pred(w4 identifier,w3 identifier).
tags(w5 identifier, PoS-tag, semantic-tag).
pred(w5 identifier, w4 identifier).
distances(w4 identifier, w2 identifier, distance in words, distance in verbs).

where, e.g., the studied N-V pair w4-w2 occurs in the 5-word long sentence "w1 w2
w3 w4 w5", pred(x,y) indicates that word y occurs just before word x in the sentence,
predicate tags/3 gives the PoS and semantic tags of a word, and distances/4 specifies
the number of words and the number of verbs between N and V in the sentence.
During this step, only a few word categories (determiners, some adjectives), which
are not considered relevant to predicting qualia or non-qualia pairs, are not taken
into account; all the other words of the sentence where the target N-V pair appears
participate to its contextual description.

   For example, consider the qualia pair *tournevis-visser* (screwdriver-screw) in
the previously seen sentence *"L'opérateur utilise les tournevis pour visser..."*
("The operator uses the screwdrivers to screw...") . This N-V pair is indicated as

being an example to ALEPH by adding the fact is_qualia(m155,m157) to the set of the examples. Contextual information about this pair is added to the background knowledge:

tags(m152,noun_masc_sg,human).
tags(m153,verb_ind_3_sg,phys_action).
pred(m153,m152).
tags(m155,noun_masc_pl,artifact).
pred(m155,m153).
tags(m156,prep,goal_prep).
pred(m156,m155).
tags(m157,verb_inf,phys_action).
pred(m157,m156).
...
distances(m155, m157, 1, 0).

About 3,000 examples and 3,000 counter-examples are automatically produced this way from the manual annotation of the qualia and non-qualia pairs in the MATRA-CCR corpus. Other information, describing the hierarchical relationships among PoS and semantic tags, is also provided in ALEPH's background. Those relationships encode, for example, the fact that a tag instrument denotes an instrument and can be considered as a kind of artifact, which is a kind of object and so on (see Fig. 19.1). This is easily written in the Prolog form:

instrument(W) :- tags(W,_,instrument).
artifact(W) :- instrument(W).
object(W) :- artifact(W).
object(W) :- part(W).
object(W) :- substance(W).
...

19.3.2.3   Learning Step

In addition to the sets of examples and the various kinds of information in the background knowledge, a hypothesis language is also provided to the ILP system. It is used to precisely define the expected form of the generated rules (or hypotheses). In the qualia extraction case, this language makes the most of the PoS and semantic tags of words occurring in the examples (N-V pairs and their contexts) and distance information between N and V (a complete description of the hypothesis language used and its consequences on the learning process can be found in Claveau et al. (2003)). For example, the rules produced, which are used as patterns to extract new qualia pairs, look like:

is_qualia(N,V) :- precedes(N,V), near_verb(N,V), infinitive(V),
action_verb(V), artifact(N), pred(V,P), goal_preposition(P).

This rule means that a pair composed by a noun N and a verb V will be considered as qualia if V appears in a sentence after N, V is an action verb in the infinitive preceded by a goal preposition P and N is an artifact. Thus, this rule is equivalent to the pattern: N artifact + (any token but a verb)* + goal preposition + infinitive action verb V. This rule covers (that is, explains or logically entails) the pair *tournevis-visser* (screwdriver-screw) in the previously seen sentence "*L'opérateur doit utiliser les tournevis pour visser...*" ("The operator uses the screwdrivers to screw...") and certainly many others in the corpus.

According to the hypothesis language, the ILP algorithm infers rules that cover a maximum of examples and no counter-examples (or only a few, some noise can be allowed in order to produce more general patterns), by generalizing the examples (Muggleton and De Raedt 1994). More precisely, the inference process follows the following steps:

1. select one example e ∈ E+ to be generalized. If none exists, stop.
2. define a hypothesis (*i.e.* potential pattern) search space H according to e and the hypothesis language;
3. search H for the rule h that maximizes a score function Sc;
4. remove the examples that are covered by the chosen rule. Return to step 1.

A precise description of the structure of the hypothesis space H, containing all the potential patterns generalizing an example, and the way it is explored to find a global optimum can be found in (Claveau et al. 2003). The score function Sc depends on the number of examples and counter-examples covered by a hypothesis h, as well as its length (shorter rules are favored). Thus, the chosen rules are meaningful generalizations of the examples and reject most of the counter-examples.

This learning step, which is the heart of ASARES, takes about 15 min on a recent Linux PC. Several rules are produced (see next section for a detailed description) which can now be used to automatically retrieve new qualia N-V pairs in the corpus.

19.4 Linguistic Discussion About the Inferred Patterns

As mentioned previously, our choice of a symbolic ML technique is mostly motivated by the fact that ILP produces general rules or patterns that are linguistically interpretable, leading to the discovery of corpus-specific linguistic generalizations regarding the concept of qualia relation. Before analyzing the performances of the patterns inferred by ASARES in extracting qualia pairs (see Sect. 19.5), this section provides a linguistic discussion about the patterns. More precisely the question raised in Sect. 19.4.1 is: what do the learned clauses tell us about the linguistic structures that are likely to convey qualia relations between a noun and a verb in the studied corpus? A comparison with manually found patterns is proposed in Sect. 19.4.2.

19.4.1 Inferred Patterns

ASARES has produced the nine following clauses from the examples and counter-examples, which we are now facing and willing to interpret linguistically:

1. is_qualia(N,V) :- precedes(V,N), near_verb(N,V), infinitive(V), action_verb(V).
2. is_qualia(N,V) :- contiguous(N,V).
3. is_qualia(N,V) :- precedes(V,N), near_word(N,V), near_verb(N,V), suc(V,X), preposition(X).
4. is_qualia(N,V) :- near_word(N,V), sentence_beginning(N).
5. is_qualia(N,V) :- precedes(N,V), singular_common_noun(N), suc(V,C), colon(C), pred(N,D), punctuation(D).
6. is_qualia(N,V) :- near_word(N,V), suc(V,C), suc(C,D), action_verb(D).
7. is_qualia(N,V) :- precedes(N,V), near_word(N,V), pred(N,C), punctuation(C).
8. is_qualia(N,V) :- near_verb(N,V), pred(V,C), pred(C,D), pred(D,E), preposition(E), sentence_beginning(N).
9. is_qualia(N,V) :- precedes(N,V), near_verb(N,V), pred(N,C), subordinating_conjunction(C).

Predicates must be read as follows: precedes(X,Y) means that X occurs somewhere in a sentence before Y. pred(X,Y) means that Y occurs immediately before X and conversely suc(Y,X) means that X occurs immediately after Y. near_word(X,Y) means that X and Y are separated by at least one word and at most two words, and near_verb(X,Y) that there is no verb between X and Y.

What is first striking is the fact that, at this level of generalization, few usual linguistic features remain. The clauses seem to provide very general indications and tell us very little about types of verbs (action_verb is the only information we get), nouns (common_noun) or prepositions that are likely to fit into such structures. However, the clauses contain other information, related to several aspects of linguistic descriptions, like:

- *proximity*: this is a major criterion. Most clauses indicate that the noun and the verb must be either contiguous (clause 2) or separated by at most one element (clauses 3, 4, 6, 7) and that no verb must appear between N and V (clauses 1, 3, 8, 9).
- *position*: clauses 4, 7 and 8 indicate that one of the two elements is found at the beginning of a sentence or right after a punctuation mark, whereas the relative position of N and V (precedes/2) is given in clauses 1, 3, 5, 7 and 9.
- *punctuation*: punctuation marks, and more specifically colons, are mentioned in clauses 5 and 7.
- *morpho-syntactic categorization*: the first clause detects a very important structure in the text, corresponding to action verbs in the infinitive form.

These features bring to light linguistic patterns that are very specific to the corpus, a text falling within the instructional genre. We find in this text many examples in which a verb at the infinitive form occurs at the beginning of a proposition and is followed by a noun phrase (found by clause 1). Such lists of instructions are very typical of the corpus:

- *débrancher la prise* (disconnect the plug);
- *enclencher le disjoncteur* (engage the circuit breaker);
- *déposer les obturateurs* (remove the obturators).

Clause 5, which is equivalent to the pattern V + : + (any token)* + [:,;] + singular N, highlights enumerative structures that are very frequent in the corpus, like:

- *Ouvrir : le capot coulissant, le capot droit...* (Open: the sliding cowl, the right cowl...);
- *Poser : le bouchon, la porte d'accès...* (Set: the cap, the access door...);
- *...déclenche : l'allumage du voyant 1, l'allumage du voyant alarme...* (... set up: the lighting of indicator signal 1, the lighting of alarm indicator signal...).

These results emphasize the ability of our technique to learn corpus-specific patterns. Indeed, when applied to other corpus, other experiments of qualia extraction (Claveau and Sébillot 2004b) or close semantic relation acquisition in the Meaning-Text theory framework (Claveau and L'Homme 2004), using the same technique have shown that most of the patterns inferred are dependent on the corpus.

19.4.2 Comparison to Manual Linguistic Observations

To further evaluate these findings, we have compared the automatic learning results to linguistic observations made manually on the same corpus (Galy 2000). É. Galy has listed a set of canonical verbal structures that convey telic information:

- infinitive V + det + N (*visser le bouchon*) (to tighten the cap)
- V + det + N (*ferment le circuit*) (close the circuit)
- N + past participle V (*bouchon maintenu*) (held cap)
- N + be + past participle V (*circuits sont raccordés*) (circuits are connected)
- N + V (*un bouchon obture*) (a cap blocks up)
- be + past participle V + par + det + N (*sont obturées par les bouchons*) (are blocked up by caps).

The two types of results show some overlap: both experiments demonstrate the significance of infinitive structures and bring to light patterns in which the verb and noun are very close to each other. Yet, the results are quite different since the learning method proposes a generalization of the structures discovered by É. Galy. In particular, the opposition between passive and active constructions is merged in clause 2 by the indication of mere contiguity (V can occur before or after N). Conversely, some clues have not been observed by manual analysis because they are related to levels of linguistic information that are usually neglected by linguistic observation (punctuation marks and position in the sentence).

Consequently, when examining the results of the learning process from a linguistic point of view, it appears that the clauses give very general surface clues about the structures that are favored in the corpus for the expression of

qualia relations. Yet, these clues are sufficient to give access to some corpus-specific patterns, which is a very interesting result.

19.5   Evaluation and Comparison of Performances

This section is devoted to various kinds of evaluation of ASARES. After a short description of the test set that makes this evaluation possible, we first present the performances of our symbolic system in qualia pair extraction. Thus, we measure the proportion of qualia pairs that the nine inferred patterns detect on a test corpus manually annotated by GL experts. We then compare ASARES's results with those of various statistical extraction methods commonly used for semantic relation acquisition. We finally compare our qualia extraction system with an entirely manual approach relying on a syntactic annotation of the studied text.

19.5.1   Test Set

To evaluate ASARES in real-world conditions, four GL experts have constructed an empirical test set. The test corpus on which the qualia-pair extraction is performed is a 32,000-word subset of the MATRA-CCR corpus. In spite of its relatively small size, it is impossible to manually examine every N-V pair to class it as qualia or non-qualia. We have thus focused our attention on seven domain relevant common nouns: *vis, écrou, porte, voyant, prise, capot, bouchon* (screw, nut, door, indicator signal, plug, cowl, cap). Of course, to prevent distortion of results, none of these common nouns were used as examples or counter-examples for the pattern induction phase by ASARES. Each N-V pair such that N is one of the seven nouns occurring within a sentence in the sub-corpus is retrieved. Then, the four experts manually tag each one as qualia or not; during this tagging phase, the eventual hypernymic links between verbs given by our semantic tagging are not taken into account; each N-V pair is examined separately. Divergences (concerning only a few pairs) are discussed until complete agreement is reached.

Finally, among the 286 examined pairs, 66 are classified qualia (each N has between 4 and 17 V in qualia relations). This test set is therefore used to compare the extraction results of our automatic system with the human expert one.

19.5.2   Results of ASARES

The nine learned rules produced by ASARES have been applied to the sub-corpus. That is, each N-V pair containing one of the seven test nouns and any verb

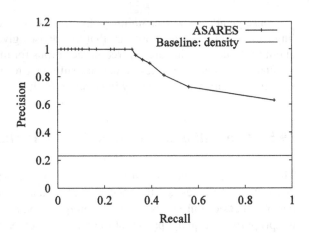

Fig. 19.2 Recall-precision graph

cooccurring with it within a sentence has been tested to see whether it is accepted by one of the learned rules. We present the results of this application of the patterns, and discuss the right and wrong decisions they have taken.

19.5.2.1 Performance

When applying inferred patterns to the corpus, we can decide to consider a N-V pair as qualia if s occurrences of this pair are detected in the test corpus by the learned rules, that is, if the context of the s occurrences correspond to the general patterns defined by the rules. Of course, if s is high, the precision rate is higher than if s is small, and conversely, for a small s, the recall rate is higher than for a high s. The recall and precision rates, measured on our test set, are thus defined (TP means True Positives, FP False Positives and FN False Negatives) according to s: $R(s) = TP(s)/(TP(s) + FN(s))$, $P(s) = TP(s)/(TP(s) + FP(s))$. To represent performances for every possible values of s, a recall-precision graph is commonly used, on which each point represents the precision of the system according to its recall for a given s. Figure 19.2 presents the recall-precision graph for ASARES on the previously described test set.

For a comparison purpose a baseline corresponding to the density of qualia couples among the N-V pairs in the sub-corpus is given; this density represents the average precision that would be obtained by a system deciding randomly whether a N-V pair is or not qualia.

In order to use ASARES, we have to choose a value for the threshold s. One way to do that is to choose the value that maximizes a certain quality criterion, that is, a single performance measure. We have used two measures of this kind: F-measure, the weighted harmonic mean of the R and the P, commonly defined as: $F(s) = 2P(s)R(s)/(P(s) + R(s))$, and the Φ coefficient $(\Phi(s) = ((TP(s)*TN(s))-(FP(s)*FN(s)))/\sqrt{(PrP(s)*PrN(s)*AP(s)*AN(s))}$, where A = actual, Pr = predicated, P = positive, N = negative, T = true, F = false) for

Table 19.1 Optimal performances of ASARES

	Recall (%)	Precision (%)	F-measure	Φ coefficient
ASARES	92.4	62.2	0.744	0.671

which a value close to 1 indicates a good result. Table 19.1 presents ASARES's results on our test set for the value of the threshold s that maximizes the Φ coefficient (this value is equal to 1, that is, a N-V pair is considered as qualia as soon as one occurrence of this pair is covered by one of the learned rules).

Results show a very good recall rate and a quite good precision rate. Thus, the learned rules seem to describe precisely enough the qualia concept. Such an ILP-based qualia-pair extraction system can therefore be used on the whole corpus to get relevant GL resources.

19.5.2.2 Extraction Performance of the Patterns

Before comparing ASARES's performances to those of other extraction methods, let us discuss briefly the kind of N-V pairs that are correctly retrieved, forgotten or incorrectly found using the nine patterns our system has produced. On one side, our ILP method detects most of the qualia N-V couples, like *porte-ouvrir* (door-open) or *voyant-signaler* (indicator signal-warn). The five non-detected pairs appear in very rare constructions in our corpus, like *prise-relier* (plug-connect) in *la citerne est reliée à l'appareil par des prises* (the tank is connected to the machine by plugs) where a prepositional phrase (PP) *à l'appareil* (to the machine) is inserted between the verb and the *par*-PP (by-PP). On the other side, only 8 pairs from the 36 non-qualia pairs incorrectly detected qualia by our learning method cannot be linked syntactically. That means that the ILP algorithm can already reliably distinguish between syntactically and not syntactically linked pairs.

The main problem for ASARES is therefore to correctly identify N-V pairs related by a telic or agentive relation—the most common qualia links in our corpus— among the pairs that could be syntactically related. However, here we should carefully distinguish two types of errors. The first ones are caused by constructions that are ambiguous and where the N-V can or cannot be syntactically related, as *enlever-prises* (remove-plugs) in *enlever les shunts sur les prises* (remove the shunts from the plugs). They cannot be disambiguated by superficial clues about the context in which the V and the N occur and show the limitation of using learning only from PoS and semantic information. However, they are very rare in our corpus (8 pairs). On the contrary, all remaining errors seem more related to the parameterizing of the learning method. For example, taking into consideration the number of nouns between V and N (with the help of the hypothesis language; *cf.* Section 19.3.2.3) could avoid a lot of wrong pairs like *poser-capot* (put up-cover) in "*poser les obturateurs capots*" (put up cover stopcocks) or *assurer-voyant* (make sure-indicator signal) in "*s'assurer de l'allumage du voyant*" (make sure that the indicator signal is switched on).

Table 19.2 Contingency
table of the N-V pair ($N_i - V_j$)

	V_j	$V_{k, k \neq j}$
N_i	a	b
$N_{l, l \neq i}$	c	d

In order to reduce the cost of manually constructing a hierarchy of semantic tags (see Sect. 19.3.1) and enhance the portability of ASARES from one corpus to another, similar learnings and evaluations have been conducted without taking into account semantic tags in the example and counter-example coding, or considering all the semantic tags except those of common nouns which is the far most populated subset. Extracted patterns and results are fully described in (Claveau 2003), which shows that, for our corpus, semantic tagging in not that important, and especially that discarding only the most expensive noun semantic tagging leads to performances quite similar to those presented here.

19.5.3 Comparison with Numerical Methods

In order to precisely evaluate ASARES's results, we have compared the performances of the patterns it has inferred to those of common numerical extraction techniques, based on cooccurrence detection (see Sect. 19.2.1). These simple techniques are frequently used in the domain of corpus-based collocation extraction or semantic information acquisition. In this framework, a N-V qualia pair is considered as a special kind of cooccurrence. We first present the statistical measures that we have tested, and then describe the results obtained by these techniques when applied on the same test set than ASARES. Note that our purpose is not to oppose numerical approaches to our symbolic one but rather to provide well-known baselines to interpret our results presented above.

19.5.3.1 Statistical Measures

We have chosen 12 well-known statistical measures to carry out the qualia-pair extraction task. All of the statistical indexes we use can be expressed with the help of occurrences of N-V pairs in the corpus; a comparison of these measures, commonly used for collocation extraction tasks, can be found in (Pearce 2002). Note that the cooccurrences of nouns and verbs are calculated in the scope of sentences and are based on the lemmas of words. With each N-V pair of the corpus, we can associate a contingency table summing up these cooccurrences as it is shown in Table 19.2. In this table, a is the number of occurrences of the N-V pair (N_i, V_j), b of N-V pairs where the noun is N_i but the verb is not V_j, c of N-V pairs where the verb is V_j but the noun is not N_i, and d of N-V pairs where the noun is not N_i and the verb is not V_j. Let us call S the total number of N-V pair occurrences, that is, $S = a + b + c + d$.

Table 19.3 Statistical methods results

	Recall (%)	Precision (%)	F-measure	Φ coefficient
Dice	33.3	88	0.48	0.477
Kulczinsky	36.4	70.6	0.48	0.414
Ochiai	42.4	82.4	0.56	0.517
MI	51.5	40	0.45	0.261
MI^3	36.4	92.3	0.522	0.52
McC	36.4	70.6	0.48	0.414
Loglike	42.4	80	0.554	0.505
SMC	100	25.3	0.385	0.17
Yule	53	41.2	0.464	0.279
Φ^2	37.9	78.1	0.51	0.464
Cosinus	42.4	77.8	0.549	0.493
Jaccard	31.8	87.5	0.467	0.467

We can now easily express some well-known statistical association criteria such as:

- Dice coefficient (Smadja 1993): $Dice = 2a/((a+b)+(a+c))$
- Kulczinsky coefficient: $Kulczinsky = (a/2)((1/(a+b))+(1/(a+c)))$
- Ochiai coefficient: $Ochiai = a/\text{sqrt}((a+b)(a+c))$
- Mutual Information coefficient: $MI = \log_2(a/((a+b)(a+c)))$
- Cubed Mutual Information coefficient (Daille 1994): $MI^3 = \log_2(a^3/((a+b)(a+c)))$
- McConnoughy coefficient: $McC = (a^2 - bc)/((a+b)(a+c))$
- Loglike coefficient (Dunning 1993): $Loglike = a \log a + b \log b + c \log c + d \log d - (a+b) \log(a+b) - (a+c) \log(a+c) - (b+d) \log(b+d) - (c+d) \log(c+d) + S \log S$
- Simple matching coefficient: $SMC = (a+d)/S$
- Yule coefficient: $Yule = (ad - bc)/(ad + bc)$
- Φ^2 test (Church and Gale 1991): $\Phi^2 = (ad - bc)^2/((a+b)(a+c)(b+c)(b+d))$
- Cosinus (binary case): $Cosinus = a/\text{sqrt}(bc)$
- Jaccard coefficient (binary case): $Jaccard = a/(a+b+c)$

19.5.3.2 Results and Discussion

All these statistical measures are then evaluated for each of the 286 N-V pairs containing one of the seven nouns. In a similar way to what we do for our ILP method, we also try to find the coefficient threshold value which maximizes the Φ coefficient for each of these statistical coefficients. Table 19.3 indicates the best results obtained.

One can notice that only a few statistical measures have good enough results to be used for automatic qualia pair extraction, and none of them matches the results obtained by ASARES. This is even more obvious when representing the extraction

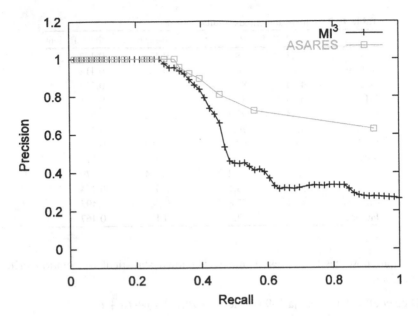

Fig. 19.3 Recall-precision graph of MI^3 and ASARES

results with a recall-precision graph. Figure 19.3 presents such a graph with one of the statistical coefficient that achieves the best performances: MI^3 coefficient. From this graph, it appears that ASARES results are more precise (*i.e.* retrieves more real qualia pairs) than MI^3 ones, whatever the recall considered; the same result holds for the 12 statistical coefficient presented above (recall-precision graphs for the other coefficient can be found in (Claveau 2003)).

Of course, the differences between our ILP-based and the simple statistical-based method results can be easily explained by the differences of knowledge used by these two kinds of techniques. Indeed, while numerical models only use word lemma occurrences, our inductive learning process makes the most of PoS and semantic tags but also needs examples and counter-examples, which is a way to implicitly add linguistic knowledge to the extraction system. Nevertheless, this comparison remains interesting from a pragmatic point of view, more particularly in the balance between the choice of a supervised or unsupervised method and the resulting performances.

19.5.4 Comparison with a Syntactic-Based Extraction Method

We have also compared our qualia extraction system with an entirely manual approach: a syntactic annotation of the studied text. Each N-V pair occurring within a sentence of the corpus is tagged as syntactically linked (that is, the noun is subject,

Table 19.4 Syntactic linkedness method results

	Recall (%)	Precision (%)	F-measure	Φ coefficient
Syntactic link	86.4	79.2	0.826	0.772

object, or modifier of the verb) or not. The underlying idea of this method is that a frequent syntactic link between a noun and a verb in a text may indicate a semantic link between this noun and this verb, for example a qualia link.

Therefore, a N-V pair is considered qualia if more than a certain number of its occurrences are detected syntactically linked. This threshold, as for the ILP-based and statistical methods, is chosen to maximize the Φ coefficient; the value found is 1. Table 19.4 gives the performances of such a system for our test set.

These results indicate a slightly lower recall rate but a better precision rate than our ILP-based method. The fact that the recall rate is lower than 100% tends to show that, in our corpus, a qualia link is more than a basic syntactic link. Much of the 13.6% qualia pairs with non syntactically linked elements are N-V couples that appear in elliptic turns of phrases, or in which N and V are separated by a strong punctuation mark. For example, the qualia pair *voyant-allumer* (indicator signal-switch on) is not considered as syntactically related in "*éteindre le voyant; allumer*" (switch the indicator signal off; switch on); neither is the couple *vis-poser* (screw-set) in "*poser l'ensemble : rondelle, vis et serrer au couple*" (set the whole: washer, screw and couple-tighten).

However, this better precision value seems to lead to the conclusion that our ILP-based method could improve its results, especially its precision rate, by considering syntactic information, and not only PoS and semantic ones. However, automatic syntactic annotation remains currently too noisy to be used without human supervision, and a manual annotation cannot be foreseen for a huge amount of texts. Here again, one should choose between high quality results and automatic or quasi-automatic extraction methods, according to one's goals.

19.6 Concluding Remarks

In this chapter, we have presented ASARES, a symbolic machine learning technique that allows us to infer morpho-syntactic and semantic patterns of qualia relations from the descriptions of some pairs of Ns and Vs whose elements are linked or not by a qualia role. ASARES, more technically described in (Claveau et al. 2003), produces efficient and linguistically motivated patterns, which are useful for the study of the corpus-specific structures conveying qualia roles. Those automatically obtained patterns can be applied to a corpus to successfully get GL resources and populate Generative Lexicons.

The portability of ASARES from one corpus to another may be considered as limited by two facts: the semantic tagging and the supervised nature of the method. Concerning the need for a manual semantic tagging, we have however shown (see

Sect. 19.5.2.2) that semantic tags of nouns, the less portable and most expensive category, can be discarded without any loss in ASARES's performances. The second point is the manual feeding of our ILP-based system with examples and counter-examples of N-V qualia pairs. We have proved (Claveau and Sébillot 2004a) that it is possible to combine a numeric and our symbolic approaches in a so-called semi-supervised acquisition technique in order to overcome this problem, keeping again the same performances.

Being able to acquire N-V qualia pairs with the help of ASARES has allowed us to test the relevance of N-V qualia relations in information retrieval (IR) applications, more precisely to expand users's requests to an IR system. We have automatically added qualia verbs learned on a corpus to the nouns contained in the requests, and have shown that N-V qualia expansion leads to a limited but statistically significant increase of the performances of IR systems, especially in the ranking of the first 20 documents (Claveau and Sébillot 2004b).

Among the next steps of our research, we shall focus on N-N pairs, which very frequently exhibit telic relations in texts, as in *bouchon de protection* (protective cap). Another potential avenue is to try to learn separately each qualia semantic relation (telic, agentive, formal) instead of all together as it is done up to now. Even if such a distinction is maybe not useful for an information retrieval application, it could result in linguistically interesting rules.

References

Armstrong, S. (1996). Multext: Multilingual text tools and corpora. In H. Feldweg & W. Hinrichs (Eds.), *Lexikon und text* (pp. 107–119). Tübingen: Niemeyer.

Armstrong, A., Bouillon, P., & Robert, G. (1995). *Tagger overview* (Technical Report). Geneva, Switzerland: ISSCO. http://www.issco.unige.ch/staff/robert/tatoo/tagger.html

Bouaud, J., Habert, B., Nazarenko, A., & Zweigenbaum, P. (1997). Regroupements issus de dépendances syntaxiques en corpus: catégorisation et confrontation avec deux modélisations conceptuelles. In *Proceedings of IC'97* (pp. 207–223). Ingénierie des Connaissances, Roscoff, France.

Bouillon, P., Lehmann, S., Manzi, S., & Petitpierre, D. (1998). Développement de lexiques à grande échelle. In *Proceedings of Colloque de Tunis 1997 « La mémoire des mots »* (pp. 71–80). Tunis, Tunisia.

Bouillon, P., Baud, R. H., Robert, G., & Ruch, P. (2000). Indexing by statistical tagging. In *Proceedings of JADT'2000* (pp. 35–42). Journées internationales d'analyse de données textuelles, Lausanne, Switzerland.

Ceusters, W., Spyns, P., DeMoor, G., & Martin, W. (1996). *Tagging of medical texts: The multi-TALE project*. Amsterdam: Ios Press.

Church, K. W., & Gale, W. A. (1991). Concordances for parallel texts. In *Proceedings of the 7th annual conference of the UW Centre for the New OED and Text Research* (pp. 40–62). University of Waterloo, Ontario, Canada.

Church, K. W., & Hanks, P. (1989). Word association norms, mutual information, and lexicography. In *Proceedings of ACL'89. 27th Annual Meeting of the Association for Computational Linguistics* (pp. 76–83), Vancouver, Canada.

Claveau, V. (2003). *Acquisition automatique de lexiques sémantiques pour la recherche d'information*. PhD thesis, Université de Rennes 1, France.

Claveau, V., & L'Homme, M.-C. (2004). Discovering specific relationships between nouns and verbs in a specialized French corpus. In *Proceedings of CompuTerm'04, 3rd International Workshop on Computational Terminology*, Geneva, Switzerland.

Claveau, V., & Sébillot, P. (2004a). From efficiency to portability: Acquisition of semantic relations by semi-supervised machine learning. In *Proceedings of COLING'04. 20th International Conference on Computational Linguistics* (pp. 261–267), Geneva, Switzerland.

Claveau, V., & Sébillot, P. (2004b). Extension de requêtes par lien sémantique nom-verbe acquis sur corpus. In *Proceedings of TALN'04*, Traitement automatique des langues naturelle, Fes, Morocco.

Claveau, V., Sébillot, P., Fabre, C., & Bouillon, P. (2003). Learning semantic lexicons from a part-of-speech and semantically tagged corpus using inductive logic programming. *Journal of Machine Learning Research, special issue on Inductive Logic Programming, 4*, 493–525.

Daille, B. (1994). *Approche mixte pour l'extraction automatique de terminologie: statistique lexicale et filtres linguistiques*. PhD thesis, Université Paris VII, France.

Dunning, T. E. (1993). Accurate methods for the statistics of surprise and coincidence. *Computational Linguistics, 19*(1), 61–74.

Fabre, C. (1996). *Interprétation automatique des séquences binominales en anglais et en français. Application à la recherche d'informations*. PhD thesis, Université de Rennes 1, France.

Fabre, C., & Sébillot, P. (1999). Semantic interpretation of binominal sequences and information retrieval. In *Proceedings of international ICSC congress on computational intelligence: Methods and applications, CIMA'99*. Symposium on Advances in Intelligent Data Analysis AIDA'99, Rochester.

Fellbaum, C. (Ed.). (1998). *WordNet: An electronic lexical database*. Cambridge, MA: MIT Press.

Galy, É. (2000). Repérer en corpus les associations sémantiques privilégiées entre le nom et le verbe: le cas de la fonction dénotée par le nom. Master's thesis, Université de Toulouse – Le Mirail, France.

Grefenstette, G. (1994). *Explorations in automatic thesaurus discovery*. Dordrecht: Kluwer Academic Publishers.

Grefenstette, G. (1997). SQLET: Short query linguistic expansion techniques, palliating one-word queries by providing intermediate structure to text. In *Proceedings of RIAO'97. Recherche d'Informations Assistée par Ordinateur* (pp. 500–509), McGill-University, Montreal, Quebec, Canada.

Harris, Z., Gottfried, M., Ryckman, T., Mattick, P., Jr., Daladier, A., Harris, T. N., & Harris, S. (1989). *The form of information in science, analysis of immunology sublanguage* (Boston studies in the philosophy of science, Vol. 104). Dordrecht: Kluwer Academic Publisher.

Hearst, M. A. (1992). Automatic acquisition of hyponyms from large text corpora. In *Proceedings of COLING'92. 14th International Conference on Computational Linguistics* (pp. 539–545), Nantes, France.

Lapata, M., & Lascarides, A. (2003). A probabilisitic account of logical metonymy. *Computational Linguistics, 29*(2), 263–317.

Manning, C. D., & Schütze, H. (1999). *Foundations of statistical natural language processing*. Cambridge, MA: MIT Press.

Mitchell, T. M. (1997). *Machine learning*. New York: McGraw-Hill.

Muggleton, S., & De Raedt, L. (1994). Inductive logic programming: Theory and methods. *Journal of Logic Programming, 19–20*, 629–679.

Oueslati, R. (1999). *Aide à l'acquisition de connaissances à partir de corpus*. PhD thesis, Université Louis Pasteur, Strasbourg, France.

Pearce, D. (2002). A comparative evaluation of collocation extraction techniques. In *Proceedings of LREC'02. 3rd International Conference on Language Resources and Evaluation*, Las Palmas de Gran Canaria, Spain.

Petitpierre, D., & Russel, G. (1998). *Mmorph – The multext morphology program* (Technical Report). Geneva: ISSCO.

Pichon, R., & Sébillot, P. (1997). Acquisition automatique d'informations lexicales à partir de corpus: un bilan (Research Report, INRIA, N°3321). France.

Pustejovsky, J. (1995). *The generative lexicon*. Cambridge, MA: MIT Press.

Pustejovsky, J., Bergler, S., & Anick, P. (1993). Lexical semantic techniques for corpus analysis. *Computational Linguistics, 19*(2), 331–358.

Pustejovsky, J., Boguraev, B., Verhagen, M., Buitelaar, P., & Johnston, M. (1997). Semantic indexing and typed hyperlinking. In *Proceedings of American Association for Artificial Intelligence Conference* (pp. 120–128). Spring Symposium on Natural Language Processing for the World Wide Web, Stanford.

Smadja, F. (1993). Retrieving collocations from text: Xtract. *Computational Linguistics, 19*(1), 143–178.

Vandenbroucke, L. (2000). *Indexation automatique par couples nom-verbe pertinents, Mémoire de DES en information et documentation*. Université Libre de Bruxelles, Belgium.

Wilks, Y., & Stevenson, M. (1996). *The grammar of sense: Is word-sense tagging much more than part-of-speech tagging?* (Technical Report). Sheffield: University of Sheffield.

Yarowsky, D. (1992). Word-sense disambiguation using statistical models of Roget's categories trained on large corpora. In *Proceedings of COLING'92. 14th International Conference on Computational Linguistics*, Nantes, France.

Chapter 20
The Semi-generative Lexicon: Limits on Productivity

Ann Copestake

20.1 Introduction

The counterpoint to any discussion of generative devices in the lexicon should be an appraisal of the counterexamples and the limitations to applicability. This is essential for several reasons. Firstly, the limits on generative processes must be investigated in order to get a better understanding of the theoretical mechanisms underlying generativity. In particular, if the concept of pragmatics as distinct from semantics has any theoretical consequences, purely pragmatic accounts of meaning generation can only be appropriate where there are no conventional, language-specific constraints on the process. Secondly, we must provide formal accounts of generativity which can allow for any exceptions which may be found. This leads to an investigation of devices such as defaults and probabilities. Finally, processing systems that aim for precision of interpretation or idiomatic generation must not overgenerate. Analysis systems that postulate massive ambiguity are of little use. One reason for the rather limited uptake of generative lexical devices in practical natural language processing systems has been the lack of techniques for control of their effects. It is much better in practice to ignore productivity and lose a small proportion of examples than to allow it and be able to process nothing!

In this article, I will go through a number of cases where there appear to be conventional constraints on generative processes. Although some of the data is quite well-known, I think it is useful to consider these phenomena together, because this sheds light on some interesting commonalities and distinctions. I will also describe a possible formal approach. This discussion follows earlier work, in particular the account of productivity in lexical rules proposed in Briscoe and Copestake (1999),

A. Copestake (✉)
University of Cambridge Computer Laboratory, University of Cambridge, Cambridge, UK
e-mail: Ann.Copestake@cl.cam.ac.uk

J. Pustejovsky et al. (eds.), *Advances in Generative Lexicon Theory*, Text,
Speech and Language Technology 46, DOI 10.1007/978-94-007-5189-7_20,
© Springer Science+Business Media Dordrecht 2013

but in this article I consider whether this sort of approach can be used in cases where lexical rules are not applicable. I will also discuss adjective-noun phrases and the degree to which a similar notion of semi-productivity might apply there.

20.2   Semi-productivity in Alternations and Sense Extension

I take as a starting point the assumption that lexical rules, implemented for instance within a typed feature structure logic, can be used to give an account of derivational morphology as well as noun-verb conversions, verb alternations and other sense extensions. I use the term sense extension to refer to any productive or semi-productive process which involves combined syntactic and semantic effects, but no morphological changes. One example is 'animal grinding' which allows a meat-denoting mass use for animal terms (e.g., *rabbit* and *lamb*). I am interested in accounts of lexical rules which allow them to be applied productively to previously unseen lexical items. For instance, *fax* and *email* readily undergo the dative alternation (*fax me this resume/fax this resume to me*). Similarly, it is quite clear that the mass/meat usage is possible even for animals which are not generally eaten: e.g., *crocodile* and *ostrich* may occur as mass terms. It seems desirable on theoretical grounds to allow such uses to be generated even though they may not have been seen before by most native speakers. Similarly, lexical rules provide a way of automatically allowing for some of the unseen usages of words in a computational implementation.

However, as discussed in detail in Briscoe and Copestake (1999) (henceforth B&C), while there have been many attempts to define narrow classes within which alternations such as dative are fully productive (e.g., Pinker 1989), it appears that even though the semantic criteria invoked may be very subtle (and difficult to test or motivate independently), exceptions always remain. For instance, *design* and *create* should be in the same class, but have different acceptability with dative in British English (Ex.1).

(1)   John designed/*created them a bridge

B&C argue that semi-productivity of verb alternations may be accounted for by assuming rules that are sensitive to both type and token frequency effects. Bauer (1983:71f), in a discussion of derivational morphology, argues that the greater 'item-familiarity' of lexical items allows judgments of relative novelty/conventionality to be built up in a way that is not possible at the sentential level because there are simply too many possibilities for the frequency of particular combinations to be assessed. For instance, we may judge that the word *thumpee* is relatively unusual compared to *appraisee* but we are unlikely to be able to reliably judge whether *we should water the begonias* is more or less frequent than *we should water the geraniums*. The argument that productivity is related to frequency applies just as well to alternation and sense extension as to derivational morphology (for detailed discussion, see B&C and also Goldberg (1995)).

20.2.1   A Probabilistic Account of Semi-productivity

The specific proposal made in B&C is to define probabilities for particular lexical entries (by which we mean structures which are either stipulated directly or derived by rule) primarily based on their observed frequencies. This is a standard approach, but the tie up with lexical rule productivity comes in the estimation of unseen uses. B&C argued that estimates of the likelihood of unattested uses must be based on the degree of productivity of the lexical rule that would give rise to them. We assume that rule productivity is defined as the ratio of possible input entries to attested output entries (see also Aronoff 1976). The unseen probability mass for a word form is defined in terms of the rules which could potentially apply to some lexeme to give that form, and the relative probabilities of each unseen entry depends on the productivity measurement for the rule which would be required to derive it. This yields revised ratios for each unseen entry which can be normalized to probabilities.

Details are given in B&C, so I will illustrate this informally with an example of noun-verb conversion (using figures taken from Copestake and Briscoe 1996). Nouns that denote paints and similar substances can also be used as verbs meaning to apply the substance. Examples include *lacquer, creosote, shellac* and *varnish*, as well as *paint* itself. A total of 38 paint-denoting words were checked and of these 25 were found to occur as verbs, giving an estimate of the productivity of the lexical rule for paint noun-to-verb conversion as 0.65. (In contrast, the corresponding figure for vehicle nouns used as verbs is 0.16.) These productivity estimates are used to estimate the likelihood of unseen uses of particular words. For instance, the word *creosote* occurs as a noun 25 times in the BNC and once as a verb. This gives an estimate of the conditional probability P(verb|creosote) of 0.038. Suppose we wish to estimate the conditional probability of the verbal use of *tempera*: the noun occurs 28 times in the BNC, but there are no verbal uses. Rather than estimate the probability as 0, we use a smoothing technique to give all the unseen uses a small probability. The distribution between the various possible lexical rules is based on their relative productivities. The specific details of the smoothing are not important here, however.

The assumption we make about processing is simply that speakers generally choose high-frequency forms to realize particular meanings and that hearers choose high-frequency senses when faced with ambiguity. Under this assumption, hearers never consider infrequent senses (derived or otherwise) unless forced to (by syntax, semantics or pragmatics). It follows that speakers will not generally use unattested forms unless they are licensed by a highly productive rule. Obviously there are exceptions. In some genres there is a value to more creative use of language which presumably causes speakers to deliberately use less likely senses. In spoken language, unattested forms may occur when utterance planning is imperfect. But in general, this principle seems rational for communication – indeed it is entirely compatible with Grice's Maxim of Manner and arguably follows from it.

Under this account, speakers do not normally generate utterances such as Ex.(2a) because there are alternative ways of conveying a highly-similar meaning which are more probable, such as Ex. (2b):

(2a)   * John created them a bridge

(2b)   John created a bridge for them

On the other hand, even though *crocodile* meaning meat might be unattested in a particular speaker's experience, there is no alternative attested lexical form conveying the same meaning. The speaker always has the option of choosing a phrase, such as *crocodile meat*, but it is likely this will also be unattested (as discussed below, it is reasonable to assume that speakers have judgments of the conventionality of compound nouns and some adjective-noun phrases). Furthermore, there is a preference for brevity.

Blocking follows from the application of this principle over a language community: if speakers use higher frequency forms to convey a given meaning, an extended meaning will not become conventionalized if a common synonym exists. This means that we do not have to stipulate a separate blocking principle in interpretation, since the blocked senses will not be attested or will have a very low frequency. And in generation, we assume that higher probability forms are preferred as a way of conveying a given meaning. Thus *beef* blocks *cow*, meaning the meat, for instance. As discussed in B&C, blocking is not absolute.

The probabilistic approach to semi-productivity might be seen as a matter of performance rather than competence and certainly has to be formalized separately from the symbolic grammar. Nevertheless, we would argue that such an encoding is a necessary part of any account of lexical generativity, though the specific details of the account may well need to be refined. The exact boundaries of the division between the symbolic and probabilistic components are difficult to determine, because it makes sense to encode some hard constraints on rule applicability. Furthermore, rule productivity might be established for well-defined semantic subclasses as well as for the rule overall. B&C discuss some of these aspects in more detail. The point of the current article is to demonstrate that semi-productivity applies in many lexical and semi-lexical processes and to discuss how the general probabilistic framework might be extended to such cases.

20.2.2   Compound Nouns

English compound noun formation is at the boundary between lexical and syntactic processes. Copestake and Lascarides (1997) propose an account of compound nouns which is based on the approach to semi-productivity in B&C. In that paper, we reviewed the evidence for limitations on productivity of the noun-noun compound rule in English, observing, in particular, the lack of direct translations for some German compounds (e.g., *Frühlingsangfang/*spring beginning*), the phenomenon of 'possessive' compounds (e.g., *blacksmith's hammer*, **blacksmith hammer*) and the different patterns of stress in compounds. We argued that to account for these effects, and for the apparent existence of conventional meanings, it was necessary to assume a range of relatively fine-grained compound schemata. Although nonce compounds which do not fit into these schemata sometimes occur, they can only do so within a rich discourse context. Compound schemata vary in productivity and we adapted the productivity measurement from B&C so that it was applicable to compounds.

This proposal is an alternative to accounts of English compound formation as fully productive, since these incorrectly generate compounds such as **blacksmith hammer*. It is also preferable to fully lexicalized accounts, which do not allow for novel compounds. We argued that compounds generally have default interpretations based either on their normal meanings (for previously attested compounds) or on meanings that are given by productive compound schemata. While novel compounds which do not fit such patterns are possible, they require a rich discourse context for their interpretation. For instance, Downing's (1977) example of *apple juice seat* does not fit one of the hypothesized semi-productive compound patterns, but could only be understood in a rich context: in the attested use, one place at a table had a glass of apple juice. But such compounds are rare in corpora, and most compounds can be interpreted out of context.

20.2.3   Ham Sandwiches

The classic *ham sandwich* examples (Nunberg 1978) involve non-conventional extended uses which are possible in suitably marked contexts. For instance, in Ex.(3), if said by someone working in a restaurant, *the ham sandwich* has to mean something like *person who ordered a ham sandwich*:

(3)   The ham sandwich is waiting for his check.

I assume that such examples may be generated by a very broad lexical rule, for instance one that converts nouns denoting physical objects to people associated with that object (there are conventional cases of such sense extensions, such as referring to musicians by instrument nouns). Although such a rule is very broad, I do not assume that any noun can be extended to denote anything: for instance, even in a marked context, using a description of a person to denote an object associated with that person seems to be impossible.

A rule such as physical-object-to-person will have a very low productivity according to the B&C formalization, at least for any normal corpus. This is reasonable, since by definition these are non-conventionalized examples. Interpretation is only possible in a very constrained discourse context, and in actual use there is probably a considerable potential for misunderstanding. Non-conventionalized examples are not infrequently found in newspaper and magazine articles, but presumably generally occur where novelty is valued and precise meanings aren't so important.

However, in a subgenre, ham sandwich examples may become conventionalized, in that the productivity measure will go up as speakers produce new examples. Clark and Clark (1979) cite at length a text where household appliances are used to denote a person who possesses that appliance. Such extended use of novel extensions is presumably to some extent deliberate word play. However, if we assume that hearers are sensitive to some quite narrow semantic class implicit in the context (e.g., menu items in restaurants, household appliances or whatever), the productivity measurement for that class would be appreciably increased, even after a very small number of examples. It is clear that other factors are also involved, but at least in general outline the B&C approach seems consistent with the possibility of non-conventionalized sense extension and at least provides an indication of how conventionalization may occur.

20.3 Syntax Rules

The examples below show a number of cases where phrases which appear to be NPs act as adverbial modifiers (see also Ostler and Atkins 1992).

(4a)   I'll meet you next week.

(4b)   We meet every September.

(4c)   I'll meet you Tuesday. (* generally for British English, although acceptable for some speakers, fully acceptable in American English)

(4d)   * I'll meet you September.

What seems to be going on here is that some temporally-denoting NPs can be used as though they were PPs. One way of achieving the desired effect is to have a rule that converts temporal NPs to PP-like phrases. Although such a rule cannot be truly lexical, because it has to be able to apply to phrases with determiners, like *every September*, it nevertheless behaves somewhat like a lexical rule, especially in that it has a very specific range of inputs and has an idiosyncratic semantic effect. There is quite clear dialect variation, as shown by the differences in acceptability of Ex.(4c) between (most dialects of) British and American English.

In formal or implementational terms, such rules do not present any great problems for a symbolic component expressed in a typed feature structure framework. In fact the LinGO English Resource Grammar (see e.g., Copestake and Flickinger 2000) implements such an approach and covers a wide range of temporal expressions. But doing this requires a rather detailed semantic hierarchy of temporal nouns, which has to capture distinctions such as day of week versus day of month and allow for the effects of determiners such as *every*. It remains to be seen whether this can be done precisely enough to capture all possible cases of modification without overgenerating and without ending up with an absurdly fine-grained semantic specification. What is most worrying is the possibility that as more and more such rules are encoded, the symbolic grammar becomes overcomplex and even more difficult to maintain.

The alternative approach, along the lines of that proposed for lexical rules, is to let the symbolic rule overgenerate and control its application via probabilities. This however runs into difficulties because we are dealing with phrases rather than words, and these may be arbitrarily complex.

(5)   We'll meet every fourth Friday that doesn't fall before a holiday weekend.

However, even though it is the entire phrase which is acting as a modifier, the distribution we are interested in concerns the core temporal NP (e.g., *Friday*) and the specifier (and a few other words including *next* and *last*). Thus it may be reasonable to assume that speakers have some degree of item-familiarity based on components of the phrase. One way of partially testing this would be to see whether we could derive appropriate constraints automatically from a realistically sized corpus.

If a probabilistic component can be used, it might be exploited in an account of dialect specificity. That is, while for an American English speaker, *Tuesday* has a reasonably high probability of occurring as a modifier, the probability would be much smaller for a British English speaker.

20.4   Logical Metonymy

Logical metonymy, discussed in Pustejovsky (1995) among other places, also shows interesting restrictions, although the data is not as clear-cut as with morphological processes. While Ex.(6a) below has both the interpretations *reading the book* and *writing the book*, putatively corresponding to the telic and agentive roles respectively, Ex.(6b) apparently only has the reading *building the tunnel* (i.e., the agentive meaning). No interpretation exists corresponding to *using the tunnel*, such as *driving through the tunnel*.

(6a)   Kim began the book.

(6b)   Kim began the tunnel.

As far as I am aware, restrictions of this type were first noted by Godard and Jayez (1993). What makes this particularly interesting is that Ex.(7) is perfect.

(7)   Kim began driving through the tunnel.

Hence the restriction cannot be explained by real world knowledge or by the meaning of *begin*. It is also worth noting that even very marked contexts do not seem to make the telic interpretation better. For example, Ex.(8b) is not a possible continuation to Ex.(8a):

(8a)   The drive to the Alps had been long and tiring, and Kim was prone to claustrophobia.

(8b)   *Therefore it was with considerable trepidation that Kim began the first tunnel.

However note that *tunnel* and similar nouns are possible with *after* and *enjoy*. The following are plausible after Ex.(8a):

(9a)   But after the first tunnel, Kim felt much happier.

(9b)   But much to his surprise, Kim enjoyed the first tunnel.

Godard and Jayez (1993) suggest that the constraint is that the telic interpretation is only possible with *begin* when the additional event involves consumption, which (somewhat implausibly, I think) has to be assumed to include reading. Pustejovsky and Bouillon (1995) discuss possible constraints involving aspect and control properties. But Verspoor (1997) demonstrates the inadequacies of both these accounts. Furthermore, the corpus data she describes show that the overwhelming preponderance of cases of logical metonymy with *begin* and a putative telic interpretation involve a very limited class of physical object/substance nouns, especially nouns denoting foodstuffs, drinks and books. The distribution is relatively similar for *finish*, which shows a greater frequency of logical metonymy than *begin*, although logical metonymies with physical object/substance noun phrases form a very small proportion of the uses of both verbs compared to the non-metonymic cases.[1]

It might be possible to attempt an account where the metonymic process, however it is encoded, applies only to a finely specified semantic class. But the data suggests that we would at best end up with a disjunctively specified class, or equivalently, with a set of subcases each concerning a very finely specified class. This has obvious analogies with lexical alternations. Logical metonymy may be sufficiently infrequent for the item familiarity story to be plausible here: although it is necessary to consider the interaction of two words which do not generally occur immediately adjacent to each other, the existence of verb-noun collocations suggest that this is plausible. Of course this means assuming that the probabilities concern the interaction of the verb and the head of the noun phrase rather than the phrase as a whole.

---

[1]Verspoor also notes that nouns like *story* and *song* occur with *begin* and *finish* in the sense of *tell/perform*. However, these might alternatively be classified as agentive. The data is also complicated because Verspoor excludes eventive nouns in her definition of metonymy, and while this distinction may be justified, it is a little hard to make precise. Her comparison with other verbs also raises interesting issues. For my current purposes, however, all that matters are the limitations on the use of *begin* and *finish* with nouns denoting physical objects or substances, since this is not predicted on a fully productive account of metonymy.

20.5 Collocations and Adjective-Noun Combinations

Collocations have been generally rather neglected within the Generative Lexicon literature, although they are a major focus of attention within Meaning-Text Theory (e.g., Mel'čuk and Polguère 1987) and there has been a considerable amount of work on them in computational linguistics. The term 'collocation' has several definitions: I will use it to mean two or more lexical items occurring together in some syntactic relationship more frequently than would be expected, given a fully adequate symbolic grammar and taking into account world knowledge. For instance, *shake* and *fist* are collocates, while *buy* and *house* are probably not. Although the latter pair co-occur more often than would be expected by chance, this may well be predictable given the role of house purchase in our culture. This definition does not lend itself to a direct test, but there is potential for investigating it via WordNet synonym sets, for instance (see also Pearce 2001). Here I will use the term collocation to refer to cases where the meaning of the phrase can be derived compositionally and there is nothing unexpected about the syntax (in contrast to idioms, verb-particle constructions and other multiword expressions). Thus the only unexpected aspect of a collocation, under this view, is its frequency. See Sag et al. (2002) for further discussion of how collocations differ from multiword expressions.

The converse of a collocation could be termed an 'anti-collocation', where lexical items co-occur less frequently than would be expected, given their semantics and hard grammatical constraints, and a phrase might be regarded as odd by a native speaker.[2] For instance, Cruse (1986:281) claims that *impeccable behaviour*, *impeccable performance* and *flawless performance* are all natural but that *flawless behaviour* is slightly odd. I will return to anti-collocations below.

20.5.1 Some Adjective-Noun Phrases

To illustrate some of the issues, consider Table 20.1, which shows frequencies of occurrence of some adjective-noun phrases. These were extracted from the written portion of the British National Corpus (BNC) and correspond to words tagged as AJ0 (adjective) followed by a word tagged as a noun (NN1 or NN2) and not directly followed by another noun. The adjectives shown are from the top 100 most frequent adjectives in these extracted phrases and were chosen because they have common meanings that broadly-speaking refer to large magnitude. The nouns are all ones which are in the top five most frequent nouns occurring with one (or more) of the adjectives: the particular 13 nouns in the table were selected from this set because they displayed limited polysemy in this context and because the adjective-noun phrases were more-or-less compositional. The frequencies given are approximate,

---

[2]Although this concept has been discussed in the literature, there doesn't appear to be any standard terminology: the term anti-collocation is taken from Pearce (2001).

Table 20.1 Frequencies of some adjective-noun combinations in the British National Corpus

	importance	success	majority	number	proportion	quality	role	problem	part	house	winds	support	rain
great	310	360	382	172	9	11	3	44	71	80	0	22	0
large	1	1	112	1790	404	0	13	10	533	108	0	1	0
high	8	0	0	92	501	799	1	0	3	0	90	2	0
major	62	60	0	0	7	0	272	356	408	1	1	8	0
big	0	40	5	11	1	0	3	79	79	196	3	1	1
strong	0	0	2	0	0	1	8	0	3	0	132	147	0
heavy	0	0	1	0	0	1	0	0	1	0	2	4	198

because of polysemy etc., but the low frequency phrases were checked manually to exclude cases which did not plausibly correspond to a magnitude use of the adjective modifying the noun. In most cases, the nominal sense will be obvious: one exception is *big number* where *number* is mostly being used in the sense of a song.

Some of these frequencies are surprising, especially the relatively low overall frequency of *big*. The BNC reflects a balance of text published, much of which is relatively high register. The point of interest here is not the relative frequencies of the adjectives but the fact that the distribution is so uneven. While it is obviously not the case that zero frequency in a corpus necessarily corresponds to ungrammaticality, some of these combinations do feel ungrammatical: for what it is worth, my own judgments for the adjective-noun pairs in Table 20.1 are given in Table 20.2.

Although there are obvious differences between the meaning of some of these adjectives when applied to physical objects, and this difference might be formalized in physical terms, some of the most common uses are with abstract nouns. There are a number of alternative ways in which this distribution might be accounted for, as discussed in the following sections.

20.5.1.1   The Denotation Approach

The simplest hypothesis is to say that the denotations of the adjectives and nouns are such that only some combinations are licensed and/or plausible in the real world. That is, these are not collocations, in the sense defined above, but adjectives with slightly different meanings. Under such an account, we might claim that the meaning of *high*, for example, just cannot be true of entities denoted by *rain*. The observed distribution becomes a reflection of real world facts and the fact that *high rain* does not occur is, on this view, no more surprising than the fact that *luxury trudge* is not found. Any formal linguistic theory could, in principle, appeal to such a mechanism, which is why I describe it as the simplest hypothesis.

This approach might be falsified by discovering another word with a compatible denotation to *rain* which does occur with *high*. For instance, rain is a type of precipitation, and *high precipitation* occurs in the BNC (once). However, it could reasonably be argued that *precipitation* actually has a use meaning *rainfall* rather than *rain* and is thus acceptable in that sense with *high*.

To take another example, *heavy smoker* and *heavy drinker* are normally described as collocations, but it could be argued that there is simply a sense of *heavy* which applies specifically to consumption. This is partly borne out by the acceptability of *heavy use* and *heavy consumption*, although it would be necessary to refine the sense to account for the unacceptability of *heavy eater*.[3]

From my current perspective, what matters is not whether it is possible to completely falsify the denotation account but whether it can be fleshed out sufficiently

---

[3]The phrase *heavy eater* is not found in the BNC: *heavy eaters* occurs once, but in a context referring to plants.

Table 20.2 The author's grammaticality judgments for adjective-noun combinations

	importance	success	majority	number	proportion	quality	role	problem	part	house	winds	support	rain
great	?										?		*
large		?				*		?	?	?	*		*
high		*	?										*
major							?		?	?	?		*
big	?			*	*	?				?			?
strong	?	?			*	*	*	*		*			?
heavy	?	*		?		*		*		*			?

Table 20.3 Some nouns occurring with *heavy* in the BNC

dew, rainstorm, downpour, rain, rainfall, snowfall, fall, snow, shower:
clouds, mist, fog: frost, spindrift, wind:
flow, flooding, bleeding, period:
sea, surf, swell:
drinker, drinking, smoker, use:
demands, reliance, workload, responsibility, emphasis, dependence:
irony, sarcasm, criticism:
infestation, soiling:
loss, price, cost, expenditure, taxation, fine, penalty, damages, investment:
punishment, sentence:
fire, bombardment, casualties, defeat:
burden, load, weight, pressure:
lorry, door, chain, boots: footsteps, thud:
loam, ground, pitch, clay, soils:
makeup, cream, oils:
cotton, tweed: belt, curtains:
medication, sedation, sleep:
odour, perfume, scent, smell, whiff:
lunch: crop: advertising: silence: infections: concentration:

to have any predictive power. That is, would it be feasible to specify a meaning for these magnitude adjectives in such a way as to account for the observed distribution? It seems clear that this would involve multiple senses for each adjective: for instance, we would need to account for *heavy rain*, *heavy sea*, *heavy breathing* and so on as well as *heavy smoker* etc. Table 20.3 shows some of the nouns that occur with *heavy* in attributive position in the BNC to illustrate the diversity found. I have tried to indicate rough groupings and I have left out phrases which seem obviously non-compositional, such as *heavy duty* and *heavy metal*.

In some cases, there are fairly clear semantic tendencies, but they do not hold uniformly. For instance, *heavy* tends to be associated with negative situations (*heavy defeat* but not *heavy win*). But *heavy support* is positive and *heavy rain* can be used when the rainfall is beneficial as well as undesirable. Some of these uses are literal ones (i.e., referring to weight of a physical object) but many are not. Some could be seen as extensions of the literal use that rely on common metaphorical patterns. For instance *heavy fine* and so on may relate to a metaphorical pattern which relates problems to physical loads. But this still leaves the question of how to specify the metaphorical use in such a way as to obtain the observed distribution and to explain why *heavy* does not occur with some apparently similar nouns. Anomalies abound: for instance, while *shower* in the weather sense is readily modified by heavy, *shower* in the bathroom sense is not, despite the fact that both refer to water falling.

Although dictionaries attempt to describe the distribution of adjectives via their definitions, none that I have seen are anything like precise enough to delimit the combinations that do and do not occur. Learner's dictionaries sometimes include hints designed to explain the difference between pairs of similar adjectives, such as *big* and *large*, but these are at best indicative and do not lead to a precise explanation of the differences.

20.5.1.2 Selectional Restrictions

There is a huge literature on selectional restrictions and the concept has meant different things to different authors. For current purposes, I will take selectional restrictions to be a refinement of the denotation account under which constraints on combination are specified in the grammar. It is normally assumed that this can be done by some finite set of features with a relatively small set of possible values. A typical example of a feature is **animate**. Under this sort of account, we could attempt to make phrases such as *high rain* ungrammatical as opposed to semantically implausible.

While selectional restrictions are generally taken to be semantically motivated, if we assume that they are grammaticized there is no formal necessity for them to correspond directly to denotation. An attractive idea would be to specify selectional restrictions in terms of qualia structure: e.g., have *heavy* etc. select for nouns on the basis of their qualia properties. But while this may look feasible for isolated examples, it does not seem possible to set up a consistent set of properties that allow for all the types of selection that might be required. For instance, if *begin* can occur with nouns with a telic role corresponding to consumption (as mentioned in Sect. 20.4) then one would hope that this notion of consumption could be consistent with that apparently found for one use of *heavy*. But we do not find *heavy reader* or *heavy eater* and hence would have to specify slightly different classes. Unfortunately, as one tries to make this sort of approach work, there are more divergences than convergences.

Of course, it is not impossible to restrict adjective-noun combination via selectional restrictions: in the limit, for instance, we could stipulate a huge feature vector on every noun with one boolean-valued feature per adjective sense to indicate whether or not this sense could act as a modifier. That is, *high* in the magnitude sense could modify nouns that have a feature **high-magn** which has the value **true**, while nouns which it does not modify would have a **high-magn** value of **false**. An equivalent encoding would be possible using types in a complex multiple inheritance hierarchy. In either case, the approach would be purely stipulative and would essentially be a variant of lexical selection, as discussed in the next section.

20.5.1.3 Lexical Stipulation

Meaning-Text Theory (MTT), as described by Mel'čuk and Polguère (1987), is one of the few frameworks that I am aware of that attempts an empirically-adequate account of the sort of data under discussion here. In MTT, the possible adjective-noun combinations from Table 20.2 could be encoded via a function

Magn (Magnitude) which is associated with a noun and specifies the adjective that characteristically indicates large magnitude. The attractive aspect of this approach is that it can straightforwardly encode the preferred combinations. It also captures the idea that the adjectives in Table 20.2 have very similar meanings. The assumption that **Magn** is a function and thus that there is a single characteristic adjective would not account for the observed data, but the idea could presumably be modified to specify a set of adjectives or we could treat some of the adjectives as pure magnitude-encoding and others as having different meanings.

Unfortunately I do not have space to discuss MTT fully here, and it clearly deserves more attention than the crude sketch given. The main problem from my perspective is that this is again essentially a stipulative mechanism. How do we account for adjective phrases which occur with productively created nouns? If it really is the case that the adjective-noun combinations in Table 20.2 are so arbitrary that the adjective(s) which can modify the noun have to be listed, it seems better to attempt an empirical approach where there is a simpler connection with the observed data and where the information can be acquired directly from a corpus.

20.5.1.4 The Frequency/Collocation Account

Much work within computational linguistics makes use in some way of frequency of words co-occurring in corpora. This is used in both analysis and generation. For instance, n-grams used in language modeling for speech recognition would predict that an input was more likely to correspond to *heavy shower* than *heavy shore*. In a statistical generation system, *heavy rain* could be preferred over *high rain* on the basis of n-grams. Most approaches to word sense disambiguation (WSD) would be able to select the weather sense of shower as opposed to the bathroom sense, given the phrase *heavy shower*: in WSD, frequencies based on a window of words might be used rather than n-grams. In contrast, more sophisticated models used for parse ranking would take account of the syntactic dependency between the words.

While it is often stated that statistical methods in current computational linguistics are compensating for the lack of sufficiently detailed real world knowledge bases, it seems quite clear that this is not all that is going on. The use of statistical techniques based on probabilities to filter output strings generated by a grammar from a symbolic knowledge representation is clearly not an application of world knowledge and there is no obvious account of the different distribution of the Table 20.1 adjectives in terms of real world denotation. Of course n-grams and more sophisticated models do sometimes discriminate between analyses in a way that could approximate real world knowledge (or rather approximate knowledge of likely topics of language, which is somewhat different) or morphological/syntactic properties, but I think we have to conclude that some proportion of the effect of statistical methods is due to collocation.

The idea of collocation implies that we could potentially account for the data in Table 20.1 on the basis of frequency in a linguistically motivated manner. That is, we could assume that all the adjectives have approximately the same meaning and that all the adjective/noun combinations are grammatical according to a symbolic grammar, but there is a stochastic component which means that because some combinations are observed more frequently than others they are also more likely to be generated. Since some combinations are not observed (anti-collocations), this amounts to saying that adjective-noun combination is semi-productive in a similar manner to compound noun formation.

As with the lexical phenomena discussed earlier, it is crucial to have a probability estimate for unseen nouns. We could do this in terms of the semantic class of the noun. This would imply that some degree of grouping of distribution by semantic class was expected.

We can also extend the notion of blocking discussed earlier: if a combination such as *heavy rain* is frequent enough that a speaker is aware of it as an established phrase, then a different phrase with a very similar meaning would be predicted to be dispreferred. Thus, in this approach, the perceived 'oddness' of anti-collocations arises directly from their relatively low frequency compared to the collocations. However the blocking effect might be expected to be weaker with phrases than with lexical items because of their lower item familiarity.

Of course this approach provides a model of frequency, rather than simply a binary grammaticality distinction. This is practically useful: even though *high importance* might be perfectly grammatical, the fact that it is relatively infrequent is something that should be taken into account in a generation system.

There are many things that remain to be specified about this proposal. For instance, what is the probability distribution being measured over? For derivation, as discussed earlier, we assumed that it made sense to talk about a probability distribution on lexical signs, with the frequency of unseen signs being estimated via a back-off that depended on rule productivity. The extension of this idea to compound nouns was reasonably straightforward since compounds are semi-lexical, but adjective-noun combinations are clearly phrasal. One problem with simply treating them in the same way as compounds is that we have to consider predicative as well as attributive adjectives. To a first approximation, for the adjective-noun combinations shown in Table 20.1, attributive and predicative frequency correlate, although there are considerable differences between adjectives in how frequently they appear predicatively.[4] This would suggest that a probability distribution over semantic relations or grammatical relations is required. Further evidence for this is that the *-ly* adverbs that are productively related to the magnitude adjectives are generally found with verbs related to the nominals. For instance: *the rainfall was heavy* vs. *the rain fell heavily*: *heavy dependence* vs. *depend heavily*.

Another issue is the estimation of the probability of unseen adjective-noun combinations: it would be plausible to assume that this was based on semantic

---

[4]Notice that the non-compositional adjective-noun multiword expressions tend not to occur in predicative form. Adjectives applying to the event in a deverbal noun are also not found predicatively, in general: *the smoker is heavy* and *the teacher is French* only have the reading where the adjective applies directly to the individual.

class rather than by a productivity measurement on the modification rule itself, but this assumes that a suitable independent notion of semantic class is available. Computational linguists generally use WordNet (Fellbaum 1998) when backing off from observed frequencies to semantic classes, but the efficacy of this technique varies considerably.

None of the existing probabilistic approaches within computational linguistics are fully adequate to represent collocation, if these factors are taken into account. In order to acquire the necessary frequencies, we would require a parsed, sense-disambiguated corpus. In order to decide what we wanted to treat as collocation, we would need to have a theory of which senses we were going to treat as synonyms or near-synonyms. Furthermore, to be really plausible, we would need a corpus which approximated the input/output of one hearer. Statistical approaches in computational linguistics routinely make use of corpora such as newspaper texts that are vaster and yet more homogeneous than is plausible from this perspective.

20.5.2   *Towards a General Hybrid Approach*

To summarize the discussion in the previous section, the first possibility I considered is that an account of adjective-noun phrases might be based on a fine-grained specification of their meaning, in which case all the potential pairs of adjective and noun are grammatical, but some are semantically implausible or impossible. This is analogous to accounting for the dative alternation by means of fine-grained semantic classes, but as in that case, I do not believe that such an account can be independently motivated and cover all the data. The second possibility is to stipulate the adjectives with which a noun can occur, which is analogous to listing all the verbs that undergo the dative alternation. Again the difficulties are similar: this does not allow for productivity, nor for the observed groupings of nouns by semantic class. The final possibility was direct acquisition of a probabilistic component, augmented with a suitable technique for estimating unseen combinations. The probabilistic approach can be seen as an extension of the Briscoe and Copestake (1999) approach to semi-productivity to the phrasal domain, but it depends on there being a core meaning component to the adjectives, minimally 'high magnitude' for the adjectives in Table 20.1. This is thus essentially a hybrid approach and one fundamental question is the balance between core semantics and collocation.

Magnitude adjectives in English may have more in common with morphological processes than other adjectives would, since augmentative affixes exist in many languages. The adjectives I have been discussing are very frequent, and thus it is plausible that speakers could develop item familiarity in the same way as for derived lexical signs, even though the phrases can be generated compositionally. There are clearly other adjectives where the meaning is quite specific and where the distribution might be adequately accounted for purely denotationally. For instance, nationality adjectives such as *Peruvian* have a more-or-less clear-cut definition: in the real world there may be border disputes, but this does not prevent the concept being linguistically straightforward.

I suspect many adjectives fall between these extremes and that in fact there are cases where there is considerable discrepancy between native speakers. For instance, *rancid* occurs with a wide range of nouns, but it is clear to all the native English speakers I have asked that its core meaning is something to do with offness in food. Different speakers have different intuitions about how it is used: for instance that it refers to dairy products, or to fats and oils, or to fatty food. The acceptability of *rancid meat* thus varies while *rancid butter* is a prototypical use for the speakers I have asked. However, there is a technical definition of *rancid*, which involves the presence of off-flavours or smells caused by fat oxidation. Some speakers have heard this definition and some others describe the meaning of *rancid* in a way which is essentially compatible with it (possibly because they have experienced the characteristic flavour/smell and can thus ground the meaning according to their perceptions). But other speakers do not apparently know rancidity as a distinct concept as opposed to a way of talking about offness in general in a particular class of food. It is therefore impossible to say whether *rancid butter* is really a collocation or whether its frequency is predictable (based on the adjectival meaning and world knowledge about food), because it seems that individual speakers have differing models. But this discrepancy between speakers is unlikely to be noticed outside a technical context.

It is worth noticing that most people will not have been exposed to a very large number of instances of the word *rancid*: it occurs only 77 times in the 100-million word British National Corpus, and many of these examples must be seen as non-core (e.g., *rancid T-shirt, rancid voice, rancid first quarter of the century*). But *rancid* is not perceived as an especially unusual adjective. This if the collocation model is to be developed in a way that is psychologically plausible, prediction of probabilities for unseen phrases must be taken seriously.

20.6   Conclusion

I have tried to show the pervasiveness of semi-productivity in lexical processes and to show that it extends to a phrasal level. I have argued that a reasonable way to account for it is to limit a fully productive symbolic account via a frequency-based mechanism. The line between cases which should be totally ruled out and those which should be dispreferred is not totally clear and perhaps never can be clear, since there is unlikely to be perfect agreement between speakers. But in the end there is no observable difference between assuming that a particular form or phrase has an infinitesimal probability and ruling it out completely.

This discussion of the limitations of generativity is not intended as an attack on Generative Lexicon theory. In fact, quite the opposite is true. Firstly, if the argument above about the nature of collocation and its application to adjective-noun phrases is credible, then the lexicon is semi-generative in the same sense as syntax is. Secondly, the only viable alternatives to the assumption of generative devices in the lexicon are approaches that leave these processes to pragmatics. The work of

Hobbs (e.g., Hobbs et al. 1993) is particularly important in providing an account of a wide range of phenomena. But pragmatic approaches have real problems in dealing with conventional limitations to generativity, especially where these are language-specific or dialect-specific. Any approach which assumes that operations like metonymy or logical metonymy are carried out at the level of logical form can only allow for conventional restrictions via operations that affect the logical form, and this just does not seem a reasonable way of accounting for most of the data described above. So, perversely, limitations on generativity provide the best arguments for a (semi-)generative lexicon.

Acknowledgements This paper is based on an earlier work published in the proceedings of the 1st International Workshop on Generative Approaches to the Lexicon in 2001, but it also includes some material presented at the 3rd Workshop in 2005. I am grateful to the audiences at both events for their feedback and also to the other colleagues who commented on the earlier paper. I am especially grateful to Ted Briscoe and Simone Teufel for their detailed comments on this version. As usual, all mistakes are the responsibility of the author.

References

Aronoff, M. (1976). *Word formation in generative grammar* (Linguistic inquiry monograph 1). Cambridge, MA: MIT Press.

Bauer, L. (1983). *English word-formation*. Cambridge: Cambridge University Press.

Briscoe, E. J., & Copestake, A. (1999). Lexical rules in constraint-based grammars. *Computational Linguistics, 25*(4), 487–526.

Clark, E. V., & Clark, H. H. (1979). When nouns surface as verbs. *Language, 55*, 767–811.

Copestake, A., & Briscoe E. J. (1996). Controlling the application of lexical rules. In *Proceedings of the SIGLEX workshop on breadth and depth of semantic lexicons* (pp. 7–19), Santa Cruz, CA.

Copestake, A., & Flickinger. D. (2000). An open-source grammar development environment and broad-coverage English grammar using HPSG. In *Proceedings of the second conference on language resources and evaluation* (LREC-2000), Athens, Greece.

Copestake, A., & Lascarides, A. (1997). Integrating symbolic and statistical representations: The lexicon-pragmatics interface. In *Proceedings of the 35th annual meeting of the Association for Computational Linguistics and 8th conference of the European Chapter of the Association for Computational Linguistics* (ACL-EACL 97, pp 136–143), Madrid.

Cruse, D. A. (1986). *Lexical semantics*. Cambridge: Cambridge University Press.

Downing, P. (1977). On the creation and use of English compound nouns. *Language, 53*(4), 810–842.

Fellbaum, C. (Ed.). (1998). *WordNet: An electronic lexical database*. Cambridge, MA: MIT Press.

Godard, D., & Jayez. J. (1993). Towards a proper treatment of coercion phenomena. In *Proceedings of the sixth conference of the European Chapter of the Association for Computational Linguistics* (EACL-93, pp. 168–177), Utrecht, The Netherlands.

Goldberg, A. (1995). *Constructions*. Chicago: Chicago University Press.

Hobbs, J., Stickel, M., Appelt, D., & Martin, P. (1993). Interpretation as abduction. *Artificial Intelligence, 63*(1), 69–142.

Mel'čuk, I., & Polguère, M. (1987). A formal lexicon in meaning-text theory (or how to do lexica with words). *Computational Linguistics, 13*(3–4), 261–275.

Nunberg, G. D. (1978). *The pragmatics of reference*. Doctoral dissertation, CUNY Graduate Center, reproduced by the Indiana University Linguistics Club.

Ostler, N., & Atkins, B. T. S. (1992). Predictable meaning shift: Some linguistic properties of lexical implication rules. Lexical semantics and knowledge representation. In J. Pustejovsky & S. Bergler (Eds.), *Proceedings of the first SIGLEX workshop, Berkeley, CA* (pp. 87–100). Berlin: Springer.

Pearce, D. (2001). Using conceptual similarity for collocation extraction. In *Proceedings of the Fourth annual CLUK colloquium*, Sheffield, UK.

Pinker, S. (1989). *Learnability and cognition: The acquisition of argument structure*. Cambridge, MA: MIT Press.

Pustejovsky, J. (1995). *The generative lexicon*. Cambridge, MA: MIT Press.

Pustejovsky, J., & Bouillon, P. (1995). Aspectual coercion and logical polysemy. *Journal of Semantics, 12*(2), 133–162.

Sag, I. A., Baldwin. T., Bond. F., Copestake. A., & Flickinger, D. (2002). Multiword expressions: A pain in the neck for NLP. In *Proceedings of the third international conference on intelligent text processing and computational linguistics* (CICLING 2002, pp. 1–15), Mexico City, Mexico.

Verspoor, C. M. (1997). *Contextually-dependent lexical semantics*. PhD thesis, Centre for Cognitive Science, University of Edinburgh.

Index

J. Pustejovsky et al. (eds.), *Advances in Generative Lexicon Theory*, Text,
Speech and Language Technology 46, DOI 10.1007/978-94-007-5189-7,
© Springer Science+Business Media Dordrecht 2013

basic principles of, 76–83
causative alternations, 89, 91
completeness constraint, 83
component of, 80
default assignment principles, 80
instrument PPs *vs.* implement PPs, 83
language-specific and construction-specific
    qualifications, 79
layered structure of clause, 77
logical structure, 78–79
non-macrorole core argument, 82
semantic units, syntactic units, 76, 77
transitivity, 80
verb alternations and optional PPs, 83–93
Lexical resources, Semantic Web
computational lexicons, 419
lexical repositories, 419
meaning, lexicons and ontologies
    commonalities, 422
    conceptual/domain nodes, 421
    conceptualization, 423
    content and multilinguality, 421
    heterogeneous lexical knowledge, 422
    implicitly structured lexical knowledge,
        422
    non-compositional aspects, 423
    polysemy, 422
    qualia structure, 423
    "shallow" semantic representation, 423
    SIMPLE model (*see* SIMPLE model)
    word senses, 422
NLP tools, 419
standardization (*see* ISLE Computational
    Lexicon Working Group (ISLE
    CLWG))
vision, 420–421
Locative verbs, 404–405
Logical metonymy
constitutive role, 134
and copredication, 53
metonymic extension, 133–134
type coercion, 133
Logical structures (LSs)
Actor-Undergoer Hierarchy, 81
RRG terms, 102, 103
verbs and, 78–79
Lytinen, S.L., 139, 140

M
Machine-learning (ML) approach, 437
Machine translation (MT) system, 429
Magn function, 473
Mairal, R., 93

Manner verbs, 378–379
Manning, C.D., 436
Manzini, M.R., 152, 153
Marantz, A.P., 15
Marchand, H., 395
Masullo, P.J., 151, 152
Mauner, G., 348
McKeown, K.R., 135
McNally, L., 4, 251, 252, 255, 256, 264, 355
Meaning-text theory (MTT), 472
Meinschäfer, J., 397, 409
Mel'čuk, I., 395, 396, 472
Mester, A., 205
Metonymy and metaphor
anomalous metaphor, 143–144
co-compositionality, 140–141
computational linguistics, 130
context, 141–143
data
    adjective, 138
    agentive role, 136
    automatic non-literal language
        resolution systems, 135
    compositional semantics, 136
    formal role, 136, 137
    GL entry fragments for (S_1'), 135–138
    semantic argument, 137
logical metonymy
    constitutive role, 134
    metonymic extension, 133–134
    type coercion, 133
one-to-one mapping rules, 140
Michaelis, L., 70, 107
MILE data categories (MDC), 431
MILE lexical classes (MLC), 431
MILE lexical model (MLM), 430–431
Miller, P.H., 152
Minsky, M., 196
Monachesi, P., 152
Monachini, M., 6
Montague Grammar, 41, 42
Montague's theory, 21
Moravcsik, J.M., 26
Morphological structure composition schema
    (MS-CS), 392–393
Multilingual ISLE lexical entry (MILE),
    430–432

N
Nakatani, K., 5
Namer, F., 6, 392, 394
Natural Language Processing (NLP), 414–415
Nishida, C., 163, 164